Y0-CAY-787

Eighteenth-Century Letters and British Culture

Eighteenth-Century Letters and British Culture

Clare Brant

© Clare Brant 2006

All rights reserved. No reproduction, copy or transmission of this
publication may be made without written permission.

No paragraph of this publication may be reproduced, copied or transmitted
save with written permission or in accordance with the provisions of the
Copyright, Designs and Patents Act 1988, or under the terms of any licence
permitting limited copying issued by the Copyright Licensing Agency,
90 Tottenham Court Road, London W1T 4LP.

Any person who does any unauthorised act in relation to this publication
may be liable to criminal prosecution and civil claims for damages.

The author has asserted her right to be identified
as the author of this work in accordance with the Copyright,
Designs and Patents Act 1988.

First published 2006 by
PALGRAVE MACMILLAN
Houndmills, Basingstoke, Hampshire RG21 6XS and
175 Fifth Avenue, New York, N.Y. 10010
Companies and representatives throughout the world

PALGRAVE MACMILLAN is the global academic imprint of the Palgrave
Macmillan division of St. Martin's Press, LLC and of Palgrave Macmillan Ltd.
Macmillan® is a registered trademark in the United States, United Kingdom
and other countries. Palgrave is a registered trademark in the European
Union and other countries.

ISBN-13: 978–1–4039–9482–0 hardback
ISBN-10: 1–4039–9482–X hardback

This book is printed on paper suitable for recycling and made from fully
managed and sustained forest sources.

A catalogue record for this book is available from the British Library.

Library of Congress Cataloging-in-Publication Data
Brant, Clare, 1960–
    Eighteenth-century letters and British culture / Clare Brant.
        p.   cm.
    Includes bibliographical references and index.
    ISBN 1–4039–9482–X (cloth)
    1. English letters—History and criticism.   2. Letter writing—18th
    century.   3. Great Britain—Social life and customs—18th century.
    4. Great Britain—Civilization—18th century.   I. Title.
    PR915.B73 2006
    826′.509—dc22   2005055289

10   9   8   7   6   5   4   3   2   1
15   14   13   12   11   10   09   08   07   06

Transferred to Digital Printing 2006

For

my family for their love

and

my friends for their inspiration

Contents

Acknowledgements

What mighty oaks from acorns grow. The acorn for this book fell when I had taken my final undergraduate exams and was pondering possible subjects for postgraduate work. I could not decide between Samuel Richardson and Dorothy Richardson and my kindest tutor gave me a book which made the difference. I thank John Batchelor for giving me that book and Ruth Perry for writing it: they helped me discover the eighteenth century.

Institutions which employed me thereafter got their pound of flesh, but I was grateful for their challenges and I thank Marilyn Butler, Stephen Heath, Roger Lonsdale, Tony Nuttall and Isabel Rivers for help and for supporting my research when there was much less to show for it. All sorts of people added to my stock of knowledge – students, colleagues, fellow scholars – and I thank everyone who knowingly or not gave me hints to work upon. My path to print was made longer and more difficult by several factors: changes to academia imposed by successive governments, principally Tory; by the strait-jacket of the Research Assessment Exercise, which has created a climate in which ideas are more imprisoned than liberated by market forces, and by certain unimaginative people.

But obstructions have made me appreciate all the more those people who have helped me. My debts of gratitude go back years and to so many people I cannot name them all, particularly students. I would like especially to thank Diane Purkiss for stimulating conversations and inspiration over many years and for friendly intellectual input in various ways, I thank Yun Lee Too, Tom Keymer, Kathryn Sutherland, Ros Ballaster, Hero Chalmers, Emma Holden, Jacqui Labbe, George Myerson, Nikki Lacey, Sally Humphreys, Justin Rosenberg, John Cornwell, Estelle Cohen, Alison Stenton, Max Fincher, Jane Darcy, Neil Vickers, Max Saunders and John Stokes. Amanda Gilroy, Tim Webb and Vivien Jones helped me think through ideas in other contexts and broadened my horizons. Jon Mee and Martin Priestman gave me a word in season, very timely for Chapter 8. Susan Whyman, whose own work on eighteenth-century letter-writing shows how much more can be said on the subject, was generous in support.

Nick Rogers and Margot Finn who read the final manuscript sharpened my ideas and put fresh heart into me; their intellectual liveliness, rigour and generosity made the last lap easier, and I am especially grateful to them, and to Paula Kennedy at Palgrave.

The bulk of my research was done in the Bodleian Library. Sometimes it was very bulky, and for cheerfully finding the right pile of boxes, week after week, year after year, it is a pleasure to thank Vera Ryhajlo particularly and Helen Rogers, David Busby and Tina King.

Overlaps between life and work are sometimes unexpectedly wonderful. To the chapter on parents and children, special contributions came from Penny Hill and Heli Webb and also from Katharine Brant. Those who influenced Chapter 3 know who they are and the depth of my goodwill.

The Oscar for Best Supporter goes to Ewen Green whose faith in this book never wavered. His devotion and witty postcards brightened many years. Sharing stories, jokes, expeditions and conjectures with him doubled the pleasures of discovery. His acumen saved me from egregious errors, and his support has been precious indeed. If only books could be released in directors' cuts, his would be both starring role and walk-on part.

A few people will know how much of Peter Carter is in this book. An impossible wish, that he could have seen it, has to become a possible endeavour, to wear learning lightly and to the benefit of others, as he did. It is a pleasure to thank all those who loved him, especially Jonty and Gill Carter, Jo and Jan Luffingham, Dick and Sheila Southern, and Donald and Elizabeth Matthew, for sharing the past in the present.

Most of all I owe a debt to those friends who in all sorts of ways have shared good times, bad times and mad times with sagacity, good humour and liberality of spirit. Many of them are great correspondents, by letter, by postcards and now by email. Vicki Bertram and Katherine Armstrong have been loyal and wise correspondents; Joann Kleinneiur taught me the art of the envelope too. So heartfelt thanks to Sarah Spiller, Alex Thomson, Jacqui Mansfield, Jo Denton, Nicky Watson, Michael Dobson, Diane Roberts, Matilda Leyser, Andy Letcher, James Waterfield, Jo Wilmott, Ros Hunt, Jo Collinge, Shirley Andrews, Amy Black, Stephen Brooke, Peter Weiler, Jon Schneer, Richard O'Connell, Andy and Gog Webb, Charles Denton, and to Sarah Murphy, Adrian Arbib, Jamie Gardner, Abi Brown and Alex Hehir for creative diversions and cheer. Veronica Ortenberg and Gordon Milne have been solicitously caring on paper and off and, chief caryatid, Gooding has given invaluable advice.

My family have been rocks among shifting sands ever since I can remember. My parents' wonderful letters have had a bearing on my academic affinity for things epistolary, reinforced by my sister Julia's lively emails and sympathy. My brother Chris deserves reams of gratitude: instead I shall simply thank him and Sarah Brant for all their kindnesses and his unfailing thoughtfulness and steadfast support.

Hence past debts turn to future prospects...thanks to Julian Loose at Faber for his patience and understanding: he should have had my book on eighteenth-century ballooning much sooner.

Finally I thank my readers, especially those who read the whole book, and open-mindedly. You were more than half the point of writing it, after all.

A Letter of Introduction

'I have not the honor, gentlemen,' said I, 'to be known to you: these letters serve to introduce me to your acquaintance, and to recommend me to your good offices:'

–Nathaniel Wraxall

A letter of recommendation to any person of fashion, secures an introduction to the most polite circles...

–William Hunter

Between 1700 and 1800, more than twenty-one thousand items were published that used the word 'Letter' or 'Letters' in their title.[1] Add to these figures the hundreds of thousands, if not millions, of letters that existed in manuscript during the period and one has a genre of extraordinary range. How can one book make sense of it all? We need to know about the norms and nuances of letter-writing in the period. Only such an analysis can show what is representative of eighteenth-century culture in its broadest sense, the way people in Britain lived – and its more specialist sense – the ideas, beliefs and representations that preoccupied them. Letters were a central part of everyday life in eighteenth-century Britain. The letter was a key medium of business and government. Letters were at the heart of free speech, symbolised by the principle of free postage for members of Parliament. Letters were the central form of communication in a world of denser contacts – contacts made denser by the growth of commerce and the state. Letters were also the key medium of communication in a world of extended contacts – contacts thinned out by distance through empire, business, travel and separations. Letters mattered not just to the very literate and the middling sort but also to the less literate, even the illiterate.[2] We know much less about these many layers of epistolary activity than we do about those few in the literary canon like epistolary fiction or the correspondence of established authors. What follows in this book are readings of different kinds of prose letters representing the astonishingly active culture of eighteenth-century letter-writing. The pool of texts to draw on is in fact an ocean.

Precisely because there was a rich diversity to letter-writing in this period, it confounds easy definitions. One is looking at innumerable texts which share identifiable markers of genre yet do not make a stable genre. To smooth out the differences between letters is to homogenize them and diminish the significance of their diversity. Letters were used in varied contexts with varied effects; adaptability underlay their appeal. They evolved through prevailing climates of wit, reason, satire, politeness, sensibility and enthusiasm; they served patriotism and party, dark ends and enlightenment, faith and madness. Letters promoted harmony in the collaboration of correspondence and discord in the clash of controversies. Letter-writing fulfilled important and multiple functions in eighteenth-century society. A full picture of those functions can be built up by treating the genre as if it were made up of small interlocking parts, for instance medical letters, consolation letters, military letters,[3] letters to the Royal Society and other intellectual communities,[4] letters of patronage, letters of dedication, the role of letters in colonialism and imperialism,[5] begging letters,[6] blackmail, even the rejection letter.[7] Then again, each of those parts is affected by the history of letter-writing as a whole, notably through the cumulative effect of more letters getting into print and being read by more people. The epistolary novel, for instance, increasingly assumes a reader is able to follow a special kind of narrative; periodicals and newspapers encourage particular epistolary conventions. People became letter-literate in new ways. What distinguishes the eighteenth century from previous centuries was the vibrancy of its letter-writing and the variety of its letter-reading. The cultural significance of letters, then, is best tracked through diversity not homogeneity. Since one book cannot hope to cover everything, the pathways I suggest are also starting points. Nonetheless, what is included goes wider and deeper than core-sampling. It amounts to cross-sectional analysis of representative kinds of letters and the contexts of their production, reception and circulation.[8] This book introduces as many letter-writers as is possible in a single book with a recommendation that they become better known not simply for themselves as writers, but as writers in the genre of letters – the most important kind of writing in the eighteenth century.

There is a substantial and growing body of criticism on the subject of letters; my book is not the first in the field. But my book does claim to be the most comprehensive study yet of letters in eighteenth-century Britain. The variety of these kinds of letters opens up the subject and establishes connections not made before. It leads to fewer easy answers, but it also avoids answers that are misleading because they arise from too narrow a research base. Diverse materials invite different perspectives so I draw on a spectrum of methodologies. In literary theory, one does not have to be chained to an –ism. Plural approaches illuminate shades of meaning and demonstrate the importance of nuance. I favour thematic clusters over linear structure in order to free epistolary complexity from some of the Procrustean beds into which it has been forced. Given the multi-directional enterprise of opening up a subject, my introduction starts by taking up zones of engagement established by historians as well as literary critics in order to explain what elements I want to carry over from both disciplines in pursuit of an approach I would rather call cultural poetics than cultural history, since my commitment is first and foremost to letters as literary objects. A principle of resonance, echo and reflections is the goal of writing cultural poetics, according to Claudia Benthein.[9] It requires more patience from readers than conventional lines of argument, but by following criss-crossing tracks rather than simplified lines one establishes a new sort of map.

Public, private and polite?

A letter of introduction opened doors in the eighteenth century. People on the move found such letters essential as a means of proving their respectability and securing invitations. It changed people's prospects, like the letter of recommendation for which it sometimes doubled and which was a common means of getting employment. This circulation of persons and letters together is a good place to begin an exploration of letter-writing in eighteenth-century culture since it combines a sense of how letters served both business and pleasure. My first epigraph suggests how the letter of introduction made connections between people, enlarging acquaintance and deploying power. My second epigraph intimates that expansion was selective; definitions of persons as fashionable led to exclusions of those deemed otherwise, contracting society into self-contained circles.[10] Both epigraphs point to a story about the letter as a form of sociability and an instrument of politeness, and so it was across Europe, not just in Britain. But there is more, much more, to the cultural significance of letters than how they served politeness.

For a start, I recommend all possible particularity when thinking about letters. It is a major aim of this book to make generalisations about letters harder – including this one. Critical arguments are too often based exclusively on one kind of letter: we need to be explicit about what kinds of letters are being discussed, at what historical moment and in what cultural context. My epigraphs, for instance, were written in the late eighteenth century by educated men, with reference to travels in Russia and Germany respectively. That context helps account for the links between letters of introduction and a polite discourse common to business and social life across Europe. Other assumptions about them are less sure. The first writer tells his audience what they should read the letters for. Is he assuming they know what he means already, or not? Is it conversation or writing which requires him to spell out their function? The second writer describes fashionable uses of letters of introduction using a language of fashion himself. Is he too being prescriptive rather than descriptive? The receivers of the letters in the first quotation are clearly gendered, and in the second quotation, less so: when and where were epistolary conditions for women the same as for men? These examples show the importance of being particular in our discussions and of paying attention to the conditions in which letters were written, read and published. As a framework for reading letters, politeness illuminates part but not all of the story; nor does it necessarily produce the fullest story. Politeness also has its own uncertain history. According to one historian, by the end of the seventeenth century, letters were the badge of membership in élite society, although in at least one family whose letters recorded the benefits of joining this club, the art of an elegant courtesy letter was something mastered by servants as well as gentry members.[11] Politeness is not attributable to any one individual or text; it evolves through changes in manners for which parents are as much responsible as philosophers.[12] Shaftesbury, Addison and Steele were catalysts in the history of politeness, but they were also part of a groundswell effect created by others and expressed through letters of various kinds, from the condensed form of the calling card to the letter of advice. Letter-writers satisfied decorum by sending letters on 'proper' occasions, using 'correct' forms of address and agreed forms of debate; they also regulated politeness by testing its compatibility with negligence, warmth and zeal.

Stereotypes of letters as products of polite society ignore how politeness breeds its antonym, a discourse of rudeness deploying irony, satire and abuse. Making elegant insults was an important part of eighteenth-century politeness. As one disaffected correspondent wrote to a lord who had not refunded business expenses incurred on his behalf, 'I have been taught to think it ill breeding, when an inferior writes to a superior to say, they are an obliged Humble Servant, and therefore with all due respect,/I have the honour to/ Subscribe myself,/Your Lordship's Most Humble Servant.'[13] In the intellectual communities that made up the republic of letters, fights frequently broke out between correspondents and courtesy went out of the window; between proponents of different beliefs, theological controversies were fought with bitterness and invective. Politeness, etymologically related to polish, was smooth and emotionally restrained: many letters of argument were openly angry and some led to physical violence.[14]

The letter of introduction is also a useful starting-point for considering terminology, an issue not as simple as it first appears. As Rebecca Earle remarks, 'There continues to be little agreement on precisely what a letter is.'[15] Thomas Beebee's definition is useful though it shies away from printed letters: 'A letter is a text which has become separated from its author and has entered the various postings and relays which will inevitably influence its interpretation and evaluation.'[16] One critic of nineteenth-century American letters favours the term 'personal autograph letter' to describe the texts he discusses, mostly the correspondence of well-known authors.[17] This suggests something in manuscript (autographs are individual, print is uniform) and something written to be sent. The term accurately describes a large body of writing that existed in the eighteenth century and indeed still does – the letter written to family or friends.[18] People in the eighteenth century tended to refer to these as 'familiar letters'. They encompassed a sense of the personal but it did not restrict them to one discourse or one outlet. Samuel Richardson's *Familiar Letters on Important Occasions*, for example, were fictional and public.[19]

Attempts to reconfigure Habermas's model of public and private spheres have led to proposals for a third site, either a zone of overlap between public and private or a realm of more uncertain relations. Reviewing some of this work, Harriet Guest observes that 'the analogy of spheres becomes a hindrance'.[20] Indeed: it compels adjustments which have become as cumbersome as Copernican calculations. Habermas's concept of a public sphere is an ideal arena of discursive engagement that does not match the complexities of eighteenth-century communicative practice: though some kinds of letter-writing fit his model of communicative action, others do not. The varied and often unpredictable circulation of letters confounds simple distinctions between public and private, and the social origins and destinations of letters are too broad to be restricted to an idealised bourgeois class. In the context of letter-writing, 'personal' is useful in that it recognises the significance of letters to individuals and to relationships. It is preferable to 'private', a term that is simply inaccurate for many eighteenth-century familiar letters, which were composed in company, voluntarily circulated beyond the addressee and frequently found their way into print.[21] True, many correspondents did not want or expect their exchanges to be disclosed to others, but 'personal' should be understood to anticipate discretion, the conditions of which were often explicit. Samuel Wesley told his son John he could show a copy of a letter to anyone interested provided they read it in his chamber, limiting its physical movement but allowing for its discursive circulation. Moreover, 'personal' is not a term of seclusion, like 'private'. It helps to break down that binary of 'private' versus 'public' which has encouraged a view of the past as more segregated than it really was. Lawrence Klein has convincingly shown that in eighteenth-century usage, these terms had more than the one meaning we tend to assume.[22] To his collection of instances of 'public' and 'private' used in polyvalent ways, I would add a description of letters being handed out 'in a private public manner'.[23] Until more people recognise the fluidity of these terms, I prefer 'personal'. It also has the advantage of suggesting a subset relationship: personal is to social as particular is to general. So personal letters articulate in miniature the concerns of a wider society.[24] Those concerns do include designating certain kinds of material as private, but they do not privilege paradigms of secrecy which have more to do with epistolary fiction than real correspondence. Even letters in cipher, an extreme form of privacy, were usually in cipher because they contained material that had dangerous public implications.[25]

Another tangle of terminology concerns letters of argument. Some were written for the press; others found their way less directly into print. Others circulated in manuscript or simply went to their addressee. The term 'public letter' needs further qualification.[26] For instance, many different kinds of letters passed through coffee houses – printed letters of argument, newsletters, periodicals featuring letters and personal post awaiting collection by individuals – post that might include unpublished letters of argument or letters that copied passages out of printed texts. 'Public' is thus as unsatisfactory as 'private' unless it includes more specific identifications of genre.

Manuscript and print

Most of the letters I discuss in this book were in print in the eighteenth century. An emphasis on printed letters gets us away from an antithesis between private and public that is all too easily converted into an antithesis between manuscript and print. Not everything in print is public; not everything unpublished is private. Archives, which started as a place where public documents were housed, have become associated with what is not public knowledge: in Derrida's terms, 'the trouble of secrets, of plots, of clandestineness, of half-private, half-publlic [sic] conjurations, always at the unstable limit between public and private, between the family, the society, and the State, between the family and an intimacy even more private than the family, between oneself and oneself'.[27] Derrida's sense of archives as speculative, as places of disclosures that are arrived at by unconscious as well as conscious motives, is anathema to those historians who, as Nicholas Rogers has observed, tend to think only the archival is the real.[28] In fact, archives are always filtered. As Amanda Vickery points out, descendants sorting and storing family letters are likely to over-represent letters between kin, and to weed others out.[29] The contents of archives are always incomplete in the sense that not every aspect of life is articulated on paper. Susan Whyman's archive-based study of letters in the Verney family observes, 'Even with so many letters, it is difficult to plumb the Verneys' political and religious convictions, for they were bred to suppress their emotions and adept at masking their thoughts.'[30] Eighteenth-century historians were conscious of the incompleteness of archives and they lamented that paper artefacts were disappearing in their own lifetimes, thanks to wilful destruction, neglect, accidents of weather and the attention of mice. These historians, however, were also often collectors. Freud's analysis of the collector's pursuit of completeness (as a defence against death-drives) helps explain some historians' attachments to the archive as a topos of fullness.

Archives are not the only repositories of the unknown, nor necessarily the best. Second-hand bookshops are also treasure-houses of the forgotten, including publications of archival research done by earlier generations of scholars. Print makes material available, selectively; it does not necessarily keep it available. In the three hundred years since some of the letters discussed in this book were written, we have had plenty of time to forget them. A letter printed in the eighteenth century has no more guarantee of being read now than a manuscript does, especially if it happens to be about something insufficiently fashionable to attract notice. What the archive represents has less to do with the intrinsically greater value of anything one might find (there are dull things in archives too) and more to do with the symbolism of archival research as something difficult – as in the term recherché, literally, researched, but figuratively, got with difficulty. Manuscripts in difficult handwriting do demand paleographic knowledge, which accounts for some value-added skill, but there is also an idea at work that represents manuscript as original in the sense of unsullied by mass reproduction, whereas print is common, therefore vulgar.[31] In privileging the archival as something got with difficulty, some historians present history as a process of excavation in which their industry uncovers hidden gems. The longevity of this metaphor, which I discuss further in Chapter 7, does not make it more convincing. In any case, survival rates of printed texts can result in published material becoming equally rare. My critique is not meant to denigrate interest in manuscripts – indeed, since letters are vulnerable to pious or prudish editing, recourse to manuscripts is very desirable. But the point remains: simply because letters have been published once does not make us more aware of them. Letters that were printed in the eighteenth century but are not circulating in modern editions or reprints exist in a limbo as full of the unknown as any archive.[32]

By giving more attention to letters in print, one can better establish the cultural significance of more kinds of letters. However, as with distinctions between archive and print, distinctions between manuscript and print can create a false dichotomy. Most eighteenth-century readers were literate in the conventions of both manuscript and printed letters. Just as many writers had a 'fair copy' hand which had the clarity of print, many printed items in the period, from title pages to trade cards, made use of several different fonts in a small space, which gave print a variability like that of script. In the hand-press period, no two printers' stock of type and ornaments was exactly the same; each was unique in its variants and identifiably so, like handwriting.[33] George Bickham's beautiful catalogue of various 'hands' used in the eighteenth century suggests differences between print and script are less than one might expect.[34] There were even 'script types', like the font specially cut for Ichabod Dawks for his newsletter. 'His Style is a Dialect between the Familiarity of Talking and Writing, and his Letter such as you cannot distinguish whether Print or Manuscript', wrote Steele admiringly.[35] Dawks supplied printed newsletters that looked like manuscript in their typeface and layout, running in unbroken paragraphs to the edge of the page rather than in columns. He advertised them in terms of manuscript conventions: 'This letter will be done upon good writing paper, and blank space left that any gentleman may write his private business.' Although he anticipated that marginalia would make his newsletters part of manuscript culture, they were emphatically also a script-print fusion.[36] This close relationship between script and print was mirrored in the way people copied correspondence into letter-books or stored it in book-like boxes.[37] Not all unprinted letters were in ordinary hands: some were in shorthand, especially after John Byrom invented his ingenious system and taught it to active correspondents like the Wesley brothers.[38]

Because letter-writing was so widely practised, it supplied numerous crossing-points between print and script. Conversion from manuscript to print involved some changes to text and much was made of this in fiction: references to blots and smudges evoked emotions too powerful for the writer's body to control. Imaged through a falling tear or trembling 'hand', these excitements wrought effects visible in script, invisible in print; the supposed loss becomes itself a metaphor of inexpressibility. But this is strategic, specific to fiction and discourses where recovery of the moment of writing helps establish a dynamic of time and place in which erotic drives predominate. There are plenty of other contexts in which letters made an unremarked transition from manuscript to print. The common practice of making copies (the writer sending a neater one) created a middle state in which manuscript features were treated as unwanted disorder (rather than, as in the novel, desirable disorder, or, the disorder of desire.) In children's letters, blots, crossings-out or interlineations were treated as imperfections, not signs of authenticity; children's texts, like their bodies, were subjected to discipline. Certainly there were manuscript features that mattered to eighteenth-century writers of familiar letters which do not all survive the transition into print: the quality and size of paper chosen, spacing between greeting and text, closing flourishes, whether the letter was franked and the choice of seal were all expressive. Writers who used epistolary form for writings intended for a public readership could dispense with these features and readers did not complain about their absence. It is true that punctuation is often altered when familiar letters are printed, although this is not a simple story of loss or additions. Print was hospitable to the swung dash favoured by sentimental correspondents in the later eighteenth century, and from the late 1760s some booksellers experimented with layout so that letters of epistolary novels were displayed for the first time complete on single pages. That these were also set typographically in double columns, unlike an actual letter, suggests an awareness of the artifice of mimesis.[39]

There are other reasons for giving extensive space to printed letters. The first is that publication gives additional meaning to a text. In some cases, the decision to print was taken by the writer; in other cases, publication was something the writer feared or opposed; in yet other cases, decisions were taken by other people after the writer's death. One can represent these occasions from the recipients' point of view or from the perspective of publishers or other interested parties who committed these texts to print:

all illuminate the cultural uses of letters. Even perfunctory adoption of an epistolary frame for a text intended for print should be noticed as a choice on the writer's part. Whatever the reasons – pious, literary, political, intellectual, commercial – they indicate motives and consequences that are part of the history of a text and the wider history of letter-writing. When William Mason printed his friend Thomas Gray's letters and argued that in themselves they constituted a life of the writer, he was contributing to a debate about the place of letters in biography in general and literary men in particular – a debate with a history of which he was conscious.[40] William Merrill Decker has argued about familiar letters, 'Because study of correspondence involves the invasion of what we perceive as someone else's privacy (albeit an erstwhile privacy, a privacy that, at a certain remove, deconstructs as an individual-centred ideology), theoretical and ethical considerations are more than usually in order.'[41] I agree, although I think what Roger Chartier identifies as 'the taken-for-granted-link between letter-writing and secrecy'[42] recreates misleading assumptions of letters as private. As discussed earlier, a dubious binary of public and private ignores letters that were read openly by multiple readers or read out to them.[43]

The expansion of print routinely cited as distinctive to eighteenth-century culture is built on an expanded manuscript base; a growth in writing precedes growth in print. But this story is too simple because print creates more writing, not all of it destined for print. People copied items out of publications to send to friends in handwritten letters; they exchanged views about books they read and annotated printed books with manuscript notes. Discussing the period 1680–1750, Roger Chartier sees letters as being 'on the cusp between manuscript and print culture'. His metaphor evokes a meeting point between two arcs coming in from different directions; I argue letters provide not only a junction or crossroad, but a whole network of routes, like the turnpikes, roads and lanes along which they reached their readers.[44] Though letters were not the only means by which people entered print, they were one of the most widespread. The relationship between script and print is emphatically simultaneous not sequential: that is, correspondence and printed letters co-existed in multiple and complex ways. To claim that epistolary fiction was the principal crossing-point is to ignore a substantial body of non-fictional epistolary writings with which many eighteenth-century readers were familiar.

Influence

Certain assumptions about influence need to be challenged. Epistolary fiction and letter-manuals are commonly invoked as landmarks for eighteenth-century letter-writing practices. On matrimonial correspondence, for instance, Amanda Vickery proposes 'formal models in letter-writing manuals and epistolary fiction abounded', although she concedes 'the mechanism by which a literary ideal informs private writing, the much touted "intertextuality" of literary studies, is notoriously difficult to substantiate.'[45] Indeed, and one critical trap to beware is the assumption that letters are influenced by exclusively by other letters. The influence of drama is important, especially concerning ideas of character,[46] and in ways we might not expect: the elegant letters of one sexually notorious woman were explained as the result of her childhood reading of songs and storybooks, and adult reading of tragedies and newspapers.[47] Moreover, 'influence' is often assumed to be that of print acting on script, whereas the reverse was also true. As I discuss in Chapter 1, manuals were not homogenous: descriptive as well as prescriptive, many of them anthologised letters not written with manuals in mind. The line between manuals and fiction was not hard and fast, since manuals offered readers many 'letters of a type that they would never themselves have to write'.[48] Chartier concludes that manuals offered 'a type of reading that, in the vast majority of cases, could hardly have been motivated by its practical utility'.[49] This is a useful corrective to the idea that letter-writers followed manuals like literate sheep. Manuals had some influence on correct forms of address and discourses of politeness, but epistolary proprieties were learnt more from fellow-correspondents. Many letter-writers kept up extensive and varied correspondences; young adults had the duty of writing to elders; low-status kin had the duty of writing to those higher up the pecking order.[50] The influence of ordinary correspondents on each other was just as important as anything they read in a book.

'Influence' is a game of two halves: writers have to want to use a certain model and readers have to want to receive it. At the start of the eighteenth century, an aesthetic of imitation gave more weight to influence whereas by the later eighteenth century, anxiety about the implications of copying had created an aesthetic in which originality was valued much more by the culture at large and literature in particular.[51] 'Influence' is also localised: as I discuss in Chapter 3, women who received love-letters were not impressed if they thought a suitor had consulted an academy of compliments or a manual. Of course a suitor could have done so undetected – 'influence' can look like originality to those not making certain connections. To make a connection between manuals and impoverished expression may be tactical – was it not better to suggest a lover had taken advice from a book than indiscreetly from his friends? Later in the eighteenth century, women seem to have minded derivation less (ironically, given emphasis elsewhere on originality); lovers who borrowed sentiments at least showed imagination in their reading.[52]

Fiction also imitated real correspondences in important ways. The complexities of origins are evident in the case of Elizabeth Rowe's popular *Letters Moral and Entertaining in Prose and Verse* (1733–4) which put romance signatures to its letters and was read by letter-writers of both sexes who gave themselves and their friends romance names.[53] This custom was around in the seventeenth century, although Rowe's book may have started the practice for some and sanctioned it for others. But more interesting than questions of influence are questions of function: why did people use personae and in texts we would think of as fiction (Rowe) and non-fiction (the familiar letter)? As Elizabeth Heckendorn Cook argues, 'studies of eighteenth-century epistolarity must begin by rejecting an anachronistic distinction between literatures of fact and fiction'.[54] The popularity of personae among women writing epistles in prose and poetry both before and after Rowe's *Letters* suggests gender played a role although as I discuss in Chapters 5 and 6, personae had important uses for men too. Recognising the interdependence of different kinds of letters leads to a literary history not limited to simplistic stories of influence.

Thomas Beebee's adoption of the term 'genealogies' is useful here, since it offers a metaphor of multiple relatedness, whilst allowing a place for chronology in how those relations are organised.[55] To foreground manuals and fiction as resources puts other important texts in the shade. The Bible under-pinned not only pastoral epistles of comfort and exhortation but also less obvious forms of letter-writing like business correspondence.[56] As I discuss in Chapter 4, errant wives deployed Christian rhetoric for supplication and forgiveness, making Milton their model, not manuals. Letters that chronicled marital breakdown also drew on the less literary discourse of legal depositions.[57] Critics need to be careful not to assume eighteenth-century readers read what we read now, or read it in the same way: giving letters a 'source' turns texts into routes of water which necessarily have a single origin and always flow downhill. If nothing else, this metaphor can hardly be appropriate for an age given to building canals.

Letters, canons and authors

Reconsidering influence leads to reconsidering the canon. It is an axiom of this book that things are not important just because 'important' people say them. Besides, since most letters explicitly acknowledge an addressee, critics should also be asking, important to whom? Rather than subscribe to the notion of literary 'value' to make selection of texts supposedly self-evident, one should remember that writers who are part of the literary canon now were not necessarily the letter-writers read at the time. For example, the young women in the West Country whose reading is ably reconstructed by Marjorie Reeves did read Pope's poetry and may have known his letters, but they refer much more to the published letters of Elizabeth Rowe, Mary Jones and Lady Rachel Russell, all of which they read, and to the as yet unpublished correspondence of Anna Seward, known to them as the friend of a friend. The one who read Sterne's letters felt moved to respond in the voice of his correspondent Eliza, not Sterne's own, which one might characterise as a negative influence.[58] Likewise, Pope's letters were widely instanced by familiar letter-writers as an example of artifice that they wished to avoid.

The immense quantity and diversity of eighteenth-century letters call into question the status of canonical authors as canonical letter-writers. Post-structuralism has provided a theoretical basis for preferring 'writing' or 'text' to 'literature', because it sidesteps politically contentious ideologies of value; feminism, new historicism, cultural materialism and postcolonialism have shown compellingly that literature is not the preserve of the literary as was once understood. The long shadow of an author-figure persists in epistolary criticism, however. One reason is the dominance of familiar correspondence, in which templates of the author as subject and subject as author are mutually reinforcing. In familiar letters in the eighteenth century, literary value was less important than pleasure, expressed as value-for-money. The simple index of epistolary worth was whether a correspondent had been sufficiently pleased by a letter to warrant paying postage for it.[59] On this count letter-writers expressed anxiety to the point of perversity, like the correspondent of Thomas Percy who apologised at length for sending him a long and therefore expensive letter.[60] Politeness had a price, sometimes too high: 'Your confounded epistle cost me seven pence; deuce take you, why did you not enclose it?'[61] Although possibly as many as one in six letters were franked, which cost the recipient nothing, and the rich, the poor and the impatient sent letters by various kinds of messenger,[62] it is perhaps surprising that labouring-class people found money for letters they could ill afford.[63] Those sacrifices are one reason to bear them in mind as letter-writers.

Foucault argued that a letter 'may well have a signer – it does not have an author', a provocative assertion which becomes less controversial in the context of eighteenth-century letters using personae.[64] Letters to newspapers now come with a full name and verifiable address; then, they avoided 'real' names. A significant proportion of eighteenth-century letters concerning politics were written under cover of a pseudonymous signature – famously unattributable even now in the case of Junius, discussed in Chapter 5. A preference for signature in certain contexts did not wholly lay to rest a desire for an author – some readers were desperate to know who Junius was. That the writer kept his (or her) secret so well suggests he perceived an authorial name to be an obstacle to discursive effectiveness: being pseudonymous was more authoritative. Generic identities were tolerated in eighteenth-century writings (more so than in any other period) which suggests readers were commonly interested in what was said and accepted some vagueness as to who said it. Many letters in print signalled their cultural place through markers of gender, class and geography with little or no reference to personal names. One should not overestimate that vagueness: to say ' "A letter to a friend" was a vehicle for anything in print' is true, but omits to mention the importance of other information often present.[65] 'A Letter from a Gentleman in Town to a Friend in the Country', for instance, was a common formula, used variously as a free-standing title, or a subtitle attached to a persona or occasionally to a real name. It diffused authorship into class, gender and urbanity; it identified a relationship, friendship, which was dialogic and sympathetic, and established a direction, the country, which was social and political.[66] Writers took pains over titles and genres that were not lost on readers; the choice of one convention over another is significant. By casting his *Reflections on the Revolution in France* (1790) in the form of a letter, Burke invoked expectations of openness and selectivity that added a layer of meaning to his subject. Collapsing different kinds of letters into the portmanteau term 'pamphlet' throws away discursive significances. Since many texts use genre precisely, why should we prefer the imprecision of 'pamphlet'?[67]

The locations of town and country were not necessarily opposites, especially for an élite class who moved between them regularly, but they gave authors different kinds of authority. Metropolitan writers informed or performed for country readers, and country correspondents showed by reciprocal refinement that interestedness was a state of mind independent of place. Town supplied *ton*, though city sophistication was linked to artifice and crime. All sorts of variations were explored: rural innocence, rustic ignorance, pastoral bliss and retirement. The relativity of these categories underpinned Tobias Smollett's study of mobile provincialism in *The Expedition of Humphry Clinker* (1771) and the influential figure of Sylvanus Urban who presided over *The Gentleman's Magazine*.[68] Symbolic of relations between nature and culture, the town–country relationship functioned like signature.[69] Its significance is lost when letters are considered only through authors.

Perhaps the most numerous kind of printed letter was the letter of theological controversy: even I have occasionally sighed as I opened yet another volume of dogged letters penned by a country curate.[70] Many of these did give names on their title pages, often followed by the writer's parish or, in the case of disputatious dons, their university position. As usual in eighteenth-century letters, this information was strategic: it signalled rank in an intellectual hierarchy or physical location in a patronage network. But this information was supplementary: doggedness, which might win the day, showed what discourse could do regardless of the writer's non-standing as an author. A country curate may seem a diminutive figure to oppose to the might of canonical authors like Pope or Swift, but our ignorance of him is at least one point in his favour.

Since letters call canonicity into question, they support an argument for literature from below, like history from below. Letters are material evidence in the case for expanding our comprehension of what counts as 'literary'. Academic interest in correspondence has been tied to authors; this is not quite the same as investment in the canon and bears some examination. Merrill Decker suggests academics turn correspondence into editions as a way of avoiding the hagiographic tendencies of a nineteenth-century genre of lives and letters. The impersonality of an editor gets round the question of value: we do not ask, what are we reading these letters for, because they come so expensively packaged the question is almost unthinkable.[71]

Apparent neutrality cloaks questions of gender, except that to feminist scholars it is a fig-leaf ill-concealing the fact that fewer eighteenth-century women have had their correspondence treated to lavish editions. Consider the case of Samuel Johnson. Two academic editions of his correspondence within fifty years confirm him as canonical author and therefore canonical letter-writer – ironically, given that Johnson disliked letter-writing and preferred to talk.[72] Decker argues that

> our own period's letter volumes derive much of their aesthetic fascination from their status as texts that say 'I'... letter-volumes preserve the idea of writing as something that emanates from a single consciousness, an author... even as they encourage a view of the letter exchange as inter-textual and multi-authorial.[73]

Feminist theory has many ways to account for why women are not supposed to be able to say 'I', which explain their under-representation. To use letters to promote authors has some advantages and many risks if editions are not linked to expansive readings of correspondence.

The history of letter-reading shows that authors were not the exclusive point of interest for eighteenth-century readers of familiar letters. Swift praised Sir William Temple as an epistolary author because he varied his style according to his addressee, 'either Men of Business, or Idle; of Pleasure, or Serious; of great or of less parts or Abilities, in their several Stations. So, that, one may discover, the Characters of most of those Persons, he writes to, from the Stile of his Letters.'[74] As I discus in Chapter 7, others read for historical pleasures, finding letters descriptive of the manners of an age (including their own). One important discourse was that of gossip, a discourse in which what is said is usually more important than who said it.[75] The letters of literary men and occasionally women were read for how they illuminated the writer in relation to the person – so readers were dissatisfied with Pope's letters because they seemed to draw attention to their writerliness. Important here were tropes of dress: letters were thought of as a kind of dishabille. Sprat refused to allow his collection of Cowley's letters to be published on the grounds that letters showed an author in a state of undress which the public should not see.[76] The conceit was an old one – Pliny used it – but remarkably durable amongst literati throughout the eighteenth century, from Farquhar in his stockings to Hester Thrale corresponding with Charles Burney in his robe de chambre.[77] In later centuries, the smoking-jacket and the housecoat served as sartorial expressions of this state of relaxation; the metaphor depends for some of its effect on a class-specific wardrobe. It may also have been resonant for authors because of a particular chain of associations that connected Locke's idea of language as the dress of thought to paper itself, which in the eighteenth century was made of rags. Divesting themselves of clothes and literary responsibilities through metaphors of epistolary undress, literary people thus expressed ambivalence about whether letters were a kind of writing outside the canon. It is after all quite a pose to draw attention to what you are not wearing as a writer. No wonder then the trope turns up in the letters of that celebrated author who had himself painted in professionally informal headgear.[78]

The politics of authorship in the eighteenth century, then, mean that would-be authors projected an idea of familiar letters as informal, intimate and spontaneous. Familiar correspondents were people you let in when you were not 'at home' to others, as opposed to more formal visits which were the equivalent of the letter of duty. Select conviviality ran like a watermark through polite society; letter-writers naturalised it through a discourse of ease and expressive language. The flip side was that those who were seen as outside polite society were characterised as writing letters that fell short of ease or expressiveness. When a seriously disturbed sea-captain bombarded the port of Arbroath, his unusual way of ending letters confirmed him as a social misfit (in case there was any doubt).[79]

A familiar text was also a plain one and letters shared plain discourse with other writings. William Cole's *A Key to the Psalms* (1788), for instance, advertised itself as 'an easy, concise, and familiar explanation of words, allusions and sentences in them...for the information of the lower class of people in particular'. Plainness increased ambiguities surrounding the literariness of letters, though it also strengthened the relationship between print culture and the lower classes, women and children to whom many such familiar texts were addressed. Associated with instruction, familiar genres became an important means of women addressing women and women writing for a juvenile audience especially in the later eighteenth century. Locke's conceit of the mind as a blank page upon which knowledge was inscribed made letters an enabling medium for women; as they filled up sheets through letter-writing, they showed their own minds were not blanks. The lesser status of letters also made them appropriate for those texts by women that, in different respects, argued for less ambitious roles for women.[80] Thus letters had liminal meanings for those in power and powerful meanings for liminal people.

People we might assume had little connection with the arts of letter-writing, such as ostlers, valets, servants, soldiers, sailors, all wrote letters, including letters which found their way into print. Actual letters co-existed in complex ways with imaginary letters written for the less literate by authors in the marketplace. Some imaginary letters fused literary discourse with an occupational discourse, for instance in specialist courtship letters which featured lovers making vows in the language of their employments. These are as much simulation as parody, so perhaps not quite a mock-genre, though the jokes are ingenious, turning on characters both well known and unfamiliar, like a schoolmaster and an oilman's apprentice, Jeremy Olive, surely related to Smollett's Peregrine Pickle who appeared in 1751. Swift's punning letter on the death of a punster was a rarefied example.[81] Fusing author-function with discourse-function, the character can only ever write in an occupation-specific language, which is entertaining but not socially adept enough to count as polite. Letters were a means of qualifying for polite society providing they were literary enough or followed the right forms. As Alain Boureau has noted, paradoxically one mark of distinction in letter-writing is to be able to ignore those formulae which manuals recommend as best practice. High and low discourses touched through a culture of politeness that needed them yet wanted to replace them.[82] To look only at individuated authors, especially those already in the canon, is to miss all this.

Adding women one by one to a canon also prevents discussion of the gendered politics of epistolary authorship. Hester Thrale's invitation to Charles Burney to be casual in his correspondence, 'as when you shut the Blinds to, & sate with me in your Wrapper', does not explicitly invoke a metaphor of undress for herself:[83] the discourse of relaxation particular to authorship is normally understood as the prerogative of men. The importance of letters for women writers was not restricted to fiction, nor even to familiar correspondence: women used epistolary form in varied ways for purposes of argument and play, alongside genres like essays and dialogues. Many *Miscellanies* published by women writers included letters, and many educational writings by women for women and girls were epistolary, defining both the proper lady and the woman writer through her letter-writing. But the distinct ways in which women used letters should not be seen in terms of a separatist literary history: although there is an epistolary version of what Catherine Gallagher describes as 'the reciprocal shaping of the terms "woman," "author," and "marketplace"',[84] the literary history of letters involves both sexes.

In doing away with canons as much as possible, I want to throw out the authorial baby and recycle the biographical bathwater. Rather than see letters only as the productions of authors, I stress fluid relations between writer, text and recipient. The history of manners and emotions are as relevant to understanding letters as any knowledge of authorial personality. Conversely, historical readings alone do not always account for the literary appeal of letters, which turns in part on the magnetism of a first-person medium. As Amanda Gilroy and Wil Verhoeven rightly observe, 'The most historically powerful fiction of the letter has been that which figures it as the trope of authenticity and intimacy.'[85] Critics of letters in biography and fiction tend to surrender gladly to the siren call of authors, without considering enough how illusions of intimacy are achieved through following conventions as much as flouting them. For instance, tropes of writing from the heart, explored in Chapter 3, are not signs of transparency; instead they are an impersonal rhetoric that fictionalises transparency deep within the body, so deep that very conveniently it cannot be examined except through its manifestation on the surfaces of paper. Quite how and why tropes like this became popular to the point of cliché, then discarded, are questions that space precludes me from following, but it shows how a study of letters through authors can obfuscate an understanding of patterns of epistolary discourse. The story-telling that best illuminates letters uses biography as a means not an end.

The power of examples

Generalisations become facile when they depend on too few particularities. As Lawrence Klein has argued, 'when...people are not found doing what the "theory" says they are supposed to do, an important question becomes: "what is the 'theory' of the actual practice?"'[86] A brake on runaway theory is valuable, but one should also see that in practice 'actual practice' is often plural. Reading for what E.P. Thompson amusingly calls 'the approved yes-words and boo-words of the time' we too often discard what does not fit just because it does not fit our assumptions.[87] Arguments about woods go wrong when they depend upon too small a sample and indifference to the particularity of trees.[88] Increasing the range of a sample can change results, and this book's commitment to wider reading in the field of eighteenth-century letters proves it contained greater diversity than has hitherto been addressed. Most of the canonical authors associated with letter-writing are discussed somewhere in this book but they are not my main concern. Instead I want to stress the extraordinary range of correspondence in the period and to show it by means of writers of whom few people will have heard – including myself until I went looking – and to stress this is still the tip of an iceberg.

We also need to be attentive to differences between and within individual texts if our readings are not to be imprisoned by the yes-words and boo-words of our own time. Hence this book's commitment to close reading as well as wide reading, taking up Klein's proposal that we pay more attention to language. As E.P. Thompson argued with reference to the history of ideas, 'one cause of misunderstanding has been an insufficiently close attention to the actual lived historical experience'.[89] If the strength of cultural history lies in its explanation of practices at a local level,[90] then literary criticism should allow a single text to have singularities and give space to discussing them. To do so is not the same as a liberal humanist return to reading the individuality of lives through letters because it unsettles ideas of a continuous human nature and insists on social forces in discourse and on the plurality of history. Another way to describe this is to say the process of approving 'yes-words and boo-words' is uneven; outcomes are not universal or consistent and such words do not always mean the same thing to their supporters and detractors.

The many examples I use are not all examples of the same thing, though they may be part of the same debate. If some of these occasions of debate seem prosaic, it is partly because the letter is the literary form *par excellence* of the everyday. Borrowing from Anthony Giddens' notion of 'practical consciousness', what Klein describes as 'the pragmatic sensitivity to place and occasion' is particularly relevant to letters, whose composition enfolds place and occasion.[91] I think it should also be extended to people: letters carry affect and what they articulate is not discourse but discourse which is meaningful to particular people at particular places on particular occasions. This meaningfulness is not located exclusively in a letter-writer or in correspondents; it can be made or contested by outside parties. Where letters were produced as evidence in trials, the meanings determined led in many cases to the death of the writer. The cases of Mary Blandy and others analysed in Chapter 4 show ideologies of classification at work in interpretations of letters, in which individuals suffered fatal effects from not conforming to societal expectations (or in the case of those defined as belonging to a criminal class, conforming too well). 'Hanging, even a hanging 200 years old, is a powerful subject' wrote Peter Linebaugh, noting 'the eighteenth-century historian needs sources of information that are as particular as the things of the eighteenth century and as concrete as the labouring history of eighteenth-century persons'.[92] Such tragedies need close reading to tease out the particularity of people's stories and epistolary histories.

Letters, sex and gender

Powerful associations exist between women and letter-writing. In the eighteenth century, as I discuss in Chapter 1, women who wrote familiar letters were figures of epistolary contradiction, simultaneously lauded as 'naturally better' writers and disparaged as naturally disorderly. It is this mixed story I want to promote, in which gendering is tactical and hence shifting. It is a story that was put about in various ways – in texts exchanged between men, in texts addressed to women that purported to teach them how to be natural, in texts by women that claimed attention. A woman writing a letter symbolises modern subjectivity, gender, even theory itself, and the scene of her writing has been linked to histories of privacy, publicity, specularity, print culture, fiction and the body.[93] 'The woman writing the letter is the figure with the power to turn allegory into myth', as Carolyn Steedman has argued.[94] These symbolic relations are constant and yet variable: the letter-writing woman of the eighteenth century gave way to the letter-receiving woman of the nineteenth. Both subjects attracted painters, expressing fascination with and fear of an imaginative world that can absorb women. The act of looking functions as a visual equivalent to that metaphor of eavesdropping used by critics as a means of confirming their own subject boundaries, as a frame does. The positioning of paper is also suggestive: the letter held above her lap, the book resting on her knees makes text and erotic body contingent. But is this the only story?

Women are even more prone to attracting generalisations than letters, which makes the letter-writing woman a harder figure to qualify. Her story is bound up with fiction, especially amatory and sentimental fiction, and the heroic epistle, and both of these have an important place in literary history.[95] But that importance has been inflated to block out other kinds of letter-writing women. Entranced by fiction that fetishised letters as substitutes for and extensions of women's bodies, to be seized, caressed, possessed, violated, critics see only erotic relations between letters and women's bodies. Especially in early eighteenth-century fiction, women and nature, letters and privacy, combined formulaically to express sincerity and passion which was artless yet half-concealed. That tension between concealment and disclosure was manifested through plots of clandestine correspondence and bodies negligently dressed. The two were linked through the key word 'betrayal' which in the classic *portugaise* version of this story is both what men do to women and what women's emotions do to themselves (and hence of interest to writers of both sexes). In reality, especially around the mid-century, paradigms of feminine passion taken from fiction were deployed in legal contexts in which the reputations of women were raked over in public, although since truth could be stranger than fiction, these paradigms were also shown to be fiction precisely because they did not fit lived experience. Yet precise interpretations were often not what emerged from contestations in court. Ambiguities abounded especially in cases like Mary Blandy's, discussed in Chapter 4. Some fictions, like Richardson's *Clarissa*, had strong paralegal components that engaged with interpretative complexity; often written by men, these stories were both critical of and complicit with stereotypes.[96]

To loosen heterosexuality's grip on the story of letters, some critical effort has been expended on finding equivalent epistolary outlets for homosexuality.[97] This expands the erotic frame but risks replacing one object with another. More interesting would be a consideration of how love was paired with business in the eighteenth century in a binary we overlook due to our own investments in romance. The link applied to both sexes: at least one male prostitute carried form assignation letters.[98] These were 'so contrived that they may either pass for a begging letter of a man in distress, or to offer his person for the basest purposes'.[99] Desiring women were able to say 'I', however much in relation to 'you' – indeed desire makes an excess of 'I'. In contrast, the letters of women of business at the time were said to cut short the first person.[100] Why? Countless correspondences show how women on the marriage market were of necessity also business women; no wonder fiction fictionalised them otherwise.[101]

Criticism's preference for the sexual body ignores alternatives that were important in the period, especially medical constructions of the body. It was still common practice in the eighteenth century for doctors to diagnose by correspondence,[102] and familiar letter-writers testified to the body's sickness as much as its sexuality. Many letters were dictated by people unable to see or too ill to write and the presence of amanuenses for the sick should remind us of less-publicised ways in which letters were mediated by auditors and scribes. The commonest excuse for lapses in familiar correspondence, sickness, gave meaning to letters: they were proofs of continued existence. Those with cure of souls also looked after bodies: many of the letter-writing ministers I discuss in Chapter 8 gave advice on health matters.[103] Letters from grateful patients helped professionalise medicine[104] and published examples were used to sell remedies in a form of advertising that has lasted to the present. Familiar letters gave women a place to discuss matters related to pregnancy, childbirth and motherhood,[105] but their role in articulating the health concerns of both sexes should complicate our fixation on the healthily desiring body. Many letter-writers pathologised their epistolary productiveness: if an 'itch for scribbling' had been a medical condition, it would have displaced gout as the archetypal eighteenth-century complaint.

It has been rightly observed that 'we forget the writing man'[106] and it is important to return him to that scene of writing which has been relentlessly feminised. One of the fictions of fiction is its presentation of the letter as metonym for a gendered private body. Here binaries proceed together, like animals into the ark: manuscript and print, feminine and masculine, private and public, or, in a subtler variation, the opposite of the feminised private body is assumed to be an ungendered public body, achieved through the decorporealising medium of print.[107] Print did not decorporealise masculinity: the citizen-critic of the republic of letters was often involved in fights in which masculinity was ever-present, and which led to men's bodies being hurt, indeed fatally penetrated, in fights which spilled off the page into duels or riots. As I discuss in Chapter 6, political letter-writing used discourses of embodiment in very particular ways. In campaigns against excise, for instance, the masculine British subject inviolate in his house was a key figure of resistance. Even where citizens used personae, which could be seen as dematerialising body into signature, traces of gender remained. 'Cato' was one of many figures with a possible sexual history. Even personae using platonic abstraction, like Philoclericus, carried associations of homosociality that allied them with social bodies of men, like clerics.[108]

Men's bodies can also be returned to letters through letters to children that advised boys as well as girls on the management of their bodies – as I discuss in Chapter 2 on parental letters of advice. In letters of advice, women shared with men a gender-neutral role of parent. There are also important areas of eighteenth-century culture in which the bodies of both sexes could be suspended: literally, in capital punishment, discussed in Chapter 4, and figuratively, in the world of spiritual experience, discussed in Chapter 8. Men and women who were 'saints of the writing desk'[109] shared equal exemplary power when writing as Christians. If gender mattered more within a denomination, class perhaps mattered more to those outside it. Women have been notably absent from critical discussions of eighteenth-century religious literature despite writing religious letters in abundance; their spiritual labours provide another point from which to critique the erotic body.[110] The body politics of religion for seventeenth-century women have been widely discussed in relation to prophecy and fasting, but hardly at all in relation to eighteenth-century women, as if the rise of the novel put religion out of women's heads as well as critics' heads.

In all these directions, one sees ways to explore the significance of bodies, sex and gender without resorting to clichés about women letter-writers taken only from fiction. What is more, 'the body' is a generalisation that hides the way particular parts of the body had symbolic functions in different areas of eighteenth-century culture. Letter-writing was an important means of making this come about, as it crossed in and out of print, and between high and low discourses. So in evangelical writings one finds the mouth is important; in political writings, the arse. Love privileges the eye, hand and skin; travel the eye and nose. My readings take up these concerns as they appear in letters. I do not claim all letters of a sub-genre show such privileging, but I propose more specific arguments about 'the body' that lead away from a body defined reductively through sex or gender.

Letters, conversations and circular arguments

It was commonplace in the eighteenth century to compare familiar letter-writing to conversation and it has become commonplace to cite such comparisons in order to highlight epistolary ideals of ease, mutuality and politeness. It has also been normal to accept the comparison at face value.[111] There is more to it than first appears. First, the face was a symbolic part of the body. 'A Letter should wear an honest, cheerful countenance, like one who truly esteems, and is glad to see his Friend': the sincere, good-natured face was supposedly legibly so.[112] Many commentators wanted this transparency for letters. Second, letters were compared to talk and reading was compared to talking.[113] Talk, however, was not compared to letters. If familiar letter-writing was so like polite conversation, why did that likeness not come to mind when people were talking?[114] In fact talking could involve writing: some advisers on the subject of conversation recommended preparing topics by writing them down beforehand. In the eighteenth century, people wrote things down as never before – journals, letters, memoranda books were in widespread use and one of their possible functions was to record and resupply conversation. For some, reading was a kind of conversation. So writing and reading were already potential precursors to talk, which at least complicates the idea of talk as a form of spontaneity that letter-writers wanted to match.[115] Conversation and correspondence shared some obvious features, such as articulation and turn-taking; they both also accommodated argument. 'A little friendly Opposition is the Life of Conversation'.[116] Beyond that we come up against what George Steiner has called 'the difficult question of the degree to which written forms ever codify the speech milieu in which they are composed'.[117] Boswell's accounts of Johnson's conversation give us some idea of how Johnson spoke but he stressed they fell short in significant ways and it is debatable whether Johnson can represent 'polite' practice. Lennard J. Davis has listed ways in which written speech differs from actual conversation – omitting silences, fillers, body language; making tempo and intonation more even than they really are; downplaying negotiations of turn-taking.[118] Davis stresses these differences reduce the anxiety of actual conversation, though I believe letter-writing retains some of that anxiety in its penchant for apologies: writers aver their letters are too short, too long, too scrawled, too dull, too anything but just right. Since we cannot really know how eighteenth-century people spoke, to assume eighteenth-century people spoke as they wrote, using letters as evidence, is a circular argument.

Two points move the argument on. One is that the comparison of letter-writing to conversation was almost always made by the writer not the recipient. True, recipients became writers in their turn, but the comparison comes out of a writer's self-consciousness, not a reader's. Writing was theorised as talking much more than reading as listening, even though letters were read aloud in homes, churches and chapels.[119] The prevalence of the idiom in familiar letters may be affected by the way leisured people had the luxury of closets in which they could write silently and alone. But they also often wrote familiar letters in company, with the writer trying not to listen to surrounding conversations.[120] My second point is that writers who describe their letters as conversational often follow it with an evocation of the recipient's presence – thus Fanny Boscawen, writing to her husband in 1748: 'I chat with you, my dear love, as if you could answer me.'[121] The conversational idiom is tied to a fantasy that the addressee will surmount absence: the point is not informality or spontaneity for their own sakes but how they enable a trope for voice. Initially, correspondence seems to dematerialise bodies, that is, letters substitute for the person of a writer who would have a physical presence in conversation. Eighteenth-century writers' liking for tropes of voice through the image of conversation can be seen as a way of dealing with the body's imperfect disappearance in letters. In face-to-face conversation, bodies are present and communicative; body language is its non-verbal adjunct. In letters, bodies are absent but they can have a phantom presence if the writer represents writing as conversation, in which voice acts as a half-way point between body and consciousness. Different writers took this up differently. Early eighteenth-century writers imagined letters from the dead to the living.[122] Later writers bypassed body language by ascribing vocal powers to the heart, as I discuss in Chapter 3 in relation to Sterne's letters to Eliza Draper. The trope also featured in evangelical letters.[123] The conversational model pressed the question of how to make intrinsically monologic letters fit into dialogue, which conversation evoked with ease:

> I never sit down to write, but I see you placed on the opposite side of the
> table, and suppose that we are just talking over the transactions of the

day; and without your presence to animate me, how is it possible that I could have had patience to write these enormous epistles?[124]

Familiar letters found ways to symbolise body language because ease was an issue in that kind of letter. Politeness offered analogous management of bodies, yet not everybody was comfortable with its formality. So William Cowper remarked on the effort required from conversationalists and letter-writers:

> As two Men sit Silent after having exhausted all their Topics of Conversation, One says, It is very fine Weather, and the other says, Yes. One Blows his Nose, and the other Rubs his Eyebrow, (by the way this is very much in Homer's Manner). Such seems to be the Case between you and me. After a Silence of some Days, I wrote you a long Something that I suppose was nothing to the Purpose, because it has not afforded you Materials for an Answer. Nevertheless, as it often happens in the case above stated, One of the distressed Parties being deeply sensible of the aukwardness of a dumb Duette, breaks Silence again, and resolves to Speak though he have nothing to Say, so it fares with me – I am with you again in the Form of an Epistle....[125]

The paradigm of politeness was powerful yet should not be assumed to be powerfully uniform – Chapters 5 and 8, on citizens and Christians, especially overturn analogies between letters and conversation by focusing on exchanges that were unequivocally shouting matches. In political letter-writing, theological debate and other forms of argument, rudeness was often allowed.

Face-to-face talk between a small number of people was not the only way eighteenth-century conversations took place. Bluestocking gatherings involved people seated in a large circle and one way of describing intellectual networks is through circles.[126] The circle was an important part of eighteenth-century public socialising, from the Ring in Hyde Park to the Pantheon. Whether in two- or three-dimensional forms, many of these circles involved time and space, like watch faces and clock dials, tours, globes and orrerys, to list just a few. The introduction of round tables for tea-taking and card-playing suggests how sociability made the circle a congenial form; it also suggests how people could join or leave a circle without necessarily breaking up conversations. The circle is a good metaphor for the circulation of letters, encompassing how familiar letters were passed around groups; how some letters were distributed (in the postman's round); how individual writers like John Wesley could function as epistolary epicentres, their letters rippling out across the country, and how groups who had never met could talk to each other, through the corresponding societies of the late eighteenth century which created and joined up circles of people. 'The image of the individual reader participating in an expanding national conversation – facilitated by print – was crucial for the reform societies.'[127] In conjunction with the straight lines of roads that saw common traffic of handwritten and printed letters, circles gave shape to the expansion of print culture and the conversations it enabled.

Character

'Who does one become when one writes a letter?'[128] And who does one become when one *reads* a letter? Conversation is performative and so are letters. With some reservations, discussed in my postscript, one can describe epistolary performances as self-fashioning and link them to that popular form of dressing up in the eighteenth century, the masquerade.[129] The subscriptive personae of many public and some familiar letters are like masquerade costumes; the connection is especially obvious in the case of Horace Walpole who loved a masquerade and used subscriptive personae wittily to underscore a theme.[130] Masqueraders had degrees of dressing up, and their masks, fancy dress and full character costumes supply parallels to the self-fashioning, role-playing and personations of epistolary writings.[131] Gay wrote to the Blount sisters in the persona of a horse; Catherine Howard corresponded with Swift in the character (and diagonal manner of writing) of a Lilliputian courtier.[132] Queen Anne and Sarah Churchill, Duchess of Marlborough, corresponded as Morley and Mrs Freeman.[133] Pseudonyms and personae were especially deployed in public writings where disguise was expedient, for instance in cases of whistle-blowing on corruption.

Letters offered a spectrum of performance. Deidre Shauna Lynch has pointed out that 'character' could be said to be an eighteenth-century invention; as 'devices for thinking about typicality', characters were important in both fiction and non-fiction.[134] In the words of one author, 'there is nothing that expresses a man's particular character more fully, than his intimate letters to his friends'.[135] His remark should not be taken to imply a notion of unmediated interiority. Quite the opposite: Hervey denoted the *particular* character, because eighteenth-century readers understood that character is found, in Lynch's phrase, 'at the interface of what is particular and what is general'. Expressed in material and literary forms, connecting polite and popular culture, character was also quintessentially part of English culture.[136] As Paul Langford observes, 'The English character was indeed a character, much more than it was ever a physical type.'[137] Part of character's attraction may have been precisely because it was a kind of act. 'It is much more difficult to converse with the World in a real than a personated Character', observed Steele,[138] but character supplied a common model for real people and fictional creation.[139] Identity was understood less in terms of psychological depth, and more through typologies of class, sex, nation, age, occupation, region, religion and the like. These may be refracted through occasion and location, which letters helpfully stress, making that active correspondent the Gentleman in Town not as bland as he first appears. 'Character' also provides landmarks in individual development and social change. It explains how the same person has different roles – how the adult may be a parent, for instance, discussed in Chapter 2.

The characters around whom this book is organised were important ones in the eighteenth century, representative and recognisable to many writers and readers. Any letter-writer can be read in terms of more than one character and the characters are open to any letter-writer, including ones not discussed in this book. The idea of character allows focused discussion of a wide range of ordinary, anonymous and pseudonymous letter-writers. It also gives a fresh perspective on the letters of 'great writers' and 'great letter-writers' by creating new awareness of discourses relevant to their letters. For example, the significance of religion for William Cowper is well known: it tends to be read as Calvinism or spiritual distress at God's abandoning him.[140] But evangelical Christians had particular conventions for articulating spiritual distress: a suffering soul used letters to cry out. Christian correspondents understood that cry in a particular way, as I discuss in Chapter 8, showing how correspondence was an active part of ministries. Cowper's delicate, self-conscious invocations of epistolary etiquette appear in a new light as one effect of trying to reconcile politeness with a rawness sanctioned in religious letter-writing.

The history of letters links up with other genres. For the traveller, journals were as important as letters; for the Christian, prayers and sermons; for the criminal, life-stories; for the citizen, newspapers. I have little space to explore these connections, but my insistence on the importance of letters in eighteenth-century culture should not be taken as indifference to other genres. Boundaries are not always clear anyway: so the letter-journal was a well-known hybrid, or more properly, the letter explicitly written over several separate occasions and posted at regular intervals is a sub-genre in itself, what Frances Burney jokingly called 'Weekals' rather than 'Annals'.[141] Letters were printed with poetry, dialogues, essays, songs, even dances, suggesting they partnered poetry's power of invocation, dialogue's play of ideas, the essay's capacity for reflection, music's harmony and vivacity.[142] The intersection of character with genre provides a narrative structure which breaks up an assumption that familiar letters or fictional letters are more important than other kinds of letters, or that the familiar letter is the *ur*-genre from which all others derive. Precisely because these kinds of letters have occupied the limelight for literary critics, I give less space to them in this book. Nor am I interested in stories of origins and expiry of the genre.[143] This book pays minimal attention to beginnings and ends of kinds of letters, preferring instead to concentrate on the story of the middle – how letters worked, who wrote them, the ways they circulated, the meanings they mediated.

The claims I wish to make for the usefulness of my schema, however, go further than its cultural representativeness and organisational convenience. The idea of character defies the critical mantra of race, class, gender and sexuality whilst accommodating readings sensitive to those categories.

It provides a form of identity politics that avoids some of its traps. Nancy K. Miller has argued that

'if identity politics has challenged bourgeois self-representations – with all its unself-conscious exclusions – speaking "as a" has emerged as an equally problematic *representivity'* ... How can any one individual – with all the eccentricity life affords each human being – possibly represent a group so heterogenous as, say, African-American women or Asian-American men, even when these composite categories hide multifaceted variants?[144]

My schema represents texts not human beings and the point of this book is to trace their eccentricities as much as their representativeness. The concept of character stresses that texts and people have disjunct as well as overlapping identities. Indeed, one of the attractions of epistolary form in the eighteenth century was that it gave writers the opportunity to imagine themselves into different personae and personae of difference. Differences can be internal to a self and relations with others may bring out similarity. Writing 'as a' makes affinity with others temporary, something which only lasts as long as the text or the moment of interpretation. It is also not an identity necessarily claimed by the writer or fixed by the critic. Writing 'as a' can be messy – Samuel Richardson wrote so much as a young lady he could hardly stop – but it is those slippages and overspills that reveal the factors which shaped eighteenth-century letters and our understandings of them. Janet Altman has argued that the eighteenth-century letter in Britain had a special relationship with empiricism, a view borne out by a large number of letters that simply reported on phenomena in a plain style.[145] But although letters had an affinity with news (not a plainly factual discourse, as critics have shown),[146] they also had an affinity with play, argument, wonder and fantasy – a spectrum of discursive colour that was just as important as factuality to eighteenth-century British culture.

Letters have a literary history of their own that is independent of particular practitioners and my selection of characters provides an outline. The device of character is part of a history of outlines which was notably rich in the eighteenth century, from the first paper profile, said to have been cut in 1699,[147] to the silhouette designs of Wedgwood or the bold outlines of caricature. The letter-writer's quill was a tool like the engraver's burin or the embroiderer's needle;[148] the letter was a way of blocking out or marking off a relationship to a subject. Like the sketch with which letters were associated at the end of the century,[149] this relationship was necessarily temporised. Some letters were closely tied to occasions – indeed, letters of condolence or congratulation helped define the occasions which produced them. Other kinds of letters were not, or their occasions were displaced into simple here-and-now, or printed in texts like newspapers and periodicals that had place and date. Even without these markers of imagined communities, letters served a need, if not a purpose, since they were the eighteenth century's most popular genre. One might account for that need by understanding letters as forms of writing which in the eighteenth century were understood to be never far from character. Even the familiar letter of friendship deals in character as it conjoins the character of friend to the subjectivities of 'I' and 'you'. The personal letter outlined subjectivity. That outline was accepted as a workable form of representation and a changeable form of representation. The significance of character – as an inscribed, contested, altered outline – differed according to context, but possible grand narratives about eighteenth-century culture can be seen in terms of how the self was regulated. Enthusiasm, politeness, the sublime, sensibility were all ways of relating to the world which tightened or relaxed the ways self was bounded. Regulation and expression, systole and diastole, were equally well served by epistolary conventions and freedoms.

Directions

What route does this book take? What texts does it address and why? I preface an outline of its contents by remarking that, since chapters are thematically organised, each is freestanding. There is no grand narrative working from start to finish. There is a continuous argument that letters are diverse and important in eighteenth-century culture, as each chapter shows with reference to a particular yet broadly defined area of experience. Demonstrating the importance of letters means taking on board experiences of reading letters as well as writing them and each chapter shows variously how different kinds of letters were read in different contexts, contexts not collapsible into categories of private or public or categories of fact and fiction. Chapters explore a succession of characters across the whole span of the eighteenth century, making one map of letter-writing, independent of other critical boundaries in literary history such as sensibility or romanticism. Indeed it would take another book to explore how letters fit and do not fit literary history built up from other genres.

Nonetheless, there is a chronological unfolding. First, the ordering of the characters. There is a loose progress from people's inception as letter-writers to the personal roles of parents writing to children and lovers writing to each other, to criminals and citizens whose letters were understood in social settings which were especially ideologically defined and contested, to two characters who share an interest in looking at the world – the traveller in terms of place, the historian in terms of time – ending with a character, the Christian, which is personal and social, one committed to trying to square here and now with hereafter. From young life to afterlife, then, my cast of characters broadly covers the several ages of people. All chapters include discussion of women letter-writers; their smaller role in chapters on citizens and historians reflects the difficulties women faced in taking up those characters. A second chronological pattern operates like book-ends. The book starts with attention to early eighteenth-century epistolary practice, casting a look at tendencies carried over from the late seventeenth century; it ends with evangelical material that was important – influential, if you want that story – in the late eighteenth and early nineteenth century. Within each chapter I have tracked characters to places of significance for letter-writing in a round-the-world-of-letters voyage that makes no claim to have put in at every port. I have occasionally reversed chronological order where I think doing so helps accentuate ideological workings of texts independently of historical developments. Besides, letters were not always published or read with chrono-logic.

Chapter 1, 'Learning to Write', starts with a close look at manuals, to argue they were as much descriptive as prescriptive, hence not examples of best practice but examples of actual practice that show how epistolary theory was full of tangles. I follow this with an analysis of tangles around gender, taking up the opinion of many eighteenth-century commentators that women wrote better letters than men, even as they were criticised for being less literate and literary. What manuals do with women's letters contributes to pinning them into categories of nature and national identity. The third section looks at how letters helped to construct 'men of letters', another gendered process complicated by market forces. The homosociality of wits, which I propose as a context for understanding the controversy around the publication of Pope's letters, is compared to the role of letters in making Johnson's life a literary commodity. Chapter 2, 'Writing as a Parent', also opens by arguing for a reconsideration of assumptions about genre and classification. The designation 'conduct literature' erases epistolary form. When you see conduct literature in terms of letters of advice, a picture of eighteenth-century parenting emerges that is more engagingly complex and open-minded than the implied didactic intention and effect of the term conduct literature. I discuss the character in relation to parents and children of both sexes and in relation to discourses about childhood and education in which letter-writing played a practical part. The final section offers a close reading of Chesterfield's letters to his son, his godson and other youths, to suggest his prescriptive advice can be better understood through a parental character that necessarily includes the complications of adult subjectivity.

The character of lover, discussed in Chapter 3, starts by relating amorous discourses in general to love-letters as their particular and privileged vehicle. The material properties of love-letters have been studied in relation to epistolary fiction; I explore them more through the equally wishful form of non-fictional desire. The eighteenth-century's most erotic woman writer was the lovelorn nun, discussed with special reference to the literary character of Eloisa, known not just through a poem by Pope but through translations of her letters and their readers' discussions, especially in the 1760s, fuelled by Rousseau's adaptation of her into his new Héloïse. Eloisas old and new were important points of reference to lovers like Elizabeth and Richard Griffith whose companionate marriage managed the pains as well as pleasures of matrimony through letter-writing. Besides contributing to a history of emotions, this chapter also proposes two arguments about the body, made visible by letters. One is that love-letters dematerialise and rematerialise the body: hence their centrality to the theory and practice of Platonic love, much discussed as a means of equalising desire between the sexes. Letters also rematerialise the body through paper's substitution for skin, a process I argue is best understood through paper-skin's evocation of a lost maternal body. It is no coincidence that tenderness was a quality highly prized in both parents and lovers in the eighteenth century. The strange re-ordering of body parts practised by writers of love-letters is discussed in relation to Sterne's love-letters and their emphasis on the heart, showing that sensibility had important epistolary origins and outlets. The character of lover is frequently one of excess, so appropriately not contained by one chapter: guilty lovers turn up in Chapter 4, as a subset of criminals, and subliminally in Chapter 8, where symmetries between divine love and earthier passions show Christians as lovers of Christ. That symmetry is a critical common-place: I refresh it by resituating it in relation to arguments about the body which show the mouth replacing skin as the signal body part in letters of religious desire.

'Writing as a Criminal', Chapter 4, tracks the character of criminal in relation to letters as a species of evidence – textual, hence open to different interpre-tations. The contentiousness of those interpretations is demonstrated first with reference to a range of crimes, especially treason and the puzzles of suicides. Letters written from prisons and scaffolds helped construct discourses of guilt and penitence that contributed to how others accused of crimes were judged. I look in some detail at three cases concerning women – two parricides and a possible suicide – to show how people's interpretations were aware of letters' material and ideological properties. Forensic readings, developed in relation to the meanings of handwriting, ran alongside social readings that rested on suppositions about women's emotions and behaviours in which probabilities were often cross-referenced to fiction. I make a case for distinguishing epistolary evidence from the categories of criminal biography and scandal into which it is too often subsumed. The chapter's final section, on letters in adultery trials in the 1770s, 1780s and 1790s, reinforces those arguments, with questions of class complicating ones of gender. How errant lovers expected and hoped servants would collude with their illicit amours shows letters as flashpoints for class difference and a moral character that crossed class lines.

The character of citizen in Chapter 5 is used to map a public world of civic life that held many secrets. Indeed one of the most vociferous complaints about eighteenth-century public life, the prevalence of corruption, was most often made through letters. A complex dynamic of hidden and open governed eighteenth-century political life, reflected in letters that made a virtue of their openness, in the sense of being openly published or appealing openly to elected representatives and electors. The opening of political secrets, scandals and injustices was performed by many letter-writers hidden under the cloak of personae. I discuss two of the best known texts, Swift's *Drapier's Letters* and Junius's *Letters*, alongside less well-known signatures like Scourge and Cato. The meanings around old Romans like Cato, a popular signature for political letters and letters to newspapers, show public life was not rational or disembodied but passionate and masculinised. My discussion of personae in this chapter explores anonymity and irony, modes that hide and expose in an inversion of the corruption at which they were aimed. In political life, epistolary personae had a history of classical antecedents and populist applications. I take up the latter with reference to the role of letters in elections, to argue for their generically distinct and important contribution, and with reference to a particular political moment, the excise crisis of 1733. Other political moments also show letters shaping political situations – the excise crisis neatly illustrates a matter of policy making and unmaking in which the significance of letter-writing has been hitherto overlooked.

The character of traveller has a global reach, so Chapter 6 starts with a discussion of how oriental personae were used to superimpose frames of east upon west, making letters a means of philosophical travel writing, especially in the 1760s. The difficulties of adapting otherwise mobile epistolary personae are discussed in relation to Ireland and India, where letter-writers engaged with colonialism more awkwardly than they repositioned orientalist fantasies. Letters accommodated doubts as well as prejudices; they are also texts that show very richly a process of identity-making. Travel literature tells us about race, ethnicity, class, colonialism, imperialism – the constituents of globalisation – and aesthetics. Travel letters also tell us about subjectivity in ways particular to letter-writing, which were different from how people unfolded themselves in journals, the other big genre of travel writing. Without forcing a distinction between different forms of first person writings – the journal-letter hybrid was popular – I argue the presence of an addressee presumed to be culturally similar to the writer allows for experiments in subjectivity. In mapping some of these, I give more space to letters from the second half of the eighteenth century when travellers were freer of empirical obligations.

The historian may seem an overly select character to include: I do so for two reasons. One is to represent the republic of letters, discussed particularly in relation to the vituperative fellowship of antiquarians. The second is because historians more than any other educated group made use of letters. Part of my design is to establish how historians came to see letters as sources and documents, a turn within historiography that has only recently (and patchily) turned again to dismantle disciplinary fences between historians and literary critics, in favour of a common ground of texts.[150] The precarious availability of seventeenth-century letters combined with a culture of contemporary letter-writing to make eighteenth-century historians sensitive to the meanings of letters. Letters were also fought over as a form of historiography – inclusive and exclusive – in class and gender terms that became especially visible in the controversy around Bolingbroke's *Letters on the Study and Use of History* (1752). This controversy should be understood in terms of a class war and the scars of old political battles, continued through a populist, middle-class and masculinist historiography epitomised by Goldsmith's *An History of England* (1764) and its competitors in the market for a readership that explicitly included women. In the differentiation of history from secret history and romance, letters played both sides of the argument. The chapter's final section pursues this argument with reference to Horace Walpole's letters to Horace Mann, analysing how and why Walpole became a self-styled epistolary historian. I use that phrase to describe his accumulation of a history of his own times by means of writing-to-the-moment, a phrase normally associated, and over-associated, with Richardson and epistolary fiction. Walpole constructs a romance through notions of nation, particularly a nation with whose foreign policy he does not identify. Walpole's epistolary history is both a history of his own times and his fluctuating opinions. In the character of historian, one can see again how much more useful are categories of personal and social than private and public.

Letters in the service of theology attracted furious arguments about readings. The character of Christian was subject to Biblical directives to meekness at odds with zeal in promotion of spiritual truth, a potential contradiction that led to arguments being conducted in particular and intense ways. The first part of Chapter 8 takes up epistolary quarrels in the province of speculative theology, on matters including the interpretation of scripture, acts of providence, miracles, holy writ, the operations of the holy spirit and the trinity. I look at debates on and off the page to show how epistolary exchanges fitted with oral forms of argument in which attitudes to writing were influenced by semi-scriptural cultures. Henry Dodwell's *An Epistolary Discourse* (1706) shows how apparently abstruse discussion of the nature of the soul became inflammatory through an epistolary medium which brought Dodwell into conflict with episcopal authority – a conflict also managed, with difficulty, through letter-writing. I then analyse one of the most under-celebrated texts of the eighteenth century, *Christianity Not Founded on Argument* (1741) by Dodwell's son, also Henry Dodwell, to show how an indeterminately ironic epistolary persona put a theological cat among very alarmed pigeons. Responses to the anonymous text by Philip Doddridge and others recognised the power of letter-writing to confuse the boundaries of reason and faith, a power handled adversarially by Joseph Priestley and Tom Paine in later controversies. Detractors and defenders of tenets used orthodoxies of letter-writing to pursue forms of reasoning in support of their beliefs.

Letters were an important means of establishing spiritual authority as well as challenging it. Many congregations were held together through letter-writing, a culture I explore through the colourful figure of William Huntington, known as the Walking Bible. Here letter-writing supplemented sermons as a genre of pastoral care. Spiritual direction, however, also took place through an active culture of ordinary Christians writing to each other. For many, self was something to shed and rise above; equally, many sank under a consciousness of sin, an emotional darkness to which letters were especially hospitable and able to palliate through the fellowship of correspondence. Discussion of this tortured world occupies the second part of Chapter 8, with particular reference to Methodist letters in the later eighteenth century. I was interested in the violence of their discourses, their disputations, doubts and despair. It is a world relatively unvisited by critics so I have used theoretical work on torture and the body to help explain how letter-writing phased in and out a body marked by suffering. Theologically related to eighteenth-century understandings of the incarnation of Christ, the semi-visible, semi-legible body in evangelical writing reveals letters as a key site for mediations between voice and body. Inscriptive properties of letters allowed and enabled a culture of utterance in which the commonplace view of letters as 'talking on paper' becomes startlingly strange.

Methodism is but one instance of how subcultures like denominations used letter-writing in particular ways and for particular ends. My book establishes the historically specific conditions of these uses whilst explaining their literary workings; along the way, I want to uncouple letters from some of the critical frameworks to which they have been attached. In turn, chapters engage with critical arguments about the literary marketplace, conduct literature and politeness, the novel, models of evidential reasoning in legal history, the extent and nature of participation in political life, postcolonial theory, the republic of letters and the kingdom of heaven as understood by differently devout people. With a chronological reach from early to late eighteenth century and an extension of critical awareness of letter-writing into many and varied areas of eighteenth-century life, the book suggests through its characters one way of combining generalisations about letters with the particularity of letter-writing practices. In a short postscript, I consider how this approach to letter-writing could offer eighteenth-century studies' fresh directions.

1
Learning to Write

Nothing is so common as to write Letters: But it is not a common thing to indite them well.[1]

Thus a typical letter-writing manual laid claim to a wide audience in need of instruction. Manuals privileged practice over theory and promoted a difference between best practice and common practice in order to sell themselves. Rules were to be taught only so they could be naturalised into proprieties; these 'proper' forms were refined, yet not necessarily identical with bourgeois politeness. To indite letters well meant more people writing confidently and variously rather than simply more politely, and to further this project many manuals included examples of letters from real-life correspondents and writings on letters from periodicals. Although writers of manuals presented their collections as instructive and authoritative, many of their examples were specimens rather than models, requiring something other than imitation from the reader. Letter-writing manuals were as much descriptive as prescriptive; they differed among themselves and within themselves. The term 'manual' is not entirely helpful: it implies a text whose function is instruction, yet books about letter-writing were discursively more complex than this. Few collections of letters used the term 'manual' in their titles, unlike handbooks of prayers; perhaps critics like it because 'manual' subliminally invokes a skill of the hand, which is certainly present in a hand-written letter.

This chapter starts by discussing some of the conventions and contradictions of letter-collections, using the term 'manual' for convenience, but arguing that the genre's didacticism works in and through cultural domains that load it with meanings beyond the practical skill of letter-writing. The most popular collections used words like 'new', 'complete' and 'universal' to describe the letter-writer they had in mind, yet their prescriptive content stressed tradition and class distinction. Socially differentiated conditions of age, sex, class, occupation and nation returned cultural difference to correspondents even as manuals subsumed them into the category of 'polite' letter-writers. I discuss age, gender and nation in particular, leading into a discussion of women as letter-writers thought to be naturally better than men, or culturally inferior to men, according to cultural imperatives that made letter-writing a site of contention between art and nature. The skills of letter-writing were symbolic and social as well as practical; they overlap with ideologies of femininity that were equally learnt behaviour. In contrast, the way men learned to correspond shows letters supporting literary status. Correspondence between wits and poets in the late seventeenth and early eighteenth century played an important part in defining the 'man of letters'. I discuss this in relation first to Alexander Pope, then to Samuel Johnson, to show that the way people learnt to read letters intersected with a market for literary biography. Learning to read and write letters were skills shaped by market forces.

Manuals

What is a letter? One manual ventured the definition 'That it is a Piece of Writing which we send to an absent Person, to let him know what we would say, if we were in a Condition to speak to him.'[2] A trope of talking on paper was popular because it smothered rather than solved the questions it begged. What is 'a Piece of Writing'? Could one comparably describe clothes as 'a Piece of Cloth'? Are 'we' all alike? What if the absent person was a she not a he? What if the writer was a lord or a child? Would that affect our 'condition to speak'? Manuals conceded complexity at once, differentiating correspondents and occasions. One common format was to divide the book into sections: one on forms of address and subscription, matters of present-ation and so on, followed by an anthology section of letters, so that best practice could be divined from actual practice, or so practice could at least be compared to theory. Another common format was to classify letters by occasions, of business, duty, courtship, friendship and so on. Manuals tried to steer round the paradox of letter-writing as something both natural and teachable by simple contradiction. 'The surest Rule is to write as we speak', declared one, after claiming that letter-writing was difficult because 'Out of a hundred Persons that speak well, scarce ten will be found that write in the same Degree of Perfection...much more Exactness is required for Writing than Speaking.'[3] Like much advice literature, letter manuals played to class anxieties, encouraging readers to adopt polite standards in order to secure a self-fashioned identity as ladies and gentlemen which substituted for a birth-based status and might exceed it by the moral authority of behaving better than born aristocrats.

Conversion of speech to writing through letters invoked anxieties even among the propertied, because epistolary ignorance showed they were unfit to enjoy the ideological benefits of their class. In Defoe's *Compleat English Gentleman*, a gentleman keen to write letters but unable to spell has to dictate to his steward and laboriously copy the script: 'I write no stile, I han't the words.' His friend reassures him that 'in ordinary conversation any thing will do. Familiar friends can be wrote to in a familiar stile', but Defoe's gentleman becomes vehement about his deficiencies: 'Look you, I ought allways to write like my self, that is, like what I should be, not what I am . . . I must write like what I am, and therefore I don't write at all.'[4] An inability to write letters threatened identity: the gentleman is and is not himself, seeming a fool because he cannot seem a man of sense on paper, unlike his scholar brother Jack. The paradox of an ignorant gentleman throws class into question but, like other compilers of manuals, Defoe's point is that education should make one competent within a class rather than necessarily move one out of it. Hence letter-writing is a key to commercial success for two young men in *The Complete English Tradesman*: the one who writes bombast rather than a 'free, plain and tradesman-like stile' will fail in business and probably turn to crime.[5] Not to be what you seemed or seem what you were in letters promised downward class mobility. There were sticks as well as carrots in learning to write letters well.

Writers of manuals treated children as a class capable of improving itself through letters. Anxious to catch letter-writers young, compilers stressed a continuous masculine identity through letters; 'from the Boy at School to the Secretary of State', males needed epistolary skills.[6] Manuals particularly pressed for juvenile observance of forms of address: 'no one should ever write to his pappa, or mamma, without beginning his letter with *Honoured Sir*, or *Honoured Madam*'.[7] Children were not to write as they spoke. The adviser here is Robin Redbreast: having caught Billy Careless neglecting this particular, he warns him that other birds will fly by to check all future letters to his parents. Avian surveillance notwithstanding, the point was to begin letters by expressing obligation, an obeisance like those bows and courtesies which children were expected to make to their elders. A rhetoric of obligation, reinforced by letters' function of articulating duty, may well have contributed to adult anxieties about epistolary indebtedness. Familiar letters between friends often had uncertain beginnings and apologetic ends, as if writers were unsure they had proceeded acceptably. The other ideological import of obligation was that children learnt the art of letter-writing as a discipline parallel to self-government. In a didactic text of the 1780s, a daughter writing to her mother is advised by her aunt to start a letter with 'Honored Madam'. The daughter is doubtful: 'I WISH I might begin Dear Mamma, for I like that much better; for you are my Dear Mamma, and I love you dearly.' Affect, however sincere, must bow to decorum. Her mother replies that personally she has no objection to 'Dear Mamma', but 'Honored Madam' is preferable: 'as that is the address customary in our country, when writing to parents, or masters and mistresses, I think you had better continue it'.[8] Epistolary form symbolised – and enacted – social conformity.

A Biblical injunction to honour parents was not consistently upheld by parents in practice. The confusions are illustrated by John Penrose, a Cornish vicar who had regular letters from his six children when he went away to Bath for a couple of months in 1766. Penrose's benign guidance was typical of many parents – encouraging in general, critical of particulars, writing to one daughter, for instance, 'it is as hard to find the Beginning of Mary's Letter, as it was to find the Exit of Daedalus's Labyrinth; one must turn round and round, as a Dog does when he's going to Bed'.[9] Penrose was happy with informal address until one day he changed his practice, as if someone in Bath had alerted him to a change in manners: 'I have said Mama and Papa, in the former Letters and the Beginning of this, but the Mode is now quite altered. The old fashioned way of Father and Mother is come round again; and we old-fashioned folks like it best.' But he could not keep it up: a week later he caught himself in a lapse, writing Mama – '(I should have said Mother: Oh! how could I be so unpolite!)' – and his letters on a visit the following year use mamma.[10]

Learning to write, then, set pleasure against duty and duty against fashion. Ordinarily familiar letters occupied the middle range between id and superego, though that middle point was often unstable, arrived at through negatives. Nominally, manuals posited a middle-class readership, addressing the readers as if they knew how to make class distinctions though not how to practise those class distinctions in letter-writing. As one advised, there were only three rules in letter-writing: '1. To take care not to be haughty in writing to Superiors. 2. Not to demean yourself in addressing an Inferior. 3. To hold an equal rank with Equals.'[11] However, manuals also reflected uncertainty about how wide the bourgeois project of politeness should extend. Letters exposed the split meaning of politeness as civility (established manners) and refinement (new manners). A letter-writer of 1738 marked one such change: 'The good old Way of writing Letters, at least to Relations, was to begin where we end, I mean, with Services, Respects and good Wishes.'[12] Genteel correspondents were anxious to improve on the courtesy of older or humbler salutations whilst conceding they served epistolary decorum just as well. One solution was to invoke lower-class practice as a paradigm of honest plainness. So William Cowper oscillated between high and low discourses in a thank-you letter:

> As servant maids and such sort of folk account a letter good for nothing unless it begins with – This comes hoping you are well as I am at present, so I should be chargeable with a great omission, were I not to make frequent use of the following gratefull Exordium – Many thanks for a fine Cod and Oysters.[13]

Cowper's self-consciousness made simplicity elegant rather than artless and hence politer. Maids are plain and so is he, but he turns that likeness into difference by identifying it in terms of classical rhetoric; educated men know a beginning is an exordium. His confident account of female servants' taste may be based on the fictions of manuals as much as experience. Middle-class unease about cross-class civility in letters could be assuaged by making plainness Roman rather than working-class and politeness French rather than bourgeois. As Cowper, ever attentive to epistolary etiquette, put it:

> I have often wished indeed, when writing to an ordinary correspondent, for the revival of the Roman custom – *salutem* at top, and *vale* at bottom. But as the French have taught all Europe to enter a room and to leave it with a most ceremonious bow, so they have taught us to begin and conclude our letters in the same manner.[14]

Ambivalence about French manners could also sanction British resistance to being à la mode. 'The slavery of French politeness was a theme which became increasingly explicit as the century wore on, even while the French remained models of fashion and culture.'[15]

Where epistolary etiquette supported more than one form, educated practice differentiated between them in terms of class, gender or nation. Writing as an English gentleman meant sounding on occasion like servant-maids or French people who were also trying to be polite. This friction between social groups differed from the forms of community found in 'the republic of letters' chiefly associated with late seventeenth-century networks of male intellectuals. As Anne Goldgar has comprehensively explored, these networks crossed national boundaries and selectively revised class borders too.[16] In eighteenth-century Britain, letter-writing was understood to be an activity involving all classes and both sexes, but correspondents stayed defined by class and sex. An educated male, the Polite Secretary popular in the Renaissance, lingered in the titles of some epistolary manuals; more gestured towards inclusiveness, as if the Complete Letter-Writer was one who comprehended all epistolary identities as well as all important occasions. Nonetheless, class divisions were upheld. Many manuals included letters playfully in personae defined through class. The complex elisions between ideological figures and supposedly real people are illustrated in *The English Letter-Writer* whose sample letters 'actually passed between People of Reputation', claimed the author, though he was not at liberty to mention their names. They echo novels in their typology of character: thus the descriptions of letters on contents pages indicate occupations or social positions which evoke class quite loosely – the sailor's letter, the sweetheart's reply, the father's answer – and their signatures mimic proper (and properly plain) names, like Elizabeth Barton and Joseph Atkins, which conventionally indicate middle or labouring class. These are fictional in so far as the author has said they are not actual names and one or two slip into comedy: the sailor is Thomas Tarpaulin, for instance.[17] In another manual, Sophia Wellbred writes alongside the personae of Euphrosyne and Mary Careful and the 'real' names of Susanna Centlivre and Elizabeth Rowe.[18] Such slippages are simultaneously democratic and class-conscious, dissolving boundaries between fact and fiction in order to promote an epistolary politeness that was not specifically middle-class, although manuals emphasised politeness was subject to class distinctions. As one put it, 'it would be absurd... to write as familiarly to a Lady of Quality, as to your Waiting-Woman'.[19] Manuals managed class tension by supposing readers to be already polite, defined through comprehension of polite letter-writing. They sold a double fantasy of becoming adept in politeness through letter-writing and through *reading* about letter-writing.

Manuals combined confidence about epistolary forms that could fix class, through tables of forms of address for dukes, bishops, baronets and the like, with an acknowledgement that epistolary discourse, like class, involved ideological overflow. From children urged to treasure letters of parental advice like talismans in fairy tales[20] to adults treating letters as a magic mirror, 'a Glass that shadows to use stronger Desires to enjoy the Person that is absent',[21] people were encouraged to invest in the symbolic properties of letters. Tropes of ore and lustre invoked enlightenment, value and preciousness regardless of use. Part of this magic came from being beyond the reach of rules or art: 'We have several Books of Letters abounding with Instructions for writing them, and yet we write not the better.'[22] This notion of epistolary perversity had a long history, from Cicero advising that 'Letters should sometimes commit Blunders',[23] to Samuel Johnson's argument in a *Rambler* essay on epistolary theory that since letters were written on all subjects and in all states of mind, they could not be reduced to rules: 'a letter has no peculiarity but its form'.[24] It is tempting to see here an analogy between eighteenth-century political liberty and epistolary freedom: 'As to subjects, you are allowed the utmost liberty.'[25] In both, a discourse of liberty in social relations coexisted with regulated activity and institutions sanctioned by usage and law. Unconstrained choice could lead to confusion, if not anarchy, which helps to explain why anxiety was sharpest in familiar letters where choice of subjects was greatest. Here, according to some manuals, rules should apply most and, impossibly, so should a natural easy manner. Managing those class differences to which manuals devoted most attention then left correspondents facing the challenge of what to say regardless of bowing and scraping. Hence the importance given to compliments, as a figure of condensation entailed on writers of lower status. Children were taught never to omit a paragraph of compliments, usually at the end of a letter; letters to aristocrats were larded with them. Between equals in letters of friendship, compliments could seem unnecessary. In a letter much anthologised by manuals, Mary Jones ended, 'I'm sick of saying for ever, I beg my Compliments to such a one.'[26] The utmost liberty did allow a freedom to experiment, including experiments of dispensing with forms.

While manuals reflected uncertainties about class, they contributed to xenophobic certainties. People learnt to write as English correspondents, reflected in titles like *The English Letter-Writer*. Manuals helped make letters clearly vernacular – not incompatibly with a legacy of classical letters since new translations of Cicero, Seneca and Pliny made old Romans sound elegantly modern in English. Manuals took relatively little interest in English letters from earlier periods: many included one from a woman parting from her husband during the Civil War, but little from the Renaissance.[27] Tradition sanctioned correct usage but provided limited examples because written English had undergone sea-changes over the early modern period: the English Letter-Writer implied a native language as well as a national identity. A stress on Englishness also countered French influence, about which compilers were ambivalent. In so far as French writers contributed to the universality of epistolary discourse in general and letters of gallantry in particular, they could not be discounted. However, French establishment of an epistolary culture at court in the mid-seventeenth century caused envy and agitation. Samuel Johnson explained that England lacked an equivalent epistolary tradition because the English were properly contemptuous of trifles. On the other hand, because he was promoting indigenous letter-writing, he did not dismiss letters as trifles: epistolary attention to daily life and its common occasions demonstrated 'how to become little, without becoming mean'.[28] Johnson located failure in French practitioners rather than the genre and attributed their undeniable success to an inferior national character: so Voiture and Scaron's letters were 'despicable...servile hyperboles'.[29] Part of the unease many readers felt about Pope's letters may be connected to nationalism, his alleged affectation read as a subliminally French idiom attributable to his borrowings from Voiture's letters.[30]

Like the relation between cookery books and cooking, the relation of manuals to actual epistolary practice is complex. Writers of manuals classified letters like encyclopaedists or post-Linnaean botanists; they did so in ways drawn from practice without necessarily determining that practice. Some classical letters became familiar from schoolbooks rather than manuals, for instance. Manuals' categories were more elaborate than the letters of business, friendship or love that occupied most practitioners and they ignored letters of political argument, religious controversy, scholarly exchange and scientific report. Constrained by questions of personal permissions and copyright, their categories of familiar letters were also selective: they studiously avoided letters of quarrels and they were surprisingly sparing with letters of condolence, despite quarrels and death being amongst the most common occasions of eighteenth-century letter-writing.[31] It is significant that one of the most popular sample letters in manuals was Pope's farewell to Bishop Atterbury on the eve of his banishment, in which Pope imagined a future correspondence though neither of them could ever write to each other again. In this anti-letter, the imaginary replaced the real, just as the manual could imply it had covered everything. As a letter that ends letters, Pope's example fitted the manuals' lack of interest in correspondence; they much preferred single or single exchanges of letters to runs of correspondence. On those interceptions to which fictional letters were endlessly prone, manuals were silent beyond condemning the practice of reading other people's letters. On forgery, manuals had little to say apart from pragmatically advising correspondents not to leave much space between the end of the text and their signature. They sidestepped staples of familiar correspondence, like news, gossip and books, preferring the archetypical to the topical.

Yet for all this divergence from readers' needs, manuals sold well not simply as a species of advice literature but as anthologies of actual letters, marketed by frames of nation and class. Less overt but equally important was manuals' projection of gender. They did show women as letter-writers, but in unrepresentative and limited ways, putting a large part of eighteenth-century women's writing in the shade, and their views of the letter as a gendered genre both drew on and contributed to wider ideologies in which learning to write meant learning to write as a gendered subject. The next section discusses writing as a woman, first in manuals and then in other epistolary writings.

Naturally better?

The Ladies Complete Letter-Writer of 1763 claimed to be the first manual for women, though it openly drew on earlier compilations. Its title page emphasised women's functions as daughters, wives and mothers; epistolary style and social duty were to be simultaneous. It attempted to establish a moral and aesthetic pattern for British women letter-writers by filtering out French rivals. But this ran into trouble. On the one hand, French women showed 'a flimsy kind of Gaiety' in their correspondence, making those manuals that printed them improper. On the other hand, that skill for which French women were extolled could be learnt by British women. So although letters revealed supposedly innate national character, national character could be properly fashioned through proper letter-writing. The art of letter-writing and the natural characteristics of nation, class and gender counterbalanced, just as the natural beauty of British women could cancel the artifice of French women. British women who used this manual would 'equal, nay exceed, the *Lamberts*, *Sévignés*, and the D'*Anois*'s of our rival neighbours, in the graces of the Pen, as much as they excel in the Charms of their Persons'.[32] A trope of natural charms artistically displayed made parallels between texts and bodies – for example, in the article of neatness, women were advised not to send out a letter with blots and interlineations, as if they were wearing stained clothes. Just as the art of dress was a way of reading women as natural or modest, epistolary theory used a double meaning of nature as something unprocessed and inherent form to associate women with natural and learnt characteristics of letters rather than freely creative writing. The compiler pitted the category of English women (potentially good letter-writers) against French women (falsely praised as good letter-writers) in order to construct a third, that category of women who could realise their true potential by becoming consumers of the manual.

Curiously, given that it promised a strait-laced moral agenda, the *Ladies Complete Letter-Writer* stressed women's erotic properties: 'Letters are an Expedient to charm at a Distance, to secure that Empire over the Mind, in absence' which their beauty had conquered by presence. The letter offered women active eroticism, '*wafting their Sighs from* Indus *to the Pole*', but women's mastery of letters via the manual entailed an ambiguous mastery over their own erotic properties. A woman could 'give a becoming Dress to her Esteem or her Fondness by Letter', or, 'by her unmeaning, ill-spelt, unsentimental scrawl' she could drive lovers away. Regardless of practice, manuals narrowed recognition of letters as an outlet for women's feelings and desire.

In learning to write letters, women's use of art was read as a metaphorisation of nature: that is, however skilfully they wrote, art usually returned them in the end to a gross nature (especially if they were French!) However, a woman's letter could represent an integrity which was not necessarily the integrity of chastity. Where the letter as material object represented women as objects, ideally neat bodies, the letter as writing could still represent her disembodied subjectivity. The complexity is illustrated by two letters that featured in numerous manuals. In the first, an unnamed lady declares her long-standing love to a gentleman; in the second, she reproves him for ridiculing her to their acquaintance by showing her first letter about. Why were these letters so popular? The manuals' fascination is not simply with a woman writing of passion, like the Portuguese Nun, or trying to sidestep scandal, but with how far epistolary sincerity might override custom. Because her letter is so well written, it wins over the reader regardless of cultural expectations about the decorum or otherwise of women showing sexual initiative. Her second, coolly indignant letter, capitalises on the attractions of letter-writing (in which the manual's reader is investing): her beloved has rejected not just her passion but her epistolary skill in expressing that passion. Her skill is an attraction which confirms her attractiveness: writing becomes womanliness. Here the letter is more a discursive object than a material object. Indeed the beloved's crime is to confuse them: rather than treat the letter as in countless fictions as an erotic object to be caressed, wept over and so on, he violates its intimacy by reading it out to his friends. It is not a private object but a subjectivity made public. Of course we the readers have also been privy to it and the popularity of this pair as samples in manuals is due to their systolic and diastolic movement of withholding and restoring epistolary eroticism. The sighs wafted from Indus to the Pole in women's letters are metonymically the wordless women and metaphorically the expressive letter. Or, letters are both the sighs and the means of wafting them. In that slippage, writing letters as a woman involved an unstable relation between body and text, discourse and agency, and an identity as both subject and object marked by gender.

A second way in which letter-writing was understood to gender women was through language. One manual claimed 'some of the best, most elegant, and useful letters in this work are the productions of female pens';[33] higher-profile critics were less gallant. Chesterfield thought spelling errors were pardonable in women's letters because they were predictable; another critic thought women quoted too much, an intertextuality made worse by being unpatriotic: 'Ladies are apt to introduce into their epistolary compositions French and Italian phrases, according to the fashion; and sprigs of poetry, and scraps of plays.'[34] Manuals' weak sense of letter-writing history meant they continued to circulate anachronisms like Swift's claim, still aired in 1796, that women could not spell.[35] True, some could not and it restricted their letter-writing: 'the truth is I can nither indite nor spell which is the reson I have never wrote to any of my friends', confided one mother to her son in 1777.[36] That lack of education which women repeatedly protested about and tried to overcome was used to belittle women's letters. Richard Griffith, who praised his wife's ability to spell, sympathetically prefaced their published correspondence with a story of a lady who wrote a business letter to a gentleman 'and thinking it too orthographical for a Woman, added an (e) to the Ende of severale Wordse, leste it should bee suspected that she had spelte by the Aid of a Dictionarye'.[37] Masculine disparagement of women's spelling and syntax had some logic, since standardisation could help that mutuality on which correspondence depended, but it mattered less to the irregularly educated or to an older generation who were used to creative spelling, like Lady Gardiner in the Verney family:

> My Lady Anne Grimston rit me word that when shee was in Wiltsher that the ill nues came of the death of my Lady Rooke to her mother, her husband is one of our Admirals. I find she was highly vallued & consequently greately lamented. I find death makes no distinction between the wise or the foolis, or the rich or the poor, all must goe to the grave & bee sure old people must goe ther forst.[38]

In the seventeenth century, spelling was used as an index of epistolary sophistication – John Evelyn remarked with surprise on his daughter Mary's 'most correct orthography';[39] in the eighteenth century, uniformity was freshly theorised, giving new weight to certain spellings as correct. Language became more visibly man made. Debates about phonetic versus etymological spelling, for instance, required a knowledge of classical languages associated with a university education; likewise, notions of ascertaining and fixing language employed the terminology of chemistry and other sciences to which women had little or no access.

Disparaging women's letters as inferior was useful to novelists: it made men writing in a female voice seem more literary, because more literate, than women would be. 'The sex... are generally too careless in their orthography (a consciousness of a defect in which generally keeps them from writing', claimed Samuel Richardson.[40] Syntax too was used as a yardstick by which to disparage women's letters: it is harder to track, though Evelyn lists 'exactness of the periods' as another mark of his daughter's epistolary talent. Just as women were slower to adopt standardised spelling, so their syntax seemed more inclined to dashes and less to subordinate clauses. Supposed defects of informality and colloquialism appear in parodies of women's letters, like Pope's 'In the Style of a Lady', 1716: 'Do you believe there is any such Place as the Elysian Fields? O Gad, that would be charming!... what do I correspond with you for, if you won't tell me all? You know I abominate Reserve.'[41] Stereotypes characterised women's letters as gushing and chaotic like their speech. In Smollett's novel *The Expedition of Humphry Clinker* (1771), the gendered comedy of misspellings dominates letters of female characters like Tabitha Bramble and Win Jenkins and the polite letters of Lydia are full of modish repetition.[42] The trope of letters as talking on paper left women's letters open to satire like their speech; even in orderly conversation, women were easily troped as disorderly. In return, women sometimes used class to profess disappointment with the letters of aristocratic men. When Sophia Baddeley's principal lover sent missives saying 'I long to here from you', her friend Elizabeth Steele commented forthrightly

> Lord Melbourne was not the brightest man of the age, as his letters sent to Mrs. Baddeley at times, will shew, and he is among many of the fashionable men of the age who are acquainted neither with good grammar nor orthography.[43]

In general, however, writing as a woman was perceived to be writing badly. When women were encouraged to learn grammar, it was to improve their ability to teach sons.[44]

Behind this apparently simple misogyny is a contradictory positioning of women in the salons of seventeenth-century France. As Michèle Cohen discusses, politeness was thought to be produced by mixed company – specifically through the conversation of women, in contrast to manliness which was produced through the company of men. Conferring politeness gave women some status but though it secured class privileges, for these women, conversation 'was ultimately productive of gender difference, not power'.[45] In England, anxieties about women as dangerously talkative meant imported ideas of polite conversation sat uneasily alongside cultural imperatives of feminine reticence. Polite women were to be modest, that is retiring in conversation. 'How could women be expected both to converse and to "talk little"?'[46] One answer is, through letter-writing. Letters enabled men to enjoy women's conversation in writing (another reason people described letter-writing as 'talking on paper') without actually being in their company. Thus men secured the advantages of women's conversation without risk of gender contamination. Conversely, women could 'talk' with men in ways that allowed them the transformative power of politeness; the price was physical separation. The predilection for nuns in early eighteenth-century fiction plays on just such a pattern of articulate women barred, literally and figuratively, from enjoying male company.

A few men argued that women were better letter-writers than men. Lack of university education was no obstacle, 'the Letters of well-educated Women, far excelling those of our *Greek*-taught gentry'.[47] Construing women as good letter-writers helped keep them out of other genres – their gift is always related to familiar letters, not to letters of argument or other forms of published letters. The reasoning behind this view was self-interested as men tried to manage anxieties about gender and genre. Letters were a genre with few rules, as manuals conceded. Although a letter-writer made specifically literary choices in selection, organisation and presentation of material, those choices could not be completely formularised and could be overridden by personal knowledge of an addressee. Ultimately, the definition of a good letter was one which pleased its reader and the simplest, crudest, most spontaneous letter could do that as effectively as the most polished and arguably more sincerely. Comparing a power to be natural in letters to the naturalised category of femininity helped reduce anxiety because it drew on deep associations between women and nature. It also left undisturbed a notion of women as a constituency who, like nature, could be improved on, not least by buying manuals.

'Beauties' and 'graces' were terms shared by admired women and admirable letters. They fuse in men's praise of women's letters – for example, Richardson's, in Anna Howe's eulogy of Clarissa:

> If you mention the beauties and graces of her pen, you may take notice that it was always a matter of surprise to her, that the sex are generally so averse as they are to writing; since the pen, next to the needle, of all employments is the most proper and adapted to their geniuses; and this as well for improvement as for amusement. Who sees not, would she say, that those women who take delight in writing excel the men in all the graces of the familiar style. The gentleness of their minds, the delicacy of their sentiments (improved by the manner of their education) and the liveliness of their imaginations, qualify them to a high degree of preference for this employment: while men of learning, as they are called (of mere learning, however), aiming to get above that natural ease and freedom which distinguishes this (and indeed every other kind of writing), when they think they have best succeeded are got above, or rather *beneath*, all natural beauty.[48]

This valourisation of women as natural obviously provided an analogue for men of little learning like Richardson (just as later women writers like Elizabeth Montagu and Ann Radcliffe cited Shakespeare as proof that literary genius did not need extensive education). But Richardson was not alone. Writing on aesthetics, John Gilbert Cooper explained the sprightly ease of Voiture's letters as a result of his friendships with aristocratic women; Balzac's letters, in contrast, were laboured because he lived secluded amongst men. Thus 'more Taste and Elegance in Writing is to be acquired in a circle of Beauties at PARIS, than in a *learned* Society of Capuchins'.[49] In part this pitted sociable court against secluded religious order so as to echo, and approve, the town-country configuration of English letters, which tended to favour urbanity as a discursive location.[50] Although that urbanity was clearly connected to the politeness of women and courts in France, its appeal helps explain why French letter-writers were so much read by a British audience which otherwise begrudged them praise. There is also a suggestive connection between British recognition of the importance of French women in letter-writing and a sexual element of epistolary theory, as if the fantasy of French women as more sexual than any other nationality made epistolary discourse resemble pornography. Beauties, graces, negligences, ease, freedom, undress, the natural and the revealing – these terms were common to men writing about women and about letters and figured the attractions of letters as heterosexual. Women noted the overlap and borrowed it back. So in 1700 one excused a hasty letter

> wanting Leisure to put it in any other than a loose Morning-Dress, not questioning but it may please you as well without the Formalities of Stile, as a pretty Woman, without Stays may some of your Acquaintance.[51]

Susanna Centlivre takes on Voiture's knowingness, and it reappears in Mary Jones' playful admonishment mid-century to Pope, that letters like beauties could be overdressed.

An alternative reading of women's letters as 'naturally better' can be found in the correspondence of the less heterosexually inclined Horace Walpole. He states on several occasions his belief that women write better letters than men. This, to the Countess of Ossory on Christmas night, 1773, is his clearest elaboration:

> Your reflection on Madame de Grignan's letter after her mother's death is just, tender and admirable, and like the painter's hiding Agamemnon's face, when he despaired of expressing the agony of a parent. No, Madame de Sévigné could not have written a letter of grief if her daughter had died first. Such delicacy in sentiment women only can feel. *We* can never attain that sensibility which is at once refined and yet natural and easy, and which makes your sex write so much better than men ever did or

can; and which if you will allow me to pun in Latin, though it seems your Ladyship does not understand that language, I could lay down as an infallible truth in the words of my godfather,

Pennis non hominis datis,

the English of which is, 'It was not given to man to write letters.' For example how tiresome are Corbellini's letters, and how he wears out the scélérat and the jealousy!

This passage has several oddities. In seeing sentiment as the distinguishing characteristic of women's letters, Walpole seems to be making the predictable patriarchal association of women with feeling, as opposed to masculine thinking. But because this sensibility is manifested in a letter – in two letters, in fact, the Countess's and Madame de Grignan's – Walpole cannot deny it a power of agency. It is not simply felt but *written.* Walpole associated that agency, however, with absence, particularly masculine absence: Agamemnon's hidden face and the painter's inability to represent emotion. But Madame de Grignan's letter evidently has been able to represent emotion, otherwise neither of her readers would have been struck by it. Walpole's praise of the Countess's reflection as 'just, tender and admirable' is predicated on incompletion: just as partial imaging is a solution for the painter, so the letter-writer chooses a veiled expression. Walpole reads this as feminine: what is unknowable and inexpressible, women comprehend. Walpole was a fervent admirer of Madame de Sévigné but peculiarly here he implies his idol, so far as we know biologically female, could not write a woman's letter, whereas her daughter can. The subtext is that as an honorary man, bereavement would have rendered her inarticulate. Walpole's bafflement at how women transform their supposedly finer feelings into epistolary aptness falls back on feminine intuition as the explanation for women's naturally better letters.

Both visible and invisible, the rules governing letters mirrored the ideological construction of femininity. Ideology was disguised as nature and epistolary convention was disguised as propriety. Laws of discourse were concealed beneath an outer dress of polite language, just as stays and laces reshaped a woman's body; the object of both was to produce an elegant, pleasing effect.[52] Ideally, pleasing effects were attributable to nature rather than art, to beauties and graces rather than labour. Ironically, it may explain why many women were at ease in letters and many men were anxious: women were already familiar with the inexpressible and elusive ideal of femininity, represented in the guesswork and silences of correspondence. Eighteenth-century ideals of masculinity were also chimerical but involved much less self-effacement and much less privileging of empathy. A cultural imperative to imagine themselves in the place of others had a mixed effect on women's position as letter-writers.

Men invoked surface rules of spelling and grammar to disparage women's letters as strategically as they celebrated women's epistolary empathy as something natural rather than literary. But the similarity between epistolary discourse and femininity, each mapped by self-disguising rules, offered women analogies with their own cultural construction – and occasional opportunities to undo it. A letter by Catherine Talbot demonstrates this. She wrote to a female cousin evoking that stoicism which educated women made part of ideal feminine conduct: 'You are at present, my dear, in a very philosophical disposition; the gaieties and follies of life have no attraction for you, its sorrows you kindly commiserate!' The joke is that the addressee is an infant, yet able to observe gendered precepts: 'You have an absolute dislike to the vanities of dress.' Irony is accentuated by Talbot's anticipation that the baby's father will read the letter out, thus underscoring how gendering is accomplished through a masculine voice. The letter wittily rewrites clichés of conduct books in which, like children, women were admonished to be silent and yet expected to run after showy attractions. Talbot points to gender inequalities as immediate and inevitable, presuming this child will soon have a brother to put her nose out of joint:

> There will be nothing to be done then but to be mighty good, and prove what, believe me, admits of very little dispute (though it has occasioned abundance), that we girls, however people give themselves airs of being disappointed, are by no means to be despised; but the men unenvied shine in public; it is we who must make their homes delightful to them; and if they provoke us, no less uncomfortable.[53]

For all Talbot's apparent acquiescence in an unequal social order, she makes a female of very limited experience into a figure of fully realised gender difference. The mismatch in their ages is countered by the mutuality of epistolary discourse and their shared fates as women, in a letter which is both a familiar letter and a parody of letters of advice. The epistolary joke shows up femininity as constructed and the letter as an ideologically motivated genre. Writing as a woman, then, was anything but natural.

Men of letters, or, learning to read

The letters of Alexander Pope were controversial for two reasons: the scandalous history surrounding the circumstances of their publication and whether they were a shining example of epistolary practice or writings tarnished by their very polish. Received wisdom is that prior to Pope's example it was not customary to publish familiar letters, that Pope's ambition occasioned subterfuges, that Curll's greed accounts for his attempts to exploit Pope. 'Pope and Curll metonymically function as opposing forces of high and low culture – "true literature" and "crass commercialism." '[54] Catherine Ingrassia's reading of their quarrel stresses instead 'the seepage of categories' and the two men's co-dependence in a relationship which 'though born of animosity, was fundamentally symbiotic. Each man invigorated the other's career.'[55] The poet and the bookseller struggled for mastery through a series of poems, lampoons and satires, not just letters. But their battle over letters has a particular context, that of a growing market. Correspondence helped construct the reputation of men of letters, which explains what made letters worth fighting for. There are two parts to this story: one about men and masculinity, the other about letters and literariness. Also important are issues of nationality, age and literary biography, particularly how a generation of writers was memorialised through letters. By restoring a sense of what was expected of letters, we can see how writing as a wit, a poet and a friend of poets had a bearing on the fight between Curll and Pope over the possession and marketing of Pope's letters.[56] The historical specificity of these configurations can be clearly seen by comparing Pope to Johnson, the most famous writer of the next generation, whose letters were also important in marketing him as a writer and in what was understood by that commodification. I discuss Pope first, with reference to a world of wits and their letters, then Johnson.

It was a commonplace throughout the eighteenth century that the lives of men of letters were devoid of incident, unlike the lives of men of action. An apparent discursive vacuum thus coexisted with a growing interest in 'great men'. Readers were curious about 'the Humours, Inclinations and secret Transactions' of biographical subjects[57] and, as print culture dispersed a court-based literary culture, in the human interest of writers' lives rather than their illustrious families. Character and conduct counted for more, circumstances and class for less. Print created anxieties about democratising and letters took some of the blame for perceived downmarket tendencies, with 'all the Sons of Wit' from coffee houses encouraged to publish 'Billets to Jilts'.[58] Restoration poets and playwrights contributed to collections including letters of wit and gallantry which played on the boundary between familiar letters and fiction, a boundary the more blurred because libertinism was understood to involve certain poses. Simultaneously, the letters of more sober men of learning were taken up as demonstrations of intellectual exchange and manifestations of their inmost characters, concerns brought together in their 'manner of conversing with their friends'.[59] Readers were reminded of letters' personal origins even as they became more widely read.

It has been claimed that to offer one's correspondence as a literary work 'was by early eighteenth-century standards unthinkable'.[60] Hardly so: for instance, in 1722 James Heywood published *Poems and Letters on Several Subjects*; in Farquhar's *Works*, in a sixth edition by 1728, letters appeared posthumously but with a high profile, as the first item in the first of two volumes; in 1721 John Dennis published his *Original Letters, Familiar, Moral and Critical*, with a candid admission it was to make people think he was not just an ill-natured critic. Where women like Katherine Philips and, a little later, Elizabeth Thomas appeared in print in personae, as Orinda and Corinna respectively, literary men like Otway and Wycherley appeared as themselves, in letters clearly part of their literary works.[61] Pope's letters would sell because Pope was an acclaimed author but also because there was a buoyant market for letters by literary men. 'Any domestick or servant, who can snatch a letter from your pocket or cabinet, is encouraged in that vile practise', wrote Pope, but his fears were about not controlling the market rather than its existence.[62] Arbuthnot's remark that posthumous publication of letters added new terrors to the grave gained force from a contrast with a world in which writers could imagine publishing their letters whilst alive.

Letters were also a recognised part of writers' oeuvres in the form of translations. Although not always included in their works, these were still authorised enterprises in which the names of English authors jostled those of French writers, especially Voiture, on a title page.[63] Understanding the significance of Voiture's letters helps explain some hostility to the content of Pope's letters, which borrowed heavily from them. Voiture's 'easy sublime'[64] did not translate neatly. There were several reasons for this. One was class: Voiture was comfortably witty with aristocrats in a way that a post-Restoration generation of professional writers, more at home in taverns than courts, were not; as one critic ventured, 'Perhaps his Manner of writing may seem too familiar, considering the Rank of Persons he writ too' [sic].[65] Another reason was gender: for all Voiture's fame as a seducer, he was intellectually at ease with women whereas English wits were homosocial, often aggressively so.[66] Steele's politeness is most comparable to Voiture's and Steele was known as an indefatigable writer of love-letters – but to his wife, so hardly a model for womanisers. Two other factors hindered Voiture's absorption into English letter-writing. The first was patriotism: English writers were trying to outdo French writers, not copy them. The second was a matter of aesthetics. In the late seventeenth century, imitation had aesthetic value. In letters, imitation was more suspect than in other genres because it clashed with the principle of sincerity. It was possible, just, to imitate Cicero, Seneca or Pliny because Romans were associated with plain-speaking; in contrast, French writers were stereotyped as insincere, making imitation harder. Hence the accusations of insincerity levelled against Pope, whose borrowings from Voiture were substantial: as Curll charged, he took over whole epistolary occasions.[67] Worse, he made these appropriations silently, rather than offering them as translations, which seemed to bypass the explicit struggle of his fellow-writers to anglicise Voiture.

The letters of English literary men shared elements with other kinds of familiar letters: demonstrations of wit and friendship, professions of sincerity and an exchange of compliments. More than other familiar letters, they were dedicated to establishing a masculinity as much at odds with hetero-sexuality as part of it and a literary-critical dynamic in which both corre-spondents' stock as writers went up. If as Pope put it the life of a wit was warfare upon earth, the domain of letters was where wits ostensibly took time out and helped each other rearm.[68] Where friendship in early eighteenth-century letters normally meant appreciation of a correspondent's good qualities, in letters between wits it meant extolling each other's literary talents. Their language of compliment borrowed most from the love-letter: 'A Friend may sometimes proceed to acknowledge Affection by the very same Degrees by which a Lover declares his Passion.' Thus Dennis listed Dryden's virtues. 'Extraordinary Esteem may sometimes make the Mind as Impotent as a violent Love does the Body': Dennis to Dryden again, tongue-tied. 'The very Thought of Mr. *Wycherley* spreads a generous Warmth thro' me, and raises my Soul to Rapture': Dennis again, aroused by another literary correspondence.[69] The violence of Dennis's mimicry of the rhapsodies of love-letters reflects Dennis's violence in general; it also shows how literary men's letters to each other used the same figures of desire as they did to their mistresses. Dennis professed himself 'ravish'd' by the verse of Suckling, Cowley, Denham and Waller until he encountered Dryden's poetry, concluding "Tis indeed impossible that I should refuse to Love a Man, who has so often given me all the Pleasures that the most insatiable Mind can desire.'[70] The heterosexual homosociality of wits' letters was further secured through the feminine figure of the Muse, with whom an erotic relation could be 'long and often enjoy'd'. First the writer possessed the Muse, then the reader, by which means the reader possessed the writer too. Enjoying a poet's works became an erotic metonym for enjoying the poet. That anxiety of influence which Harold Bloom so productively read as oedipal – specifically, the rivalry of younger writers with paternal figures of the previous generation – was in early eighteenth-century literary correspondence between men troped as pleasure in order to sublimate anxiety. As new mechanisms of criticism like the periodical joined old ones of satires, squibs and lampoons, early eighteenth-century male writers manifested anxiety in fraternal rivalries rather than paternal ones.

The early letters of Pope, especially ones to Wycherley, certainly have an undertow for which psychoanalysis seems helpful. A remark in a letter of 1714 suggests a desire to be an anti-oedipal subject: 'To follow Poetry as one ought, one must forget father and mother, and cleave to it alone.'[71] But to older men he clearly took up a feminine position: 'I know it is a common opinion that a young scribler [sic] is as ill-pleas'd to hear truth as a young Lady.'[72] Responding to Sir William Turnbull's compliments on his writings, Pope adopts a girlish role to make himself desirable to his literary forefathers. The versatility of oedipal triangles in managing sexuality has been explored by Kaja Silverman, who elaborates on Freud's suggestion of a negative oedipal triangle as a base for homosexual desire. In a heterosexual oedipal triangle, a male subject identifies with his father and desires his mother. In a negative oedipal triangle, a boy behaves like a girl and is affectionately feminine to his father and is jealous of or hostile to his mother. 'The relative intensity of the two identifications in any individual will reflect the preponderance in him of one or other of the two sexual dispositions.'[73] These tendencies can regroup and polarise, so the triangle is not static. For understanding Pope's epistolary identity, several possibilities present themselves. In a heterosexual oedipal triangle, Pope would be identifying with his literary father and desiring the mother – a fecund Muse. In a homosexual oedipal triangle, Pope would be desiring his literary fathers and identifying with the Muse. 'A maternal identification apparently translates... not only into sexual receptivity, but narcissism and exhibitionism'[74] – of which there are traces in Pope's letters, and which echoes Curll's summary of Pope's correspondence with Wycherley: 'There is little more to be seen in these Letters, but that Mr. *Pope* rubs the old Bard's Back, and he in return chucks our young Poetical Saplin under the Chin.'[75]

Models for reading literary men's letters are complicated by how one genders the Muse, a feminine figure who presides over a business men think of as masculine.[76] For all the discussion of mistresses in letters between literary men, women's allure was limited by the supposed impossibility of their being able to possess the muse as men did. A discourse of jealousy in relation to the muse at this period is important here: men figured their possession of the muse as exclusive, but not hers of them, thus explaining the inconstant inspiration of poetry. In so far as other men of letters were also rivals for the muse/mother, a heterosexual oedipal triangle can make Pope feminine; it also fits with a version of Bloom's model in which other poets are brother poets – like siblings, in a parallel subject position of desiring the muse, but also, like siblings, competitively so. In a homosexual oedipal triangle, Pope's sense of himself as already precociously possessing the muse (in his phrase, 'I lisped in numbers') would establish a maternal identification, with older poets representing that masculine subject-position ostensibly completed by age – 'the *man* of letters' – which is both desired and feared, lest it come between Pope and his incorporated muse. Kaja Silverman notes that the negative oedipal complex has a capacity

for challenging and subverting the heterosexual imperative, and for scrambling the socially acceptable temporality and narrative sequencing of normative human sexuality. More importantly, it might be said to negate the most fundamental premise of male subjectivity – an identification with masculinity – and in doing so obstruct paternal lineality.[77]

An identification with masculinity is, I contend, hard for poets to complete where their identity as poets is accomplished by means of a feminised figure for poetry. Hence the necessity of 'men of letters' as a term and the absence of an equivalent for women until the adoption of 'bluestocking' (a term said to be invented with reference to a man). In characterising Pope's playing both sides of the triangle in order to become and postpone becoming a man of letters, I recognise the problems of historical difference involved.[78] But as

Mark Breitenberg observes, 'if . . . it is ahistorical to posit heterosexuality and homosexuality in the early modern period (indeed, neither terms even exists), then it need not be the case that hetero and homoerotic discourses or representations of desire are themselves necessarily discrete'.[79] My use of the term homosociality argues for such an overlap.

Turning oedipal rivalries into fraternal attractions did not stop poets from jostling for primacy. When Pope fell out with Addison over alleged criticism of his translation of Homer, he compared Addison to the Grand Turk. The point was to represent Addison not only as a tyrant but as anti-fraternal: he 'can never bear a Brother on the throne'.[80] If brother poets were not love objects, they were necessarily rivals in a primogeniturist system. Familiar letters had a special role to play in trying to reconcile these extremes, for they were thought to accommodate sincerity more than other kinds of writing. First, the letters of a sincere friend 'showed his Temper, natural Disposition, and Frame of Mind by his very Expressions, for *Epistola est index animi*'.[81] Second, the reciprocity of correspondence allowed two-way criticism. Again one can see Pope narcissistically bending conventions by threatening to break away from the exchange-rate of compliments: 'a man, for hearing a great deal more than his due said of him by another, must afterwards say a great deal less than his due of himself'.[82] Third and most importantly, love and rivalry were controlled by asking the friend to be the critic. As if to pre-empt public criticism or offset its violence, poets stressed how the relative privacy of familiar letters could provide a just and sympathetic forum of correction. The liminal but still literary status of letters made criticism seem disinterested: thus 'a Friend's reprimand often shews more Friendship than his compliment'.[83] This difficulty of getting the balance between public acerbity and personal emollience created a new anxiety, aired in the safety of semi-parodic letters like that from one wit to another: 'Our Correspondence hitherto, methinks, looks as if we were seasoning a Sallad between us: I am for softening it with Oil, and you are still souring it with Vinegar.'[84] (Taking his cue, he wrote more acidly.)

Writers' use of familiar letters played with a public–private divide. As Wycherley put it, 'the best Mark of a Friend, is telling his Friend his Faults in private, so the next is concealing them from the publick, till they are fit to appear'.[85] Often unable and indeed unwilling to keep letters concealed, men recognised the market value of familiar correspondence. The image Wycherley used about a complimentary poem to Pope on his *Pastorals* applies equally to his letter: 'like an old City-bawd's attending a young Country-beauty to Town, to gain her Admirers, when past the Hopes of pleasing the World herself'.[86] Familiar letters helped make writers marketable more subtly than in the open alliances of complimentary poems or dedicatory epistles. Letters also supported the construction of masculinity and its commodification because the more men performed the identity of men-in-letters, the more writing seemed a man's business. Some trace of this may be seen in epistolary novels around the mid-century, in which the heroine has a romance name and her confidante a plainer name, as if men like Richardson unconsciously recognised a connection between writing letters and aspirant literariness. It was the harder for women to break the glass walls around writerly identity because women were stuck in a discourse of suspicion of men's language. As William Walsh observed, 'to commend a Man for a Wit to the Women, is like commending him for a good Protestant to the Fathers of the Inquisition ... They love a tame, easy, governable Fool, and fancy all Wits ill-natur'd and proud.'[87] Pope likewise was anxious that Lady Mary Wortley Montagu should read his letters to her as ones of esteem not wit. There were two women letter-writers in print with a positive literary reputation: Katherine Philips who was not part of the London literary marketplace and Elizabeth Rowe whose commitment to Christian otherworldliness also kept her out of competition with male wits.[88] Voiture had proclaimed that women make the best judges of wit, but when Madame de Rambouillet took up his game he was frightened,[89] and in Britain men preferred to exclude women as judges where possible. The one advantage for women was that an increase in *Miscellanies* after the mid-century allowed them to publish familiar letters as legitimate works.

By the 1730s, epistolary conventions that served to allay the anxieties of an older generation of male writers were worn out. Pope, as its last productive survivor, became trapped in the very epistolary market he had helped to create. Curll's pursuit put a damper on Pope's letter-writing – 'you will not wonder if I should forswear writing a letter again while I live', he wrote to Bethel, but he still recognised the allure of self-commodification, adding, 'I could publish my own heart too.'[90] Moreover, Pope recognised that Curll was the agent of a wider constituency avid for his letters: 'If you please to reflect either on the impertinence of weak admirers, the malice of low enemies, the avarice of mercenary Booksellers, or the silly curiosity of people in general; you'll confess I have small reason to indulge correspondences.'[91] This generalising of epistolary interest is important for understanding the significance of the publication of Pope's letters. Though Curll vowed to win the last round (by outliving Pope and publishing all his letters in a *Life*), Curll also threatened to displace Pope as a market leader. Going beyond that convention of printing letters on both sides which confirmed correspondence as a homosocial club on paper, Curll included letters by people like Prior, the Duchess of Ormonde and Henry VIII. This is not evidence of Curll's lack of discrimination, his rapacity or revenge, but another agenda. He was cynical about Pope's claims to be above the market and knowing about ideologies of masculinity (interestingly referring to editorial excisions as castrations). Most of all, he wanted to expand the market for letters. This wish is articulated in a dialogue between Curll and a customer, Squire Brocade, who complains that Volume II of Pope's *Letters* is a rip-off because it is full of letters by people other than Pope. Curll responds that his purpose in printing them is to show that other people's letters are better than Pope's. A canny attempt to play the market? Yes. Curll put forward two candidates in particular: Delarivière Manley and Lord Lansdowne. The letters of the former are 'very pretty... full of true Humour, perfectly picturesque, in a genteel unaffected Style, natively pleasant, and, as *Horace* says, *simplex munditiis*'.[92] He sets a discourse of amiability against wit and a 'natural' woman against the class of male writers. Praising Granville's letters seemingly without irony, he pits an ideologically loaded identity against an inferred self-interested class of men of letters:

> the Patriot, the *Englishman*, the Christian, the Tenderness of the most humane Mind, the politeness of the finest Gentlemen, the Dignity of the *British* Peer, are here united, and shine forth with full Lustre in the utmost Propriety and Perspicuity of Language.[93]

Curll's eulogy is puzzling. George Granville, Lord Lansdowne, was better known as a peer and patron than a writer. He wrote technically assured and conventional poetry; two of his plays were successes. Pope had dedicated *Windsor Forest* to him in 1713 and in 1715 he had been imprisoned for Jacobite activities. In 1732 he published a handsome volume of his works including some elegant letters of advice to the newly elevated Lord Bath. He was also the author of a character of Wycherley which fixed them both as players on the literary scene, and perhaps readers understood too the force of Granville's plain-dealing in a letter to his father at a politically sensitive moment. The frontispiece provides another possible clue: an engraving of a portrait by Kneller, it shows Granville in a soft cap – as William Hoare's portrait of Pope did – and a significantly unbuttoned shirt. In the state of undress that indicated intimacy between poets, Granville was ahead of Pope.[94]

Moreover, the letters Curll refers to are allegedly volunteered by a high-minded member of the public keen to promote taste. This public source transforms a personal feud between Curll and Pope into a patriotically motivated struggle over what letters were to represent: the writer as producer or the writer as product. Curll saw Pope's commodification of himself as a writer through letters both as fair game, commercially, and as a manifestation of homosocial exclusivity in which the literary marketplace was taken over by bourgeois but élitist men, leaving less room for aristocratic or women writers. Swift's resistance to Pope's project of publishing his letters may also be seen in this light: Swift was too misanthropic to be homosocial and too much a journalist to invest much in witty or polite writerly identities. The stakes were high because homosociality, as it materialised in letters, was the key to an Augustan identity for Pope and others. It was explicitly challenged in a *Memoir* of Wycherley attributed to Charles Gildon and printed for Curll (who may have had a hand in it). Wycherley was an interesting case for the markets: in and out of debt, a writer of some widely acclaimed comedies, he might have been an example of the independent writer whose wit leads to commercial success. Instead, according to the *Memoir*, he made the mistake of printing a folio edition of his works in 1704, doing it himself rather than dealing with a bookseller. Its relative failure led to coolness with other poets, which explains why he became friends with Pope. Trying to square Wycherley's talents with the opportunism of this friendship, the *Memoir* starts to unravel the whole literary scene in which poets vaunt their unworldly friendships with each other over dealings with booksellers. The poets' claim to Augustan distinction is based on intimacies which they compare to the friendships between Virgil, Horace and others in Augustan Rome. The *Memoir* refutes these claims to a special status:

> this Clamour of our little Writers and Poets amounts to no more than this, that several Men of Wit and Poetry were very well acquainted, and very good Friends. And so it happens in all Ages and Nations, where there are at the same time many of Figure in the same City, frequenting the same Places of Resort.[95]

Urbanity is returned to a topographical coincidence. Letters remained awkward evidence for poets' claims for Augustan-style friendships and literariness mutually reinforced through the literary friendliness of correspondence.

Readers of letters desired these pleasures as much as addressees and public thirst for letters changed their value. Curll wanted them to fit a biographical and literary market; Pope wanted them to show, or show off, the writer's power to be writerly in all contexts, neither a poet by rote nor a wit by accident. The scintillation of these familiar letters was to serve the altruism of brilliant friendships – and vice-versa. As Wendy L. Jones observes, 'the correspondence constituted the "story" of a close-knit coterie characterised by its mistrust of "Party-spirit" and by its preoccupation with how one may lead a "good life"'.[96] Epistolary celebrations of virtue countered a much less flattering interpretation of the Pope-Swift-Gay-Bolingbroke world elsewhere in print culture.

The power of the meanings of letters can be seen in the relative unimportance of their textual authenticity; then as now, readers were interested 'irrespective of whether one letter goes back to an early holograph and another to a late printing'.[97] The tangling of authorised and unauthorised editions of Pope's correspondence was important not because purer texts came out of it, but because it showed the cultural value of letters being wrested into new meanings with new commercial applications. In the second half of the eighteenth century, these meanings changed again. Literary markets were less interested in wit; sentimental fiction promoted empathy. By letters, 'we are admitted into the closets and the confidence of the great and good, we imagine *ourselves* their friends and correspondents' (my italics).[98] The change can be seen in the 1780s, when commodification of Samuel Johnson was, if anything, more intense than Pope's.

By his own account Johnson was not a keen letter-writer: 'I fancy that I write letters with more difficulty than some other people.'[99] His most recent editor Bruce Redford believes it was his friendship with Hester Thrale which provided an epistolary vocation, a view supported by a letter to her of 4 November 1772: 'We keep writing to each other when, by the confession of both, there is nothing to be said; but on my part I find it very pleasing to write.'[100] Prior to that, he had difficulty with interiority: 'I have risen and lain down, talked and mused', he told one correspondent – and refused to elaborate.[101] Yet he equated letters with vitality, pointing out that we shall receive no letters in the grave and encouraging the ultimate in epistolary plainness: 'if you know any thing, write and tell it; if you know nothing, write and say that you know nothing'.[102] In an early letter to Richard Congreve, an Oxford friend, he stressed the opportunities for pleasure and improvement which correspondence afforded but presented them as general, not egotistical or even necessarily literary. The letters of Swift and Pope did not impress him: 'what looks at first like dignified independence comes to look to Johnson like...a kind of solipsistic self-regard'.[103] Self-conscious rather than self-seeking, Johnson's choice of correspondents, like his choice of household members, favoured unglamorous people. His democratic attitude to letter-writing was evident in a letter to his six-year-old goddaughter which he took the trouble to write in a large round hand resembling print so she could have the satisfaction of reading it herself. When Queeney Thrale was stuck for material, he encouraged her to draw on her own cultural repertoire, telling her that the books of a morning or the talk of an evening were both fit subjects for a letter. Young girls could join the republic of letters; appropriately it was a woman who first made Johnson's letters available to the public and reshaped perceptions of him.[104]

Although it was ultimately Johnson's conversation that commodified him as a writer – Hester Lynch Piozzi's *Anecdotes of the Late Samuel Johnson* (1786), Sir John Hawkins' *Life* (1787) and Boswell's *Life* (1791) – Johnson recognised the market value of letters. He grumbled to Boswell that it was so much the fashion to publish letters that he put as little as possible into his own. One letter by Johnson shows the power of letters mid-century to fix the construct of a writer and the means by which a writer might control that process up to a point. Johnson's letter to Lord Chesterfield rejecting his belated offer of patronage for the *Dictionary* is the most famous letter of the eighteenth century. In it Johnson asserted bourgeois labour over aristocratic favour:

Is not a Patron, My Lord, one who looks with unconcern on a Man struggling for Life in the water and when he has reached ground encumbers him with help. The notice which you have been pleased to take of my Labours, had it been early had been kind; but it has been delayed till I am indifferent and cannot enjoy it, till I am solitary and cannot impart it, till I am known and do not want it.[105]

Johnson distanced himself from that lordly ease which earlier men of letters had made their own through wit. There were gendered connotations too: on hearing of the letter, Bishop Warburton sent Johnson compliments on his 'manly behaviour' in rejecting Chesterfield's condescension.[106]

Johnson's letter to Chesterfield is arguably most significant for its curious textual history. Its addressee treated it as a semi-public literary text: he kept it on a table and showed it to visitors. To the publisher Robert Dodsley he said 'This man has great powers' and pointed out the severest passages and observed how well they were expressed.[107] So the letter became celebrated without being printed and indeed Johnson withheld it from public circulation. Boswell badgered him for years for a copy; only in 1781 did Johnson give in and dictate one. He refused a copy to another friend in 1784, though he gave one to Langton with instructions that if it were to be printed, it should be from that text. Boswell first published 'what the world has so eagerly desired to see' in 1790, at the high price of half a guinea.[108] Johnson tended to distinguish between publishing and printing – the former a process, in the Biblical sense of making available, the latter a product, a literal object issued from the press. He seems to have kept this letter out of print as a way of resisting his own commodification at least until after his death. Boswell thought Chesterfield's reaction was an affectation of indifference; a later biographer thinks it shows Chesterfield accepting the rebuke with good nature and being 'quite impressed' with the letter.[109] To my mind, Chesterfield's reaction is that of the rejected patron still acting out approval as if, whether or not money was involved (Johnson had in fact accepted £10 from him), he was entitled to treat Johnson as a commodity for criticism.

That Johnson knew the metonymic power of letters to market writers is illustrated by an experience in 1755, the same year as the letter to Chesterfield. An admirer 'had conceived such a reverence for him, that he urgently begged Dr. Burney to give him the cover of the first letter he had received from him, as a relic of so estimable a writer'.[110] This fan asked only for a cover, not a letter; other devotees were less delicate. Where commodification is now measured by fans *writing* mail, admirers of eighteenth-century writers invested affect in reading their idol's letters. Public interest was not about gate-crashing a writer's privacy; letters were sold more as *authentic* texts, like the modern celebrity interview. As one editor observed, Cicero corresponding with Atticus showed his character more genuinely than Cicero debating in the forum. Character was operative across both public and private domains; the proper comparison – and not an antithesis – is between personal and social discursive contexts.

The context of Johnson's letters represents a late eighteenth-century tendency more elusive than bonding letters to a private sphere: an interest in the transience of texts. Like those manuscripts and scraps of paper whose accidental fates set in motion episodes in sentimental novels, letters represented the power of writing and its fragility. That anxiety which earlier surrounded literary status and masculine identity for men of letters was diffused into an anxiety about mortality as letters became part of literary remains. So Sir John Hawkesworth introduced a new edition of Swift's letters with a declaration that reading correspondence 'most forcibly impresses a sense of the vanity and the brevity of life',[111] a sentiment applicable not only to Swift as a moralist and a divine but to any epistolary collection. Hawkesworth pushed empathy to the edge: reading the letters of eminent men to their friends,

> we live with them, we hear them talk, we mark the vigour of life...we see the scene gradually change; hope and expectation are at an end, they regret pleasures that are past, and friends that are dead...we lose them in the grave.[112]

He makes the letter akin to the elegy, with correspondence allaying and articulating the inevitability of death. One critic has argued that after Gray's *Elegy*, 'the fortunes of Elegia rose considerably', to the point where 'written wailings' became almost preposterous.[113] The danger of preposterous writing could be converted into proprieties of reading. Reviewing peoples' lives through their letters was a properly melancholic engagement with personal 'remains'. Here the market for literary letters was supported by a market in Christian letters, in which epistolary remains had long been thought edifying and comforting.

Enthusiasm for transience, then, fed markets in familiar letters and biography and in literary conversation. Johnson argued in a *Rambler* essay that 'incidents which give excellence to biography are of a volatile and evanescent kind'.[114] Letters counted both as incidents and as evanescent. The market for trifles about eminent people attracted some criticism – one satirist compared Boswell to a watchful cat who had sat for twenty years mousing before the hole of Johnson's mouth[115] – but wit had shifted to a more narrative form compatible with a politer society: the anecdote. Anyway recognised as 'talking on paper', the letter helped establish that market for trifles out of which grew collections of anecdotes and later table-talk.[116] The publication of more familiar letters by women put a squeeze on literary men's promotion of each other's correspondence within letters and they moved more into preserving and collecting correspondence. Homosociality turned to editing letters as letters became no longer just 'works' but a form of the men themselves. William Mason's *Life of Gray* (1775) re-established the man of letters through the disappearance of the editor: Gray's letters 'will give a much clearer idea both of Mr. Gray and his friend Walpole, at this early period, than any narrative of mine...In a word,

Mr. Gray will become his own biographer.'[117] Boswell, beaten by Hester Thrale Piozzi in the scramble to get Johnsoniana to press, struggled to bring Johnson as a letter-writer within his homosocial reach: the title page of his *Life* links letters to 'conversations with eminent persons'. In contrast, although Hester Lynch Piozzi was confident that a letter-writing Johnson was an authentic Johnson (a confidence which extended to the inclusion of some of her letters to him, at the publisher's request), she seemed uneasy about whether Johnson commodified through letters really resembled her friend. She compared the effect to something uncanny, like 'waxen figures modelled from the life, and dressed with such minuteness of propriety – they startle while they please'.[118]

Whether biography through letters involved misrepresentation or the perfect representation which Mason promised his readers, the coupling of lives and letters was assured. Curll was ahead of his market in suggesting that Pope's letters would make a perfect life; the next generation caught up with him.

2
Writing as a Parent

We may give advice but we cannot inspire the conduct.

– La Rochefoucauld

The character of parent acquired new importance in the eighteenth century. Fiction often put parents at a distance or dropped them out of the picture; actual children pointed to the importance of their start in life. Many valued parental advice. Unpublished letters from mothers and fathers show how parents interpreted their role as advisers; they also show that the character of parent was relatively gender-neutral, yet gendered in particular circumstances. Letter-writing gave mothers a voice and some authority, a much more active role than that represented by many writings on motherhood.[1] This chapter examines letters of advice first from a wide range of ordinary parents to children to show how letters helped create and uphold the character of parent. I look at some of Hester Thrale's letters to her daughter to show the character of parent under threat. Then I discuss Lord Chesterfield, the most controversial writer on youthful behaviour. Letters offered advantages as a means of giving advice, not least a greater likelihood of being attended to than sermonising and weighty tomes. The advice on offer needs to be understood in relation to the value of reason for children and ideas about education. Parental advice co-existed with other sources of advice – the periodical, for instance, made advice-seeking and advice-giving a major area of interaction between writers and readers and was often premised on an age difference between protagonists. Friends offered advice too.[2] For children, however, parents provided the first port of call and letters a familiar medium. Grown-up children continued to seek – and sometimes dodge – parental advice in letters.

In sampling this large and diverse area of writing, I want to detach it from conduct literature, proposing instead a context of relationships between parents and children – not quite the same as the history of childhood. Since letters establish and maintain relationships, they are good expressions of eighteenth-century attitudes to parenting and being parented. Whilst

I argue that the term 'conduct literature' needs to be more sensitive to genre, I do not wish to homogenise parents or children. Letters show how variously people approached the inculcation of precepts. Nonetheless, letters between parents and children illuminate arguments about relations between polite society and civil society. The letter helped frame questions: was human nature good or bad? Were generational conflicts inevitable? Could parents teach by precept as effectively as by example? Personae were roles; parents were role models. They were also, like their children, human.

Letters of advice

A Mother only knows a Mother's fondness. – Lady Mary Wortley Montagu

The term 'conduct literature', which has dominated criticism of advice literature, is a blunt instrument. Whereas advice can be taken or not, 'conduct literature' assumes didactic intent, if not effect. Though parents promote do-as-I-say, advice aims to benefit a child more by reasoning than by hectoring and hence allows greater empathy. Familiar letters were eminently suitable since they assumed some tailoring to the needs and interests of an addressee. 'Conduct literature' erases differences in genre, so that sermons, essays, homilies and letters are lumped together. It has been understood predominantly in terms of gender and class: 'Conduct literature addresses an audience of, almost exclusively young marriageable, women who are either already members of, or who aspire to join, the leisured classes.'[3] So says the modern editor of four eighteenth-century texts, first published as a collection in 1790. It is true the compilation aims at an audience of young ladies through its title but the picture is not quite as straightforward as it looks. One text is a selection of fables for the female sex; the other three are epistolary. Of those three, one is by an early eighteenth-century Frenchwoman who wrote a long letter of advice to her son as well as to her daughter; the other two are by a respectable Scottish father and a cast-out English mother. Each had its own publication history before being subsumed into a portable production whose title projects an ideal readership defined by age, class and sex: young ladies. Without wishing to quarrel with the significance of this cultural construction in 1790, I do wish to point out that it obscures the fact that three of these texts are letters of advice from parents of both sexes. This context is still relevant in 1790. Their explicitly gendered repackaging for young ladies should not be allowed to block out other ideological concerns, such as the eighteenth century's construction of youth as a class, parents as their guides and the relationship between them as one of watchfulness – as the subtitle of this collection, *Parental Monitor*, suggests. It is important to understand the particular cultural pressures involved in turning girls into young ladies but equally important to understand the pressures on young people as a group. The formation of polite society involved more than constructions of femininity.[4] Important as these are, we should not make them more important than they were. There were as plentiful books of advice for young men and much conduct literature concerned itself with entry into civil society for both sexes. For instance, *The Young Gentleman and Lady Instructed* of 1747, two handsome volumes authorised by George II, did treat some matters as specific to women, but its contents were mostly unisex, its title inclusive and it included parents amongst its intended readership.[5] Since learning was so often designated as polite, books of education also simultaneously instructed youth in conduct: thus Robert Dodsley's much-imitated *The Preceptor*.[6] This volume had a dedication to the future George III, connecting it to a long tradition of special instruction for princes going back to Xenophon's *Cyropaedia*; it was also explicitly designated for a schools' market. Youth, then, included young persons of different ages, capacities, classes and sexes – a rather broader readership than the niche market for young ladies allows.

Certain assumptions look different when one particularises conduct literature into letters of advice and writers into parents. One is about class. In tracking the evolution of early modern courtesy book to Enlightenment conduct book, Jacques Carré declares 'The middle classes...had pride of place in the new media of conduct. They were inevitably tempted to redefine manners in a way that would confirm their own hold on urban society.'[7] Yet if one thinks not of authors prescribing conduct but parents offering advice, the ideological reproduction of class becomes less important to bourgeois hegemony. Parents wanted children to uphold moral standards but these were not necessarily class-specific; indeed, ideologies of politeness stressed a moral equality that treated class differences as accidental. This is not to deny that ideologies of class still operated, but to stress they became more noticeable when writings by parents were read by children other than their own. As Carré also notes, two of the most read authors, Halifax and Chesterfield, were aristocrats who neither wrote for publication nor claimed authority from their rank. Instead they attributed their authority to fatherhood and worldly experience.[8] Of course letters in periodicals blurred the distinction: they often featured familial personae such as parents writing in to complain of children and vice-versa,[9] but the importance of this category of bourgeois reproduction should not obscure the existence of others with different dynamics. As Carré comments, 'The often modest status of the writers on conduct as fathers, mothers, tutors, clergymen, or simply persons of experience, offered them sufficient justification for giving advice, without recourse to social eminence.'[10] One might even argue that it is when people have less authority through the family that they are explicit about class: thus Wettenhall Wilkes put 'Genteel' in the title of his published advice to a niece. Even so, he noted people had been curious about whether he really had a niece – which suggests they suspected he was superimposing a public constituency of advice on a pre-existing category of familial writing.[11]

A 'friend of the family', like clergymen, helped smooth a path between family and wider social sphere. Likewise the agony aunt (an eighteenth-century invention)[12] is nominally the sibling of a parent. Nonetheless, parents had pre-eminence. Parental control of correspondence could be relaxed; many allowed children to correspond with approved elders like godparents who offered advice whilst being at one remove from the family.[13] Letters invite critics to be precise about who is saying what to whom; 'conduct literature' does not.

Conduct literature has been subject to some rethinking. Vivien Jones suggests it could produce a resisting reader or even a perverse reader: warnings against libertines might put ideas *into* young ladies' heads.[14] The imaginative power of descriptions of vice was evident in the liking of young ladies for Richardson's Lovelace and fiction showed young readers mocking moral books prescribed by their elders. One such scene set in a bookshop in Buxton has a group of young women wanting to buy something to read; when the bookseller offers them *Filial Piety*, they just laugh.[15] Owning a conduct book did not necessarily mean reading it or putting its advice into practice. One should be careful of reading fiction as if it simply reflected actual practice – the scene above is satirical – and one should consider advice literature in relation to a complex and contested area of family history. The term 'conduct literature' foregrounds the child as object of ideology and we know relatively little about children's responses to the processes by which they were socialised. As T.G.A. Nelson observes in a study of children and their relationships with parents in early to mid-eighteenth-century novels, 'The child figure appears more often as an object than a subject, and on those occasions when a first-person narrator is made to tell the story of his or her childhood the account is often tantalisingly brief.'[16] Historians are divided: some see child-rearing as increasingly progressive with the eighteenth century as a turning point; some see it as a story of continuous emotions with historically distinct moments. 'The history of childhood has become an embattled topic.'[17]

It is useful to recognise that the history of childhood is simultaneously a history of parenting and that the role of parent is a construction: one must learn it. In this sense, parents are as much in need of advice as their children. In the twenty-first century, there is much advice available to adults about how to parent, but even in the eighteenth century, advice literature had a double market in that it advised would-be advisers, parents as well as children. The Marquise de Lambert's letters of advice to her son and daughter were retranslated in 1749 by a man who lived at Deal in Kent. Among his list of subscribers was a large number of sea-captains – at least eighteen. One might explain this as support for a local author and suppose the copies were given to their children to read, but it is also possible that men away from home might be interested in a book that could advise them how to give advice to children, perhaps in their own letters.[18]

The term 'conduct literature' tends to mask uncertainties in its producers. The onus of duty was as much on the parent as the child; in writing, the parent fulfilled a duty to instruct the child. Biblical dicta to train up a child in the way it should go[19] were taken up by one of the most popular books of the eighteenth century. It elaborated the duties of a father in rhapsodic prose:

> Consider, thou who art a parent, the importance of thy trust; the being, thou hast produc'd, it is thy duty to support.

> Upon thee it also dependeth, whether the child of thy bosom shall be a blessing, or a curse, to thyself; a useful, or a worthless member of the community.

> Prepare him early with instruction; and season his mind with the maxims of truth.[20]

A father should teach his son obedience, gratitude, temperance, justice, diligence, science and religion, the text argued. It differentiated men's conduct into roles of husband, father, son, brother; women were specifically addressed in a section titled 'Woman'. It seems to presume a male reader-ship (and a male child) but that does not necessarily produce a gendered reader. Given its extraordinary sales I think one can assume both sexes read it. Gender in children was also bound up with other qualities, like intimacy or vulnerability: so Sarah Pennington's daughter was identified in her mother's letter of advice as an absent daughter, Miss Pennington, and 'my dear Jenny'.[21] Letter-writers' power to define an addressee allowed them to add colouring to gender.

Advice letters like Pennington's could double as a vindication; not all were morally motivated. Eugenia Stanhope published Chesterfield's letters to his son because she needed the money; the mysterious appearance of fourteen letters to his godson in *The Edinburgh Magazine* was likely to have been the work of the godson's recklessly impecunious tutor Dr Dodd. The power of the market was illustrated by one mother and son in 1765: exasperated by his never answering any item in her letters, she proposed sending him a blank paper,

> as he wou'd see by the directions it came from me; and that if he pleas'd he might answer them in the same manner – that after we had carried on this curious correspondence for some time, we would publish a Book under the title, of Letters between a Mother and her Son; in which should not be one wrong expression, one word of bad English, nor one false narration and I added to be sure the World would be in vast admiration at our Genius'es.

Her son replied enthusiastically: 'When shall we publish these Letters between A Mother & her Son? when we do I hope to get a little Money, for

I am sure I want some much.' (This cheekiness charmed his mother into sending some money.)[22] It is clear that many children separated from their parents longed to hear from them: 'in some measure to make up for your absence, let me have the consolation of hearing from you every post', wrote Catherine Hutton, aged seven, though she feared being troublesome – 'I shall write to you so often that you will dread post day as I shall long for it.'[23] This child imaginatively comprehended parental guilt; some parents showed little understanding of their offspring as feeling beings. In these cases, correspondence became a medium through which parents fulfilled their obligations with formality. Tutors complicated relationships, as third parties meant to serve parental authority but often its imperfect instrument. Lady Mary Wortley Montagu and her husband had a farcical correspondence nominally with their son, but really with each other:

> Mr. Wortley drafted, usually word for word, the letters to Edward ostensibly written by Mr. Gibson [their son's tutor]; now in return Lady Mary was taking in hand the drafting of Edward's reply to Mr. Gibson. Thus, in sober fact, husband and wife were gravely enacting the comedy of exchanging pompous paragraphs of good counsel with one another – over the signatures of their son and his tutor.[24]

Their son was now in his thirtieth year: the role of advising was compelling for some parents.

Letters of advice were not all unsolicited: the readership was active. The impecunious son cited above wrote to his father at length about joining in a rebellion at Eton. The letter sought not advice – it was too late – but approval: 'pray tell me in your next if you do not think I was in the right for going as all the other Boys did?'[25] Active correspondence, however, does not necessarily mean people who received parental writings actually read them. John Martin, who grew up to be a Methodist preacher, reverenced his mother so much that he carried her letter of advice in his pocket till it crumbled, before he had dared to read it. 'Her letters I preserved with care; but her good instruction I soon forgot. This, I believe, is a common case...'[26] Letters given to children, like books, were often defaced or lost. Arabella Davies' grieving husband reported that he had pieced together a publication from copies of letters mutilated by his children.[27] To prevent children's carelessness, parents stressed that an advice letter was 'a Token of my parental Care'.[28] Susanna Wesley, who took immense pains with her children and compiled a manual of advice for them, asked her son Samuel to transcribe her letters; copying entailed re-reading, hence possibly remembering. Her precautions were sensible: a youth who evidently paid attention to his mother's advice and at times asked for it, Samuel nonetheless lost some of her letters at school.[29] An example from a later period shows that parental letters continued to be symbolic. The artist Samuel Palmer thanked his small son (aged two and a half) for a letter:

> I take care of it – and suppose that you also will take care of my letters – for when you grow up to be a young man – I shall die and my body will be put in a hole and you will never see me again while you live in this world – and perhaps then you will look at some of the letters I have written to you.[30]

One should be wary of taking particular parents as representative of their era, but certainly many eighteenth-century parents preferred a kindlier writing than this.

Letters were not necessarily in competition with other genres as vehicles of ideology because in their manuscript form they were not for sale and because most parents could write a letter but not, say, a sermon. There was a conservative flow of information backwards: the Marquise de Lambert drew heavily on Fénelon and Chesterfield drew on La Rochefoucauld. The sequence of fourteen letters to his godson started out as an essay, and in turn Chesterfield's letters to his son were turned into a digest, which by 1850 had become an Encyclopaedia.[31] Just as educational books promoted duty to parents, advice letters often contained reading lists. People writing letters copied from books,[32] and letters became books. This free interchange between manuscript and print culture was assisted by the letter's flexible relations with other genres. Likewise within correspondences, parents measured their children's progress by setting them mini-essays on moral themes and sought to entertain them by sending drawings.[33]

On the other hand, epistolary form offered advisers particular advantages. Children were understood to be best instructed by degrees; they should be 'argued into their duty by fair and mild remonstrances'.[34] Letters allowed parents to put a frame of concern and love around advice and dispense that advice in small, letter-sized doses. 'Graver discourses like galenical medicines, are often formidable in their figure, and nauseous in their taste.'[35] Education was also often described through agricultural or horticultural metaphors. George Savile, Marquis of Halifax, imagined his daughter as an Eve-figure who needed to be protected from the bite of a spiteful world, but also as nature in need of nurture:

> Such an early sprouting Wit requireth so much the more to be sheltred by some *Rules*, like something strew'd on tender Flowers to preserve them from being blasted. You must take it well to be prun'd by so kind a Hand as that of a *Father*.[36]

Parents who laid aside authority for kindness in writing were figured as tender and tenderness between parent and child was imaged through the mutuality of correspondence. 'Whether my skill can draw the Picture of a fine Woman, may be a question: but it can be none, That I have drawn that of a kind Father', wrote Halifax.[37] Parents could get it half right at least by using letters to convey themselves as ideal. This ideal was familial: one of the many reasons Mary Wollstonecraft disliked Dr Gregory's advice to his daughters was that he sounded too much like an author and too little like a father, thus wasting the advantages of an easy familiar style which she thought suited the tenor of his advice.[38] Mindful of child mortality, parents tried to prepare their children for the next world as well as this. Arabella Davies, who lost several children, primed them all for death in her letters. It seems they took her advice to heart: one son, who died aged 17, wrote in his Bible '*There is but a short step between me and death.*'[39] In the natural course of events, children might reasonably expect their parents to die first; ahead on the road to futurity, parents' letters were thus allied to the genre of letters from the dead to the living whose admonitions could teach 'that which the Living dare not, or care not to say to Us'.[40] Mothers wrote letters for children when they faced childbirth; fathers too wrote letters to be given on their deaths to their children. The solemnity of death in the eighteenth century meant such letters were usually treated respectfully as remains.

Some writers recognised that children could find it an effort to honour their parents and suggested that children keep in mind the role reversals of age. Elderly parents' infirmity mirrored children's physical dependence; the garrulity of old age echoed the tedious prattle of infancy. Children should therefore be patient with parents as they aged since parents had been patient with them when young. This reasoning made duty sound wholly reasonable, reinforcing what advice letters also promoted – an idea of the child as to be reasoned into duty. In letters, equality of reason, albeit suited to different capacities, was supplemented by a love peculiar to parents. Arabella Davies wrote to her son Ned, 'remember you are writing to a Parent, who, though she expects attention and respect, desires you will write with the utmost freedom' and reassured him of her tenderness, 'never think, my love, as youth is too apt to do, that every piece of advice is meant as a reproof'.[41] Parents reminded children that they were eager to be pleased in language which came from the heart, not conduct books:

> IT is not easy to express the Emotions of Hearts that Parents have, when they see their Child do a Thing that's laudable and Praise-worthy. Their Love gives an *Importance* and many Times a *Merit* to Actions and Things, which others are ready to pass over as indifferent and insignificant.[42]

Pleasure could become pressure, exerted for instance through subscriptions. A typical model letter of advice written to an errant son 'rather as a warm friend than an angry father' ends with an emotional plea: if the dear child reforms, it will bring pleasure to the aged heart of his indulgent and affectionate father.[43] Contrition could be made material through children's replies, like a carefully written letter from a child in 1736: 'I own my fault and ask mama's pardon for doing any thing against her orders.'[44] Older children were offered less didactic parenting: 'So far as I think you ought, and believe you do, remember me as your real Friend', wrote Lady Mary Wortley Montagu to her daughter. Parental success was measured by its coincidence with the non-parental character of friend.[45]

Repetition was forgivable in letters to children because it inculcated duty, which was a matter of repeat performances. Correspondence was itself an educational tool: following explanation and verbal examination, children could learn by conversational exchanges, spoken or written, 'with able and virtuous characters, whereby we may polish and sharpen our minds, like iron from the effects of the files'.[46] Dutifulness was expressed through regularity of writing. Thus Arabella Davies enjoined her daughter Nancy, 'You will be very punctual in writing to us... and indite your own letters.'[47] Interestingly, letters are still seen as a help to parent–child relationships: an advice book published in 1984 urges its young adult readership to 'Cultivate the precious art of letter-writing. It will certainly strengthen your communication links with your parents.'[48]

Letters allowed parents a degree of subjectivity that compensated a little for tension between their duty and their feelings. When older children took up dangerous professions, many parents were torn between solicitude for their person and concern for their conduct. Death could strike suddenly in battle or at sea leaving offspring no time to prepare, so parental advice about principles was necessarily urgent. The balance between glory and safety was tricky. One father warned against imitating 'the precipitate temerity of the horse, which rushes into the battle'; what he desired instead was 'a race of pious, temperate and hardy soldiers, who would meet death with a rational intrepidity'.[49] Rationalising by a child in danger was complemented by parents' imaginative effort in approving, from safety, the child's choice. So Jane Davis struggled with feelings of loss when her son went to sea, writing to him, 'I hope I shall most cordially coincide in your determination.' She recognised a good sailor had to be brave: 'I would not be thought to encourage a pusillanimous or cowardly temper', but just in case, wrote to the captain to ask him to keep her son from unnecessary danger, not simply to comfort his mother but so the son could live to serve his country.[50] What Chesterfield rudely described as a womanish concern for the person was a more complex labour of love to sustain a dual discourse of offspring as child and citizen, a labour expressed and preserved through letters. 'I have no motive in view but your welfare', wrote Davis,[51] a word whose resonance can be understood if one remembers that the welfare state was originally defined in explicit contrast to the warfare state.

Letters from parents to children going far from home traversed an imaginary space, a beyond often empty as yet of narrative, and hence full of precepts.

Fiction reshaped this space a little to make parents into examples of uncomprehending readers or well-intentioned readers whose hopes and fears for the child reflected a moral code whose idealism was tested. Thus in Richardson's *Pamela*, the heroine's parents comment on events like a chorus, prayerful but not exactly practical. Some fictions recognised the state could act for parentless children. One example concerns a good girl, Alice, who goes to live with an aunt who runs a nursery. The aunt's childminding is a nightmare and Alice writes to another relation about her plight. The letter is dropped, found and taken to the authorities, after which Alice is rescued and the repentant aunt sent to Bridewell. Here a child seeking advice gets prompt action from the state.[52] Other fictions used letters to underscore the value of advice in family circles. These circles, like the actual group around Richardson who listened to his novels, tended to be composed of marriages between friends and siblings. The formula minimised friction between families and communities by extending families into communities through correspondences. One such is *Sophronia* (1761) in which an unfashionably happy and sensible married couple inspire others to overcome problems and imitate them. Ideological networks are kept up by correspondence that recounts their progress and passes on their experience: 'Your letters are the rule of our living', writes one ecstatic spouse.[53] It is hard to know if novels were creating a demand for advice from peers rather than parents, or cashing in on it. Novelists directed morals at parents too, famously in *Clarissa*, but there is a sense that the power of parents' advice to daughters waned a little in conjunction with fiction's waxing.

Letters from parents to children in reality crossed gender lines rather than simply enforcing them. Children were not straightforwardly gendered in the image of their same-sex parent. John Wilkes had one child, a daughter whom he adored. 'The greatest blessing which Heaven can bestow on any man, is a daughter like you', he wrote, adding '– unless, indeed, it be the favoured mortal who can call you his by a still closer connexion, and be perpetuated by another resemblance of yourself and him; which would complete my happiness, as a father.'[54] The oedipal moment is unusual: more characteristic were invocations of her happiness with no further definition or qualification. These abstract gestures towards her autonomy co-existed with a practical commitment to her pleasures: he frequently sent her gifts of food, expressing care for her person and that health which is a precondition of happiness. Michèle Cohen has argued that the Grand Tour became popular as a means of detaching sons from their mothers and making men of them.[55] Correspondence accommodated contact and separation simultaneously. Many parents of both sexes worried about the health of offspring on their travels;[56] tender parents regarded letters as expressions of care in themselves. When Lord Beauchamp set off on the Grand Tour in 1742, his devoted parents consoled themselves for his absence with the thought that it would improve him and benefit the nation. They missed him acutely, especially his mother, rejoicing in his letters and organising theirs to maximise the days he would hear from home. In some respects the correspondence was gendered: Lord Hertford tended to write of public news, affairs of state, military clashes, politics, and Lady Hertford wrote in detail of life at home – people, places, animals, anecdotes, seasons, the weather. But for the nobility, public identities were manifested at home too: 'since your Papa has taken the news which relates to greater matters out of my hands I choose rather to entertain you with the memoirs of a nursery than say nothing', she wrote. But she qualified apparent belittlement: 'to speak truth I am not sure that they are of less importance than things which make more *éclat* in the world, since I am not sure but that many both of our virtues and vices as often spring there, as they proceed from our first formation...'[57] What made her son so cherished was that he had a strong moral sense and entered into a domestic world, familial rather than feminine. If any difference mattered, it was age:

> My dearest Beauchamp,
> It is impossible for me not to begin a letter to you on the appointed day; whether I have materials to fill up my paper with or not, my fingers naturally take up the pen and my heart dictates that I cannot be at a loss to find something to say to a son so deservedly dear to me, and whose good-nature interests him in every occurrence which happens in his own family; and who at so great a distance can share not only in their pleasures and pains, but can hear with pleasure the recital of their amusements, which are far from being of the sprightly kind which most young people are fond of...[58]

That child is grown up who no longer aggrandizes parents, nor yet belittles them. Significantly, Lady Hertford follows this paragraph with one reporting that her father-in-law, the Duke of Somerset, is gravely ill. He had shown unremitting and intense hostility to Lady Hertford; part of the letter she wrote to her first child, Lady Betty, when preparing for childbed, was given over to emphatic advice not to continue this feud into another generation.[59] That Lady Hertford trusted her son with her unease about her in-laws is not so surprising, but the occasion is notable for her reinforcement of moral lessons even as she acknowledged the Duke of Somerset was an unnaturally severe father: 'I cannot be insincere enough to pretend to any other tenderness for him than what is inspired by the duty I owe him as the father of my Lord.' The mother does not simply teach duty but explicate an ideological tangle in which feelings, moral beliefs and duty have to co-exist. Letters of advice are in this sense free not to be didactic. She tells him in case the grandfather dies, in which case her next letter would have to use a black seal and her son might think his parents or sister have died. Letters enabled parents to show they were attentive to children's feelings and small things manifested this. Advice could be implicit, concerned with how to manage feelings as well as duty in a world in which both adults and children needed to reconcile sincerity and social convention.

That the character of parent was textual as well as biological can be seen from the strange case of Hester Thrale. Her marriage to Henry Thrale had little warmth and after his death she fell for her daughter's music teacher, an Italian called Piozzi, causing consternation among her family and friends. What Frances Burney described as a violent breach of decorum involved several factors: a mature woman's open sexual desire; attraction to a Catholic foreigner; putting herself before her children. Friends conceded Hester might well be swayed by romance after years without it, but the unusual resentment at her remarriage was exacerbated by the way the mother behaved like an adolescent. Passionate, obstinate, resistant to remonstrance, she became ill. The rights and wrongs of the frustrated mother versus her abandoned children are absorbing, but I am interested here in how correspondence expressed a curious upset of roles: the mother pleaded for her eldest daughter's understanding of an affair which placed the daughter *in loco parentis* to her own mother and her siblings. Hester Thrale (to keep the complications of naming simple) was a woman with literary powers who was known to be compiling a book on her friendship with Johnson. Her home at Streatham had been a significant background for her friendship with Johnson;[60] now that home was publicised (not least by her servants) as a site of passion at odds with decorum, revelations about Johnson were seen as likely to be indelicate. The literary woman who was loose became represented as loose-tongued (p. 109). Frances Burney, who had been a close friend, wrote letters to the eldest daughter Queeney exclaiming against her former intimate: 'that Such a Mother should desert her Children, & leave them to the mercy of the World, & the errors of youth unprotected & unadvised!' (p. 86). She recast the mother as daughter-like in her need of advice, taking as understood the convention that advice in this context related to the management of desire, and she offered the daughter advice as a friend, about how to manage the scandal. This advice, which recommended discretion to others yet encouraged Queeney to show her relevant correspondence, the mother saw (with some reason) as mischief-making. The family split up in 'a dispersion of Mother from Children, & Sister from Sister' which made Burney shudder theatrically (p. 93). Though there were other legal guardians besides her mother, Queeney de facto assumed care of her sisters. They parted from their mother on the road to Bath, thus avoiding an appearance of open rupture, and Hester Thrale married Piozzi.

Queeney's point of view has not survived on paper; accounts of her by others refer to her as reserved. At the time of her mother's remarriage in 1784 she was nearly twenty. Her father had died in April 1781; her mother had been close to Piozzi since 1780 and wanted to marry him since 1782.

Family opposition led to emotional scenes, conferences and partings, after one of which Gabriel Piozzi put into Queeney's hands her mother's love-letters. What the daughter made of this symbolic act is unknown: was it evidence of renunciation or its impossibility? Finally, isolated at Bath with a mother increasingly frantic and close to collapse, the embargo on Piozzi's return was lifted and he came back. Hester Thrale's state improved and the daughters considered their own position, in Burney's tactless phrase, as 'Orphan Girls of fashion' (p. 86). News of the marriage was filtered out through their mother's letters whose deliberate misdating of them supports a critical reading of them as performances although they profess a sincere desire for the daughters' love: 'My poor Heart is in a State wholly undescribable; *saltando, balzando,* &c. Let me have your dear Friendship continued to me; there is nobody's on Earth which I esteem more highly, exclusive of the Tenderness we have some right from each other' (p. 145). In a curious reversal of that epistolary surveillance which parents felt entitled to exert, she enclosed to her daughter copies of letters to Johnson and the guardians. 'Dear, precious, charming Queeney, accept my truest, tenderest Thanks' (p. 167): gratitude for her daughter's concession was mixed up with epistolary self-consciousness as she boasted of how the King knew Johnson had cried over her letter. Attributing Queeney's reserve to the intrusion of other people reading their letters was a more flattering explanation than the possibility that the daughter did not want to be caught up in the mother's authorial machinations.

Relations remained strained. When Hester travelled with Piozzi on the Continent, she wrote letters she defined, again self-consciously, as entertaining, while her daughter wrote irregularly and coolly. Finally the mother snapped: 'in short treat us as We are treated by others every way your *Equal* at least, or do not continue any longer a Correspondence in which enters neither Confidence, nor Respect' (p. 211). The difficulty was partly temperamental: the mother frequently urged the daughter to be gay, especially since she had the excuse of youth to enjoy those rational pleasures which even Johnson saw as central to life. Gaiety would minimise the difference between the daughter and her lively mother. The tension was also connected to letter-writing. Hester remarked on her daughter's dislike of her new name (p. 214), as if the initials with which she signed off symbolised how Hester Lynch Piozzi was no longer the mother of Miss Thrale. The mother who sent letters full of her literary successes (though tactically silent about her forthcoming book on Johnson) was more author than mother; perhaps in revenge, Queeney withheld her letters from her mother's publication of letters to and from Johnson. Since at one time her mother had shown some jealousy over Johnson's epistolary attention to her eldest (p. xxv), this non-cooperation punished mother and author simultaneously. When their quarrel came to a head, ostensibly over Queeney's plans for her youngest sister Cecilia, letters were again the instrument. Hester Piozzi took exception to her daughter's use of the 'kingly' idiom 'we', although she herself had used it when reproaching Queeney and her sisters for not writing to her. The law allowed Hester to remove Cecilia from Queeney's care and the breach lasted six years. Each had struggled to keep the maternal character for herself: for the daughter who had mothered her mother through a personal crisis and the mother who hoped that mothering would make her daughter into her friend, there were strange reversals. On paper, the maternal character could more easily be assumed by the older woman; having surrendered it with her love-letters, her parental authority collapsed.

Conduct literature simplified relationships between mothers and daughters, figuring them both as subjects to be advised and giving the mother authority according to how actively she transmitted advice or acted on it. Advice on behaviour to husbands was not just for newly weds: just as the daughter was to be wife and mother, so the mother was often still daughter and wife. This multi-identity collapsed differences between women, replacing subjectivities with roles. As a parent a mother could know best, but as a female parent she could be returned to the category of women who were much less knowing about the world than men. The Marquise de Lambert told her daughter, 'in endeavouring to cultivate [solid reflections] in you, I instruct myself'.[61] Male writers appropriated the power of the maternal persona, handling it anxiously: thus Richard Murray in *Alethia* (1747), an over-egged concoction of allegories in letters. He describes the letters as written for a young lady, and himself as a family friend. In the letters Selima, Empress of the Turks, writes to her married daughter Isabella in Cairo, a scenario that combined Madame de Sévigné with Arabian fantasy. A necessary change of religion presented few problems, although the text chokes up in trying to reconcile Selima's roles as a chastely devoted wife and a mother who lives in a seraglio. Sovereignty solves it in part: Selima is an Empress and one who teaches her daughter self-government. But she is really a medium for another teacher, a dervise whom she consults about one of her visions. Although the dervise addresses her as 'great Madam', class does not cancel gender; Isabella is to read 'these general Hints with the same Pleasure that I, thy Mother, have heard them', applying them to her own use.[62] The text has some surprises – a section on the law of contracts – and many conventions, like warning against pride as a woman's special vice. One inset story tells of a prince who rebels, thus grieving his aged royal parent. Murray's friend's daughter was presumably unlikely to overthrow anybody's kingdom, and indeed this proves to be an allegory about how passions upset parents that daughters everywhere might take to heart. Tropes of self-government compensate for a lack of material power. Murray uses the mother as a trope for feminised care: 'you will forgive a Mother's Anxiety, when I consider you as a human Creature', writes Selima on the first page and this care gives the mother some authority. It is mediated through masculine authority, the dervise, premised on teaching. Murray, a man, writes as a woman passing on to her daughter what a man says. Maternal authority is supplementary.

Real mothers writing to daughters worried about self-control, but more in terms of spending sprees, extravagant habits and gambling. The most famous mother–daughter correspondence, that from Madame de Sévigné to her daughter (Madame de Grignan's letters have not survived), was known to eighteenth-century readers in a version 'corrected' by its editor, Denis Perrin. According to a recent critic, his 'polite' emendations 'deprived the letters of their vibrant, vivid, inconsequential character'.[63] One recurring topic was money: 'Pleas, advice and exhortations pour out on that subject'.[64] One can track a fascinating parallel course of mother–daughter relations across three generations: Georgiana, Lady Spencer, her daughter Harriet, who became Lady Bessborough, and her daughter Lady Caroline Lamb. Lady Spencer, a widow for thirty years, tried hard. Harriet wrote her long letters about Westminster politics; she said she would have been better pleased if they had been on sermons.[65] Late in life she feared she had failed: 'Who knows, if I had had more firmness, how much it might have operated upon your dear sister's conduct & your own, & what bitter regrets it might have saved us all.'[66] But she had written two or three times a week, full of exhortations about conduct (and complaints about her daughter's handwriting), and there was much love as well as severity. In 1780 Lady Harriet married a man of her parent's choosing and wrote to a confidante: 'I wish I could have known him a little better first, but my dear papa & mama say that it will make them the happiest of creatures, and what would I not do to see them happy.'[67] To mark the occasion her mother wrote her a special letter of advice, which cautioned about the dangers of admiration and too-intimate friendships (with both sexes), counselled her about how to behave to her husband and in-laws, warned her strongly about gambling debts and recommended her to the practice of religion. Yet for all its conservative precepts, it was not unaware of the kind of world her daughter moved in – for instance, that sensibility was likely to make friendships blow hot and cold, or that what custom had been to her in the 1750s, fashion was to her daughter in the 1780s. As advice it had little effect – Harriet had many admirers, two illegitimate children and constant enormous debts. She also had a happy marriage and became a very affectionate mother. Her daughter Lady Caroline told her husband-to-be William Lamb, 'judge what my love must be, when I can leave such a mother as this for you', and her mother wrote, 'Your letter made me cry & then laugh at myself for crying. The truth is we are two simpletons, & unlike what mothers & daughters ought to be.'[68] When this child had her troubles, the grandmother comforted the mother and approved her performance of duty. The older woman sometimes struggled with new definitions of acceptable feelings, for instance teasing Lady Bessborough about excessive solicitude for her nearly grown son: 'after his travels in Russia & Spain your enquiries about his journey to St. Alban's was a little like Genl. Wolfe's mother begging him to take care how he came down Shuter's Hill'.[69] Maternal care was not lost on the children: 'I love you in my heart of hearts', wrote Lady Caroline Lamb,[70] and they were grief-stricken at her death.

Letters from parents reconnected old homes with new homes. There was special anxiety about one kind of child away from home: the apprentice. 'We should acquit ourselves according to our condition', wrote the Marquis of Halifax,[71] but apprentices were in transit between a condition of what has been described as 'close to slavery'[72] and independence. Apprentices were taken in 'as a member of the family, as an unpaid servant, and as a trainee for the relevant trade. Rags to riches was possible under the system but for the most part this was a motivating myth rather than a reality.'[73] The ambiguities of their position can be seen in the history of Samuel Richardson's *The Apprentice's Vade Mecum* (1734), part two of which was originally a letter to his nephew Tom. Advice is dispensed within a familiar frame, given to a 'dear' nephew from his 'affectionate Uncle and Friend'. Kindliness disappears from the printed version which instead 'demonstrates the desire of a master to establish control, both over the text and over the worker'.[74] A benign master–servant relationship had parallels with father–son, goodwill being cemented by marriage to the master's daughter which kept business in the family and the family in business. In reality, apprentices were often exploited, maltreated and prevented from learning enough to become rivals in trade: no wonder they were restive. In loco apprentice was an innately uneasy situation. Letter-manuals made prescriptive epistolary forms commensurate with proscriptive advice on conduct. Model letters from apprentices to absent masters informing them of customer developments ran alongside concerned letters from fathers warning their sons not to be at fault: 'It is so much a master's interest to use his apprentice well, that I am inclineable to think, that when they are badly treated, it is oftener the effect of provocation than choice.'[75] Economic loyalties fought for precedence over blood-ties, although apprentices who caused trouble were figured as doubly disturbing because they disrupted their master's personal life too. So one father expostulated with his son:

> What can you mean by breaking the rules of a family you had bound yourself by contract to observe? Do you think it is honest to break through engagements into which you have so solemnly entered; and which are no less the rules of a corporation you are one day to be free of, than those of a private family?[76]

The combination of personal and social immaturities in the person of the apprentice created confusions exacerbated by a fusion of family and workplace. Moreover, the apprentice was a figure of riot and disorder who could stand in for the potentially rebellious son. For example, one allegorical letter from the 1790s used apprentices' supposed predilection for bad company as a metaphor to denounce reformist associations and their concomitant radical politics. The riotous apprentice who demands a vote offends both his industrious father and his paternalist king; the father can only hope the apprentice will turn prodigal son and repent.[77]

The rebel child who shames his old parents by being a bad citizen was a powerful trope because the eighteenth century was discursively unclear about adolescence. 'Boys and girls – or were they men and women? – between the ages of twelve and twenty should behave, eighteenth-century commentators suggest, with the compliance of good children; alternately, with the common sense of grown ups.'[78] Hobbes' view that youth was a state of natural drunkenness was still quoted, supplemented by Locke's opinion that after the age of about fifteen youth entered a 'boiling boisterous part of life'.[79] It was unclear at what age children should become independent: an age of majority did not always translate into financial independence. Boswell and his father, for example, fought for years over a complex entail. As his biographer notes, Boswell was rarely subtle about his desires: ' "Give Your Son His Will" was the title of Boswell's early attempt at a comedy.'[80] But for every rebel child there was often a tyrant father who exerted sway long into adulthood. 'Age is not the Measure of Truth and Falsehood. Threescore-and-Ten may be in the wrong, and Twenty-five in the right', as one handbook put it.[81] Well-intentioned children struggled against neglect and hostility. John Aubrey, who said he felt about his parents as a slave about his torturers, tried to educate himself: 'My studies (geometry) were on horse back, and [in] the house of office: (my father discouraged me).'[82] This lonely child mourned the absence of books and conversation; luckier children had parents whose letters supplied an additional means of improvement.

The history of parent–child relationships can be understood as a history of surveillance. Looking after children translates as keeping them in sight. Although the parental gaze is often emotional – tender, proud – it is also simply watchful. Eighteenth-century children were reminded that God's eye was always on them, even in darkness or privacy, and encouraged to believe 'that you are at all times under the immediate notice of a self-existent, righteous, and omniscient GOD, in whose sight every evil disposition and action is offensive'.[83] When William Cowper tried to commit suicide as a young man, he was terrified at being under the eye of God.[84] This eye was also internalised in the monitoring power of conscience which had to be instilled in children: 'Teach them to be doubly diligent when no eye overlooks them.'[85] Hence the popularity of the term 'monitor' in conduct literature especially for women, who were advised by conservative moralists to keep out of the public eye.[86] Sight became a paradigm for control in the public sphere, expressed most chillingly in the development of the panopticon.[87] Before technologies of video and close-circuit television, which have familial analogues too,[88] surveillance mechanisms mixed verbal and visual resources that included letters. These could substitute for watchful parents or provide advice in their own right. I want to discuss a selection of these in some detail because they help explain the functions and power of letters of advice – and also because they can be misunderstood. Modern critics have been appalled, for instance, at Chesterfield's surveillance of his son. 'I will set a hundred Arguses on you', he told the boy, and asked those of his correspondents who had seen the son in person to make full reports. Class decorums were temporarily suspended: the boy's valet was interrogated about his size, health, bearing, dress and so on – all physical matters on public view, but still personal. Modern sensibilities regard this as heartless and it is ironic given that young children are taught it is rude to stare, but a comparison with a novel of 1768 suggests how looking closely at people ensured a social order thought by some to be more important than individuals. *Sophronia, or Letters for the Ladies* has an inset story about a duke whose marriage is in trouble and who pursues various amours. These are mysteriously frustrated – by his friends, as it turns out, who want to reclaim him: 'we had a committee that sate upon you every week; knew all your motions, and counterplotted them, and picked your pocket as often as we could. Your very tradesmen were employed to watch you.'[89] The aristocratic male's privileges are suspended; potential humiliation is allowed because surveillance can pre-empt deviance. Modern genres favour the spy, the detective and the private eye (sic!) for comparable ideological ends.

Besides the eye, another symbol played an important part in discourses of moral improvement. The mirror had a long history as an image for representation: texts claimed they held a mirror up to nature. Letters also promoted the mirror as an entity that could create an ideal for the real to try and reflect. This reverse imaging could be achieved by self-searching, or reflection in the sense of clear thought, and was especially prevalent in discourses of education – hence a mirror for princes. Thus the mirror simultaneously shows how things are and how they should be. In a less Platonic way, mirrors had mythological connections to vanity via Venus and her looking-glass which led moralists and parents to counsel against them. Affected women lived by their looking-glasses, George Savile warned his daughter.[90] Mirrors were increasingly significant in eighteenth-century interiors: large pier-glasses adorned the ends of entertaining rooms, public and private, and among the middle and upper classes more young women had mirrors where they dressed. Mirrors enabled subjects to see themselves as objects, thus replicating the objectifying gaze which for women in particular carried various meanings. Where these concerned female consciousness of beauty they were regarded with suspicion, but where they manifested a gaze of self-scrutiny and surveillance they could be turned to moral account. As one aunt advised her niece, 'Your observation must now be directed to the actual conduct of those around you; and as you will, in turn, be subject to the observation of others, learn to imitate what is most amicable in them.'[91]

One author who wrote a letter of advice purporting to come from a parlour looking-glass drew analogies between material aspects of the mirror and a brittle female viewer. This mirror is also a clear trope for sincerity, telling Angellica 'I perceive you are apt to view yourself with too great pleasure, and grow proud and conceited.'[92] A periodical devoted mostly to matters of education and manners, called *The Mirror*, featured as its eighth number a long letter from Vitreus about a magic mirror given to him by a dervise. The mirror acts like an eastern persona, defamiliarising appearances in morally predictable ways: it shows people as they really are. An alms-giver is bloated with ostentation; the physician poring over his watch is counting guineas, not his patient's pulse. But the mirror does more. Vitreus is especially amused by its ability to show people as they wish to be – dull fellows become amazingly clever – and to show people with the talents they think they have – a merchant becomes a fox-hunter, a mechanic's wife turns into a Countess.[93] The mirror becomes almost an allegory of writing: like glass, the medium of representation is supposedly transparent, or, reading dematerialises just as glass creates an image of reality which is not-real, is ideal. Vitreus's mirror, used properly, will not exhibit broken, distorted or unnatural images. This fitted the symmetries of letters of advice in which paper substitutes for parents, or the voice of experience, and advice acted as a metonym of proper conduct. Don't do as I do, do as I say: the discourse of parents was imaged in and by mirrors and supported by epistolary reflection.

Chesterfield

It is impossible to please all the world and one's father. – La Fontaine

It is widely recognised that eighteenth-century advice was predominantly concerned with politeness. What has been less explored is the relationship between politeness and openness.[94] I want to look at this in detail with reference to letters of advice from Philip Stanhope, 4th Earl Chesterfield, to his son because their publication sparked a controversy that involved major arguments about manners and dissimulation. Eighteenth-century readers knew some of Chesterfield's letters to his godson too but not his collected correspondence which provides a fuller context for his letters of advice. Readings and misreadings of Chesterfield's letters to his son also turned on shifts in social behaviour: what was sagacious in the days of George II seemed sinister in George III's era. Thus the arguments about Chesterfield's advice reveal new paradigms of socialisation dominated by sensibility and sincerity. Part of the controversy around Chesterfield's letters came from the shock of realising a parent had been advising a child against the grain – that letters could warp and subvert parental standards.

Truth-telling was taught early to eighteenth-century children. Many had it beaten into them: Boswell was beaten by his father for lying and Boswell in turn beat his son.[95] Some preserved honesty despite beatings: one much-flogged child protested to an Eton tutor, 'I dont Lie whoever say I Lie Lies.'[96] Lying and politeness, both described as arts, were also both departures from plainness. The Marquise de Lambert advised her son, 'The true Use of Speech is to make known the Truth', but acknowledged a potential slippage between being and seeming polite: the air of politeness 'shows a Man without, such as he *ought* to be within' (my italics).[97] Early and late eighteenth-century writers agreed that politeness involved pleasing others and that this involved effort or study. Duty had to be taught which meant it could always be seen as something learnt rather than voluntary, although its ideological power was premised on being natural. This tension could be resolved through sincerity or belief in learnt behaviour: 'friendship, filial duty, and parental affection, are founded in Sincerity'.[98] Complications persisted. The most important, predictably, concerned women. Women were not encouraged to speak their minds or indeed speak at all in so far as modesty presumed reserve: so the Marquise de Lambert told her daughter (but not her son) 'NOTHING is more becoming a young Person than Silence'.[99] Women, like children later, were advised it was better to be seen than heard. If a wife had criticism to make of her husband, she should keep it to herself: 'Your inward thoughts must not hinder the outward payment of the consideration that is due to him', Halifax advised his daughter. Reserve, he thought, was a guard to good women: though it might be a disguise to bad women, 'those ought to use it as an Artifice, who refuse to practise it as a Virtue'.[100] He recommended a courtier-like civility: 'the surest and most approved method will be to do like a wise *Minister* to an easie *Prince*; first give him the Orders you afterwards receive from him'. To behave in a polite and politic way, women had to become politicians. Politeness was also not clearly sincere for men, because where women were unable to be equal in company for fear of being thought forward, men had to initiate and sustain polite conversation. The Marquise de Lambert told her son, 'The means of pleasing is not to make a show of Superiority, but to conceal it. There's a cunning in being Polite.'[101] That this theme's appearance in Chesterfield was construed as a unique recommendation of hypocrisy seems surprising. La Rochefoucauld had observed in the previous century that hypocrisy was the homage vice paid to virtue and earlier eighteenth-century letters from parents had acknowledged that politeness required self-management. Like women, would-be wits were also cautioned to exercise self-command, to forego the pleasure of saying a fine thing if it risked being impolite. It was a mark of Chesterfield's reputation as a wit that, according to Colley Cibber, 'his sharpest Replies [had] a mixture of Politeness that few have command of'.[102]

Other qualifications of politeness concerned adolescents. On the one hand, children were to be taught candour, construed as 'frankness and ingenousness of temper'. On the other hand, if children's self-expression manifested humours, conceits and passions, they were not to be indulged.[103]

With adolescents, emergent sexual feelings were approved if they could be channelled into socially respectable ardour but repudiated if they led to autonomous sexual activity. T.G.A. Nelson traces the problem back to Locke who defended children against being married off too young by proposing 'some kind of induced latency period during which the child is simply kept from learning about sex'. Nelson offers a compelling reading of a novel about sexual awakening in which the adolescent protagonists defend their sexuality against adult control by hiding their true feelings – not because they think of them as crimes, but because they realise their elders disapprove.[104] The acculturation of adolescents meant moderating desire regardless of its sincerity. Moreover, adolescent manners were naturally impolite in so far as puberty made their body language awkward. Inelegance was a constant preoccupation in Chesterfield's letters to his son and his stress on the boy's need to cultivate grace was gleefully taken up by parodists. But other writers also lamented adolescent embarrassment or 'a sheepish, awk[w]ard bashfulness; which occasions young people to hide their faces, hang down their heads, to blush and seem confused when they are spoken to'.[105] Youth had to be trained to hide its impulse to hide especially in conversation, the principal domain of politeness.

A fear of polite behaviour's potential for insincerity was increased by uncertainties around how it was learnt. Young people should be exposed to good examples, all agreed, but the process was one of contagion which made it dangerously like vice: 'there is something that can never be learnt, but in the Company of the Polite. The Virtues of Men are catching as well as their Vices', wrote Robert Dodsley.[106] He had been a footman and one of his poems concerns a footman who learns the laws of politeness from hearing them discussed whilst waiting at table.[107] This situation rewrites some of Swift's anxieties about servants although, as Solomon notes, satirists used the aspiring footman as a popular trope for false politeness. The problem was partly that politeness had been too obviously learnt, or class difference could not be as easily assimilated as age difference, and partly that politeness was meant to work like a footman, covertly, silently. Directions for polite behaviour at table, for instance, refined upon those services of helping others (to food) which might otherwise be the duties of footmen.

Politeness, then, was coloured by questions of gender, age, class and nation.[108] It was not a straightforward prerogative even for privileged men. Educators wished to inculcate politeness as habitual whilst recognising it could be learnt only by practice. This opened the way for practised men whose politeness to women was sex-specific and sexualised. Politeness was held up as in reach of all, not least because it expanded the market for advice literature, but universal politeness meant an overlap between men's considered behaviour to women and men's strategic use of politeness as a cover for seduction. Advice literature and novels warned women continuously against men's insincerity. Here letters were particularly implicated. The second

Earl Chesterfield, instructing his daughter on letter-writing (another 'art'), observed coolly, 'it is usual to say in a letter that wee can not flatter when at the same time we doe it the most'.[109] Polite letters were open to being read as insincere on grounds of class as well as gender. When Dr Dodd wrote to Chesterfield's godson, his former pupil, Chesterfield commented 'this letter of Dr. Dodd's is in my opinion the utmost effort of human cunning'.[110] Letters were a medium in which writers could deploy insincerity in the name of social ideals such as politeness. Parents had an edge as authors since the parental persona allowed divergence from full subjectivity without risking dishonesty. Moreover, as parents gave their children advice letters written by other parents, the parental character became confirmed as something simultaneously personal and impersonal.

Critics need to enter Chesterfield's world quite deeply in order to see beyond the obvious. This is true of many letter-writers but it is especially true of Chesterfield because he explicated a code of politeness dedicated to veiling the obvious. Colin Franklin suggests a very helpful analogy when he remarks of Chesterfield's polite world of smiling and seeming, 'This form of falseness has shifted in two and a half centuries, from court life to television.'[111] One should also remember the dangers of selective reading: Chesterfield wrote to his son first as a small boy, then a child, then a youth, then a man – a younger man. As Franklin observes, 'A modern educational assumption, that a child's character should have been understood rather than created, would have struck him as most peculiar.'[112] Condensing the relationship as it unfolded over thirty-odd years of correspondence, one seeks a way of explaining Chesterfield without necessarily judging him, tempting though it is to redress the balance against an apparently relentlessly judgemental parent.

Chesterfield himself thought relationships between fathers and sons were generally unhappy (and made worse by quarrels over money) but told his son, 'You and I form, I believe, an exception to that rule.'[113] At various moments Chesterfield explicitly laid aside paternal authority in favour of friendly advice, or the experience of a man of the world who could guide an inexperienced youth:

> I know how unwelcome advice generally is; I know that those who want it most, like it and follow it least; and I know, too, that the advice of parents, more particularly, is ascribed to the moroseness, the imperiousness, or the garrulity of old age. (p. 776)

But he wanted to be able to return to the paternal character as a licence for reproof. Where novels promoted same-sex confidants as friends and moral monitors, Chesterfield argued 'nobody but a father can take the liberty to reprove a young fellow grown up, for those kind of inaccuracies and improprieties of behaviour. The most intimate friendship, unassisted by the parental superiority, will not authorise it' (p. 1615). Letters were a medium in which such reproofs could take place discreetly, as the textual equivalent of a fireside chat (p. 1234). Ironically, their unauthorised publication by Philip's widow ensured that all the world knew the son's imperfections.[114] Readers could also feel the weight of the father's ambitions – literally, in two large and elegant volumes, and metaphorically, as the letters poured out advice in what even Chesterfield acknowledged was a compulsive flow 'which my fears, my hopes, and my doubts, concerning you, give me' (p. 1069). Chesterfield's understanding of the paternal character pointed towards the more gender-hard nineteenth-century paterfamilias: claiming that natural affection was an invention of fiction (p. 1070), he repudiated concern for the child's well-being as a womanish concern for the person.[115] Instead, fathers should concern themselves with culture, not nature: 'My object is to have you fit to live' (p. 1070). Yet he did not always police the divide, worrying about his son's illnesses in later life and advising on medicines. There was equality too in his familial contract:

> I think I offer you a very good bargain, when I promise you, upon my word, that, if you will do everything that I would have you do till you are eighteen, I will do everything that you would have me do ever afterwards. (p. 1066)

Demands for obedience did cease: Chesterfield changed his form of address from 'My dear Boy' to 'dear Friend'. He still looked for a return: 'when I reflect upon the prodigious quantity of manure that has been laid upon you, I expect you should produce more at eighteen, than uncultivated soils do at eight-and-twenty' (p. 1446). But this horticultural trope was common amongst parents and it should also be remembered that in retirement Chesterfield took to growing melons – which do require prodigious manuring and were not common or garden plants. So too the boy was to be a fine specimen. Other eighteenth-century fathers fantasised about their sons – compare Boswell in 1775: 'I wrote several letters to announce my son's birth. I indulged some imaginations that he might perhaps be a Great Man.'[116]

Chesterfield's letters to his son start in 1737 when the boy was about five. One should bear two points in mind: the child was illegitimate and Chesterfield's only contact with him until he was an adolescent was through letters. Many of the early letters were in French, Philip's mother-tongue, and they function as a kind of correspondence course: the father sent back letters with corrections (p. 322); set exercises (p. 412) and essay topics (p. 463) and asked for transcriptions of ten or so lines from good authors, to be chosen by Philip, in every letter (p. 696). His own letters instructed the child in good habits: he must shun injustice, lying, pride and avarice (p. 327); he must ask questions (p. 47) and not learn like a parrot (p. 359); he must pay attention (p. 461); he must also look after his teeth (p. 336). There are stories from Ovid; a little on geography, chronology and poetry, accompanied by appropriate reference books; and a sequence on Greek and Roman history. Throughout Chesterfield stresses the importance of play – 'divertissez-vous bien' (p. 307) – and offers praise and encouragement: if the child learns well, he will be loved by Chesterfield and all the world (p. 320).

Chesterfield emphasises letter-writing, through which the child can learn how to spell correctly and how to write with ease – for instance to his governess (p. 329). Simple advice, but there is also more to it. To paraphrase a letter devoted to the topic: if the child writes often, and in Chesterfield's manner, he will not treat him as a little boy but as a youth who has ambition and loves to learn. He should pay attention not just to substance but also to spelling and style, because it is very important to know how to write letters well: one needs them every day in business and in pleasure and only women are excused from faults of orthography and style. When the boy is older he will read the epistles of Cicero which are the best models for good writing. Chesterfield adds a paragraph on Cicero's oratory and politics, and ends by reminding the boy if he does not understand a word in his letters, to look it up in a dictionary or ask his mother (p. 332). Letters become both the paradigm and the means of socialisation: the child can reach maturity by writing in a mature manner. Letters show both his potential (his ambition and willingness to learn) and a means of achieving that potential (Chesterfield puts in words he thinks the boy will not know, to stimulate his curiosity, and the boy's replies are free compositions). Through letter-writing, he learns manners, or politeness expressed through epistolary correctness, and the conventions (spelling) that mark him as a properly masculine subject and, eventually, a man fit for public service. Chesterfield proposes himself as a temporary model who can equip the boy to benefit from Cicero as an example of public service (saving the Republic of Rome from the bad ambition of Mark Antony). Epistolary propriety doubles for intellectual precision and moral justness; epistolary exchange becomes a medium of correctness and politeness which doubles for a worldly style that combines ease with decorum. The medium was the message.

Equality between correspondents was less certain between parents and children because children's letters were often supervised, short, and shaky. But the child did have a voice and a point of view which was not necessarily scripted by an adult. Frederick Ponsonby, for instance, aged nine, wrote to his mother from school about marbles and toy soldiers.[117] Philip Stanhope's letters to Chesterfield have not survived but there are instances of Chester-field entering imaginatively into his son's world. Again this is imaged through letter-writing.[118] Pleased with his son's efforts, Chesterfield encourages him to expand his notions, to imagine himself writing as if he were talking. This leads to a letter as if by Philip, describing success in his studies, running and playing till dinner, eating then like a wolf. It figures the child as untamed and also attentive, real and ideal (p. 381). On another occasion, Chesterfield tells the boy to translate a letter as if from himself to Chesterfield:

> My dear Papa, It is true you give me praises, but it is also true you make me pay for them, because you work me like a galley slave to acquire them. Never mind; one cannot buy glory too dearly. So thought Alexander the Great, and so too thinks Philip the Little. (p. 388, my translation)

Chesterfield recognises himself as a hard taskmaster, but justifiably so in the service of classical ideals. The witty persona for the child is not exactly mock-heroic, because the child's recognition of parental ambition and adult self-fashioning puts him on a par with classical heroes. Where is the irony, if the child is to imitate the hero? Letters become an express line into civic identity.

The civic identity that occupied Chesterfield's time during this stretch of the correspondence was politically uncertain. Frustrated at the failure of attempts to get rid of Sir Robert Walpole, he was disenchanted with politics. This inflects the significance of Roman history as recommended to his young son. He preferred it to Greek history, he told a friend, and he filleted from it conventional moral lessons. Thus the Romans (and Lacedaemonians) exemplified how

> the ambition of a man of sense and honour is, to be distinguished by a character and reputation of knowledge, truth, and virtue; things which are not to be bought, and that can only be acquired by a good head and a good heart. (p. 431)

In Chesterfield's world this was no simple thing. Men like Walpole whose hearts were bad had created a murky world of intrigue and corruption which disabled principles. When Chesterfield wrote to his son in 1739 asking him to consider the example of Cato and answer the question, is a man obliged to contribute to society, the reply would have supplied him with the juvenile equivalent of 'answers on a postcard' concerning his own situation. To retire from the fray might seem Roman but it also created the suspicion of flight: so he wrote to Bubb Doddington, 'I will either fight or run away, as you shall determine' (p. 470). One judicious critic has described Chesterfield's letters as 'a book of tough political self-fashioning, geared with remarkable range and prescience to the historical situation of the aristocracy, if not to the abilities and provenance of their addressee'.[119] But Chesterfield really only knew the son through his letters (which we cannot read): the *idea* of him or his existence in text would be as powerful a representation as stories from Roman history. His choice of stories for his son can thus be read in terms of an adult political agenda. In another letter of 1739,

Chesterfield writes to his son of Roman virtue, with stories of three generals. One refuses a bribe, one returns home to grow vegetables and one treats a prisoner generously and hands her back untouched (p. 396). In each case, people stay unchanged, uncorrupted. It is as if the adult unconsciously projects a longing for a simpler world. What one critic has described as Chesterfield's craving for parenthood[120] may be read as a desire to be released into an ideal and necessarily imaginary child's world, realisable through letters.

Against this utopian drive one can set Chesterfield's preoccupations with politeness. He laid out the rudiments before the boy was ten, expounding it fully in letters written during the boy's teens. The point was for the son to arrive at 'what I reckon to be the perfection of human nature, English knowledge with French good-breeding' (p. 526). The French *honnête homme* combined an honest man with a civil man; like an upright Roman, he was the same everywhere, a model of politeness and good-breeding who could speak to kings or peasants with ease. Chesterfield explained the rules – how to speak politely, how to behave at table, with examples of best and worst practice, how to move gracefully (pp. 446, 459, 461, 464, 525). It could be copied from life: 'I repeat it again to you, observe the French people' (p. 525). One reader commented it seemed Chesterfield would rather give up the Thirty-Nine Articles than the Three Graces, except that in Chesterfield's book there were more like three hundred graces.[121] Chesterfield's favourite verb for the process was *décrotter*, literally to get muck off, figuratively to polish. Some of his prescriptions have been derided, especially his injunction never to laugh, but some of his advice concerning grooming, clothes, posture and voice is given today to adults entering the public worlds of the media or politics whose common cultivation of image makes them increasingly the same world. It was not enough not to be rude, declared Chesterfield and some agreed, like the mid-eighteenth century adviser who declared there were rules even for sleeping with a good grace.[122]

The arcana of fifty-three years' experience had a number of parts – just as the polite man was a man of parts. Moral probity and knowledge was to be assumed; for this Chesterfield paid tutors, whilst including information in his letters about Europe's history, geography and political past. He arranged introductions into polite society and begged his friends to superintend social opportunities. Most of all he lectured Philip in letters outlining well-bred behaviour. The graces gave one a *je ne sais quoi* (p. 1115) which was pleasing to others. Chesterfield used the same phrase as Burke describing grace: 'In this ease, this roundness, this delicacy of attitude and motion, it is that all the magic of grace consists, and what is called its *je ne sais quoi*.'[123] Burke describes gracefulness as 'an idea not very different from beauty'; since neither Chesterfield nor his son was good-looking, it was the more important to cultivate what some people still term 'beautiful manners'.[124] Young Stanhope's illegitimacy also meant he had to overcome prepossession against him if he was to make headway in his planned career as an envoy and statesman like his father and for which his education had been designed – including modern languages and history. 'The trade of a courtier is as much a trade as that of a shoemaker', Chesterfield wrote (p. 1908),[125] and his son's apprenticeship was a composite of practical experience supplemented by paternal advice concerning the workings of courts. Politeness here was dynamic, an active mode of pleasing that involved calculating behaviour: 'Wherever you would persuade or prevail, address yourself to the passions' (p. 726). A 'complaisant indulgence' (p. 1038) of people's foibles and weaknesses, which made them pleased with themselves, should be extended into flattery so that they would be pleased with you. This tactical insinuation would enable a foreign minister to know the secrets of men and women 'which are easily got out of them by proper address' (p. 1235). The successful diplomat would give nothing away himself: 'The height of abilities is, to have *volto sciolto* and *pensieri stretti*; that is, a frank, open, and ingenuous exterior, with a prudent and reserved interior' (p. 1248).

This part of Chesterfield's system appalled many eighteenth-century readers. Chesterfield's argument that it was a matter of manners not morals to recommend that a man of the world must be like a chameleon (p. 1249) reassured few, although some conceded that the world of diplomacy supported the two-faced. Others argued hopefully that 'The sincerest christian, paradoxical as it may seem, would perhaps be the best courtier in the world: honest . . . faithful . . . sincere',[126] and noted that ambition had displaced conscience in a lord who showed little concern for religion.[127] Readers bore in mind too Chesterfield's distortion, as they saw it, of letters of advice in which parents commonly recommended virtues not graces and discretion not duplicity, and in which socialisation of the child was more important than self-advancement.[128] One explanation is that Chesterfield's letters clashed with the dominant taste in the 1770s for fictions of sensibility – Mackenzie's *Man of Feeling* was selling well[129] – in which doing good to others was promoted above doing yourself good; sensibility offered a virtuous glow which went deeper than the shine of graces. A parental persona was understood to involve an authority which rested on difference from the adult's full subjectivity. But Chesterfield's letters encouraged his son to develop a dissembling persona submissive to his parent but to no higher authority. Such deception contaminated all social relations, argued Chesterfield's critics, not just the specialised world of courts: 'Our noble writer is certainly a complete Machiavelian in politics, in friendship, and even in love.'[130]

Chesterfield's views of women caused most indignation. To his son he described women as 'only children of a larger growth' (p. 1209) although he kept up a long and elegant correspondence with the Marquise de Monconseil and believed that mixed company was the best company. Women gave men their reputations and could help polish awkward youths. They had two ruling passions, vanity and love (p. 1469), and affairs with married women could be useful. One should make polite advances and if one was repulsed one should try a second, third, fourth time. Critics were aghast at these 'lessons of lewdness given professedly and coolly by a father to his son... containing instructions on how to w——re with discretion and credit'.[131] For all sorts of reasons, men responded in women's defence and it may be no accident that there was contingent on the publication of Chesterfield's *Letters* a wave of advice letters by women, in their own persons, written to young women.[132] Links were made with Lovelace as an example of a man who was both polite and wicked,[133] and a novel-length critique of Chesterfield's letters had as its antihero an aristocratic youth who treats the advice as his Bible and sleeps with it under his pillow. He fatally seduces the wife of Horace Homespun and nearly causes the death of virtuous Fanny whose family both respect her privacy and are tenderly concerned for her happiness. Set against this wayward youth is a noble father whose children emulate him because they adore him, in a conservative process of example and imitation. Personal desire, linguistic trickery and misogynist dissimulation are set against sensibility and social responsibility contained in the bourgeois family.[134] Anxieties about both top-down and bottom-up encroachments are imaged through the Chesterfieldian lord and his footman, who imitates his employer's 'polite' seductions. Ironically, Chesterfield himself tested class-transference of politeness through letters in a correspondence with the Countess of Suffolk, in which he took up the persona of his footman writing to her maidservant. The 'sort of second-hand good manners from keeping good company' are both approved and mocked, as if the logic of imitation available to servants was less secure than that available to children who had been instructed in the theory via letters.[135]

Lord Chesterfield's title misled some readers into reanimating stereotypes of the aristocratic seducer. More to the point was the significance of courtly bodies. Chesterfield represented politeness as sexual: 'men are taken by the same means...that women are gained; by gentleness, insinuation, and submission'.[136] The wise minister had to hide his learning, as women were advised to do. 'Turn over *men by day, and women by night*. I mean only the best editions' (p. 1708). Some construed this advice as rampant heterosexuality, imagining the letters inspiring a community of unrestrained voluptuousness and indiscriminate sex like that supposed to exist in Tahiti.[137] But it was also a cover for homosociality: the polite man was often in danger of being thought a fop and although fops were feared for their heterosexual attractions, they were simultaneously derided as effeminate.[138] Openly acknowledging the value he set on vanity, Chesterfield wrote to his son advising 'Practise all the arts that ever coquette did' (p. 1974): to be seductive was to be actively feminine. The 'ministerial shrugs and *persiflage*' had to be practised too because they prevented one being seduced in turn (p. 2251). A minister's body is subservient yet expressive – he bows, deferentially, and yet acts as a blank; the *volto sciolto*, devoid of laughter lines, defies interpretation like a mask.[139] But the body returns in letters, especially Chesterfield's as he tries to train his son's body into a gracefulness seductive to both sexes. When the son wrote diplomatic correspondence to be seen by the old king, Chesterfield advised him to write a big, dark hand (p. 2240). Philip's crabbed handwriting was taken as evidence of an ungraceful body (p. 1563). Advice letters offered children 'hints' which they were to improve upon; likewise diplomats worked with similarly incomplete discourses. Letters were a way of sending and enlarging upon 'hints': the feminine seductiveness which can make the son a polite man also makes him a good minister, because Chesterfield thought 'Princes in general . . . are about the pitch of women' (p. 1438). His own experience of negotiating what became the Treaty of Vienna involved para-sexual skills: 'treating with about two hundred sovereigns of different tempers and professions is as laborious as treating with one fine woman who is at least of two hundred minds in one day' (p. 220). Moreover, sex-distinctions blurred as ministers could get power over kings through queens (thus Walpole, p. 308); princes also resembled women in being badly educated (p. 1982). In practice, then, the polite body was trained to be both open and closed in subtle ways. On paper, a simpler body could return. As one of Chesterfield's critics put it, 'HA! ha! ha! There is no law against laughing in a *letter*, as there is neither a vulgar noise nor a ghastly grin attending it.'[140]

Chesterfield's efforts to reproduce politeness in his offspring's body were insistent.[141] Vices like drunkenness and gluttony which altered the body's boundaries were inveighed against.[142] He was less sure how to contain and direct sexuality. His letters inquired about his son's amours and regretted reports of an apparent lack of interest in women even as he acknowledged it was none of his business. The oedipal aspects of sexual competition were displaced into an oedipal romance in which the father returned to a scene of conception. In 1751 when Chesterfield was planning to meet the boy again in England, he wrote, 'I look upon that moment as a young woman does upon her wedding-day; I expect the greatest pleasure, and yet cannot help fearing some little mixture of pain' (p. 1730). The father becomes the woman about to conceive a son; his letters took up the labour of reproduction.

Chesterfield also wrote letters to another young man, Lord Huntingdon, whom he considered as a son. This correspondence, not available to eighteenth-century readers, supplied advice to a legitimate aristocrat, a suave young lord on his travels in Europe. Chesterfield was deferential, apologising for 'impertinent' letters (p. 1520), and though he advised on delicate career moves he said much less about the arts of pleasing. 'There must be, to be sure, a *dessous des cartes*' (p. 2211): he recommended being poker-faced, as we would say, not using a courtier's mask.[143] To his son, Chesterfield asserted a father's privilege of correcting his defects; at the same time, he described himself as a father-figure to Lord Huntingdon in a correspondence devoid of criticism. Lord Huntingdon had sent him some verse on a lady; Chesterfield approved the subject. 'Desires are natural to youth and warm blood' (p. 1617). Chesterfield could approve sexuality when it was polished through poetry, when it came in the person of a youth of high rank, or when he could invoke worldliness to separate sex from love: 'Is there another Berenice to be dismissed when you leave Caen? The more, the more easily they are parted with' (p. 1540). When Lord Huntingdon went to Paris and had an affair with an actress, Chesterfield simply advised him to use condoms (p. 1931). When Lord Huntingdon went to the country, Chesterfield imagined him pastorally in pursuit of sex: 'I do believe that youth, exercise and good spirits may dignify, Dryadise and Naiadise, the Squire or the Curate's plump daughters, or even the cherry-cheeked milkmaid. And why not?' (p. 2234). The best pleasures were imagined or literary. As Johnson observed, the true effect of politeness was ease rather than pleasure.[144] Chesterfield proclaimed that his godson at the age of eleven had no idea of sexual difference and no thoughts of sex, conveniently overlooking his weekly subscription to a charity for ex-prostitutes, the Magdalen House (pp. 2789, 2803, 2815). Of his godson's sexuality he proposed avoidance. At the age of fourteen or fifteen, when 'appetites and desires begin to be busy...I would transport him' to Geneva: 'In that little, well-regulated republic, no indecorum escapes the knowledge or the punishment of the diligent magistrates' (p. 2437) and if there were vices, they were secret. Describing himself as a magistrate and censor over his son's republic (p. 1447), censoring not least his body, Chesterfield recommended culture should pervade even calls of nature, approving the example of a gentleman who read Horace on the loo. Philip Stanhope's response was to enjoy a secret marriage that produced two sons, in an ironic rebellion of hidden desires.

One can, however, see Chesterfield's adult civic persona complicating his character as a parent. Love has kingdoms; Chesterfield was a republican. Aristocratic men were supposed to seduce women whilst being femininely seductive to men and women. Chesterfield's marriage (to George II's half-sister) was one of convenience and amity: courtiers should exploit passions not have them.[145] The good father acted as a magistrate over the son's body but the good courtier acted as parent even to a most abject form of child. To illustrate *complaisance*, Chesterfield told his son a story of how he had cultivated a Dutch count and his wife. They were very fond of their little boy so Chesterfield was too, even wiping the child's snotty nose with his own handkerchief (p. 1900). The letters beg the question why, if a courtier could have a womanish concern for the person, Chesterfield could not be a more tender parent; they also suggest the answer, because the persona of courtier was at odds with the persona of parent.[146]

That letters were a kind of mask Chesterfield knew from his roles as Envoy to the Hague, Secretary of State and Lord Lieutenant of Ireland. A complex system of 'secret and apart' letters ran alongside pro forma correspondence which could be used to keep information back or oil relationships. Chesterfield knew its refinements, sending the Earl of Sandwich a letter he could show but with 'a more mysterious and confidential manner than usual' (p. 852). When Chesterfield retired, he sent his friend Solomon Dayrolles an explanatory letter he could show to people, followed by a personal letter outlining his real reasons. But there was little difference. In a world in which old friendships could be dissolved by half a crown (p. 522), Chesterfield had unusual integrity. His correspondence is full of polite refusals to write job recommendations and he took nothing from his employments apart from his official salaries: 'A good conscience is to my mind a better thing than the best employment' (p. 489). It is hard to reconcile the adult who is both principled and cynical with the parent who recommended equivocation. 'Remember then, as long as you live, that nothing but strict truth can carry you through the world' (pp. 1007–8), he instructed his son. Strictness in morals had to become a strict command of the body because the world existed in shades, not primary colours: 'Truth, but not the whole truth, must be the inviolable principle of every man' (p. 1868). Chesterfield's contemporaries glossed the letters as '*An entire Code of Hypocrisy and Dissimulation*'[147] and sifted Chesterfield's other writings for evidence, especially a paper in *The World* proposing in irony that code of simulation which the letters recommend in earnest.[148] Even more perplexing is Chesterfield's petition to George II written in 1752 which replaced courtly professions with downright rudeness: this satire, printed with the letters, reads like an outburst of contempt and rage, the heavily repressed returned through heavy irony.

Yet Chesterfield reiterated his world-view in letters of advice to his godson, another Philip Stanhope. Letters were again instrumental in teaching politeness – Chesterfield sent lists of words for the boy to learn which taught French vocabulary and social distinction simultaneously (e.g. *parvenu*, p. 2425).[149] The boy had a propensity to anger which Chesterfield encouraged him to hide through artful self-management (and threats of sending him to a madhouse), but he did well enough to be entrusted, aged nine, with the induction into politeness of Lord Herbert, aged five (p. 2589). Although the godson was also Chesterfield's relation and heir, ideological reproduction mattered more than kinship: 'I supremely despise that *postero-mania*' (p. 2807). There were important differences between the situation of this Philip and Chesterfield's son: he had a father, whom Chesterfield was careful to consult about 'our boy', and he visited Chesterfield often. The godson also had a sister who was being educated at home. Clearly cleverer than her brother, she outstripped him academically and socially, behaving at thirteen, as Chesterfield reported with approval, like a well-bred woman of twenty (p. 2581). 'If I had a daughter, I would give her as much learning as a boy', Chesterfield wrote to her father, but this was because learning kept women at home 'out of harm's way' (p. 2679). Her future was of no import: 'Miss Stanhope, I dare say, will do as well in her way' (p. 2375).[150] As Michèle Cohen argues, 'while there is no space for the achieving girl, girls' achievement itself continues to create the space for the fiction of boys' potential to be sustained'.[151] The courtier in a feminised body had to keep women out of the public sphere even as he recognised that women's presence was necessary to make a polite society in which the courtier could shine.

When exhorting the godson in person to control anger, Chesterfield developed a special body language to fix his attention: he held the boy's face in his hands and set one foot on the child's two (p. 2511). This motion is the physical equivalent of the parent's power to compel in letters of advice. It foreclosed some kinds of replies – the godson's best bet is to nod – but it did hold the child in focus. It is also an attitude that requires the adult to hold a position, which the character of parent helped. Letters showed how children were made, not just born. They occupied several time zones, like the child. The time-lapse between the world in which adults acquired experience and the world they anticipated the child moving through was well managed by letters, which connected different moments – the writing moment, dates of postage and delivery, the reading moment, even the re-reading moment in the case of letters of advice. Education is both process and product; so is letter-writing. Letters collapsed experience into reading: they bridged gaps, including the generation gap. They also trusted to children as reasonable readers, unlike newly popular stories for children which showed them listening to advice rather than reading it, or dialogues which scripted children's questions and answers in full, or tales of exemplary bird-parents who predigest matter for their offspring. Letters of advice also showed adults in process, the parent as a cultural construct.

The genre required that parents should advise their children on two counts: how the world works and what should be unchanging in a world that changes. These agendas were sometimes in conflict although politeness was supposed to minimise the difference between pragmatic and moral behaviours. 'A conformity and flexibility of manners is necessary in the course of the world' (p. 1024) opined Chesterfield, and Halifax likewise advised his daughter to conform to current best practice. Parents moulded children to fit, to conform, but they were less able to explain how society changed. 'Do everything in minuet time', Chesterfield advised his son (p. 2692) as if the world would always accommodate that even beat. On this point, politeness was helpfully detached from fashion; old-world courtesy never goes out of date. Tensions between primitive and polite behaviours were expressed in the socialisation of children. As Chesterfield observed,

the golden age of native simplicity will never return. Whether for the better or the worse, no matter; but we are refined; and plain manners, plain dress, and plain diction, would as little do in life, as acorns, herbage, and the water of the neighbouring spring, would do at table. (p. 2061)

So Johnson, discussing 'made' dishes, noted that the Scots had milk, eggs and sugar, but few of them 'know how to compound them in a custard'.[152] Politeness transformed a child from something 'raw' to something 'cooked'.[153] The letter of advice sustained the process.

The character of parent, then, was varied. Benign parents advised in the character of a friend; authoritarian ones sought to impose advice. Chesterfield's letters show how parenting was grafted on to adult character, not always organically. Hostility to his letters shows that however people promoted politeness for themselves and children, theories of it needed a moral framework: the duty that parents were expected to inculcate included unworldly principles or otherworldly beliefs through religious observance. Seventeenth-century analogies between fathers and kings, responsible for good government of family and state, gave way to more varied and thoughtful direction, with the letter as a medium of encouragement and reproof. However, letters of parental advice do not constitute a Whiggish story of progress towards a modern model of understanding children. Then as now some parents were tender, imaginative and enlightened, and others were not.

3
Writing as a Lover

Heaven is unchangeable. who can say so of love and letters?

– John Gay

The struggle to write about love is also a struggle to write about language. The lover is an unstable figure governed by paradox. As Barthes put it, 'I can be understood by everyone (love comes from books, its dialect is a common one), but I can be heard (received "prophetically") only by subjects who have exactly and right now the same language I have.'[1] Protestations of exclusivity and vows of constancy amongst eighteenth-century lovers testify to the roving, protean aptitude of the figure. Love-letters express love; they also express demand and need. Late twentieth-century critical interest has concentrated on their relation to desire, but this may not always mean what we think it means. The love-letter can be an anti-love letter, at odds with words of love, as in the case of the lover who 'unsaid all he had wrote'.[2] Whereas plots of rivalry were popular on stage and stories of abandonment in poetry, the prose letter favoured frustration. Moreover, the dramatic or poetic lover was more contained by the form of dramas or poems, whereas the epistolary lover was a figure of excess. Rousseau advised that one should start to write a love-letter not knowing how it will end; correspondence's resistance to closure emphasised the boundless potential of love – and vice-versa.

One of the primary paradoxes of love-letters is their desire to individuate their object and passion whilst being obliged to share a discourse with other lovers. 'It is an unsupportable misfortune that all declarations of love should be alike, and yet the passion itself so very different.'[3] This play between originality and conventionality was accentuated in the eighteenth century by customs that structured courtship and marriage. People had freedom and choice but not always freedom of choice.[4] Love-letters might be either a prelude to marriage or an escape from it; in both cases they provided a contrast to the more ideologically rigid institution of marriage. The character of the lover might merge into that of a husband or wife or be at odds with it, an ambiguity which made the character unstable. Further instability came from a traditional view of the lover as mad, translated into Enlightenment discourse as a figure of excess (extravagant, frantic, non-rational), and another traditional image of the lover as false, again updated by eighteenth-century culture as a figure of linguistic deception (the liar, the smooth-tongued seducer). Both these deviants accentuated qualities present in the typical lover, who experienced love as a passion at odds with reason which called into question the truth of the world as it was to one in love and how that differed from the perceptions of people who were not in love. Letters manifested these problems, allowing lovers, beloveds and readers alike to learn the languages of love – languages of happiness and hurt.

It is perhaps anomalous to talk of non-fictional love-letters because so many involve fancies, but the term draws attention to the existence of love-letters outside the novel. Critical emphasis on amatory fiction might suggest people learn how to write love-letters by reading novels. This is not necessarily untrue but it is simplistic. Where 'the letters of many eighteenth-century epistolary fictions generate a phantasmatical erotic body, a kind of prosthetic compensation for an absent lover',[5] they were doing so in ways shared with other contexts. Love-letters outside fiction could be fantastical: in the 1740s, 'some sparks in the navy took it into their heads to pacquet all the young ladies in Plymouth'. The postage cost three shillings and sixpence for what turned out to be 'a rhapsody of nonsense and bombast' with a lewd signature that outraged at least one mother. The daughter in question was an admirer of Richardson; she had no expectation that any of her suitors would write in the Richardsonian manner.[6] Manuals and fiction suggested available discourses but they were not the only options. Courtship manuals existed alongside relationships as letter-writing manuals did alongside letter-writing – that is, frequently with no connection at all. Love-letters by all sorts of people in and out of print provided other resources.

This chapter discusses some of the landmark correspondences whose publication in the eighteenth century made available a variety of models and a variety of responses more complex than simply imitation. My first section discusses the body in love-letters, its powers to wound and its vulnerability. Eyes and hearts had central roles in love-letters as speaking parts of the body. Sensibility and wit gave them different things to say, a difference I discuss with reference to Platonic correspondence, which treated the body as ambiguously attractive, and to the love-letters of Laurence Sterne. I also discuss how love was distinguished (by kind, by degree) from friendship and how this concerned letter-writers. Psychoanalysis is helpful here: many letter-writers played with similarities between paper and skin which suggestively evoke erotic contact with a lost maternal body. The lover is an unstable character and so appears in manifold contexts. Literary and legal aspects are discussed in 'Learning to Write' and 'Writing as a Criminal'; in this chapter, the focus turns to mid-century on, especially the 1760s and their particular constructions of gender. My second section, on nuns and lovers, takes the letter-writing nun in love as a starting point to explore the significance of the figure of Heloisa, principally for Rousseau who made the lover's vow a precondition of a political contract in which the potentially anarchic lover became a model citizen. The letters of Richard and Elizabeth Griffith show how Heloisa had cultural resonances beyond fiction, as a prototype of the lover as educable woman, which was important in companionate marriages. Heloisa's veils act as a metaphor for writing itself, a trope of incomplete articulacy with which the sighing lover was all too familiar. Expressions of love in letters get entangled in questions of language, as lovers occupy, abandon and negotiate subjectivities that are exclusive and present-tense. As Barthes suggests, 'I love you' can be heard only by others who share exactly and right now the same language.

Love and friendship

> Heavens, what a wide Sea of Perplexities do we launch into, when once we embark in Love. – Eliza Haywood

Writing as a lover meant taking up discursive complexity.[7] The most intractable problem of writing as a lover was how not to write like every other lover. The character had a generalising force even as it depended on being able to articulate its uniqueness. Books of advice for lovers and epistolary manuals both offered solutions to the problem and suggested it was insoluble. 'I AM in the utmost despair, to think that all professions of love are alike, whilst there is so wide a difference in the sentiments of lovers. My passion for you is beyond what was ever conceiv'd; but my address does not differ from any vulgar lover.'[8] At the popular end of the market, manuals suggested codes as a way for lovers to avoid being predictable. Mostly simple codes that substituted one letter of the alphabet for another, they allowed the simply literate to enjoy love's discursive perplexity in the form of a riddle. More literary lovers, also continuing seventeenth-century conventions, used imagery. Similes formed the backbone of those compliments which made the character of the lover immediately recognisable – compliments not only in its modern sense of praise for attributes, but also as an expression of willingness to do service (ironically a sense which survives now in business correspondence, in compliments' slips). Extravagantly allusive letters frequently assumed a female reader unimpressed by hackneyed imagery, whom a lover could interest either by more ingenious extravagance or by ironic self-consciousness:

My charming tyrant

THO' you expressly forbid me to repeat suns, rocks, mountains, earthquakes, which are as essential to a letter of this kind, as gilt-paper; yet you forgot to except against sighs, prayers, vows, tears, and the many other little reliefs the unhappy fly to...[9]

Paradoxically, a woman able to appreciate a lover who knew '*how to rank and file your complements* [sic]' would have heard it all before: '*you men can play the* Proteusses *at Pleasure*'.[10] Especially in the early eighteenth century, discriminating women readers had power as lovers. Compliments were often lifted from French texts,[11] which educated women might spot, although the iconography was overdeterminedly natural and elemental or Christian in a way that involved no theology, using tropes such as heaven, hell, the sun, brightness, fire, hot and cold.

Women's cynicism about compliments was reinforced by an older generation who warned daughters against flattery: 'my mother told me men had deluding tongues, and bid me never trust them'.[12] Witty men made a virtue of imagery's predictability. Farquhar turned his habitual tipsiness into a metaphysical compliment to his mistress: 'I retired to the tavern where methought the shining glass represented your fair person, and the sparkling wine within it looked like your lovely wit and spirit.'[13] Compliments were mocked as the unimaginative lover's first resort but they continued to appeal because they manifested the 'foolish fancy' of love itself. Similes enacted a displacement felt by an absent lover, who consoled himself with the power to bring other terms together. This industry of substitution could be mocked as lower class, like the courting shopkeeper writing to his mistress: 'Oh! what a pleasure it is to him to ransack all the academies of compliments for fine tropes and figures to adorn his stile with.'[14] The anarchy of instinct which love set free had to be contained: hence the continued popularity of tropes of academies of compliments and schools of love – not just as a continuation of the old classical idea of *ars amatoria* or the idea that teachable skills enhance love, but, in a more early modern outlook, the idea that the pupil who learns a master's discipline can master passion. The formulaic nature of compliments gave stability to amorous rhetoric; so too did a language of the body which, evolving from the erotic blazon of earlier love-literature, was one of the main constituents of early eighteenth-century love-letters.

If one signal part was the tongue, especially for men, another was eyes. The young George III showed his interest in Lady Sarah Lennox through '*langage des yeux*', according to one witness.[15] Again this foregrounds substitution: one part of the body 'speaks' for another, creating a satisfying trope of love as a power simultaneously expressive and imperfectly articulate. What one handbook described as 'the language of...looks'[16] was not straightforward, however. Male periodical writers used figures of the gaze – The Spectator, The Observer – as shorthand for dispassionate survey, although in tandem with figures evoking the tongue – The Tatler, The Pratler. The gaze has been read by Kristina Straub in terms of the licence accorded to men to treat women on (and off) stage as sexual objects.[17] Playgoers' licence to stare at women was powerful in eighteenth-century ways of looking but it should not be allowed to block out the glance, a more equal expression of desire between the sexes. One allegorical description of the Kingdom of Love featured an inn called '*alluring glances*' where both sexes mingled.[18] Steele's periodical *The Lover* devoted a whole number to a comic account of 'The Battle of the Eyes' between Mrs Lucy and Tom Whiffle; it involved an intricate repertoire of glances, looks, stares, peeps and so on.[19] Manuals catering for a popular audience were explicit about the licence allowed to women by the glance: 'where a languishing and bashfull Maid desires, and is not understood by the dull Animal she adores, though Words in strictness are denied, yet her Eyes may speak'.[20] This ambiguity translated into letters: the languishing maid is promptly given an example of a letter she could write, covertly mingling 'a touch or two of love' with business. That desire which eyes spoke contradicted the cultural constraints on women: 'natural' desire competed with ideological pressure to restrict women's desire. So one clever young woman anticipating a royal proposal wrote to her sister, 'I am allowed to mutter a little, provided the words *astonished, surprised, understand,* and *meaning,* are heard.'[21] The contradiction is just that of modern misogyny, which feminism's 'no means no' has tried to answer by stressing language over and above body language. Novels of sensibility entrenched the confusions: 'Her eyes, in their silent state (if I may use the term), give the beholder every idea of feminine softness; when sentiment or feeling animates them, how eloquent they are!'[22] In the early eighteenth century, manuals like *The School of Love*, predominantly aimed at a male readership, instructed female readers in the 'art' of managing reluctance as a cover for willingness:

> As for Maids & Widows, if they like a brisk Man, and are bashful, they may use dumb Signs, which is called *Cupids silent Language,* gaze on his Face, &c. Then when he perceives it, suddenly take of [sic] your Eyes, turn your Head aside, blush naturally, start a little, as if you were surprized: if he takes you by the Hand, grasp his with a little trembling, and seem to withdraw your Hand again as uneasie; if he kisses you, stay your Lips on his a while, with some Advance, and he is dull indeed that will not take these for signs of tender Love.[23]

Although these instructions might seem to mark a woman as a coquette, men seemed willing to surrender eye-power to women on the page because it allowed them a discourse of injury in which women had to make amends. So Dick Easy wrote to Miss Eyebright: 'You, Madam, like the murderous Basilisk, destroy'd me with your Eyes...you who gave the Wound, should also perform the Cure.'[24] The trope was spread further by seeming transhistorical: so a translation of Aristanaetus's letters which purported to show 'How women lov'd a thousand Years ago' characterised its female protagonists as having

'Eyes that destroy with their Light, and sparkle with irresistable Brightness.'[25] This business of eyes put women at odds with the Enlightenment: if men were dazzled by women's eyes, they were not able to operate by the light of reason; hence men need not bear the responsibility of abandoning reason for love.

Men were not caught like rabbits in headlights for long. They had several defences. First, eyes were frequently filled with dimming tears: just as the articulating power of the mouth was condensed into the sigh, so the expressive power of the eye was condensed into tears.[26] Second, sensibility undid some of the equality of the glance, turning it back into a gendered gaze, although a reversely gendered gaze was also possible. So in one imitation of Goethe, it is Werther's eyes which are expressive and Charlotte who remarks it: 'I see the ardour of his passion, I learn it only from his eyes; his tongue is silent.'[27] Third, especially in the early eighteenth century, women's injuring glances gave men an excuse to write letters complaining of love – 'complaint' being a term shared by literature and medicine. Men's pain was reannexed to a heroic discourse of injury in battle: as one manual put it, lovers should endure fatigues, like soldiers; as another advised, 'they that are hurt in service are permitted to shew their wounds'.[28] This militarism differed from a misogynistic discourse of courtship as siege and sex as invasion, especially popular among libertine poets of the Restoration; here, injury was the prelude to women showing mercy. Vulnerability (a word etymologically linked to wounds) thus partnered aggression in men's love-letters, inviting women's responses to be curative. A gentleman dying for love could be relieved by a 'balsamick Letter'.[29] An emphasis on the male body as prone to harm did not damage masculinity but paradoxically reasserted it. It has an analogue in westerns in which the hero is wounded then tended by a woman before successfully returning to a narrative climax.[30] Disarray becomes a temporary precondition for a reinvigorated masculine subject. In love-letters this harm was rhetorical. A collection of rejection letters purporting to be by women suggested that were women really to look at men, they might anatomise them unsparingly. To a gentleman hopelessly in love, one correspondent replied

> tho' you have a Hatchet-Face, Sugarloaf Crown, Saddle-Nose, Blub-Lips, and Wall-Eyes; I have new cast your Face in a Cherubim's Mould; I have also flatted your Shoulders, brought your Elbows within compass, pull'd in your Bum, set the right ends of your Legs upwards, corrected the waddle of your Gate, and erected your whole Fabrick...[31]

She (or he-writing-as-she) defuses the fantasy of her power to inflict grievous bodily harm with a counter-fiction of a grievous male body.

This semi-presence of (men's) bodies in epistolary discourse helps explain eighteenth-century interest in Abelard as the exception who proved the rule or the lover who could not be healed. Again reconfigured a little by sensibility, men's propensity for masochism moved letters centre-stage. Off-the-page dynamics of looks could be changed into the rapt and eager gaze of the letter reader and the letter acted as a substitute for the writer's body even as it dematerialised the other lover into discourse. Masochism connected page and body; the page connected sympathy and body: 'she who was not to be seduced by the fine figure of her lover, was lost when she reflected on the sufferings he had endured for her'.[32] Sufferings in this case include smallpox which has marked St Preux's skin: marks both superficial and permanent, like the fragile but preservable letter, they suggest an analogy between writing and the body or more precisely between paper and skin. As Judith Halberstam has argued, 'Sometimes skin ... forms the surface through which inner identities emerge and upon which external readings of identity leave their impression. The cultural constructedness of these readings and identities is stressed by Carol Clover in her description of gender as a skin-like permeable membrane.'[33] Likewise Barthes, discussing how Werther brushes against Charlotte, sees erotic exchange as skin-orientated: 'Every contact, for the lover, raises the question of an answer: the skin is asked to reply.'[34] Though no longer made literally of skin, writing materials in the eighteenth century still resembled its impressionable surface.

What of the heart in eighteenth-century love-letters? Deep under the skin, yet audible and palpable through it, the heart is both a literal place of vital forces and a figurative place of truth. Lovers who pressed letters to their hearts in countless fictions, illustrations and real-life correspondences made them another layer of skin, enacting both a desire to incorporate the beloved and its impossibility. The heart miniaturised love's pains for both sexes when connected to writing: as one heroine put it, 'I find my Tortures arise when I write: My Heart sometimes dissolves into Passion, then boils with Frenzy and Desire.'[35] Men's letters could be curative objects for women: 'How I press your Letters to my Breast as the greatest relief to my aking Heart!'[36] Broken hearts could be imaged through torn texts – famously in Richardson's *Clarissa*, in the distraught scraps written by the heroine after being raped, and also in the lesser-known *Love Fragments* by John Robinson. A heartbroken heroine does not stop writing – far from it. Even and especially at death's door, 'Her pen is seldom out of her hand, and she frequently enquires for the post-man.'[37] They continue to write because they court a new suitor, Death.

The lover was an especially compulsive letter-writer. Horace Walpole heard of two lovers in Paris of whom the man, rather than talk to his beloved, tossed billets to her over a screen placed between them. When Jonathan Swift wrote to Stella, he often finished one letter and promptly started another and his letters give much space to the mechanics of corre-spondence as a subject in itself.[38] Bad conversationalists could compensate by being good letter-writers – indeed, they more than compensated: they became peculiarly desirable. 'I am much pleas'd with the fond Folly of a Lover, who, on the Point of being Shipwreck'd, wrote a tender Billet to his Mistress, tho' he expected the next Wave would swallow up both himself and the Letter.'[39] Is this celebrating an addiction to love or to writing? To both: epistolary compulsion marked the true lover because 'Like the lover, the writer is alienated by his desire.'[40] In love-letters, one stood in for the other: 'the lover finds himself caught in a tension between distance and presence equivalent to the paradoxical situation of the correspondent'.[41] In the examples just cited, the protagonist is male and the symmetries between a correspondent unable to possess writing and a lover unable to possess the object of desire may depend on gender. Equally it may not: there are many instances of men and women falling for each other through their letters. It was a commonplace of early eighteenth-century amatory fiction. One of the strangest real-life examples was a story put about for George III. The *Annual Register* respectfully reported that he had fallen for the charms of Princess Charlotte after reading a letter she had written to the King of Prussia, nobly reproaching him for an invasion of her cousin's territories. In fact the monarch and his mother thought of her as a candidate after spending an evening going through a continental directory of princesses.[42] The epistolary legend made better copy than the facts.

For both sexes, then, letters reached the parts other texts could not reach. Hence the eighteenth-century appetite for stories in which love-letters foiled prison bars and guards and spies, like Helen Maria Williams' accounts of the stratagems used to get love-letters in and out of prisons in revolutionary France, tucked into food or carried by a trusty dog.[43] The stories would mean less were the letters not love-letters, because love and letters reinforce each other's powers to elude laws of time and space. Love-letters even evaded the enclosure of tombs; epistolary testaments to bodily affections were poignantly juxtaposed with the mouldering corpses who had written them. *The Tatler* printed correspondence unearthed by a sexton in which Sir Thomas Chichely courted the woman he later married, and in whose grave they were found. Most of the letters had crumbled away but two ardent letters were entire and printed thus, as if textual completeness imaged or even resurrected corporeal wholeness.[44] Steele reported that the company present at the discovery became melancholy, but he sought no explanation of why the lady was buried with her love-letters. It needed none: readers understood how love and bodies and letters went together.

The eighteenth-century correspondent most associated with the heart was Sterne – ironically, given that after his death his heart was for many years accidentally interred separately from the rest of his body. The civil, good-humoured, nonsensical discourse of Tristram Shandy that was meant to do good to all readers' hearts was supposedly carried over into his letters too, which according to Sterne himself showed 'the easy carelessness of a heart that opens itself, any how and every how'.[45] Sterne tends to evoke the heart impersonally – it is a heart, or the heart, not *his* heart – and this reluctance to own his own subjectivity contributed to the complex textual history of Sternean letters. To be heartfelt like Sterne, one did not have to be Sterne; hence the proliferation of imitations of Sterne, with various degrees of honesty.[46] Even now it is hard to untangle Sterne's productions from those of his imitators. Authenticity here is not so much a matter of authorial name as of the sensibility for which Sterne's name was a byword, especially in his *Journal to Eliza*.[47] Yet as this text shows, sensibility had a worldly counterpart. Sterne's rhapsodies to Eliza were written at the same time as he tried to avoid correspondence with his wife about a financial settlement during their separation: 'thrice a week this last month, has the quietest man under heaven been outraged by her Letters – I have offer'd to give her every Shilling I was worth, except my preferment, to be let alone and left in peace by her – Bad Woman!'[48] Love was connected to business.

Confidence, the key to Sterne's manner, was readily converted into epistolary confidence tricks. Sterne's manner could be passed off through the Yorick persona as authentic, though unauthorised. Even his beloved Eliza Draper was his imitator: 'I have in my writings aimed as much as possible to be Yorick.'[49] The picture was further complicated by Sterne's daughter Lydia, who had a bad press from later editors for messing about with Sterne's texts, even commissioning the radical and libertine John Wilkes to write letters in her father's manner to swell out a posthumous edition.[50] Inviting other authors to sound like Sterne was not so different from Sterne's practice of raiding his old letters to sound like himself – for instance, when he wrote to Eliza Draper, he recycled courtship letters originally written to his wife.[51] Moreover, authentic and inauthentic Sterne are hard to tell apart, as in the following letter of c.1761, to Elizabeth Vesey:

> O Lord! I would give away my other Cassoc to touch you – but in giving this last rag of my Priesthood for this pleasure You perceive I should be left naked – [nay] if not quite dis-*Orderd*: – so divine a hand as *yrs* would presently get me into Order[s] again...[52]

Published in 1775, this letter was thought to be spurious until a copy was found in Sterne's letter-book. His description of his letters as 'loose touches of an honest heart' was barely metaphorical and created unease among some readers similar to that distaste felt for parts of *Tristram Shandy* as lecherous and vulgar, although it also suggests Lydia's invitation to the libertine Wilkes was a shrewd move. The persona of Yorick played with seriousness; intermittently he assumed the role of spiritual instructor, telling Eliza to bind up his letters to make a book of advices (which she did and promised to wear them next to her heart). He also aired some unchristian fantasies, for instance anticipating how his wife's death would free him to marry Eliza. (Decently, she replied she hoped Mrs Sterne would continue to live.)

Sterne-as-Yorick wanted his amour to be literary: 'Not Swift so loved his Stella, Scarron his Maintenon, or Waller his Sacharissa, as I will love and sing thee, my wife-elect!'[53]

Sterne was too obsessed with possessing genitalia to draw on the castrated Abelard as a model, but he did play at being a different sort of priest – a Brahmin. This subscription located him in the Anglo-Indian world of Eliza Draper but from her point of view it fitted ill with his kindly jester persona of Yorick. 'I was almost an Idolater, of His Worth, while I fancied Him the mild, Generous, Good Yorick', wrote Eliza to a friend.[54] She associated the Brahmin with a more painful sensibility: 'Yorick shall heal the sorrows the Bramin gave.'[55] Her metaphors seem like standard paramedical imagery: Sterne-Yorick is the physician of her mind, bringing the cordial of sentiment. There is also more to it. In his letters, Sterne typically uses the heart as both the object sensibility worked upon and the subject whose response proved sensibility's presence. Others before Sterne declared they were writing 'from the heart': the phrase is one Richardson's Pamela uses about her letters. Yet her avowal was disbelieved and recast by Fielding as deceit in the letters of Shamela. In Sterne's letters to Eliza, the possibility of self-deception could not be tested so long as the heart in question was a votary of love whose delusions were imaged through multiple personalities. Paradoxically, personae implied more sincerity. The fusion of heart as subject and object was repeated in an emphasis on tears as process and product – something produced by the heart and something leaving the body. Visible against skin, rolling tears imaged moving emotions.[56] Tears' translucency acted as an analogue for the transparent heart, just as epistolary formlessness acted as an analogue for the heart's lack of premeditation.

For early eighteenth-century lovers, hearts, tears, sighs and kisses were exchanged through the medium of letters. Eroticism was understood to involve a certain cost, often figured as self-surrender or given a transcendent value: 'Lovers... divest themselves of their own Souls, that they may more happily be fill'd with others... by *Love we do not Sell*, but Exchange ourselves.'[57] Sensibility refined the transaction: as Draper put it, 'I feel as you felt, when I read what you pen.' It also made sympathy more aggressive and aggressively corporeal. As she continued,

> when your page compels the tears from my eyes, and makes my heart throb – I will say; Here my Bramin wept – when he penn'd this passage, he wept – let me catch the pleasing contagion from each heart-felt sentence, and bedew the leaf with mutual streaming sorrows.[58]

Sensibility comprehensively appropriated the lover's body and its products in order to dissolve ego-boundaries which other amatory discourses respected more. Draper was often uneasy about Sterne's letters. Left to her own devices, she offered him super-ego and id, prayers and dreams:

My Yorick, my friend, divides my thoughts with the dear name that duty binds me to [i.e. her husband]. I often dream of you – remember me in your prayers – think of me waking, and let me, like an illusion, steal through your fancy, while you sleep. – I am yours – I am yours.[59]

Sterne's version of sensibility pressured Draper to melt her ego into his, a move disguised as the more rewarding mingling of hearts. She clearly found it seductive to be valued for her being rather than her body: when Sterne told her bluntly she was plain, she responded that she was happy he was attached to her for sentiment, not beauty.[60] But this seduction was damaging as well as alluring. Sterne's advices mostly consisted of telling her to have more self-esteem; a double epistolary persona, of kind Yorick and cruel Brahmin, helped him wound and comfort her sense of self.

Sterne's letters were written when the market for letters on love was heating up. The 1750s, 60s and 70s saw numerous writers take advantage of this, especially women whose miscellanies often included sentimental letters and essays which debated the nature of love and its difference, if any, from friendship. Some writers made definitions of desirable love part of the duties of friendship – thus Mary Masters advised a semi-fictional female friend to be less romantic.[61] The idea that satisfaction in marriage depended on esteem, or love depended on friendship, has been described as 'one of the theorems of eighteenth-century life'.[62] Naughty girls like the young Catherine Jemmat or Elizabeth Gooch seemed to outdo the stratagems of fictional heroines in securing secret correspondence with bold suitors: Jemmat pulled up pacquets to her room by her garters; Gooch persuaded a gardener to attach her beau's letters to a stick outside her window.[63] For them, effort was an index of esteem quite unlike ideas of esteem promoted by conduct books and novels. Love and friendship were both staple ingredients of letters, leading Elizabeth Griffith to remark disapprovingly that silly girls only stayed in love because they wrote letters to each other about love.[64] Correspondence offered a model for reciprocity and a medium for mutuality; hence it was formally supportive of those dynamics of likeness and difference that create relationships of love and friendship.[65] Love and friendship intertwined when 'Women readers wrote the Richardsonian text'.[66] Since women were Richardson's friends and correspondents as well as his readers, one could equally say Richardson was imitating women's texts. Alarmed by competition from women writers, Sterne disparaged their texts as overly crafted and hence not from the heart. To Mrs Fenton he wrote, 'I promise to send you a fine set Essay in the Stile of your female Epistolizers, cut and trim'd at all points. – God defend me from such, who never yet knew what it was to say or write one premeditated word in my whole life.'[67] But Sterne also contemplated exploiting this market, telling Eliza, 'when I am in want of ready cash, and ill health will permit my genius to exert itself, I shall print your letters as finished essays, "by an unfortunate

Indian lady." [168] In order to understand the commercial success of women's contemplations on love, one must backtrack a little to the mid-century to pick up the threads of one of the most debated notions of the eighteenth century: was Platonic love possible? Could friendship between men and women be both rational and passionate? If Platonic friendships inevitably became sexual, were they the more passionate for having been repressed?

The ever-amorous Robert Burns declared memorably that love and friendship go together like strawberries and cream. Few other writers were so cheerfully hedonistic about Platonic friendship, preferring to see it as a domain that offered women intellectual pleasures rather than sensual ones. As *The Lover's Pacquet* put it, 'we believe, that to treat of *Corporeal Love* will be distasteful to the *Platonick Sect*, who totally reject every thing in Respect to *Flesh and Blood*, and intrance themselves in Admiration of the Ideas of Virtue'.[69] Especially up until mid-century, Platonic love was seen as a risky business, perhaps surprisingly since it offered a temperate zone between passion's heats and chastity's coldness, although this was also the zone where prudes were thought to lurk: 'a Platonick Lady has lain with her humble Servant out of a refin'd Friendship, when she would not listen to a Declaration of Love'.[70] The cultural history of how homosocial philosophical dialogue became a paradigm for asexual heterosexuality is not my concern here,[71] but two points are relevant to eighteenth-century epistolary culture. First, in Britain, Platonic love was seen as a model of reciprocity, worryingly close to equality: 'You see there was a reciprocal Confidence. Nothing is more dangerous: It is the high Road to Love.'[72] Since correspondence was both reciprocal and an exchange of confidences, letter-writers of different sexes were predisposed to Platonic relations. Second, although Platonic love was mocked as a self-deluding discourse, associated with faux-naifs and prudes, it was not subject to inarticulacy. Rather, it borrowed from philosophy a pleasant confidence in words even as it demanded examination and clarification of terms. Rational argument was a means even when the end was not rational, for instance if friends became lovers or lovers broke up. If the mark of love was that, as one manual put it, all parts of the body become vocal except the tongue, in Platonic love the tongue functioned just fine. Hence Platonic discourse was particularly appealing to women: it required them to be articulate and intellectually alert, in contrast to other amatory discourses that confined them to cynical wit or silent expressiveness.

One Platonic correspondence that was also a literary success was Martha Fowke's *Epistles of Clio and Strephon* (1720). Fowke (otherwise known as Sansom following her marriage to a lawyer) was much admired and desired by men in the circle around the writer Aaron Hill in the 1720s. The *Epistles* further endowed her with literary attractions. These were letters, some verse, some prose, to William Bond, a dramatist and writer, the later editions of which were prefaced with a glowing critical essay by one John Porter, who thought 'Clio' excelled Ovid. The couple only meet at the end of the text so their relationship (which was succeeded by others for Fowke) was strictly a-corporeal. In consequence, the lovers' attractions are both imagined and displayed by the text, which substitutes for their bodies. Porter reads their dematerialisation as refinement – as he puts it, 'A Woman's Love, which begins in her Eye, is of a coarser Mold than Love, which begins in her Mind.'[73] But this refinement only semi-detaches the body which is constantly present as a point of comparison. Of Clio, Porter rhapsodises, 'she indeed plainly appears to be the *Fair* one in *Mind* as well as in *Sex*...her Mind was surely formed to Excite such an intellectual Courtship'.[74] His comment is oddly reminiscent of pornography, in which bodily eroticism is redirected to writing; here, letter-writers share with lovers and readers pleasures of the flesh made word. The critic too can reread the letters back from text to body. So Porter shows excitements that are not exactly intellectual: 'Did ever so much fearful granting, retracting, blushing, trembling, bewitching, Modesty appear in Action, as there is here lively painted in Expression?'[75]

Fowke uses the Platonic letter to celebrate her escape from a double standard: in the eighth letter, 'when her *denying* is so *faint* that it *may pass* for *granting*', Clio appears to discourage Strephon:

> Thus speaks my Soul, but it alas! is join'd,
> To human Clay, which is to Rules confin'd,
> And thou thy Self wou'd chide it if too kind,
> Yet whatsoever rigid form attends,
> Let us at least – Eternally be Friends,
> And I intreat thee, Oh! my charming Spright,
> In Verse to Visit CLIO ev'ry Night.[76]

Poetry defies decorum: one may be ravished by it. Letter-writer, lover and reader share a desire to be seduced by writing. Fowke also uses dream tropes to create an etherial body able to enjoy sexual pleasures, pleasures that decorum denied women the right to seek out in the real world. Platonism preserves decorum because Clio rejects a male body in favour of the Soul as a locus of erotic pleasure:

> You may admire me, all the Ways you can,
> Give me the Lover; but keep back the Man:
> Yet even him perhaps my eyes cou'd bear,
> Because thy Soul, (who is my Friend) lives there.[77]

Platonic correspondence was popular because it allowed lovers to flirt and fantasise under the pleasurably transparent cover of a transcendent discourse which both allowed the body in and kept it out.

Platonic love was also indirectly supported by moralists and novelists promoting the idea that women could say no to suitors of whom they disapproved. Hugh Blair argued that a principled woman could 'always convert a lover, if she cannot give him her affections, into a warm and steady friend',[78] a conversion aided by epistolary ease and politeness. This notion did not allow women a positive yes, but led to space for Clarissa's 'conditional kind of liking' for Lovelace. Two factors came together: first, arguments in favour of women as rational creatures who deserved to be educated; second, the dwindling influence of French romances which made heroic love appealing to witty women.[79] Combined with female interest in Stoic writers such as Epictetus and Marcus Aurelius and the growth in published miscellanies by women which included thoughtfully argued essays, by mid-century women were increasingly associated with reason. Hence the popular image of the companionate marriage, which successfully combined love and friendship. Platonic love might, however, be a threat rather than a prelude to such relationships: companionate marriages could be wrecked by wives' friendships with clever men, or husbands' with other women, especially younger women, either class of whom might reasonably enter the household in the guise of friendship.[80] Platonic love's combination of reason, refinement and literariness made it dangerous because it fitted all the criteria of the 'polite' by which the upper-middle class sought cultural hegemony.

After the mid-century and especially post-Rousseau, the picture diverges. The idea of the companionate marriage is a troubled one but people did look to the arts, especially 'polite' literature, to provide common interests for husband and wife. Notions of subjectivity for each spouse, or what Lawrence Stone has termed affective individualism, were as much about rescuing women from commodification in the marriage market as really exploring their world-view and granting it cultural validity. Letters were crucial here because they purported to delineate that world-view, however much they were packaged as fiction. A novel like Richardson's *Sir Charles Grandison* (1753–4) debated frictions between love and duty without suggesting its nature as a fiction would make it less relevant to real women – quite the opposite. Thus for all her Italian trappings, Clementina is anxious to do the right thing in a way consonant with British pragmatism. 'Politeness was a tool which a well-born woman could use to extend her reach', observes Amanda Vickery, noting that letters, along with periodicals, pamphlets, papers and novels, provided women with a means of laying claim to wider cultural horizons.[81] For women aspiring to politeness, passion was best encountered not as a *rude* shock. The fiction of Rousseau and his inheritors challenged the primacy of courtship plots: they showed the 'correct' choice of love-object in marriage was not necessarily final; seduction was a repeatable event. This pattern entailed painful recognition but was also expansive since pain expressed growth (in both sexes). For much of Rousseau's *La Nouvelle Héloïse* and Goethe's *The Sorrows of Young Werther*, Julia and Charlotte are promised to one man and beloved by another. As heroines they are committed to duty, but the knowledge they could make a husband happy is not enough, finally, to distract them from the question of whether it made them happy – which adds to their charms in the hero's eyes. Passion becomes untameable: not necessarily destructive, it is difficult to live with and challenges all the characters to respond. Their response, moreover, is formal as well as figurative: it is significant that many of these novels were epistolary. In corresponding, characters need repress nothing.

The Rousseau-style novel usually started with the meeting of two young people whose affinity is laid out in correspondence. The attraction between them depends on soul-felt sympathy akin to Platonic idealism, although the situation is also familiar from countless novels of less idealistic seductions. Hence a curiously old-fashioned note:

> the young unmarried woman, who suffers herself to commence an epistolary correspondence with a man her own age, is guilty of a great imprudence; but that, if she writes one letter to him on the subject of Love, she risques her undoing.[82]

Condemnation, however, is compatible with irony, as in Rousseau's warning that unmarried women would be undone if they opened his novel (a transgression necessary to read his warning). One needs to be equally careful about positive statements on friendship's metamorphosis into love and its acceleration by letters. Sounding cautiously utopian, Henry Mackenzie's novel *Julia de Roubigné* (1777) suggested that, providing consummation was out of the question, 'the friendship of one of each sex...has that combination of strength and delicacy which is equally formed to improve and delight'.[83] This view, however, is expressed by one of the many imprudent mothers in sentimental fiction. Their own marriages often less than satisfying, they encourage their daughters to explore equality with non-domineering men. The daughters duly fall in love but in obedience to their father's wishes marry older and less imaginative men. Then they pine. Obstacles that thwart the young lovers symbolise social relations from which women are not free and which they do not necessarily want to abandon. It has been suggested that *La Nouvelle Héloïse* is a generic hybrid: 'the first half is a scandalous fiction of illicit love, the second half is a moralising work of philosophy and social comment that seems to expunge unregulated desire'.[84] The politics of the personal challenges this distinction: who legislates on forms of love, making some 'illicit'? The philosophers who moralise against desire: co-opting women onto the side of philosophy helps their cause but in the process exposes it as ideologically motivated. The personal connects with the social by means of letters, a genre common to love and philosophy, joined at the point of a friendship that can go either way.

Rousseau and some of his imitators used multiple correspondence to break down that structure of principal love interest and subsidiary friendship which normally constituted epistolary plot and subplot. In *La Nouvelle Héloïse*, Julie's confidante becomes such a good friend to Julie's lover St Preux that Julie suggests they would make good lovers. Having struggled to make a good friend of her ex-lover, Julie seems to confess at the end that after all he was her true love and offered her a passion that her companionate marriage to Wolmar could not supply. Sensibility was caught in its own trap: if love inspired benevolence, then prohibiting love after marriage shrank its utopian social effects. Some fell back on friendship: 'though that love only can be pure, which glows for one; yet holy is that friendship which glows for all'.[85] A woman could choose the virtuous glow of duty to her husband or the glow of passion outside marriage, but she could not have both – except in fiction, where it was promptly cut short by death. Writers tried to shortcircuit the opposition through virtue as a term common to duty, love and friendship: as Rousseau put it, 'we shall be guilty, yet we will be in love with virtue'.[86] Rousseau himself favoured paradoxes as a way of inscribing without resolving ideological tension. As Mira Morgenstern succinctly explains,

> Love can be seen as doubly ambiguous. It is constructed of seemingly contradictory elements that are both Self-regarding and Other-directed. Reaching out to the Other, which is supposed to promote our happiness, may wind up destroying our Selves. On the other hand, not even trying to love is, as Julie discovers, to condemn that same Self to death.[87]

In Platonic relationships, correspondence was the medium of an idealist affair; in sentimental fiction, an instrument of passion that served lovers. Letters were agents of corporeal love, not its substitute: St Preux does not fall in love with Julie through her letters.

In fiction, the love-object of love-stories may be less obvious than plots suggest. Within even simply heterosexual plots, definitions and alignments can be in process, in ways that evoke pre-sexual intimacies. Adult desires may have traces of previous dyads, particularly a mother–child dyad, as a precursor of, if not a foundation for, adult intimacies. Tania Modlieski has persuasively read the Gothic romance as a genre that covertly stages a female Oedipal plot. She argues the genre shows young heroines negotiating their sexuality in relation to parental figures: the father is obviously present in the lover, often a dangerous or forbidding figure, the mother is conspicuous by her absence. In Gothic, a genre running parallel with epistolary fictions of sensibility and overlapping with it, the mother may be represented by location rather than plot – compare Roger Dadoun's reading of the Gothic castle in film as the domain of a phallic mother, most familiarly embodied in the vampire,[88] or, less ingeniously, the matrilineal aspects of other, safer houses, like Emily St Aubert's chateau, La Vallée, in Ann Radcliffe's *The Mysteries of Udolpho* (1794). Epistolary fictions share this discourse: in *La Nouvelle Héloïse* and many other novels, the mother is killed off part-way through the plot, leaving a grieving daughter in a state of melancholy that merges with mourning for her absent lover. Plots also make daughters into mothers, stressing women as naturally reproductive objects: Lovelace's fantasy of Clarissa and Anna Howe as mothers of his children; Julie's first pregnancy, ended by an accident, and subsequent family; Charlotte's circle of children. My interest is in mothers in discourse rather than plot – although St Preux's dream of a veiled Julie tending her dying mother is a powerful representation of how daughters are wrapped up in a relationship with their mothers that is simultaneously fantasy and threat.

I think the eighteenth-century love-letter in sentimental fiction evokes mothers through language. Consider Rousseau's description of

a letter really dictated by love. [It] will be tame, diffuse, prolix, unconnected, and full of repetitions...like a natural fountain [it] flows continually without being exhausted. Nothing brilliant, nothing remarkable; one remembers neither words nor phrases; there is nothing to be admired, nothing striking: yet we are moved without knowing why.[89]

Rousseau's description uncannily fits Julia Kristeva's concept of the semiotic, that world of infant expressiveness before entry into language, in which utterance expresses bodily drives without being reducible to grammar, logical structure or signification through a symbolic order.[90] Critics have taken up Kristeva's semiotic as a pre-verbal place from which to critique entry into the symbolic order; I propose that in special circumstances the semiotic is open to adults – to mothers and lovers. Sweet nothings between adults echo low maternal murmurs. Rousseau expressly makes its appeal intuitive: 'our hearts, in spite of ourselves, sympathise with the writer'. It is not that lovers aspire to baby talk, though many lovers are comfortable with it, but that subliminally love-letters draw on pleasurable infantile memories of prelinguistic rhythms and inexhaustible maternal love. Like lovers, mothers coo and babble. Neither pairing needs meaning or syntactic boundaries to express affect, pleasure or desire: '*you*, and *I*, are two words prohibited in the lover's language. Two lovers are not two persons, but one.'[91]

An amorous discourse of guilt can be read in the light of a maternal ghost. To be sure, the 'stolen kisses' so often celebrated by male lovers are marks of conscious (and defiant) guilt at infringing on another man's property rights, either the father's right to dispose of his daughter or a husband's right of exclusive ownership. But their guilt may be shaded with unconsciousness, as the lover competes with the mother to be the provider of bodily pleasure. There are two ways to break the daughter's pre-conscious bond: first, to make her a mother, literally or figuratively, servicing her lover's own pre-conscious memories; second, to change the focus of the lover's memory from latent and infantile to conscious and adult. Rousseau offers both in a letter from Julie to St Preux, licensing him: 'listen then only to your own desires, follow only your own inclinations, and think above all on the growth of our infant affections'. Just as Rousseau's educational writings argued a child should be unfettered, so in his fiction the lover should be free to pursue love like a child. Julie continues: 'So long as the remembrance of those delightful moments of innocence shall remain, it will be impossible that you should cease to love that which renders them so endearing.'[92] Desire is innocent for adults insofar as it resembles infantile unselfconsciousness. Paradoxically (for this is Rousseau) innocence is recaptured through a very conscious act of remembering. Repeatedly Rousseau stresses his lovers are figures who remember: of St Preux, Wolmar observes, 'Deprive him of his memory and you destroy his love.'[93] Wolmar's way of curing St Preux is to overlay romantic memories with sociable ones. But St Preux cannot give up his investment in the world as the repository of memory. Returning with Julie to the scene of his letter-writing at la Meillerie, he tells her,

> Here is the stone where I used to sit, to reflect on your happy abode at a distance; on this, I penned that letter which moved your heart; these sharp flints served me as graving tools to cut out your name; here I crossed that frozen torrent to regain one of your letters which the wind carried off; there I came to review and give a thousand kisses to the last you ever wrote to me...[94]

Letter-writing inscribes not simply separation from the beloved but a complex dynamic in which things are moving, fixed, recoverable. Text is obviously one of these things; memory, another. Layers of memory are imaged out as physical locations and the pattern of loss and reunion, letters lost and held close, is very suggestive. Here, there; possession, dispossession: as in Freud's fort-da scenario, the lover-child both controls and cannot control the lover-mother. Since both are adults, the game is enacted through writing rather than orally; since this is an epistolary novel, readers have the satisfaction of ostensibly possessing those letters of which the characters' grasp is uncertain.

Fictions of author as editor make this possession semi-conscious; analogues between a heroine's letters and the body of text relocate it in the politics of heterosexuality. Readers of novels have to enjoy second-hand the abundant fantasies offered by manuscript letters. For instance, lovers who press letters to their breast make paper simulate skin in an adult erotic desire to incorporate the beloved. This gesture, common in eighteenth-century illustrations of lovers, can also be read as an infantile fantasy of closeness to the maternal body. In the late eighteenth-century, the word 'breast' is not sex-distinct, but it was being used more to refer to a woman's breast. Extravagant kissing of letters can similarly be read as lovers acting out a maternal role of caring and a child's role of being cared for. Pressed close, kissed, cherished, love-letters look back through adult desires to infantile pleasures in which touch and orality are privileged.

Nuns and lovers

Part of the appeal of eighteenth-century love-letters was their connection to regressive pleasures. Not all readers relished this; one editor classed love-letters as 'amongst the most embarrassing topics of correspondence which can be imagined'.[95] Just as important as the needy ego was a discourse of the superego which was transcendent but not asexual. Many writers noted the overlap between secular and divine love; some cultivated it. 'Those souls, which by love were converted to tinder, / Catch flame at religion, and burn to a cinder.'[96] The nun was a crucial nexus for ideologies of femininity, inscriptions of desire and dramatisations of epistolarity. Two figures dominated the eighteenth-century literary imagination: the Portuguese Nun and Heloise. The former's five letters to a cavalier, possibly by an author neither Portuguese nor female, sparked debates then and now about authenticity but, like many eighteenth-century heroines, the question was less about whether she was real or fictional and more about how she was plausible.[97] Ostensibly trapped by narrative in a convent's enclosed world, the nun shows a dynamic, demanding subjectivity pleasurably at odds with a plot of abandonment. Heloise, a real woman with a colourful history as Abelard's pupil, wife and soul-mate, was also unquestionably a mediated figure: translated from Latin across six centuries of historical difference, her letters were remoulded by poets.[98] The most famous representation was Pope's verse epistle, *Eloisa to Abelard* (1719), though Pope's canonical status now should not be allowed to block out other versions. 'The letters of ABELARD and ELOISA are in the hands of every person of taste': John Hughes's prose translation of 1714 was the more important text.[99] Nor should it be assumed that Pope's version was uncontested, from Joseph Berington, who argued that Pope had downplayed Eloisa's reasoning powers and presented her 'in the true stile of a boarding-school Miss',[100] to John Matthews, who in a parallel text parodied Pope's ponderous couplets with deftly facetious dactyls.

Representation of Eloisa or what Pope called 'this tumult in a vestal's veins' proved suggestive for love-letters. Rousseau's novel *La Nouvelle Héloïse* made her a type for saintliness and desire, although his title hints that Julie's predecessor, the old Heloise, needs updating. In contrast, Richard and Elizabeth Griffith, who published their correspondence before and after marriage, use the personae of Eloisa and Abelard to reflect upon their reversible roles as pupil and preceptor, reflections which link to debates about women's education and the professionalisation of women writers. Different uses of Eloisa in the 1760s show her as an ideologically malleable rather than contested character; writers rewrote her, drawn to her explicitly amorous character and her investment in letters as a writerly medium nonetheless manifesting the declamatory power of speech. Linda Kauffman has argued that amorous discourse is written as if it were going to be spoken to the beloved: Eloisa upholds this principle and qualifies it. As she argues in her second epistle, letters 'have all the Softness and Delicacy of Speech, and sometimes a Boldness of Expression even beyond it'.[101] Like prayers and confessions with which nuns were naturally associated, love-letters were potentially oral whilst textual.

The nun is an unstable figure in that not all women in convents took vows, or having taken them kept them. Eighteenth-century novels made the most of these distinctions by playing with a double discourse of constant lovers and broken vows. The nun could be a woman who made a promise to God following a lover's broken promise to her or who abandoned her convent in order to be constant to a man. The solemn ceremony of taking vows that disturbed many British travellers was formally irrevocable but not discursively final: like Heloise, one might be an abbess and still in love. Paradoxically convents, like prisons, tempted lovers to defy enclosure by writing. Physical obstacles tested the heroism of those immured: 'Love will find wings to top your lofty walls.'[102] The convent was a place of non-desire which love could penetrate; it was also a place of heavenly desire where lust might be cherished as well as repudiated. As Kamuf observes, Heloise's text dissolves distinctions of inside and outside: 'These letters stage a confrontation between, on the one hand, a system of mirrored oppositions which cloisters the sexual object and, on the other, a generalised economy of desire in which the suspension of such oppositions is the scene of erotic pleasure.'[103] The convent was also a trope of otherworldliness which figured ideological difference as well as sexual attraction; as the locus of error and superstition, convents sucked in the impressionable, imagined as young women. Although many Gothic novels had anti-hero monks who were unable to repress their lusts and eager to corrupt the vulnerable, few of them write, whereas secluded nuns are constant writers. The Portuguese Nun's addressee is a significantly uncloistered and silent Cavalier. That literature made secluded nuns into constant writers seems to associate letters with a feminised private sphere, swapping a closet for a cell, except that it was so very public; more writers crowded into Eloisa's space than Abelard's. Rather, the convent, like the brothel with which it had links, functioned as an inside-out trope for the family. The authority of parents becomes the religious order's hierarchy; the good nun is a daughter obedient to God – and potentially a mother superior.

What made a woman a nun was taking the veil. As Eve Kosofsky Sedgwick has shown, the veil alerts to the presence of ideological masking even as it covers up a material object.[104] Aesthetically it reinforced that simplicity of garb which made nuns a turn-on: the veil hides nothing and 'sets off everything'.[105] Veiling simultaneously enacts a spiritual renunciation of flesh and the impossibility of making bodies wholly invisible. The veil is like skin in being a fetishisable surface of desire between the nun and her heart; it is unlike skin in being materially detachable. 'The permeable boundary of the cowl or veil becomes a borderline between denial or repression on the one hand and sexual fantasy on the other, projecting both desire and its interdiction in the same figure.'[106] A veil turns a lover into a religious devotee, with the tease that this might be reversible. So hoped one fictional lover, who anticipated that his pensive nun could be transformed into a woman of the world by displaying her veiled charms, 'which were divine under every disadvantage of dress, and when seen through a grated window'.[107] In the convent mis-en-scène, veils, grates and walls function as obstacles to the gaze, making it pleasingly thwarted.[108] Veiled female forms, like a barred space, are objectified: what it feels like to the nun to look out through a veil is not represented as an experience; rather, imperfect perception is represented as emotional confusion. Rousseau was keen on these allegorical tendencies, especially to mystify. On Julie's married state, for instance, her husband comments, 'A veil of wisdom and honour makes so many folds about her heart, that it is impenetrable to human eyes, even to her own.'[109] Morality screens passion, is the inference: the veil is a sartorial advance on the fig-leaf of bourgeois morality.

The veil drew rhetorical power from Eloisa's frankness about the contrast between outward observances and her true feelings. Indeed, she turned Abelard's correspondence into a kind of alternative veil, a talisman of her real passion to protect her love against redirection to the divine: 'When I pronounced my sad Vow, I then had about me your last Letters, in which you protested you would be wholly mine, and would never live but to love me. 'Tis to you therefore I have offered myself.'[110] His letters are a veil of pleasure which she takes willingly, in contrast to the nun's veil of penitence and masochism: 'O Vows! O Convent! I have not lost my Humanity under your inexorable Discipline! You have not made me Marble by changing my Habit.' Paradoxically, her love becomes a veil that Abelard cannot renounce: 'You must bear with my passion, as a thing . . . from which you can no Ways be disengaged.'[111] Conversely, in his reply to her, his passion reawakened by her letter, he turns her into a kind of veil: 'in your Holy Habit thrust yourself between God and me, and be a Wall of Separation'.[112] There are three veils: the one she wants (his letters), the one she wants each to be to the other (a fixed love) and the one he fears she is (an obstacle to God's love). The veil is thus a site of reworkable meanings and a site of penetration: men, who don't wear veils, get wrapped up in its allegorical propensities.[113]

In narrative terms, the veil should mark the moment when lovers turn away from past lives. But its figurative instability also makes it a medium through which they return. Memories can pass through the materially filmy veil that otherwise divides lovers; in this they resemble letters, which unite lovers across time and space. Much of Eloisa's letters are given over to remembering the passion between her and Abelard; these letters threaten the veil because they give a textual and recoverable form to memory. One writes something down precisely in order not to forget it. By recalling origins and enshrining past exchanges, including epistolary ones, letters' power of activation is at odds with the veil's power of closure. The do-you-remember-when conversations of lovers are close to the you-must-remember-this of the Eloisa-type lover – for St Preux, as for Abelard, too close, too painful.

Rousseau's novel has explicit parallels with the Abelard and Heloise story: the affair between tutor and pupil; the philosopher who cannot conquer his passion; the integration of lovers into a community and the conversion of desire into service. Kamuf cites the Bibliothèque de la Pleïade editor's view that 'the suggested analogy of the title was a kind of afterthought which points only to a loose set of parallels thrown over the text in a superficial fashion'.[114] I see the analogy as Rousseau's tease, a veil whose lightness should not be mistaken for superficiality. The revelation at the end that Julie has found contentment but no real happiness so long as she denies her love for St Preux privileges sensibility over sociability; in one sense this rewrites the original ending, in which Abelard and Heloise stopped writing and returned to religious life, although it also confirms their status as myths, their fame for love rather than duty. Other eighteenth-century interpreters also wanted a reunion: John Hughes, for instance, recorded that when Eloise was laid in Abelard's grave some twenty years after his death, his body reached out to embrace her.[115] This alleged miracle fuses happy-ever-after with hereafter. A pre-Cartesian belief in the unity of mind and body connects with a post-Cartesian wish that mind and body should act consonantly. Medieval and Enlightenment writers alike look to the lover to escape lust's mortality through literature's immortality. In the medieval story, transmogrification happens when Abelard abandons philosophy to compose poems and songs which make Eloisa famous; in the eighteenth century, the process is intertextual, looking to a symmetry between Abelard and Eloisa's correspondence and the epistolary novel. That Hughes and Berington argued respectively that Eloisa was more and less imaginative than the heroine of an epistolary novel shows they were attuned to the comparison, even if they could not agree on the degree of similarity.

Rousseau's assumption of readers' familiarity with the Abelard and Heloise story was rammed home to British readers by the translator, who calls Rousseau's heroine not Julie but Eloisa. St Preux compares Julie to Heloise as pitiable, since she has a heart made for love (I, 79). Like Abelard insinuating himself into Heloise's household in the guise of her tutor, St Preux becomes Julie's teacher and then lover, but with little suggestion of premeditation. Eighteenth-century Englishmen tended to blame Abelard for undermining family values; typecast as 'a base seducer', he had gone looking for an affair, whereas love stole up on St Preux. Although Julie's mother denounces St Preux for betraying trust, Julie's deathbed conclusions give him the benefit of the doubt: 'He made use of the specious insinuating language of virtue, by which a thousand base men daily seduce our sex; but perhaps he only of all mankind was sincere.'[116] Julie resembles Heloise as lover and voluntary nun: although Abelard's insistence that Heloise should take the veil has been seen by Linda Kauffman as coercion, Heloise in her letters nonetheless describes it as a self-determining act. Heroically calm during the ceremony, she writes about it afterwards in distress. Julie's account of her marriage vow is a Gothic scene of coercion, shot through with horror, terror, gloom and shivers, but she then becomes calm: 'I made the promise not only with my lips but with my heart, and I will keep it inviolably till my death.'[117] Rousseau's plot thus shadows and inverts key moments of the medieval romance.

The second half of Rousseau's novel explores that tension between love and religion which dominates the historical Heloise's letters – in particular, her third letter, which starts with a declaration that God has indeed and at last displaced Abelard in her heart, then turns to fantasy, recounting erotic dreams in which Abelard is again potent. Where Heloise played with a religious vocabulary as antithesis to her passion, Julie means it, renouncing St Preux except as the lover of her soul and invoking God as a chaperone. St Preux complains, 'I found the divinity always between us.'[118] But like Abelard cut off from physical satisfaction, he relocates desire as non-phallic: 'My heart is become, if I may so express myself, the organ of all my wants.'[119] Julie and St Preux's conversion from passionate lovers to passionate Christians takes up Abelard and Heloise's useful but dangerous disentangling of love and devotion. Julie even offers St Preux a fiction of Heloise as her alter ego: 'Do I not even give you an Eloisa? ... let your heart fulfil with her all our former engagements.'[120] Where Abelard advised Heloise to fast and pray as aids to forgetting him, Julie recommends prayer to St Preux: 'Slaves by our weakness, we are set free by prayer.'[121] But St Preux (echoing Heloise) is still wedded to letters and the material world they represent: 'the form, the fold, the seal, the superscription of your letter call to my mind those very different epistles which love used to dictate'.[122] The heart of his resistance is that Julie, or the new Heloise, is too emotional in her religion: 'beware Eloisa of becoming a mere devotee'. Rousseau adds a note explicitly comparing St Preux's views on prayer with Abelard's. Prayer should involve effort: 'we acquire strength in confessing our weakness. But if we ... turn mystics, instead of raising ourselves to God, we are lost in our own wild imaginations.'[123] The characters' complex identifications with reason and passion shift again, until on her deathbed Julie shows both 'the fortitude of a philosopher and the mildness of a christian'. Intimate confessions to each other through letters become confessions to heaven through prayer. Both letters and prayers offer a language of the heart made rational through literary convention – for letters, the relative order of disordered letters (the clarity of frantic lovers) and Rousseau's intertextual use of the Heloise story (his lovers are characters who have written before, as it were).

Besides a counterpoint of character and discourse through committed letter-writing, Rousseau draws on the old Heloise story to keep the reader in mind of a key issue: what can we learn from lovers? The struggle of Abelard and especially Heloise to be reconciled to their communities staged the question of how lovers fitted in, or not, to society. For Rousseau, the self-centred lover was the opposite of the socially conscious citizen. In Julie's words,

> The intent of matrimony is not for man and wife to be always taken up with each other, but jointly to discharge the duties of civil society, to govern their family with prudence, and educate their children with discretion. Lovers attend to nothing but each other...[124]

On the other hand, precisely because the lover has a relationship with another self-centred person, the beloved, a lover knew better than a citizen how to deal with lovers. Thus St Preux listens dutifully to the model citizen Wolmar, but is not really persuaded by his arguments. What moves him more is Julie's sensibility: 'that pathetic eloquence which dictated by the heart, flowed in persuasive accents from her tongue'.[125] Sensibility seems to associate women with passion – and letters – making Julie another Heloise or Portuguese Nun. But it is not that simple. Julie can also turn citizen Wolmar into a lover. Two pages on from St Preux's tribute, Wolmar pays his own: Julie, he says, 'argues so affectingly that I cannot help embracing her at every reply'. His demonstrativeness is not a shut-up-and-kiss-me response to end dialogue but a reward for her reasoning, which he links back to St Preux: was not it St Preux who taught her this line of reasoning? No answer is given, but if the reader supposes yes, there is an analogy with Abelard the philosopher-lover who creates Heloise the lover-theologian. Educating women leads to re-educating men. If the reader supposes no, Julie did not need to be taught either reasoning or sensibility by St Preux, there arises a contrast with Heloise which sheds light on what is new about Julie. Abelard advised Heloise to end her predicament by cultivating particular virtues: 'Have the Purity of Virgins, the Austerity of Anchorites, the Zeal of Pastors and Bishops, and the Constancy of Martyrs'.[126] If she does so, she will be a comfort to herself and an example to others. Julie's qualities as St Preux's pupil enable her to teach him how to be a citizen and a Christian. Unlike Heloise, she just has to be herself. She can even be wrong: as Rousseau teasingly asks about his lovers,

> is not the importance which they give to their romantic notions more amusing than all the wit they could have displayed. They speak of every thing; they are constantly mistaken, they teach us nothing, except the knowledge of themselves; but in making themselves known, they obtain our affection... Their errors are more engaging than the wisdom of the wise.[127]

Lovers' self-deceptions, for Rousseau, are interesting and affecting; their struggles, to know who to love, how best to love and the price to pay for that love, teach us indirectly about humanity and social relations.

Appropriately, Rousseau's final volume marks this recognition of lovers as teachers by metaphors of veils. After dreaming of a veiled Julie with her dying mother, St Preux runs in a panic to tell his friend Lord B, who rebukes him for being unmanly and takes him back to Clarens to see Julie. In fact he does not see her: he hears her voice behind a hedge and is calmed. He then tells Lord B 'that veil which has so long hood-winked my reason' has been drawn aside. One can read this symbolism several ways, but I suggest that St Preux means the veil described by Julie in the dream as too sacred to be removed, and which represents religion and motherhood, often described in the eighteenth century as a sacred duty.[128] That is, Julie can be a productive member of civil society, a Christian, and *still* a lover. Finally, there is one more veil in the story – the one in which Julie is buried. Brought back by St Preux from his travels, made of gold and pearls, this veil is just a veil, or, it functions at last as a simple metaphor for something, someone, precious.

Accounts of the reception of Heloise's letters in the eighteenth century have over-emphasised her association with emotion. R. Adams Day, for instance, claims Hughes' translation, which first appeared in 1713, 'seemed an echo of the passionate letters of the [Portuguese] Nun'.[129] Hughes does say that Heloise's letters are the most passionate extant and that women write more naturally tender and passionate letters; his claim that Heloise's letters were superior to the Nun's may be attributed to competition – not incompatible with imitation. But his Abelard is passionate too – 'I sigh, I weep, I pine, I speak the dear name *Heloise*.'[130] There are echoes of Hughes, possibly conscious, in Judith Madan's epistle from Abelard:

> Alas I rave! nor grace, nor zeal divine,
> Burns in a heart oppress'd with grief like mine.
> Too sure I feel, while I the torture prove
> A feeble piety, conflicting love,
> A black despair my forc'd devotion built,
> Absence, to me, has sharper pangs than guilt.
> Yet – yet, my *Elois'* thy charms I view,
> But yet my sighs, my tears pour forth for you;
> Each weak resistance stronger knits my chain,
> I sigh, I weep, love, despair – and all in vain.[131]

Abelard is soft, trembling, indecisive and miserable, like the post-portugaise Eloise, but the point was not to effeminise him as a way of countering Pope's too-pathetic Eloisa. Rather, to some writers the lover was a figure of emotional vicissitude regardless of sex. Gender returns through letters: Madan's Abelard is responsive to Eloise as a letter-writer in ways that sound like others' Eloisas. Heloise may be unable to control emotions but both she and the Nun control language in articulating those emotions, which is why poets were drawn to the one and novelists to the other. A reductive association between women and emotion helps explain men's interest in Heloise, but we should also ask why they drew away from Abelard. In part it was because Abelard's dual role as scholar and lover did not fit with the homosocial world of eighteenth-century learning (and Heloise's arguments against marriage foreground the intrusion of domestic life on serious study). Hughes suggested hopefully that scholars make the best lovers (ah yes – all that attention to detail...) but the libertine in the library, a figure who frequented early eighteenth-century fiction, was associated with sexual education that corrupted young women: his books were pornography not philosophy. Abelard's lessons included beatings to show Heloise's uncle he was good on discipline, beatings which Heloise implied they treated as an erotic game, but which hardly seemed a progressive contribution to women's education or converse between the sexes. Berington stressed Heloise's learning and heroic strength but was completely unable to deal with Abelard, 'a selfish eunuch', suggesting Abelard's castration made him an impossible role model. The impossibility was compounded by an epistolary silence, particularly the lack of a reply from Abelard to a letter purporting to be from his friend Fourques, who suggests the scholar might find some benefit in being cut off from passion. As Hughes commented, ' 'Tis great Pity we have not *Abelard*'s Answer to this delicate Letter, the Matter then would look like one of *Job*'s Dialogues with his Friends.'[132] But even Job's afflictions did not encompass a mutilation which psychoanalysis posits as the root of masculine identity and sexual difference.

Yet not all men were compelled by Heloise and repelled by Abelard. The correspondence of Richard and Elizabeth Griffith shows how two writers took up the personae and the epistolary relationship in productive ways. They looked to Abelard as potent tutor and Heloise as adept pupil, personalising the mid-century debate about women's education. This debate involved Elizabeth Griffith on two counts: first as a companionate wife and second as a writer who contributed to the family income by publishing for money (at times more successfully than her husband). Heloise was a useful model because although her learning had little market value per se, she was marketable as a lover for attractions including intellect, shown through her letters. When the Griffiths published their love-letters to make money, it was significantly Elizabeth Griffith who found it difficult to continue to write intimately in letters destined for print: she thought 'that printing of Love Letters is almost as indecent as embracing each other in public'.[133] Yet the plan to publish seems to have been hers, a contradiction not edited out of the printed correspondence and which mitigates her otherwise conventional middle-class women's anxieties about the decorum of publication. The letters *are* equivalent to embracing in public. Here Heloise was useful as an antecedent or a pre-text for imitation; she was an unequivocally sexual woman who did not write for publication. Moreover, because Heloise wrote in Latin, she was exempted from the frivolity associated with French female letter-writers like Madame de Sévigné, whom Elizabeth Griffith disparaged in the usual way.

The dozen or so references to Abelard and Heloise in the Griffiths' correspondence serve powerful agendas. Most important was Heloise as a figure of the educable woman,[134] especially in the early days of their relationship when 'Henry' was avoiding marriage but offering 'Frances' love and friendship, that is, more than a Platonic correspondence. He compliments Frances on having 'the wit of *Heloise*, without her prophaneness'; in return, she defers to his intellectual authority: 'you are my *Abelard*, my only orthodoxy in speculative points'.[135] Using these personae makes the correspondence literary; it allows Frances to show she is at ease with high culture and provides a point of identification with a famous woman writer. The companionate marriage acknowledged women's potential in return for enclosing it within the husband's authority; Frances concedes masculine superiority in return for the fantasy of being taught. Henry was unusual in arguing that Frances, unlike Heloise, could teach herself. Possibly emotional laziness on his part, it touched a nerve. Like many eighteenth-century women with intellectual aspirations,[136] Elizabeth Griffith had been encouraged by her father and his death had shaken her confidence. Henry was not consistently patient with her self-doubt, but he made their letters a literary medium which consciously challenged her to read, think and write: 'I often tempted you to try your Strength, or sound your Depth: Was this Sarcasm, to allow you both Strength and Depth? ... you may reprehend my Manners, which are, I confess, liable to Censure: But blame not my Sentiments, which are faultless in regard to you' (I, p. 289). She found his challenges taxing on occasions, as if love-letters had to be essays, although he rewarded her with praise. When she dutifully wrote up her thoughts on virtue after reading Brown's *Characteristics*, he gave her full marks: 'extremely clever and just ... really surprizing for a young woman upon so abstruse a Subject' (II, p. 259). Both Griffiths seem to have been prone to depression, but her unhappiness about enforced education used a suggestively infantile imagery: 'the little Understanding I am Mistress of, may be compared to an Infant just weaned from Leading-Strings, afraid to make a Step without a Guide' (II, p. 311). An encouraging father was preferable to a critical husband because fathers, being the object of other female fantasies of seduction, made more seductive teachers. Henry's recognition of this was acute as well as patronising: 'I have always behaved to you, as to a favourite Child; cherishing you for your own Advantage, and thwarting you only for your Good' (I, pp. 209–10). The Griffiths' correspondence showed that daughters' oedipal plots could only be defused by companionate marriages following a struggle.

The Griffiths, however, saw Heloise as more than a seduced pupil: she was also a seductive inspiration. Henry repeatedly stressed an intellectual component in their compatility: their correspondence shows 'how our Studies, Sentiments, and whole Turn of Mind, were adapted for each other'

(II, p. 298). But he also represented Frances as his teacher. What she teaches him is love and virtue. Previously something of a ladies' man (a past which made Frances suspicious, even jealous, in the present), he becomes wholly committed to rational friendship as the basis of desire: 'what is my Love to my dearest *Fanny*, but that Taste for *Virtue*, . . . and that high Admiration for Beauty, Harmony, and Order, which is the proper Contemplation of the truly philosophic Mind?' (II, p. 68). He promises the equality of Platonic love within the heterosexuality of marriage and it dominates the middle years – or volumes – of their relationship. It is as if Abelard and Heloise had been able to be happy and interested together. Lawrence Stone has argued that 'the open inclusion of eroticism in marital relations' affected only the landed élite 'and hardly affected the bourgeois and professional classes'.[137] The Griffiths' form of domestic affection was openly, if platonically, erotic on paper; it included physicality in part because Henry, an admirer of Sterne, cultivated sensibility's passion for touch, hugging a cat, for instance, when he could find no human outlet for his benevolence. Both partners were ill, she with arthritis, he with a stomach complaint, ailments that the letters include as part of the texture of their daily life. They also had children, which returned some discourse of the body to an intellectual correspondence. Reluctant to separate mental activity from bodily identity, they offer unusual compliments. Henry tells Frances, 'there is indeed, in your Understanding, so little of Effeminacy, that I frequently consider you, not only as a Man, but a Man of Letters too . . .' (II, p. 234). A rational woman enables gender to be reworked through letters, by writing as a lover and an intellectual in the context of a marriage whose companionacy was physical in the material form of letters – they were otherwise often apart. In the penultimate volume, Frances offers an equivalent compliment, telling Henry that since he is stoic about his own pains and sensitive to others', 'You are a Sort of philosophical *Hermaphrodite*: A Man's Mind, with a Woman's Heart' (V, p. 261). The man who shares intellectual pleasures with a woman and who incorporates feminine sensibility is not emasculated like Abelard but doubly sexual. Mutual intellectual pleasure need not smother amorous dalliance. Heloise, as lover and pupil, remained a touchstone for Frances, alluded to in the Ode on Love she dedicated to her husband (V, pp. 17–18). Earlier references to Henry as her Abelard allowed her the pleasure of paying extravagant compliments (tricky for women) and the eroticism of role play as the knowingly submissive pupil.

Like Rousseau, the Griffiths were drawn to Heloise as a woman inspiring a pious community. Henry owned some property in the country which he called the Paraclete after the foundation established by Abelard and led by Heloise. Frances left this allusion alone, perhaps because rural retirement was more of a male fantasy and one that had little appeal for a young woman often left in Dublin alone, pregnant or unwell. The Griffiths' relationship had difficulties – Elizabeth broke off the correspondence for a while when

Richard implied she could be his mistress but not his wife and their marriage was secret so as not to offend an uncle upon whom his prospects depended. But in later life though their finances and health were often precarious they saw their marriage as a model to which others could aspire. In another teaching fantasy (V, p. 193), Henry proposed they establish an Academy for lovers using their letters as lectures. Where Rousseau looked to Heloise to help him puzzle out how to integrate lovers into the community, Richard Griffith proposed dividing society into twos, improving each couple as lovers. Congratulating themselves on keeping love fresh for so long, the Griffiths noted the absence of model lovers of mature years (Penelope and Ulysses had some appeal) and decided to fill that literary space themselves. In Henry's words, 'We are, indeed, my amiable Woman, the most extraordinary Couple that ever lived; and our Loves will hand us down to Fame.' Fame was to be realised through the letters, 'the natural Prose of my Heart', like Abelard and Heloise, and unlike other lovers made famous through poetry. The point was not for others to imitate the letters per se, but to proselytise by letters their ideal of married love as democratically attainable and experientially unique. Lovers join the pantheon of those famed for love by allusion rather than imitation – because legendary love must seem unique.[138] Where Heloise fantasised about Abelard coming to her deathbed, Henry, quoting Pope's Eloisa, imagines dying first and waiting for his wife in the next world: 'I sometimes shudder at such Thoughts as these: "Thy Image steals between, &c"' (VI, p. 234). In reply, Frances neatly averts blasphemy by arguing that Henry is one of God's works, so she can love one through the other: 'I flatter myself that the Thought of thee but assists my Devotion; as I never address the Almighty with such enthusiastic Fervour, as when I pray for your Health, your Life, or Happiness' (VI, p. 237). The Griffiths exceed Heloise's unstable reconciliation of love and piety precisely because allusions to Heloise do some of their discursive work. The power of Heloise as allusion rather than model allows those who draw on her to escape, in turn, becoming models and attracting scrutiny which reality might not bear. In Berington's words, 'I hold her up not as an example to call imitation, but I view her as a phoenomenon, which has my admiration and my wonder.'[139]

Both Heloise and the Portuguese Nun were important because they gave voice to women's amorous frustrations. Male lovers' complaints were a staple of pastoral, but it was letters in the eighteenth century that aired both sides of lovers' quarrels. As the opposite of compliments, complaints were often raw expressions of need: you never say you love me, Frances wrote, 'except to put your subsequent Unkindness or Censure in a stronger Light' (I, p. 161); 'You wrong me', Henry replied, 'my Actions are crossed, or restrained by your's, which are governed by Caprice, and a Temper bizarre' (I, p. 162). Frances responded to unretractable words by trying to make words more tractable: 'I may have misconstrued Friendship into want of Tenderness; and you deemed that Caprice, which was Excess of Love' (I, p. 193). Her concession implies an elegant writer must be a polite lover; love-letters can allow literary equality to override gendered faults. Many lovers' quarrels invoke cultural stereotypes of women as inconstant, peevish and perverse, and men as fickle, heartless and selfish. Henry puts masculine analysis (his) above feminine complaint (hers): 'Now observe, ma Seule, et chère Mignonne, that I am not scolding, but only philosophizing' (II, p. 173). Educating a companionate wife in her faults, the companionate husband offered intellectual privileges as compensation for personal attack. The process puts gender into what would otherwise be the equality of quarrelling or what Henry calls their tendency to *'faire la Guerre'* (I, p. 103).

The convention that love-letters tested sincerity affected the whole of the Griffiths' correspondence and its censorship, especially once they knew what they were writing was destined for print. In the preface, Henry took up this question as a textual one of completeness and regularity, claiming to have been tempted to burn some letters to make the whole look more natural, that is irregular. But roughness was present as conflict, with a nod to stage conventions, as in Henry's identification of the pair with Benedict and Beatrix, 'too wise to woo peaceably' (VI, p. 234). Where the symmetrical repartee of stage lovers showed that to be well-matched in wit was to be well matched, the Griffiths' letters are a kind of picturesque, with uneven jolts and smooth interludes. Epistolary rupture added force to quarrels by supplying a formal repertoire of hurt: letters sent back unanswered, reconciliations postponed to another post, chilly subscriptions, cool or stiff language in place of warmth and ease. Both Henry and Frances used these devices whilst relying on the centrality of letters to their relationship to ensure neither can have the last word.

The Griffiths' letters are an exceptionally substantial portrait of a marriage, in which the character of the lover shines through that of spouse. The epistolary lover was extravagant – with time rather than with money, usually measured by hours invested in writing or waiting for a post. Henry kept a go-between waiting for five days until his peaches were ripe enough to send with a letter to Frances. Willed romanticism lay at the heart of the companionate marriage; a desire to please displaced duty as the driving-force of partnership. Social approval mattered in complex ways: since the Griffiths' marriage was initially secret, publication brought letters forward belatedly as proofs of virtue. Coy about third-party readers and silent about the market value of their correspondence, the Griffiths stressed their literariness. Henry reports compliments on Frances' letters with pleasure and each praised the other's letters as superior. Their children, a bond but also a barrier between the exclusive couple, feature relatively little. There is some sense of what else each is writing besides letters – her translations and dramatic adaptations, his novels – but not enough to diminish their primary identity as lovers. Since both were authors, their stress on romance prevents them becoming rivals. Letters thus gave them a common identity (as lovers), a shared purpose (as letter-writers) and, importantly, a separate space. Frances remarks 'frequent Absences encrease our fondness' (III, p. 98), unlike a suspicious acquaintance at Bath who, having written to her husband only once in three months, cannot understand how the Griffiths correspond three times a week. Lovers in fictions, especially bereft women like Eloisa or the Portuguese Nun, stressed correspondence as a means of reunion: the love-letter could bring the lover back, though narratives got the maximum out of desertion. Real lovers like the Griffiths sometimes celebrated letters as a medium of unity that crossed distance but did not necessarily benefit from abolishing it.

Elizabeth Griffith's letters represented a letter-writing woman as a woman writer. Richard Griffith's letters represented a man of letters writing as a lover. A common complaint about eighteenth-century husbands of all classes was that they became inattentive; the complaisant lover turned into the complacent spouse. After marriage, Richard Griffith continued to pay attention to his wife – *epistolary* attention. Partly a matter of volume (he thought it a crime to miss a post), quality mattered too: proper attention should be elegant and ardent. Its vital ingredient was tenderness, a significant term in love-letters and understood at the time to be compatible with masculinity. Men with long and happy marriages wrote as tender lovers. Elizabeth Griffith singled out tenderness as Richard's best quality; male lovers knew its importance. Writing at the same time as Henry and Frances, the middle-aged William Pitt, in his passionate letters to Lady Hester Grenville, repeatedly describes his feelings as tender – in one letter, four times.[140] Suggestively like that maternal love with which it was elsewhere vigorously associated, tenderness was boundless and inexhaustible: 'when I have writ whole sheets of Paper, I seem to have said but the smallest part of feelings too tender and too deeply rooted for my pen to reach'.[141] Tenderness mediates between solicitude and joy. The ardent lover absorbs everything about the beloved: all the senses stretch. When Pitt got a letter from Lady Hester, he wrote back: 'it is a bliss but one degree from that of seeing you, looking at your lov'd charms, hearing your voice, catching your every word, and gathering a thousand ways, a thousand graces and delights that accompany everything you do and everything you say'.[142]

Tenderness was not only heroic but also domestic and everyday. A tender lover attended to little things, even trivia. The polarisation of little and great upon which so much eighteenth-century satire depended is turned into domestic heroism, a middlebrow fusion which especially appealed to the middle classes. Steele, for example, made a speciality of it in plays like *The Tender Husband* (1703), a play whose eponymous hero is not much in evidence in the action but whose attitude to women is thoroughly endorsed: ' *'Tis less to conquer, than convince, the Fair.'*[143] It was by Steele's 'tender fondness' that he recommended himself to his future mother-in-law and his subscriptions to his wife are explicit, from 'the warmest, tenderest Heart' to 'tenderly...thine'.[144]

In Steele's marital correspondence, tenderness is partly epistolary – 'write no cross stuff' – and partly a moral creed: 'The main thing is to preserve allways a Disposition to please and be pleased.'[145] Compliments come in again, but attached to cheerfulness rather than wit. Tenderness was a form of sensibility in locating sensitivity in self as well as other and in figuring masculinity as open. The tender lover was one who understood the power of touch, a relief from an older amorous discourse which privileged sight (all those ogling or wounded eyes). As material objects, letters were tactile; impressions left by the pen were like the impressions treasured by lovers and remembered through letters. Writing and the body connected through tenderness. Thus Pitt responded to Lady Hester's calling herself 'yours': 'how often do I read and kiss the word you say you love to repeat because I love to read it?' Tenderness allowed men to express sensitivity and vulnerability. While it relaxed control, its association with elegance protected men against charges of disorderliness attached to women's amorous discourse. It also mediated between love and friendship. The *Tatler*'s story of Lady Chichely's love-letters, exhumed from her tomb and read to a company including her daughter, is prefaced by a significant tribute from the fictional Jenny Bickerstaff. She confides to her brother that her husband Tranquillus is all she could wish for: 'I . . . enjoy in him (what indeed you told me were to be met with in a good Husband) the Fondness of a Lover, the Tenderness of a Parent, and the Intimacy of a Friend.'[146] Sir Thomas's love-letters from the seventeenth century are then read and approved in this light: tenderness, like love, seems timeless.

Writing makes an impression on paper which lovers imitated by imprinting kisses on each other. Judith Halberstam has observed that 'skin, or outward appearance, becomes the fetishised signifier for a heterosexual culture'.[147] In the eighteenth century, the love-letter's imitation of skin assisted fetishisation; it also recalled infantile pleasure in maternal closeness, coded as 'the tenderness of a parent'. These complex erotics shadow pronouncements on heterosexuality, such as a declaration in *The Lover's Secretary* (1692) that friendships between people of the opposite sex were either too cold or too hot. One might take this to be hiding a recommendation of same-sex friendships as relatively temperate and in a sense it is, but it also implies the perfect temperature would be blood-heat, reminiscent of a maternal body. In evoking this body, through epistolarity and the materiality of letters, eighteenth-century lovers kept it available to literature.

4
Writing as a Criminal

The criminal is a character keenly contested: in the eighteenth century, many people died in consequence of its attribution. It should be understood to be both a legal category and a discursive construct, with complex relations between the two. I use the character of criminal in a loose sense to cover cases in civil law as well as criminal law on the grounds that they share discourses of guilt. Whilst acknowledging the significance of documenting and quantifying crime,[1] my interest is in neither the history of crime nor the literature of crime but in letters' role in crime and criminal literature, separated out so one can see how letters were handled materially and textually as a specific form of evidence and how ideas about letters affected verdicts. Attributions of criminality were often contentious and many letters presented to courts raised more questions than they answered. The way letters were discussed drew on and contributed to assumptions about epistolary practices at large, mixing up legal thought with cultural norms. Since court contexts made letters available to the public, the history of letter-writing in relation to law is also one of letter-reading.

The cases I discuss come from life, not fiction, yet the ways in which 'criminals' were constructed relate to fictions, some of which presented ostensibly 'factual' writing. As others have noted, the literature of crime had ideological uses: these included frightening the middle classes, titillating them and selling them criminal biographies.[2] 'By the range and inventiveness of its coverage of crime, and its confusing mix of fact and fantasy, the eighteenth-century press resists a uniform interpretation and refuses to be controlled by a neatly restricted typology.'[3] The generic term 'criminal biography' has its attractions but, like the term 'pamphlet', it masks the roles played by a specific culture of letter-writing. Judges, juries, witnesses, law-breakers and readers all drew on epistolary culture to help define criminals and differentiate them from figures like the rogue. In doing so, they made and remade discourses about letters and criminals simultaneously. 'Criminal biography' assumes a relatively unproblematic teleology: the narrative must fix the criminal in order to write the biography, even with exemplars like

Defoe's Moll Flanders, whose preface expresses remorse and reformation and whose narrative exhibits vicissitudes. Actual juridical literature can be less fixed than verdicts of guilty imply; doubts linger. A comparison of responses to two cases recorded in Lady Sarah Ponsonby's diary shows how letter-writing and reading was part of constructing the criminal character. The first, in 1788, concerned a young woman accused of infanticide. Lady Sarah was sympathetic, even more so when the accused wrote to her. 'Letter from the poor unfortunate Creature in Ruthin Gaol. What can we do for her?' A lenient judge let the woman off, in spite of compelling evidence.[4] In 1789, a convicted sheep-stealer got short shrift: 'He writes to us, to entreat we will get him off from Transportation. Threw his Letter in the fire as we cannot consider a noted Sheep Stealer entitled to much lenity even had we interest to get him off.'[5] The process of justice and appeal went beyond courts, in part thanks to letters.

The first part of this chapter discusses cases which fit the figure of the criminal as traditionally understood – people represented in criminal biographies, including thieves, murderers and fraudsters. I include some suicides and Jacobites, whose criminality was partly controversial because self-murder and rebellion could have a basis in reason. I discuss several murder cases in which letters were crucial, showing how letters complicate arguments about a growing reliance on circumstantial evidence rather than testimony: I argue that letters functioned as both. Trials concerning middle-class domestic murder showed simultaneously care in reasoning and assumptions about class and gender that were clearly ideological. Fiction had a shadowy presence in representations of issues of character and motive; the crime of passion had more than a nodding acquaintance with the literature of sensibility. Then follows a section on the importance of letters in trials for adultery. It may seem strange to discuss these in relation to 'writing as a criminal' rather than 'writing as a lover', but my point in doing so is to highlight how guilt was frequently established through letters in cases of divorce. Most (but not all) of the letters involved were self-evidently love-letters; what made them criminal was that the writer was married to someone other than the addressee. Many guilty lovers showed awareness of this at the time by writing in code; others showed the strength of their passion by refusing to hide, by daring to speak their love's name. These choices had implications in court. Letters in adultery cases also qualify a picture of love-letters derived from novels, manuals or courtship correspondences. They flout some conventions and bow to others. In many cases, letters also overspilled the courtroom to involve a wider reading public. Like disaffected citizens who appealed to 'the tribunal of the public', many people protesting their innocence fought lonely battles, seeking help from persons of influence or a broader groundswell of public opinion.[6] This chapter explores the character of criminal as constructed through letters, but one should not forget the innocent as the criminal's double, a character whose possibly unjust sufferings made interpretations more important.

Legal uses of letters in the eighteenth century underline the interdependence of personal and public worlds. To send a personal letter, most writers had to use a public postal service or the agency of other people. Secret communications like notes between lovers or treasonable messages were vulnerable to surveillance and interception. The story of letters failing to arrive at their destination becomes here a story of letters falling into other hands: one would say, the 'wrong' hands, except that in legal contexts, wrong-doing is allowed to interceptors acting for certain ideological interests like the safety of the state or the sanctity of marriage and 'wrong' is reflected back onto letter-writers. Models of 'secret' versus 'open' readings, or single versus plural readers, are more useful here than categories of public and private; 'secret' versus 'open' also accounts for secret intelligence in state correspondence, to which access was a measure of power.[7] The law and the press have been described as the two central generators of ideology in early eighteenth-century England;[8] letters were among the principal genres to be found where they intersected.

Letters had unstable meanings in court. Reports of current events might be unproblematically political or dangerously treasonable depending on circumstances extrinsic to epistolary discourse. Before looking at ideological instability, one needs to understand how courts paid attention to material aspects of letters. Courts understood that letters might be forged or fraudulently signed. Authenticity was a primary concern. A forger was someone who wrote as a criminal without quite becoming an author, except as an author of his or her own doom. Forgers used writing as a medium of crime, which made them fascinating to other writers. Class sensitivities were particularly evident; many forgers were respectable. Paul Baines has shown that the meanings of forgery change during the eighteenth century and proved 'how very inclusive the category of forgery can be: forging letters, meddling with texts, misquotation, political propaganda and editing' were all 'cognate with criminal forgery'.[9] In forgery trials, guilt was proved by a script's inauthenticity. Verification was important in many sorts of trials, however, because writing was proof of certain illegal actions provided writing itself was 'proved'. Proving meant matching samples, for instance through close comparison of the formation of letters. This process seems simple enough but in practice the law was inconsistent. 'The most common defence against a charge of forgery was an assertion of the natural variability of handwriting, and the standard prosecution of the charge was an assertion of its natural sameness.'[10] Comparisons should in fairness be made between two samples from the same period of time, argued the defence for a man convicted of manslaughter following the death of his adversary in a duel. An assignation note was central to the evidence – 'Mr. Thornhill's servant swore that he believed this letter to be his master's handwriting, but Mr. Thornhill hoped the jury would not pay any regard to this testimony, as the boy had acknowledged in court that he never saw him write.'[11] Servants were quizzed closely over the identification of employers' handwriting because class politics made their testimony suspect and also because courts distinguished between seeing someone write a letter and seeing a letter someone had written. John Moody, a footman, gave very detailed and convincing evidence to incriminate Mrs Rudd, charged with the Perreau brothers in a celebrated case of a forged bond for £15,000. He testified to the differences between two scripts and two kinds of paper, both used by Mrs Rudd, and her instructions to say one set of letters he said he saw her write had been delivered from outside the house.[12] But the split between process and product was usually too great to convict upon unless it could be re-enacted in court. This was the case in Francis Charteris' famous conviction for rape. His defence was that the woman involved had consented and that he had love-letters to prove it, but they were in a radically different script from the hand she wrote in court and so were assumed to be fraudulent.[13]

The common view was that 'Similitude of Writings is a Species of Evidence in itself extremely uncertain, vague and trifling'.[14] In some cases, discontinuities were strangely disregarded even where there were compelling reasons to attend to them. Material questions about provenance and authenticity were affected by cultural pressures, of gender, for example. Mrs Rudd was surprisingly acquitted, although the forged bond was presented with a letter from a Mr Gilbert Adair, which she later claimed Daniel Perreau had forced her to write. When challenged on the spot by the bankers, she told them she had written the bond. One told the court, 'My brother said, that it was a masculine hand, and he did not think a woman could write it: she proved it, by taking a bit of paper and shewing us she could write it.'[15] This paper was burnt and Mrs Rudd was not asked to repeat the performance in court – perhaps because the court recognised that anyone able to write two hands might well be able to act not being able to do so. Forgery was not just a matter of mimesis but the effrontery of a performance not necessarily contained within text. Credibility also turned on audience expectations: where the subject involved matters normally assumed to be out of women's range, ideological shock waves suspended logic. Not that illogic was predictable: a converse gendering was assigned to sexually explicit poison-pen letters circulating in Bath in 1767. They were attributed to a respectable woman despite, or because of, being written in a 'strong, bold, masculine hand'.[16]

Other material aspects of letters besides handwriting came under scrutiny. Provenance was part but not all of authenticity: a text might be a copy, so materially different from an original. Best practice legally was to accept as a true copy a reproduction made from an original, ideally where the two had been compared side by side by a copyist to eliminate discrepancies. In the last resort, parole evidence as to the contents was acceptable.[17] Courts connected absent originals and reproductions in imaginative ways, for instance in the singular case of James Sheppard, executed in 1718 for high treason.

Sheppard having conceived the idea that it would be a praise-worthy action to kill the king, wrote a letter, which he intended for a non-juring minister of the name of Leake; but mistaking the spelling, he directed it 'to the Reverend. Mr. Heath.'[18]

This letter, offering his services as an assassin, seemed to Mr Heath 'most villainous', and he threw it on the fire. Sheppard returned for an answer and was arrested. A copy of the letter was found in his house: its contents were debatably unbalanced, but Sheppard's ability in court to recall the letter and write out a 'copy' of it was fatefully lucid.

Care about the material aspects of letters can be seen in a case saturated with epistolary significance. Two men robbed the Bristol mail in 1722, 'a crime of so enormous a magnitude, that we are at a loss to find language in which to express our abhorrence of it'.[19] One man, Simpson, had written an anonymous letter turning in his confederates; this was shown to the other prisoner, Hawkins, who then confessed. But their conviction turned on a receipt said to be forged because part of it was written in ink of a deeper colour than the rest. One of the jury then noticed that the shorthand writer seated in front of him was producing differently coloured script after dipping his pen in fresh ink. This recognition of material discontinuity in an otherwise to-the-moment text nearly produced an acquittal.

It was accidents such as these that made a forensic approach inadequate in securing the truth-telling powers of letters. And yet, paradoxically, accidental aspects of letters were also read as providential. Letters featured in countless cases as the means by which malefactors were trailed or exposed. James Bradley was caught after robbing the Earl of Harrington's house in London because he left a pocket-book behind a mirror at an inn in Chester with a bank-bill traceable to the Earl. He was discovered when he wrote to the landlord to claim it and, in a not uncommon twist, forgot the false name he had given. The Earl's steward commented with satisfaction that even the best-planned robberies could be exposed by 'activity, perseverance and vigilance'.[20] Letters provided vital and random clues: in cases where justice was thought to be done, they were treated as stable texts by participants and publishers. This confidence upped the ante in other cases featuring epistolary evidence.

Since letters aided detection in almost supernatural and also local ways, they matched the symbolic role of law itself as an ideologically charged but everyday system. Already a familiar part of British culture, in legal contexts letters were recognised across all classes and regions as potentially incriminatory texts that tied persons and acts together through text. The success of Charles Gildon's early epistolary fiction *The Post-Boy Robb'd of his Mail* highlighted the allure of letters for illicit purposes – both theft and unauthorised readings. Although the latter might be the preserve of gentlemen in fiction, in reality people of all classes committed 'literate' crimes. Where criminals used letters for conspiracy, agents of justice used them for detection, control and prosecution. These meanings created violence in a double murder which shocked contemporaries by its brutality.[21] Daniel Chater, a Sussex shoemaker, was able to identify a smuggler passing through his village. The Customs Office sent William Galley to accompany him to the local justice to give evidence. The smugglers were warned and at an inn plied the pair with drink. Once asleep, their clothes were searched and letters of instruction found on Galley which the smugglers determined to destroy. But the synecdochal relation of letter to writer – or in this context, carrier – meant that the persons had to be destroyed too. Bodies and texts were conflated by the evidential role of letters. The two men were separated, mutilated and buried, possibly alive. The smugglers' sadism seems to have come from panic after a hostage plan went wrong, but their tortures were not aimless. Perhaps it is not over-literary to see it as a desperate attempt to unwrite a text by dismembering the body that carried it. Detection was also epistolary: the gang were caught thanks to an anonymous letter to a magistrate.

Criminal biography, like fiction, imbricates the typical and the singular.[22] The protagonists' rise and fall is formulaic, but the paths they take are distinctive in their details. Letters fitted this pattern well, with their durable and recognisable conventions and their space for subjectivity. They counter-pointed oral aspects of justice (like testimony they usually conveyed some narrative, but might stray in colourful ways) and in the chaotic world of prisons and public executions they were often one of the few ways a prisoner might be heard.[23] 'Newgate is a dismal prison ... a Tower of Babel where all are speakers and no hearers.'[24] The relative power of texts to cross distances can be seen in the way last words were written down by diligent bystanders and papers thrown into the crowds by the condemned. The last communi-cations of criminals were so frequently published that anyone writing a farewell letter might reasonably be supposed to anticipate an audience beyond the addressee; publication made these letters familiar to a wide readership even as they served an individual's family.[25] Illiterates got others to write for them, though the role of clergymen as amanuenses frequently meant that violent men sounded godly in their final messages. A group of twenty-six pirates executed in Rhode Island in 1723 had letters written for them to relations in Britain and America. Those with children wrote to them; those without, to siblings' children. 'Divers of them lamented their Disobedience to their Parents, & their Prophanation of the Name, Day and Word of God & their ungodly company keeping; & warned Young People, To keep clear from those Crimes.'[26] The consistency of such formulae, internalised by penitents and sold to readers, can be seen from a letter written in plainer terms in 1776 by William Davies, a forger, to a lad who had worked for him: 'Never tell lies. – Go to church or meeting as often as you can. – Never come to see any body in Newgate. – Be a good boy, and God will bless you. Farewel!'[27]

The universalising power of letters also had specific class inflections. They could demonstrate in writing for the satisfaction of a middle-class readership the otherwise non-verbal skills of the criminal mastermind. The brilliant escapologist Jack Sheppard, on one of his daring break-outs from Newgate, 'went to Black-friars, to the house of Mr. Applebee, printer of the dying-speeches, and delivered a letter, in which he ridiculed the printer, and the Ordinary of Newgate, and enclosed a letter for one of the keepers of Newgate'.[28] The first letter vivaciously defies the genre of last words; the second suggests a more friendly alliance between gaoler and prisoner. Such friendliness could involve mockery, but being directed against a social system that divided people into law-enforcers and law-breakers, it realigned class distinctions. So one fraudster wrote in 1792 to his old gaoler, 'Your sudden departure excited just regret among those who tasted of your conviviality the preceding evening.'[29] The gentility is partly a bourgeois joke at the expense of those who distinguish between criminals and polite society, groups whom the courtesies of letters reunite.

Epistolary eloquence could get people in and out of trouble. John Stanley, executed for stabbing his lover, 'had a free and genteel Stile, with several brilliant Turns of Thought and of Expression, such as Nature, not Art, must furnish. After he had loaded himself with Misfortunes, these Endowments were needful to him.'[30] William Smith 'too strongly presumed on clemency, through the delusive expectations of influencing the Regency with the tender and pathetic Elocution of his Pen, his genteel Behaviour, and Denotations of the sincerest Penitence'.[31] The sample given by his biographer combines Biblical quaking with a more modern anatomical dysfunctioning; his letters petition auditors 'to pity the silent Sobs which my feeble Soul sendeth forth, surprized with Fear, and to regard the broken Voice which my trembling Tongue addresseth to them'.[32] Epistolary conflation of body with voice allowed letters to substitute for persons in displays of physical symptoms of remorse that were authentic because, ironically, they were inaudible. Smith plays on epistolary writing as a substitute for speech that can be read without intruding any noise, though it mimics the physiology of voice production.

Letter-writers faced difficulties here. The exaggeration necessary to emphasise abasement of the fallen created strain. Smith wrote crawlingly to the highly placed Henry Pelham, 'you are the greatest Man breathing; as such, a poor Wretch in the deepest Disconsolation and Anguish, prostrates himself at your Feet'![33] Where letters of friendship usually assumed equal status, letters of supplication emphasised the gulf between writer and addressee, providing vertical and vertiginous rhetorical spaces which the benefactor's condescension would traverse. To inscribe this moral falling might prevent the literal drop entailed in hanging. The temptation to appear sincere for strategic reasons is considered less than one might expect, partly because last things were taken seriously and partly because compilers of accounts of the condemned needed to promote their sources as unchallengeable. Exclusivity was essential. The triple claim of Thomas Harris's title – *The Real, Genuine, and Authentic Narrative* – helped to fend off a rival who also claimed to have secured the papers of Captain James Lowrey, executed for murder after striking one of his troublesome crew a fatal blow.[34] The criminal, whose character was often defined by dishonesty, had to be represented as honest at the last in order to give force to examples and to stabilize representation. In the awkward business of telling crime stories, providential guidance and revelation could convince readers of the 'truth' of what they read.[35] Familiarity with letters also shaped readers' sense of scepticism and belief.

Public belief in letters as a true representation of the mind was encouraged by two factors. One was an overlap between consciousness of the body and soul felt by people anticipating death. Samuel Orton wrote pathetically from prison to a minister that he was too cold to pray. The three letters included in the account of his life, crimes and death are notably ephemeral – 'wrote with pencil on the blank leaves of a book'.[36] Two beg a minister to accompany him in the coach to execution. What makes them even more tragic documents than usual is that the minister revealed at the start of the text that the coach had failed to collect him, so a reader reads the note already aware of Orton's desperately lonely end. Criminal biography's retrospection meant readers supplied hindsight (the protagonist had usually been executed) and anticipation (the protagonists had written with their doom awaiting). After material authenticity, narrative teleology was the second factor that supported letters' truth-telling.

Where events were doubtful, letters could illuminate whether their writer was criminally inclined by establishing character and motive. These concerns were fostered by the novel but the novel is not their only or even prime source. Letters had their own well-established market. Overlaps with fiction point to an influence of letters on fiction as much as fiction's influence on letters, for instance in a feud in the Douglas family after Lady Jane Douglas privately married Colonel John Stewart, to whom her brother had an aversion. She produced two sons whom her brother refused to accept as his legitimate heirs. Public opinion supported Lady Jane[37] and an epigraph to a selection of her letters presented them juridically: 'This is a Jury Cause, where every body will judge for themselves, and also judge those who judge it.'[38] The sons had to prove they were not impersonators, which they did by proving their mother was not a liar through the honesty of her letters. 'As perhaps there never was (even in romance) a more affecting story, the world will no doubt be anxious to know it intimately; towards which the following letters will contribute more than volumes of proofs and memorials.'[39] The human complexity of the case was best served by a humane medium. The letters' narrative is organised around an emotional plot rather than strict chronology; disjunction from the story taking place in court confirmed a sense of intimacy. Instead of foregrounding the setbacks and advances of the legal action, the letters demonstrate an exemplary domestic absorption. Lady Jane is endlessly sympathetic to her husband who was languishing in prison for debt: 'only what concerns you, dear Mr. Stewart, and these two little babes, Archy and Sholto, robs me of rest and ease'.[40] The sympathy she shows for him in barely being able to afford food creates sympathy for her in the same unspoken situation, even as she blames herself for his hunger: 'owing to your parting too freely with your few shillings to me, which I took from you with regret'.[41] Her husband's inability to provide for his family is touchingly rewritten as an act of generosity. Her epistolary tact even extends to her possibly insane brother, to whom she writes affectionately and submissively. Punctual, considerate and supportive, she is the perfect epistolary wife. Lady Jane's pious cheerfulness is clearly willed, though this does not make it necessarily insincere since duty sanctioned moral performances. But the strain in the face of destitution and family separation told on her body: she died emaciated before the case was favourably ended. Her tendency to fast, ostensibly on religious grounds, was also a contraction of bodily space which in the context of a prison correspondence is arguably a specific kind of anorexia.[42] Lady Jane reorders her geographical world in order to share the legally enclosed domain of her husband; becoming ill, she turns physical separation into psychic union by a disembodiment also reflected in letters.[43]

From Boethius to Gramsci, a prison location has given writing poignancy and intensity. The writers' seclusion places them outside society but not beyond it, especially in the eighteenth century when prisons were crowded and many of those imprisoned were not criminals.[44] Particularly where debt and forgery were connected to the failure of respectable business, commentators recognised degrees of moral abandonment. Imprisonment called into question the nature and immutability of laws; it made possible the idea of excarceration.[45] The literary equality of correspondence could cast doubt on unequal legal procedures. Moreover, correspondence could get in and out of prisons, making letters a form of freedom. Liberty meant freedom of the body which included a sense of enlargement of the mind, well-expressed by letter-writing: 'the power of writing...can soothe, in some measure, the black desponding hour, and enable me to hold an imaginary correspondence with you.' Thus an exile in Botany Bay found a little consolation in sending pathetic letters to his beloved old aunt in Scotland.[46] Conversely, letters from those at liberty could reproach the confined with the freedom they abused. A penitent highwayman, James Maclaine, was given a letter from his brother only when he was in a fit state to appreciate that its compassion and morality epitomised those social values he had abandoned.[47] Minds, hearts and souls were not restrained, but the body bordered free thoughts and feelings. 'There was not a dry eye among us', wrote the clergyman attending Maclaine as he read his letter. Like bodies, letters gave material shape to ideological meanings.

The reader too can get in and out of prison by reading prison correspondence. The pleasure and edification of spectacles of suffering involved both objectification and sympathy. On the one hand, letters and last words, however formulaic, personalised criminals; on the other hand, they could show the subject falling to pieces. A complicated representation of subjectivity about to be extinguished, yet flickering intensely through letters, was devised by Sir Herbert Croft. His material came from a celebrated crime of passion in 1779 when James Hackman shot the mistress of the Earl of Sandwich, Martha Reay, with whom he was in love. She stayed distant so he became frantic. Planning to kill himself at her feet, he shot her dead and only injured himself. There were actual letters between the couple; Croft opportunistically made up more. Although his sensationalist inventions under the title *Love and Madness* have been described by John Brewer as fitting into 'a recognisable genre of works whose appeal lay in their effective crossing and re-crossing the boundaries between the genres of history and fiction',[48] they should be understood in relation to the explanatory power of letters in relation to constructions of a criminal character. In the this light, reference points are less ones of history and fiction and more a discourse of last words through letters. In order to explain last words, an epistolary sequence establishes passion's windings and tangles. Most readers at the time believed in Croft's fictionalisings, which Brewer explains as the gripping power of sentimental clichés.[49] Epistolary framings, however, helped make them plausible.

Croft represents Hackman, or 'Hackman', scribbling a letter in his last moments. This visible commitment to communication emphasised the subjectivity about to be extinguished, or at least gestured to something beyond spectacle, as unfinished as 'Hackman's' letter. Letters struggle to articulate his coming dissolution:

> Were these scraps of paper to be seen by any other eye than yours, common people would wonder that, in proportion as the moment drew nearer, I got further and further from myself. It may be contrary to the rule of critics, but so it is. To think, or to write about myself, is death, is hell. My feelings will not suffer me to date these different papers any more.[50]

Croft printed these fragments separately, reminiscent of Clarissa's semi-coherent meditations after being raped.[51] What Croft as 'Hackman' called 'the picture of a heart'[52] is framed by recognisable conventions that are not simply literary but *epistolary*. The process of writing could make subjectivity coherent – 'When I finished my last scrap of paper, I thought I felt myself composed, resigned'[53] – but it did not guarantee protection against derangement up to the last moment. Hence letters offered a plot of suspense even when the outcome was irrevocable death: would the condemned go quietly?

Hackman's letters, like those of Lady Jane Douglas, invited readers to assess whether their author was a criminal and if so, what kind. Croft's invented letters placed the murder in high culture; 'Hackman' implies his is a noble crime by alluding several times to *Othello*. Hackman's actual story could be made to sound lurid: Horace Walpole called it a shocking murder but added, 'The poor criminal, I am persuaded, is mad, and the misfortune is the law does not know how to define the shades of madness.'[54] Literature did, on the other hand, as 'Hackman' is constantly aware: 'What a tale it would make of woe! Take warning from me, my fellow creatures, and do not love like H.'[55] Tragic romance accounts for some of the letters' sense of doom: the day before the murder, Croft has 'Hackman' writes wildly to a friend that his passions were 'a pack of bloodhounds which will inevitably tear me to pieces'.[56] The drive is mythic rather than modern; like Actaeon, he is caught up in bloody forces. But although rhetorical violence was present in sentimental fiction, actual, impending violence was latent in letters by the condemned. Ironically, Hackman himself was judged not insane (though he had no wish to evade death by pleading so) because along with pistols in his pocket he carried a letter at the time of the shooting, whose coolness and deliberation showed no mental disorder.

The question of responsibility that focused readings of criminals' letters became a question of sanity in relation to the letters of suicides. Self-murder was in theory both mad and bad. In practice, contemporaries puzzled over instances that suggested otherwise.[57] The death of Richard Smith, his wife and daughter in 1732 was coolly chosen in the face of poverty. The letter they left explaining their reasons 'was altogether surprising for the calm resolution, the good humour, and the propriety with which it was written'.[58] This decorum was not unique. A suicide letter sent by its author to a newspaper in 1771 offered similar pleasantries and reasons: 'it is a folly to think that men must be cracked, or *non compos* to put an end to themselves; no such thing; I am as much in my senses now, as ever I was in my life'.[59] Hackman's predicament was that in wanting to die, he had killed another, so in being punished by death, he was getting his desires as well as his deserts. The disorder of madness disguised this logic: madness, traditionally associated with poetry, distracted from the poetic injustice of the state's decision to execute someone who wanted to kill himself. Letters by 'Hackman' were peppered with stories of suicides and framed by Croft with three more. One was famously the death of Thomas Chatterton, whose letters Croft had implanted into Hackman's. This strange conjunction has been explained on commercial grounds: Croft invented correspondence between Hackman and Reay as a vehicle to sell the Chatterton material, clumsily linked by a letter about Chatterton that Croft pretended was written by Hackman.[60] The conjunction can also be explained in terms of literary forgery of which Chatterton is now the focus, though the letters purporting to be by Hackman express interest in other contemporary controversies about authenticity, including that of *Ossian*.[61] Forgery, however, is not the only frame for interpretation. Croft presented Chatterton as a genius driven to suicide by rejection, a myth which has had a long literary shelf-life but needs to be re-read in the context of Hackman's entanglement with murder and would-be suicide. Croft links Hackman and Chatterton as men rejected – Hackman by a woman, Chatterton by the world. Yet the letters of both men defy simple stereotyping, as Croft conceded, commenting on Chatterton that 'The motives for everything he did are past finding out.'[62] Creating letters by Hackman, Croft supplied motives in abundance but still they did not quite explain him. The letters of suicides and desperate types made love and madness more complicated than in fiction.

Suicides seemed to register the seriousness of their actions through humour, which readers found curious. They brought irony to that composure which those obliged to die by the law were expected to muster. Character here was clearly constructed for a performance with rules. James Foster who attended the Earl of Kilmarnock before his execution in 1746 had many earnest conversations with him about the decorum of public death. The 'most just and decent' behaviour, he concluded, 'must surely be resigned, but awful; free from an extreme of dejectedness, but not eager and rapid to meet death'.[63] Some condemned people welcomed attendance of clergy and an opportunity to rehearse the manner of their deaths. All death was violent, observed Thomas Potts before his execution, but 'there is a great mercy in the foresight of death, and in having time to prepare for it'.[64] Last letters made visible the criminal's turning towards eternity. Epistolary disembodiment helped people leave flesh behind. Since cultural specificity was left behind with wordly concerns, imprisonment literature could cross national borders. Hence the translation of the last letters of an infantry captain who had offended the King of Prussia.[65] These turned loss, farewell, resignation and Christian composure into universals. The Emperor's oppressive royalty gives way to God's merciful majesty: writer and reader look to another world, one that recognised not subjects but sinners. So although letters helped construct the character of criminal, the letter as last words often demonstrated a repentance that eluded ideologies of earthly punishment.

Like suicides and mad lovers, Jacobites had a contradictory relation to criminality. They challenged one authority (Hanoverian) but upheld another (Stuart); they also had links with the Irish and Irish strikers who counted as criminals in many English eyes.[66] Still, many Jacobites impressed contemporaries by the dignity of their deaths. One who did not was William Paul, a non-jurying clergyman captured at Preston in 1715, who was patently terrified of death. He wrote frantic letters that pleaded innocence, begged help, implored mercy and promised penitence. Receiving no replies,[67] he became less conciliatory and more desperate, writing to the Archbishop of Canterbury, 'What Confession the Court would have from me, I can't tell . . . I humbly desire your Grace to consider your poor afflicted

Servant, and take him from this nasty Prison.'[68] These letters were widely circulated and condemned as hypocritical after Paul denounced the Archbishop and unrepentantly upheld rebellious views from the scaffold. (His last speech was stopped as 'grating to Loyal Ears'.) Letters also made the Earl of Mar's change of mind look nearly hypocritical: he wrote professing loyalty to King George I on 30 August 1714, but by 9 September he was writing to his tenants with threats to make them join him in the rebellion.[69]

In many treason cases, the character of criminal collided with that of citizen – a rebel was a good citizen in a bad cause. Rebels wished to overthrow particular rulers or governments, but they were also defined more loosely as an oppositional class, the subversives of the moment. The rebel was simultaneously a lonely figure who had to be ideologically isolated and a conspirator spreading contagion to others. Letters were a practical medium of conspiracy that troubled distinctions between public and private. 'Happily, we can now sit quietly, and write our sentiments in our own houses, without being liable to have our papers seized by the arbitrary mandates of a secretary of state' (which general warrants earlier had allowed), wrote a commentator in 1779.[70] Confusions between secrecy and openness were activated by letters, as a case from 1704 shows. Some gibberish letters were intercepted in Edinburgh and baffled decoders. An anonymous letter to the Duchess of Queensbury named David Baillie as someone who knew what they said. The Duke interviewed him and was not satisfied with his answers. Baillie then wrote to the Duke of Hamilton complaining that the Duke of Queensbury was trying to bribe and threaten him to incriminate Hamilton and others. By a complicated route, Baillie was brought before the Privy Council who asked him to depose against the Duke of Hamilton. He referred them to his letter; they insisted he repeat its contents. Unable or unwilling to do so, Baillie claimed he could not remember what he had written five weeks earlier. Since the letter recalled events five years previous, the court disbelieved him; they also discounted his argument that because the letter was private, it could not count as calumny. Baillie was found guilty and banished. The court's decision should be understood in relation to an established history of associations between letters and treason, especially plotting by Catholics, which re-focused Protestant fears almost every generation of the early modern period.[71] 'Letters give the enemy a name and a voice revelatory of the opposition's secrets.'[72] They made the personal into the political and vice-versa.

In Baillie's curious case, the superfluity of signs aroused most suspicion. Paradoxically, signs of loyalty were read as signs of subversion. Comparing Baillie to other traitors, the commentator remarked, 'these Gentlemen had nothing more frequent in their mouths, than *Encomiums* upon her Majesty, and Protestations of their Zeal for her Person; when at the same time they were carrying on a Conspiracy against Her Government'.[73] Patriotic expressions become giveaway signs of a conspiracy. This anxiety about disguise underlay a specifically eighteenth-century obsession with cant, but it also required a peculiar way of reading letters, less perverse than it seems at first in that plotters did use normality as a screen. Paul Monod has commented that 'The closer one examines Jacobitism, the more one doubts the existence of "ordinary", "typical" or "average" people in eighteenth-century England.'[74] Letters contributed significantly to the surrealism of Jacobitism. On the one hand, the person responsible for intercepting seditious letters at the Post Office was 'a highly placed Stuart agent'; on the other, the person in charge of Jacobite affairs in the 1730s believed Sir Robert Walpole was a secret Jacobite and so delivered treasonable correspondence straight to him.[75] Monod argues that 'it was easier to write than to act', which accounts for a Jacobite liking for anonymous letters, 'a sort of wish-fulfilment rather than a real weapon' and typically full of 'wild promises, vague menaces' and vehemence.[76] Political fantasisings were also disguised as mundane communications, however, and two cases from the middle and end of the century demonstrate that paranoid readings were not unreasonable.

The case of William Jackson, tried in Dublin in 1795 for high treason, turned entirely on the interpretation of a correspondence between Jackson and some friends. They used rather transparent false names – W. Stone became W. Enotts – and the subjects appeared to be manufacturing and a family lawsuit. But, argued the prosecution, 'through the course of this correspondence, terms are strangely and enigmatically used, for instance; – you will find terms of trade where trade was not concerned',[77] and he proposed that the letters secreted an account of the political and economic state of Ireland intended to be of use to those in France considering an invasion route to England. The defence countered there was no evidence to show that references to a sister-in-law meant the kingdom of Ireland: 'the idlest correspondence might be strained to any construction; and for that which men had written in the moment of harmless gaiety, they might be obliged to pay the dreadful forfeit of their lives'.[78] Jackson's sudden death in court meant no verdict was given, but the tension between these two ways of reading was too great to be resolved.

Of the case of Florence Hensey, the Solicitor General commented, 'I do not remember ever to have heard a Charge of High Treason better, more strongly, or more consistently made out.'[79] Hensey, an Irish doctor living quietly in London, was convicted but thanks to some string-pulling by his brother reprieved and deported. Twenty-nine letters identified as being in his handwriting were produced, some intercepted via the Post Office, some taken from a bureau in his lodgings. They reported in French on troop movements, giving crucial information about the (disastrous) British expedition to Rochfort. The defence worked hard to find exonerations: did posting a letter necessarily constitute an intention? Were Hensey's letters sent before a declaration of war that turned open public news into secret military intelligence? Could intelligence be treasonable if the letters never arrived? They were defeated by the weight of evidence of the letters' material appearance. Like Jackson's later, Hensey's were directed to neutral or allied countries, a circumstance that might be innocent but which was read as suspicious. Unequivocally guilty was their wide spacing: the ink text was spread out to allow secret lemon juice letters in the gaps. Since the contents were plainly treasonable once their disguise had been exposed, the case was significant for showing how private communications were open to scrutiny by officials and self-appointed vigilantes, in this case the postman. Sorting letters one night, he held one up to his candle and saw it was written in French. Xenophobia roused his patriotism:

> the Letters I received of Doctor *Hensey* were generally directed Abroad and to Foreigners; and I knowing the Doctor to be a Roman Catholick, and as I imagined in the Interest of the Pretender, I advised the Examining Clerk at the Office to inspect his Letters, telling him, that I had some Suspicion, that the Writer of those Letters was a Spy.[80]

The cosmopolitan correspondence that gave fictional spies cultural breadth became in this case friction between religious faiths and political creeds. Though the postman plainly enjoyed his knowledge of gentlemen's affairs, he was also only following standard orders from the postmaster general to employees and servants that, in times of war, all suspected letters should be stopped. Letters thus criss-crossed between home and state, with household servants and post office employees providing the body politic's means of regulating its members.

For all that public interest seemed to determine that epistolary secrets would be exposed to society by the law, the double-sided nature of correspondence meant that there were often two viewpoints to be considered, thus reinforcing the division of case law into a two-sided process, *Rex versus x*. The openness of letters made them a suitable medium for an individual at odds with the law to put a case to the public and for the public to add personal material to published representations of malefactors. The power of letters to weigh in on both sides of a case and to fuse personal and social spheres is clear in the shady case of Mrs Rudd and the Perreau brothers from whose forgery she successfully dissociated herself. That signature was not coterminous with authorship was ironically the point of the forgery case and compounded the play between open and secret aspects of letters under the law. 'The public entertains various opinions of the conduct of Mrs. Rudd', wrote one memoirist with understatement;[81] in the snowstorm of texts competing to establish her as victim or vindictive female, there were hostile anonymous letters which she attributed to the Perreau brothers,[82] and sympathetic ones attributed to her and signed with her name. Whilst letters revealed criminal behaviour, they did not perfectly explain it – indeed, letters often showed how mystifying and secret other people's lives were.

Particular cases showed public familiarity with the material import of letters and fascination with their power to conceal as well as reveal the springs of human action. Definitions of 'bad' that accrued to the character of criminal were often accompanied by awareness of other paradigms, like 'mad', allowing for polarised and ambiguous readings simultaneously. Within a context of recognition of the material significance of letters, ambiguities surrounding their interpretation, and their relevance to securing ideological frameworks governing the actions of individuals, I next explore three murder trials in detail to show how people looked to letters for explanatory narratives and how letters made explanations murky.

Women in the dock: three cases

The case of Mary Blandy, accused and convicted of poisoning her father, was widely argued about at the time. Her case has attracted some notice from critics interested in the predicament of women under the law and the development of circumstantial evidence as a force in legal reasoning.[83] These discussions, however, have little to say about letters, which were at the heart of the case. They were vital evidence in the relation between Mary Blandy and her lover, Captain Cranstoun, between him and his wife in Scotland and in events surrounding her father's death, when an ambiguous letter from her was construed as evidence of her guilt. 'On the whole, because of the love interest and parricide, the following for *R v. Blandy* was more literary than legal.'[84] Although medical evidence formed part of the trial, letters invited spectators to be readers of epistolary evidence. Interpretations of character and motive turned on letters and spilled outside the trial into the press, when letters to, by and about the protagonists dominated public debate. Restoring the visibility of letters in the case alters arguments about gender and proof.

How one represents the 'facts' of a case obviously colours it, but in this case the facts were pretty much agreed – only one point was under dispute. Mary Blandy was the only daughter of a gentleman who lived in Henley-on-Thames. She was well-educated, lively, affable and apparently well treated by affectionate parents to whom she behaved respectfully. Her father wished her to marry well and in order to catch a better class of suitor, he put it about that his daughter would have a fortune of £10,000. His unwise move drew mercenary suitors, though 'Miss was naturally of a gay and coquettish Humour'[85] and made her own appointments. Her father left her at liberty to favour Captain Cranstoun, whom her mother strongly liked. Captain Cranstoun was small and scarred by smallpox. He was the younger son of a minor Scottish nobleman and joined the army to improve his prospects. He became involved with a woman called Miss Murray who bore his child. He later claimed he had never married her, but in Scots law cohabitation was treated as marriage so she was entitled to call herself his wife whether or not they went through a ceremony. She had some money, but the prominence of Jacobites in her family damaged Cranstoun's prospects. He met Mary Blandy on a recruiting trip to Henley; cynics said he was after her money, but she at least was persuaded there was more to his attraction than that. If a fraud, he was at least assiduous: when apart, they exchanged letters almost every post.

In order to free himself, Cranstoun wrote to his wife and asked her to copy a letter disowning him as her husband. She was eventually persuaded:

> No sooner had the Captain got this Acknowledgement under her own Hand, but with a Baseness and Ingratitude that can hardly be parallel'd, he sent Copies of her Letter both to her Relations and his own in *Scotland*; which so alienated their Minds, that both the one and the other withdrew their Support from her, whereby she was reduced to the utmost Poverty and Distress.[86]

On the basis of this letter he sued for divorce. She then produced the letter in his writing which he had asked her to copy, moving the court to rule in her favour. Someone warned the Blandys that Cranstoun was still not single; Mr Blandy subsequently behaved to Cranstoun with coolness on some occasions. Mrs Blandy and her daughter wrote to Cranstoun to ask him what the situation was; his response was satisfactory enough to make Mary Blandy declare she would wait for him, though she refused to marry him privately.

Two incidents show how crucial letters were in revealing information and concealing character – often simultaneously. That Cranstoun was accepted as part of the family can be seen on the occasion of the mother's death, when he wrote condolence letters to Mary Blandy and her father and sent his own footman to deliver them express. Mary Blandy recorded this epistolary respect as a positive point for Cranstoun's reputation:

> When my Father opened his Letter and read it, the Tears ran down his Cheeks, and he cried out, 'How tenderly does he write!' Then he gave Mrs. *Mounteney* the Letter to read, who, having read it, said it was as pretty a Letter as could have been wrote on such an Occasion . . .[87]

Their intimacy takes place in a context of familial propriety established through letters. His female relations also wrote civilly to her, which impressed her, like Richardson's Clarissa who placed much stock on civil letters written to her by Lovelace's female relations. If Cranstoun was not sincere, his insincerity was highly skilled. Not long after this, however, Mary Blandy went into his room and found 'a letter from a Hand I knew not, tho' he used always to give me his Letters to open, and that unasked by me. This I opened to read, and found it to come from a Woman he kept.'[88] Many commentators expressed shock that she could continue to see him after this discovery. They attributed her infatuation to physical obsession, diabolism or, more romantically, to 'the Violence of Love'.[89] 'Love, all powerful Love, found her his Votary, his Slave.'[90] By countenancing his correspondence with a mistress, she showed a passivity in keeping with a role as his dupe in later unhappy events.

These events are doubtful and a modern reader finds no benefit from hindsight. What nobody disputed was that Mary Blandy gave her father some white powders, first in his tea, then in his gruel. He suffered agony and the powder, spotted by an alert doctor, proved to be arsenic. Servants who had tasted leftover gruel on earlier occasions were also taken ill. Mary Blandy confessed she had given the powders, but said she had been given them by Cranstoun and she thought they would have a benign effect. A letter she had given to a clerk to post, and which was sealed with an unusually large number of wafers, was opened. It read,

Dear Willy
        My father is so bad that I have only time to tell you that if you do not hear from me soon again don't be frighted. I am better myself. least any accident sd happen to your letters take care what you write my sincere Compts
        I am ever yours[91]

The letter was unsigned and the handwriting more rough and unsteady than Mary Blandy's usual script, but the clerk testified she had given it to him, like others to Cranstoun before, and she never disowned it. The letter seemed damning. She was arrested, taken to prison in Oxford, tried there and hanged. One of the clergymen who had written sympathetically to her in prison conducted her funeral in Henley.

The literature of this case is typical of the genre in its fascination with minutiae in the last days, hours, moments of a human being whose life was to be ended by law. The prosecutor limbered up, oratorically, by attributing the mesmeric effects of murder to empathy: 'Who ever beheld the ghastly Corpse of the murdered Innocent weltering in its Blood, and did not feel his own Blood run slow and cold through all his Veins?'[92] But this fellow-feeling also chilled many observers of executions, especially those conscious that the condemned might be innocent or that, even if guilty, death might be too cruel a punishment. As Mary Blandy pleaded, 'Let me be punished for my Follies, but not lose my Life – Sure it is hard to die for Ignorance, and too good an Opinion of a Villain!'[93] Many were uneasy that Blandy went to her death protesting her innocence. Doubts persisted long after her death: 'she was certainly either the most unfortunate, or most wicked of women'.[94]

'It is an awful Thing to trifle with the Almighty', wrote one commentator, but Blandy's performance persuaded him of her innocence: 'her Story was uniform, her Spirit calm and resigned, and her Sense of Religion lively and strong'.[95] Blandy's slide between respectability and criminality is illustrated by an engraving: the top part shows a three-quarter length portrait of her posed like a Reynolds or Gainsborough sitter in the pink of felicity and prosperity; below is a much more crudely drawn scene of a female figure with a sack-like covering over her head, dangling from a scaffold. One of the case's piteous ironies was that the executioner agreed to Blandy's request that she be 'turned off' from a low drop 'for decency's sake', but when she was cut down she 'was carried through the Crowd upon the Shoulders of one of the Sheriff's Men in the most beastly Manner, with her Legs exposed very indecently for several Hundred Yards'.[96] Middle-class proprieties were at least maintained for her in prison: the same source complained she 'was indulged to an unparalleled Degree; for no Person, without her previous Consent, from her Commitment to her Death, was permitted to see her, tho' very extraordinary Sums were daily offered for that Purpose.'[97] What one critic has described in an unfortunate phrase as 'the glamour that hung about the murderess' involved appropriating her privacy and parading her as spectacle.[98] Blandy's seclusion put more emphasis on letters as a way of gaining access to her.

Blandy received various letters whilst in prison. Several clerics wrote to ask if she was a freethinker. She replied piously; the answer was important. Atheists, being less impressed by religious sanctions against perjury, were considered more likely to lie; hence doubt could be cast on their testimony. The work of divines would change too. As one said of a highwayman he was attending, 'If he had taken Shelter in Infidelity, I had his Judgment to Inform, and his Prejudices to remove; if not, my Business was only, by Divine Assistance, to endeavour to awaken his Conscience.'[99] But Mary Blandy acted soberly, attended services and at all times professed Christian beliefs. Her narrative starts '*Oh! Christian Reader*'.[100] This decorum in religion was mutually supportive of propriety in gender and class too. Her case and her identity were synonymous: in both, she was to be 'Consider'd as a *Daughter*, as a *Gentlewoman*, and as a *Christian*'.[101]

The prominence of letters in Blandy's case distinguished the protagonists from a stereotypically less literate criminal working class. It also enabled literate people to have an opinion about the evidence. 'In the various lights this transaction may be viewed, there is room for the divine, the casuist, the lawyer, the naturalist, the physician, to take each an important province'[102] – and one could add the literary critic to this list. On the other hand, texts were also a liability: they were scrutinised for inconsistencies and Mary Blandy's written account was openly attacked. She 'appears fond of Evasions', wrote one commentator;[103] another took issue with how she represented her father 'as a Man of a hasty, passionate, uneven Temper'.[104]

The trial was held in Oxford – not at the Town Hall, which was being rebuilt, but in the university's Divinity School; it drew an undergraduate audience and increased a sense of Blandy's case as intellectually challenging, socially genteel and ideologically dynamite. Letters were crucial to the evidence. The unsigned note sent as Mr Blandy lay dying needed to be explained. 'Much stress is laid on Miss Blandy's letter, a letter no person here would have dictated in her circumstances, nor have advised her to entrust with the clerk at that time.'[105] Only one writer tried to give it an innocent construction. The rest thought it ominously unfeeling:

> She had beheld his Tortures; she knew that, whether innocently or not, she had caused them; and yet in this Letter she writes so coolly in Regard to him, as if there were nothing in his Case, dreadful as it was, to affect her.[106]

Blandy's explanation that terseness was an effect of distress did not convince readers, who objected to specifics as well as to the general tenor. 'She cautions him to beware of what he writes! Why, if the Correspondence was not a vicious one?' This critic concluded she showed a murderer's sang-froid: 'There is no difficulty in conceiving a Woman, who could write this in such a Situation, capable of any Wickedness.'[107] A more compassionate but equally damning reaction took its cue from Mr Blandy, to whom the clerk read the letter as he lay dying. He 'smiled, and said, "Poor Lovesick Girl! What won't a Girl do for a Man she loves?" '[108] Interpretation of the letter was crucial in deciding if the accused was calculating or foolish.

Alexander Welsh has tracked the mid-eighteenth-century emergence of circumstantial evidence as a category of legal reasoning; first celebrated by the prosecution in criminal cases, it became a favourite kind of proof because, in William Paley's famous aphorism, 'Circumstances cannot lie'.[109] Welsh sees a divergence between direct testimony, made by people (who of course can lie), and indirect testimony, frequently drawn from things, objects that are mute until read as signs, when they becomes expressive. One of the advantages of circumstantial evidence is that the conversion of things to signs takes place after a crime has been committed, Welsh argues, so 'the ambiguities are all confined to later interpretation, which looks backward in time without the danger of being misled by anyone other than the interpreter'.[110] Complications, however, arise in respect to letters, because letters are 'things' when understood as material objects and 'people' when understood as forms of expression. Moreover, letters are always signs in the sense that they are text. Letters in cases like Blandy's represented both 'people' and 'things' depending on what would be most damning. Interpretations based on new models of circumstantial evidence, or letters as 'things', were helped by old-fashioned ideas of Providence. The patchy evidence against Blandy was thus not imperfect but supernaturally selective: as one of the prosecutors put it, 'For what, but the hand of Providence, could have preserved the paper thrown by her into the fire, and have snatched it unburnt from the devouring flame?'[111] There is an obvious alternative answer, since human hands had saved other parts of the evidence. Again, this had special meanings for letters. The *Gentleman's Magazine* declared 'the unseen hand of God must uncover what the unseen hand of the accused has already wrought'.[112] The order of trumps put the hand of God above the hand of the accused (in the sense that it was by her hand that her father died); the hand of the accused as it appeared in her handwriting was thus self-accusing. Mary Blandy claimed that her warning to Cranstoun to write guardedly referred to an earlier letter from him that had disclosed his family secrets. But here she was trapped: she could not produce this letter, because she had burnt it and the rest of their correspondence. At her trial she insisted that the letters would have provided evidence to hang him and acquit her. But in conjunction with the unsigned note, few were convinced: 'This indeed was a strong Argument to prove her Consciousness of Guilt; for had the Correspondence between them been perfectly innocent, there had been no occasion to destroy his Letters.'[113] At best imprudent, at worst a sign of her guilt – sexual or criminal – Blandy's conflagration thickened ambiguities.

The evidence was gone but critics were haunted by the letters. Blandy's staunchest defender looked to romance for explanations: 'Did ever Lovers yet exist, who would not chuse that their Letters should be seen by none but themselves?' Alternatively, he suggested, 'these letters she knew would make her appear ridiculous; besides, at the Time she burnt them, it was no wonder that she was a little disordered in her Senses'.[114] With a choice of romantic, satiric or tragic plots, at least two authors were drawn to supply letters to fill the gap, one sympathetic to Cranstoun and one favouring Blandy. Both treat the administration of poison as the climax, but with different implications. Blandy's own story at the trial had been stranger than fiction. As relations between her father and Cranstoun deteriorated, she claimed, 'He got his Mother and Sister to write to my Father, and seemed to do all in his power to force him to love him.'[115] When these letters failed, Cranstoun proposed a Scottish remedy, a sort of love potion, which was said to create good feeling in the recipient towards the supplier. On one occasion he told Blandy he would use it and her father was subsequently cordial. He sent this powder to Blandy and supposedly so as not to spoil the charm he labelled it as powder to clean some Scotch pebbles he had sent her as a present. This labelling paper did exist: it was saved from the fire. To some commentators, this story was incredible, particularly since Blandy was a bright woman who might reasonably be supposed to have little truck with the mumbo-jumbo of love potions. But Cranstoun cultivated fey Scottish airs: there had been talk of supernatural music presaging deaths and instances of second sight – a phenomenon not wholly discredited, as

Samuel Johnson showed by asking about it whilst in the Hebrides.[116] So besides tracking the story of two lovers divided by a parent, the fictional letters that stood in for the burnt correspondence had to address the uncertain topic of Mary Blandy's gullibility and the euphemisms surrounding the powders and their purposes.

Captain Cranstoun's Account[117] includes three letters leading up to the last dose. The 'editor' claims they set 'that whole tragical affair in a true Light' and that they come from the Captain's trunk in his room in Flanders. There was indeed such a trunk, though Cranstoun's papers had been returned to his family in Scotland after his death. Like the letter Mary Blandy gave to the clerk, these are unsigned, 'yet, by their Contents, they plainly shew from whom they were sent'.[118] A prefatory narrative blames Blandy, alleging it was she who demanded a private marriage, that she lured Cranstoun with promises of money and that although he proposed the method of death, she knew exactly what the powders were and agreed to use them. The three letters take up the oblique mode of Blandy's known note, so that again what is not said becomes eloquent. 'When you write, let it be as mystically as you please, lest an Interception should happen to your Letter, for I shall easily understand it.'[119] The need for code reveals the existence of nameless deeds about which she cannot be open. The second letter declares, 'I particularly understand what you mean' with no referent;[120] her adeptness at reading between the lines becomes between-the-lines testimony to her deviousness. The criminal mind is represented as a combination of chilling efficiency – 'I am going forward with all convenient Speed in the Business' – and gothic derangement – 'tho' I suffer more Horrors of Mind, than I do at this Time, which I think is impossible, I will pursue that, which is the only Method, I am sensible, left, of ever being happy together'.[121] Her abstraction and euphemism are discursive absences that distract from the more material absence of his letters and whatever they might say to balance her guilt with his. Touches of conscience remind the reader of the moral edification in reading letters written by a person subsequently hanged to a correspondent whose death seemed marked by the hand of Providence, though not the long arm of the law.[122]

In contrast, *Original Letters To and From Miss Blandy and C——C——* is cheerfully sympathetic to Blandy as a victim of villainy. '*These are the* LETTERS *supposed to be burnt, and which she gave to her intimate Friend a few Days before her Execution*', begging her to publish.[123] The twelve letters spiral from tender to bitter: 'My dearest Willy' from 'Your loving Polly' becomes 'Cursed C——' from 'M.B.' Eschewing the moral ambiguity of anonymity for emotional forms of subscription and address from fiction, this text mimics novels in its emphatic use of signature and its collision of viewpoints. The effect is curious – as if Clarissa and Lovelace were arguing about whether to murder Mr Harlowe. The parallel might well be a conscious one: both this story and *Clarissa* feature a clever woman deceived, an unstable father and close attention to epistolary codes. The collection plays out melodrama and sentiment to the final letter, in which 'M.B.' curses Cranstoun and laments her ruin.

This text takes an ambivalent line on whether Blandy knew about the poison, but it is more concerned to exploit possibilities than authenticate facts. In one letter, 'M.B.' breaks from the sentimental discourse of the romantic heroine and accuses Cranstoun of dealing with an old hag, the drug supplier who means to harm her father. In a clever twist, 'C' is able to persuade her to continue giving the powders, on the grounds that if she *stops*, her father will die, according to the infallible foresight of old Mrs Morgan. But the author's boldest move was to include the actual unsigned letter that Blandy gave the clerk:

> N.B. – Here we hope it will not be disagreeable to our Readers, if we insert the following Letter which was produced upon her Trial; tho' there was no Copy of it found; yet there seems to be a Connexion with the former.[124]

By casting doubt on its authenticity, provenance and coherence, the only real letter in the collection is made to look fictional!

That discourses could be so altered by rewriting their contexts is made easier in letters where the single letter also has an identity in a sequence. The instabilities, however, also connect to a larger plot about gender. There was more to reimagining Mary Blandy than simply her situation as a criminal condemned to die. She was a woman who had been convicted of parricide, an offence stigmatised as unnatural not least because it struck at the heart of patriarchy.[125] Attempts to reimagine Cranstoun also connected monstrosity and sexual politics, but they were fewer and more conservative in literary terms. They looked back to Biblical archetypes – 'the *Fawning Serpent* plies her with a kind of *magic Inchantment*, tortures her into a belief, that it is quite Innocent, and lures her to this 𝕷𝖆𝖇𝖞𝖗𝖎𝖓𝖙𝖍 𝖔𝖋 𝖂𝖔𝖊'.[126] Black-letter type indicated blackguardism. Alternatively Cranstoun became demodé, a Restoration libertine and freethinker. One writer has him say,

> Men of Honour and Extraction scorn to be tied by those Shackles which they have made for their Inferiors and Slaves...Marriage I always consider as a Thing no farther necessary for a Man, than to continue his Name and Inheritance in his Family; and that his Wife is no other than a domestic Utensil which he keeps for that Purpose. This being secured, he is at full Liberty to range the Female World, and crop every Virigin Flower he can lay his hands upon.[127]

Stage villains and satanic characters traditionally condemn themselves from their own mouths and the military stereotype was also associated with oral swagger. These analogues distract from the absence of any actual words from Cranstoun. Again, although the literary associations around Blandy took sentimental fiction as a reference point, bearings were established through letter-writing practices shared by fact and fiction. One analyst described her story as 'Delicacy in Distress', anticipating Elizabeth Griffith's 1769 novel *The Delicate Distress*. An anonymous correspondent explained the romantic impulse which moved him to write to her in prison: 'I dare say you have often wept at Distress in a Tragedy or Novel, where, perhaps, every thing was fictitious – much more may I at your too real Tragedy.'[128] The literary appeal of Blandy's story was sustained by her own literary activity. For one author, she was too active in her own cause: 'being unwilling that her Name should be transmitted to Posterity with so foul a Blot, she has employed too much of her Time, since her conviction, in writing Letters to be published, to vindicate her Innocence'.[129] This pro-active, public writing he construed as aggressive and unfeminine, and hence evidence of the unnaturalness of a parricide.

That letters, class and gender interacted in powerful ways can be seen in a comparison of Blandy's case with that of Elizabeth Jeffryes. She was a woman from Walthamstow who conspired with a man called John Swan to murder her uncle. Both were hanged in front of a large crowd in Epping Forest, within a few days of Blandy's execution. They had tried to make the murder look like a burglary gone wrong, but facts were swiftly established thanks to a servant who had refused a bribe to join them. Medical evidence clearly proved that the uncle died slowly from a shot fired by Swan, but the few writers drawn to the case preferred to make Jeffryes a lurid death-dealer: 'one Thing is certain, that she entered with great Coolness into the Conspiracy, prosecuted it with Spirit, and in the closing Scene shook off all that was Woman in her Nature, when with her own Hand she gave the finishing Stab'.[130] Despite this totally fantastical reference to Lady Macbeth, in all other respects Elizabeth Jeffryes was not at all lady-like, nor her behaviour in prison genteel enough to attract sympathy. Her memoirist claimed 'she would drink very excessively, was extremely passionate and vindictive against any one whom she conceived an Ill-will to, swearing and using horrid Expressions against them'.[131] Jeffryes had some sympathy in that nobody mourned her uncle: he had brought her up and sexually abused her, leading to a miscarriage and an abortion. The murder had poetic justice for some: 'And here we may admire the dispensations of Providence, in permitting this unhappy, this ruin'd Creature, to be the Means of destroying that Man, that had before destroyed her Virtue.'[132] Less poetically, Jeffryes' motive was that her uncle had threatened to alter his will in favour of a servant with whom she had found him in bed. She was having an affair with her accomplice, Swan, and after all her uncle had put her through, to be cast off financially was intolerable. Justice was very rough in this case; Jeffryes struggled violently on the way to execution and Swan's body was hanged in chains.

At first glance the cases of Blandy and Jeffryes seem to demonstrate entrenched social differences: Jeffryes uneducated, abused and materially struggling; Blandy educated, loved and comfortable. But there were similarities, beyond the obvious one of conviction for the killing of male relatives who met ghastly deaths. Both women, had they secured funds from their male relatives, would have been free to follow their sexual inclinations (which in Jeffryes' case were said to have ranged beyond Swan). Though Blandy's motive could be represented as love rather than money, self-determination issues were as clearly involved as for Jeffryes. One text which compared the two ended with qualified support for young ladies' choice of husbands. This freedom was fenced in by class considerations: choice might be possible for young ladies not carried away by passion but could not be condoned in the amours of working women. The irony that lower-class women were thus freer to choose their lovers but more vulnerable to being forced or cast off was not lost on Mary Blandy, who hinted at a common cause with Jeffryes:

Soon after Miss *Jeffryes*'s Trial was published, Miss *Blandy* read it, and said, *It was barbarous, but I am sorry for her...* A Day or two after this, she said, *A Bill was going to be carried into Parliament, for a Law to hang all the sensible Women, and let none but Fools live.*[133]

As convicted murderers, both women were not simply victims. But they were disadvantaged at law by patriarchal attitudes that insisted on proper behaviour for women. The author who quotes Blandy's perception of Jeffryes is the same author hostile to her writing letters to vindicate herself; he also sees positive remarks she makes about women as evidence of an arrogance that confirms her guilt. Blandy's resemblance to a lover in a novel of delicate distress meant she might be the more capable of writing her own fiction in letters: 'one Thing is certain, her good Sense is the greatest Argument against her'.[134] Rational women should not be so naïve as to believe in Scottish folklore. Both Blandy and the reader were caught up in a mystery which could be solved by reading the evidence aright: for Blandy, was Cranstoun a villain? And for the reader, was Blandy guilty? The textuality of the case both sharpened reading skills and confounded them.

The ways in which literary expectations of gender were read onto actual women's writing can be seen in an earlier case where the literary model was more obliquely fictional. In 1699, a woman's body was found floating in a river in Hertfordshire. She was Sarah Stout, a Quaker. Much of the trial was taken up with forensic questions: is it the presence of water or the absence of air which makes a body drown and how much of each element will allow a body to float in fresh water?[135] The answers would determine whether Sarah Stout had been strangled on land and her body thrown into the water or had thrown herself in and drowned. The principal defendant was a lawyer, Spencer Cowper, who had left Stout's house late on the night she disappeared. He defended himself, which is not surprising, but the case had an epistolary twist. His defence was that Sarah Stout's death was not murder but suicide. For this he had to establish a motive or a relevant state of mind. The evidence existed, he said, but he was reluctant to use it because things written down can become indelible and he was aware of what this might mean to a woman's reputation:

> I shall give the clearest Evidence that was ever given in any Court, that she murthered her self; when I enter upon this Proof, I must of necessity trespass upon the Character of this Gentlewoman that is dead, I confess this is a tender Point, 'tis a thing I would willingly be excus'd from, and 'tis not without a great deal of Reluctancy and Compulsion forc'd from me...[136]

He conceded that 'in Honour I ought to conceal the Weakness of this Gentlewoman' but that he had to expose it to save his co-defendants. Before making this revelation, Cowper first established that he left the house to go to another lodging and his witnesses and experts challenged the prosecution's interpretation of the autopsy. Letters were the final and conclusive piece of evidence. Their appearance was prefaced by testimony that Sarah Stout was melancholy and had confided to an acquaintance that she was in love with a man she could not marry. This person, Cowper suggested, was himself. She had sent him a handful of letters under cover via a mutual friend, a form of address that itself testified to covert passion: 'For her to direct to me at a Coffee-house might make the Servants wonder, and the Post-man might suspect.'[137] Various witnesses reported that Cowper had showed them the letters when he received them. Such confirmation, as in modern harassment cases, showed Cowper understood how a paralegal frame would fit the letters.

Cowper and Stout had become acquainted when he lodged with her mother during sessions at Hertford Crown Court. She was also friendly with his wife. Her letters invited him to stay again, in personal terms: one began, '*I am glad you have not quite forgot that there is such a Person as I in being, but I am willing to shut my Eyes, and not see anything that looks like Unkindness in you*'.[138] Another letter followed – too quickly?

> *I Writ to you by Sunday's Post, which I hope you have received; however as a Confirmation, I will assure you, I know of no inconveniency that can attend your cohabiting with me, unless the Grand Jury should thereupon find a Bill against us, but won't fly for't, for come Life, come Death, I am resolved never to desert you, therefore according to your appointment, I will expect you*...[139]

This mix of humour and hopefulness had alarmed Cowper, but he had to work to persuade the court since 'one or two of the Jury seem to doubt whether the Letters are sufficiently proved'. Among the witnesses he called to swear to her handwriting, her family proved uncooperative.

> Mrs. *Stout*: How should I know! I know she was no such Person, her Handwriting may be counterfeited.
> Mr. Bar. *Hatsell*: But if they were written in a more sober Stile, what would you say then?
> Mrs. *Stout*: I shan't say it to be her Hand, unless I saw her write it.[140]

Her brother made the same distinction between body and language which graphology collapses: 'it don't suit her Character'. Her relations struggled to preserve her as a person not a thing, by refusing to recognise her letters as signs that replace her subjectivity as they knew it. Handwriting, like signature, is a sign taken to be contiguous with person; Cowper turned this metonym neatly into euphemism, an incompletion sanctioned by delicacy. The letters, he suggested, make it so obvious why he had to leave her house in a hurry that he need not spell it out: 'I had rather leave it to be observed, than make the Observation myself.'[141] Through the letters, the jury became active readers, persuaded by an interpretation they make for themselves but which, he inferred, they cannot help making. Having thus established Sarah Stout's transgression of sexual propriety, he piled in with character witnesses for himself, mostly legal colleagues from the Temple who confirmed him as an upright gentleman of superior morals. Using her letters as circumstantial evidence of her sexual guilt proved his innocence.

Decorums of class and gender, however, emanated from other sources besides clever lawyers. As a Quaker, Sarah Stout had a public identity as a modest woman unlikely to be sighing after married men. Though the prosecutor argued 'she might be a virtuous Woman, and her Brains might be turned by her Passion or some Distemper',[142] her friends objected to the use of anonymous letters to destroy her reputation. They argued in court and in print that the letters matched neither her character nor specifically her Quaker character. In part this was a question of epistemology – if someone nurtured a secret passion, how could you know? But it was one affected by fiction – you could know, because people would reveal it in letters, as they did in novels. In legal contexts, ironically, the more letters equivocated, the more they tended to be read as revealing the truth. To put it another way, textual ambiguities encouraged ideologically motivated interpretations. For women, these constructions were consistently hostile to self-determination in matters of sex and finance.

Where women wrote frankly and satirically, they were openly denounced as scandalous. But at least letters provided a means of publicity in which what blazed was also their anger at the injustices they faced.[143] Men's treatment of women's letters in criminal cases showed comparable tactics. Where women showed deference to decorum by writing codedly, their indirectness was construed as criminally devious. What euphemism did for Mary Blandy, innuendo did for Sarah Stout. Both were guilty because both wrote with an evasion which could only be guilty. So the impropriety of Stout's desires shifted sympathy to Cowper as the object of harassment; what had to be proved is not his guilt but hers. Because she did not write in 'a sober Stile', she was as drunk in her way as the visibly disorderly Elizabeth Jeffryes. If Sarah Stout was not what she seemed, she might be unstable enough to be a suicide. This logic was powerful enough to override questions about Cowper's behaviour, including that of who was responsible for the letters' circulation since 'the Printers, who at the Trial did not take them in Short-hand, were favoured with them – to be exposed to the whole World'.[144] Sarah Stout's case made only a local stir, unlike Mary Blandy's, but its ordinariness is eloquent and sad. A pamphlet that took Cowper's part claimed that his story, had he told it immediately, would have sounded incredible and mad.[145] That he could make it plausible enough to persuade a doubtful jury to acquit him showed the immense power of letters in reconstructions and explanatory narratives. Evidential reasoning around epistolary texts has a history that diverges from circumstantial reasoning around material evidence.

Guilty lovers

The double-edged ability of letters to testify to 'facts' and to create character played an important part in trials for adultery. Looking at a range of trials between the 1770s and 1790s, one can see arguments about readings contributing significantly to the confusion of divorce law and the marital mess of most cases.[146] On the one hand, letters were marked as formal exhibits in court; on the other, they were usually intimate, erotic and emotional, testimony to desire and subjectivity. The same letters were typically seen in two ways, as in the trial of Katherine Earle for adultery with Charles Holland. She had seen him on the stage and 'boldly sent him a written challenge, inviting him to combat on the field of love'. Her discourse of chivalry jarred with the language of the formal indictment which declared that she 'did commence, by letters and otherwise, a lewd and adulterous intimacy and correspondence with one Charles Holland'.[147] This friction was echoed in arguments between those who took a conservative line on divorce and those who felt marriage was a human institution that could be improved upon, not least by easier divorce. Adultery cases exemplify how 'the "local" character of the law is distinguished by its dual nature as both instrument of protection and oppression'.[148] As in other kinds of cases, adulterous letters established narrative, motivation and guilt; they also expressed passion unsocially at odds with reason or reason run amok in the service of passion. This duality meant rational readings were not necessarily right ones.

Letters were the first thing suspicious spouses looked for to prove an affair. John Wilmot, proving an affair between his wife Fanny and their footman Edward Washbourn, searched Washbourn's lodgings. They found various presents but no letters and he had to be content with a formal declaration from his wife that she had written and sent some, and from her lover that he had received them and burnt them the previous day.[149] In cross-class relationships or where both parties were middle or labouring class, letters were likely to partner more solid mementoes. When Mrs Conner, who helped her husband run the Mitre Inn at Barnet, had an affair with William Atkinson, a Cheapside linen-draper, so that business fell off, it was deduced by one witness 'that great intimacy subsisted between them; for that she sent him an hundred times, presents consisting of *hams, geese, ducks, hares, partridges*, and other things.'[150] Plaintiffs hunted for letters because letters outlasted edible proofs of affection. In this instance, there was one, unsigned but in Atkinson's handwriting, which 'contained professions of familiar kindness never known but between lovers'.[151] Since Mr Conner had gout and was not mobile enough to catch the lovers together, the letter was accepted as proof of irregular relations.

Letters were not the only proof of adultery. People around protagonists at the time of alleged affairs were invited, both in and out of court, to sift the significance of a variety of signs. These ranged from incontrovertible marks of guilt to less certain traces where codes of decorum and probability could not always clarify doubts. Most bodily signs were read as empirically secure: pregnancies where dates of conception coincided with husbands' absences (usually overseas), ocular testimony (often from voyeur landlords who bored holes in walls and wainscots to overlook lovers) and the reports of servants in households and inns about telltale stains, rumpled sheets, unrumpled beds, tousled hair and disordered dress, traces of powder and pins at one end of a couch matched by dirt from shoes at the other. Behavioural signs were less secure: Catherine Cade passed her lover Lord Aylmer off as her brother, but witnesses thought they kissed too ardently for siblings.[152] Women's instructions about not letting in company other than a particular man, or of being at home to him any time, were understood – not least by servants – as signs of intrigue. The public learnt a language of strange signs: an account of how Lady Abergavenny was seen walking with her skirts held out stiffly puzzled listeners in court until it was explained that she was returning from her lover's room and wished to prevent anyone overhearing the rustle of her silks.[153] Such evidence testified to how the other half lived: a combination of material difference (literally, for those unaccustomed to wearing silk) and human likeness. The plain-clothes classes hearing about aristocrats' liaisons (not all with other aristocrats) could contemplate social difference in detail. Ideas of social difference were relevant to people's ideas of refinement on paper; there was an epistolary equivalent of silk even as adulterers proved that the politest people had animal appetites.

Often a case involved a range of signs that had to be fitted into a legal framework of proof. The case of Lady Ligonier, for instance: she had an affair with a Piedmontese nobleman called Count Alfieri who visited her in the country in disguise. A big hat and old coat made this red-haired Count partly less conspicuous, but a sharp-eyed post-boy noted his smart shoes and clean white stockings and his feet betrayed him again when he left prints, later spotted by servants, outside the house windows. His inability to speak English made him an intriguing figure at the local inn, though it was not until an inn halfway to France that Lord Ligonier's emissary formally secured evidence that he and Lady Ligonier were lovers. The point was not in doubt, especially since the husband had already called out the lover for a brief duel, but it made adultery a witnessed fact as well as a human situation. Both were fully articulated by five letters produced in court. The two from her are conventionally amorous – 'my last sigh shall pronounce your name!' she exclaimed[154] – and his are passionately frantic – 'you love me, your dear letter, which I have just been reading over and over again, assures me so; I kiss it, I sprinkle it with tears, I turn fool; cruel woman!'[155] He contemplates death with voluptuousness: his final epistolary embrace is morbidly erotic, as he signs off 'PHANTOM BODY'.[156] For all the comedy of Count Alfieri's letters (better in their original French, perhaps) they did alter the nature of the case being heard. They restored subjectivity and some dignity to lovers whose intimacies otherwise looked foolish or were reduced to a catalogue of stains; they made adultery a union of hearts as well as bodies. Court records do not supply much evidence about reactions in court, but they suggest letters were not simply a means of shaming: letters also distributed sympathies.

Letters were highly instrumental in fixing ideologies of gender for women, even though adultery trials involved lovers of both sexes. The affair between Viscountess Bellfield and her brother-in-law, Arthur Rochfort, came to light because a letter from 'Philander' to 'Sylvia', containing 'the most passionate expressions that ever man made to woman', was misdirected to her husband. Lord Bellfield received it coolly. After breakfast,

he, without betraying the least emotion, took the letter out of his pocket, and handing it to her, calmly said, 'pray madam, do you know anything of that paper?' She no sooner saw the criminal lines, but struck with the force of her own guilt, she fell down on her knees and cry'd, O my lord, kill me yourself, but do not discover me to my father. She then gave the keys of her cabinet, where there were several dozens of letters with the same name and character, as well as some rough drafts of hers to Mr. Rochfort, containing a compleat evidence against themselves, and in some of them it appeared that my lady had entertained a desire to poison my lord, and wanted to bring Mr. Rochfort to the same end, with regard to his wife.[157]

Letters provide both the narrative climax – the spectacle of her confession – and a condensed narrative. The story is both a tableau of guilt based on the single letter and a bundle of guilty secrets: there is both more and less to the letters than first appears. Discovery, confrontation and confession are not the end of the story, as they might be in fiction. Fiction sanctioned adulterous passion insofar as it exploited it, but it was rarer to make sensationalist capital out of death. Lady Bellfield's 'criminal lines' expand adultery into suggestions for multiple murder; her destructive power continues to be amplified through letters. Lord Bellfield wrote to her father who read the news with tears in his eyes. The weeping reader and the grieving father were both powerful figures in sentimental fiction: although the original letter incriminating Lady Bellfield was not written by her, it made hers doubly offensive.

While letters clearly disclosed guilt, they also testified to the messiness of human behaviour. Ambivalence was compounded by two factors. First, letters had a double existence as material objects that substituted for the lover's person and as immaterial text that spoke from, and to, heads and hearts. In erotic contexts, bodies, hearts and minds were all subsumed into co-dependency in *feelings*. The very confused letters written by Theophilus Cibber to his errant wife Susanna show a dissolution of tropes that goes beyond even his usual excitability:

> Ah! my Life, I wish not to cure the Wounds of your dear Mind with Corrosives; I would pour the Balm of Comfort, tho' I am mentioning what is a Dagger in my Heart; but thy kind Hand can remove it, and I will draw a veil over it...[158]

A sterner letter to her lover William Sloper shows similar overlaps in his mind, 'not a little ruffled' as he considers whether to fight a duel. After being stabbed through the heart, he wrote, 'you are welcome to a fair Opportunity of shooting me thro' the Head, or running me thro' the Body'.[159] For a spouse who felt bodily betrayed, the mind was physical and the heart metaphysical. The confusions have that logic of madness which made adulterous love seem criminal because it deranged virtuous husbands.

The second factor besides disembodiment that made letters inherently ambiguous in adultery trials was that signs of true passion were also signs of dishonesty. The truer lovers were to each other, the more they deceived their spouses and families. Lady Sarah Lennox wrote regretfully to her French lover Lauzun, 'All this that I am doing must be very wicked, since I try to conceal it, and I, the most truthful woman living, am obliged to lie and to deceive two people whom I esteem so highly.' She dared not trust this letter to a servant, but bribed a waiter at the inn to post it.[160] Lady Grosvenor feigned a pain in her side in order to remain in London to be close to her lover, the Duke of Cumberland. To him she wrote, 'Only think how wicked

I am, for in reality I'm already as strong and as well as ever I was in my life.'[161] In exposing this duplicity, her letters take on some of the untrustworthiness of their writer, even physically: when her husband was away, her lover could write in ink; on other days, she told him to use the less detectable medium of lemon juice.

Possibilities of deceit gave letters a symbolic potential regardless of what they actually said. This was often exploited in court to add a criminal tendency to the uncertainties available in many texts, especially those written in passion and haste. One case where letters played this role, and unusually for both plaintiff and defendant, was that of Lord Augustus Fitzroy, sued in 1742 by Sir W——M——. The circumstantial evidence was suspicious but not conclusive: Fitzroy and Lady L had stayed up most of the night together at an inn, perhaps just talking, perhaps not. That Fitzroy at least had strong feelings was evident from his declaration, in a paper styled 'The Solemn League and Covenant', that he would always defend her against calumny and peril.[162] The husband's lawyer sneered at this as 'a genteel and fashionable Way of writing and thinking';[163] Fitzroy's lawyer defended it as a piece of gallantry that proved nothing criminal. Both sides reached an impasse over Fitzroy's letters and one expression in particular:

> The next Letter says, *That he had not recovered the Injury that he did himself by the last Journey.* – Pray can any-body infer criminal Conversation from these Words? I am sure they cannot... The most that can be made of any Expression in these Letters, is that they only shew the Assiduity of the Defendant, to gain the Lady's Favour[164]

an assiduity, added the defence, that the lady might repel. But the plaintiff's lawyer insisted that 'the INJURY I DID MYSELF' referred to a specifically sexual complaint. It was

> a plain Reference to *the Fatigue he underwent that Night*, in the Criminal Conversation with the Lady. It was not an Injury *that he received*; but an Injury *that he did himself, that Night*. In that Letter he begins and makes his Address to her, thus *My Angel*, and concludes thus, *I long for the Expiration of these next five Months, and when I hope to be with you. Adieu, my Angel...* Is this Language proper to be writ by a gentleman to a married Lady? That very Letter speaks the Criminal Conversation between them...[165]

Showing himself to be an ingenious lawyer – and a bad literary critic – he concluded dramatically, 'to endeavour to make it clearer would be but lighting a Candle at Noon-day'. Rather than any particular words, what the letter 'speaks' is a general amorous discourse which becomes a literary equivalent of sex. Apostrophe, which makes absence presence through rhetoric, is read over-literally as a recuperation of bodily possession. Correspondence is thus not only a substitute for sex but also a memory of it. The same lawyer was equally adept in switching the focus between epistolary phrases and their broader cultural charge when the defence produced two letters from Sir William. Both were bitter and unhappy and blamed his wife for keeping bad company at Bath: *'I once loved you to Madness, but your Scorn and Contempt of me, have made me withdraw my Affections in great Measure from you.'*[166] The defence described these as evidence that the marriage had broken down independently of the accused, who therefore could not be considered as depriving the husband of the comfort and society of his wife as a verdict against him would require. The plaintiff lawyer conceded 'there was no one that heard them read, but what was moved by them', but argued that silence about Fitzroy should be interpreted as a discursive space with an end other than blame in view: 'tho' he writes to her, That he was resolved to part, yet are there such Marks of Affection and Tenderness towards her in the Letters, that there was Room left for bringing about a Reconciliation betwixt him and his Lady'.[167] Both sides raided the same letters to support competing readings. They used letters as evidence of a specific act, adultery, and to interpret a general situation – a failing marriage. Verdicts turned on these responses – here, £5000 was awarded against Fitzroy – and they contributed in turn to a climate in which letters could be scrutinised more confidently.

Involuntary disclosures of adulterous relations had to be set against willed deceptions in letters. Several cases in which women caught in adultery pleaded penitence by letter showed how they were led by financial desperation to stage a sincerity that may have been fake. Lady Maria Bayntun, for instance, had an affair with her husband's nephew. He and she were seen too often leaving the outdoor toilet at the same time; eventually the footman, nursemaid and huntsman reported their romps and rendezvous to her husband's father. Her husband requested the return of her wedding ring and left the house. In 'great agitation of mind', according to the maid, Lady Maria wrote him a letter. But

> before it was possible for her servant to return from him with an answer to it, and notwithstanding her professions of sorrow and repentance expressed in such letter, she, very soon after her writing the same, dressed herself, put on her riding habit, and went to the Greyhound at Bromham, to the said John Allen Cooper

having, agitation notwithstanding, sent on a clean pair of sheets.[168] Her disappearance changed a possibly sincere letter into a performance, though it is important to remember that for many women in this situation the script was not wholly of their choosing. Indeed scripts were foisted on them by the press because spectacles of penitence sold well to a readership versed in sentimental fiction. When Lady Sarah Lennox left her husband Sir Charles

Bunbury, *Town and Country Magazine* published a 'fulsome epistle' of contrition supposedly by her but wholly invented.[169]

Lady Maria's letter is pathetic – and literary. She describes her daring to write as 'an impertinence', but promises she is telling her husband 'the real sentiments of her heart', especially her remorse: 'I am not, Bayntun! so far gone in vice as to glory in it. I hate and detest myself.'[170] Rather implausibly, she declares that his noble behaviour on discovering her crime has made her fall in love with him all over again; despair at losing his love has made her contemplate an overdose. Were he to forgive her, 'no power on earth, or even an angel dropt from heaven' should seduce her from virtue. Despite her confusion about angels – he is both an angel, and something from which an angel or devil might tempt her – she at least offers her husband a sublime terrain for anger and forgiveness. The Miltonic imagery is tricky since it evokes the duplicity of Eve's descendants, a liability she acknowledges: 'Perhaps you will say, that the love of deceiving mankind is my motive for writing this letter.' Misogynist discourse about the unreliability of women in general implied particular errant women were simply true to type.

Wives expelled from marital homes could hardly cast them as Eden: why then would they have strayed? But their investment in penitential letters was more than metaphorical. These were begging letters. Having behaved as free women, penance required them to take up voluntarily and with enthusiasm that submission to husbands they had abandoned. Glimpses of the fear that spurred Elizabeth Draper for one seem not to have compromised the performance. 'I have heard with horror to my soul, that if I am removed from hence you design me a place of confinement', she wrote in one of four pleading letters to her husband.[171] She had had a slew of affairs with young working men and frequently had two or three in tow. One of these, William Penfold, an apprentice, wrote to Draper begging forgiveness too: 'O my much injured master, I know not what to do with myself, nor what to say for myself.'[172] He balanced this plea of inarticulacy with a punctilious attitude to prepositions: he had never been *to* bed with Mrs Draper, he said, because 'my *conscience* would not let me; but I have been upon the bed several times with her, and enjoyed her'. The sexual detail of his confession of course did not help her cause. In contrast, she had to rid herself of physicality as though the most authentic self was that farthest from her transgressing body: 'Think not, my dearest love, I have any one to write or even to *coppy* for me, it's from the bottom of a heart overflowing with gratitude and love.'[173] Her guilt is registered not by phallic stabs of conscience, but by promises of a life of atonement in which the husband has a god-like role: 'suffer me to make my peace with God and you, in the course of a sober and virtuous life'.[174]

The instability of penitential letter-writing can be seen in the desperate example of Arabella Heatley. The fall-out from her affair with John Jolly was aggravated by her passing on a venereal disease and by separation from her infant son. Her twelve penitential letters labour to reverse the 'pretty free declaration' she had written to her lover: 'Jolly, I do more than love you, I adore you, both your person and your mind; I had rather be your mistress than the empress of the world.'[175] She even anticipated the economic hardship of leaving her husband: 'If he turns me out of doors I will not complain – I have not been *ust* to work, but I will try . . . one smile of your's will pay me for all I have or can suffer.'[176] Her trust was misplaced: her lover vanished, leaving her destitute. Her letters range through strategic moods, from melodrama – 'A villain, curses on him, seduced me from you' – to Senecan plainness – 'I have confessed my faults, and am truly sorry for them.' But bitterness and impatience start to show through: 'shut up here without a creature to speak to; uncertain what must become of me——How can you use me thus!'[177] The effort of sustaining a penitent spectacle became too great, given a husband for whom Old Testament powers of justice were untempered by New Testament qualities of mercy.

In the printed texts of Draper's and Heatley's letters, spelling mistakes are italicised. This orthographical emphasis suggests the authenticity of an unpolished text; it also stigmatises variant spellings associated with women and the labouring classes. It also highlights key emotional terms, especially in Draper's text; *forgit, upbraide, pitty* and *releave* form a micronarrative in themselves. The tenderness so prized by lovers takes on a spiritual dimension: 'To Mercy, Pity, Peace, and Love / All pray in their Distress', as Blake's poem 'The Divine Image' put it. Its register of Innocence and Experience, neither quite what they seem, is also strangely like Blake. Heatley's letters read like a *portugaise* sequence in their mood swings: like a novel, they have an emotional plot; like legal discourse they foreground crime and punishment. They bring out aspects of writing in sorrow and in anger that test the law and which show human subjects chafing under particular paralegal restraints – here, the punitive responses of patriarchy when women put personal desires before marital duty. Reinstating the moral and Christian codes abandoned by adulterers, these penitential letters are generically close to hymns.

Studied disorder in letters served the metamorphosis of criminals into forgivable sinners. Orthographical deviance served other ideologies besides gender, as one can see in the letters of Samuel Oliver. He had forced himself on his young sister-in-law who became pregnant. He sent her pills so she could miscarry. She then became very ill and showed his self-pitying and remorseful letter of instructions to her mother. Oliver then wrote to her father, not to confess, since the facts were known, but somehow to account for them. As he put it, 'the thing itself will not bear any defence, therefore I shall not attempt any'.[178] The bewildering enormity of incest and abortion left discursive gaps with which Oliver grappled:

> In whatever light you may look on the fatal transaction, you cannot look at it in a more *horrable* one than I do . . . but God's mercy is great,

and I hope, by a sincere repentance, to obtain that from him I cannot expect from man.[179]

Playing divine mercy against human justice, he evaded condemnation by putting his case before a higher tribunal. The criminal becomes a *sinner*, no longer different from faulty humanity in kind, but only in degree. After assaulting his father-in-law and wife when they served a writ on him, Oliver wrote to the family from Bridewell that he was again tormented by conscience, a power before which men declared themselves helpless in ways comparable to women throwing themselves on the mercy of patriarchs. Oliver offered them the spectacle of himself subjectively penitent and objectively disgraced, pre-empting their vengeance by representing himself as already suffering all that they might wish:

> View me one day respected, esteemed, now neglected, despised and justly persecuted. View me at once in favour with a virtuous and affectionate wife; by her deserted and abandoned; see me in prison with ironed felons, nothing but oaths of the most horrid nature uttered, fearful of being *robed* even in bed, rats ready to devour me as I lay...[180]

Rhetorical masochism dilutes the sadism of his crimes. In this context, spelling errors are signs of moral errors: his 'horrable' act is linguistically deviant. This is not to propose that Oliver deliberately misspelt. But interestingly his spelling improves: by his last letter 'concience' has become 'conscience'. 'N.B. I hope my distress will be an excuse for any *inaccuraces* that may appear in this letter':[181] his apologetic postscript is suggestively aware of disorder.

Epistolary decorum reflected social propriety; hence indecorum served social boundaries such as that between criminals and the insane. The case of James Altham, a priapic clergyman from Essex, was complicated by the consideration that passion was rarely rational. Among fifty-odd affairs, Altham had seduced a woman called Ann Saunders, to whom he had written a letter for whose return he had been persuaded to pay £60. According to one witness, this letter was 'full of strange unconnected and inconsistent language',[182] its whim and caprice the textual equivalent of his bodily hyperactivity, in which he was subject to fits of dancing, capering and boxing. It was said he had been sent mad, periodically, by a local song about him. The letter helped to assess the disturbed state of his mind. It

> contained many strong expressions of love and regard; and, if the said James Altham was to die he would leave her two hundred pounds; and that, if his wife died, he would marry her, if he had not a quarter of an hour to live.[183]

When did a lover's extravagance become insane? Lord Grosvenor's lawyer raised a great laugh in court by ridiculing the Duke of Cumberland as a correspondent: 'the *incoherency* of his letters plainly proved him to be really a lover'.[184] Was Altham mad to commit adultery or was he a mad adulterer? The mental fitness of men was also tested through letters in the trial of Andrew Bowes in 1789 for adultery and cruelty. Besides the beatings and threats practised by – and allowed to – many eighteenth-century husbands, this one burnt his wife with hot food, forced her to translate his love-letters and stabbed her tongue with a quill pen. The Countess of Strathmore, as she was known, was unlucky in love. She hated her first husband so much that she had S struck out all of the household plate at the first opportunity, which may explain why she sought comfort in the arms of other men and the company of animals. One witness claimed that Lady Strathmore 'declared that she loved her cats better than her children; wickedly calling the former, her blessed angels; and adding, that she hoped never to go to Heaven unless she were to meet them (meaning her cats) there'.[185] A letter, Exhibit A, was produced in support. In it she writes about a kitten:

I expect your condolence on my fourth and only remaining Bambino, at Mrs. Moor's, who is gone loaded with the mange to Heaven; and I do not doubt there is an incessant scratching of angels, and picking of their wings, which will rather unharmonize the psalm-singing.[186]

Exhibit B, which follows in the printed account of the trial, is a polite note from her husband to someone concerning the education of her children. The juxtaposition promotes him as civil, responsible and stable; her jeu d'esprit looks frivolous. But perhaps remembering Donne's congruity of fleas and angels, if the court thought her mad, they thought him bad; for all the attempts to discredit her, she got her divorce.

There are unusually clear intersections between class and gender in adultery cases because of the disturbances to households which adultery brought, which was part of the context in which letters were read. The degree of this disturbance was an index of criminality because it revealed a disregard for appearances. Not all errant mistresses neglected their domestic duties like Sarah Worgan whose extravagance was resented by her servants not least for jeopardising their jobs. It was their evidence as much as the letters supplied by her lover that secured her husband a divorce. As one servant who was sacked put it, 'if she does not give me a character, I'll give her one'.[187] Working-class testimonials could be traded for middle-class reputation; both had a market value. Lady Grosvenor's maid left her after the trial because, she said, her character was all she had to live on and it would be compromised by her ladyship's notoriety. Servants invested in virtue out of necessity, or rather, they had to choose how far it would not pay them to go along with vice. On the one hand, Arthur Gray's coachman was promoted to the post of gentleman for services that included secretly delivering letters;[188] on the other hand, after helping the Duke of Cumberland's amour with Lady Grosvenor in the persona of 'Trusty', Robert Giddings was dismissed, ironically at the united request of his fellow servants.[189] Immediate rewards varied: on more than one occasion, Quentin Dick gave his lover's maid half a guinea and her manservant half a crown. Perhaps it was the discrepancy which motivated the latter to gather evidence clinically; the husband had been away when he was hired, so his loyalty may have been on principle.[190] Abraham Allec's motives were clearly personal when he wrote to his master, an infantry captain with whom he had travelled from South Carolina, to tell him that the wife he was daily expecting in Jamaica was dallying in London with a lover.[191] Conflicts between class and gender can be seen from servants' perspective as making them choose between master and mistress. Letter-related activities could tip the balance.

Some servants may have resented the extra work adultery entailed, including letting lovers in and out at odd hours, keeping track of extra candlesticks and cleaning up after sex. The colourful Harriet Errington, who gave locks of her pubic hair as keepsakes, had constant visitors and correspondence which servants had to deal with. She would pose in the window of her lodgings and hopeful men sent over letters; those whose looks she liked, she arranged to meet. The servants wearily decided that letters which arrived in her absence should be returned unopened.[192] Servants were more interventionist in the case of Harriot Brooke who was married to a doctor often away from home. When he suspected an affair, she gave Samuel Tattel, his servant, a letter for her lover:

> But on his going into the kitchen, and informing his fellow servant, Catherine Spencer, of the commission he had got from his mistress, she desired to see the letter, on which she broke it open, and Spencer not being able to read, he read it to her, and found it contained in substance as follows, '*Every thing is discovered I am ruined and undone and am to go into the country in the morning, but do not know where so adieu.*' After reading it, Catherine Spencer told him that he should not carry such a note, on which he threw it in the fire.[193]

It is interesting that Catherine Spencer opened the letter even though she could not read (she may have expected to make out key words). Her gesture inscribes both the undercover nature of adultery and the way its signs can be recognised even by illiterates. In other circumstances, it would be unthinkable for servants to open their employers' letters. These two would iconically mirror the guilty pair of lovers were it not that the gendered significance of adultery takes precedence over the class implications of tampering with the post. Adultery was then the more heinous for turning servants into censors.

Tensions between class and gender interests can usefully be viewed through a passage in Henry Fielding's *The True Patriot*:

> If we lose our Characters, we shall lose our Places, and never after be received into any other Family. Herein our Situation differs from that of our Betters; against whom no Profligacy is any Objection. And if by Treachery they happen to be discarded in one Place, (for that is the only Crime they can be guilty of), they are nevertheless received with open Arms in another. How many Men of Fashion do we know, whose Characters would prevent any Person from taking them into his Family as Footmen, who are as well received, caressed and promoted by the Great as Gentlemen.[194]

Fielding makes a notable overlap between amorous discourse and employment but his irony depends on the subjects being masculine. Adultery involved women in losing their places and their characters, ironically because they had been received with open arms and caressed. Though obviously adultery exposed men too and courts required them to pay compensation to husbands, yet women tended to come off worst. As one sympathiser put it, 'The ladies who have committed matrimonial *faux pas*, have been so unmercifully handled in a variety of late publications... the ladies only have been exposed.'[195] His explanation – 'Because the men have been the editors and publishers!' – shows the importance of print for circulating scandal aired in courtrooms. The *Ramblers Magazine* printed trial accounts as a salacious subgenre of pornography. Servants had an ambiguous role here. One critic deplored 'the absurd formality of making coachmen, footmen and postilions, depose', as the law required, whether they believed carnal knowledge had taken place.[196] His anxiety is partly about working-class men exposing middle- and upper-class men. It is also specifically textual:

> It is indeed shameful to think that, from such gross improprieties being admitted into the depositions taken in the spiritual court, the publications in Doctor's Commons, when republished in Pater-noster-Row, are bought up like the most licentious ribaldry, and devoured by the vulgar with the utmost avidity.[197]

Ironically, trial literature could be converted into pornography precisely by making servants moral agents. Even as servants defended their master's property and family honour against adulterers, they could turn into sexual consumers. The pornographic frisson of disclosed letters could have been worse. One of the many tortures that Isaac Prescott inflicted on his meek wife Jane was to lift her skirts, hold her down and summon their servant. Illustrations to this case, which appalled contemporaries, show the servant coming into the room, but his gaze is not quite lifted. On the verge of seeing his mistress naked, he is excluded from the full view available to the reader.

In fact it was often servants who provided the evidence that protagonists had been 'naked and alone' (though as one writer tartly observed, lovers were rarely naked and, if together, never alone!) In some cases, servants were sole witnesses. There was only one witness, Elizabeth Bentley, in the case of Captain Gambier; the defence tried unsuccessfully to prove she was motivated by revenge against her employer, Lady Knowles, who had an endearingly playful affair with the Captain. There were also four letters, 'very surprising and romantick', between 'Torrismond and Leonora'.[198] Since Bentley shared a passage back from Jamaica to England with them, she seemed a well-placed witness. Some servants became confidantes, like Mary Osborn to Catherine Degen, who read to her extracts from her lover's letters.[199] Verbal evidence, however, could be doubted, especially from upper servants possibly on the make. But a report of an accidentally dropped remark, like an accidentally dropped letter, could persuade as evidence because it was a sign of disturbance.

Textual and verbal evidence came together in the trial of the Marchioness of Carmarthen in 1779. When her young lover, Mr Byron, was spotted emerging from her bedroom, she asked her maid if she thought the other servants knew. When the maid said yes,

> her ladyship then cried very much, and said farther to the deponent, *Sally, Will you go downstairs and tell them* [meaning the servants] *not to mention what has happened, and I will take care that it shall never happen again.*[200]

Her contrition lasted three weeks; then Byron returned. Late one night the maid bumped into him on the landing: 'she could not help looking him in the face, and she said, pretty loudly, *My God!*, but he took no notice; and seemed to be perfectly easy, as if he had been the master of the house'. The lover shows a shamelessness often rebuked in servants who did not 'know their place'. The footman likewise made it clear to the lover he had intruded, telling him 'Every servant in the house will be bound to rue the day, or hour, when you first came into the house.'[201] Like opening letters, his challenge would be impudent except that adulterers forfeited privileges. When Lady Carmarthen asked him to say nothing, the footman commented, 'he was very sorry that Lady Carmarthen had put it in his power to hurt her'.[202] Such saturnalian reversals of mastery are important not simply as illustrations of how knowledge is power, but of how power is demonstrably a form of knowledge. The point is not just to know, but to show you know – a Weberian rather than a Foucauldian inflection. Without necessarily knowing what was in a letter, servants often worked out what letters signified. The question then was how they acted on that significance.

Divorce and adultery trials shed interesting light on how not very literate people understood the power of writing. Lady Carmarthen's maid could report the dates Byron stayed 'because she, of her own accord, set it down in a little almanac at the times the same happened'.[203] In the case of Elizabeth Campbell in 1777, crucial evidence to prove her often noisily sexual relations with William Wade came from her servant Joseph Harris. She would give him letters to post addressed to her tailor or maid; he, suspecting them to be a cover to her lover, opened them, read them and kept them for a week before giving them to a business agent of her husband's. He and the second maid listened at doors; she took notes and the coachman kept memoranda of when he saw Wade go into Mrs Campbell's bedroom. Even though this record-keeping may have involved ringing a date rather than full writing, between the three of them, they intercepted letters and provided corroborating records of her sexual activity. Their testimony was both accurate and bureaucratic. Knowing that texts counted in court, servants made documentation part of their surveillance. Hence they contributed actively to the growth of that written culture which feeds print culture and to a milieu in which the interpretation of letters was democratic.

One of the most publicised adultery cases in the eighteenth century showed how class and gender decorums were established through letters. The affair between the Duke of Cumberland and the beautiful Lady Grosvenor was conducted through letters, sent secretly via her milliner and his perfumer, and later published in newspapers and several trial accounts. The pair were exposed when Lord Grosvenor was alerted, possibly by anonymous letters from a 'Jack Sprat'. He intercepted their correspondence, had copies taken and followed their arrangements to meet at an inn in St Albans, where his servant confronted them:

> His highness found himself quite unmanned at the servant's boldly declaring, that neither his name nor quality were unknown to him; and he, who but a minute before would not have deigned to look at so mean a person, was, by this stroke of fortune, obliged to bear his keen reproaches...[204]

According to one source, the duke panicked, tried to escape and protested 'on his BIBLE OATH' that he had never been in the room – a response greeted with contempt. When the case came to trial it was peculiarly resolved in that though Lord Grosvenor sued for divorce, his wife brought in a countersuit, called a recrimination, which the judge decided meant no divorce was possible. Damages were demanded of £100,000, but only £10,000 awarded, perhaps because, as cynics noted, any sum would be borne by the public purse.

Even by eighteenth-century standards the case was lively and letters were at the heart of it. They served many of the usual purposes: they proved the relationship was sexual; they set a general tone for the case (farcical rather than shocking); they shed light on the husband's behaviour and character (correct and dull, though there was some criticism of his interfering with her post, and if half the allegations in her recrimination were true, he was the more unfaithful) and they showed how the lovers were equally guilty. Plaintiff's counsel read them out in court which may have afforded some revenge for Lady Grosvenor's satire at her husband's expense – 'as you may imagine a Tête à Tête subject', she wrote.[205] Critics have noted that trial literature resembles drama in how it prints dialogue; when these letters were read out, the sense of performance and entertainment was strong.

The lovers had been assiduous correspondents. The Duke wrote everyday whilst at sea, including this report of his fantasies:

> I got to Supper about 9 o'clock but I could not Eat, and so got to bed about 10 – I then prayed for you *my dearest love kissed your dearest little Hair* and laye down and dreamt of you had you on the dear little *couch* ten thousand times in my arms kissing you and telling you how much I loved and adored you and you seemed pleased but alas when I woke I found it all dillusion *no body by me but myself at Sea.*[206]

She was more blunt: 'They are bawling about supper so farewell; I'm ashamed of my letter'.[207] But it was his letters which were described as 'miserably illiterate and vulgar'.[208] When Lord Grosvenor showed a stray letter from the Duke to Lady Grosvenor's mother, she marked it as lower class: 'with a prudence and foresight peculiar to herself, she told his l——p that it was certainly intended for one of the servant maids'.[209] The implication was she guessed for whom it was intended, but used a class-based imputation of vulgarity to put her titled daughter above suspicion. Literate aristocratic seducers who wrote letters to servants had to decide whether to use polite or familiar language or something in-between. Aristocrats discussing affairs between themselves often favoured pastoral as a way of coating class difference with literariness.

The friction between duty and pleasure in the letters was striking. The Duke mentally abandoned those obligations of royalty which, like wifely duties, underpinned a public identity. 'To-morrow at six o'clock I'm engaged with you know whom, to go to Woolwich, to see the launch of a new seventy four gun ship. Alas! I had rather be witness to another kind –', he wrote to his lover.[210] He could, however, resume public hauteur at will. When she complained she had not heard from him he replied peevishly

> it ought not to be attributed to any alteration in my sentiments, but to a sense of the importance of the commission with which I was charged, which would not admit of my thinking a moment on any other subject. Excuse this freedom, Madam, in an Englishman and a subject...[211]

Vulgarity is an effect of his shedding class-based responsibilities, although to facilitate their rendezvous at various inns he did adopt 'low' disguises. At the Red Lyon in Whitchurch he wore coarse clothes, an ill-fitting wig and spoke peculiarly. His companion, alias his servant 'Trusty', explained he was a fool travelling for his health. When they retired, having ordered tea, pen, paper and ink, the ostlers and maids suspected they were highwaymen or sharpers.[212] At other places he pretended to be Welsh, a farmer or a squire. The performances convinced nobody, though they did draw attention to the performativity of class. Reaction was indignant: it was 'absurd... preposterous... meanness' that a prince should be 'skulking about in sheds and hovels and hiding himself behind trees, like a deer-stealer'.[213] Readers not present at these scenes could savour their comedy and find traces of their lack of dignity in the prince's letters.

Lady Grosvenor escaped class limits in a more imaginary way. A conversation with her personal maid, Mrs Birch, after Lord Grosvenor had taken her letters, sheds remarkable light on how letters crystallised tensions between class and gender. It is helpful to quote it in full:

> Lady Grosvenor... said, that if she had been a servant, she could have been trusted to have conveyed a note, she need not have put herself in other people's power; and added, that she was in many people's power; that she had often thought of mentioning this to this deponent, but that she expected this deponent would fly, and make a great noise and exclaim against it, which would be very disagreeable to her. On which this deponent said, that she would have been very sorry to have disobliged her Ladyship, and that she did not know well how to refuse carrying a note, if her Ladyship directed her; but that if such a note was in her opinion improperly directed, that she should have refused carrying it though she had been turned out of doors for refusing; and she the said Lady Grosvenor said, she expected as much, and was therefore forced to put herself in other people's power; and added, that when a woman is determined to proceed in that way, it is not in a servant's power to prevent it; and this deponent replied, she believed not, but that if she could not prevent, she would not encourage it; for that she believed the easier those things were done, the more it encouraged such proceedings.[214]

The limits of freedom are gingerly mapped out through the symbolism of what counts as a proper letter for a virtuous woman to write and a respectable woman to carry. 'O lust, what a leveller art thou!', exclaimed one observer on the Grosvenor case.[215] The aristocrat trapped by propriety and the servant trapped by exigency both had to live within structures which confined them as subjects. For both, it was through letters that they measured the flow of power.

Criminal activities – adultery, theft, treason, murder and other crimes – involved readings of letters that superficially fixed the character of criminal. But neither as material object nor as interpretable text were letters stable.

Divergent readings of letters meant epistolary evidence was often ambiguous and controversial, influenced by cultural assumptions about what people could or should write. Readers and juries referred behaviours to romance and novels as a rhetorical gesture – that is, a way of acknowledging truth was stranger than fiction, rather than implying the stories disclosed were like fiction. Because criminal behaviour was taken seriously in relation to both earthly and heavenly punishment, discourses of penitence and contrition in letters expressed sincerity in ways consonant with Christian norms. Lying, the sin thought most likely to lead to crime, was evident in letters; conversely, letters could restore truth-telling to situations in which their writers had lapsed into error and sin.

5
Writing as a Citizen

'The genius of this nation is, to be either too much *asleep*, or too much *awakened*.'[1] Jonas Hanway's formula offers a path through the complex world of eighteenth-century politics. Throughout the period, people from all points of the political compass saw writing as a means to rouse, warn or restrain the public. Of course they disagreed about what fears were groundless and how to head off threats, but eighteenth-century political writing has a curious *discursive* consensus. The British lion was rarely perceived to be going about business as usual: it was too asleep or too awake. Agitation and lethargy were held up as states from which the good citizen was saved by being properly active, not improperly hyperactive, careless, gullible or indifferent. Writing became a rousing or warning activity, valuable even though it led to vehemence seemingly at odds with rationality in the public sphere. Linda Colley has argued that 'Informality and improvisation bred new opportunities' for political activity.[2] This chapter shows how letter-writing helped create those new opportunities and broaden political awareness.

Here one needs to consider briefly some aspects of recent thinking about the public sphere in the eighteenth century. For Habermas, the public sphere was a place of rational debate. Its success as a bourgeois stronghold turned in part on its sensitivity to the rationality of those it historically excluded, like women and labouring classes, which led to its being more inclusive. Questioning this optimistic model, Paul Keen argues that 'Ideas about the capacity of different social groups for rational enquiry provided the ammunition for the reinforcement, rather than the correction, of structural exclusions.'[3] My concern here is to explore the part letters played in defining and testing those limits; by examining particular occasions of debate, one comes to understand more general patterns of representation. Letters show that inclusions and exclusions were uneven: the public sphere was not smoothly rounded, like a globe, but rough-edged, variegated, textured, like the earth close up. Habermas represents letter-writing in the public sphere as a means of unfolding subjectivity. Letter-writing shows subjectivity to be culturally volatile, political and open to rewriting. Jonas Hanway's title, for example, flags its author by a contracted actual name and an occupational designation: 'J. H-y, Merchant'. In his other publications, many epistolary, Hanway uses different markers to describe himself, including an advocate for public welfare, a father, a farmer, a citizen, a member of the Marine Society, an author of travels, his full name (with and without esquire) and no name. Such variations can be explained as natural in a prolific writer, but they are also evidence of the mutability of social identity. Hanway's different tags are not just nuances of class but also signs of how class is a textual construct.

Surveying critical disputes about the relation between classical republicanism and individualism and which of these paradigms was more powerful in eighteenth-century social ideologies, Paul Keen suggests that

> many expressions of what we might now describe as an eighteenth-century middle-class ideology were hybrids of these two views, fusing a commitment to the self-motivated individual with a nostalgic belief in public virtue. However incompatible they may have been theoretically, they were fused together within the heteroglossia of cultural change.[4]

In part, as Keen notes, interpretations depend on what evidence one selects in support. In the immense field of letter-writing, there is certainly evidence of the kind of fusion Keen identifies – for example, in the letters of William Cowper, a self-absorbed poet with a social conscience. On 21 May 1785 he wrote to a friend, 'I seldom grumble against the State or the Climate because I can mend neither of them' but complained, 'The frost makes it necessary to burn coals which are risen in their price, and the same frost that makes such costly fuel necessary, has cut off my kidney beans. Oh what a climate! Oh what a Government! Who can feel these things and not wish himself a Turk or a Hottentot?'[5] Taxes on fuel offend the civic-republican; ruined beans offend the gardener-individualist. Cowper elegantly fantasises himself outside polite society, a controlled environment like the public sphere which leaves him shivering by his own fireside. Cowper's letter demonstrates reasoned debate; it also draws force from exclamation. The rational citizen is a feeling, wishing citizen too.

As critics have observed, what counts as rational is often disputed, especially in the 'seething cauldron' of eighteenth-century politics.[6] Letter-writers won arguments by silencing opponents as well as by persuading them. Many eighteenth-century writers used reason as a flag of convenience, and in politics certain feelings – like loving one's country or hating its enemies – were meant to be close to hand. 'So I would not have engaged in public position-taking if I had not, each time, had the – perhaps illusory – sense of being forced into it by a kind of legitimate rage, sometimes close to something like a sense of duty.'[7] Bourdieu's description provides a useful parallel for the emotions that motivated many eighteenth-century letter-writers. Bourdieu too has a wish – that the logic of intellectual life, a logic of argument and refutation, would govern public life; instead, 'it is often the logic of political life, that of denunciation and slander, "sloganization" and falsification of the adversary's thought, which extends into intellectual life'.[8] Bourdieu's distinction of a rational ideal that can be filtered out from other aspects of public life is politically idealist; likewise in the eighteenth century, an ideal of reason survived market-driven practice. But although reason was seen as at odds with the market or above it, it was also caught up in it as a force against luxury and corruption, both seen as appetitive, greedy, corpulent. However, the relationship was not simple opposition: Bourdieu shrewdly makes the connection in describing 'the consumer, the commercial *substitute* for the citizen' (my italics).[9]

The citizen, then, is a character who plays a part in ideologies of class and capital, and whose activities and writings may be read as describing, even delimiting, the public sphere. I use 'citizen' as a broad term, compatible with others like Hanway's advocate, farmer, merchant or author. Although the word acquired demotic and demagogic overtones in relation to the French Revolution, it was otherwise widely used as a self-respecting self-description. The citizen is also a character with a major part in the cultural history of letter-writing. This chapter looks at letter-writing by citizens in relation to parliamentary business including lobbying and elections; corruption, a half-hidden aspect of the public sphere; personae like the Drapier, Cato, Junius and others less well known. The chapter ends with analysis of letter-writing's forceful role in a specific political moment, the excise crisis.

Letters were important as a medium of political participation not least because the dialogic nature of correspondence matched the interrogatory nature of political exchange. Writing a letter, like asking a question, presumed there could be a reply. Correspondence, like arguments, had two sides; hence it represented well a model of reasonable enquiry. In politics, however, a predominantly two-party system turned on antagonism: as one writer put it, *'we have played the Fool with throwing Whig and Tory at one another as Boys do Snow-balls'.*[10] Party politics throughout the eighteenth century seem to settle repeatedly into a dualist track: Jacobite versus Hanoverian, Court versus Country, Pitt versus Fox and so on; even groups like patriots and radicals were defined as much through a dynamic of opposition as a self-set agenda. From Swift's parody of bipartisan differences between Big and Little Endians and Low and High Heels in *Gulliver's Travels* to an anonymous dialogue of 1771 that amusingly pitted Wigs against Nightcaps in two-party argument, writers recognised the ideological attraction of opposites.

The ways in which parties were polarised were affected by the relationship of party to nation. For obvious tactical reasons, government supporters often claimed that party opposition threatened national unity. As one observed darkly, 'The most Successful Arms the Turks ever us'd against the

Christians were their own Divisions.'[11] National identity was in part defined through the continual contest between parties as to which was truest to the practice of that liberty on which Britons, especially Englishmen, congratulated themselves as the envy of the world. The rhetoric of nation was in the foreground of much eighteenth-century political discourse and it compensated for a shifting sense of what the public was. On the one hand, 'the public' looked back to the Roman *res publica* and to forms of government associated with oratory, made familiar to Englishmen through their education. Continuities with classical discourse were actively sought: 'The same Principles of Nature and Reason that supported Liberty at *Rome*, must support it here and every where.'[12] On the other hand, there were glaring differences between republican Rome and enlightenment Britain. Commentators slid past the awkward difference of religion, preferring to be impressed by Roman moral standards especially under the republic, but many stumbled over the technological gulf between ancients and moderns. The growth of print culture did not just increase the volume and circulation of texts but made a qualitative difference to ideological reproduction. This reproduction was often troped as uncontrollable. So Joseph Galloway, attacking Charles James Fox as a modern Catiline, claimed that Fox was more subversive than his predecessor because he had access to 'that source of delusion, public fraud and sedition, the *licentiousness of the press*'.[13] Conservative writers like Galloway were predictably silent on the irony that they were using the press to denounce the press, though their critics were quick to spot it. Print thus made it possible to imagine the nation and simultaneously fractured a fantasy of that nation as unified.

A free press was universally agreed to be the guardian of British liberty. But given unease amongst progressives about government powers of censorship and propaganda, unease amongst conservatives about how licence could become licentiousness, and cross-faction confusion about how writers should make money from political writing, print culture was not perfectly synonymous with a politically legitimated public sphere. 'The press' was really many presses, owned and operated by people of different political beliefs. Printers filtered letters as they streamed in – the printer of the *Gazettee* claimed in 1764 to have received 861 letters in four months.[14] Printers shaped as well as selected: the persona of 'Cato' was attached to Trenchard and Gordon's letters by the printer, not the authors. That the term public opinion becomes meaningful in the eighteenth century has been attributed to the expansion of the press and the growth of newspapers. Both are valid links, but should be understood as considerably enabled by a letter-writing culture in which people became used to airing their views and responding to other peoples' in manuscript as well as print. Dror Wahrman has extended the notion of 'political language' from J.G.A. Pocock and other historians of political thought to stress the 'proper multi-layered and historicized political and linguistic contexts...for the shaping of the social consciousness of large groups of people'.[15] I wish to argue for literary contexts too, especially awareness of the significance of epistolary genre. Political intelligence was a staple of much personal correspondence, some of which was printed and helped create a sense of public opinion by circulating opinions plurally.[16] News reports in eighteenth-century newspapers came from epistolary sources – a convention which went back earlier and survives even now, so that news reporters are described as 'foreign correspondents' long after news turned non-epistolary. Many of these factors were in place throughout the early modern period.[17] What was new in the eighteenth century was the volume and visibility of these debates. More literate than the shouts of crowds yet as democratic as the address or petition, letters represented the views of citizens as individuals and groups.

Letters in newspapers became a significant and visible form of political argument in the eighteenth century. Plurally they created a spectrum of argument. As one editor put it,

> Every argument of consequence, on both sides, is here handled with that comprehensive brevity, which tends to give a full view without fatiguing the mind: So that any Gentlemen, by means of this, may become master of all the parts of the controversy in an hour or two.[18]

Letters' power to argue made them suitable for attacks on policy and critiques of administration. They were frequently the first choice genre for accusation and investigation, especially into corruption, and a preferred form of communication between electors and their representatives. As someone wrote to Pitt in 1789, 'SIR, AS you are a public character, I have a right to address you in a public manner.'[19] Some correspondents used letters to advance political neutrality in the public sphere; thus Capel Lofft wrote in 1788 to the people of England that his reasoning '*whatever it may be, is at least unalloyed by Party. I offer it as one of the Community: and I trust it has its source in PUBLIC REASON*'.[20] Readers assessed manifestations of civic ideals by the way a letter was written: a commitment (however nominal) to candour and moderation made epistolary convention stand in for social decorum. Shared civic values were of course not exclusive to letters, but letters visibly expressed them through forms of address and signature. Letters targeted an audience and specified an origin, giving the text simultaneously a simple direction and a complex dynamics. A Letter from a Farmer, a Merchant or a Freeholder located the views expressed in relation to a particular interest group and hence to a system of lobbying that was a critical part of parliamentary activity.[21] Expressing interests and resistances, letters both partnered and rivalled the genre of the address. The address was a formal and collective expression of the people's will; the letter was usually individual and less formal, often not associated with an authorised constituency. This independence was a virtue. 'If we seek for the *voice of the People*, we are not to look into addresses from venal corporations and boroughs, but collect it from the general sense of the People.'[22] The letter took up a middle ground between organised interests and populist disorder, especially from the mid-century on when urban experience registered 'a growing middling presence in national politics'.[23]

'The people', however, were gendered. As Kathleen Wilson observes, 'the accessible "universal" identity cultivated by newspapers was in fact a particular one that recapitulated the self-representations of the urban and upper middle classes, and especially their male, white and English members.'[24] The singleness of a letter kept it symbolically free from group politics, but it thereby entrenched the public image of the citizen as male, rational and propertied. Like letters in periodicals, letters in newspapers were ideologically charged and directed.[25] 'Manliness' was proclaimed by that tireless correspondent, An Independent Englishman and his cousins, A Gentleman and A Free-Born Briton. Although women wrote about politics extensively in their personal correspondence and were active in court and extra-parliamentary politics, the public political letter was constructed so as to keep women and the unpropertied out. These barriers were breachable: anonymity and pseudonymity provided cover for some women writers[26] and unpropertied voices were present too, albeit distorted by the mimicry of bourgeois writers. Seventeenth-century notions of symmetry between state and family faded, though they never wholly disappeared; letters show how notions of masculinity shifted and were tested. Male sexual appetite had been politicised (again) at the Restoration and a fresh liaison between discourses of liberty and libertinism took place around Wilkes in the 1760s and Charles James Fox in the 1780s.[27]

The emptying of femininity from political letters was achieved in several ways. Old-fashioned types used crudely gendered symbolism, like the correspondent who wrote to an MP that '*Liberty*, like a Woman's *Virtue*, is only to be *preserved* by keeping its Enemy at a Distance'.[28] More usual was a subliminal gendering like that of the writer who condemned Fox: 'WHEN the Constitution is assaulted, and the Rights of Parliament threatened with invasion, it is the duty of honest men to exert themselves, and endeavour to obviate the impending danger.'[29] The point is not that the body politic is feminised – sometimes it is – but rather that the militarist register connects masculinity and civic identity. Protection of liberties is work for heroes. Rousing the nation from sleep, to return to Hanway's formula, was done by men; what threatened it was most often figured as foreign invasion or the instabilities of populism in which class and gender barriers collapsed together. This correspondent is especially furious with Fox for bringing 'English Ladies' into politics – 'You have taught them to associate with shameless prostitutes, and drunken voters'[30] – but femininity had to be expelled whether or not actual women were present. In a complacent circle, men constructed public roles for themselves by writing publicly to each other.

Historians' frameworks for interpreting eighteenth-century politics offer, broadly speaking, a choice between continuity, conservatism, challenge or centrism.[31] For all the overlap between politics and religion visible in, for example, the Sacheverell affair, attempts to repeal the Test Act, the upheavals of Jacobitism or Priestleyan radicalism, the predominant patterns of letter-writing favour a focus on the politics of challenge and protest, though also of *advice*, in which ideological tensions are variously *diffused*, rather than defused, through epistolary conventions. Letters blurred personal and social: they attacked politicians as well as policies. Eighteenth-century political letter-writing was adversarial, with a rhythm of claims and put-downs which made communicative action a matter of contradiction. An ingenu observed,

> When I began to apply myself to the public Prints I was surprised by finding what was one Day positively asserted in one Paper contradicted the next Day, with the same Assurance, in another...I laboured under the same Difficulties in my private Conversations; what one Man affirmed to me in the Morning was pronounced absolutely false by another before Night.[32]

The fantasy of irrational citizens becoming rational readers was less wild in the context of letters where persuasion was often fictionalised as polite. 'IT will be readily granted that every Briton is a reasonable Man, however *irrationally* some *Britons* may act', wrote one letter-writer hopefully.[33] Civility and citizen shared a common etymology in *civis*; hence epistolary civility helped define civil society.

Access to open-minded readers became the more desirable because political writing was so patently partisan. As one commentator put it, 'A free, unprejudic'd, and impartial Writer is a Kind of Solecism in Politicks', adding that the two parties (here Court and Country rather than Whig and Tory) were like John Lilburn, of whom it was said 'That if there was no other Man in the World, that *Lilburn* would quarrel with *John*, and *John* with *Lilburn*.'[34] Still, hope persisted that the rational reader existed, that 'people unprejudiced are fond of being rightly informed'.[35] Published letters deferred proclaiming their politics insofar as titles stressed participants and topic rather than slant. It is hard to anticipate the political views of A Letter from a Gentleman in Town to his Friend in the Country, a common formulation in the first half of the eighteenth century, or of A Letter from a Gentleman to a Member of Parliament, a common formulation in the second half. Even where topical knowledge linked writers to lobbying groups, simple titles and attributions made interested views seem more disinterested. *Two Letters on the Flour Trade* (n.d.) by a Person in Business and *Three Letters to a Member of the Honourable House of Commons* by A Country Farmer (1766) are plain about their affiliations with mercantile and agrarian interests, which associates them with plain speaking. One should not assume, however, that such interests were necessarily uniform. Published letters like these were not always as headed towards politics indoors as they appear: *The Farmers' Address to their Representatives* (1768) was recommended to 'Every Honest Man in Britain.' As one farmer pointed out, 'special' interests were often hardly that: every man ate, so every man's interests were concerned in corn prices. Farmers expected MPs to read tracts on the corn trade and they applied pressure by writing openly to the public as well. Just as party writers could use multiple addressees to fend off charges of faction, so special interest groups widened debates through letters.

Franking, or the privilege of free postage for MPs, symbolised the importance of free parliamentary speech – literally free. Hence letters symbolised how writing itself was a political act, and increasingly people expected 'vox populi' to appear in writing. By the 1760s it was axiomatic that 'STATESMEN may be corrected in their blunders, or chastised for their villainy' by the press.[36] Not all ministers read these rebukes, but all political publications were supplied to the Treasury and a stream of prosecutions for libel shows someone was reading them on government time.[37] Great men might read letters when they would refuse to see a petitioner: in what was described as 'this reading age',[38] letters could prevent the common scenario of hanging about a great man's levées only to be turned away by his servants after hours of fruitless waiting. In the 1770s as the reform movement gathered pace, it was observed that the king was insulated from his people by advisers who stopped petitions getting through to him. But they let him read newspapers, so opinions voiced there by letter could reach the royal ear. One such letter in the *Morning Chronicle* pretended to come from George II in the Elysian Fields, reproaching his successor for making a mess of being king.[39] Such epistolary familiarity was encouraged by 1770s radical fraternising but it existed earlier too. In the 1730s, one writer complained that recent civic letters of congratulation to George II had forgotten 'all the Care, all the Circumspection, the Observation of the strictest Rules' attendant upon writing to a sovereign; instead,

> some of them undertook to direct him how he should proceed in the laudable Designs he had undertaken; while other applauded him with the same Rudeness of Joy, with which they would clap one of their boxing Companions on the Back, and cry, Well done, my *Lad!*[40]

Familiarity was the price paid for that singleness of epistolary voice, even in a corporate letter, which dissociated the genre from dangerous mass politics.

The democratic potential of letters, however, resurfaced in connection with the body politic. Some writers considered it a mechanical body but conventionally the trope evoked an organism governed by medical metaphors. Political activity was represented in terms of fevers or diseases for which treatment was blooding, purging, amputation and so on. Puns on constitutions kept the metaphor alive throughout the century, perhaps assisted by the fact that many physicians still diagnosed patients by letter. Letters mediated material and metaphorical identities of the body politic: the people had a material existence beyond the expression 'the people', as the letter had a page for its words. The single citizen who could be appealed to by intellect was thus collectively engrossed: 'we atoms are singly endued with such efficacy of reason, as cannot be expected in an aggregate body, where we crowd and squeeze and embarrass one another'.[41] Epistolary familiarity, a plebeian slap on a king's back, was expressed through images of the body and two kinds of repressed bodies returned: those of correspondents and the political mass. Political liberty was represented as bodily freedom; a pen was no use in a manacled hand.[42] Excessive liberty was bodily, wanton and licentious – though not as straightforwardly sexual as those terms suggest. Letters were normally understood to tolerate mixing value with waste, so in the context of politics they readily accommodated the metaphorical entanglement of political and physical bodies. This mix can be seen in a story of Lord North who was always losing State papers: 'A Letter of the first political importance, addressed to him by the King, which he had lost, after a long search, was found lying wide open in the water-closet.'[43] The alarm is not just over where the letter is, or who might read it, but the combination and to what use the king's letter might have been put – by North (who was famously short-sighted) or anybody else. As levelling as Swift's 'Celia shits!', the story showed how those with bums to wipe were no respecters of royal persons embodied in letters.

Questions of liberty governed relations between people and sovereign. Questions of corruption characterised relations between people and parliament. The two merged in that a corrupt parliament neither represented the people nor mediated properly between them and the king. In helping themselves rather than the nation, the corrupt exposed the difference between the theory of the constitution, in which monarch and parliament and people had balanced powers, and the realities of government. The trouble with corruption was that it was simultaneously obvious to its detectors and hidden from everyone else. Chesterfield defined corruption as taking a sixpence more than your salary, but in a system of patronage it was often unclear what distinguished illegitimate emoluments from perks. A sea-captain who took his share of prize money at source rather than wait to be paid by the Admiralty at its convenience was nearly subject to criminal charges; the published correspondence put him narrowly in the clear, not least because his willingness to make papers available implied a clear conscience.[44] A voluntary appearance in print suggested honest disclosure. So a 1751 anthology printed a letter from Jeremiah Finger-Cash, a lawyer's clerk who felt guilty for making – legitimately – fifty pounds a year in fees. The cash flow described was believable; the letter's comedy lay in the character's unlikely guilt. In reality, people were less abashed. In 1769 a letter was produced in court in which Samuel Vaughan offered the Duke of Grafton £5000 for a clerkship in Jamaica. Such an offer was not illegal, but Vaughan's lawyer conceded it was not strictly gentlemanly or honourable. Public trust in officials presupposed those officials would act as trustees of public property, a notion of common trust broken by corruption.

In the muddied waters of corruption, smaller fish of placemen and pensioners were easier to catch, especially after the leviathan of Sir Robert Walpole escaped from a parliamentary enquiry. Writers tracked quarry through accounts, often involving letters of business. John Robins ingeniously calculated a set of alternative costings to support his claim that directors of his local water company had put up prices to line their own pockets. (The company cut him off, but he moved to a house by a river and supplied himself.) Robins stressed his limited education and his belief in collective action; his appeal for customer solidarity echoed radical political discourse, as did his title.[45] The personal form of letters could engage a reader on the side of an ordinary citizen confronting a heartless corporation, alias avarice, tyranny and oppression. Then letters became the opposite of accounts: literacy described what numeracy concealed.

Bourdieu suggests corruption stems from a decline of confidence in the public good; corruption is an index of the rulers' lack of respect for the people, which in turn stimulates religiosity among the people, who despair of temporal remedies.[46] As Kathleen Wilson comments, 'belief in the transformative moral and rhetorical powers of printed texts transected the society, being shared by religious enthusiasts as well as coffeehouse politicians'.[47] Eighteenth-century citizens, however, took up letter-writing as a remedy with a resilient confidence in its power. Letters had particular uses when an investigator was an interested party, especially in the lucrative world of government contracts. The same influence that let an official cream off benefits could be used to persecute a whistle-blower. The use of pseudonyms or epistolary personae was a prudent if primitive defence, given that courts convicted writers of libel on as slender a basis as identifying targets by three initial letters of a nickname. The case of 'Selim' is a perfect example of the problems. Selim placed letters in the *London Evening Post* in 1771 claiming malpractice at the Board of Ordnance. The charges were standard ones: appropriation of government monies for private uses; passing over able candidates, here in favour of raw recruits and useless engineers, and interference in contracts for personal gain. As Selim saw it, the problem was not these practices *per se* but their extent. Eighteenth-century metaphors of corruption tend to be fluid, perhaps in relation to London's waterways and rubbish-filled ditches. Corruption rises, oozes and cannot be contained, and exposés incline to the rambling. Besides applying serial pressure via a newspaper, 'Selim' published the correspondence halfway between a Board of Ordnance enquiry and a parliamentary enquiry. Although 'Selim' got some satisfaction from General Conway after the Board advertised for the author to come forwards, he found himself literally out in the cold when he went to give evidence: carpenters, plumbers and masons who appeared for the defence waited in a comfortable room with a large fire whilst Selim and his friends shivered in a passage. The letters redressed that imbalance in that witnesses were augmented by members of the public who wrote to the paper in support, although some sound suspiciously like Selim, despite his claim to have chosen a newspaper on the grounds that it offered a variety of readers, all (naturally) unprejudiced. Given that internal enquiries had both doubtful legal status and doubtful integrity, whistle-blowers turned to newspapers as a tribunal they could hope to influence.

A striking case in which a citizen pressed the case against corruption was that of 'Scourge', whose letters appeared in the *General Advertiser* and were published as a collection in 1781. 'Scourge' accused one Christopher Atkinson of supplying the Commissioners of Victualling with overpriced and underquality malt. He criticised the transaction in detail and on seemingly good information, though he kept quiet about how he got hold of those accounts that showed irregularities. Scourge was most fired up by two letters. One was from the Commissioners to their superiors in the Admiralty, announcing they had got the cheapest grain available and were wholly satisfied. The second was a letter offering the same Commissioners cheaper terms and better quality grain. Not until significantly later in the collection do you learn that this letter came from Scourge, alias W. Bennett, a cornfactor. This discovery creates a tricky moment: for most of the text, the author promotes himself as a Scourge on behalf of the public, not a disappointed business rival. At one point he even disingenuously writes under the signature of Bennett in support of Scourge, as if they were different persons. But as Scourge he lashed out particularly at Atkinson for a letter to the Commissioners complacently declaring ' "nothing would ever induce me to supply a commodity inferior to the best, and more than a common commission I never wish to gain" '.[48] Supposing Atkinson intent on personal gain, Scourge declared this to be 'Matchless effrontery!' – it was not just the deed but its representation which was offensively corrupt. Lies were something to be hidden as well as something which hid the truth: thus after the débâcle of the South Sea Bubble, Sir Robert Walpole was known as the Screenmaster General. In eighteenth-century idiom, truth was masked and lies were bare-faced. This paradox helped writers using personae: it was understood that they put on a mask in order to expose a cover-up. Normally this under-standing was on offer to persons writing in newspapers in the public interest – to the citizen, in other words. When Scourge exceeded those limits, he was in trouble.

Believing that Atkinson was motivated by a need to make back money he had lost in election expenses when becoming an MP, Scourge demanded a parliamentary enquiry and to that end sent a circular letter to all MPs (except, awkwardly, Atkinson). This unwisely moved the scene of corruption away from government contracts to Parliament, where election expenses were regarded sympathetically. Scourge attempted to recover a public platform by writing, as Bennett, to the Commissioners via the *General Advertiser*:

> The Public, a valuable portion of whose dissipated treasure maintains your Lordships in the splendid luxury of employments, enjoy a right of animadverting to these abuses; and I, as a member of that Public, conceive myself intitled to exercise, as an individual, the privileges of which *they* may not avail themselves, *collectively*.[49]

Then a backlash overtook his avenging sobriquet: as Bennett he was briefly arrested, his house ransacked and his papers seized, on the strength – ironically! – of a supposed anonymous letter which accused him of having set fire to Newgate. Shaken, Bennett fought back: when Lord Stormont, who issued the arresting warrant, refused to let him see this letter, he set off in pursuit of an author better hidden than he had been. Unable to trace this invisible (and possibly non-existent) letter, he pursued Lord Stormont by letters for all of the next year and annually thereafter. One can see him as obsessive but his persistence was admirable and if he attracted obstruction from every quarter, it simply strengthened his case that the Establishment looked after its own.

Scourge's case is unusually rich. It supplies comparisons between person and persona as writers; between newspapers, courts, boards of enquiry and Parliament as forums of investigation and redress, and between all the different kinds of letters involved in exposés, with their power to audit, verify, incriminate, explain and denounce, singly and in sequence. Corruption, general and particular, was a major catalyst of eighteenth-century political writing, but it has not hitherto been seen as a field of force that drew letter-writers into the public arena. Two personae have been recognised as significant in political journalism, but despite their star status, Swift's Drapier and Junius were not lone voices crying in the wilderness. The next section places them alongside less well-known writers to amplify epistolary contexts of eighteenth-century politics.

Personae

A pseudonym indicates 'not a received, historical self but a conceived, textual self' and 'Finding a name entails defining – and knowing – the self', says Deborah Baker Wyrick.[50] Slippages of meanings between different selves have intrigued critics especially in the case of Swift, whose skill at remaining authorially elusive adds to his status as a canonical author: 'the peculiar elasticity of Swiftian anonymity'[51] occupies literary critics with his aesthetic complexities. Conversely, historians are interested in the political import of personae: thus Hannah Barker has discussed epistolary personae in the late eighteenth century, pointing out that people writing to newspapers stressed their constitutional standing through terms such as 'freeholder' and 'elector'.[52] But letter-writing is central to the history of personae. In travel writing, epistolary personae were used to defamiliarise political subjects; in political writing, the epistolary persona tended rather to project an identity in possession of something authentic. It can be compared to the curious logic of masquerades whereby costumes were understood to convey both a disguise of the wearer's identity and a fantastical identity that nonetheless expressed a hidden aspect of the wearer's identity. Thus Richardon's Pamela combines sobriety and sexuality when she goes to a masquerade dressed as a Quaker, but heavily pregnant.[53] Epistolary personae had unconscious resonance, from their repression of writers' names; they also made conscious, imaginative claims on meaning. Many personae were taken from different planes of history: names like Cato, Brutus and Alfred 'were used to add authority to a cause in a society which used historical precedent as an ultimate sanction',[54] although the dissolution of historical difference as those names were imported into the present can be read as a disturbance of the border between past and present, akin to the popularity of ghosts in eighteenth-century culture.[55] Personae could be place-specific, like 'Nathaniel Glasgow' who urged the magistrates of his home town to share that civic consciousness promoted by his signature: 'throw off all parties of great Men, let the good Town of *Glasgow* be your Party, and nothing else'.[56] No address could be attached to the name: Junius was contactable only via the papers in which his letters were published; his printer Henry Woodfall had to follow a series of cryptic signals to leave communications at a coffee house designated by Junius.

Use of a persona was not tantamount to ownership: half a dozen different people might use a name at any one time and writers might use more than one name at any one time. That liberty of class mingling which made masquerades so alarming to moralists was also acted out in political correspondence. Personae subliminally reminded readers that lords and labourers were equal before the law and that so long as labourers were nominally propertied they had a vote and power. Personae letters also resembled masquerades in mediating between high and low to blend a distinctive set of codes that drew from both street and salon. Their cultural shorthand drew on iconic figures like John Bull and Britannia and famous people like Jack Ketch, a public hangman, whose name was put to a number of letters satirising the rewards open to public office-holders.[57]

The reversals of high and low discourses in Gay's *The Beggar's Opera* or Fielding's *Jonathan Wild* provided a well-understood form of irony through which to attack Sir Robert Walpole and corruption. Letters worked a little differently. Since letters could be high or low anyway, the point was not to exchange those registers (as in ballad opera) or fuse them (as in mock-heroic) but to use them as counterpointing voices which could cooperate or disrupt. In this pattern, letter-writers mirrored politicians' fictions of independence and facts of coalition. It is sometimes possible to anticipate a letter's political stance from its persona: thus Cato was unequivocally associated with liberty.[58] But since liberty meant different things to different people, 'Cato' was used by Patriots or Tories as a sign they were contesting Whig discourses of liberty.[59] Moreover, a textually consistent signature was compatible with changeable views, as in the shifting party allegiances of the two writers who made Cato a famous persona in the 1720s. Paradoxically, consistency of signature helped articulate the inconsistency of political terms: 'Indeed, I can't see what we differ about...the honest and wise Men of all Parties mean the same Thing, and ought to lay aside and forget the old Names, and become one Party for Liberty.'[60] Though personae seemed to resist party borders, they sustained political divisions by building associations around particular names. In the early to mid-eighteenth century, political letters reverse associations customarily made between Tory poets and the ancients, thus unsettling a literary canon based on Pope and Swift that celebrates them as Augustan writers representative of the age. In political letters, it was Whig writers who looked back to Rome, but to Rome as a republic not an empire. Hence the label Augustan is wildly misleading as a chronological term since much early eighteenth-century political journalism promoted the values of the republic and stressed the failings of the empire.[61]

Letters in personae are pseudonymous in that the name used is not 'real' but it may be true; likewise, although the signature may be a type rather than a name, it has an attributive function that makes such texts not anonymous. The very common signature 'A Freeholder' was popular because it indicated a class-entitled identity. Those owning property whose freehold was valued at forty shillings or more were entitled to vote; since this part of the electorate expanded thanks to inflation, a flexible identity represented their interests – and their differences. The term was 'a rhetorical tool to conjure up images of the ancient constitution in which landed property should determine power and freeholders possessed a "legendary integrity"'.[62] It denoted political identity of the broadest kind: no party loyalty could be assumed from it. Although some local papers charged partisan letters the rate for advertisements,[63] the *signature's* neutrality offered welcome relief, albeit temporary, in a climate in which intimidation of voters and activists was common. So one Freeholder involved in a quarrel with his MP refused to put a name to his letters for fear of being persecuted. He also wanted to disconcert his addressee, who had supposed him a clergyman: 'It matters not who, or what, I am. Turn to the observations.'[64]

Writers were keen to avoid not only the long arm of libel law but also the personal vengeance of duellists, though some belligerent writers chafed against the protection of a generic signature. An Honest Man was faintly regretful that he could not challenge Son of Candour after an exchange in 1766. Hinting darkly he was a military man, his eye was on alerting readers' class-consciousness as much as on intimidation:

I should think it very imprudent, and beneath myself, to give him the satisfaction, or mortification, to know who I am, without previously knowing who he is, in order to judge whether he deserves it or not.[65]

Invisibility made letter-writers vulnerable to constructions which could not be challenged off the field: 'This anti-candid Son of Candour sets out with his guess-work, of who, or what I am; makes of me what he pleases, and then makes me write and think what I never wrote or thought.' The Honest Man claims Son of Candour used a persona to hide his scurrility, whereas he, the Honest Man, did not want to appear in print: the original letter attacked by Son of Candour was a private communication sent to a friend in the country and published without his consent. A private letter with a name becomes a published letter with a persona. The persona encodes an assurance of integrity, a moral wholeness that covers over the discursive gap of the lost name. Often printed in attention-seeking capitals, signatures in printed letters are placed last, if not always read last, so the assurance is also a reassurance. Loss of name is not loss of self-definition.

For all its passion, much political writing was not the fruit of conviction. When Matthew Concanen and his friend John Sterling came to London and took up hack work, they decided by the toss of a halfpenny that Concanen should defend the ministry and Sterling oppose it. Personae were a tactic in the business of seeming honest so it was an enjoyable irony that James Macpherson used the signature An Independent Englishman when he was in fact a dependent Scot. As Thomas Cooke explained when he signed himself 'Atticus', 'the Reader is not to suppose that I imagine Myself capable of reaching those Excellencys which I admire in him; but while I had him in my Eye I could not descend to what is mean'.[66] Personae in letters indicated an aspiration to virtue.

Readers were of course familiar with personae from periodicals, like *The Spectator* or *The Female Tatler*. Miscellanies often featured short pieces with humorous personae who resembled small parts from the stage, especially city comedy; the ruminations of types like Will Sharpsight, Peregrine Ramble and Paul Poorwit made letters and essays overlap.[67] A signature like Humphrey Oldcastle, used by Bolingbroke in *The Craftsman* between 1728 and 1731, drew on a typology of naming familiar across the literary spectrum. Letters thrived, however, partly because the Stamp Act reduced periodicals and allowed newspapers to expand and partly because letters broke away from theatrical kinds of comedy in favour of jokes simultaneously more bookish, more populist and more politically urgent. Personae allowed public reason to be playful: 'we can't forgive a real Author acting or thinking oddly or idly, though our Entertainment arises from thence, because we consider him as a reasonable Man, and obliged by a superior Duty to another kind of Behaviour'.[68] Whereas 'proper names' required 'proper behaviour', letter-writers in personae could play the fool. Since fools had originally held posts at court, epistolary foolery reconnected with politics. Earnest opponents were ruffled by frivolity. In 1782 *The Caledonian Mercury* printed correspondence on church patronage dominated by Philanthropos who solemnly investigated scriptural precedents for congregations electing their pastors, with explicit parallels to the reform movement. Various people wrote in with comments, including Obolus who criticised Philanthropos's translations of Greek. Philanthropos responded that 'he is much obliged to Mr *Obolus* for his remarks; but cannot think the insinuation, conveyed by that gentleman's signature, is very charitable; and it makes nothing to the point in debate'.[69] An obol (in Greek, *obolos*) was a small coin in Athens, which also served as a voting token, so Obolus's half-pennyworth of argument was wittily and light-heartedly political. This mis-taking was a common discursive move. Citizen letter-writers had little control over the flow of argument in replies and as respondents enthusiastically joined debate with each other, foolery could involve multiple mis-takings.

Attacking a writer's choice of signature was one way to refuse to find foolery funny or to challenge the ideological appropriation of values implicit in the signature. One critic complained when 'Sir Walter Raleigh' wrote in *The Craftsman* that Raleigh had loved his country, was loyal to his Queen and had benefitted the world by his writings, whereas 'Raleigh', a.k.a. Bolingbroke, had abused his queen, opposed the peace, never faced an enemy, nor written anything of use. This outline, however, identified exactly those parameters of patriotism and statecraft to which Bolingbroke aspired. Regardless of authorial performance, a persona publicised a political value system.[70]

Anyone could put on a persona but not everyone could carry it off. Humourlessness did not help, as Joseph Galloway showed in his *Letters from Cicero to Catiline the Second* in 1781, which berated Charles James Fox for inflating political insult to Miltonic proportions:

> The epithets 'corrupt, treacherous, traitorous, tyrannical, despotic,' and, as if this world, with all its wickedness, did not afford a quality sufficiently foul, either for their mouths or for their pens, they have travelled into the regions below for the word 'diabolical'.[71]

Galloway's curious solution was to resort to faith in the signature of Cicero as a sign of that eloquence needed to triumph over the linguistically hyperactive Foxites. Historically a winner, Cicero's power came from plain speaking:

> And what has this Cicero done more? Nothing. He has only called Treason Treason, and a Traitor a Traitor. 'A Cat a Cat, and Dick a Knave.' 'J'appelle un Chat un Chat, et Ricard un Fripon.'[72]

Issues of allusion and translation condensed in the signature of Obolus here make the persona bilingually opaque. However plainly Cicero spoke, he never spoke French!

One politician declared that a letter-writer was worth twenty placemen in putting government views to the people.[73] The press can be seen as a revolving door connecting parliamentary politics with politics out of doors; writers believed in the power of writing to direct public opinion even as they attacked their competitors for making people easily led. Like a whale preceded by a pilot fish, 'the Mob was like a great tractable Monster led about by a popular Scribbler'.[74] Despite the contradiction of figuring the lawless mob as passive readers, letter-writers frequently put a political argument to the whole people: 'Writing is the one mode by which alone we can appeal to a nation.'[75] An epistolary format reached a wide audience that included, because it could not exclude, the shadowy presence of the politically disaffiliated.

The Drapier, Cato and Junius

One nation unequivocally galvanised by letters was Ireland; the occasion, Swift's *Drapier's Letters* (1725). The particular occasion was a patent granted, in 1722, to William Wood, an English merchant, to produce small change for Irish coinage. The inferior composition of 'Wood's halfpence' was more generally a token of English impositions on the Irish, especially in matters economic, against which Swift had long protested. Critics have placed the Drapier's letters in the contexts of Swift's satire and Anglo-Irish politics; my discussion stresses Swift was part of an epistolary debate, not a lone figure. The Drapier's letters need to be understood in terms of public letter-writing, taken up by Swift in response to his antagonist's use of the press. It has been said that Swift was ultimately writing for an audience in London – specifically Lord Carteret, brought in halfway through the controversy as Lord Lieutenant and an old friend of Swift's.[76] To propose a metropolitan readership downplays the letters' populist and nationalist context. In Swift's shadow, moreover, are other less famous letter-writers who were equally committed to resisting English imposition of the coinage of impoverishment. 'Cato Ultonensis' addressed a letter to the collectors analogous to the Drapier's letter to the shopkeepers. Cato uses a rhetorically high register, comparing economic infiltration to national invasion: 'I hope therefore upon this occasion, we are all prepar'd to Fire our Beacons, our Pens and Tongues, and dispute every Inch of Ground with this grand Invader by dint of Law.'[77] Sympathetic to the collectors' dilemma – if they accept Wood's money, they ruin their country, if they refuse, they ruin themselves – Cato gave the collectors symbolic importance as defenders of the nation: 'you are the Persons who at this Iuncture guard the Avenues, and keep the Passages, and the Enemy can't enter into the City without your Compliance'.[78] As Raymond Williams has observed, 'in many villages, community only became a reality when economic and political rights were fought for'.[79] Community here is both material town and symbolic polis; the humblest citizens have the highest responsibilities. These, like the writer's persona, gain demotic force by echoes of classical heroism: they could as well defend the Capitol in Rome as capital in Ireland.

Swift's populism draws on the discourse of sermons, a genre as much autocratic as democratic but still recognisably populist. *A Letter to the Shop-keepers* is marked on the title page 'Very Proper to be Kept in every Family', like an advice manual or moral compendium. Particularising the effects of Wood's halfpence as they affect different groups, Swift works his way up the social chain, combining hearty collectivism with that abjection which associated expulsion of waste with freedom: 'Therefore my *Friends*, stand to it One and All, refuse this *Filthy Trash*.'[80] The title page of Swift's letter has both a Latin motto and a Biblical quotation – marks of educated and general culture. The noble addressee, the Rt. Hon. Lord Viscount Molesworth, has to share the text with a popular audience: the Drapier asks his printer to circulate the letter as well as send it to Lord Molesworth. His 'excuse', that the letter is written in a feigned hand which will not be legible enough for Lord Molesworth to read, foregrounds one kind of disguised identity, a feigned hand, in a cheeky pretence of consideration for Lord Molesworth; flirting with the seditious implications of epistolary disguise, he supplies a place and date, 'facts' to match the 'feigned' handwriting. The irony is that personal, signed letters to politicians do not necessarily carry more weight than public, printed ones. Swift's joke – if he could write legibly, he would write in his own name – is a conservative one, nostalgic for a community disturbed by print. Swift's persona, it should be remembered, is not simply 'The Drapier': it is 'M.B., Drapier'.[81] The initials supply the remnant of an identity not defined by trade. The persona is also the ghost of a person.

The Drapier is both a writing tradesman and the writer as tradesman. According to the letter, the supposed draper, after an apprenticeship in London, kept a woollen shop dealing in black and white material approved by this lord, until the poor people demanded a coarser stuff to protect them against incessant east (i.e. English) winds. The draper-writer supplies some, though he gets no money by it and it does not protect the gentry. This overlap between fabric and text, the black and white stuff, brings together an experiential world and abstractions of policy. Writing could protect people in an economically hostile climate. Swift's attack on Wood's coinage may be 'thoroughly materialist in his understanding of currency',[82] but it is also idealist about text as a commodity. Political letter-writers countered specious scrip with script.

In his letter to the nobility, the Drapier, a simple person, is able to answer every paragraph in the Privy Council Committee's report because 'there was no great Skill required to detect the many Mistakes contained in it'.[83] A plain persona turns epistolary writing into plain reason. An ability to distinguish different values in specie demonstrated reason; numeracy could even define sanity.[84] Making the letter-writer a figure of reason is commonplace; what is unusual about this letter is its struggle over the place of representation. The Committee's report had been published by Wood in an unauthorised appropriation of parliamentary discourse. It had come from London via the *London Journal*, a pro-government paper, rather than via the official *Gazette*. The Drapier concedes that anger over textual issues 'may seem a strange Way of discoursing in an illiterate Shop Keeper',[85] but to an experienced political journalist like Swift, Wood's manoeuvres were loading the discursive dice. The press is a site of struggle as much as the pockets and purses of the Irish people. Money, Swift (and others) noted, is neither Whig nor Tory. The battle was not only between the Irish people and the English government as to what money the Irish should be compelled to use, but also between newspaper journalism and political letter-writing as a means of representing the coinage clash: '*Wood* prescribes to the News-Mongers of *London* what they are to write.'[86] The two issues merged, of course, in that Wood's influence over news allowed him to add insult to the injury of poor coinage:

> I am informed that *Woods* is generally his own News writer. I cannot but observe from that Paragraph that this Publick Enemy of ours, not satisfied to Ruin us with his Trash, takes every Occasion to treat this Kingdom with the utmost Contempt.[87]

The Drapier imagined that if the Irish people could read the pamphlets published at London by '*Wood* and his *Journey-men*...they would convince you of his wicked Design more than all I shall ever be able to say.'[88] The Irish people were not reading the pro-Wood case; the English were given access to nothing else. Some chose bias: 'I have reason to believe that no Minister ever give himself the Trouble of Reading any papers written in our Defence.' Indignation, ignorance, indifference all framed the written argument. Hence political letter-writers tried harder to reach people – Swift urged Harding, his printer, to sell the letters as cheaply as possible – and their power was recognised. Lord Carteret's secretary wrote to a civil servant that it would be amusing to have the unofficial correspondence of ministerial employees: 'a volume of Daily Posts written in the days of Augustus would at this day outsell as many Roman Gazettes published by authority'. His remark suggests official recognition that populist discourses could win arguments against government-sponsored reports – that letters could make history.

The Drapier's success can be measured by revivals of the persona, who reappeared in print in 1729, 1731, 1745, 1754, 1760, 1767 and 1778. The Drapier was almost invariably Irish and nationalist pride in the persona can be seen in the republication of Swift's letters under the title *The Hibernian Patriot* in 1730.[89] Subsequent Irish patriots took up Swift's theme of the politics of representation: in 1785 William Drennan, firing up the Irish against English despotism, urged them through *The Belfast News-Letter*, 'If you be MEN, to whom I address myself, MAKE NEWS.'[90] The alternative was to allow English newspapers to set the agenda: 'Must a mighty nation stand gaping for the wind which blows them the news of one man going into a *closet*, and another man coming out?'[91] An Examinator, locked in argument with a pro-government Country Gentleman, echoed Swift on the need to combat long-standing misrepresentations of Ireland: 'Lord Sheffield tells us, that we have got more than we expected or looked for, and therefore least [sic] we should get into a habit of asking more, what we have got ought to be wrested from us.'[92] Though people questioning policy through the press had variable success, Irish printers won victories in the paper war by publishing pirated editions.[93]

Where the Drapier was a homespun type used by a political sophisticate, 'Cato' appeared to be an experienced politician who told home truths. The letters by John Trenchard and Thomas Gordon under that signature in *The London Journal* in the 1720s, published as a collection in 1724, are less well known than Swift's but highly significant for political journalism. 'Cato' marked out an independent space coloured by nationalism that was close to, but not identical with, a Patriot agenda of opposition.[94] Rather, political independence and intellectual independence were to be mutually sustaining: to be properly patriotic, one had to be suspicious of Patriots. Two dramas from the previous decade laid ideological foundations important for Trenchard and Gordon's use of the Cato persona. Joseph Addison's startlingly popular *Cato* – 8 editions in 1713 – made Roman history available for British self-mythologising: 'Be justly warmed with your own native rage', as Ambrose Phillips put it.[95] Fascination with Cato was curiously masochistic: as Pope's Prologue put it, 'Who sees him act, but envies every deed? / Who hears him groan, and does not wish to bleed?'[96] Cato's violence and suicide were acclaimed as heroic in contrast to the more obviously martial Caesar who was associated with tyranny, and with brute force as against Cato's powers of rational persuasion. Through Cato, debates in the Senate of Rome could be referenced to the British Parliament, and Cato's personal courage combined with antimilitarism chimed with British memories of internecine civil war and anxieties about an uncontrollable standing army.

The popularity of Cato was not exclusive to letters and some of the signature's resonance came from other writings. In particular, Addison's play gave the character a sexual politics, which Julie Ellison has persuasively argued had powerful consequences in how masculinity was represented.[97] My interest here is less in gender and more in sexual politics, or how Cato helped the citizen letter-writer reproduce. Addison's Cato is 'stern, and awful as a God, / He knows not how to wink at humane frailty' [sic]. The degenerate age deserved his severity; where Cicero's eloquence was succinct, Cato's was austere. Circulating in Britain alongside Addison's play was *Cato of Utica* by Deschamps and the two were much compared. They had differently improbable plots – mistaken parentage in Deschamps and repressed passions in Addison – but both divorced the Roman hero from domestic complications experienced by his children. In these plays, parents do not grieve for children slaughtered for the sake of Rome. Being Roman becomes a matter of loyalty not blood, a political affiliation which must be willed by imitating a male Roman parent. Patriarchal reproduction requires sons whose obedience is measured by assimilation to a value system. What is odd in these plays is that the daughters are successfully assimilated: they require their suitors to show Roman values rather than romantic ones.[98] Elsewhere Addison wrote in panic about politicised women, denouncing discontented matrons conversant in matters of state, a situation illustrated by a woman and her maid falling out over the Habeas Corpus Act.[99] For Addison, women might appear to be members of the body politic by taking an interest, like Roman daughters, but they could not count as political subjects because their minds were too feeble to respond to 'solid Arguments and strong Reasonings'. Addison partly gets in this tangle because he is writing against *Tory* women: 'the Passions of our States-women, and the Reasonings of our Fox-hunters' can be ridiculed by men of sense regardless of party. Ideological reproduction, figured as intellectual activity, could not be done by women.[100]

This drive created sexual politics in republican personae like Cato. A linguistic expression of desire – eloquence – replaces heterosexual desire. Reproduction is thus accomplished not through figures of children but through masculine friendship: republicanism is male and (self)-reproductive. Hence Boswell made a gift of *Cato's Letters* to the Corsican patriot General Paoli. Homosociality through Cato also has a class bias: the classics are presumed to be the fruit of that education from which the labouring and many of the middle classes were excluded. So 'Philaleutheros Anglicanus' wrote a letter in support of John Almon, the radical bookseller prosecuted for selling Junius's letters, confident that Almon's politics showed 'the enthusiasm of liberty, which young men contract at the university, from reading the republican authors of Greece and Rome'. In fact Almon never went to university: inspiration for his politics was more likely to have come from his apprenticeship in Liverpool at a printing shop where Benjamin Franklin had also worked.[101]

Classical homosociality was elusive in a world of political unfriendliness – Cato's bookseller had dozens of offers to write against him. But it was visible when Cato split into two identities after Trenchard's death and Gordon mourned his friend at length in a panegyric introducing the collected letters. Julie Ellison argues that 'Trenchard and Gordon signify political virtue through rage rather than the manly friendship of other Whig subcultures',[102] but the memoir makes up the difference, touchingly. Wanting to be sincere and dependable, Trenchard would not make friends lightly, controlling his body language lest he be misunderstood:

He thought he never could be too plain with those he had to do with...he us'd to foresee...partial Constructions, and fix everything upon full and express Terms...though he was very civil to every Body, he order'd it so that the Forms of his Civility appeared to mean no more than Forms, and could not be mistaken for Marks of Affection, where he had none...[103]

Explicit language co-exists with volatile signs. Gordon wants to make Trenchard's life seamless, so that personal practice, political principles and writings all dovetail, like Cato's domestic life, public life and speeches. The account is unbalanced by the gradual return of that body erased both by an epistolary persona and by death. Body language merges into idiolect: 'He had indeed vast Variety of Images, a Deluge of Language, mighty Persuasion in his Looks, and great Natural Authority.'[104] You learn he had a manly face (of course), fair complexion, dark eyes, a passionate nature; you even learn he died of a kidney ulcer. The surprise these details create can be compared to the blankness surrounding Junius, about whom we know nothing personal or physical.

What difference does this return of the body make to how one might read the Cato *Letters*? 'His Character was as little known as his Name was much':[105] how does attaching a character to a name, and in such an unusually full and humane way, alter it discursively? Joining an eighteenth-century memoir of the everyday with a classical model of eloquence produces a narrative wholeness that stands in for moral integrity. It is a little like the doubled identities of twentieth-century superheroes whose public derring-do needs a quieter domestic life to complement it: hence Batman and Bruce Wayne, Superman and Clark Kent. But Trenchard, like Cato, is the same everywhere: 'I have often heard him make as strong, fine and useful Discourses at his Table, as ever he wrote in his Closet.'[106] The dangers of misconstruction which lurk in political journalism, especially around epistolary personae, are resolved by the power of friendship: 'Many sorts of Men and Causes combin'd to misrepresent him...but no good Man that knew him thoroughly cou'd be his Enemy.' Homosociality neutralises political hostility.[107] Gordon made Trenchard sound like a nicer Cato, as part of a new expression of sensibility connected to Whig self-authorising and masculinity.[108]

In *Cato's Letters*, Trenchard and Gordon together made the Roman polis a congenial model for Britons. Rome was an inspiration – its liberty, glory, empire – and a warning – its decay, decadence and slavery. Its fall was the fault of corrupt magistrates who strongly resembled British placemen, against whom much of Cato's energies were directed. 'Every Ploughman knows a good Government from a bad',[109] Cato claimed; like Cincinnatus, who famously preferred ploughing to politics, a British labourer possessed that honesty needed most in politics. By means of universal moral standards, politics could be class-inclusive. They then became gender-exclusive and women appear in passing in the letters, usually as figures of tyranny. Anti-monarchism was added to conventional figures of Rome as a bastion of masculine rationality against eastern sloth and tyranny. Turkish emperors took up where Roman emperors left off: 'a Monarchy of Ministers, and Parasites, Pathicks, Buffoons, Women, and Butchers, rule for him, and over him'.[110] Women, slaves and eunuchs were to be abjected by freeborn Englishmen. There is one letter in which Cato responds to a question about a woman not rich enough to secure a suitor: conceding political philosophy should acknowledge women's oppression – 'With their Cause, the Cause of Liberty is blended' – Cato is too ingrained in gallantry to pursue it.[111] Women may be bought and sold, like voters, but because some waste money, their plight as consumed object is overshadowed by their own ruinous consumption. Trenchard liked and respected women, according to Gordon, but Cato could not stretch political discourse to address women as subjects.

As in the early periodical and the novel in which men assumed feminine voices,[112] political journalists occasionally adopted female personae. One, 'Junia' (possibly Caleb Whitefoord), wrote to Junius, whose reply faltered into flirtation. This radical scourge of ministers could offer only reactionary metaphors:

> It is true I am a strenous advocate for liberty and property, but when these rights are invaded by a pretty woman I am neither able to defend my money nor my freedom. The divine right of beauty is the only one an Englishman ought to acknowledge, and a pretty woman the only tyrant he is not authorised to resist.[113]

Sexual innuendo replaced political debate: 'I should be glad to furnish her with one a subject more fit for a lady to handle, and better suited to the natural dexterity of her sex.' Explaining that 'Politics are too barren a subject for a new-married couple', he implies politics have to be homosocial, not heterosexual. This letter, described in those editions that print it as a delicate double entendre, was left out of Junius's own edition; in others his letter is included but Junia's is omitted. Junius's seductive effects on men did not have to be suppressed. When he wrote privately to Wilkes, Wilkes felt an erotic thrill: 'a line of applause from him gives the same brisk circulation to my spirits as a kiss from Chloe'.[114] In life, Wilkes was hyperactively heterosexual but in homosocial politics a generic female figure from pastoral was as close to real women as correspondents wanted to get.

An interest in public crime became a staple of political letter-writing. Satirists were interested in this too, of course, but it was expected of them, whereas the enormity of public crime taken seriously did not obviously fit into the register of a letter, even when referenced to public letters rather than familiar ones. Where poets satirised individuals through types or transhistorical examples,[115] Cato used group identities which could be particularised – a corrupt and wicked ministry using vile instruments to pillage the people.

192 Eighteenth-Century Letters and British Culture

That sense of community which provided identification in letters here gave readers a lazy pleasure, a sort of civic schadenfreude:

> Thus, without ent'ring into the Merits or Truth of the Matter, the Reader takes the same Delight in it, as those that are in the dry take in looking on those that are in the wet; they care not who they are, as long as they themselves are out of the Weather.[116]

What mattered to Cato was not investigative journalism – uncovering secrets, analysing causes, proposing remedies – but rousing indignation. Like much eighteenth-century political writing, his register draws on popular and polite discourses, combining metaphors of sexual violence recognisable to a fiction-reading public with chapbook iconography and heraldic devices of the street: 'To our deathless Shame, we are the Conquest, the Purchase of Stock-Jobbers. The *British* Lions crouch to a Nest of Owls!'[117] Stockjobbers were harpies, vermin, leeches, pillagers, rogues, ravens, crocodiles, cannibals – but also a modern kind of robber not found in the Bible, fable or natural history. Characteristically (being a double act) Cato tested out two alternatives, important for their expansive effect on letter-writing by citizens.

The first model Cato offered was an old one, a theory of ruling passions whose central injunction of self-government made civic government a plural version of virtues which individuals should be practising. Bourdieu suggests large-scale corruption 'is simply the extreme case of all the ordinary little "weaknesses" ';[118] likewise, Cato and others saw it as the product of unconstrained personal greed which required individual not systemic cure, though publicity could catalyse remedies. 'What is the Publick, but the collective Body of private Men, as every private Man is a Member of the Publick?'[119] Stockjobbers, who were rifling the public, should be subject to the same penal code as highwaymen or robbers. Elsewhere Gordon spread the blame for the South Sea Bubble more evenly than in the Cato letters; some directors were villains, but the people were greedy too. Epistolary dynamics of intimacy and publicity were well placed to explain how public figures' private passions could be made worse by the private passions of the public.

As the South Sea fiasco faded and Walpole's policy of selectively screening those involved deflected calls for justice,[120] Cato became increasingly fascinated by the Romans, who seemed to have streamlined passions and principles.[121] When Trenchard and Gordon wrote to an MP they offered 'some Instances of the good Oeconomy, and the steady and unbiassed Virtue of the Romans, since it was by these, and by these alone, they became so great and powerful'.[122] Not everyone warmed to these parallels. 'Our Condition and Story, and that of the *Romans* then, are not alike . . . I wish such Practice were less *common*', wrote one politician fed up with advice from the ancients.[123] Cato's critics raised questions of accuracy: '*It is a wrong way of arguing . . . unless all Things in both Times did agree*' – and the whole principle – 'What are the *Romans* and the *Lacedaemonians* to us?'[124] Another observed sagely 'there's no Government without its Inconveniencies' and suggested Cato was too idealist: ''Tis unreasonable to expect, that Men, who live in *Foece Romuli*, should act as if they were in *Republica Platonica*.'[125] But given the ideological pull of Roman republicanism for Whig writers, epistolary personae offered a literary bridge between past and present. 'The name of Cato is the signature of the oppositional citizen.'[126] 'Cato' was a signature through which the parallel lines of real and ideal might indeed converge.

The identity of Junius was the eighteenth century's best-kept secret. That Junius was unusually committed to invisibility can in part be attributed to the crackdowns of administrations made nervous by the reform movement; partly too to the tenacity and precision with which he derided ministers and the subtlety with which he insulted the king. His letters, printed in *The Public Advertiser* from 1769, suddenly dried up in 1772. The invisible man fell silent. Wraxall passed on a story that the king, out riding with General Deaguliers, told him, 'we know who "Junius" is, and he will write no more',[127] but the general was too much a courtier to press him further, leaving every reader since to enjoy what in the late eighteenth century was recognised as the ambivalent pleasure of being in the dark.[128] Alongside this biographical mystery is a bibliographical challenge. Since Junius's letters were so popular, booksellers made up collections as they appeared; editions proliferated even after Junius organised an authorised edition for his own printer's benefit. This emphasis on the who and the how distracts from the *Letters* themselves, which Wraxall praised as more elegant than Bolingbroke's writings and as forceful as Swift's satire. My interest is in how Junius used and developed letter-writing as a tool of citizenry. Junius offered an insider's view, literary thermal imaging compared to letter-writers like Cato who removed scales from the public eye. Junius's letters ran against the grain of that plain speaking promoted as political truth by John Bull types and radical orators alike:

I AM a freeborn Briton, and an independent man; I have no place or pension; never was at court, nor ever intend to go there. I know neither the ministers, nor those who oppose them. I have a right to think and speak for myself, and will do so; and I call upon all true Britons to hear what I have to say, and then judge for themselves.[129]

Junius patently had been at court and claimed to know its subtleties dispassionately. He repudiated the violence of opponents like Zeno who wrote through *The Public Advertiser* on 15 October 1771,

Sir, when you are only puerile, blundering, inconsistent, and absurd, I treat you as you deserve, with ridicule and contempt. But when you assert positive falsehoods, the mildest usage you can expect is to have them crammed down the foul throat from which they issued.

To this Junius tauntingly replied, 'I will not call you *liar, jesuit*, or *villain*; but, with all the politeness imaginable, perhaps I may prove you so.'[130] If bodily violence, or threats of it, constituted the bottom of a rhetorical hierarchy, Junius did not adopt that irony usually put at the top; rather, he perfected an art of polite name-calling which was not a substitute for political analysis but a form of it. There was certainly savagery lurking nearby; as his principal target Sir William Draper brilliantly observed, his weapon was neither the rapier nor the hatchet but the tomahawk. In private correspondence, Junius could be blunt. He wrote to Woodfall, 'Having nothing better to do, I propose to entertain myself and the public with torturing that poor bloody wretch Barrington.'[131] In Junius's public letters, sadism was refined.

Junius's letters had tangible effects – one was said to have pushed the Duke of Grafton into resigning. But they are significant for the power they accrued to letters discursively rather than practically. In politics, critics frequently disparaged opponents by accusing them of stirring up the people. Their subtext was that such writings had a power of affect that exceeded their referent. This anxiety differed from the perennial ambivalence about eloquence in politics in that it exposed class consciousness. Thus Samuel Johnson commented on Junius: 'It is not by his liveliness of imagery, his pungency of periods, or his fertility of allusion, that he detains the cits of London and the boors of Middlesex.'[132] This was wishful thinking, expressing Johnson's desire that this might be the case, regardless of evidence about radical reading practices. Johnson, a Tory, wanted literary resources to be the prerogative of a conservative government, to be both beyond the reach and the comprehension of radicals. To this end he associated radicals with literary barbarism: supporters of the Bill of Rights were, he wrote, responsive to bawling and harangues, not dextrous compositions. The politics of representation again shape the representation of politics.

Tension seems greatest over metaphor. Though Johnson's critique of Junius is best known for its crisp comment, 'it is not hard to be sarcastic in a mask', most of it is heavy with metaphor. Junius, he wrote, is an archer; Jack the Giantkiller; a comet that will burn itself out; a comet that will plunge its followers into a bog; a monkey, and a pseudo-Roman subversive who imperils the state on a Shakespearean scale: 'he cries *havoc* without reserve, and endeavours to let slip the dogs of foreign and civil war, ignorant whither they are going, and careless what may be their prey'.[133] Johnson uses Mark Antony to rewrite Tory foxhunters and deny civic responsibility to radicals. He may be parodying Junius's adroit turns of metaphor; I think it more likely he was being competitive. Junius had described the Duke of Grafton as Blifil and Black George rolled into one, a high-low scoundrel fused from two characters in Fielding's *Tom Jones*. Johnson became zoomorphic: the opposition were vultures and *phthiriasis*, an infestation of crab lice that arises from dirtiness and causes intolerable itching.[134] Suspicious of metaphor's power to simplify politics for supposedly simple minds, Johnson found himself snared onto the same territory.

The graphic language of metaphor should be considered alongside the iconography of political prints. By the 1760s, this had evolved a rich idiom of beasts, fables, puns and allusions; it had also dropped the practice of deleting names. Prints are usually associated with popular culture but there were also high-cultural caricatures in which unsparing portraits were placed in genteel settings. 'The graphic character must differ somewhat from its literary counterpart. It cannot rely (or at least limit itself to) verbal skills: the well-turned phrase, the witty conceit, the clever epigram.'[135] One such print from 1746, entitled *A Collection of Modern Statues and Characters*, shows a semi-circle of seven modern political figures on pedestals, like statues.[136] Faces and bodies are individuated and on each base is a classical name, a parallel which the text below explicates. Bolingbroke is Proteus, Pelham is Atticus, Pitt is Museus and so on. Junius plays with this idiom: the ministers he challenges are individuals, though as ministers their office requires them to set aside personal foibles and adopt the character of public servant. The signature of Junius stamps the character of citizen on each letter. His aim is to knock undeserving politicians off their pedestals; he reserves to himself the allure of classicism. Concerned like Cato with public crime in the form of ministerial incompetence, complacency and deceit, he stretched the boundaries of public accountability to include even the king. That George III was domestically virtuous cut no ice with Junius, who shrewdly saw that the sovereign as uxorious family man was part of the problem of royal domination of ministers at parliament and people's expense:

> Ministers are no longer the public servants of the state, but the private domestics of the Sovereign. One particular class of men are permitted to call themselves the King's friends, as if the body of the people was the King's enemies...[137]

Although Junius's brushes with ministerial defenders like Sir William Draper threatened to become personal feuds, he persisted in an argument conducted by himself but shared by many of his contemporaries, that oligarchy had gone wrong.

Junius used all the proven resources of writing as a citizen. The brevity of his letters proved he did not write from vanity. He did omit a shaky first letter from his authorised collection so as to make an entrance with éclat, but his manifesto was consistent:

> I do not presume to instruct the learned, but simply to inform the body of the people; and I prefer that channel of conveyance which is likely to spread farthest among them. The advocates of the ministry seem to me to write for fame, and to flatter themselves, that the size of their works will make them

immortal. They pile up reluctant quarto upon solid folio, as if their labours, because they are gigantic, could contend with truth and heaven.[138]

His anonymity made motive irrelevant: it was up to the people to decide if he was motivated by personal malevolence, political opposition or defence of the laws – whatever his motive, he implied, it did not affect the truth of the charges. His use of ironic address to the Duke of Bedford, though not new, was perfectly performed, like a compulsory figure in a skating competition:

> My Lord,
> You are so little accustomed to receive any marks of respect or esteem from the public, that if, in the following lines a compliment or expression of applause should escape me, I fear you would consider it as a mockery of your established character, and perhaps an insult to your understanding.[139]

His hypothetical address to George III likewise resembles letters from the dead but goes far beyond that genre in articulating political discontents and advising remedies.

Junius's improvisations combined a radical's political intensity with literary skills supposed to be the preserve of gentlemen and often described in terms of gentlemanly culture – rapier wit, polished periods, refined style. Precisely because Johnson was a Tory but not exactly a gentleman, the politeness of this rebel discomfited him. Junius's aristocratic targets were frustrated by his anonymity. His letters were the more unsettling because they suspended signs of class difference by which gentlemen could dismiss libels as 'impudent'. Sir William Draper claimed that 'People cannot bear any longer your *Lion's skin*, and the despicable *imposture* of the *old Roman name* which you have *affected*.' This outburst concealed two issues. One was that, unlike Cato, Junius was not a name attached to a famous historical figure. Ideologically, it was uncertain, though as a name shared by Brutus and Juvenal the persona fused associations of liberty and satire which the letters articulated at length.[140] The second issue was that, without knowing who was under the lion's skin, ministers looked stupid or guilty if they did not respond to Junius's accusations. Thus the letter-writer set the agenda. Though others wrote with wit and vehemence, Junius made writing as a citizen proactive, and sustainably so, through the power of a persona.

Letters and elections

Letters played a significant part in politics out of doors. One could track this through personal correspondence;[141] here, I discuss letters in elections, where they were publicly visible and affected outcomes. My analysis builds on Nicholas Rogers' account of eighteenth-century electoral experience in

Whigs and Cities and how his emphasis on crowds challenges interpretations based on reading politics from the top down.[142] Besides this broader understanding of the social base, Rogers also proposes an expansion of the centre, especially in urban politics from the mid-century. 'Through the new medium of journalism, urban festival reached an expanding audience.'[143] Letters were crucial here. Through common practices of letter-writing, top and bottom met and the middle mediated both. But letters were important not just to the dissemination of class in politics but to its formation. The special conditions of elections brought latent issues to the surface, making participants conscious – at times nervous – about how they used cultural forms like the letter to mobilise or suppress these views. 'Historians have become increasingly aware of the cultural affinities of riot and ceremony in the predemocratic era':[144] since letters could be riotous and ceremonious, even both at once, they should be closely investigated by anyone interested in eighteenth-century politics.

The following section shows letters on the hustings and in voters' hands in a variety of elections. It has been suggested that political writing made little difference to results: 'It was a basic fact of eighteenth-century politics that in the great majority of constituencies public opinion could play either a very limited role or no role at all.'[145] Although Paul Langford's case for this being so in the elections following the Excise Bill is persuasive, the contested nature of so many eighteenth-century elections shows voters believed in the power of challenge. Some politicians seem to have enjoyed it as a sort of sport: the Duke of Norfolk was alleged to have said he wanted the thrill of winning an election by a single vote.[146] The big picture has regional variations: 'it is clear that the big cities were electorally more contentious in the Hanoverian decades than in the Augustan, hitherto enshrined as the great age of political vitality'.[147] Without claiming that contested elections necessarily give a more representative picture than uneventful ones, they do show letter-writing playing a forceful role.

My choice of electoral locations overlaps with Rogers' partly for good historical reasons but also because in these cases election literature was not simply ephemeral – it was printed in collections for a wider public and so had more than local significance. Elections in Westminster famously staged both the parochial concerns of the nation's most populous constituency and the symbolic register of issues relevant to that political nation of which it was metonymically the centre. 'Geography allowed Westminster to press on the nerve of politics.'[148] Westminster elections were notoriously turbulent in the 1780s but earlier contests also showed acute class tension. Bristol and Norwich were major economic centres – Bristol the hub of transatlantic shipping and slavery, Norwich the heart of trade in textiles with the Continent. Both cities also had unusually broad constitutions; social diversity amongst voters was explicit. Political activity in Norwich in 1784 can also be compared to trends in the county election in Norfolk the same year, providing one model of town–country (or county) relations. I discuss an election in two smaller country towns: in Cirencester in 1753 because it shows the percolation of anxieties surrounding the Jew Bill and in Shrewsbury in 1796 because it shows characteristics of family quarrelling. In both instances, letter-writing by citizens was significant in determining outcomes.

My account is not an overview of history or politics but a study of how letters fit into cultures of electioneering at different times and places in eighteenth-century Britain. Letters were a principal means by which citizens communicated with each other and with candidates, and at elections the character of the citizen took on ideological power as a figure through whom political community was articulated, especially a community premised on a notion of public good, a notion less fissured by class difference than at other times. Before looking at specific elections, certain atmospheric conditions of the political climate need to be established. 'With the advent of Hanover, the political calendar became a calendar of riot.'[149] Like the original saturnalia when Roman slaves ruled briefly over their households, carnivalesque linked politics and festival. The ferment of a general election licensed all the community: 'All the World is in Motion on this Occasion; the very Children take Sides, and the Women are mere Firebrands of Parties.'[150] Transgression of decorum co-existed with excess, of which the top-down kind was loose money.[151] The costs of elections were legendary: an author in 1767 claimed he had been offered £4000 to get one MP returned (£6000 was the going rate for two).[152] According to Rogers, the candidate returned for Bristol in 1713 was said to have spent £2257; few candidates after 1750 could expect to get away with less than £10,000. In Bristol in 1754 the Whigs alone spent £30,000; in 1734 Sir Robert Walpole allegedly spent £10,000 in Norfolk only to lose the election by six votes.[153] It was seriously suggested that rich men made the best MPs because they could refuse bribes, but in practice, the rich made the only MPs anyway. The line between bribery (illegal) and treating (legal and indeed expected by voters) was often uncertain. At the 1749 Westminster election, the Duke of Bedford funded his brother-in-law's £4900 costs for tavern entertainment (this compares with £500 spent by the court party in 1762 when candidates were returned unopposed).[154] Election drinking, defended as patriotic because it helped the beer trade, was also attacked for creating addiction and disorderly habits the year round. Though the voteless were hardly great readers, with the literate frequently drunk it was no wonder that so many election letters closed with slogans in capital letters, to survive slurred speech and blurred vision.

In elections, letters mediated 'facts' and principles. They laid out the social boundaries of a constituency and made a collection of voters from different walks of life known to each other and to the candidates. They gave the voting public opportunities to create public opinion – like public meetings, which not all voters could leave off business to attend. Hence the importance of 'hearing' those opinions voiced in writing, either as separately circulating texts or in newspapers, local and national. Letters also laid out what was expected of an MP. An MP needed 'a head to plan and to project, a tongue to enforce and to persuade, or at least a pen to explain' or, for a plainer readership, 'a *wise head*, and *honest heart*, and a *well hung tongue*'.[155] These qualities were put on display through an MP's speeches and letters to electors. Letters also reminded MPs they were supposed to protect constituents' interests by reading relevant papers and turning up for business (which many did not). It was a public sign of Wilkes' commitment to parliamentary democracy that when a duelling wound failed to heal in time for him to face charges in the House of Commons, he made sure an earnest letter of excuse reached the Speaker – and a printer.[156] Election letters particularly addressed an ambiguity in the function of MPs: whether an MP was obliged to voice the views of his constituents or could exercise his own judgement on controversial occasions. Voters too had to determine their functions as well as their allegiances. Voters in Westminster in 1749 were given three categories with which to identify: '1st, *The Sons of Liberty*. 2d, *The Abject Slaves*. 3d, *The neutral Drones that don't deserve the Liberties they won't defend*'.[157] These informal categories were translated into official party language and vice-versa. For many, it made little difference in that their votes were spoken for by employers, landlords, patrons or customers; still, many others bravely resisted threats and bribes. Bribery seems venal, but honesty might well seem a luxury to the poor old men who were offered an income for life if they stayed away from the polls in 1722 in Hastings, where independent voters posted neighbours in front of their houses to keep out tempters they might not withstand.[158]

There were about a dozen different points at which letters played a part in elections. Preliminary letters would be sent privately between potential candidates and local figures to see how the wind blew. Private conversations were equally a place for this. Conventionally candidates declared themselves in a public letter couched as a response to an invitation to stand.[159] A candidate might then approach voters in the way described by a satire of 1768:

> His letters are filled with assurances, how much he will exert his endeavours to promote the interest of that ancient borough of Guzzledown if he shall have the honour to represent them again: He talks mightily about liberty, and hath promised to have the parish engine new painted, the streets paved, and to reduce the price of corn: He hath got the promise of an exciseman's place for the mayor's son, and hath assured all the aldermen, that their wives and daughters shall not be forgotten when he comes down.[160]

Candidates then solicited votes, personally, by agent and by letter. To pitch correspondence correctly at this point could make a big difference to a campaign. When Sir William Jones stood as a Whig candidate for Oxford University in 1780, his 'hectic, colourful, but seriously misjudged campaign' went awry through an arrogant circular letter on his behalf.[161] Having declared a platform (sometimes with policy commitments, but usually a more general party affiliation), the candidate was challenged on fair grounds, sent as an open list of queries, or through jokes, jeers and sneers. Opposition writers (who were simultaneously defending their candidate) raised anxieties about the platform and doubts about the candidate's character and history. Overlapping with these challenges was a wave of epistolary hostility in which rival supporters attacked each other, adding local enmities to national divisions. Again these letters used both serious and comic tactics. In a second wave came volunteer accounts of voter intimidation and the candidates' distant past, in letters usually politically nastier and more wildly humorous. When polling took place there were last-minute warnings, exhortations and complaints. In most elections, winners declared their grateful acceptance and thanks, losers their gracious regrets and thanks; both promised service, by either speech or letter or both. If a result was contested, there would be further correspondence, both official and unofficial.

Canvassing was mostly done in the flesh but historians' emphasis on crowds needs a little literary counterweight. In some respects, letters in newspapers mimicked public meetings by situating an address in a public context, but they also allowed solitary, silent and private readings. In a world where votes were publicly recorded and elections were shaped by family interests, letters' mix of public argument with personal voice fitted uncertain boundaries. On the one hand, letters were part of an ephemera of texts that denoted the social sphere – hence the visual litter of texts in political prints, including treaties, parliamentary bills, bankbills, lists, bills of fare, correspondence and so on. This tide of paper was swelled at elections by handbills, invitations, announcements, advertisements, letters, cards to be tucked into hatbands and so on. On the other hand, letters had power to filter people in and out of representation; hence they became emblematic of political community as something select (or self-selecting). Candidates courted the public, but political letter-writing is meaningless if read in the terms of privacy and fictionality attendant on the love-letter. Affect *is* present, but as the erotics of publicity, not intimacy.

It is difficult to establish exact readerships for people writing as citizens. Letters with the pragmatic function of persuading voters in an election were delivered in various ways – by hand, by print, by flyposting. Others with local provenance circulated in the press for more general political ends. Others were written for publication in national newspapers which were distributed throughout the provinces. Readerships intersected: people got information and opinions from newspapers and personal correspondence.[162] Some personae were impersonations, especially in the 1780s when writers on both sides were anxious to capture popular voices. Although impersonations were often based on occupation rather than class, some satiric letter-writing is proof that 'Parody was knocking away continually and uncontrollably at the notion that language reflected class and social position . . . When commandeered by radical propagandists parody may become an act of linguistic acquistion and simultaneous subversion.'[163] Parodic letter-writing shows this process was active well before the 1790s.[164]

Letters and songs were often printed together in collections of election literature. According to one historian, folk songs 'draw on wisdom that can rarely be attained by persons acting singly', which echoes the letters' voicing of political community; they also 'exist commonly in the major . . . seldom or never in the minor', which matches the carnivalesque tendencies of political letters.[165] Authors of folk songs, like political letter-writers, are not claiming fame for themselves but expressing, they hope, a shared point of view. Letters in personae at elections brought traditions into contact with current events, a double frame shared by election songs in which new and topical words were set to familiar tunes. Folk melody mixed with satire in song just as memory mixed with scepticism in political letters. In both genres, anyone could join in; as one voter wrote to a candidate, 'At this interesting period, the meanest individual amongst us is not only justified in forming his political sentiments, but may declare them with peculiar propriety.'[166]

At first glance letters seem to be just one of a crowd of election genres, like those listed on the title page of a 1784 collection: essays, songs, epigrams, cards, reasons, strictures, prophecies, letters, questions, answers, squibs, queries, addresses, replies, rejoinders &c. This list is printed in three columns, but whether you read them across or down, letters are in the centre like the best square in noughts and crosses. Moreover, letters had a certain decorum from their associations with print elsewhere. Though a raucous song on the street might metamorphose into a clever pastiche on the page, letters kept a more consistent value across different contexts. Consistency was important in elections where print was selectively used to oppose vocal din on the streets. On the other hand, print could spark fresh trouble as one group took exception to the terms another used to describe it. In Norfolk in 1784, an MP standing for re-election was punished by a reduced majority for blaming a stormy public meeting on the 'canaille' and their 'hissing, hooting, and other expressions of party madness'.[167] An anonymous letter to the freeholders soon followed with an indignant gloss of 'canaille':

> This it seems is a French word, signifying the *rabble, the rascally people*, the lowest, the basest, the dirtiest of mankind. Yet was this meeting composed of Norfolk *Freeholders*, once a respectable and respected body of men; and who now have sense and spirit enough to resent the insult; it sinks deep, and will not easily be obliterated.[168]

Part of the problem was that cheering caused as much uproar as jeering; 'order' and 'disorder' were hard to distinguish. In contrast, written cheers and jeers were clearer signs. That made mistakes harder to retract and comparisons easier to make. Nobody could heckle a letter – except by another letter.

Crucial to voters was the character of an MP – part personality, part principle. Tested through letters and speeches, candidates who asserted their independence could clear themselves of negative associations with corruption and placemen, but they risked alienating voters. In Norwich in 1784, William Windham misjudged the balance in his initial address:

> Scorning the mean arts of dissimulation, I have planted myself before the judgment of my friends, and the prejudices of my enemies, in open day. I may offend the unwary, and even the well disposed, but I cannot deceive them . . . as to popularity, I disdain to court it . . .[169]

This provoked many letters criticising his arrogance. A few defences were ventured: 'A Citizen' wrote, 'He has addressed you in terms not "high and haughty" but manly and open.'[170] More amusingly, some locals staged a comic version of *Coriolanus* which parodied Windham's pride (the performance was stopped in case it unduly influenced electors). Part of Windham's problem was that his fellow candidates were polite to the point of obsequiousness. As one, Sir Henry Hobart, wrote,

> Educated amongst you, long ambitious of conciliating your esteem, deriving also some degree of hope from the preference by which you have been pleased to distinguish our family in some remote, as well as more recent instances, and above all most respectably encouraged by my friends, I again address you for the favour of your VOTES and INTEREST at the ensuing election.[171]

Hobart's polished flattery was restrained compared to a candidate in an election in Bristol three years earlier who addressed voters in terms which could come straight from a love-letter: 'The singular tokens of esteem and confidence, with which I have been honored [sic] are my glory, and they impress me with every sentiment of gratitude and respect.'[172] A quasi-erotic discourse (we still talk of wooing voters) links politics to fiction through sensibility expressed in letter-writing.[173]

At elections, citizens asserted their power against oppressive class interests even as that power required them to choose someone whose ability to represent them partly turned on social difference. The candour and gratitude required from candidates in letters and speeches were shorthand for a discourse of conciliation that was important in elections but less relevant thereafter. The contradictions can be seen in a letter from 'A Baker' during the Bristol election of 1781:

> Mind your own business, be diligent, sober and thankful to those masters, merchants and others, who have never ceased to give you and

your families a comfortable living, and will still continue to do so. – See for yourselves, judge for yourselves and be no longer the dupes of designing men...[174]

Especially in the 1780s, sexual politics could stand in for tense class politics: like heroines, voters are prey to designing men. The Bible supplied a useful lingua franca – the Baker writes against an evil one who tempts voters into the error of liberty! But the Baker's advice of social quiescence and mental alertness showed how uneasily conservatives reconciled the electoral privilege of enquiry with not questioning their betters. Letters' mix of deference and self-expression fitted the restricted self-assertion of voters.

Comparing the Bristol elections of 1754 and 1781 reveals some differences in the parts played by letters. In 1754, the campaign turned on the candidates in ways that reflected agitation felt nationally over the 1753 Act (later repealed) to naturalise Jews. Agitation was expressed through open anti-semitism – at Cirencester, one correspondent tried to frighten voters with a prospect of a synagogue in the local landowner's park – but anxiety was also oblique.[175] In Bristol, it coalesced with anti-Catholicism and anti-Jacobitism to dominate the agenda. The candidates were Sir John Phillips, an old-style independent Tory landowner, and Richard Beckford (brother of William), who declared on a platform of encouragement of trade and opposition to the Jew Bill. They stood against Robert Nugent (later Earl Nugent), a political fixer who had done well under the current establishment and was also pro-trade. Beckford did not feature much. The real showdown was between Phillips and Nugent, carried on in a paper battle between their supporters. Phillips was unable to scotch a ludicrous rumour that he had worn a plaid waistcoat and hence was a Jacobite sympathiser; nor could he allay suspicions about his membership of a semi-secret society. Probing into these areas became so obsessive and frivolous that eventually Sir John wrote an exasperated letter of self-defence: the Sea-Serjeants Society provided innocent mirth for gentlemen from Wales; he had prosecuted anti-Jacobites, but because they had raised money illegally; he was emphatically not a Jacobite. 'And this Declaration I make only for the Sake of my Friends, who for want of knowing me better, might be induced to believe these Calumnies.'[176] But the teasing did not stop: a mock-vindication promptly appeared, clearing Sir John from having written that false apology which was obviously 'a *Jesuitical* Artifice to blast his Character'.[177] Nugent had problems too. Having supported the Jew Bill, he had to face wild claims about the general naturalisation of foreigners some feared would follow it and which would supposedly force the wages of Bristol voters '*below Two-pence a Day, and a* Clove *of Garlick*'.[178] Nugent had the support of some local politicians; churchmen, however, were suspicious.[179] The twists of religious argument were hardly rational. Nugent, a convert from Catholicism, might still be a Catholic; as an ex-Catholic, he was still associated with Catholicism, and as a friend to Jews and foreigners, was anti-Protestant. Phillips was a suppressor of anti-Jacobites, therefore pro-Jacobite and so pro-Catholic. Hence a bizarre conclusion: the ex-Catholic Nugent was anti-Protestant; the Protestant Sir John Phillips was pro-Catholic.

In their refusal to assume wholly serious discourses, letter-writers showed comedy's power to deflate complacency and to vent deep fears. Nicholas Rogers observes that 'The Bristol contest of 1754 turned out to be a raucous, scurrilous affair, full of party invective and caustic aspersions about caucus politics.'[180] Rogers' description does not quite fit the *epistolary* picture, which showed not the violence of political discourse but its inventive tenacity; for every letter from a 'William Plain', one from 'William Hint' would appear. Letters allowed voters to be *wittily* abusive. Populist persistence also characterised the 1781 election literature in Bristol. Political clubs played a greater role this time. After the ruinously expensive 1754 campaign, 'gentlemanly agreement became the order of the day'.[181] In 1781 it went too far: the Whig Union club proposed to the Tory White Lion club that they take turns to nominate candidates, which some voters resented as an infringement of their prerogative. Xenophobia had mutated from anti-French feeling (though one candidate, Daubeny, was said to be secretly French, D'Aubeny); now it was fear of American republicanism. Cruger, the Foxite candidate, was thought to be the author of a sympathetic letter to a republican in Philadelphia and published in newspapers there. This letter accused the English of being indifferent to liberty and happy in their supine vassalage.[182] It was neatly parodied by 'Yankee Doodle' in a letter which insulted the electorate and pleaded for their votes – an ironic treatment of the reversals of power in elections and election letters.

The question of whether Cruger had written this letter or (merely) posted it became a focus for different views on liberty. Another key means was through epistolary personae. Bristol's electorate included a large artisanal class and letters appeared as if from various journeymen. It is unlikely that the Shoemaker, Carpenter, Pipemaker, Sailmaker, Cooper, Hatter and Barber were all actual journeymen; still, they sounded like voters rather than party hacks. The purpose of these letters was to warn each other of attempts to cheat them out of proofs of their right to vote; to make being pro-American republicanism an equivalent of being anti-British trade, and to imply that workers' interests were better served by gradual self-advancement than by class revolution. As a Journeyman Shoemaker put it, 'it is by honest industry alone that we can be truly independent, for by that we may become in time masters ourselves'.[183] Insofar as this discourse put change in the hands of the people, it was radical; insofar as it made changing their condition a matter of joining a more propertied class, it was conservative.

These texts anticipate Hannah More's political writings in the next decade: she lived in the Bristol area and must have known these discourses aimed at that same constituency of 'honest poor' with which she was so concerned. There are clear resemblances between these letters and *Village Politics*, a dialogue between a blacksmith and a mason ostensibly written by a carpenter, Will Chip.[184] A Journeyman Shoemaker, for instance, uses Aesop's fable in which limbs rebel against a body that by starving them makes them weak, so 'being thereby made sensible of their folly, chearfully returned to their labour again'.[185] That Hannah More uses the same strike-breaking fable is not in itself conclusive – Aesop's fables were widely read – but she too uses it to preface a reminder to the poor that ' 'tis working, and not murmuring, which puts bread in our children's mouths' and that 'few are so poor but they may get a vote for a parliament-man; and so you see the poor have as much share in the government as they know well how to manage'.[186] Forelock-tugging in letters in Bristol elections shows the democratic significance of letters: 'I AM a plain man, not used much to writing, and may not express myself very properly; yet I hope you will indulge a working man, in a few words to his fellow tradesmen.'[187] It is not that defiance makes a persona authentic (and Whig activists may equally well have written in journeymen personae), but deference to epistolary conventions of apology shown by these Tory-inclined personae functions very conveniently as a form of class deference. Via plain-speaking but with that hesitation supposed to be proper as the plain approach the polite, these personae promote letters as a form of persuasion opposed to Whig force. As a Journeyman Hatter puts it,

> I love freedom as well as any man, being a true Englishman; but whilst my comrades talk of it they will knock a man down, or ruin him, if he dares take the freedom of thinking of it in any other manner...these liberty-boys argue best with a clinched fist or a short stick.[188]

A constituency that normally inclined to the Whigs supposedly reports its disillusion; class-based epistolary personae are used to break up class-based politics.

The same double pull between the pleasures of fiction and ideological conviction can be seen in mock-letters. Mock-genres generally were popular in election literature, with mock-advertisements in particular supplying some of the best jokes. Especially popular were letters from Jesuits or Popes expressing joy that their underhand campaigning for Tory candidates was proving successful (or dismay if not). Here a language of excess associated with parody was reinforced by languages of excess associated with Catholicism and the effusive thanks of election candidates. So the Bristol Tories supposedly replied to Pope Pius VI, ' 'TIS not in the power of language to express the exquisite raptures we felt on the sense of the unspeakable honour conferred on us by your very acceptable and superexcellent epistle.'[189] Such letters were obvious spoofs but since letter-writers in elections really were diverse, they were comically not impossible. As Freud observed, jokes often turn on a clash of discourses.

Besides comedy, letter-writers used pathos. In the Westminster election of 1784, the usual personae were busy: A True Briton, An Impartial Elector, A Free Citizen, An Independent Elector and so on. At the end of the campaign, John Churchill, who was chairman of the committee for electing Lord Hood and Sir Cecil Wray, Fox's opponent, published an appeal for donations to pay for a scrutiny of results. His appeal elicited a reply from one Tim Flanagan: 'I AM a very poor chairman too, as well as yourself; and God knows I stand in as much need of public charity.'[190] With a starving family and an injured back, he represents the unskilled, voteless Irish labourer whose limbs supported aristocratic chairmen in more ways than one. Elections do not alleviate his poverty, but he is as meek as Hannah More might wish: 'all I would *axe* and desire is, that you will think of my distress, and put my name down with Lord Hood and Sir Cecil Wray's, for some little share of that same collection you are going to have'. The pun is surreal rather than witty: a chairman who wants political donations meets, in letters, a chairman who needs a charitable donation. This election was full of financial issues – questions of taxes and corruption, of Fox's large debts, of the East India Company's profits – hence this epistolary comedy is also serious in its appeal to remember less literate citizens. An Irish joke about miscomprehension becomes a way of including the voice of the poor.

Political dynasty made families self-evidently part of the public sphere. The 'family interest' of so much eighteenth-century politics kept the world of fathers, sons and brothers visible in public life; it also muddied distinctions between family business and public record. Letters were crucial in stirring and settling the waters, for instance in Shrewsbury in 1795 when a controversy arose between two uncles and a nephew as to who should be MP. This story stars the colourful Sir Richard Hill who with his brother John, the MP for Shrewsbury, was an executor for his young cousin, the Hon. William Hill, who now wanted to stand for Parliament without waiting for a general election. The plot turned on whether John Hill had promised William's father Lord Berwick that he would give up the seat when one of his sons came of age. All parties had to tread carefully since it was a country-wide axiom that 'A Seat in the House of COMMONS is NO MAN's INHERITANCE.'[191] Whatever the realities of pocket boroughs, it was impolitic to put them on paper. Sir Richard, who had an earlier career as a theological controversialist, denounced his nephew as a Biblical prodigal – 'O Absalom my son, my son!!!'[192] – and a Gothic villain. Both the Hill family and the town of Shrewsbury were in danger:

> that restless spirit of ambition or envy, or both united, after having been long undermining and working underground, forming secret combinations and alliances, yet hardly daring to stalk abroad, except by night, as if ashamed that the sun should be witness to its transactions,

having now thrown off all disguise and restraint, appears under a thousand hideous forms...[193]

This combination of the Monk and Frankenstein's monster was a youth of smooth address and sly civility.[194] In the epistolary battle between himself and John Hill, William lamented that his uncle has introduced 'into our correspondence, the too frequent, but unnecessary, ill temper and illiberality of election controversy' and insisted his own letters showed 'no traces, I flatter myself, either of ill humour or ill manners'.[195] John Hill, though no great rhetorician, seized on William Hill's mannerist concession that his pen was unfledged to ask his readers whether his genius might be too unfledged to cope with Parliament. He also deflected criticism of his letters: if the glitteringly oratorical nephew considered his style to be 'long verbose *leaden periods* void of grace',[196] it was because he could not appreciate plainness. Both men were careful to insult each other's letters; their texts both are and are not themselves.

Sir Richard published these public letters as an appendix to his own denunciation, but someone else then published a supplement of 'elegant extracts', which turned out to be the most abusive bits from both uncles' letters. Few stones were unturned: old correspondence in which Sir Richard professed affection to Lord Berwick was exhibited as hypocritical in the light of recent events, as if public integrity depended on epistolary consistency across seven years. This text, clearly authorised if not authored by William Hill, was sarcastic about the 'rage militaire' of Sir Richard's letters and tried to nail John Hill, quoting as undemocratic his expression in a letter to Lord Berwick, ' "I am WITH YOUR PERMISSION, *likely to become member for Salop."* '[197] The author is nervous about whether Lord Berwick's reply sounds too seigneurial – he *thought* it *possible* that John Hill *might* stand – but the proprietorial suggestion of a joint candidacy is masked over by comments on epistolary style. The correspondence

> passed in private from a young man to his relation. It was written in confidence, and without the most distant idea of laying it before the public. This circumstance will at once apologise, if any apology be necessary, for inaccuracy of expression, or carelessness of composition...It is well for Sir Richard, if his private letters will stand the test of public scrutiny with so little disadvantage to their author...[198]

Textuality soaked up political irritants. John Hill's physical rejection of the letter shows its substitutive power: 'He threw it on the table with rudeness and indignation, demanding an explanation of the word *coalesce.*' The indelicacy of producing family letters to insult a senior family member is made an ingenious though again nervous excuse for the text's anonymity.

Besides the family letters about election prospects, an important role was played by a conversation between Sir Richard and a local gentleman, Edward Burton, the details of which were also contested by letters. According to Burton, they had spent a Sunday together in the course of which they discussed John Hill's alleged promise to stand down for his nephew. Sir Richard disputed Burton's version of events and Burton substantiated it, in letters expressive and evidential: these added to arguments about temperament and suggested how people corresponded was indicative of their honesty. Sir Richard had to apologise for misquoting one of Burton's letters: by a Freudian slip, this devotee of literary warfare turned Burton's claim that when violently attacked we must defend ourselves, into when violently attacked we must violently defend ourselves. When Burton pointed this out, Sir Richard breezily dismissed it as irrelevant, the consequence of writing in a great hurry. Insisting that the letter was not *printed* in a great hurry, Burton eventually secured a grudging retraction. Sir Richard sneered at Burton, an anal type who kept notes of conversations in his pocketbook, whereas he relied on memory. Unfortunately his powers of recollection were as foggy as Oliver North's and he was careless with texts. John Hill, less literary but more politic, patched up his differences with Burton through carefully punctilious letters which were also carefully publicised.[199]

The fusion of family quarrels with political differences made commentators remember civil war: 'Vollies of rancour, malice and envy were fired off, and many were wounded in the conflict. Fathers, sons, brothers, friends, were enlisted on either side, and every social bond broken or destroyed.'[200] Letter-writing between citizens was important in establishing communities of interest and connecting them; equally important was the process of agreeing readings. Political communities, like other imagined communities, identify themselves through difference from others. In doing so, they probed character and family in ways that show letters melting distinctions between public and private, and carrying political heat into contexts simultaneously domestic and national.

The excise crisis

Like elections, the excise crisis shows how politicians and citizens understood the uses of letters and how letters in politics were publicly debated. The excise crisis of 1733 is well known in the history of high politics; it has its own definitive study.[201] My aim is to recover the literary specificity of letters, which has been overlooked in generalisations about 'sources', or what one historian discussing the excise crisis refers to as 'A plethora of printed material'.[202] I choose this case of policy making and unmaking because it shows arguments about the nature of government; it is also one important example, among many, of how political moments were shaped by letters. 'It was the Theme of Coffee-Houses, Taverns, and Gin-Shops, the

Discourse of Artificers, the Cry of the Streets, the Entertainment of Lacquies, the Prate of Wenches, and the Bugbear of Children.'[203] If the excise crisis was universally a topic of discussion, it was also a time when reading and writing took on ideological heat. Literacy was both important and imperfect in this struggle: as a pro-excise writer put it, 'It was common to hear Men, otherwise very reasonable Men, declare that they would read nothing on t'other Side. What wonder then if the Vulgar and the Many were totally bewitched?'[204] With political tides running across class lines, the literacy that traditionally separated gentlemen from mob had to be reimagined.

According to Paul Langford, 'The excise crisis is an outstanding example of the whole political nation at work',[205] including women and children. It is important to remember that one (larger) part was working against Robert Walpole's proposed extension of excise duties and one (smaller) part was working for it. It is also important to remember that much of this work was textual, ensuring written arguments reached people. Not all these writings were epistolary but letters were critical in three respects: as the form chosen by Walpole to defend his policy to the public; as letters of instructions to MPs, and as a genre in which resentments about the failure of 'proper' reading practices were expressed.

The literature showed uncertainty about how far public opinion was scriptive and how far oral. One might read a pamphlet but still be 'deaf' to its argument. Terms of speech in titles pressed their claim to be *vox populi*: an appeal, an advocate, a word to, an answer to, join the usual inquiry, considerations, observations and review. Letters, already associated with conversation and with print, featured on both sides. They served special interest groups afraid that new excise duties would harm their business, like a distiller who published pessimistic projections in detail in the form of a letter to an MP. Letters also served to express general indignation at the excise's potential encroachment of civil liberties, principally from the 'army' of excise officers who would have to collect it. The excise campaign created unlikely coalitions between landed gentry and merchants, leaving anti-excise freeholders to berate Walpole and his scribes for addressing the gentry

> as if they took them for a Mob, an *unthinking, inconsiderate* Mob, and treat them with such Arguments of *private* Gain and Interests, distinct from those of the Publick in general, as would hardly be capable to influence the *very meanest* of the Populace *itself.*[206]

In fact that public appeal which contemporaries assumed was written by Walpole himself was very careful about class. It was set out as a letter to friends in the country, projecting an audience sympathetic yet not well informed thanks to their unavoidable distance from the truth. It also set itself up as a reply, expressing surprise and concern at the constituency's unhappiness about the excise plan, and evoking a fiction of dialogue with it. This courtesy slips with the suggestion that their letter looks like a copy of an advertisement sponsored by wine and tobacco merchants, but this is a temperate lapse of tact given that elsewhere Walpole complained frankly that 'The most part of the people concerned in those clamours did not speak their own sentiments, they were played by others like so many puppets.'[207] Walpole uses an epistolary premise of mutual interest to work back to a common ground of basic political theory on which both sides can agree: 'IT might look pedantick in me', and it is 'unnecessary to men of your under-standings', but he explains nonetheless how taxes are necessary not evil since they pay for governments to protect people from injuries, which he then illustrates.[208] The case is carefully suggestive: 'let me suppose a case which may happen'; the new excise on wine will prevent adulteration which endangers public health. But the temptation to score political points by insulting his political opponents proved irresistible and the postscript became a to-the-moment response to an attack in *The Craftsman* the previous week. The voice of reason was after all the voice of spleen; as one respondent noted amusingly,

> Methinks I see you in your Closet, while you are writing this elegant Passage, knitting your brows and muttering to your self...you immediately drop the smooth, cajoling Style, and losing all your Temper at once, call every Body about you, JACOBITES and REPUBLICANS.[209]

Epistolary inconsistency was interpreted to be a sign of Walpole's ultimate indifference to public opinion.

Many constituencies sent tough letters of instructions to their MPs with orders to vote against the Bill, using various epistolary arm-twists. An MP in Kent was sent a report from a local farmer bullied by an excise officer even before the new laws were in force. The town of Woodstock tried menace: if excise officers increased, the town would not be free to elect their MP again. The town of Reading started with modern science: 'You, Sir, like a good Physician, will oppose the very Beginning of a Disease' and shifted aetiology of the body politic into Hobbesian prophecy: 'we need not remind you of the prenicious [sic] Consequences from this overgrown Monster, this great LEVIATHAN, the EXCIZE, nor need we urge how sensible our Ancestors were of the dreadful Effects it would bring forth'.[210] MPs tried various stalling tactics – they could not promise to vote either way until they knew the Bill's exact terms, or until they were sure the people's apprehensions were well founded. The Corporation of Colchester was one body unimpressed by such wriggling: 'Nothing in your Answer hath in the Least alter'd our Thoughts; and if you vote for a Bill of that Nature...you can't reasonably expect our Approbation.'[211] These correspondences were published in national and local papers, but questions arose as to how representative they were. As Paul Langford discusses, some were contested. In Rochester, the mayor and the corporation were at odds; there was also 'a tendency for merchants to pass themselves off as representative of the general feeling of their town, especially where they lacked the support of their municipal corporation'.[212] The difficulty of defining public opinion became more acute when what people wrote claimed to speak for non-writing groups and when opinions were wilfully misrepresented. In the end, Walpole withdrew his proposals, but the arguments rumbled on. One writer of a letter purporting to be from an MP to a Lord exploited the social equality of correspondence to be freely scathing about popular misconceptions. The Lord, an ex-MP, is metaphorically in proximity to the MP, though removed from the action; they are neighbours in the country, supposedly. The MP argues in detail that excise officers would have had no new powers, but it is too late; 'The Thing was lost for not being generally understood',[213] and because the literate have misled the illiterate. The people 'only listened to their own Fears and to the Voice of Clamour'.[214] The author can denounce electors' stupidity without giving direct affront and can salve a political defeat by reworking a class alliance between gentry and aristocracy, MP and Lord.

This MP saw losing the argument as a case of orality overpowering literacy. The excise crisis had in fact occasioned an intense print campaign. The Post Office withheld newspapers from the ministry's opponents and supplied names of coffee houses who were then sent papers to display.[215] Private families also received mailshots. People complained that 'the *Post-Office* was never before prostituted in such a Manner'.[216] The opposition, who also used newspapers, devised equally inventive ways to reach readers:

> Little *Hand Bills* were dispersed by thousands all over the City and Country, put into Peoples [sic] Hands in the Streets and Highways, dropped at their Doors, and thrown in at their Windows; all asserting that Excise-men were (like a foreign Enemy) going to invade and devour them.

Letters insinuated themselves into liminal space as if imitating the invasiveness of excise-men; methods of delivery became politicised. To the terms politics indoors and out of doors one might add politics through the window and the post box.

Writing as a citizen meant participating in a culture of letter-writing that had a widely recognised power to represent, misrepresent and contest political processes. Readers became sophisticated, even cynical, about politicians' use of printed and unprinted letters. Shades of publicity in their authorised and unauthorised disclosure made letters an index of the fiction of the transparency of government. These nuances inform the London Corresponding Society's choice of a name, more than the necessity of letter-writing arising from a prohibition on meeting. Writing as a citizen was nominally a socially inclusive practice. Yet the body politic, as in Aesop's fable, included members at odds with each other. Their co-existence and competition was articulated through letters as a medium of new political force in the eighteenth century. A significant part of newspapers and a staple of political life, letter-writing gave the public a sense of itself even as it demonstrated that 'public opinion' was rarely homogenous. It helped sketch in a cultural background of the civic good and national identity through the personae of old Romans and others. Epistolary costuming resembles masquerading but can be compared to a more specifically political dressing up. This was perhaps most visible in Whig circles in the later eighteenth century, in the buff and blue colours borrowed from Washington's army which became a Whig badge, almost a uniform. It was also evident in the strange and practical gear worn by men high up in government who won and lost fortunes at Brooks's club. These serious gamblers, who included Charles James Fox, put on heavy coats, leather sleeve-guards, high-crowned hats adorned with flowers and masks.[217] They could be seen through the window by passing members of the public: disguised, purposive, serious about play. Their appearance creates a powerful image for the worldly yet slightly surreal effect of epistolary personae, the period's most characteristic form of writing as a citizen.

6
Writing as a Traveller

Letters played a major part in eighteenth-century travel writing. Many kinds of letters presume a geographical separation between writer and addressee which is akin to the distance involved in travel; as Donna Landry observes, 'the letter writer is always travelling, explicitly through time, and either explicitly or implicitly across space'.[1] This chapter explores issues germane to travel writing with reference to letters as one of its most significant forms. This means crossing some familiar critical territory but seeking epistolary landmarks. The chapter starts with a discussion of imaginary travellers, mostly Far- and Near-Eastern personae, since one of the most popular uses for *epistolary* travel writing was to present not accounts of 'abroad' but critiques of 'home' seen through the eyes of supposed foreigners. These foreign personae were shaped by ideas of the East tangled up with real travellers' tales in ways that defy separation into fiction and non-fiction.[2] That travel writing combined empiricism and fantasy was understood at the time. It was common for travel writers to disparage predecessors for inaccuracy;[3] it was also common for writers to invent for their own ends. Travel metaphors mediated new or strange concepts:

> I shall carry at first a heavy trot through rough unbeaten ways, entertaining you unpolitely, with Discourse quite foreign to your way of Thinking; such as passed in Correspondence between me and a Friend...In the Progress of our Travels (which I honestly must tell you, will only touch upon, not terminate in, Fairyland) I shall carry you into an unknown Country, where everything is real, bright, and transporting...[4]

The protective relationship between addressee and letter-writer licensed discomfort in the cause of exploration. Letters moved readers easily between realms of myth, lands of fable and real countries; letters in personae fused and confused national identities.

My second section discusses letters by British writers on their travels, especially around Europe. Beginning with an analysis of those formal properties of letters that made them a key genre for travel-writing, I then discuss discourses of identity. Letters suggest that variations *within* the self are as much in evidence as differentiation from others, and the notion of 'otherness' needs to be read alongside consideration of relationships with addressees. My argument is not that affinities between letter-writer and addressee made letters a vehicle of cultural similarity – rather, that cultural similarity between letter-writer and addressee made letters a space in which people could test their identities. Travel puts identity in motion; letters were a genre that allowed the borders of self to be renegotiated. Letters were not simply a medium for establishing cultural difference, but for questioning it, qualifying it, overcoming it, updating it and erasing it.

Both sections of this chapter show letters in the service of complex identifications. Philosophers in the republic of letters critiqued nationalism and European complacency through mask-like personae. Travellers' letters show enquiry testing prejudice and familiar frames of identity dissolved by cultural difference. Both sections show how letters enabled travellers to look outward to the world and inward to themselves when trying to comprehend cultures. Inward and outward are terms that show yet again a dynamic of public and private is misplaced in relation to letters.

Oriental gentlemen

The frontispiece to Edward Young's *The Centaur Not Fabulous* (1755) shows a centaur standing with a woman, a harlequin, a Chinaman, a Turk and some musicians on the edge of an abyss, at the bottom of which are some lost-looking souls. The centaur represents profligates, in whom brutish pleasures run away with human attributes, and the text deplores sins in vogue in Britain, like infidelity and luxury. The illustration brings popular characters together. The Near and Far Eastern characters' proximity to the woman suggests the effeminacy of orientalism; the proximity of all three to the harlequin and musicians makes sexual and cultural difference performative. The contingency of gender, race and theatricality invites the assumption that the spectator is, in contrast, white, polite, male and heterosexual – like Addison and Steele's prototype Spectator, although this assumption is just that – an assumption. In the context of a moral fable, the figures represent the instability of women, foreigners and performers; in the context of travel fiction they represent the difficulty of separating deception from perception, which makes otherness entertaining and challenging. As Young puts it towards the end of the book, 'Man is the most noble study of man/ To himself he is a Theatre immense.'[5] Shades of difference in the typology of characters, however, show there were precise scripts to be acted.

Letters cross-fertilised philosophy and satire in eighteenth-century travel writing. Shaftesbury imagined an Ethiopian transported to Paris or Venice at carnival time and mistaking people's masks for European complexions.

Europeans may laugh at this reading, he writes, but the joke rebounds on them because they are the people who have invested in surface, by adopting masks.[6] The relationship between nature and art, skin and mask, stands in for a relationship between nature and culture in which 'civilisation' is relative. One cannot change skin colour but one can mask it. Race does not exactly disappear as the guarantor of culture – the Europeans are still 'fair' underneath – but it disappears from view temporarily. Cultural difference thus becomes open to interrogation through relativity. Representation rather than race becomes the site of culture: so Voltaire imagined a Chinese man in a European bookshop enquiring after a volume titled *Universal History* which proves to say nothing about Chinese history. Since Voltaire was the author of a work with that title, his criticism of Europeans' complacency, their inability to imagine a universe beyond Europe, is comic. His irony, however, is universalised: the Chinese man wants the book to read about his own culture. All civilisations naturalise their own limitations, Voltaire implies, but some more than others.[7] It was one of the purposes of epistolary personae to expose the limitations closest to home. For some critics now, the persona is a threadbare device: 'the foreigners were little more than . . . enlightened Europeans in exotic dress'.[8] I agree personae can be clichés, but their function in epistolary travel writing shows many were intriguing and culturally significant acts of costuming.

Epistolary personae functioned like masks, distracting from essentialist issues of skin. It could be said that masks can only function as a denotative surface when racial community can be assumed – that is, white people dressed up in oriental costume because they were not Orientals and because they did not anticipate oriental people being present at their masquerade or carnival. White has been naturalised as a colour to the point where it seems colourless: 'whiteness as race resides in invisible properties and whiteness as power is maintained by being unseen'.[9] Europeans writing in Eastern personae do not anticipate readers mistaking them for Orientals; there always remains an awareness that this is a game. To use Homi Bhabha's phrase, the persona is *'Almost the same but not white'*.[10] But although impersonation may involve a confidently colonialist appropriation of otherness, it does so for ends not usually recognised as within an occidental outlook: to critique the mindset that assumes West is best. It is true that oriental personae were related to countries like China that were not colonies of the West and one should note that the power to expose Western shortcomings is manifested through Asian and Arab characters – not white, but not black either.[11] Where colonial discourse construes colonised peoples as degenerate on the basis of racial origins,[12] epistolary personae use stereotypical characters from non-colonised cultures as plausible critics of European mores. Bhabha observes that 'the stereotype is a complex, ambivalent, contradictory mode of representation', which in colonial discourse involves fear and desire, phobia and fetish.[13] Personae do not deploy these polarisations; rather, they set in motion a relativity whose ambiguities involve reason as well as emotion. Even so, they fit some aspects of Bhabha's model of colonial mimicry: 'mimicry is like camouflage, not a harmonisation of repression of difference, but a form of resemblance' that produces 'an erratic, eccentric strategy of authority'.[14] Even as they critique the mindset that assumes West is best, impersonations through personae reinstate Enlightenment values by promoting Europe as a civilisation that can be improved. Belief in amelioration distinguishes them from that other antithesis to a corrupted Western civilisation, the noble savage.

The geographical distance between China and Europe provided an obvious spatial metaphor for cultural difference:

> How would a Chinese, bred up in the formalities of an eastern court, be regarded, should he carry all his good manners beyond the Great Wall? How would an Englishman, skilled in all the decorums of western good breeding, appear at an eastern entertainment? Would he not be reckoned more fantastically savage than even his unbred footman![15]

Yet intellectually the Chinese could be counted on: they were 'curious in their Enquiries, penetrative in their Observations and sagacious in their Judgments'.[16] Goldsmith discarded a Turk or Persian character for his Citizen of the World because 'A Chinese ... being equally advanced in the scale of civilisation, could pass an opinion on all he saw better than the native of a more barbarous community.'[17] The Chinese persona was always male, which reinforced its associations with reason and philosophy. European incomprehension of religion in China led to a stress on Confucian philosophy which supplied the gloss of moral seriousness necessary to satire. The *general* tenor of this system, moreover, allowed writers to invoke it in general ways. Charles Johnston's *The Pilgrim*, for instance, is subtitled simply 'a Picture of Life.'[18]

Eastern personae were especially popular around the mid-eighteenth century as writers joined a vogue for chinoiserie. 'The furniture, frippery and fireworks of China have long been fashionably bought up. I'll try the fair with a small cargoe of Chinese morality.'[19] The attraction of personae was not novelty – in any case pre-empted by the Marquis D'Argens' *Lettres Chinoises*[20] – but the pleasures of self-conscious fiction. Where personal correspondence was often anxious about egotism, philosophical travel letters exaggerated writers' self-estrangement into mannered fictions. 'The Chinese are often dull' declared Goldsmith's Editor self-parodically, criticizing one letter of his own letters for being 'little more than a rhapsody of sentences borrowed from Confucius'.[21] The Far East seemed able to enlighten the West, but also to frustrate or disappoint it, an uncertain familiarity that fits Bhabha's observation on mimicry: 'Like the mirror phase "the fullness" of the stereotype – its image *as* identity – is always threatened by "lack".'[22] *The Monthly Review* grumbled that there was nothing Asiatic about *The Citizen of the World*. Goldsmith's absence of local colour was conscious: 'what signifies what am I?' asked the Citizen of the World and Johnston's Pilgrim likewise declared, 'As for myself, I am a perfect blank among them.'[23] It has been suggested that chinoiserie offers a surface aesthetic that 'tends to...evacuate any suggestion of a viable foreign subjectivity'.[24] Emptiness of the oriental persona gave fullness to something else – not the occidental satirist as an individual but a textual community of author and reader through letter-writing.

A sense of China as an imperial society was useful for writers who wished to venture beyond classical models. There were overlaps: significantly, Goldsmith included part of a real travel letter describing Chinese students making excellent Latin orations.[25] Confidence in Britain as an international power was expressed through the device of a foreign observer not simply for complacently patriotic ends but also to explore possibilities of global utopia implicit in the Enlightenment. The Pilgrim, for example, surveyed the resources of a British shipyard, marvelled at its indications of power but concluded in despair:

> Good Heaven! what beneficient purposes might be served by a right application of the treasure expended here for the destruction of the human kind? My soul sickens at the thought. I no longer admire a power so horridly abused.[26]

Though the alien subject voiced alienated opinions, epistolary personae worked more for dialectic than heresy, inviting readers to respond with reasoned debate. Through identification with addressees, readers were disassociated from national origins, making it easier to call prejudices into question. Epistolary form therefore helped defamiliarise the European world whilst simultaneously hardening fictional conventions of orientalist outlook.

The supposed vagaries of post to so distant a destination as China allowed for even greater disconnection between topics than usual. *The Citizen of the World*'s 119 letters were not initially numbered, so probably not planned as a series when they first appeared in the *Public Ledger* in 1760 and 1761. Like periodical essays they addressed a wide range of topics, using allegory, narratives, anecdotes, didactic tales, histories, sermons, satire, ethical essays, philosophy and social commentary. Goldsmith's subtitle, *Letters from a Chinese Philosopher, residing in London, to his Friends in the East*, indicates the race, place and discourse of the letter-writer; like many real travel letters, it promises a proper empiricism derived from the sustained observation of a resident. It also counters the limited horizons of a static observer by its metropolitan location and its cosmopolitan conjunction of writer and subject cultures. The Chinese writer critiques English customs sometimes openly, sometimes implicitly, and sometimes by accepting them at face value. The reader supplies that irony which undercuts Lien Chi's enthusiasm for English medicine, for example: 'Few physicians have to go through the ordinary courses of education, but receive all their knowledge of medicine by immediate inspiration from heaven.'[27] Comic naïvety depends on erasing cultural difference – so Lien Chi assumes that because in China the great retinue of a Mandarin is always a mark of great respect, the same must be true in England. The joke invites readers to relativise in a double perspective: because it is not the case in England that those with large retinues are always respected, it may well not be the case in China either. 'The truth is, the Chinese and we are pretty much alike.'[28]

In reality, truth seemed relative even to those otherwise committed to absolutes. One Jesuit missionary, who became as Chinese as his race and religion allowed, wrote to his father of the efforts of assuming this new identity: 'The Usages and Customs of this Empire are so different from ours, that an *European* must quite new mould himself, as it were, in order to become a perfect Chineze.'[29] In a short, influential satire of 1757, Horace Walpole insisted that the Chinese and English were not alike. Xo Ho looks blankly on the English because they are incomprehensible: 'There is no Rule for judging of this People . . . I do not understand this Nation.'[30] Walpole satirises English practices as straightforwardly astonishing to an intelligent observer. He targets topical crises such as the execution of Admiral Byng and the lack of a ministry – 'can the King of *England* unmake his Ministers and not make them? Truly I know not how that is'[31]– though he also points to general mysteries, like why the English call chilly weather summer. His defamiliarising requires the reader to exert reason in puzzling over a known process or object made strange; it focuses attention on the rationality, or lack of it, in politics, and on the role of cultural difference in relativising reason. 'Reason in *China* is not Reason in *England*', Xo Ho declares.[32] Implicit harmony between personal correspondents contrasted with other social relations, especially the chaos and deceit of political faction.

Eastern personae flourished in the wake of Montesquieu's *Lettres Persanes*, translated as *Persian Letters* in 1722.[33] Sixty years later John Andrews was still recommending it to travellers on both literary and moral grounds, claiming that 'all the sensible people in Europe were charmed with that ingenious review of the manners and notions of the times, and with those instructive and well-founded strictures, with which it is so judiciously interposed'.[34] Readers were charmed by both the fiction and its transparency. Its ideological reversibility – Europe as corrupt and worth improving – was especially visible in matters of religion. Notions of Mahometanism as a strict religion associated Moors and Turks with probity whilst their reputation for barbarism assumed a familiarity with cruelty that made their responses to European injustice all the more forceful. On the other hand, religious difference could be used to praise the benefits of Christian toleration, more evident in

England than elsewhere in Europe, according to many writers: 'The Principles and Practice of Toleration prevail very strongly in this Country: I myself have felt the effects of it very much to my Advantage', as one 'Persian' put it.[35]

Reversability became more ambivalent on the question of liberty, one of the central themes of eighteenth-century travel writing. Foreigners could not be assumed to be familiar with the usual terms of debate so arguments had to be made afresh. The letters of Lyttleton's Persian are prefaced by a declaration that *'they are certainly the Work of a perfect Stranger. The Observations are so* Foreign *and* out of the Way ... *that it is hardly possible any* Englishman *shou'd be the Author'*.[36] In part a standard joke about fictionality and its pathways to *a priori* positions, the persona also makes a serious claim to be freer from bias than a native: 'it is plain the Man who wrote them is a Lover of Liberty; and must be suppos'd more impartial than our Countrymen when they speak of their own admir'd Customs, and favourite Opinions'.[37] This disclaimer of national prejudice signals distance from party politics. Lyttleton's survey of contemporary life in fact takes an emphatically Whig view of political institutions past and present. Several letters discuss the British constitution, its strengths and weaknesses, especially corruption. Paradox is paramount: 'All the Electors swear not to *sell* their Voices, yet many of the Candidates are undone by the Expence of *buying them.*'[38] Like Horace Walpole, Lyttleton uses orientalism to defamiliarise politics; cultural otherness ironically becomes neutral. Or rather, racial otherness becomes a cipher which turns otherwise familiar political parties and arguments into something culturally other. The effect is not apolitical since the estrangement leaves readers more open to the persona's direction. Lyttleton's criticism of the excise crisis of Robert Walpole's administration in 1733 and his more general view of government had partisan implications not lost on an anonymous Tory. This writer appropriated Lyttleton's persona to serve his own agenda, barefacedly acknowledging the Persian's volte-face: 'I see no Reason why I may not bring my *Selim* back to his Senses, and let him retain a due Regard for *Monarchy.*'[39] Eastern mystification could be reconverted to Eastern autocracy.

The Persian Letters Continued interleaved rebuttal of Lyttelton's arguments with a romance, the history of Hyempsal, King of Numidia, which Selim's wife wishes him to send to Persian ladies. The inclusion of romance imitates Montesquieu,[40] but other factors are also at work. First, commercial: romance was market-tested. Eastern sensuality made courtly intrigue novel by removing it to a setting simultaneously strange and recognisably erotic. The epistolary reader's role of confidant became more exotically voyeuristic. The formulaic floweriness of supposedly Eastern rhetoric was also helpful to writers in a hurry, as this one admitted he was; thus Goldsmith complained it was a maxim that every Oriental 'must express himself in metaphor; swear by Alla, rail against wine'.[41] Second, as Ros Ballaster has convincingly shown, intricate relations between parliamentary politics and sexual politics in this period doubled fiction's discursive functions.[42] In Selim's case, pro-monarchy arguments are supported by the heroics of a King of Numidia. Romance also draws attention to codes of reading that link travel letters to other letters. An orientalist frame supposes revelations – the West turned inside-out, the mysterious East divulged – mirrored in epistolary fiction's manifestations of confession or disclosure.[43]

At their simplest, Near-Eastern personae were figures of wisdom.[44] More complexly, like spies, they communicated secrets.[45] Legitimate observation was close to covert investigation, especially that obtained by associating with suspected wrongdoers.[46] A role as ciphers was reassuring since by seeming to pass on only information, orientalist personae avoided some troubling issues of language which their stagily literary idiom could not fully absorb. Many of these texts express anxiety about political oratory and its power to seduce and corrupt. Lyttleton, for instance, spends three letters on the proposition that politicians' eloquence damages the constitution.[47] Hence political writers were attracted to romance which had well-established admonitions about the duplicity of men's amorous language. Letters were useful here, suiting equally affairs of state and the heart. However, segregation of the sexes in the East made men-only spaces for oriental personae to explore truth-telling between men. *The Life of Cassem* declared in its preface, 'The bold metaphors and noble simplicity almost peculiar to the Orientals add a lustre to their compositions, not to be rival'd by the greatest orators of Greece and Rome.'[48] Eastern oratory is civic, public and part of world history.[49] A subjoining letter from Cassem to his preceptor, however, also characterised by 'oriental simplicity', is personalised: it 'contains his most private sentiments, which he freely unbosoms to his friend'.[50] Truth-telling was confirmed through epistolary form supported by masculinity.

Besides the 'promiscuity and violence (or cruelty) [which] eventually established themselves in Western eyes as the main characteristics of all Muslims',[51] Turks and Arabs from the north coast of Africa (including 'Barbary') were associated with sodomy.[52] Horace Walpole exchanged his usual masquerade outfit, women's dress, for a Persian outfit in order to deliver a risqué letter to his old flame Lord Lincoln. He 'bowed three times and knelt at his feet, with a letter written on a long sheet of red paper, folded and wrapped in silk, balanced on his head'.[53] Lincoln was persuaded to read this letter to the company. In the persona of Thamas Kouli Kan Schah Nadir of Ispahan, Walpole sarcastically celebrated Lord Lincoln's heterosexual potency, ending 'May thy days be as long as thy manhood'. Orientalism naturalises the single homoerotic relationship though epistolary intimacy and collective homosocial discourse through epistolary reportage.

Eighteenth-century British writers directed plentiful satire at Italian castrati but were more coy about the emasculation of eunuchs.[54] Though they distanced themselves from what they figured as the rampant masculinism of seraglios, epistolary personae allowed them to indulge misogyny.[55] Early to mid-eighteenth-century writers tended to contrast, often satirically, European women's opportunities for sexual choice, both in and outside marriage, with Eastern women's situation as objects of polygamy. As Lyttleton's Selim put it,

> THERE is nothing more astonishing to a Mussleman than many Particulars relating to the State of Matrimony, as it is managed in *Europe*: Our Practice of it is so totally different, that we can hardly think it possible for Men to do or suffer such Things as happen here every Day.[56]

The pose of astonishment allowed masculine fantasies of the overlap between Eastern potentates and sexual potency to co-exist with celebrations of English women's freedom. Such a double-edged view in the extensive debate about how free English women really were or should be was challenged by Lady Mary Wortley Montagu, who suggested with rather different ironies that Europeans had all sorts of self-interested misconceptions about Eastern women. She argued that veiling provided Turkish women with a handy disguise for intrigues: 'This perpetual Masquerade gives them entire Liberty of following their Inclinations without danger of Discovery.'[57] The growth of more mutually contracted relations between the sexes in Britain increased the fervency with which writers repudiated the sexual enslavement supposed to characterise Eastern affairs. As William Hunter declared in 1792, 'The prejudices which the Turks entertain against their women, are, indeed, one of the great causes of their own inflexible barbarism.'[58] Sympathy for women kept out of view inclined English male writers to criticise domestic forms of tyranny as straightforward signs of Eastern despotism – a co-dependence of politics and sexual politics to which they were not necessarily sensitive at home. But as if to downplay the significance of seeing women as oppressed, many epistolary texts by actual travellers switched to female addressees when describing matters to do with women, implying formally that women were the proper audience for women. Epistolary personae involved writers in a masquerade of race which managed issues of gender awkwardly.

Although Persian personae were used to discuss British politics, in general, oriental personae put into play a broader occidental world. Even when critiquing courts or churches that could be particularised back to national institutions, the philosophical Chinese persona helped to create a *European* discourse. Within the book trade, these satires travelled easily between European countries, with the pleasure of selective schadenfreude – that is, English readers of Montesquieu could conveniently remember they were English when his satire of European manners came too close. The detachment of oriental personae from politics was also secured by their identity as citizens of countries not (yet) touched by European colonising. In this respect, personae were emphatically not part of colonial discourse. Indeed epistolary personae partly refute the argument made by some historians that African and Asian societies seemed 'vastly inferior' to Britain.[59] Discursive boundaries are never neat, however, and personae played a small but significant part in mediating representations of English power in Ireland and India.

Not quite a colony, Ireland was a touchy subject.[60] English bigotry, ignorance or, in the later part of the century, aestheticising, blanked out acknowledgement of oppression. As Thomas Campbell put it,

> I am persuaded, that here in England, we know less of Ireland, than of the more remote parts of the Empire. We look upon it as a spot over-run with lakes and bogs, where nothing is worth notice but a Giant's-Causeway, a Killarney, a Dargle, or a Salmon-leap...[61]

Two personae – one openly exotic, one carefully disguised – showed how fictions of travelling challenged English complacency. The first, *Letters from an Armenian in Ireland, to his Friends at Trebizond* (1757), was unequivocally hostile to English rule. English control of appointments was scathingly accounted for, 'as if it were better that the king should have but one instead of two flourishing kingdoms'.[62] Aza's letters to Abdallah foreground political topics such as the constitution, judiciary and trade; they also include social and some romantic material. Defamiliarising's potentially delicate ironies become sardonic, as blunt and inescapable as the colonialism being anatomised. 'Thou askest me what are the respective Conditions of the Lord and of the Peasant in this remote World: Know therefore that they are, in general, the Conditions of the Master and Vassal.'[63] The usual conversion of oriental discourse into Western idiom cannot be performed because English despotism is not metaphorical: thanks to economic exploitation, the Irish really are in a feudal relation to England.

Though *Letters from an Armenian* ends with a paean to universal reason, it prefers polemic to persuasion. In contrast, Thomas Campbell's *A Philosophical Survey of the South of Ireland* (1777) patiently reasoned its case without recourse to the surrealism of injustice. The letters have a time, date, place and an apparently real addressee ('John Watkinson M.D.'). They looked with care at everyday life: 'one must listen with attention, and assent with caution', he writes.[64] His conclusions were often questions: for instance, on whether Catholic practices are irrational and superstitious, he asks 'What multitude is philosophical? What vulgar is rational? The bulk of all persuasions believe they know not what, and practise they know not why.'[65] As the title suggests, politics is displaced by a broader-minded philosophy. But for all his temperateness, Campbell makes English oppression plain – in his succinct antithesis, Ireland has 'the richest soil, the poorest people'.[66] He appeals to English self-interest with a utopian prospect of mutual prosperity. Regretting English restrictions on Irish trade, he argues liberty for the Irish would create liberality from which the English would benefit: 'if Ireland were suffered to export, at all times, it would soon be allured to a systematic industry and become a perpetual granary to our manufacturing country'.[67] Campbell's defence of Ireland has passionate moments but his indignation is softened by a mournful elegance:

> We keep the Irish dark and ignorant, and then we wonder how they can be so enthralled by superstition; we make them poor and unhappy, and then we wonder that they are so prone to tumult and disorder; we tie up their hands, so that they have no inducements to industry, and then we wonder that they are so lazy and indolent.[68]

The evolutionary narrative of letters is used to symbolise changes of heart for himself and to mark the conversion of his reader: 'you tell me I have made you see some things in a new light'.[69]

Campbell writes like the most likeable kind of English traveller. He was in fact Irish. The text assumes the persona of an Englishman as a clever device to revise the sympathies of English readers without appearing to challenge their imperial identity, though Boswell for one thought this device the book's one fault.[70] Campbell's subtle and convincing mimicry plays a more dangerous game than Smollett's better-known personation of a Welsh squire to celebrate the achievements of his native Scotland in *The Expedition of Humphry Clinker* (1771, six years earlier). It and the Armenian's letters are like the sun and the wind competing for the traveller's cloak: Sexton storms, Campbell warms. The tactic seems to have been a success in practice: two years earlier in the course of a visit to England, Campbell noted in his diary, 'I find the first method of conciliating an Englishman, is to praise England.'[71]

The transformation enacted by a persona is not always a simple matter of signature, as the example of Campbell shows, and not all transformations involved the drama of assuming a radically different persona. Running against the grain of stereotypes, such texts showed up that grain more clearly. Some colonisers came to question cultural difference through a sympathy that could become empathy, an elective affinity usually shored up by ideologies of class and gender.[72] The process was often gradual, suiting letters – a matter of incidents accumulating, beliefs shaken, imagination awakened. Balanchandra Rajan has argued that between 1785 and 1810, there opened 'a moment of understanding between peoples' as Orientalist scholarship made India's past look elevated,[73] and William Dalrymple's study of colonial administrators in late eighteenth-century India confirms active dissolution of differences.[74] Two texts about India, not coincidentally from that period, show how letters were especially hospitable to reconstructions of identity. Where personae reversed Western subjects into objects of investigation, in the decolonisation of consciousness 'subject peoples' become 'people of subjectivity', helped by the letter as familiar medium for the traveller. One text shows an English aristocrat becoming disenchanted with English rule abroad; the other shows a Bengali footsoldier enthusiastic about English culture but conscious of European ignorance of Indian life. The first, *Genuine Memoirs of Asiaticus*, sounds like a fictional title and starts like a sentimental romance, written with the elegance one might expect from an author sharing a name with Lord Chesterfield. Leisurely delights of life for the English in India gradually disappear after Stanhope chooses to command a regiment for the Nabob of Arcot and finds himself increasingly at odds with official British forces led by Lord Pigot, whose cruelty he likens to Pizarro's to the Incas. The nadir comes when the Nabob's Brahmin agent is forcibly dragged from his garrison – an act of violence and humiliation which shocks Stanhope as an officer, a gentleman and a European alert to the significance of touching in the caste system. This scene, 'unexampled in the annals of English tyranny',[75] illustrates Stanhope's disillusion with colonial maladministration; it is made vivid by epistolary form's combination of personal testimony and detailed day-to-day reassessments. With the detachment of an insider cut loose, Stanhope's grim care in distinguishing between human brutality, colonial greed and imperial insensitivity makes both politics and philosophy relevant to understanding the cultural differences laid open by personae in travel writing.

Where Stanhope chose life in an Indian regiment, Sake Dean Mahomet begged to be taken into the English army. Like Stanhope he explains Indian customs both civil and military – retrospectively since the letters are composed after he has accompanied his patron back to Britain. Though the title proposes the author as 'a native of Patna in Bengal', his travels reposition him in a different culture far removed from his place of birth, literally and figuratively, which undercuts his biographer's account of his voice 'as an Indian, in contrast with travel narratives by Europeans of the time'.[76] Perhaps one should call him an Indian-Anglo. *The Travels of Dean Mahomet* (1794) neutralises cultural difference through the aesthetic blandness of a universal picturesque idiom – a description of gentlemen's seats along the Ganges might as well be set on the Thames. His grasp of Milton assures him civilised credentials in English eyes, which he enhances by a fascination with European architecture that is flatteringly imperial. Glass, iron, brick and stone used by the English transform local buildings as loftily as Roman marble.[77] He confronts colonial hostility uneasily, invoking supernatural forces to teach racist Europeans respect: so an English lieutenant who urinates on a holy tomb at Peepaharea meets a sudden death moments later. But, most notably, he uses his position as a cultural insider to explain in meticulous detail the meanings of those Moslem ceremonies where Europeans most often projected orientalism. In his account of the famed 'nautch' dancers, for instance, he explained how their dances told specific folk stories – a recognition of narrative skill missing from the accounts of

Englishmen mesmerised by the performers' lasciviousness. His account of Hindu beliefs exemplifies a will to cross-cultural understanding, appealing to a moral ground held in common by all races and religions, including his English readership: 'However strange their doctrines may appear to Europeans, yet they are much to be commended for the exercise of the moral values they inculcate, namely, temperance, justice, and humanity.'[78]

The examples of Ireland and India show how writers used angry and reassuring epistolary personae to put troubling material before their readers. They show the complications of colonial identity: an Englishman sincerely in sympathy with Indians is compelled to a kind of fiction. Alternatively, one can read 'Asiaticus' as a voluntary designation that reinvents the individual as a singular type, but one who may attract a community of like-minded others. Comparable personae in explicitly political discourse, like 'Hibernicus', were identities open to being assumed by more than one person – indeed, the cultural resonance of these signatures depended upon nobody owning them.[79] Using such signatures becomes a way of asserting freedom discursively.[80] Orientalist personae investigated nation; patriotic personae like 'Hibernicus' imply ethnicity. All personae were ideological, but their connotations were nonetheless compatible with the republic of letters. Two kinds of personae, however, had inferences that led out of the republic of letters and towards a new world order. Jesuits had no country, nor even a common national identity; Americans were forging a new nationality. The tribe with no nation and the newest nation produced personae who had a different relation to place, which in turn led to a different relation to time. Hence some notable science fiction of the eighteenth century, starring Jesuit and American personae.

Jesuits were not detached from the material world. Far from it: 'he who rules the soul, rules everything', as John Shebbeare put it.[81] Since Jesuits made many of the early reports of China, they were instrumental in representing oriental ideas. At its simplest, the Jesuit persona was synonymous with an ideologue: Shebbeare pretended to be a Jesuit, Battista Angeloni, in order to explore connections between political and religious freethinking. Angeloni believes 'That the Whig idea, of every man's possessing a right of deciding for himself in matters of religion, is destructive of true liberty.'[82] Readers who missed the play on the character's name, with its threat of baptising the English, could hardly miss the play of bigotry. Shebbeare neatly turned the devil's advocate into an epistolary persona.

Actual Jesuit letters were published in collections throughout the eighteenth century. Bowdlerisation by translators who excised accounts of conversions, persecutions and miracles[83] made them even more gripping reading as the protagonists ventured into unexplored territories, meeting all sorts of dangers with honed intellectual skills, physical courage and spiritual persistence. 'I believe it will be granted, that no Men are better qualified to describe Nations and Countries than the Jesuits', suggested John Lockman,[84] noting their knowledge of languages, arts and sciences, their commitment to living in remote countries and their ability to glide into courts. Jesuits paid special attention to customs that could aid or jeopardise their missions – one reported from China that the husband of a potential convert had been told by local priests that Jesuits pulled out sick people's eyes in order to make telescopes.[85] Disinformation such as this gave factual support to the defamiliarisation performed by Eastern personae.

Several other reasons made Jesuits important to travel letters. First, their religious order replaced national identity. Since 'a true state of any kingdom is not to be expected from any of the natives',[86] they were able to offer a non-national perspective. Second, their global ambitions created a complex role for them in international relations. Although they were stateless (the kingdom of heaven notwithstanding), they appeared, especially to suspicious Protestants, to operate a para-state apparatus, particularly in the field of intelligence gathering. 'Our Jesuits may be considered in two very different lights. In the one they appear as celestial Ministers, in the other as infernal Spirits.'[87] Jesuits were linked to a string of dualisms: the double sense of discipline and order; the difference between Catholicism as a proselytising religion and catholicism as tolerance of diversity, and between imperial and papal Rome. Hence Jesuits became a trope through which to address both the possibly utopian consequences of a highly organised state and the dystopian effects of surveillance and stifled dissent. Third, the term 'Jesuit' alerted readers to rhetorical skill: 'the Jesuits are acknowledged to be fine Painters'.[88] The covert nature of Jesuit reports offered readers the pleasures of secret histories and stealthy ideological incursions whose triumphs they could share in as fellow Europeans. Fourth, since actual Jesuit disguises could involve extraordinary transformations of identity, Jesuits represented an extreme form of mimicry in the assimilation of cultural otherness. Yet paradoxically, Jesuits went 'native' in order to persuade the locals to turn Catholic, so even as they blended with cultural otherness they were motivated to change it. Their disguise compared interestingly with imperial and colonial hidden ambitions; it also made their sincerity to locals performative and their letters home more confessional. Fifth, Jesuit missionaries were not only members of an order but also its lonely emissaries. They had a group identity yet were cut off from that society which defined them. In this they epitomised all travellers, who leave behind their original society only to find themselves representing it.

Like Jesuits, diplomats were also trained observers and formal letter-writers from abroad. The overlap was explored in the futurist fiction of Samuel Madden's *Memoirs of the Twentieth Century* (1733), which purports, humorously, to be a collection of state letters from the late 1930s, mediated through a celestial spirit who tells the editor his descendant will be the last British Prime Minister, under George VI after whose reign the world ends. Ambassadors from Constantinople, Rome, Paris and Moscow report to the

Lord High Treasurer in London who replies periodically with friendly advice and official instructions. Changes since the eighteenth century are connected to the growth of Jesuit power: in its shadow the Turks are more secular and less warlike; the French are wavering towards its influence under a weak king, Louis XX, and Greek Orthodox priests need subsidising in an otherwise politically quiet Russia. Britain is the last and best obstacle to papal power which, following the conquest of Italy in the nineteenth century, radiates out through puppet kingdoms and cultural domination. Jesuit success is sustained by a network of correspondence: 170,000 Jesuits send weekly written reports which are filtered back to the Pope, who shapes policy accordingly. This scenario of epistolary bureaucracy is only partly parodic.

Madden uses multi-correspondent epistolary form to present conflicting readings of the Jesuit programme. The ambassador in Rome reports a sale of Jesuit relics that occupies 24 satirical pages: 'with what Indignation! with what Resentment! with what honest Scorn! must every considering Christian...look on such horrid Trifling both with our Religion and Understanding?'[89] The ambassador in Moscow offers more qualified criticism:

> I admire the great Talents, Learning and Wisdom of that prodigious Society as much as any man, where they are applied (as they ought solely to be) to the good of Mankind, and the glory of our Creator. But to see such excellent instruments turn'd to corrupt our Morals, to wound Religion, and raise Factions, Schisms, and Rebellions in the earth to serve their own ambition, must raise every one's indignation.[90]

The Society of Jesuits is emblematic of civil society in general: capable of benevolent practices which lead to peace, prosperity and piety, and also of self-interested ends which increase suffering. This trope had a national as well as a universal application. The absolute authority of the Pope provided a model of unchecked power which Madden compared unfavourably to a limited monarchy as in Britain. The ambassadors show reverence for the king they serve and confidence in the Lord High Treasurer with whom they correspond. Focus on Jesuit persecution of those who thought differently likewise allowed Madden to congratulate British readers obliquely on their enjoyment of a freer press and freer speech.

Madden seems torn between celebrating the heroic virtues of British imperialism – in his story, the only check to Jesuit world domination – and the superior morality of sensibility, which values national conquest less than individual sacrifice in the cause of equality:

> After all, the building up noble Families, or founding great kingdoms, are in the eye of reason as trivial performances, as the baby-houses and

puppets of Children, in comparison of those generous schemes and foundations, wealth and power might provide, to relieve the distressed and the miserable, the poor, the sick, and the unfortunate part of Mankind, and to instruct the ignorant, or reform the savage, the brutal or the wicked among Men.[91]

The Lord High Treasurer, whose views these are, confides 'we may trust such a dangerous truth to a private Letter' – a transparent fiction, but one made plausible by the letter's ability to articulate both individual beliefs and social ideologies simultaneously, even when contradictory. Letters signed by the state representative are representative of the state yet personalised in that such officers still carry a name: at this crux, and for the first time, the Lord High Treasurer subscribes himself also as John, Earl of N-m.

The fictional *Letters from an American in England* (1769)[92] evokes a futurist scenario more bleak than Madden's Jesuit dystopia. The author gives minimal space to characterisation in order to reflect the dehumanising effects of a corrupt society. England is desolate and depopulated: anyone of talent has gone to America; national monuments are broken up; trade has collapsed; public institutions are ruined (the Royal Society has become a fishmarket); military skills have given way to manic politicking; the absence of a high church leaves a way open for low life and low morals to take hold. In a neat reversal of fortunes, the Scots lord it over the English, who cannot afford to own property in their own country and are arrested for speaking ill of the Scots. A young American correspondent picks his way about these cultural ruins in company with a 'Corporal Trim', crustier than his original in Sterne's *Tristram Shandy* but equally old-fashioned. The letters depict a society surreal, sinister and sordid. It has been argued that the eighteenth century was an age of cities and the nineteenth century an age of nations,[93] and this tale set in 1799, in the twist of time between centuries, shows the persona in crisis: normally a vehicle of transnationalism and progress, it collapses beneath tribalism.

All personae have a potential secretiveness, like the underside of a mask. Stuart Sherman relates Mr. Spectator's secretiveness to his disclosure through periodicity, like 'a diary turned inside out...a wholly secretive sensibility imparting itself in print, to be read...at the running moment, of its making'.[94] Letters share this fluid periodicity, emphasised by the way many orientalist fictions gave letters dates from a lunar calendar. Travel-writing in personae called into question relations between global values and local politics: it mapped ideology onto space, the countries left behind, the countries visited. Through the place-and-date combination of the letter, an epistolary here-and-now existed in relation to utopia, things as they should be, or dystopia, things as they should not be. Like characters in masquerades, epistolary personae mixed up time and place: travel slipped easily into time travel.

Genre and the borders of self

'A orderly mind is the foundation of all intellectual requirements.'[95] Writing was such an important part of eighteenth-century travelling because it visibly ordered experience. This section discusses first some formal properties that marked letters out from other genres, then reviews letter-writing travellers in the light of those properties. In his guide for young gentlemen setting out for the Continent, John Andrews uses epistolary format to give a vocative dimension to his imperious advice: 'We are sent abroad not only to see, but to reflect; the first of these is the threshold to the second.'[96] His terminology is standard and other genres besides letters, such as diaries and journals, provided space for observation and reflection. But letters had distinct properties which should be recognised. Motion was not the same as direction: 'It often happens that a man's person is continually on the wing, and his thoughts as perpetually rambling.'[97] Letters offered fixed points in that the figure of the addressee was a constant object at least for the duration of a letter. An addressee stabilised epistolary rambling without necessarily restricting it. Where many journals were annotative or introspective, letters were explicitly communicative; because observations were nominally directed to another person, letter-writers' reflections were cast into sociable form. Conversation is not a wholly helpful analogue here in that it has been too closely tied to the adjective 'polite'; rather, letter-writers were talkative in varied ways – some intimate, some experimental, some rude, some urbane and sometimes all in the same letter. The high numbers of travel writings cast in letters in the eighteenth century suggests epistolary form usefully concentrated wandering writers' minds. That concentrating power was compatible with a mental expansiveness that allowed minds to explore territories of self.

How did letter-writing fit eighteenth-century travel writing's requirements? Charles Cordiner's *Antiquities and Scenery of the North of Scotland* (1780) turns into a journal after warm and personal letters addressed to his fellow-traveller Thomas Pennant. Cordiner initially suggests epistolary form will sharpen his attention: 'CONSIDERING myself as always in your presence, holding converse on the occurrence of the day, I shall be inspired with closer observation, and more steady attention, to all the subjects of enquiry enjoined me.'[98] Concentration is an effort: it is perhaps to relax from this effort that Cordiner takes up diarising. Barthes has noted that many journals syntactically omit the first person; in contrast, letters are normally dialogic. They supplied literary companionship in the remotest places and, when published, often proclaimed sociable motives like patriotism, altruism or entertaining others. 'Observation' was properly a process of looking-and-writing and it gave travel writing serious virtues:

> To observe the variation of manners, the force of customs, the utility of laws, or the effects of climate, renders a much more essential service

to your country than to set a new fashion, teach a new air, or give a new dish.[99]

Service to a wider intellectual or scientific community gave an excuse for publication to an enthusiast like John Williams, who hoped to 'move the curiosity of the Learned' with his investigation of vitrified forts in the Highlands.[100] His carefully neutral projection of reader response inscribed hope within diffidence: 'I KNOW not what effect reading the account of these old ruins has upon you; but they appear to me so very singular and extraordinary, that the more I see and consider them, the more I am astonished.'[101] The open form of a letter was a formal analogue to that open-minded spirit of enquiry supposed to characterise travel; the mobility of correspondents symbolised progress. Letters made solitary interests more sociable.

Pressure of friends was repeatedly invoked to explain the contradiction between publication and professed authorial reluctance. Here epistolary form was helpful in two ways. First, the presence of friends within the text as addressees legitimised that pressure; second, because the genre was relatively rough, vanity publishing was supposedly less likely. 'I hope you'll pardon the Incorrectness of my Style, and want of Method in putting things together', wrote Thomas Windham at the end of a letter about glaciers to a scientific friend.[102] Writers constantly invoked the irregularity of letters:

> I do not pretend to systematise or dogmatise in any thing: and even my arrangements must be chiefly casual. I must, in all respects, plead the privileges of epistolary correspondence, free and wild, above rule or art; though faithful to truth and nature.[103]

Throughout the period two characteristics were constantly asserted: the right to leave things out and the freedom to include what interested the writer. This distinction between incompletion and selection was significant, like the description of a glass as half-full or half-empty. In travel writing, tension between writerly desire and readers' expectations was reduced by a widely used trope of writing as travelling, which refigured both writers and readers as subsidiary to travel. 'The miscellaneous nature of a traveller's letter is continually making violent transitions necessary from one subject to another, of a species totally different.'[104] Epistolary ease offset that violence. Some writers celebrated the freedom of familiar genres: 'I detest formality...The reader who looks for connected accounts, Ciceronian epithets, and polished expressions in these rambling pages, will be greatly mistaken in the intention of the author.'[105] Elegant apologies were partly simple insurance against criticism, but the loose form of letters structured the unknown and restored surprise to well-trodden paths, such as parts of Italy whose familiarity left writers with a sense of déjà-lu as the century wore on.

Incompletion represented discursively the inability of any one person's experience to be comprehensive. Letter-writers humorously excused themselves from repeating information already in the public domain: 'I need not trouble you with a recital of all the laws of the Alcoran which you have most likely read.'[106] Nor need they include what correspondents might not want to know: so Lady Mary Wortley Montagu neatly avoided explaining to a friend the technicalities of military fortifications.[107] Authenticating sources was less important because 'it was inconsistent with the nature of letters, to interrupt the reader by perpetual references to authorities'.[108] Anxiety about detail was complemented by an approval of hints: this put letters forward as interactive rather than performative. Although good acting also turned on hints,[109] development of *ideas* through hints related travel writing to scientific deduction and historical proof. As John Williams put it, trying to relate vitrification to local legends,

> I would not insist so much on these points, which rather belong to an able historian, than to me, who should only give you an account of what I see in viewing these remarkable ruins, but that I want to give you all the hints I can, which I hope you will correct, and give me your opinion, as I know you to be a much better judge of these matters.[110]

Giving the reader something to work upon was desirable in all forms of correspondence. In travel writing, common ground was tested by geographical displacement. Space for response let the addressee or reading public add value to a text. Hints allowed value to be created variously: 'they serve as first principles for the mind to work upon'.[111] Letters made the process explicit whereas journals did not; they connected travel to philosophy through a common consciousness of epistemology. Struggling with a description of a Roman amphitheatre, one correspondent hoped 'to communicate, as entire as possible, the same impression I myself shall receive, without descending too much to particulars'.[112] Deriving from Locke's notion of mental transference and graphically expressed by Sterne's image of a servant girl impressing a seal into wax, impressions affected first the traveller, then the reader receiving those impressions from the traveller's letter.

Epistolary incompletion could be made more positive through artistic terms, especially the sketch,[113] more metaphorical than literal, though some writers did send drawings with letters. So John Lettice puzzled over how to organise his information about Edinburgh into 'a slight and impressive sketch':

> Though I am far from intending you a 'Tableau d'Edinbourg,' correctly designed and coloured; yet I would willingly attempt something beyond the meagre outlines of a map: Suppose my essay then a sort of aqua-tinta drawing: This, could I fortunately touch it with due spirit, might perhaps

be that sort of representation, beyond which a traveller's letter ought not to aspire.[114]

Even thematically specific writers evoked the sketch, like Sir John Talbot Dillon who lamented that his study of poetry in Spain 'only traced the skeleton of a gigantic figure'.[115] Visual analogues of epistolary form were compatible with tropes of touch: after all, writing involves the hand as well as the eye. John Lettice celebrated letters as 'a sort of writing meant to convey information, as it were, by a single stroke or touch of the pen; which is all that a traveller almost continually progressive, or in motion, can successfully aim at'.[116] He fretted against its limits, yearning to dissolve an epistolary frame into sensurround:

> to shew not only the time and season, but each successive place of the traveller's tour, *its form and pressure*; that so the reader may be almost persuaded that he himself exists and moves in each real and local circumstance, in which he finds the tourist and his companion actually moving, and persons and objects in motion about them, with which they happen to be engaged. This, it will be said, is something like an attempt to infuse substance, colour, life, and motion into verbal representation.[117]

Rather touchingly he concluded that this project to collapse representation back into the real might require more imagination than he has. It is an almost pathological extension of epistolary empathy.

Writers alternating between the material world and subjectivity explored the possibility of speeding up that alternation. The epistolary sketch raised the possibility of moving pictures – not unlike the melting effects of the sublime, which dynamically disrupted the distinction between viewing subject and viewed object. When letter-writers were stuck for something to say, they often turned to the self in motion. An episode in Alexander Drummond's letters illustrates this. He writes of driving along a cliff road with a sheer drop that frightens him. Afraid his fear will endanger him in the event of an accident, he reflects

> had my chaise been overturned, while I remained in a state of stupefaction, incapable of taking any step for my own safety, I must have been dashed to pieces long before I should have reached the bottom; whereas, had I preserved that presence of mind which becomes a man, I might have sprung out in time, and been probably quit for less than a broken arm: and, indeed, this experiment I several times tried with success, in very rugged roads, when the carriage jolted so much I thought it in danger of being overturned.[118]

The imaginary crash, as an event, is no different to a reader than Drummond's reports of acts of leaping in and out of his chaise. That gendered presence of mind which is the principal feature of Drummond's bizarrely proactive attitude to road safety merges bodily fear and reaction with anticipation and reason, to make a coalescent sense of self. Mental activity replaces narrative vacancy. Drummond writes this passage after lamenting that 'a modern traveller labours under the misfortune of writing upon subjects which are supposed to be well nigh exhausted'. He proposes that novelty be supplied by subjectivity: 'every man is an original in his own remarks and adventures; and that, as such I shall continue to transmit myself, until my correspondence is declined'.[119] Interior landscapes took over from exterior ones. Travellers who kept journals also crammed in observations, but letters differed from journals in that letters were sent to a reader who became a witness to the writer's authority and subjectivity. The letter involved double jeopardy: one might look more interesting or informed, but one might also be judged to have failed.

Letter-writers regularly expressed mistrust of what books reported – ironically, given that many letters were themselves published. The contestation was not so much between print and script culture as between eyewitnessing and reading. Here the relatively low standing of letters allowed writers to evade charges of misrepresentation attendant on literary ambition, even as epistolary independence increased expectations of authenticity, because readers relied on letter-writers to supplement and correct other sources. Correspondents deployed political metaphors in which the liberty supposed to be enjoyed by British subjects acted as a guarantee of independent thought. As William Coxe put it,

> I promise you that I will describe nothing, of which I have not been an eye-witness. The remarks I shall transmit to you, will be the genuine result of my own feelings; and I had even rather be frequently wrong in my sentiments and reflections, than servilely follow the observations of others.[120]

Letters often included copies of documents as supporting evidence. The conversational properties of letters made them hospitable to oral report, but writers were cautious in the service of proof: 'I will defer giving you any account of the government until I am better informed', wrote William Coxe from the Vallais in Switzerland.[121] Sources and methodologies had to be accounted for: 'I endeavour to ascertain the truth of these informations, by procuring as many as I can from persons of all ranks, by laying them together; and then comparing them with the written accounts, if there be any.'[122] Christopher Hervey ended his account of Christian slaves capturing a Turkish sloop: 'This is the best relation I can get you of this affair, which, indeed, I flatter myself is tolerably authentic.'[123] Often delaying information until he could verify, amplify and update it, Hervey was also exact about the provenance of his own letters, dating them not only with day, month and year but also with the day of the week and even hour of composition.

Precision about origins overlapped with historical paradigms of proof. The traveller, however, could authenticate where the historian could not. Time and place were constantly foregrounded in a trope of 'on the spot': 'I am this moment returned from visiting the spot.'[124] Regardless of revisions for publication, many books claimed composition *in situ*, like William Hunter's *Travels*, 'written on the spot whence the respective Letters are dated'.[125] Writers also claimed authenticity through residence: 'whatever forms the true character of a people, can only be known from residing amongst them; from being admitted familiarly into their houses; from viewing them in the social and unguarded hours of domestic retirement'.[126] Residence, familiarity and the familiar letter supported each other in the idea of day-to-day observation, even where the author spent less time indoors than in motion.[127] Journals may specialise in the quotidian, but letters invited comment on the process and its uses to writer and reader.

Letter-writers' inclusiveness could seem a rational exercise of faculties: 'in committing my remarks to paper, I find my memory much more deeply impressed by every object I have seen, than by a superficial view'.[128] Ideally, writing made travellers think for themselves and not rely on books. In amplifying memory, it produced use-value: so William Coxe thought that the extra attention involved in corresponding would create 'much greater profit to myself'.[129] Alternatively, one might look to psychoanalysis to explain the eighteenth-century compulsion to the point of neurosis to write things down. 'I was so fearful of misrepresenting the truth, that I immediately committed it to paper', wrote one traveller, denouncing Italian sermons as vulgar: his fear seems to be a displacement of a threat to ego boundaries from something he thought was lower class.[130] Narcissism was a motive too: 'There is a flattering and virtuous pride which we cannot avoid feeling from the consciousness, or at least the hope, that we are opening scenes of liberal knowledge, and elegant curiosity, to our listening friends.'[131] A discourse of friendship stood in for social likeness in general, by which the letter-writer was approved. In return, the letter-writer accepted a moral function of friendship: friends did not lie and friends made efforts to discover the truth.

Friendship on paper could conflict with friendliness in person and sometimes the traveller had to choose between them. Travellers wrote letters self-consciously in a variety of locations. The 'mechanical traveller' sat and wrote regardless: rather than talk with his companions or the locals, he

> casts a look of pity, blended with contempt, upon his fellow-travellers; exhibits an enormous common-place-book; draws out his scale and compasses; falls to measuring the length of an old church, or the height of a mutilated statue, and scribbling alternately; all this he does with the most unrelaxed solemnity of phiz. He introduces his vade-mecum at his meals; he sips his tea with a gravity quite edifying, then writes, looks wise, and writes and sips, and sips and writes by turns. In vain do we

attempt, by the introduction of a nonpareil burgundy to call him off... he fills his glass, passes the bottle, drinks, is silent, and writes on. When he is disposed to be what, in a stage coach is called *pretty company,* he will read to us his travels.[132]

For the satirist, these writings are of course dull and moralising. Here script is associated with repression, in contrast to the unhampered divulgence of secrets from wine-loosened tongues. Compulsion to write things down could be figured as anal, except that unlike diaries and commonplace books, letters nominally release information to one other person at least. 'There is perhaps no pleasure greater, than that of communicating pleasure received', wrote Nathaniel Wraxall from Normandy.[133] For discontented travellers, letter-writing compensated for unpleasant or dreary experiences. Anne Grant wrote from Fort William, 'O! this is a bad country for a butterfly, a bee, or an enthusiast, to expatiate in; but it is the best place in the world to remember an absent friend in.'[134] Letter-writing reduced friction between emotional and geographical landscapes. Grant confided after going to church in the Highlands, 'all the way home, I was lost in lofty meditation, and to own the truth, writing this letter in idea'.[135] Defining the 'foreign' often depended on comparing it to something at home. Chloe Chard has noted that eighteenth-century travellers characteristically 'construct oppositions between the foreign and the familiar even when commenting on relatively trivial aspects of the topography of foreignness'.[136] Most of her supporting sources are epistolary and it is not a coincidence: letters put travellers in mind of the familiar. They may even have preferred epistolary form because it linked them to their 'home' country. Although George Bogle wrote as a colonial merchant and a sentimental traveller, he thought of 'correspondence itself as a chain to link to the other country, a guarantee of national identity, and a kind of *aide-mémoire* for the affections'.[137] Explicit address to friends made letters symbolic mediators of home thoughts from abroad. 'Whatever may be the novelties and pleasure arising from travel, the mind naturally preponderates towards home.'[138]

Like the term 'rambling' which made writing a species of travel, the concept of reading as 'transport' enabled representation and experience to fuse. 'Adieu! fellow-traveller', ends one letter from Anne Grant, 'for such you may be accounted, if you are as willing to be informed as I am to inform you'.[139] Letter-writers interpolated readers into scenes, like Edward Topham enthusing over Edinburgh views: 'But before I proceed any further, I must entreat you to take a view of the prospect from the top of the Castle.'[140] Nearly twenty years later, John Lettice was in the vicinity offering his correspondent 'a distant and cursory view' of public buildings: 'conceive yourself following me, with a telescope in your hand, up to Calton Hill, or Authur's Seat' [sic].[141] Representation was figured as tiring as travel itself:

'Our voyage, even thus made on paper, has unavoidably taken up some time ... I must beg leave to rest.'[142] The unpredictable nature of travelling matched the miscellaneous nature of letters: excusing himself for a letter that might have bored his readers, Joseph Cradock told his correspondent, 'Have patience, Sir, a reader must sometimes, like a traveller, put up with bad as well as good accommodations.'[143] It is not that letters alone had this advantage – after all, the same trope structures Henry Fielding's comic epic novel *Tom Jones*. But just as the pleasure of travelling could be increased by hospitality, so the pleasure of reading could be increased by writerly effort which letters promoted: 'if the landlord does his endeavor to please, his guest ought to be satisfied'. Small narrative courtesies, such as putting readers in media res, kept letters politely less fatiguing. 'Not to keep you continually in inns, I ... will seat you with me in the chaise upon our journey the next morning.'[144] Such fictions showed how friendly and polite manners went globe-trotting through letters.

Travel-writing could be contentious and, as in other letters of controversial import, writers wrote readers into letters as devil's advocates. Joseph Cradock's *Letters from Snowdon* had a prefatory 'Letter from a Friend to the Author' which criticised Cradock for treating the Welsh with asperity and not being sentimental enough; Cradock rebutted the charges of this possibly fictional friend. Not all objections were so stage-managed. An English lord politely corrected the 'mistakes' of de Muralt's *Letters describing ... the English and French Nations* (1726) in two letters that became attached to the text. Some remarks in Jemima Kindersley's *Letters from the East Indies* (1777) about the conversion of negroes in Brazil incensed one clergyman who wrote angrily to the *London Chronicle* that negroes could not be called Christians if they had become Catholics. In an apoplexy of anti-popery, he berated Kindersley for mildly suggesting there might be some merit in confession as a practice: 'Blush, Madam, at the recollection of having ever written a word which could even be twisted to praise such a system as popery.'[145] (The thought then occurs to him that *she* might be a Catholic, which goads him into three more letters.) Correspondents handled conflict in different ways and textual outlets: respondents claimed the right to quarrel from the form's openness; writers defended themselves through protective devices of form.

Reader objections were commonly pre-empted by an explicit contract at the start. Most expressed a willingness to inform and a wish to entertain, however imperfectly, a recipient assumed to be benign. 'I wish to amuse you; and as charity covers a multitude of sins, so friendship can hide a multitude of faults.'[146] Others were less insouciant. For one traveller, the obligation was 'Hard task upon us both. Upon you, in the article of patience; and upon me, in that of perseverance.'[147] Another traveller offered a reductio ad absurdum:

All I engage for, is to daub a sheet of paper over with a black fluid called ink; reducing it into certain hieroglyphical characters called letters; which letters shall be put together into little packets called words; and this is all I promise: reserving to myself the full and absolute power of writing in what language or style I please; intelligible or not; good, bad or indifferent.

Despite a stable discourse of liberty and tyranny, this deconstruction of epistolary contracts points to the ambiguous standing of both letters and travel as randomly productive.

Although letter-writers stressed the miscellaneous nature of their productions, many published texts had a geographical or thematic focus, frequently justified in relation to the character of the traveller. Samuel Sharp concentrated on drama: 'When I am in *Italy*, I seldom fail to be present every evening at the Theatres, as being the place, where next to good company, a traveller is best enabled to catch the manners of a people.'[148] Certain subjects were widely discussed: national difference, religious difference, trade and politics – what one might call the constituents of civil society. These formed the staples of travel writing, along with 'the productions of nature, the monuments of art, and the manners of the inhabitants', as the subtitle to Thomas Broderick's *Letters from Several Parts of Europe and the East* (1753) put it. These elements are certainly not exclusive to letters. But in two respects letters differed from other genres. First, whether published or unpublished, they specified a readership. Second, their dialogic aspect made them sensitive to voices of doubt or dissent. Letters were thus a significant form not only of communicative action but also of communicative *reaction*, especially if 'Communities are to be distinguished, not by their falsity/ genuineness, but by the style in which they are imagined.'[149] In the context of travellers' letters, imagined communities were personified through an addressee whose relation to the writer was not usually imaginary. The traveller's self was defined in relation to two 'others': people living in the place travelled through and people written to, with whom some cultural similarity could be presumed – commonly, in a shared language. Fellow travellers from the same country occupied a middle ground. Otherness is not *only* foreignness.[150]

Community between writer and reader made questions of national and religious difference especially relevant to letters. Insofar as difference turns on a paradigm of 'them' and 'us', letters supplied an 'us', based on cultural likeness, which could be broken down into 'you and I', making difference manageably personal. Where cultural likeness existed in terms of language or nation but not, say, class or gender, a relationship with otherness was structured through formal aspects of letter-writing. Tutors who went on the Grand Tour worked out a repertoire of such choices when they wrote home to their employers.[151] At the same time, the sequential nature of correspondence allowed changes of mind that destabilised 'us' beyond the anchoring power of the recipient. Travel led to new scenes that could estrange travellers from those at home; equally, letter-writing maintained ties. Tensions ran three ways: between ideologically charged senses of identity, between open-minded efforts of enquiry and between prejudices about race, gender, religion and class that could be confirmed or shaken by travel. Without apologising for eighteenth-century complacency, it is vital to stress that it was different from nineteenth-century bigotries. Reason and irony are much less visible later. National stereotypes had to fit with ideas about human nature. Difference was often troped as natural throughout the century: 'Mankind is every where the same: like Cherries or Apples, they may differ in size, shape or colour, from different soils, climates or cultures, but are still essentially the same species.'[152] Discourses of race, nation, class, gender and religion played a key part in defining likeness and difference.[153] Layered and variable, these discourses repay close reading. Their complexity is a challenge: 'Often we must learn to read these terms with regard both to their conjunctions with one another and their internal disjunctions.'[154] As Linda Colley remarks, 'Identities are not like hats. Human beings can and do put on several at a time.'[155]

Letter-writers stressed travel created opportunities for comparison that stimulated political consciousness. They underwrote pride in constitutional advantages, supported by close enquiry into mechanisms of liberty in other countries, concerning their state, church, taxation and press. Chloe Chard reads these comparisons as affirmations;[156] I question this. Travelling through Switzerland, William Coxe commented, 'it is impossible for an Englishman to observe, in his travels, the governments of those countries, without becoming a warmer and more affectionate admirer of his own'.[157] His observation, however, is sandwiched between praise of the Swiss polity and critical comments on the state of prisons in England, where people acquitted could nonetheless be ruined by prison expenses. Letters allowed for internal debate and ideological conflict. 'The English are mild and generous', declared William Hunter,[158] a rather hollow claim since he has just discussed the rapacious cruelties of Cornish smugglers of whom he has been reminded by Mediterranean pirates. Nationalism in travel letters supports a view of the English as always given 'to speak ill of all other nations, incessantly boasting of their own', as the French writer Dupaty put it.[159] But trumpet-blowing was not always unthinking. A characteristic passage by Hunter exposed the mental labour involved in ideological activation:

> Englishmen, whilst at home, are so familiarized with the blessings of a good king and a free constitution, that they often appear to be almost indifferent about their possession; but when they are in foreign parts, where circumstances are continually arising which lead them into investigation, and dispose them to draw comparisons between the

advantages which they enjoy and those which obtain in other countries, they feel a new train of ideas enlighten the mind, and a new train of emotions warm the heart; and when any particular day arrives which places these various sensations in a full point of view, and calls them into the plenitude of action, they are as much surprised at their past apathy as they are delighted with their present sensibility.[160]

Hunter is driven by a patently wishful desire to overcome discontinuity between the English at home and the English traveller by making both active citizens. Epistolary form supplied community, allowed it to be read as a fiction and to stand as an inspiration.

Nationalism was also open to irony: 'I think I shall love *England* the better for having quitted it.'[161] Critical of travellers from the same nation, Lady Mary Wortley Montagu's complaint about callow English youths on the Grand Tour was widely echoed (here residents grumbled about tourists). Cultural difference between women was erased by a sexuality common to all women, according to male writers. One pontificated that

love of admiration is the universal propensity of the sex: and, *perhaps*, it is displayed here [in Greece] in more lively colours, only because the restraints on nature are not so severe, or the artifices and refinements so numerous, as in the polished countries of Europe.[162]

Ironically, his letters are addressed to a woman and, more irony, this reader is only intermittently gendered – so when Hunter discusses commerce he stresses the subject should interest all minds regardless of sex.[163] Gender difference could be neutralised by epistolary community. Eyles Irwin's *A Series of Adventures* were also addressed to 'a Lady'. As he made his way across the Red Sea, up the desert and home via Cairo, Irwin faced many dangers; ironically the most helpful people he met were a band of robbers. He counts on the addressee's sympathy obliquely until the end, when she is acknowledged as a source of sensibility: 'To be a serious member of a thoughtless tribe, is no less an honor to a woman, than to possess a refined heart in a depraved and dissipated age.'[164] Her sex acts like a racial identity, fixing her in a tribe. Women's uncertain national identity was reinstated when writers were on familiar ground.

Religious difference seemed if anything even more intractable to eighteenth-century English letter-writers than gender difference. 'Errors' and 'superstition' were widely paired but ultimately distinct charges: that Catholics had wrong beliefs and a wrong way of believing. Some places were, in Peter Clarke's phrase, distinctly overchurched,[165] but three things created particular friction: religious orders, relics and ceremonies. English suspicion of religious orders was historically entrenched since their dismantling in England under Henry VIII; it was also topical because convents, like harems, were seen to deny women freedom of movement. Alexander Drummond, who became consul in Aleppo, sampled a range of religious spectacles around the Mediterranean. Relics aroused particular ire. About the supposed spurs of Antenor on show at Padua, he wrote, 'It is really surprising to see with what success they trump up such absurd fables, that are in direct contradiction to the truth of history and common sense.'[166] He went to see them though, in spite of his own devotions to accuracy (he thought nothing of lying on thistles to copy inscriptions). His passion for historical geography committed him to proofs of age and provenance which most relics lacked; his indignation turned on a kind of competition. In Padua, he watched a gala for the Virgin and decided it was 'mummery...a disgrace to religion'. Part of the problem was hostility to personnel: some years later, Drummond visited the pillar of St Simon Stylites and scoffed at 'this aerial martyr...Saint Wronghead'.[167] Perversely, anti-Catholics had no trouble with the pluralism of pagan iconography. Cultural difference in the staging of public spectacle was not confined to worship: Drummond was disappointed by both a Venetian wedding (he thought black gondolas were funereal) and a state parade in Smyrna: 'no order, decency, taste, or any thing truly grand appeared'.[168] Drummond's taste in processions was probably affected by his enthusiastic freemasonry (after this pageant he promptly founded another lodge) but his views show how anti-Catholicism was rarely just that.

Letters allow critics to contextualise prejudice in relation to drives that emanate from places other than their apparent sources. Matters of religion illustrate how letters mobilised latent as well as overt identities. Religion showed letters attuned to drama. Contact with the numinous allowed a temporary suspension of reason and its guards upon fear and desire; descriptions of this were self-consciously theatrical. Samuel Sharp normally found Catholic ceremonies 'a trial for the patience of reason'; nonetheless, he watched St Januarius's blood liquefy and joined the throng to have it applied to his front.[169] William Eddis sent a fascinating notice from America of ceremony as masquerade: on St Tamina's day, certain New England colonists dressed up as Indians and rushed into a room war-whooping.[170] Religious ceremonies created structured spaces in which many travellers experimented with their own subject boundaries. Chloe Chard has explored how male travellers were drawn to women as spectacles in whom subject boundaries broke down;[171] I suggest there was a parallel dynamic of temporary and cathartic absorption through religious ceremonies. Letters then acted as confessions. Patrick Brydone confided to William Beckford his response to those who venerated saints:

> I own I have sometimes envied them their feelings; and in my heart cursed the pride of reason and philosophy, with all its cool and tasteless triumphs, that lulls into a kind of stoical apathy these most exquisite sensations of the soul.[172]

He stresses the saints are female: significantly, the sensuality of Catholic worship is figured as a heterosexual moment in which he and his addressee are outsiders, though he swiftly reinstates class otherness: 'don't you think so too, that this personal kind of worship is better adapted to the capacities of the vulgar...?'[173] Thomas Gray also joined in Catholic ceremonies, writing from Genoa to his friend Richard West, 'I believe I forgot to tell you, that we have been sometime converts to the holy Catholic church.'[174] Their satisfactions are almost erotic: like a masquerade, Protestant played at being Catholic and queer played at being straight through theological cross-dressing. Letters allowed impersonations, including camp ones. Wishful ideas of nation, sexual identity and religious identification were explored experimentally by many letter-writers. Journals that were more than memorandum books were hospitable to fantasy too, arguably more so, yet having an addressee meant putting fantasy in a communicative guise. 'Private' ideas became sociable ones through letters.

Letters both confirmed and tested prejudice. Their first-person medium tolerated and encouraged subjectivity; their second-person relationship via an addressee meant opinions, however strong, were placed in a domain beyond the self. Alexander Drummond, helping a fellow consul in Cyprus, had his anti-French prejudice activated by commercial rivalry: 'The French are a restless people, incessantly employed in working some politic point, to gain which, they use truth and falshood indiscriminately in their insinuations; and, when the deceit is detected, they are never out of countenance.'[175] Epistolary 'ease' smoothed transitions between the particular and general, making prejudices seem naturalised. Drummond describes this letter as 'a talkative fit...communicating what is now in my mind, especially as my own character is concerned in my reflections.' Epistolary intersubjectivity assumed an 'us' that allowed an 'I' to explain or confess its ideas of difference to a 'you' assumed to be sympathetic. Where only one side of a correspondence was printed, difference was understood as culturally compatible – we do not read any reply to Drummond to disagree or challenge. The reader slips into the position of the addressee, invited to recognise the workings of prejudice rather than just their expression.

Drummond came from Scotland but politically he identified himself as English. The slipperiness of national identity and the complexity of identifications with nation are subjects I can only touch on here,[176] to make the point that many letter-writers employed variable identities, often with unstable moves between the serial identities of English, British and European. Location made a difference. Out of Europe, people from different countries found themselves homogenously described as Europeans. In the Middle East they were simply 'Franks' and became themselves spectacles of otherness. 'The first arrival of a Cherokee Indian in Europe, could not have begotten half the wonder that our appearance did here', wrote Eyles Irwin from the eastern shore of the Red Sea.[177] Conversely, in colonial contexts European identities both melded and separated out like colours in a chromatograph. From Antigua, John Luffman reported that 'thirteen islands under the different powers of England, France, Denmark, and Sweden, may, in clear weather, be distinctly seen and numbered'.[178] Cultural geographies could be simultaneous: ancient met modern for Jemima Kindersley when Indians put her in mind of Israelites.[179] In Europe, Britons were simplified back into Englishness. From Rome, Christopher Hervey wrote amusingly about a play he went to see in which four suitors, an Englishman, Frenchman, Spaniard and Italian, courted a heroine. The otherwise very Euro-minded Hervey gives details only about the Englishman – to please a parochial recipient? – 'Lord Roastbeef' is unsociably laconic but lavish with presents. The heroine, unsurprisingly, chooses the Italian. Hervey says the costume is not proper English taste but English travelling dress, 'resembling that of no nation at all'.[180] Accuracy was irrelevant: national caricatures did good box-office.

Many letters, however, show national considerations set aside in favour of a utopian drive. This was Eurocentric in that it proposed technology and trade as agents of progress, and colonial in its condescension and pathways. In her account of the manufacture of fine muslin in India, Jemima Kindersley lamented the slow but exact needlework done by men by hand:

> One is at a loss which to wonder at most, their patience in completing any piece of work with such tools, or their stupidity in not inventing others; or lastly, their obstinacy in refusing to adopt a better method when it is pointed out to them...[181]

Her bafflement also included genuine distress, albeit paternalist, at seeing poor people with no access to amenities. Utopianism served capitalism in its promotion of material comforts but it did not define liberty as only the freedom to consume. So William Coxe surveyed the shores of Lake Lugano:

> From Porto the traveller may observe, with satisfaction mingled with compassion, the strong contrasts effected by the influence of a free and of an arbitrary government: the borders of the lake subject to Switzerland studded with a succession of villages, houses, and gardens; this part of the Milanese desolate, and almost unpeopled.[182]

It was thanks to travellers, argued Thomas Nugent, that 'the public is indebted for those useful discoveries which have contributed to improve the conveniences and elegancies of life, and to render human society more happy'.[183] Measurement of this was uppermost in many letter-writers' minds:

> In travelling through different countries, the first idea that suggests itself is, whether the laws and customs which prevail, are such as tend to make

the people happy; and in forming this estimate, we are but too apt to measure their feelings by our own.[184]

Consideration of the collective good in a moral sense led to goods in a material sense. Travel and trade went hand in glove. Commerce was widely recognised as the vanguard to colonialism: an Ottoman edict banning Christian ships from trading round Suez cited India as a cautionary example of countries where Christians first claimed to be merchants and then conquered and enslaved.[185] Travel books frequently devoted 'special issue' space to commerce; one exclusively concerned with it was Alexander Cluny's *The American Traveller* (1769). This text shows business letters and travel letters in overlap. Cluny was 'an Old and Experienced trader' analysing imports and exports down the eastern seaboard of America. There were two markets involved, native peoples and colonists, and more than one agency, though his discussion focuses on the Hudson Bay Company. Cluny argued that the British should encourage colonists in agriculture and manufacture so they made enough money to become consumers without necessarily becoming competitors. His view of relations with native peoples is simultaneously more cynical and more idealistic. Hostile to the Hudson Bay Company because he thought they wasted opportunities secured exclusively to them by charter, he conceded that profits were not compatible with justice, since what the Company bartered were shoddy goods, 'the cheapest and worst of their Kind'.[186] The Company also set a variable rate of exchange for furs whose fluctuations always favoured the Company. 'Such an Imposition was too glaring to escape unnoticed even by *Savages*', he commented.[187] In return, they squeezed supply. Cluny regretted that the unequal benefits of trade were premised on social injustice and he urged better treatment of native peoples not wholly from self-interest: 'In their Natural Dispositions they are brave, honest, generous, and friendly; and as grateful for Benefits, as revengeful of Injuries.'[188] His solutions tried to be neutral, gesturing vaguely to a fair rate of exchange.[189] Cluny's letters show there is more to commodities than profits and that travellers were attuned to cultural capital – not least because their letter-writing was part of a flow of information and opinions that interacted with and helped direct a flow of peoples, goods and labour.

Letters allowed traders travelling on business to address a wider audience with little anxiety about performance. Letter form made arguments manageable for readers, 'the most indolent, or inattentive, seldom having so little Curiosity, or being so soon tired, as to stop before they reach the End of a Letter of moderate Length'.[190] If readers can consume at a pace that keeps them fresh, they can consume more: epistolary form becomes a paradigm of capitalism. Cluny keeps his aristocratic addressee respectfully in view not simply to add social cachet to an otherwise utilitarian text though it helps, giving him 'a Voucher to support my own Credit'.[191] It becomes an analogue for international relations: the initially unlikely friendship between Cluny and the unnamed Earl is a metaphor for the friendship of countries where colonial dependence has turned to the mutual advantage of trade. Cluny begins his second letter,

> It is an old Remark, that the Value of a Friend is seldom known, 'till he is lost. I most sincerely wish, this may not be the Case of Great-Britain with Regard to the American Colonies. While we went on smoothly together, we enjoyed the Advantage of our Intercourse, unequal as it was...[192]

Cluny was right to worry, given how economic issues affected international relations. The metaphor of countries as friends is not exclusive to letters, but it gains force from an epistolary setting. His letters promote epistolary commerce as a metaphor for commercial traffic – a free and fair exchange which capitalism has mythologised as its own best practice. 'Mutual Advantage is the most solid basis, the strongest Cement of Union, in all Connections, whether political or private.'[193] Epistolary plainness also symbolised the transparency of ideal trading relations. As the author of a study of trade between Britain and Portugal put it, none too modestly, 'the Publication of these few Letters has filled our Country with Astonishment! Men have seemed to start, and awaken as it were out of a Dream, and declare they never comprehended rightly the Ties the two Nations had to each other before'.[194]

A number of genres handled the abstractions of capitalism and their very material exchanges, but they were at home in letters, a genre that foregrounded its constituent materials of paper and ink and which also dematerialised the world into script. There were many letters, both published and unpublished, from travellers and emigrants who moved through new worlds and tried to explain them to people at home. British emigrants to America were advised to arrange a correspondence with someone from the old country. Home ties to abroad were sustained through letters; people at home travelled in imagination through letters. How readers responded to travel letters can be generalised as a suspension of self – not exclusive to letters, since readers reported thrills from non-epistolary travels too. But the intersubjectivity of letters gave travels an extra cultural charge and one that resists turning solely on difference. When Edward Clarke set off on a three-year tour of northern countries and the Near East in 1799, he wrote frequently to his friends in Cambridge. One reported their excitement when his packets arrived: 'The first letter began with these words: "Here I am, eating strawberries within the Arctic Circle." We were so intent on his dessert that we forgot our own.'[195] Their untouched food symbolises recipients' appetite for the intricate and subtly various process of difference, similarity, presence, absence, connection, displacement and strangeness staged by travellers' letters. The familiar form of letters helped readers acclimatise to strangeness too.

The attentiveness of epistolary form was compatible with experimentation, especially concerning the ways self inscribed itself into that world of changeable differences encountered through travel. Rather than seeing difference located solely or predominantly in the world, I propose it was also located in writers. The traveller is one of the most diverse characters imaginable and one whose diversity should be protected from simplification. Such diversity makes it hard to relate travel letters to other forms of letter-writing, even though many can be seen as extensions of familiar letters, simply written on the road rather than at home. One way to is alter taxonomy, even the useful taxonomy of character, to propose travel letters as a form of letters of argument in that they advance certain criteria as a basis for understanding the world. Observation, information and opinion in travel letters operate like arguments. What was best practice? Actual practice? Where letters of argument usually deployed reason and persuasion, travel letters framed enquiry through description that acknowledged empirical obligations and the subjective basis of evaluation. Another way to describe what the character of traveller especially brought to letter-writing was an awareness of 'conditions of possibility'. The phrase is Kathleen Wilson's in relation to empire's work of transculture, as people – and commodities – moved around the world in the eighteenth century. Wilson proposes that gender and national identities emerge as 'an uneven, ambiguous and more troubled process than is usually supposed – marked by indeterminacies rather than radical departures, and refusals as well as affirmations'.[196] Whilst a cultural history of identities defined through gender, race and class is valuable, letters suggest travellers also wanted to define themselves in relation to humanity intermittently undifferentiated by nation, race, religion, gender, class and other frames. To see only these frames is to attend to group difference at the expense of sameness between peoples and difference within people. Wilson suggests 'Travel through the space–time continuum of the globe thus held out the possibilities for self-realization for explorers and explored alike.'[197] Letters allowed travellers a space in which to feel comfortable with uneven identities, to explore subjectivity and to account for their outlooks to recipients and readers who were familiar with how letters accommodated unevenness in all identities.

7
Writing as a Historian

> I know, by experience, that from my early youth I aspired to the
> character of a historian.
>
> – Edward Gibbon

'The poet and the historian diffuse lustre on the age', declared Oliver
Goldsmith.[1] Neither character was one open to all comers, despite an
expanding print culture. Where would-be poets could be dismissed as
hacks, dunces, scribblers or poetasters, historiography had equivalent
false or bad characters: romancers, fabulists or creatures of party. This
chapter argues for the significance of letters in defining the nature of
history and policing the character of historian. To demonstrate how
letters fit in, I want first to sketch in some cultural politics of eighteenth-
century historiography.

Opinions about what qualities a historian needed were plentiful in the
eighteenth century. The question led straight to another: what was
history? Tests for poets turned on skills of versification or arguments
about 'genius'; defining history also generated anxiety. Some saw disciplinary boundaries as rigid: 'IT is usual to treat law, manners and government,
as if they had no connection with history, or with each other.'[2] Others
preferred permeability. The most important purpose of history, according
to a professor at Edinburgh in 1782, was 'the tracing events to their
causes, the detection of springs of human actions, the display of the
progress of society, and of the rise and fall of states and empires'. Thus
history could link psychology and narrative, as letters did, and encompass
clearly ideological territory: 'particularly ... the manners of nations, their
laws, the nature of their government, their religion, their intellectual
improvement, and progress in the arts and sciences'.[3] The historian
appears as a neutral instrument, or rather, disappears as a human instrument; the weight shifts from producer to product, as if to compensate for
the ideological nature of the material being explained. Where poets could
talk of laurels as a metonymy that linked person to product and let them

inherit a classical system of acclaim, those writing history were caught up in a project in which differences between ancient and modern methodologies were all too obvious. Added to this was a growth in new markets that aggravated competition between eighteenth-century writers of history. It has been suggested that 'Books of history were written by literati, clerics, antiquarians, journalists, and political propagandists, but rarely by full-time professional historians. History in the eighteenth century had not yet become a specialized academic discipline.'[4] Whilst agreeing that historians in this period are diverse, I see rather the contrasting singularity of 'history'. As the popularity of the title 'universal history' indicates, writers rejected plurality: 'history' was the real thing in a way 'histories' could never be.

Letters played an important part throughout the period: they helped democratise the study of history. Using letters as sources enabled historians to track affairs of state day by day, a familiarity at odds with the elevations of majesty, and one that had to be differentiated from the confidently personalised world of secret history. Epistolary exchanges between historians helped to sustain and extend the republic of letters; equally, correspondence contributed to the fragility of scholarly community, as can be seen from looking at antiquarians. Their quarrels and arguments were often bitter, even as they acknowledged that antiquarians needed to stick together against the amused condescension or open contempt with which more worldly people regarded them. I then discuss frictions between historians who targeted wider audiences, especially between gentlemen amateurs and scholars with new ideas of professionalism in the controversy surrounding Lord Bolingbroke's *Letters on the Study and Use of History*. I discuss this text in terms of historical methodology rather than the deism for which it is better known because it is a good example of how the significance of letters can be overlooked: contemporaries were responding as much to the epistolary medium as to the deist message. One can see the different ideological ends of epistolary form by comparing Bolingbroke to Goldsmith and William Russell as writers of history for a middle-brow audience. Comparing them in turn to Catharine Macaulay, Catherine Talbot and others shows how the masculine conservatism of much history writing was challenged in different ways, although the ideological reproduction expressed through letters from fathers to sons about history had considerable purchase as an idea. In more informal historical writings, represented in the last section of this chapter by some of Horace Walpole's letters, correspondence provided a medium for reporting daily life as it supplied, minutely and ephemerally, the constituents of history. In this sense, the letter can be read as a conscious form of historiography, related to the memoir but differentiated from it by its inclusion of an addressee whose reading is also historicised by taking place in a time-frame separate from that of the writer.[5]

Discourse, documents and historiography

In order to understand the eighteenth century's interest in letters as both historical sources and historical medium, one must first go over the ground of definition – often treacherous, because ideological splits and commercial pressures made rivals of writers even in the same interest group. One needs to understand the difficulties around historiography, because then one sees better the meanings of letters within it. Francis Squire's ideas of a good historian seem straightforward enough:

> He must have Patience to compare his several Materials together, and Discernment to reconcile the seeming Contradictions; he must have right Notions of the Original of Government, and be well acquainted with the civil Constitution of his Country; he must have a cool Head, an honest Heart, a sound Judgment, a Purity of Diction, an agreeable and perspicuous Manner of expressing himself, and an inviolable attachment to Truth.[6]

Ideals about history were rarely disinterested: Squire's were aired in the context of an attack on Thomas Carte. He was the author of a gigantic history of England, a tome so weighty anyone trying to lift it risks industrial injury. Even so Carte lamented its unfinished state. For Squire, Carte's devotion to scholarship was as nothing because he had too many 'fine-spun speculations *a la françoise*'.[7] Squire's advertisement even proclaimed that his epistolary remarks had persuaded one young admirer not to part with twenty guineas for Carte's *History*. So the ideal and the material were bound together. Eighteenth-century metaphors for historiographical activity are revealing in this context. These acted wishfully: they made labour visible and gave it value. As for many eighteenth-century intellectual activities, construction images were popular, explaining how work became *Works*: Gilbert Stuart declared in his *History of Scotland* he aimed 'not to raise a monument to my prejudices, but to build a Temple to Truth'.[8] After more ruins were unearthed at Pompeii, excavation imagery was especially common: thus Voltaire appealed to fellow historians, 'let us endeavour to dig some precious monuments from under the ruins of ages'.[9] Analogies with archaeology seemed straightforward but on closer inspection it was not always clear what was being dug up nor what to do with it. 'My materials were buried in the midst of rubbish, were detached, and unequal. I had to dig them up anxiously and with patience; and, when discovered and collected, it was still more difficult to digest and fashion them.'[10] Hence the popularity of images of mining, in which what was dug up was self-evidently precious. One antiquary titled his labours *Aurum ex Stercore*, or gold from dross.[11] William Hayley's poetic epistles to Gibbon figured history as effortlessly fecund: 'O History! whose pregnant mines impart / Unfailing treasures to poetic art.'[12] Gold or gems satisfyingly combined the organic and durable, but the trope left little room for human intervention. Hayley turned to natural history with its framework of collection and classification to restore concepts of labour and value.

> As eager Fossilists with ardour pore
> On the flat margin of the pebbled shore,
> May pay the labours of their long pursuit;
> And yield their hand the pleasure to display
> Nature's neglected Gems in nice array:
> So, GIBBON! toils the mind, whose labour wades
> Thro' the dull Chronicle's monastic shades,
> To pick from that drear coast, with learned care,
> New shells of Knowledge, thinly scatter'd there...[13]

Social narratives of quest and organic narratives of self-realisation converged in objets trouvés or, in reverse here, Nature's neglected gems. The move is characteristic of the way historians represented history-writing as a meeting point between nature and culture.

Besides establishing value, imagery was used to make criticism seem natural. So one critic represented Gibbon's 'deviations' from truth as violations of cosmic order:

> one of the satellites of Saturn, relinquishing its master-orb, and running the round of the solar system; or the moon, deserting her duty of attendance upon our earth, and losing herself in the wilderness of space; can alone image forth the strange excursiveness of Mr. Gibbon in history.[14]

The 'dark' secrets of history were also associated with winter nights. Both Thomson's *The Seasons* (1730) and Cowper's *The Task* (1785) portray history as a winter-evening occupation, that is, one where light was supplied artificially by lamps and fires. The image could be simple: when one implacable critic of Burnet called him 'a *Winter-Night Historian*', he meant the bishop was boring.[15] The metaphor usually suggested historians themselves were not in the dark: they were illuminating the past. So David Erskine, Earl of Buchan, urged the foundation of a Scottish Society of Antiquaries in terms of a metaphor of winter reading.[16]

Metaphors showed writers trying to fix history imaginatively even as they unfixed it through a proliferation of conceits.[17] More precisely, they tried to fix the role of imagination itself. In 1755 the Marquis D'Argenson told the French academy that historians needed some imagination as well as exactitude. The imagination he had in mind was 'sage, & fleurie', decorous but 'quelquefois avec feu'.[18] This concession of possible heat left room for argument about an imagination expected to both blossom and blaze. Metaphors of climate took up the theme of heat. Stylistic luxuriance (bad) entwined with ideological fervency (also bad) to create a tropical zone which self-styled temperate writers feared for its femininity and foreignness. Placing themselves, naturally, in a temperate zone, writers criticised fellow-historians for desiccation especially. Conceding that 'THE barrenness of events, and their incident circumstances in ancient times, generally produceth a dryness in the narration', Thomas Carte was unusually direct about how he had used imagination; after doing his research, he 'judged and wrote of ancient ages, as if I lived only in them'.[19] John Oldmixon added musty to dusty in his suggestion that history written by clerics 'generally smells of the Cask'[20] and John Evelyn, writing in 1699, deplored avaricious law students uninterested in history: 'who are they among this crowd...who either study, or vouchsafe to defile their fingers with any dust, save what is yellow?'[21] The scholar, the amateur and the populariser were all wary of dust. Since letters were associated with both reportage and reflection, they were potentially more dust-free than other genres.

The horror of dust has some unconscious fear in it. Like dirt, dust evokes pollution and category violation.[22] Historians' alarm was wired to two conscious fears, however: one, that their discipline might be dead and unusable and two, the opposite, that scholarly pursuits served modern political agendas all too easily. Letters were helpful here: associated with ease and openness, they were less likely to be the form preferred by antediluvians or ideologues.[23] History in the form of letters became popular because it put gender at the forefront, through the format of fathers writing history for sons. Male historians constantly reassured each other about their proper gender. Clarendon's style was praised for being 'masculine, elegant and persuasive'; Smollett was 'manly and sensible'.[24] Gibbon's admirers defended his style in terms nervous about gender: one reviewer ventured, 'Perhaps the sobriety of the Historic Muse suits not with so bright a glare of ornament' but he surrendered erotically to its headiness – 'it is a paradise of sweets almost too powerful for the sense'.[25] Anxieties about gender ran through all historiography, but especially after the mid-century when more women published their writings in epistolary form.

Debates about what constituted 'proper' and popular history writing were complicated because historians were trying to ring-fence history within a spectrum of writings that competed with history whilst sharing its interest in the past. Secret history and novels gave the term 'history' meanings that were troublesome to historians using epistolary form. Readability required an elegant style, argued Oliver Goldsmith, by which he meant one not cluttered up with footnotes. This argument meant he could use letters as a relatively informal medium, dispense with the signs of scholarship and still claim to be as much a historian as those who preferred original research to third-hand compilations like his. Hence his praise of Smollett, like himself a conservative populist, as manly and sensible. Commercial pressures to produce 'an history that may be purchased at an easy expence...delivered in a style correct yet familiar'[26] were disguised by his allusive misogyny. 'The ancients', he wrote, 'have represented history under the figure of a woman, easy, graceful, and inviting; but we have seen her in our days converted like the virgin of Nabis into an instrument of torture'.[27] Goldsmith alludes to a contraption modelled on Apega, wife of a Spartan tyrant in the second century BC. Those unwilling to give money to him were pressed against iron spikes in her arms and breasts until they changed their minds or died. Goldsmith's version of ease, ostensibly a matter of literary style, invoked a wider ideological domain whose sign of being trouble-free was to have no women in it or to have women whose only purpose was to provide pleasure for men. Scholarly history comes to seem repellent through its association with the monstrous-feminine. Goldsmith altered his sources in two significant respects: he made the woman of Nabis a virgin, whereas the ancients described her as a wife, and he suppressed the associations with extortion. These alterations show how his history constantly used misogyny to distract from its commercialism.[28] Letters here came loaded with subtle gendering.

That women, children and foreigners were consistently disassociated from eighteenth-century history can be seen in the ways historians differentiated history from romance, fairy stories and oriental tales. An exception was Horace Walpole: unusual in writing all of these, he declared that 'History in General is a Romance that is believed, and that Romance is a History that is not believed.'[29] More typical was Alexander Campbell's differentiation. He spans the full range of narratives that threaten history in his discussion of the 'fable fiction and romance' of the ancient histories of all nations:

> when a man dips into the accounts we have left of fabulous and ignorant ages, he seems to be transported into another world as it were, he treads on enchanted ground where other laws obtain, and where neither human nature, nor the nature of things appear to be the same they are now known to be; at every step, he meets with miracles, prodigies, supernatural events, and appearances of Genii, fairies, &c. But as he approaches to the more enlightened ages of knowledge and learning, they disappear by degrees, and at last, entirely vanish.[30]

This model might be explained psychoanalytically as the process of adult repression of infantile pleasure; even in the eighteenth century, it was suggested that antiquarian interests awoke people to their own earliest memories. Separating from romance meant securing history as the preserve of adult, male, European subjects with a bourgeois hostility to fantasy and aristocratic tales of chivalry. By figuring credulity as oriental, feminine or juvenile and locating transience and untruth in these representations of otherness, historians tried to persuade readers that their own work, in contrast, was believable and durable. An opponent's historical system was thus not proper history, but 'merely the fading fabric of an eastern romance, rising in a night, and vanishing in the morning'.[31] The stakes were raised because historians wanted indelibility for themselves and feared it in others.[32] As one commented, '*he looked on Falshoods in History as the Worst sort of Lying, both the most Publick and most Lasting, and still worse if persisted in after a Discovery*'.[33] A generation later, Johnson worried likewise (he had Voltaire in mind), 'Many falsehoods are passing into uncontradicted history.'[34] Epistolary form fitted in to this struggle in ambivalent ways. On the one hand, letters were a more obviously first person form than traditionally impersonal forms of history-writing, so their claims to impartiality and truth were weaker. But they allowed authority to be staged in other ways – for instance through a persona – which deflected that vituperation normally heaped by writers on historians they disliked. Less formal letters could also escape some burdens of scholarly proofs.

Letters, however, were sleeping with the enemy. They had a well-established place in two of the genres that many historians considered simultaneously rival and beneath them: fiction and secret history. The roots of secret history go back into the seventeenth century: 'by the early 1640s, certainly, epistolary discourse had developed strategies of address geared to revelation, to making state secrets public'.[35] In seventeenth-century discourses, the oral properties of letters played a significant part in history, thought to be accessible through ear-witnesses.[36] Especially popular in the early eighteenth century, secret histories encrypted real people and events into political and amorous contexts lightly glossed by feminocentric fantasy.[37] In Aphra Behn's *Love Letters between Polydorus the Gothick King, and Messalina, Late Queen of Albion*, Mary of Modena (James II's wife) looks to the French King for refuge. Between his 'growing Extasies' and her 'fervent Boilings',[38] historical questions about the fate of dispossessed royals are transmuted into a fiery narrative of passions, uncertain aristocratic affections and plebeian faithlessness. Secret histories were associated with changes at court especially when supercharged politics made history harder to follow.[39] Court intrigues involved women, and many secret histories besides *The Fair Concubine* featured 'a Petticoat Plotter',[40] which allowed women to enjoy romanticised versions of history – and also to write them. Hence the titillating title *Court Secrets, or The Lady's Chronicle, Historical and Gallant* (1727) was used for a collection of Madame de Sévigné's letters.[41]

Romance and secret history parodied professional historical argument.[42] The author of *The Secret History of an Old Shoe* set at defiance 'the whole Possee of defunct Historians' and delighted in upsetting 'Mr. *Historiographus of Cambridge*' who thought history should be written only 'in a plain strong easy Stile'.[43] Minuteness associated with historical scrupulosity became in romance intimate or illicit details, with disconcerting mimicry: '*History* and *Biography* may appear to be Twin Sisters in the Eyes of some People'.[44] Historians did not want wholly to cast off fiction, however, since they shared its interests in narrative, character and morality. Though novelists and historians agreed in denigrating romance, fiction's increasing strength compounded historians' problems with discursive boundaries, blurred by the practice among novelists of calling their stories histories. When novelists like Henry Fielding wanted to differentiate their kind of fiction from romance, they aligned themselves with history, a separation that repeated the gendering of romance as low because feminine.[45] Even after the mid-century when the market for history increased, thanks to the success of Robertson and Hume, competition between history and fiction continued. When Goldsmith reviewed Madame de Maintenon's memoirs, he denounced 'amphibious productions...in which History wears the face of Romance, and Romance assumes the appearance of History; where the Writer's endeavours are equally exerted in rendering trifles important, and subjects of importance trifling'.[46] But when writing biography (and when there were no troublesome women about), he was happy to promote memoirs above history:

> There are few who do not prefer a page of *Montaigne* or *Colley Cibber*, who candidly tells us what they thought of the world, and the world thought of them, to the more stately memoirs and transactions of *Europe*, where we see kings pretending to immortality, that are now almost forgotten, and statesmen planning frivolous negociations, that scarce outlive the signing.[47]

Letters could go either way: to writers of secret history, they had confessional appeal; to historians, they offered links to biography and ear-witnessing.

The directives governing history – to expose the truth, to trace causes of events, to promote morality, to be neither too dry nor too luscious – seem plain. History's inseparability from politics, however, meant historians quarrelled endlessly about the rights and wrongs of the Restoration and relations between monarchy and liberty in British history, going back to prehistory. In this context, letters had special uses. They provided fresh and extensive sources for the seventeenth century, that era most immediately contended. The abundance of such materials made people careless of them even as their growing historical value made scholars avid for them, and letters came to epitomise the vulnerability of records generally. In 1699 John Evelyn wrote to William Nicolson deploring the patchy safeguards for collections in the Paper Office: thanks to riflings and neglect, by the Restoration, 'it was almost as if there had never been any correspondence abroad before...abundance of those papers and dispatches you mention, and which ought to centre there, have been carried away'.[48] Evelyn blamed ministers and ambassadors who left letters to their heirs, 'as honourable marks of their ancestor's employment', turning state property into family possessions. Evelyn's own losses included letters from Mary Queen of Scots, which he lent to Burnet for his *History of the Reformation*; Burnet, he reported disbelievingly, claimed his printer had lost them.[49] Some later historians like

Hume showed more cooperation, but that too stressed the symbolic function of letters and documents: 'they held a potentially divisive group together and, when invoked in the new historical texts, they signified the assumptions that united that group.'[50]

Trust and cooperation between historians were all the more valuable because history was an expensive and exclusive pursuit. One historian complained that London was

> the city in the world where it is most difficult for a private and obscure man to get access to books of real learning and antiquity, and that it would have required a princely fortune to afford to buy what I should have wanted to consult on this subject, and a palace to lodge them in afterwards.[51]

Recommending folio volumes of state papers and letters, one self-improvement guide noted the class weighting of historical study: 'these collections are more suited to a nobleman's Library, than a moderate Collection'.[52] Writers who aimed to make general history affordable admitted they cut corners.[53] Research then, as now, cost money. A representative case was that of Foote Gower, who worked on a large history of Cheshire. In 1771 he proposed a subscription of six to ten guineas by 200 local gentlemen to defray his estimated costs of £3000. Gower was lucky enough to own some of his material, including five folio volumes of the correspondence of Sir William Brereton, a Parliamentary general. But this was a drop in the ocean of sources which included 'the almost incredible number of 268 LARGE VOLUMES' amassed by a local family.[54] By 1773 Gower's proposals had swelled to three folio volumes; the project was 'already too alarmingly expensive for a single and a private hand'.[55] Even with copies and extracts from public records promised by supporters, he anticipated consulting 400 volumes of private manuscripts, 'all of which must be completely perused and partially transcribed'. If he used a specialist amanuensis, his costs would spiral; if not, his labours would lengthen.[56]

The situation was eased by intermittent publication of substantial collections of documents, letters and other papers.[57] But institutional resources were limited: 'The British Museum was not opened until 1759 and there was no British equivalent to the Academie des Inscriptions, established by Louis XIV to promote historical study and to preserve historical remains.'[58] Frequently access to materials depended on owners approving scholars, especially on political grounds. John Cotton denied Burnet entrance to his library of manuscripts on the grounds that he had too little respect for the royal prerogative. Only after a sympathetic relative smuggled him in was Burnet able to work, clandestinely, on those papers. (Cotton relented and gave him official access in time for his third volume.)[59] That Burnet discussed this in print suggests how scholars were becoming less willing to be subject to the controls of patronage, even though they were still tied to the aristocracy for materials.[60] Although politics supposedly had no place in the republic of letters, claims of bias flew about because historians were often clearly partisan. The Duke of Ormond's family gave Thomas Carte extensive Stuart correspondence because of his Jacobite sympathies.[61] Some of these letters were used by James Macpherson in his *Original Papers; Containing the Secret History of Great Britain, from the Restoration, to the Accession of the House of Hannover* [sic]. He printed Stuart and Hanoverian papers for each year, an even-handed approach reflected in benefactions to him. Macpherson paid tribute to 'the peculiar condescension and liberality' of two gentlemen who let him use their Hanoverian collections but he was also scathing about the non-cooperation of other owners:

> Men having become distrustful of the principles of their ancestors are, from selfish views, interested in their reputations. With a preposterous view of attachment to their progenitors, they seem to think, that to conceal their actions is the only way to preserve their fame.[62]

Secretion of sources reflected the profound generational tension of the Civil War which helped make father–son motifs important in historiography too. As Matthias Earbery put it, *'no Man likes that History, so closely pressing upon the Present Age, should be all Masquerade, that none can know, with all their illustrious Blood, their Fathers or nearest Relations'.*[63] Claims to legitimacy made historiography as riven as the monarchies it chronicled.

These inescapably partisan aspects of history made readers want records and letters published in full:

> the World desires nothing so much as to see the Truth of Things, as they were really Design'd and Acted, rather from some Original Papers, than from the Collections or Extracts of Persons of whose Fidelity or Judgment they were not well assured.[64]

A shift from history such as Livy's, in which an author might make up speeches, to an increasingly text-based history, changed historians' labour from rhetoric to research.[65] Some were unhappy: Goldsmith fearfully anticipated a Shandean nightmare in which the transactions of a single year took folios to write, and cited an actual history of the world which by 1763 had reached its 61st volume.[66] Others saw new possibilities opening up. William Nicolson, who knew better than anyone how many papers were potentially available, suggested that letters and journals could supply biographies of statesmen.[67] As an example, he praised John Strype's *Life* of Sir John Cheke, who died of a broken heart in exile from Mary Tudor's rule, noting 'There's a good Collection of Letters to and from this unhappy great Man.'[68]

Nicolson was particularly excited about the wealth of Tudor letters, in part from relief at the human dimension supplied by letters in otherwise overwhelmingly large series of public documents. Nicolson had seen in the Cotton Library alone over 400 volumes of treaties between the English and the French;[69] such material could be animated by focusing on the people involved in these negotiations. The correspondence of diplomats was especially valuable because they were often as conscious as historians of sources, facts and biases. Nicolson instanced the letters of Roger Ascham, secretary to Edward VI, Mary and Elizabeth as examples of dispassionate assessment: 'THE grand Advantage and Light that accrues to History, from the Epistolary Remarks of Men of Sense and Business, is so very obvious and apparent, that I shall need only just to touch upon it.'[70] In analysing their uses, he balanced the interests of old and new history: 'In these we have all the fine Variety of Language that's proper for the rendring of either a Petition or Complaint the most agreeable; and (withal) a deal of very choice Historical Matter, that is hardly preserv'd any-where else.'[71]

It was not only foreign policy that letters illuminated. Thomas Carte used the (predictably voluminous) correspondence of the Noailles brothers, consecutive French ambassadors to Mary Tudor's court, to discuss the politics of her reign. His praise of them as 'men of excellent parts, judgment, merit, and integrity' showed the masculine bias in transhistorical community between diplomats and historians.[72] Historians argued that 'Men of Sense always spoke like Men of Sense'.[73] It took one to know one, they meant. Burnet's account of Mary's reign also used letters in new ways. He tracked the epistolary machinery of government by which Mary oversaw political allegiances and religious persecution, through letters of thanks to supporters, letters of intimidation to opponents and letters of instructions to lords, gentlemen, sheriffs and mayors. These letters showed state, local and personal functions. They stabilised the dubious historical value of hearsay by the security of attributable writing. Eye-witnessing replaced ear-witnessing.

Reservations about the importance of letters were rare: Macpherson was a lone voice in suggesting some letters were boring or duplicated public records. He made extensive use of the papers of Nairne, an under-secretary to three successive ministers to the Stuarts, but argued that most letter-writers had

> a very imperfect idea of the whole system of national affairs and the intrigues and secrets of a system. A writer must stand, as it were, in the very point where informations from all parties unite and concentrate, to judge of transactions and of men with precision.[74]

This vantage point he thought was best reserved for historians rather than letter-writers. Those who wrote up their own times were both historian and historical subject, but virtually all the criticism this genre attracted was for its political colouring rather than its narrative perspective on events. People agreed that letters, being to-the-moment, could represent a historical moment. As in epistolary travel writing, a trope of 'on the spot' was used as a mark of unassailable authenticity. This view was upheld by Horatio, Lord Walpole, even as he took furious exception to Lord Bolingbroke's account of Queen Anne's reign. Blissfully ignoring the irony that both he and Bolingbroke had participated in the same epoch but had radically different versions of it, he, like most eighteenth-century historical commentators, wanted unproblematic relations between epistolary trees and historical woods.[75]

Symmetries between letters as historical material and history written in letters made them the medium as well as stuff of history. A sequence of seventeenth-century letters could be read as a narrative by an eighteenth-century historian. Since both writer and reader built up the story bit by bit, letters became a symbol of historical narrative. Time lapses between letters were the formal equivalent of epistemological gaps but less troubling precisely because they were literary signs. The letter-writer unable to write everything would select salient information; so too would the historian. Thus epistolary method was not only a happy medium between dry and swampy extremes but also 'best calculated to preserve the Chain of Events' whilst still allowing both detail and reflection, 'which many consider as the chief Merit in History'.[76]

That letters, like chains, had gaps as well as links explains their popularity amongst amateurs like Rupert Green who, aged eight, was probably the youngest eighteenth-century historian. His conservative *Abstract of the History of England* (1779) fitted each reign into the compass of a letter that apparently took him on average a fortnight to write. But since epistolary form made assertions as well as concessions, it should not be read too quickly as uncertain. Its accessibility made it a favourite medium with populist historians, writers like Goldsmith and Russell whose works sold well between the 1760s and 1780s. Publishing her history in the same decades, Catharine Macaulay might be supposed to have chosen letters as a relatively female-friendly form. That she did not until 1778 when she published a more popular version shows epistolary form acquired associations with middle-market history which scholars rightly suspected of inadequate research. Macaulay owned a very impressive library of seventeenth-century tracts, but sought a broader audience for her *History of England from the Revolution to the Present Time in a Series of Letters to a Friend* [the Reverend Dr Wilson] (1778) than for her *History of England*. Using no footnotes and sustaining a broad narrative sweep,[77] she makes use of her addressee to figure at least one respectable person taking her seriously and sharing her devotion to liberty. This could be read conventionally as a gendered defence against public hostility to women writing history, although by 1778 Macaulay was surely inured to detraction. Rather, her choice of epistolary form at this juncture can be read as a radical appropriation of the letter as a democratic medium needing to be rescued from misogynist Tories and monarchist juveniles.[78] In her epistolary history she ventured up to the present. Noting 'it is not safe for an historian to draw a very just and accurate description' of principal players, she invoked her addressee's supposed encouragement. Letters allowed her to analyse individual and systemic factors: Queen Anne was a bigot, a slave and a victim, but 'The vices of her reign were the vices of those by whom she was governed'.[79] Weak monarchs are bad, because being weak they are ruled by bad advisers. Macaulay's attack on monarchy and Tories gains force from the gendering of historiography at this point. Macaulay had observed in 1763, 'The general education of the English youth is not adapted to cherish those generous sentiments of independency, which is the only characteristic of a real gentleman.'[80] Providing a test case, the young Rupert Green ended his epistolary history, published the year after Macaulay's, with a Postscript professing loyalty to the current king, George III, as if dateable letters updated traditional sentiments. The use of letters in to-the-moment history was an important ground of contention between Whigs and Tories, scholars and amateurs, misogynists and women.

Among the antiquarians

The microcosmic world of the antiquarians shows how letters helped define intellectual community. Eighteenth-century antiquarians saw themselves as bringing the Enlightenment into dark periods where there were few texts and patchy material remains.[81] Stuart Piggott argues that antiquarian studies were in decline in the early decades 'but some were going down fighting'.[82] Certainly many were busy fighting each other. Because evidence was limited, interpretation was contentious. Pages of controversy turned on how best to decipher eroded inscriptions. Specialist skills such as knowledge of old languages or antique coinage tended to fan rather than settle disputes; etymologies, for instance, could be tortured any number of ways.[83] In this small world, friendships were nurtured by letter. More than that, scholars cultivated what in the republic of letters was known as *commerce des lettres*: 'regular, arranged correspondence, sometimes between strangers – with colleagues elsewhere. Through a commerce they could find out what works were in progress, which in press, who was in controversy with whom, and what other people thought of new publications.'[84] Correspondence served as a model of the exchange and evolution of ideas, in script and print. As Edward Lhwyd wrote to Henry Rowlands, who printed the letter as if to state his own commitment to open-mindedness, ' 'Tis the happiest Temper a Man can be Master of, not to be too tenacious of his Conjectures'.[85] Publications favoured provisional, conversational titles – *Discourses*, *Remarks* and *Conjectures* seemed to uphold a communicative ideal which in practice involved much wrangling. The dialogic aspects of letters allowed authors to address rivals' errors and though challengers were not obliged to propose counter-theories, many did so. Since resources were even more limited than for other kinds of history, letter-writing was the more symbolic as a medium for sharing. As William Nicolson put it, organising an amiable exchange with Lhywd, 'I do not understand the humour of making discoveries of this kind, purely for a man's own private information. And yet I see that is the sordid pleasure of a great many of us sullen antiquaries.'[86] This sharing created a kind of trickle-up history, so to speak, in which specialist information was obtained by active correspondents who directed it to appropriate outlets. In 1724 Thomas Hearne wrote enviously of the antiquarian Anthony Wood, compiler of a biographical dictionary of Oxford authors, 'indeed, 'tis almost incredible what came to him by letter, I mean, lives drawn up for him, and Catalogues of the respective Authors' Writings'.[87]

In the antiquarians' strained world of touchiness and diffidence, letter-writing was full of pitfalls. 'The unwritten rules demanded that those high in the scholarly hierarchy deserved especially respectful treatment', but the pay-off for that respect could be 'Reflected Glory'.[88] One case illustrates the risks.[89] In 1738 Francis Wise published *A Letter to Dr. Mead Concerning Some Antiquities in Berkshire*. Though Wise, an Oxford don, noted gloomily, 'Every science has it's [sic] discouragements, and none perhaps more than that of Antiquities',[90] he also hoped antiquarianism could attract national support, perhaps by reviving the Saxon Olympics. His main topic was the White Horse at Uffington, a stylised image cut out of the turf on a chalk ridge. It was a Saxon battle emblem, he suggested, a monument to commemorate King Alfred's victory over the Danes at Ashdown in 871. Ashdown had no confirmed location: Wise tortuously proposed linguistic corruptions that would make it the village of Aston. His explanation of why Alfred should have such an unconventional monument was equally ingenious: Alfred was too busy beating Danes to commit time and resources to having anything built. In 1739 'Philalethes Rusticus', thought to be a Mr Asplin (dubbed Mr All-spleen by one of Wise's friends), demolished Wise's arguments. Aston was probably a corruption not of Ashdown but 'East-town' and the Saxon battle horse – which anyway may have been a dragon – was rampant not galloping like the White Horse. Why, he asked, should the monument have been preserved but not the memory of its occasion or maker? Because his intemperate title, *The Impertinence and Imposture of Modern Antiquaries Display'd*, attacked a whole community, another scholar, George North, stepped in to defend Wise and to tell Philalethes he should 'not try and refute a well-wrote Piece by Abuse and Scurrility: but answer Argument by Argument, like a Gentleman and a Scholar'.[91] Letter-writing reinforced the connections between those two identities.

Nonetheless, North evaded two charges that reflected on the antiquarian community. One was that Wise had used Mead's name to sanction a weak argument. North brushed this aside, arguing Mead was a community figure-head who was not obliged to read all letters addressed to him. Epistolary form, he implied, enacted a symbolic relation between scholars which made their personal acquaintance, or lack of it, irrelevant. It is noticeable though that Wise silently dropped Mead as an addressee in his *Further Observations* on the subject in 1742. But the point remains: letter-writing allowed a scholar to claim a relationship with a more famous scholar, as if the addressee's status would rub off on the apprentice like gilt. That this relationship might be unsought on the senior's part was understood but unimportant – indeed, it was part of the ritual of struggle as youth locked horns with age. So Gibbon corresponded as a very young man with the Swiss professor Breitinger: 'the combination of aggression and deference in the presence of authority... is an early milestone' in his professional development as a historian, observes one biographer.[92] Corresponding in Latin demonstrated learning and invoked a classical hierarchy, but 'the formulas of classical deference make tenacity possible'.[93] By keeping company with veterans, the recruit lost rawness.

The Wise–Mead–North exchange aired the issue of authority through correspondence and also a discourse about kings to which letters were relevant: first as a genre with potential levelling properties, and second as a means of debating national character, sometimes accentuated through personae. Wise's sequel discontinued acclaim for Saxon heritage, which suggests Philalethes' rather mad accusations of popery had hit home. To Philalethes, antiquarian nationalism undermined modern patriotism. He invented a paranoid old Whig who keeps asking, 'What is it to him, whether the *Saxons* thrashed the *Danes*, or the *Danes* thrash'd the *Saxons* 800 Years ago?'[94] Not only were the Saxons not English but because King Alfred had been to Rome they were tainted with papist idolatry. Admiration for King Alfred was thus covert Jacobitism and disloyalty to King George. Philalethes' illogic shows how eighteenth-century historians used the past to wage political battles with special reference to the monarchy. 'THE greatest part of mankind form their political opinions on the usages of past times', argued one.[95] Though all periods could be politicised thus, the seventeenth century most obviously obliged historians to side with one of the 'Two Armies of Epithets', pro- or anti-monarchy.[96] Contentions were doubled by there being two royal families to choose from. The contortions are nicely illustrated by a text which argued that William of Orange was the most English king because it was an English tradition to import foreigners as kings; furthermore, if Englishness was defined as a belief in liberty, a Hanoverian who upheld the constitution was, though German, more English than a Stuart who imposed royal prerogatives on an otherwise free people.[97] Paul Langford's observation that 'Englishness is a term much employed by historians' applies with added irony to eighteenth-century historians' interpretation of an Old English past.[98] Precisely because letters were nominally open to anyone, reflections on national unity took on ideological heat. Agreeing to be gentlemen and scholars united letter-writers up to a point; disagreements about the political colouring of national character divided them again.

Considerations of class difference also informed epistolary history. At its simplest, for instance in children's eyes, history was about kings.[99] More sophisticatedly, it dealt with royal policy on a daily basis – literally so in the case of Burnet, who pointed out that he had had 'much free conversation' with five monarchs.[100] It was part of the remit of history not to be awed into panegyric: as Hayley put it, the historian required 'An eagle-eye, that with undazzled gaze / Can look on Majesty's meridian blaze.'[101] Even reactionary historians were beguiled: 'what can be more entertaining than ... to constitute ourselves judges of the merit of even kings?'[102] One clever parody of historiography noted the anxiety induced by such 'Familiarities, not nicely regardful of *Distinctions*': 'There is also something *levelling* in these Enquiries; where we find Rottenness and Corruption, Dust and Ashes, to be equally the Fate of the Emperor and the meanest of his Vassals.'[103] Publication of royal correspondence meant that others besides historians could familiarise themselves with monarchs: 'every Man has Liberty to look into the Cabinets of the great'.[104] Since the past defined national identities, old letters supplied historical slurs. Hence the Pope used to show visitors to Rome Henry VIII's love-letters to Anne Boleyn, hoping to shame the English.[105] Letters passed on royal gossip and irreverent anecdotes. A Hanoverian envoy wrote home about Queen Anne that she 'GOT DRUNK every day, as a remedy against the gout in her stomach.'[106] The letters of William of Orange to his grandmother were stately enough[107] – though plebeian old ladies can be imperious too – but to his uncle Charles II he sounded cynical; his subscriptions invoke affection coldly. The editor celebrated his heroic subject with all possible respect, yet these letters exposed the personal manoeuverings of princely discourse. For perhaps the first time and with long-running implications, royal families sounded like any other.

Epistolary form created communities that were partly closed, which suited gentlemen-scholars, and partly open, which suited popularisers. Yet as both source material and medium, letters introduced new voices, grating to old ears, in which class and methodological differences overrode common masculine interests. One prime example of this can be found in the controversy surrounding Lord Bolingbroke's *Letters on the Study and Use of History* – to which I turn next.

Bolingbroke and history

Henry St John, Viscount Bolingbroke, was a political maverick: leader of the Tories, minister to Queen Anne, sometime political partner of Harley, orchestrator of the Peace of Utrecht in 1714 and, following the Whig ascendancy, organiser of Jacobite interests before returning to the Hanoverian fold. A friend of Pope and Swift, he cultivated a philosophical role not least because it lent purpose to the periods of exile and retirement that chequered his career. *Letters on the Study and Use of History* was written in 1735–36, but not published until 1752, after his death. The letters were addressed to a young nobleman initially unnamed but evidently expected to participate in national affairs. He turns out to be Lord Cornbury, later Lord Hyde; as the grandson of Clarendon the historian, he represented a historical dynasty. Like Wise writing to Mead, Bolingbroke's choice of correspondent laid a symbolic claim to authority. The *Letters'* core was an attack on the orthodoxy of accepting parts of the Old Testament as historically accurate. The genealogies of the Book of Genesis, for instance, could hardly be taken as a full history of the twenty centuries that they spanned chronologically. Bolingbroke was theologically slippery, seeming to uphold the deist notion that at least parts of the Bible were not sacred writ. There were thus two controversial matters to respond to: the Bible's integrity as a sacred text and the historical methods that might sift fact from fable. Also open to challenge were Bolingbroke's general remarks on history, the encouragement his views gave to deism and an account of his own times at the end.

Predictably, churchmen rushed in to defend Biblical purity. One argued that the Bible must all be true because Moses would not lie. Another wrote that whether or not it was true, he wanted the comfort of belief.[108] A hefty refutation was mounted by Robert Clayton, Bishop of Clogher, using his own peculiar cosmology.[109] More orthodox was James Hervey's *Remarks on Lord Bolingbroke's Letters* (1752), a response ostensibly written in obedience to the commands of an anonymous lady of quality. Hervey was well known for mildness and his letters humbly beg her ladyship's compliance with his instruction. But for all his modesty Hervey clearly recuperates theology from history by replacing Bolingbroke's young nobleman with an addressee equally aristocratic, but debarred by her gender from any civic and historical destiny. Deference to aristocrats paradoxically enhanced the authority of scripture because her ladyship's quality required a politeness based on volition, rather than the intellectual kowtowing which lordships imposed.

Almost the only defender of Bolingbroke was Voltaire who proposed that, since history was open to the enquiry of the learned, philosophers had a right to be heard.[110] But the élitist associations of princely philosophers whom Voltaire admired grated on English ears. As Thomas Hunter put it, 'when Nobles commence Philosophers...they put themselves on a level with the people'.[111] Many were offended by Bolingbroke's manner: 'he dictates like a prince to his slaves', complained one,[112] with some justification since Bolingbroke described those involved in historical spadework as peasants (implying that theorists like himself were their generals). His lordship's conceit was attributed to class rather than simply personality: if his talents – which nobody denied he had – were individual, his rank gave them authority. Because the nobility would be sure to support one of themselves, to bring Bolingbroke down required commensurately aristocratic methods. An author should choose 'the *Rapier*, which will do the business every bit as well, certainly was more becoming his Lordship's Character, and Rank in

Life than the *Pole-ax* of the Butcher'.[113] In this pamphlet, the rapier consisted of increasingly ironic encomium. Other writers used sarcasm less politely: one commented of Bolingbroke's blunders that 'his Quality requires the Word "trips" or makes "faux pas" '[114]; another made a witty dig at Bolingbroke's limited reading – 'This remark may be thought only to impeach his Lordship's knowledge in title pages.'[115] Most responses challenged Bolingbroke not only about his accuracy and arguments, but also about how he had infused class prerogatives into letters in order to lord it over professional historians. For example, Bolingbroke habitually invoked his addressee at controversial moments. In personal correspondence, his care not to tire his addressee with detail would be considerate; in historiography, it let epistolary form shake off burdens of proof. It was a humourless version of John Oldmixon's tongue-in-cheek argument that he had deliberately left his footnotes incomplete so as to test the scholarship of his critics. Here, Bolingbroke's 'talking so fluently, quoting so familiarly'[116] was the *sprezzatura* of a courtier whose grasp of essentials was proved by his neglect of details.

Hostility to Bolingbroke was not just a reaction against arrogance. Underneath ran resentment at how he had commandeered a communicative form, using letters for exclusion, not community. Critics were offended at the letters' posthumous publication, which pre-empted dialogue: one, angry at 'this cowardly way of bequeathing Writings', set out to dig Bolingbroke up from the grave metaphorically, like any common regicide.[117] Dialogue was restored by the notable preference for epistolary form among Bolingbroke's critics. One author went further and included a formal dialogue in his critique. Alexander Campbell agreed with Bolingbroke that the Old Testament was a procrustean bed for sacred history. Scornful of clerical devotees of the Bible's integrity who 'recommend it so earnestly to the constant perusal of their dear, believing lords and ladies',[118] he was equally suspicious of aristocrats who appropriated history for cultural capital. Partly mediating between Bolingbroke and his opponents, he invoked the republic of letters as a cultural field in which ordinary people had a stake just as much as aristocrats or clerics. The author is challenged by a tradesman character who tells him 'your volumes are so valuable, that I have not money to buy them, and were you to give them to me for nothing, which you do not seem disposed to, they are so vast, I have not time to read them'.[119] His wife and mother persuade him to buy a popular history, issued in parts, but he knows this is not the real thing. The author is sympathetic to 'this worthy and virtuous citizen' because he represents a lower middle class alienated from knowledge by controversy. He is shut out by a lack of resources and because he is expected to believe what he is told. In this way, what might seem arcane arguments about sacred history become ideologically central as evidence of the powers of the first estate over the second and third. Sacred and contemporary history are connected by Christian controversialists: troublemakers since ancient Rome, they have finally been abashed by the glorious Revolution of 1688. Campbell wanted Christianity to be devolved away from theologians and historians and entailed on a wider society constituted by reason. At Judgment Day, he argued,

> I hardly think it shall be asked of me, whether I have been a christian, a jew, or a mahometan, these are circumstances which depend on the external accidents of place, time, and education, with which I have no concern; but if I be asked, how I have behaved as a master of a family, and a member of society? I hope I shall be able to give a satisfactory answer...[120]

But this attempt to dismantle dogmas of class on which Bolingbroke depended, and dogmas of creed on which his opponents depended, does not question the patriarchal powers of the paterfamilias who displaces the aristocrat and cleric. Even in relatively open forms like dialogues and letters, history was not neutral in gender.

The introduction of a Bill to naturalise Jews in 1753 (later withdrawn) made the Bolingbroke controversy topical. If Jewish history could be detached from sacred history, the case for Christianity became thinner, which might encourage Jews empowered by new property rights to resist conversion. Campbell was unusual in not caring about maintaining separate creeds; far more common was a investment in ideological reproduction, literal and figurative, so that differences were not solved by rational argument but bred out. Repeatedly writers used letters between fathers and sons to dramatise the ideological inheritance which history made available. The fathers are almost always noble, though the authors are not. This fiction borrowed from Lord Chesterfield's posthumous reputation as an educationalist.[121] The association of history with masculinity gave it cross-class appeal even though aristocratic protagonists made it class-specific: 'the knowledge of affairs in antient and modern times, is the highest qualification of any man, from the senator down to the mechanic'.[122] The prospect of senators communicating with mechanics was possible in dialogues, a form that mimicked conversation, but less so in letters where differential literacy would strain exchange, so sons stepped in as recipients. *The Roman History*, for example, is addressed to the son of an unnamed nobleman, destined to make a distinguished figure in 'the British senate'. 'Frederick' has already read – and admired, naturally – the anonymous author's earlier volume, *The History of England*. Now at university, Frederick corresponds with his father to demonstrate his capacity for an active civic role. In fact the father dominates, though he tries to temper paternal authority with affection so that the son can be free to make mistakes: 'I have nothing but your interest and benefit in view, and therefore do not imagine that I am going to act the part of an imperious dictator.'[123] The son may even surpass the father. 'You are too dear to me, to suffer jealousy to take place in my mind on account of your superior abilities.'[124] Expertise in history offers a male reader the pleasurable fantasy of peaceful resolution of oedipal rivalry. Personal affection will prevent the acrimony of professional historians, while epistolary exchange between males of different ages creates limited democracy.

The double act of fathers and sons sold well – understandably, since it combined fictions of class and gender. In Goldsmith's *An History of England*, another anonymous nobleman writes to his son Charles, also at university. Goldsmith tried to make the aristocratic persona bring together two markets: the élite world of his protagonists and the humbler world of schools.[125] The letters, he pretends, have been circulating in manuscript; their author, who has managed to compose them in between his public duties, has permitted the editor to publish them and give offprints to selected schools. The letters inform more accessibly than the question-and-answer format traditionally preferred by schoolmasters, claims Goldsmith; he dismisses an objection that they may be 'above the capacity of boys' with the curious response that 'those who are rising up to manhood, should be treated as men'.[126] A doubt about age-groups slides onto the securer ground of a gender-group. In case anyone misses the point, he repeats it: 'Children can never be too soon treated as men.'

This gendering of correspondence debars girls, who might otherwise think of themselves as children. In fact, females of all ages were advised by conduct writers to read history as an alternative to fiction. The publisher John Murray wrote sneeringly in 1783 that female readers skewed the market (and successful historians had sold out to them): 'To make a saleable work it should be addressed to the Mob of Readers, to literary Amateurs, & to Smatterers in taste ... If you are able to entertain the ladies your business is done.'[127] One girl happily inspired by reading history was Catharine Macaulay:

> From my early youth I have read with delight those histories that exhibit Liberty in its most exalted state, the annals of the Roman and Greek republics. Studies like these excite that natural love of freedom which lies latent in the breast of every rational being, till it is nipped by the frost of prejudice, or blasted by the influence of vice.[128]

'Every rational being' may escape gendering, but only momentarily: 'A good citizen is a credit to his country, and merits the approbation of every virtuous man.' But Macaulay feigns neither nobility nor paternity; when she used epistolary form she wrote as herself. In fact, she opposes family affections to civic commitments, praising patriots who sacrifice personal ties to social interests. Though she claims inspiration from 'our illustrious ancestors',[129] she associates father–son relationships with autocratic rights of succession which, in the case of the Stuarts, have made the monarchy an oppressive institution. This association between families and royal families only made epistolary paradigms of fathers and sons more attractive to male and Tory writers of popular history.[130]

Catharine Macaulay minimised gender in order to reclaim history from conservative men; Catherine Talbot's less well known contribution to *Athenian Letters* returns to secret history in order to let women in.[131] *Athenian Letters* is a compound epistolary text; it drew on Thucydides, the *Turkish Spy* and seventeenth-century diplomatic correspondence. Its famous characters overlapped with those in Crébillon fils' *Lettres Atheniennes*, which it disparaged as *'petit maîtres* [sic] *and petites maîtresses'*.[132] Written by different people, the letters included history, geography, literary criticism, philosophy and religion, comparing ancient and modern rivalries, treaties and wars. Athens, Sparta and Persia are the England, Prussia and France of the day. In antiquity, power is not balanced but oscillates between vacuum and vortex. It is prevented from becoming unstable so long as statesmen are committed to resolving differences honourably rather than fomenting them. Wars start because of individuals' moral failings. The text takes a strong stand against corruption as the site where psychology, history and politics fuse to warp personal integrity and national interests. Different political systems are debated at length: Cleander, a Persian protagonist, upholds absolute monarchy but encounters alternatives as episodically as *Star Trek* – the democratic Athenians, the republican Spartans and a variety of ancient governments, all in a polite guise.

The first edition was ushered in by a preface which claimed the manuscript, originally in Spanish, came from a Jew who had access to rare Arabic versions of Greek and Latin authors in the library at Fez in Morocco, who left it to an English consul at Tunis. Progressing round the Mediterranean, the text's geographical masquerade leaves little room for women anywhere. Nonetheless, of the 179 letters shared between 13 writers, 4 were written by Catherine Talbot, a friend of the project's prime mover, Lord Hardwicke, and better known as a friend of the scholar and writer Elizabeth Carter. The book's high moral content could allow a woman to join in the fiction but its idealism was heavily gendered. A letter paying tribute to the memory of an honourable courtier, Hydaspes, makes integrity didactically masculine: 'Nor did he ever express a zeal in any cause, to which he was not by honour and principle most firmly attached. In this address and behaviour he shewed a becoming ease, a manly gracefulness; nothing effeminate, nothing fantastical.'[133] Talbot wrote two letters that fitted this agenda – a sober account of the Eleusinian mysteries and an anti-corruption letter in which she avoids gendered bodies thanks to sensibility's emphasis on hearts. More interesting in terms of historiography are her other two letters, from Sappho to Cleander. In the first, Sappho is offended that Cleander has written an ode about her; in the second, she upbraids him for having betrayed some unspecified confidence. A 'Translator's note' emphasises the obscurity of their relationship but stresses its probity, since nowhere else does Cleander show any tendency to womanise. 'Our Ephesian understood how to converse with the ladies for political purposes, without proceeding to gallantries; which shews him to have been a most complete master in the most refined insinuation.'[134] In other words, Cleander is a better diplomat because he talks to women and because he talks to them about politics rather than amours. Normally, secret history makes sex part of politics and romance part of history. Talbot repudiates the role of mistress (and hence *petite-maîtresse*) for Sappho, who shares Cleander's moral vocabulary: 'We both have been deceived by names: Faith, Honour, Constancy, Discretion, Tenderness, these too I find are empty names.'[135] The vocabulary can apply equally to matters of love or politics, but since Cleander's betrayal is disassociated from sex, Sappho's idealism is linked to civic as well as personal integrity. Rather than drawing men into the feminised world of gallantry, Talbot uses the overlap between history and secret history to give women a voice in a moralised civic world.

Athenian Letters does briefly address women's place in the ancient world and with an eye to modern arguments. In a discussion at Aspasia's house, Cleander argues that 'a single national tyrant makes many family ones',[136] but his conclusions are not liberal: Spartan women are too bold, Persian women too secluded, Ephesian women too worldly. Aspasia points out that in Egypt women are too exploited – men sit around and women do all the work – but otherwise Cleander's views are unchallenged. In this context, Catherine Talbot's shift of the gendered ground of history is more than fractional. In one of Talbot's dialogues, 'reading abundance of history' is one of the summer resolutions an eighteen-year-old woman makes (and light-heartedly fails to keep).[137] That an author as relentlessly polite as Talbot should contribute to a historical fiction in terms of secret history shows how constrained the options were for female historians.

Horace Walpole

Was Horace Walpole an historian? And if so, of what? Peter Sabor argues Walpole has been seen as a source rather than a writer of history, paradoxically because his letters are such a good source for historians now. Timothy Mowl likewise notes his irresistibility as a source. Calling him respectively a 'bottomless mine' and a 'treasure trove', they return us to tropes of history as self-evidently valuable but semi-processed.[138] Sabor makes a persuasive case that 'Walpole, despite his many claims to the contrary, was a historian of art, architecture, gardening, literature and politics, and that his formal historical works, long overshadowed by his correspondence, should not be regarded merely as source material.' This case turns on certain publications, including *A Catalogue of Royal and Noble Authors* (1758), *Anecdotes of Painting in England* (1762–71), *Historic Doubts on Richard III* (1768) and *An Essay on Modern Gardening* (1771). The letters are explicitly counted out:

> Walpole's depiction of his memoirs as raw material for subsequent historians does accurately characterize his letters, which were immediate reactions to contemporary events, frequently written before outcomes could be known and thus possessing the advantages and disadvantages of 'to the moment' accounts.[139]

The distinction between 'immediate reactions' and historiography was already confused in the genre of the history of one's own times; where history traced causes, letters offered reflections which had a shorter reach but were no less analytical. In the *Memoirs*, Walpole described his material: 'I am no historian; I write casual Memoirs; I draw characters; I preserve anecdotes.'[140] Historians proper, he continued, could take it or leave it. But their choice was made possible because of what contemporaries preserved. Mowl describes Walpole the letter-writer as 'a professional friend'; Sabor, more helpfully, describes Walpole the historian as 'amateur but not dilettante'.[141] Between the two is a category of a writer of history in letters, which I propose to apply to Walpole in this section. The dedicated collector and cataloguer – both of which Walpole indisputably was – are lower in the academic food-chain than the historian, but they are interdependent life-forms. Moreover, with the growth of museum studies, what used to seem a natural practice of object gathering has turned into a cultural science of culture. 'Preserving' is an act which participates in the making of culture, not just its saving.

There were also ideas in eighteenth-century philosophy relevant to what kind of historian Walpole was. Clifford Siskin has shown that disciplinarity has a history. Describing David Hume as a philosopher and a historian separates into two disciplines a band of thought that, besides being unified by the person of the author, was perceived differently within eighteenth-century modes of intellectual researches: 'History... became, by the middle of the eighteenth century, a central feature of the experimental philosophy we know as political economy.'[142] Hume's enquiries promote observation of experience – either philosophically, by investigating the present, or historically, by using experience from the past. History, Hume wrote,

> is not only a valuable part of knowledge, but opens the door to many other parts... [it] extends our experience to all past ages, and to the most distant nations; making them contribute as much to our improvement in wisdom, as if they had actually lain under our observation.[143]

Siskin points specifically to the door history opens into political economy, but also stresses more generally the methodological force of 'empirical observation of experience extended through history, alternating with general propositions'. It produces 'the extraordinary outpouring of knowledge' we associate with the Enlightenment; 'in the slightly longer term came the separation of knowledges that characterize modernity'.[144] Walpole suggests future historians of Britain will use his data to support their more philosophical enquiries, but that suggestion is cast using the terms of a methodology he shares with them. The character of the historian was closer to that of philosopher than modern usage of those terms implies. The genre of 'history of one's own times' is where understanding of the past meets awareness of modernity; the genre of letters is where 'outpouring' meets 'separation', especially in Walpole's prolific and regular correspondence to Mann.

Walpole thought he had a place in the history of letter-writing. As he remarked in 1784 about the more than eight hundred letters he had written to Horace Mann, 'A correspondence of near half a century is, I suppose, not to be paralleled in the annals of the Post Office!'[145] It induced geographical awe in his editor: 'The Mann correspondence is the great Andean range of the Walpolian continent, stretching from 1740 to Mann's death in 1786.'[146] Since Walpole and Mann did not meet during the correspondence, their paper friendship had to be tended even as Walpole settled into the character of epistolary historian. The half-century frame of the correspondence with Mann also involved changes in discourse – not just the conventions of epistolary writing, nor even the absence of conventions of writing epistolary history, but those broad shifts in mentalité which take place over any half-century. Between the 1740s and the 1790s, the premium placed on wit fell and sensibility rose, making Walpole consciously awkward about certain idioms. One can also see less conscious resistances to change which can, with caution, be keyed to the psycho-historical alterations of an ageing adult.

In singling out particular behaviours as illustrative of contemporary mores, Walpole reworked definitions of history to suit an epistolary medium. He explored the tensions between himself as a historical subject, prone to indeterminacy, and himself as historian, able to escape flux by anatomising it. 'My mind is a little one, and apt to fluctuate', he told Mann, but 'though my letters may have been affected by the weather-glass, the sum total has been uniform. I have hoped or feared, but always in the same spirit, the liberty and happiness of England.'[147] National identity and national idealism supplied consistency in a climate as changeable as the English weather.[148] Patriotism allows those not living in their native land to revisit it mentally; 'the liberty and happiness of England' offered Mann the opportunity to pledge simultaneously, like a toast. Escaping the constraints of time and space through the medium of letters, Walpole brought historical constancy alongside political instability.

Walpole has been seen as a ruthless epistolary artist who matched correspondents to his interests; if by disagreement or death some disappeared, they were rapidly replaced. This model turns eighteenth-century correspondence into a kind of fantasy football with Walpole needing on his dream team an antiquarian, a literary person, a political animal and so on. Conversely, Walpole has been seen as an epistolary chameleon, changing his manner according to his correspondent – trying to be on his friends' dream teams.[149] Author-centred paradigms are attractive as a way of generalising about Walpole's mind-bogglingly large correspondence. But his letters to Mann shows the usefulness of reading letters according to character: the most relevant dynamics are the historian's drive to stabilise and the wit's delight in discrepancy. Walpole's consciousness of possible future publication does complicate his professions of insignificance, but epistolary loyalty doubled for political integrity: 'I can learn to feel no friendship, but I cannot learn to profess one where I have it not.'[150] He is detached from his subject not from his friend: the warmth of familiar letters ironically supports, not undermines, his claim that 'Disinterestedness is my passion.'[151]

Walpole's interest in historiography was active. He told Gibbon he had often thought of writing about that 'wonderful period in which the world saw five good monarchs succeed each other',[152] but he was no simple monarchist. Congratulating Gibbon on his synthesis of rival traditions of 'érudits' and 'philosophes', Walpole admired the latter (in Voltaire) though he is usually associated with the former through antiquarianism. He disavowed a public character as a scholar, correcting Mann

> Pray, my dear child, don't compliment me any more upon my learning; there is nobody so superficial. Except a little history, a little poetry, a little painting, and some divinity, I know nothing. How should I? I, who have always lived in the big busy world; who lie abed all the morning, calling it morning as long as you please; who sup in company; who have played at pharaoh half my life, and now at loo till two and three in the morning; who have always loved pleasure... How I have laughed, when some of the magazines have called me *the learned gentleman*![153]

But the life of a dilettante ironically qualified him as a social historian, one using letters for both eye- and ear-witnessing.[154] He told Mann 'a bon mot very often paints truly the history or manners of the times'[155] and adduced a causal relationship between manners and history so as to blur the distinction, remarking to the Earl of Buchan, 'the manners of the times... are very often the source of considerable events'.[156] With few precedents, Walpole represented himself as an iconoclast, 'a person who collects the follies of the age for the information of posterity';[157] his letters to Mann were 'the annals of Bedlam'.[158]

For those who wished to turn ephemerality into history, the generic options were confused:

> Times of party have their great outlines, which even such historians as Hollingshead or Smollet can seize. But a season of faction is another guess thing. It depends on personal characters, intrigues, and minute circumstances, which make little noise and escape the eyes of the generality. The details are as much too numerous for a letter, as, when the moment is past, they become too trifling and uninteresting for history. I can only endeavour to preserve the thread, but it is impossible to develop all its windings.[159]

Besides letters, another genre accommodated to-the-moment uncertainties: memoirs. Memoirists too were doubtful about the historicity of their writing. Thus Lord Holland: 'I now come to the recital of what has happen'd these last five months, & come to my knowledge, not likely to be the subject of history, as too minute.'[160] The confusions are illustrated by Nathaniel Wraxall's *Memoirs*. These are epistolary, though not published for twenty years, which formally enacted the gap between acts of recording and facts of record which would-be historians worried over. Wraxall argued

it is only from cotemporary authority we can derive the most authentic, as well as curious materials of history. The minute and personal anecdotes of illustrious men soon fade under the touch of time and are obliterated. In order to be preserved and transmitted to posterity, they must be transmitted at the moment.[161]

Walpole got back his letters to Mann at regular intervals; to-the-moment history, preserved, became history. Here the idea of a chronicler (rather than a historian) was helpful. Review of memoirs tempted authors to burn, a fate that befell several desirable texts.[162] Walpole could have written a compound history-journal, as Boswell did in his *Account of Corsica* (1768) and of which Johnson thought the history necessarily dependent and the journal preferable, thanks to 'that difference which there will always be found between notions borrowed from without, and notions generated within'.[163] Letters allowed most free play to notions 'generated within'. Besides, satire benefits from peer response. Walpole thought history restricted comedy: 'yet shall I not check a smile now and then at transient follies; nor, as much appropriated as gravity is to an historian, can I conceive how history can always be faithful, if solemn'.[164] Letters were recognised as historical documents and as texts of wit. They also accommodated that subjectivity which Walpole wanted in history. Again medieval metaphors, here of tapestry, were helpful. He wrote to John Pinkerton, a Scottish historian and antiquary,

I am not overjoyed at your wading into the history of dark ages, unless you use it as a canvas to be embroidered with your own opinions, and episodes, and comparisons with more recent times. That is a most entertaining kind of writing.[165]

Relieved by epistolary transience from a mission to inform, he was free to entertain. Nominally, personal letters required traces of warmth at odds with that coolness supposed to signal objectivity amongst historians. Walpole found it difficult to appear aloof: 'I must become a less valuable correspondent. Indifference is not a good ingredient in letters, I think, in nothing; no, not where it is demanded, and commonly pretended, in history.'[166]

Detachment posed difficulties for the epistolary historian. Walpole's letters to Mann frequently avoided even those reflections which letter-writers were entitled to make. 'I will not proceed upon the chapter of reflections' he declared; the facts 'will supply your thoughts with all I should say'.[167] This erased the authority of the historian in favour of the cordiality of corre-spondents, secured against disagreement by evasion. Moreover, detachment was present naturally in the correspondence because by the time Mann's replies arrived they were out of date:

> BY the tediousness of the post, and distance of place, I am still receiving letters from you about the Secret Committee; which seems strange, for it is as much forgotten now, as if it had happened in the last reign.[168]

Walpole was representing a temporality that slipped from topical to historical: as Stuart Sherman puts it, 'Chronography is chameleonic.'[169] The slippage between news and history was evoked in the names of newspapers like *The Historical Account* (1695), the *St. James's Chronicle*, even *The Times*.[170] It was not that political change was too rapid for a historical response – rather, when Walpole sent Mann news turned into history, it was still news to Mann when it arrived. Walpole's difficulty, in return, was how to keep what was history from what was passé. Mann was removed from the action, like a confidant in an epistolary novel. Walpole could compensate by aligning him with posterity, but since posterity's responses are necessarily unknown, this muted Mann again. Walpole as letter-writer was then obliged to guess the response he might count on as a historian. Projecting Mann's interest in the execution of Lord Ferrers, he concluded

> If I have tired you by this long narrative, you feel differently from me. The man, the manners of the country, the justice of so great and curious a nation, all seem to me striking, and must I believe do more so to you, who have been absent long enough to read of your own country as history.[171]

The parameters of epistolary history – 'personal characters, intrigues and minute circumstances', in Walpole's phrase – are staples of epistolary fiction and Walpole is like a character caught in an unknown plot. This he accepted and was occasionally excited by. Writing to Mann about rumours of an assassination attempt on the French king, he comments, 'We are quite in the dark still about that history: it is one of the bad effects of living in one's own time, that one never knows the truth of it till one is dead!'[172] He told another friend, 'they who can be spectators, cannot be readers, for the story is not written till they are dead'.[173] Walpole is not the author of the main plot but he can impose miniature narrative structures on inchoate events. Where epistolary fiction interlocked letters to make plot and consciousness continuous, Walpole had to limit consciousness in order to make plot intel-ligible: '*you* want information, not a rhapsody on my sensations'.[174] But the erratic flow of verifiable information made epistolary history resemble fiction again. Frequently Walpole stayed a letter for the post in case it brought fresh intelligence. Half-relishing suspense, he wrote to Mann

I may be able to unfold a little more of the drama by Tuesday's post; but I have long left off guessing, for in all public events, I have observed, that the turn things take, depends upon persons and accidents that start up in the midst of the story, and have nothing to do with the reasoning on which one builds conjectures – so for the present I leave this chapter in the dark, which is conformable to the suspense that artful tragic writers use to increase the interest and curiosity of their readers.[175]

Both writer and recipient are prey to flux but able to find detachment via literary archetypes: life's unpredictabilities are like fiction's predictabilities.

Walpole used fiction to give structure to epistolary history and to show up its lack of structure. He was more ambivalent about newspapers as an analogue. Initially the comparison appealed:

I cannot help smiling at the great objects of our letters. We can never converse on a less topic than a kingdom. We are a kind of citizens of the world, and battles and revolutions are the common incidents of our neighbourhood. But that is and must be the case of distant correspondences: kings and empresses that we never saw, are the only persons we can be acquainted with. We can have no more familiarity than the *Daily Advertiser* would have, if it wrote to the *Florentine Gazette* – Adieu! My compliments to any monarch that lives within five hundred miles of you.[176]

Epistolary gossip has involuntarily turned to history. When the Earl of Hertford was posted to Paris as Ambassador, Walpole sent him the news by post: 'I am very glad to be your gazetteer...I should be ashamed of such gossipping, if I did not consider it as chatting with you *en famille*.'[177] Letters, newspapers and chat invited lower expectations of accuracy; letters and newspapers overlapped in being impermanent like conversation – like throwaway remarks, one might say. But in later life Walpole denounced newspapers: 'not only all private history is detailed in our newspapers, but scarce ever with tolerable fidelity!'[178] They turned reality into literary fantasy: 'how the Houyhnhnms would have stared if they had been told that in a certain country there were daily courants to inform the public of what every old Strulbrug was *not* doing'.[179] His anxiety on this occasion was inflamed by an inaccurate and embarrassingly complimentary paragraph in *The World*, which he sees as symptomatic of how newspapers will mislead future historians. This is not simply a public–private opposition. Newspaper material, or what he refers to as the importance of nobody to everybody, competed with epistolary material, or the importance of anybody to somebody. The impersonal medium of print took over functions previously mediated by the personal medium of correspondence. To read about yourself in the papers is like meeting yourself in masquerade – a kind of mimicry. It is significant that Walpole presents the paragraph as excessively complimentary.

Modesty shrinks ego-boundaries; it also dissociates him from an aristocracy whose activities are of 'public' interest to the general public. Post-Bolingbroke, aristocracy was a liability to the historian. Walpole sees newspapers as invasive in the cause of democratic information:

> to give those historians their due, nothing comes amiss to them – and lest they should defraud their customers, they keep open shop for everything true or false, or scandalous, or ever so private, or ever so little relative to the public. Ancient annalists thought nobody game below a monarch, or a general, or a high priest. Modern intelligencers have no mercy on posterity; and not considering how enormous the bulk of events is grown, contribute all in their power to store the world with the history of everybody in it.[180]

Walpole's mercantile metaphor points to literary rather than social exclusivity: newspapers have an indiscriminate readership fed by their invasive practices. Journalists' indifference mimics the historian's detachment. In contrast, so long as letters kept the personalised direction and limited circulation of manuscript, they could be excused from print's omnivorousness.

Like Goldsmith with his Shandean nightmare, Walpole worried about the expansion of print culture. But he welcomed the democratisation of history in terms of demystifying the monarchy:

> They tell me Mr Hume has had sight of King James's journal; I wish I could see all the trifling passages that he will not deign to admit into history. I do not love great folks till they have pulled off their buskins and put on their slippers, because I do not care sixpence for what they would be thought, but for what they are.[181]

A playful and informal historian, Walpole was unthreatened by romances. A ludicrous world has no call to exclude fantasy. Outraged by Lord North's belated and complacent confession of 'faults' over America, Walpole parodied his own habits of comparative history:

> no parallel instance is to be found in ancient or modern history, whether Ammonite, Jewish, Chaldean, Egyptian, Chinese, Greek, Roman, Constantinopolitan, Frank, French, British, Saxon, Pict, Ossianite, Mogul, Indian, or English (all of which I have carefully examined this morning to no purpose) – nay in the *Tales of the Fairies*, in which I am still more deeply versed, I find nothing similar.[182]

Walpole often chooses medieval mock-heroic to explore events through fantasy – for instance, writing to Mann about the secret and supposedly punitive expedition against the French naval base at St Malo, which turned out to be 'making a bonfire and running away':

I WRITE to you again so soon, only to laugh at my last letter. What a dupe was I! at my years, to be dazzled with glory! to be charmed with the rattle of drums and trumpets, till I fancied myself at Cressy or Poitiers! In the middle of all this dream of conquest, just when I had settled in what room of my castle I would lodge the Duke of Alanson or Montpensier, or whatever illustrious captive should be committed to the custody of Seneschal *Me*, I was wakened with an account of our army having re-embarked...[183]

The delusions of an innocent self show up an ineffectual and corrupt administration. Both share nationalist myths: the historian's folly is harmless, the politician's is culpable.

In turning contemporary culture into history, Walpole focused on the frame of 'this age', an idiom that allows a historian to age gracefully too. 'There is nothing more like than two ages that are very like':[184] by comparing his age to the heroic age of Roman republicanism, he was using a staple of political discourse. Alexander Pettit has argued that the 1730s saw an attempt 'by writers hostile to George II and his de facto prime minister Sir Robert Walpole to control the recasting of history as analogy and thus its conversion into partisan political rhetoric'.[185] If 'analogic historiography was the dominant opposition trope of the 1730s', there is a nice irony in Sir Robert's son appropriating this discourse subsequently for Whig purposes. Alternatively one could read it as a discourse that lets Walpole engage with politics without being implicated in the ebbs and flows of party politics. Classical comparison allowed him to satirise, moralise and philosophise so as to reinforce the production of historical knowledges, to use Siskin's terms again.

I must go and hear Caesar and Pompey scold in the Temple of concord. As this age is to make such a figure hereafter, how the Gronoviuses and Warburtons would despise a senator that deserted the forum when the masters of the world harangued![186]

The similarities between letters and conversation relaxed conventions. Walpole defended to Gray the phrase 'tinker up' in his Preface to *Historic Doubts on the Life and Reign of King Richard the Third*, 'I own I think such a low expression, placed to ridicule an absurd instance of wise folly, very forcible. Replace it with an elevated word or phrase, and to my conception it becomes as flat as possible.'[187] Where satire mixed high and low for trans-gressive effect, letter-writers could use bathos more freely than historians.

Most often Walpole invoked previous ages in order to interrogate the assumptions of his own. Rhetorical questions made history philosophical:

The age, it is true, soon emerges out of every gloom, and wantons as before. But does not that levity imprint a still deeper melancholy on those who do think? Have any of our calamities corrected us? Are we not revelling on the brink of the precipice? Does administration grow more sage, or desire that we should grow more sober? Are these themes for letters, my dear Lord? Can one repeat common news with indifference, while our shame is writing for future history by the pens of all our numerous enemies?[188]

This perspective gave Walpole's epistolary history a longer shelf-life than much overtly political writing. It also enabled him to rewrite the conservatism of Augustan-inspired satirists of the previous generation. Paradoxically, modernity was best addressed through antiquity. As he mused to Mann, 'The times immediately preceding their own are what all men are least acquainted with. A young man knows Romulus better than George the Second.'[189] The classics turned topicality into history for the next generation – and posterity.

Walpole was ultimately ambivalent about the relation between England and Rome. Philosophical detachment was hard to sustain when history involved fresh follies or simply repeated follies. Concluding his account of the fracas when John Wilkes was shot in a duel, Walpole asked Mann, 'Do you think me or your countrymen quite distracted? Go, turn to your Livy, to your history of Athens, to your life of Sacheverel. Find upon record what mankind has been, and then you will believe what it is.'[190] If human nature was constant, human society could be predictable: 'Nations at the acme of their splendour, or at the eve of their destruction, are worth observing. When they grovel in obscurity afterwards, they furnish neither events nor recollections.'[191] But he could not decide if Britain was on the brink of triumph or ruin. The Pitt administration's activities abroad made Walpole proud: announcing the conquest of Martinico to Montagu he exulted

I shall burn all my Greek and Latin books; they are histories of little people. The Romans never conquered the world, till they had conquered three parts of it, and were three hundred years about it; we subdue the globe in three campaigns, and a globe, let me tell you, as big again as it was in their days.[192]

But he doubted the moral value of such conquests and his own reaction to them: 'Well! say I to myself, and what is all this to me?...yet self-love makes one love the nation one belongs to, and vanity makes one wish to have that nation glorious.'[193] What Walpole passionately believed to be the North administration's gross mishandling of the American colonies made him hostile to British triumphs at the expense of others' freedoms. Finally he became sickened by imperialism. He wrote sombrely to Mann,

Europe has a mass of debts to pay to the other quarters of the globe, which, on the merit of having improved navigation and invented gunpowder, we have thought we had a right to desolate and plunder – and we have been such savages as to punish each other for our crimes. The Romans havocked the world for glory – the Spaniards, Portuguese, Dutch and English, for gold – but each nation thirsted to engross the whole mass, and became scourges to each other. Attila and Hyder Ally are at least as innocent as Julius Caesar and Lord Clive.[194]

The free association of letters led Walpole to some free-thinking. Letter-writers can turn a subject over from various angles and still be sanctioned by the premise of spontaneity. The play of subjectivity is protected in a friendly correspondence, not exposed to public criticism as it would be in formal history. A benign epistolary context allowed Walpole to explore contradictions in his identity, as imperial subject and imperial critic:

My Whig blood cannot bear to part with a drop of the empire of the ocean. Like the Romans I would have Rome domineer over the world, and be free at home. The old man in me is sensible there is little equity in this, and that a good patriot is a bad citizen of the world...I am persuaded that a good justice of the peace, who confines himself to his own parish, is a more beneficial member of society than Brutus or Cato – however, there would be nothing but Tarquins and Caesars, if there was nothing but justices of the peace; and therefore one must not refine too much. I never did give loose to my own disquisitions, but I found it as well to come back to my own common sense, and to the common routine of thinking.[195]

Imperialism seduced Walpole, but letters drew him away from some of its orthodoxies.

The role of capital in imperialism alarmed Walpole. Where his contemporaries Adam Smith analysed the wealth of nations and Gibbon chronicled the decline and fall of an empire, Walpole outlined the decline of a wealthy nation. Worship of money created disorder as effectively as barbarism and religion. In one sense this was ritual breast-beating: as John Sekora observes, 'by the middle of the century the condemnation of luxury was practically unanimous among the traditionally privileged groups of England. While such opposition did little to define one's position, it did signify one's quarrel with the present age.'[196] But in two respects one can go a little deeper. One was that the topic had been grounds of contention between Bolingbroke and Sir Robert Walpole: are the son's laments over luxury laced with unconscious elegy for paternal power? The other was that Walpole puzzled over how imperialism was now economic rather than epic:

If the Romans or the Greeks were beat, they were beat; they repaired their walls, and did as well as thy could; but they did not lose every sesterce, every talent they had, by the defeat affecting their Change Alley. Crassus, the richest man on t'other side Temple Bar, lost his army and his life, and yet East India bonds did not fall an obolus under par. I like that system better than ours...How Scipio would have stared, if he had been told that he must not demolish Carthage, as it would ruin several aldermen that had money in the Punic *actions*![197]

Walpole deplored the huge gambling debts of young prodigals like Charles James Fox.[198] But capital as historic force struck him as more significant than as excess:

> I pray for an end to the woes of mankind; in one word I have no public spirit, and don't care a farthing for the interests of the merchants. Soldiers and sailors who are knocked on the head, and peasants plundered or butchered, are to my eyes as valuable, as a lazy luxurious set of men, who hire others to acquire riches for them; who would embroil all the earth, that they may heap or squander; and I *dare* to say this, for I am no minister.[199]

The interests of capital create wars; imperialism fuels violence, greed and social divisions – and this in England, the nation supposed to benefit from it! This letter has a topical occasion – Walpole observes sardonically 'Beckford is a patriot, because he will clamour if Guadaloupe or Martinico is given up, and the price of sugars falls' – but its analysis is explicitly historical. Walpole continues

> I am a bad Englishman, because I think the advantages of commerce are dearly bought for some, by the lives of many more. This wise age counts its merchants, and reckons its armies ciphers – but why do I talk of this age? – every age has some ostentatious system to excuse the havoc it commits. Conquest, honour, chivalry, religion, balance of power, commerce, no matter what, mankind must bleed, and take a term for a reason. 'Tis shocking![200]

Contemporary critics of the slave trade often argued that it damaged imperial nations both economically and spiritually. Walpole is neither pragmatist nor moralist so much as pacifist. His letters to Mann often end with invocations to peace, as if the end of writing represented the end of violence. Language is the pretext for war – the 'term for reason' – and also the opposite of war. Jaw-jaw defers war. In substituting for conflict, dialogic forms such as letters stand in symbolically for conflict. War becomes the sign of history – the excuse for historically continuous havoc, under different names.[201] Peace is an undifferentiated condition, so it has no history. Hence Walpole writes himself into silence: peace and epistolary closure overlap.

Besides peace, Walpole promoted ambivalence through tragicomedy:

> I have often said, and oftener think, that *this world is a comedy to those that think, a tragedy to those that feel* – a solution of why Democritus laughed and Heraclitus wept. The only gainer is history, which has constant opportunities of showing the various ways in which men can contrive to be fools and knaves. The record pretends to be written for instruction, though to this hour no mortal has been the better or wiser for it.[202]

Letters allow the historian to think and feel. Modulation between humour and gravity need not be inconsistency but rather spontaneity or variety. For Walpole, who rarely took himself seriously, letters let him be playful to his friends and absolved him from moralising. Initially too much in tune with his age to castigate it deeply, in later years Walpole no longer enjoyed writing about it ironically and took refuge in epistolary conventions which let him disengage. But if the present age disappointed, there was always the future. Having everything to tell posterity, Walpole turned gossip into history and observations on his age into transhistorical psychology.

> Babylon and Memphis and Rome probably stared at their own downfall. Empires did not use to philosophize, nor thought much but of themselves. Such revolutions are better known now, and we ought to expect them – I do not say we do.[203]

Personification connected historical constructs to historical subjects – including the historian, whose life, as Walpole observed, did not necessarily overlap with a historical period. Like Gibbon, Walpole related the collective psychology of an empire to its significant characters, though he used a more conservative typology than Gibbon's model of causation. Gibbon attributed the fall of the Roman empire to demographical changes and sociological influences – the triumphs of barbarism and religion. Walpole represented figures of the day by historical analogues who shared their ruling passions: 'A country is undone before people distinguish between affected and real virtue ... Every Clodius of the hour takes the name of Cato to himself, and bestows his own name on the enemy.'[204]

The concept of character combined personal traits with their representation in writing. Walpole was ambivalent about the historical power of text. In one gloomy letter he remarked, 'Writings impel, but can restrain nobody'; in another, he told Mann, 'I don't believe this age will be more read than the Byzantine historians.'[205] An enthusiastic reader of letters from the past, Walpole knew that letters by himself and his contemporaries were sources which the long-lived might enjoy as history: 'The transports I allude to, are living to see the *private* works, sentiments and anecdotes of one's own time come to light.'[206] The significant distinction is not simply between public and private history – Walpole foresees that private will become public – but between one's own time and a future free to treat it as past. Thanking Sir David Dalrymple for a present of letters from the reign of James I, Walpole remarked, 'nothing gives so just an idea of an age as genuine letters; nay, history waits for its last seal from them'.[207] The metaphor gave a common reader to historians and letter-writers: Walpole made the epistolary historian a significant character in the eighteenth century.

8
Writing as a Christian

To write as a Christian in the eighteenth century was to write in a complex identity. The prevalence of polemic in eighteenth-century religious literature has been recognised,[1] but not the significance of letter-writing. Whether writing to a fellow-struggler in the same faith or to an opponent on a point of theology, questions of address, content and circulation acquired religious significance. To whom was it necessary to write? What was it acceptable to say? What kinds of friction arose between religious imperatives and secular decorums? Did Christians have special epistolary conventions? In religion, a difference of opinion could have the status of heresy. For some, this meant a righteous hunting down of error; for others, a test of forbearance and love. Here Christians were potentially subject to contradiction: enjoined both to enlist under the banners of a faith which promoted aggression towards weak belief or unbelief, and to uphold ideals of mildness, compassion and meekness, letter-writers enacted tensions between justice and mercy inherent in Christian doctrine. Christian letter-writing also had a national context: Acts of Toleration or Test and Corporation Acts helped shape climates of opinion in which certain kinds of intolerance were formally promulgated. Within the established church too, politics were at work in the appointments of bishops and the dispensation of livings and preferments. Writing as a Christian was an identity bound up with secular power and coloured by denominational preferences.

For all the complications of eighteenth-century religion, letter-writers of different faiths frequently described themselves as writing as Christians. Part of the use of letters was to clarify a context for exchanges between people so that either their letters served a community (or a would-be community) or they were clearly engaged in communicating across theological lines. Complex titles spelt this out. Yet when many people wrote to those outside their imagined community, to people-not-like-us, it was in the hope that they might become like-us. Letters clarified enemies without and enemies within. Epistolary aggression often partnered the hope that believers could subscribe to basic principles that would unite them in the face of worldly scorn. John Wesley promoted the idea that Methodists were like other Christians in that

281

they believed in God, an after-life and Christ; these beliefs distinguished them from Jews, Moslems and infidels. Such appeals to common Christian principles were as much a pious hope as a reality since eighteenth-century Christians were not all agreed on the significance of Christ and their disagreements gave rise to differences as profound as denomination. It would be most historically accurate to discuss eighteenth-century religious letters in terms of distinctions used at the time – deist, Antinomian, Arminian, Socinian, antipaedobaptist – and to some extent I shall. But the perplexities of doctrinal arguments co-existed with a widespread affirmation of a Christian identity and letters had an important role in making that co-existence possible.

The first part of this chapter explores a selection of key doctrinal controversies so as to show the significance of letters in their construction. I start by discussing some religious societies that promoted theological debate and letter-writing and articulated best practice for conducting arguments. Theological disputes often became controversies because of how they were conducted: violation of letter-writing decorums turned contentious ideas into inflammatory ones. Four themes are explored: how controversy fitted (or not) with ideals about Christian fellowship; how spiritual authority, especially that of bishops, was exercised and challenged through letters; how reason rubbed along with faith, often uncomfortably, and how ministers of the gospel used letters to tend their congregations. For the latter I use William Huntington to show how abusive letters promoted religious truths and to show how people made up paradigms of epistolary authority where there was little or no tradition to sanction them. 'Sanction' in the sense of 'influential encouragement' is an eighteenth-century usage; its older sense, of a force that compelled obedience through penalties, continued. Huntington's letters illustrate how discipline and devotion were both promulgated through correspondence taken to print.

The second part of the chapter discusses devotional practices and how letters expressed, shaped and spread them. Letters were highly influential in sustaining religious community and individual faith. The division between speculative and practical religion was not hard and fast but it was widely recognised and provides a useful way of discussing an immense area of writing. I give special attention to Methodism because John Wesley's letters have been described as 'the marching orders of the Evangelical Revival',[2] and because although Methodists did not leave the Church of England until 1797, they used letters distinctively to draw in adherents and tend a particular kind of evangelism.[3]

Letters and speculative religion

> On the whole, *Controversies* relating to *Christianity* are endless... – Philip Doddridge

Theological writings make up probably the greatest percentage of eighteenth-century print culture in general and epistolary writings in particular. My selection of texts has been made less to illustrate a history of religious thought than to show how letters served controversy. Many eighteenth-century controversies are intricate and voluminous; they lead to some strange territory. My aim is not simply to add to the history of religious ideas but to suggest different histories through a common form – the letter. For instance, the charismatic and now nearly forgotten William Huntington published one hundred books and was described in 1813 as 'the most indefatigable and voluminous religious writer of the present century'.[4] Like the better-known John Wesley, he was also a writer whose use of letters to police his congregation, promote his doctrines and fend off critics was canny and tireless. Using denominational identities is unhelpful in that they suggest that to be an Anglican, a Dissenter, a Baptist or a Huntingtonian is to sign up to a fixed set of tenets which in turn fix adherents; in fact, every denomination had its own internal differences and controversies. Other identities like nationality also complicate the picture: so an account of religion in Scotland at the end of the eighteenth century began with the plausible generalisation that 'a Scotsman always stands as an antipode to the Pope', but subsequently struggled with an intricate, even surreal history of splits and secessions. For instance, following a controversy as to whether bread for communion should be blessed on the table or after it had been lifted up, Stirling, which was home to several different kinds of Presbyterians, further divided into 'Lifters' and 'Anti-lifters' (reminiscent of the Big Enders and Little Enders in *Gulliver's Travels*). A set of modern disciples in Edinburgh, determined to adopt primitive Christianity in all its forms, argued about the apostles' injunction against men wearing long hair and nearly came to blows over whether pigtails and periwigs were permissible.[5] Christian letter-writing often took place in contexts of violent behaviours.

Religious societies that allowed debate were careful to lay down rules that committed members to common tolerances: 'We shall carefully avoid stiffness or positiveness in our opinions, and sharp or virulent expressions, or reflections on the sentiments of others who differ from us.'[6] A society devoted to religious polemic in the 1790s set up penalties for invective in debates in person and letters.[7] Its printed proceedings end with a cautionary tale addressed to a pious youth who is thinking of studying predestination. The subject leads people to become bigots, sceptics or universalists, he is warned, and he is told about two neighbours:

the one a Calvinist, and the other an Arminian, who had long been in the habit of settling differences as referees; but who, finding it troublesome, had fairly agreed to change sides, so that he who was nominated by the plaintiff should plead the cause of the defendant, and *vice versa*. This was attended with good consequences, for harmony was kept up, friendship increased, and the contending parties were generally pleased. These friends, seeing the good effects of changing sides, proposed to defend their respective tenets in the same way; but now they charged each other with not doing justice to the cause they had respectively undertaken. Bad blood ensued, a duel was the consequence, and the whole neighbourhood suffered.[8]

For all its humour, this story points to a no-win situation. Is the point that rational methodology can be defeated by passionate belief or that some issues, like predestination, simply cannot admit compromise? People struggled on paper with questions of tolerance. Those of uncertain status found letters useful as a plain genre free from sophistry: indeed, in an evangelical context plainness could overturn clerical authority. The case of Mrs Talbot illustrates the power of letters. She was the widow of a vicar in Reading: when the new incumbent fell out with his flock, it was to her house that they went to pray.

Highly offended at such conduct, he vehemently remonstrated. Various letters passed. To all his bitter reproaches, she returned answers so full of meekness and wisdom, that, at length, he fell at the feet of accumulated kindness, humbled and subdued; and, to the last moment of his life confessed, to the praise and glory of God, that Mrs. Talbot's letters and example were the principle means of leading him to the saving knowledge of Christ.[9]

Letters allowed women opportunities to do spiritual work from which their communities formally excluded them and to 'advise, teach, argue with and sometimes stubbornly resist' men.[10] For all their ideals of brotherly love, it was common for controversialists to revile each other for unchristian tactics. Print was seen as inflammatory. By moving disagreements into a public realm that attracted attention and other disputants, writers asserted a right to a fair hearing but under a banner of wrath not meekness. John Wesley, a selective controversialist who was unafraid of criticism but unwilling to enter fights in print, often tried to avert a public dispute by sending a private letter of correction.[11] Those who attacked Methodism publicly were treated to public replies but emphatically by letter since Wesley thought it wrong to use the pulpit for controversial reproofs.[12] He recommended forbearance to others, advising one correspondent beset by disputants to 'simply say, "I believe otherwise; but I think and let think"',[13] and he practised it himself. When Zinzendorf placed a notice in the *Daily Advertiser* announcing that the Moravians thought the Methodists erroneous but would not quarrel with them, Wesley wrote to Zinzendorf that this was provocative – 'you strike a man as hard on the head as you can, and then declare you will not fight' – but that he would refrain from controversy: 'Your unusual conduct does not hinder me from still embracing you with candour and love.'[14] Archbishop Secker, believing that some controversialists wrote out of necessity, sometimes gave distressed authors money to deter them, although he also paid other authors to answer them. His biographer praised him as an active writer of letters promoting the interests of the Church of England 'not by warm and violent Counsels, but by Methods of Tenderness and Brotherly Kindness' – a forbearance the more striking given that Secker had a short temper and was often in agony from a bone disease.[15]

This discursive ideal of tolerance, more honoured in the breach than the observance, was promoted through several key terms. First was candour, a term much appealed to in secular disputes but which took on special overtones in theological disputes, perhaps because its etymology (from the Latin for 'whiteness') evoked a holy colour. Second was zeal, a worthy quality in itself which became bad in excess, thus leaving room for disputants to accuse each other predictably of excessive zeal. Third was heat, which also could be good or bad: it was acceptable as warmth, but if intemperate, showed a serious departure from cool reason. These terms were relatively stable throughout the eighteenth century although they had local inflections, for instance of class: candour was a term of appeal between gentlemen. The role of letters in religious controversy was relatively stable: used in early and late decades, local and national disputes, widely taken up by writers of different classes, letter-writing by Christians expanded like print culture itself. But Christian letter-writing should not be read exclusively through the paradigm of print. Rather, letters were one of several genres of religious discourse that existed on the page and as something voiced. Like sermons, prayers and hymns, letters had oral overtones. Christians wrote letters in contexts already saturated with ideas about reading and writing that were circulated and changed by print culture, certainly, but fed by other sources too. Different denominations assigned different meanings to text, to the roles of reason and revelation in interpreting it, and to that interpretative community supposed to be influenced by it. Whether manuscript or print, letters were a form of faith that linked text in the form of scripture and text in the form of believers' writings. Whilst letters put faith on paper, faith was bigger than any paper form.

The complex traffic between manuscript, print and public debate in theological controversy can be seen in two controversies involving Quakers in eastern England at different ends of the century. Quakers cast doubt on directives in scripture taken as read by other groups – in particular, the divinity of Christ and the necessity of baptism. They were sympathetic to prophetic discourse, which was oral as well as written. The controversy of 1701 started when Henry Pickworth, a Quaker, wrote a letter complaining of the errors in a book by Francis Bugg. Pickworth addressed this letter to a kinsman of the Bishop of Lincoln – that is, he pitched it into the Church of England's hierarchy. Bugg claimed to have answered the charges in another book but Pickworth wrote again, this time to Bugg himself. So too did concerned local clergy. Bugg burnt a letter delivered by two Quakers; after this literally inflammatory act, Pickworth advertised a debate in the town of Sleeford. In a printed acceptance, Bugg agreed to debate provided the loser would suffer his writings to be publicly burnt. The controversy involved a complex osmosis between manuscript, print and speech; between protagonists, third parties and the public; between bodies and heretical letters; between heated texts and fire. Bugg drew up terms of debate and organised himself a platform in Sleeford's largest public building; he advertised it with a notice drawn up by the local writing master – that is, in script that looked like print. Then both protagonists busily spread printed letters around Sleeford accusing each other (Bugg was an apostate and atheist, said Pickworth; Pickworth was a rapist, claimed Bugg). The debate, refereed by a justice sympathetic to Bugg, focused on whether Quakers despised scripture, denied the divinity of Christ and valued their own writings more than scripture. Bugg quoted from George Fox's works to prove the charges, giving page references; he treated books as legal exhibits and made sure the audience saw them. Pickworth counter-argued that Quakers did not write books: they produced doctrines that happened to appear in ink on paper. Writers were scribes for the spirit of God, not authors of books. Bugg cited an exchange in which a Quaker who denied authorship of a book was forced by a Cambridge librarian to 'own' it – an ambiguous expression, implying both that it was his property and that he admitted it was his production. Any injurious effects from the doctrine could be blamed on the material object, the book. Controlling its circulation as a commodity could limit the spread of its ideas. In contrast, Pickworth treated ideas and their paper form as separable. Bugg was declared the winner, so a selection of Quaker books was burnt at Sleeford's market cross – a monument that stood for commerce and religion.

In some ways, the outcome was confusing in that Bugg (who published forty-one anti-Quaker works) suggested Quakers were wary of text, yet part of his evidence was a set of written records kept by Quakers. The ambiguities were mirrored in the medium of letters, unstable because they accommodated both inspirational and empirical arguments. Inspiration (from the Latin *spirare*, to breathe) suggested an oral dimension to representation that was captured by the 'talking on paper' aspect of letters. Bugg won because he persuaded his audience and readers that writing was best served by a scholastic apparatus of page numbers, footnotes and so on. This apparatus anchored arguments, made quotations reliable and was to be preferred to Pickworth's idea of text as an evanescent medium. Letters were a form that could serve either view. The protagonists squared up like Old Testament champions and fought with epistolary weapons. Letters got the process going, stoked it and supplied a personal frame to a methodology of documentation of which they were also themselves part. They also marked out a local territory – here the town of Sleeford – in which people could be persuaded by print, by letter-writing and by debates that mimicked academic conventions of written argument. A formal debate between a Baptist and a Quaker in Norwich in the 1780s combined denominational differences about text with a general appeal to a Christian temper to be recognised by readers and applied to letters, argumentation and public disputation. Again the apparent victor published an account of the debate, held in a crowded Baptist chapel, and again print was used to extend the argument retrospectively to exchanges prior to the debate. Joseph Proud, a Baptist minister, had become friendly with John Bousell, a Quaker unsure of his affiliations. Proud invited Bousell to address the Baptist congregation, but his repetitive delivery and his ideas of baptism (as something enacted by the Holy Ghost through fire rather than water) made him a dubious prospect and Proud suggested he find another audience. To begin with their relationship was friendly, thanks to a correspondence in which differences were articulated and contained: 'notwithstanding our *freedom* both in conversation and writing, yet we neither *took offence* or *fell out* with each other'.[16] But a different view of scripture created a rift: Proud told Bousell his last letter 'hurt my mind'. The correspondents then hesitated. Bousell proposed a debate and Proud agreed; their letters expressed a desire for both to continue 'in christian temper', partly achieved through epistolary conventions such as amicable subscriptions – Bousell signs off as 'thy real friend' – and timing of replies – 'Thy answer within a week will oblige . . . Expect an answer this morning.' The debate in person, supposed to be conducted with coolness, Christian temper and candour, quickly collapsed into uproar since Bousell read out passages of scripture which Proud thought was not proper arguing. When someone proposed that the debate should go to press, Bousell called out ' "I will print first" ', suggesting a knowingness about polemic on the page which he had not shown in speech. Proud's printed text projected more sorrow than anger and claimed impersonal motives: 'I stood forth as a gospel Minister, to defend a positive institution, a divine ordinance appointed by Jesus Christ', making 'an humble and friendly address to those who differ from me in their judgement'.[17] Protesting his commitment to Christian unity, Proud defined his opponent's productions as unchristian – hence he need not show him any Christian love. One letter, evidence of Bousell's abusiveness, Proud said he would not print. This seemed like Christian forbearance, except that Proud then summarised it in a footnote: 'The following are specimens of his abilities and kindness in the B-ll-gs-te [Billingsgate] way: "Full of darkness" – disturbed brain – seeking the praise and honour of men – no true believer – ignorant, to write to thee is but casting pearls before swine' and so on.[18] With wonderful irony Proud took to the moral high ground – 'I hope I shall never forget to treat with candour and christian affection those who differ from us in their judgment' – before launching into his own abuse of Bousell's 'poor

feeble efforts...a thousand degrees below reason or good sense...his inco-
herent, heterogenous, and absurd jargon is below the *abilities* and *language* of
a *decent school-boy*', contrasting his own 'silent contempt' with Bousell's
'*noise, nonsense,* and *hodge-podge divinity*'.[19] His contempt was of course not
silent, except so far as it was unspoken in the debate. Letters played in the
space between oral and print culture.

Like many controversial writings, Bousell's response crammed polemic
into a long title as if to impose a sense of conviction on readers who might
not last the whole dispute. Where Proud had represented himself as coolly
reasoning, Bousell attributed zealous warmth. He reinterpreted Proud's
authority as a minister as a trap of worldliness with Biblical antecedents:
'Priests in all ages have been the greatest stirrers up of persecution.'[20] Where
Proud used 'B-ll-gs-te' elisions, Bousell used poetic ellipses – 'the men of this
world are like the waves of the sea, I do not say raging waves that cast up
mire and dirt'[21] – puns on Proud's name and oblique threats to despoil his
congregation: 'I must publish the letters I have written to thee [which Proud
had mostly edited out of his text]...they will tend to the awakening of
some of thy flock.'[22] But what made Bousell such a frustrating opponent for
Proud was his indifference to educated opinion and reason: 'a man's own
heart will tell him more than ten wise men', Bousell proclaimed. Like his
fellow-Quaker Pickworth, he was suspicious of scholastic writing. Of what
use was it? Scripture made one a passive reader, no wiser; writing was only
of use if words flowed from God through the writer, a process supposedly
demonstrated by Bousell's letters. Because the writer surrendered authority,
or gave it all to the letter not the letter-writer, there was none left for
readers, who should become simple, child-like, receptive: 'These gospel
truths have occurred to me while writing; receive them therefore in that
love that is gentle, and easy to be intreated; receive with meekness the
engrafted word that is able to save thy soul.'[23] As the ultimate riposte to
'men of letters who can persuade the blind that black is white', Bousell even
wrote briefly as God, expressing displeasure with the Baptists.[24] An Old
Testament preference for voice over text was not necessarily a losing ploy
(one newspaper reckoned that nobody had won the debate) but it was a
minority one.

Controversialists were often at odds not simply because they disagreed
but because they could not agree how to disagree. Accommodating both
polemic and critical commentary, letters kept an opponent personally in
view whilst allowing impersonal refutation. They were widely used because
they combined a favourite form of discussion between scholars with a
paradigm of address that was recognised both as friendly and hostile. In a
religious context, however, the rational dealings of the republic of letters
took on an additional and complex dynamic according to the participants'
understanding of the relevance of reason to faith. Baptists, for example,
tended to write for their cause using persuasion rather than polemic,

because their raison d'être was that the commitments of a Christian should be made by reasoning adults rather than by infants incapable of understanding the significance of baptism. One such text by a West Country Baptist arose, typically, from a confrontation with a local clergyman who had refused to bury two infants, much to the distress of their Baptist mother. The letter began, again typically, with a struggle to contain indignation at what the writer saw as discrimination and the clergyman's return of his polite letter with a curt note saying he had done only what law and duty required. Although the Baptist skirts the edge of invective – the clergyman Mr Collins is a zealot, a Pharisee, one who strains at a gnat and swallows a camel, and unchristian in his refusal to allow decent Christian burial to other believers – most space is given to rehearsing the arguments in favour of adult baptism. These depend on church history, scriptural exegesis and linguistic analysis, typically examining passages in the Bible referring to baptism, inferring that immersion is to be preferred to sprinkling and that it was reserved for adults. A key player here was Lydia, who was said to have been baptised with her household. Some argued that 'household' must include children; others argued that inference was wrong, especially since there was no mention of a husband. Lydia and her possibly non-existent children presented a textual puzzle, like Lady Macbeth and hers. The letters are inspired by a local incident but flow into an area of debate with nationally recognised conventions and frictions.[25]

Christians writing on doctrinal differences had to negotiate another force-field besides those of enmity and friendship: respect. If brotherly love in the plural led to Christian unity, it still had to accommodate differences in authority between church fathers or elders and those they were appointed to lead on earth. Although bishops, ministers and parishioners might be equal before the Lord, spiritual authority on earth was not to be compromised lightly. A number of tangles with lords spiritual show how writers used letters to further their case. A letter from George Whitefield to the Bishop of London shows the problem of hierarchy at its simplest. The Bishop had drawn up a list of charges against the Methodists; these charges were printed and circulated privately and anonymously to other bishops. Whitefield's counter-attack starts, like so many, on the title page, with a pointedly chosen epigraph from the Psalms: *'False Witnesses did rise up; they laid to my Charge Things that I knew not…'*[26] But his letter opens respectfully: St Peter's command to answer with meekness and fear is all the more relevant to one responding to a bishop (albeit one who will not sign his name). He volunteers a confession of his own fallibility and his complaint is polite: 'it is not quite fair to *give Stabs in the Dark*'. Printing copies of his correspondence with the printer and the bishop (who did not deign to reply) showed the substantiating power of letters as documentary evidence. To the main charge, that Methodists are disruptive because they practise field-preaching, he invites the Bishop to reflect upon Christ's example: 'Was not the best

Sermon that was ever preach'd deliver'd on a *Mount?'*[27] The Bishop's alarm about outdoor sermons was common, although usually remarked on by those denounced from indoor pulpits (Wesley's advice to Methodists was to bear with it, or, in extreme cases to file out in silence but be sure to return next week). As another uninterruptable form, prayers could generate resentment: so in 1740, a Presbyterian objected to some words in an extempore prayer which he took as reflections upon himself. Battling against detractors, he like Whitefield used a secular language of character assassination – 'they chuse to deal with me in secret insinuations and in the dark' – and made the visible, legible and signed form of the letter a Christian medium protecting against diabolical craft. Letters here challenged oral forms of authority: 'I'm afraid you'l scarce venture in Print what you bellow out in the Pulpit.'[28]

The eighteenth century saw changes in the ability of churches to control doctrinal arguments. It is tempting to connect this with the growth of letters rather than print culture *per se*, or, to see the networks of debate set up by letters as an ideological constituency whose power competed with the church. One early eighteenth-century controversy is intriguing in this context. Henry Dodwell was a highly respected scholar with a history of ideological detachments: he declined to take orders (thinking the office too sacred and himself too lowly) and he refused to take the oath to King William and Queen Mary. In 1706 he published a book that attracted much criticism. Five hundred pages of what Gibbon rightly called perplexed prose on how the soul became immortal through baptism seems unpromising stuff, but it was taken as evidence of how academic arguments might undermine ordinary Christians' faith, a danger increased by the growing sense that reason was the prerogative of all. In this case, Dodwell could give comfort to libertines who need only be baptised to secure salvation. Locke had run foul of a similar line of resistance in his theological writings, partly because his name was synonymous with reasoning and partly because his prose was lucid; these factors made his silence on the subject of Christ doubly expressive. Dodwell tried to historicise his detachment: whereas in the past churches debated spiritual differences between themselves, now it could be done by private persons, 'provided *they* do *not* exceed the liberty *allowable* to their *Station'* of only collecting materials.[29] This distinction between preparing neutral materials and developing controversial doctrines was impossible to sustain in divinity, even though Dodwell offered the church a fantasy of full and final authority: 'the *less Authority* the Collectors have, the greater *Liberty* others will have to *discover* their *Errors* where they may prove mistaken. And, when all is thoroughly debated, *Authority* may then the more securely *judge* of the Testimonies produced on all sides.'[30] Dodwell's view was that he was not trying to win an argument but put a case. In the early eighteenth century, to promote your cause as reasonable was to set it up as a winning argument, but here it ran into the question of how far the province of theology should be open to philosophers. Although

Dodwell protested that he had no desire to weaken church authority, he attracted widespread condemnation, partly because his title seemed to suggest to careless readers that the soul perished with the body. It was also reinforced by his use of epistolary form: *An Epistolary Discourse* is not quite the same as A Letter. The text is all one letter, with a shadowy addressee whom Dodwell does not know personally. The title's namelessness implies modest subordination to church authority; the scholar answering letters acts as a trope of reluctant engagement with controversy. But the epistolary first person allows the proponent a nominal subjectivity precisely to protect the argument as dispassionate. The first person becomes a medium for anybody to argue rationally.

Hurt by attacks and the lack of a fair hearing, Dodwell defended the *Epistolary Discourse* mutedly. His most persistent critic was the professional controversialist Samuel Clarke. At the core of their differences was a Lockean problem of language. Dodwell tried to argue that they understood key terms differently; Clarke, a commentator on Locke, saw common terms as a constituent of common reasoning and sarcastically dismissed Dodwell's definitions of consciousness as unstable: 'If so, it can be to no great purpose for us to dispute about Any Thing: For, before you receive my Reply, you may happen possibly to be entirely changed into another Substance.'[31] No doubt to prevent this evasion, Clarke published a sequence of brusque letters aimed at Dodwell; to what another, gentler critic called '*one of the greatest Innocence of Life*'[32], support became precious. Unexpected aid came from John Norris, who observed that church fathers might be wrong: '*I don't find but that they are to be read with as much Discretion, and liberty of Private Judgment, as other Writers.*' The famously pious Norris also shared Dodwell's concern about the souls of heathens: were God to annihilate pagans, 'It would be a kind of Massacre in the Intellectual World, for which it would be hard to give any good Account.'[33] In the republic of letters, Christian philosophers could express concern for their pagan predecessors. Dodwell was grateful but still beleaguered; how seriously can be seen in an exchange of letters with Gilbert Burnet, then Bishop of Sarum. He had denounced Dodwell in a sermon and called for his excommunication as a heretic. Dodwell wrote anxiously to the Bishop protesting his loyalty to the church but still defending his arguments. He Bishop became fierce: 'that you are one of the most conceited Men of the Age, is too visible' and the book had given more comfort to infidels than any published in the last thirty years.[34] He then refused further correspondence. What made the matter tricky for Dodwell, besides the threat of expulsion from the church, was that he wanted his son to be confirmed and as a subject of the bishop's diocese he needed the bishop's co-operation. Hostilities were defused by Dodwell's sending a book of which the Bishop would approve (a criticism of incense); in return the mollified Bishop sent copies of his explications of catechisms to Dodwell's children and cordially closed the subject. This collection got into print and no wonder: it showed the possibilities of the sins of fathers descending to their children, but being averted by an exchange of books. For Dodwell and the Bishop, letters aggravated their differences; they could resolve conflict only by using symbols. 'I see you are a Master in every Argument you undertake':[35] the Bishop's concession to Dodwell as a controversialist was made possible by Dodwell's submission of his son to the Bishop's authority – in a very Old Testament way.

Power held by high-placed churchmen was coloured by questions of seniority and politics. Some letter-writers were openly insolent, like George Sewell who conducted a vendetta against the Bishop of Salisbury. Burnet's excuse for troubling the world with his thoughts was that he was seventy and not long for this world; Sewell commented sarcastically that this excuse would licence 'every Splenetic Old Gentleman'.[36] His resentment was partly political, as Burnet implied only the older generation had a right to reflect upon that glorious revolution of which they had been part, and partly professional, since Burnet cast aspersions on the ability of the universities to train a younger generation of clergy. Youth's resentment of age in the churches was exacerbated by the elders' control of preferments and by political differences between seniors and juniors irrespective of age. One such exchange between the Tory Bishop of Exeter, Dr Offspring Blackall, and the Whig Benjamin Hoadly, who became a bishop in his turn, showed both sides using letters cannily. Hoadly took to print first after a sermon by the Bishop which glanced in his direction; he laid on politeness with a trowel, insisting on his reluctance to criticise, his veneration for the bishop as a person and his wish to remain, 'with a very high degree of *Respect* and *Esteem*', his lordship's '*most Obedient Humble Servant*'.[37] The Bishop continued his pulpit insinuations so Hoadly tried another letter. In it he distinguished between the Bishop's person and office: 'when a Person, whose *Character* is Great and Powerful, Publickly asserts the same; the more Veneration is paid to his *Authority*, the more necessity is there, in proportion, publickly to examine the *Arguments*'.[38] Hoadly was keen to be seen as a fervent supporter of the Hanoverian succession; the more lukewarm Bishop had a see in the West Country, a traditional home of foment, and his politics were country rather than court. On the other hand, Blackall's appointment was sanctioned by royalty and Hoadly risked being seen as disloyal. 'I am, for the whole, now represented as an *Enemy to Government*; of *Levelling Principles*, and I know not what.'[39] Hence he stressed his Christian forgiveness of his enemies, although he saved a postscript for a quick attack on one of his attackers. A key point of friction was whether the Bishop had said her Majesty's title was a successful usurpation or, since he had not used those words exactly, whether his principles could bear that inference. What Blackall denounced as innuendoes, Hoadly defended as syllogism – a defence likely to appeal more to a younger generation closer to their university training. The ethics of paraphrase, like the ethics of quotation, inflamed controversy as participants quarrelled about how they had been represented.

Hoadly complained in the politest terms that his superior publicised his correspondence as 'a violent assault'. Blackall's reply was written from Bath: preoccupied with his health, away from his books, he sounded querulous and verbose. But a trenchant counter-attack emerged in which his bluntness trumped Hoadly's card of deference. Politeness did not necessarily win epistolary battles. To pious cavils, the Bishop was deflatingly practical – he would tell his bookseller to alter offending phrases, if Hoadly insisted – and sardonically alluded to terms favoured by logic-choppers: '*Dato, non concesso*' [I give, not concede]. Declining to pursue his adversary with a libel action (but reminding him of the possibility), he stood so little on ceremony that Hoadly's deference to his authority comes to seem a pose and his jovial informality became provocatively casual, as if Hoadly was not worth bothering to be polite to: 'I tell you plainly, that I an't at Leisure, nor I shan't be at Leisure, nor I won't be at Leisure, to write to you so much as one single Line about such matters.'[40] Writing off a serious charge as a squabble effectively squashed his challenger; authority bestowed a right to belittle.

One of the most extraordinary texts of controversy appeared in the mid-eighteenth century and at the heart of debates about the relevance of reason to faith. *Christianity Not Founded on Argument*, by another Henry Dodwell (son of the Henry Dodwell discussed above), is a masterpiece of irony that deserves to be as well known as Defoe's *The Shortest Way with Dissenters* (1703) or Swift's *A Modest Proposal* (1729). Where those texts have become famous for embedding ironically savage solutions (hang Dissenters, eat Irish children) in polemical logic, Dodwell's used an epistolary persona to persuade a correspondent simultaneously of the necessity of belief and its rational absurdity. Moreover, unlike Defoe or Swift, Dodwell was not a controversialist identifiable with a cause and readers attributed his real beliefs very variously. Some thought the author was a deist, some a sincere Christian, some a dangerously clever parodist. John Wesley's opinion was as usual shrewd: 'It is a wonderful proof of the power that smooth words may have even on serious minds that so many have mistook such a writer as this for a friend to christianity.'[41] Given Dodwell's well-kept anonymity, the dozen or so writers who responded had only the text to go on.

First, some context. Ridicule was an accepted weapon against hypocrisy. Insofar as it exposed false religion, true believers accepted it: 'Ridicule and Reason are admirable auxiliaries to one another.'[42] Insofar as ridicule served secular thought, Christians were suspicious of it. Ridicule was usually used by controversialists in the form of personal sarcasms against their adversaries. It was very unusual to read a text in which ironies accumulated into ridicule of belief *per se*. Those most given to irony, the deists, were normally associated with a rationalising faith and some made sport with what they saw as the ludic, even ludicrous, aspects of the Trinity. So one of the livelier controversialists writing in Dodwell's wake joked about the three persons of the Trinity being a concept the mind could not grasp; one might as well talk about the three somewhats.[43] But deists had little to lose and could plume themselves on their own reasonableness. The history of relations between reason and revelation has been explored by others;[44] suffice it to say that when Dodwell published in 1741, the deist case seemed to be waning and revelation was being taken up with new vigour, although many Methodists still paid tribute to reason. One might see the history of reason and revelation not as a history of opposites but as a history of partnership in which their due weight had to be tested both conceptually and experientially; in this light, Dodwell's letters both dissolve the partnership and cast doubt on what kind of tests are possible, since to choose a test is already to align with one side or the other. Moreover, Dodwell introduces a distinction between that reason nominally supposed to be the prerogative of all and the kind of intellectual scrutiny that follows on from education. This distinction was a touchy matter for Christian and academic communities: they overlapped but were unsure of their relevance to each other.

Christianity Not Founded on Argument starts with two epigraphs which enact the divergence between plainness and learning: one, a simple quotation from the Psalms, 'I believed and therefore spake' and the other an untranslated quotation from Cicero. The letter's addressee is a young gentleman from Oxford – that is, a person destined by class for the highest education available but still a pupil and hence impressionable. The connection between universities and the Church of England implied a predestination towards orthodoxy, although Wesley had secured a foothold for Methodism in Oxford in the 1730s, and the eminent Dissenter and educationalist Philip Doddridge thought that *Christianity Not Founded on Argument* was an artful attempt in the persona of a Methodist, but made by a deist, to subvert Christianity. As so often in published letters, the author and addressee have supposedly talked beforehand; the letter simply extends their conversation. The addressee proclaimed that his reason was 'the only Guide you could depend upon to come at the Knowledge of every Thing your Maker design'd you should know'.[45] This view sets him up as a deist and the author's dismissal of it as profane babbling marks him as a representative of orthodoxy. But like the Calvinist and Arminian neighbours who agreed to argue each other's case, the writer suggests he will become 'your unexpected Advocate' (p. 6) and he starts with the premise that reason cannot lead everyone to think alike: 'an Infinity of Sects...is but the natural and unavoidable Consequence of every Man's thinking for himself' (p. 8). This point played cleverly on British anxieties about a history of dissent in multiple forms; so too his next point, about how infants incapable of reason were admitted to its privileges through baptism, went to the heart of long-running controversies about the reasonableness or otherwise of paedobaptism. Again, a widespread suspicion that reason led to scepticism lay behind his suggestion that a Christian who reasons must necessarily hesitate about the truth of the gospel. Some popular lines from Young's *Night Thoughts* disputed the point:

'Are passions, then, the Pagans of the Soul; / Reason alone baptiz'd, alone ordain'd / To touch things sacred?'[46] It is important to recognise that Young asks a question. Dodwell's letters were disturbing precisely because they played out an answer in the negative. Letters enforced the dislocation, because writing to the moment supports what one might call sceptical time, a counterpart to what Walter Benjamin has described as Messaianic time – 'a simultaneity of past and future in an instantaneous present'.[47] Messaianic time structures visions: the visionary's sense of worlds coming together requires a moment of perception that is simultaneously intense and infinite. In contrast, sceptical time offers a moment of perception that the here and now is all one can know.[48]

Ostensibly, *Christianity not Founded on Argument* was committed to belief:

> the Difference betwixt us is evidently not the Truth of Christianity; that main Point we both unanimously allow: The Connexion and Justice of the Inference, that because it is true, therefore all Men are bound to believe it, is the Circumstance I so justly except against. (p. 20)

Again Dodwell played cleverly to a readership that prided itself on toleration. In a country in which religious liberty was discursively important, the idea of being compelled was anathema – even by reason, as powerful a shibboleth as liberty. Dodwell's protagonist takes up the notion that a rational faith is a contradiction in terms – faith is powerful precisely because it bypasses the mind and goes straight for the soul (or to evangelicals, the heart); equally beside the point were phenomena like miracles which were often advanced as empirical proof of supernatural agency. The drawbacks of reason are examined – it cannot ever be satisfied, it does not convert people, it cannot control our passions, it is fallible and, most importantly, it is not universal, since those most capable of reasoning – the educated – are too narrow a constituency for a religion intended for everybody. Could anything replace reason as the basis of religion? How about the Holy Ghost? – an infallible guide who would irradiate souls with conviction 'and perform more by one secret Whisper, than a thousand clamorous Harangues from the Schools' (p. 56). The Holy Ghost was potentially universal, instantaneous and incorruptible, where written scripture was perishable and adulterated: 'Now, what a very different Prospect this, and Ground of Security from the empty Notion of mere manuscript Authorities and Paper-Revelations?' (p. 60) But again, this is teasingly put as a question. One might well reason that whispers are no more secure a medium for divine utterance than writing and doing away with scripture and scholarship would lead to only a temporary relief from textual complications. Representation, even of whispers, would have to use writing at some point, and hence one would be trapped back into text. Like a post-structuralist for whom language is unstable, Dodwell suggests a religion in which holy writ made through writing is open to deconstruction: 'The Foundation of Philosophy is all Doubt and Suspicion, as the Foundation of Religion is all Acquiescence and Belief' (p. 70). And yet the arguments become paradoxical: scripture is a text that can only be properly understood by the learned, yet Christianity enjoins its adherents to become like children, not philosophers, to show 'the Impotence and Impuberty of a dutiful Understanding' (p. 70). Academic disputation about divinity raised more questions than it solved and in any case argumentation in the academy was bounded by the premise that Christianity was true, restricting free enquiry. Universities both upheld orthodox belief and taught men methods of critiquing it; Christians required people to debate on their own terms – in instance of which the protagonist cites Bishop Beveridge, 'We must have a sight of spiritual Sight, before we can behold spiritual Things' (pp. 103–4). Is he mocking this circular argument or offering it as a paradox more productive of piety than reasoning? The ambiguity is perfect and teasingly offered: 'It is evident that Religion knows no such Situation as that of a Moment's Neutrality' (p. 111).

Dodwell's case could have been put in some other form than letters – dialogues, for instance, very popular amongst writers on religion because they allowed doubts to be both aired and corrected. Letters were a common medium of controversy offering plain-speaking or erudition, so it was appropriate to use them in an analysis of the frictions between them in religious belief. Letters also encouraged readers to think about why some people held the ideas they did through the character of the addressee. The young gentleman represents a sex and class whose education and training befit them for a career as Christians; if Christianity is not founded on argument, all this is a waste of time. So the text ends with a provocative injunction: 'Be content then, in God's Name, to be even as good a Christian as your Sister' and to remember that your pious mother is as entitled to pronounce on religion as 'the well-glossed Heresies of a letter'd Clarke' (p. 114). With a final irresistable twist, the letter ends with 'a Father's Concern' – an imitation of letters of advice, or a travesty? – in which the father–son axis of Christianity is both parodied and played straight: '*My son, trust thou in the Lord with all thy Heart, and lean not unto thine own Understanding*' (p. 118).

The responses to *Christianity not Founded on Argument* took issue with it in several ways. Some, quite reasonably, objected to its polarising of reason and faith;[49] there was plenty of reasoning in the Bible[50] and faith did not have to be blind: 'in Scripture it is all along supposed, that there are different degrees of Faith and Knowledge'.[51] Some were puzzled by the critique of education: 'Are Ignorance, Positiveness and Presumption, such amiable Qualities, as to deserve all possible Encouragement?' and (this from a letter-writer in Cambridge) were the educated necessarily better thinkers?[52] Education could instil prejudices as well as remove them, as illustrated by deists who were always made not born and who could be seen as prejudiced against the prejudices of their Christian upbringing. A Christian education was also defensible as an antidote to worldly prejudices against piety; it prevented gentlemen from being too enamoured of a character *'rational, polite,* and *ingenious'*.[53] Readers puzzled over the author's motives: '*It is true, indeed, it is a very hard matter, in several instances, to fix his meaning, or be sure that you have his real sentiments.*'[54] The two smartest replies were by readers who took up the implications of Dodwell's epistolary game. One took on the persona of Dodwell's addressee and, as if in a tutorial, argued the case against reason: reasoning could come in many forms. So working people operated by logical premises and conclusions in daily life. Scholars' evidence might be more extensive but not necessarily more rational and even the most learned had to accept things on the authority of others. The Oxford Gentleman's reply falters a little on the question of education.[55] Poised like Johnson's *Rasselas* to make a choice of life, the student represents both potential reason and emotional vulnerability. It was precisely Dodwell's point that in deciding between rival authorities, or between reason and revelation, one is subject to both. Moreover, although the student is a product of class and gender privilege, his ideological affiliations are not yet closed – by being a Christian he might forego some advantages and turn out like his sister and mother. The Oxford student recognises the critique of his class privileges and can only reject it outright:

What is this to ME? If my Father's Groom or Footman is not qualified to examine his Religion; I hope his Son may, upon whom he has bestowed a liberal Education. Why must I pin myself down to their Measure, and be that by *Choice* which they are by the *Necessity* of their Condition?[56]

But he recognises this is not a great argument; conceding he lacks 'the necessary between Helps to qualify me to decide upon this Question', he can only suggest he might find them if he is let alone.

The most extensive counter-arguments were put forward by Philip Doddridge who as an eminent Dissenter and educator had more reason than most to be alarmed by Dodwell's book. He perceived the adroitness of Dodwell's epistolary persona as a mask:

By this means also you have artfully enough disarmed your Adversary of the Weapon called *Argumentum ad Hominem*, a whole Magazine of which might otherwise have presented. Were you to be attacked that Way, you would no doubt laugh very heartily, to see an Adversary so fairly bit, in a grave Expectation that you should be solicitous *cum Ratione insanire*, to appear a cool-headed, consistent Enthusiast.[57]

Recognising a complex picture of religious emotions, Doddridge chose simplicity instead. Conversions were achieved differently and not always explicably; minds might be struck by some aspect of the word of God in a way that was not straightforwardly rational but led to deep thought. He drew on his experiences as a teacher of mathematics at Dissenting academies to argue one might teach labourers to reason and in any case, the satisfactions of religion did not require infinite enquiry. 'You argue, as if there were *no Medium* between an *implicite* [sic] *Faith,* and perpetual *Scepticism'*:[58] instead Doddridge pointed out there were reasonable objections that might be rationally answered and degrees of proof that included revelation. Class identity was irrelevant – 'I esteem the Evidence, not the less, but the more, because *Day-labourers* might enter into it, as well as myself.'[59] But identity was important, because the case for Christianity was supported by good Christians, whereas deists tended to shelter behind anonymity or the disguise of an ambiguous epistolary persona. Doddridge was so concerned by *Christianity Not Founded on Argument* he replied to it in three separate letters. In his second, he took up Dodwell's valedictory blessing as a shocking impiety which blew apart any case for sincerity and in his third, he pointed out that the enemies of Christianity were rarely men of impressive morals. This returned an *ad hominem* argument to Dodwell regardless of his persona – or, because he had used a persona, he was to be considered artful, but still pernicious.[60]

Issues of class and exclusion were particularly discussed in letters because they were open to all. Letters by Joseph Priestley and Tom Paine show how 'radical writing in the 1790s... sought to contest the authority of hegemonic texts and their established readings', especially the Bible.[61] Some of the controversies in which they were involved demonstrate 'how far radical bricoleurs... were prepared to cross scholarly boundaries between irrationalism and rationalism, the vulgar and the polite'.[62] Though the genre of dialogues became more popular in the 1790s because it allowed both radicals and reactionaries to stage debates between educated and vulgar characters, letters encompassed both territories and were especially useful in manning crossings because they showed up addressees as gatekeepers for vested interests. Priestley took over from the deists a hostility to the Trinity, although it is proper to call him a Unitarian. His proactive spread of this belief was indefatigable and he wrote letters extensively to whoever might be persuadable.[63] From Priestley's many controversial letters I select four that appeared in print collectively as *Defences of Unitarianism for the Years 1788 & 1789.* The differences among the four addressees showed that Priestley had an answer for everybody, that he could shade questions about the Trinity according to the concerns of his addressee and that he was consistent as a controversialist. The run of letters establishes a character for him, like a character in an epistolary novel or a periodical, as a tireless reasoner, a man scornful and impatient at times but committed to ideals of truth and candour. The year 1789 was significant in that a Blasphemy Act was passed by Parliament which denied toleration to persons writing against the Trinity; hence Priestley's pointed comments upon the relation between civil power and established religion. The 1789 collection is similar to others he published in 1786 and 1787 (1788 was a slack year).

Introducing the letters are sketches of Priestley's adversaries which predetermine a reading: thus Dr Horsley, Bishop of St David's and Priestley's most loathed opponent, is said to be one of the poorest figures in the history of controversy; Knowles and Barnard are weak on early church history, but bright enough to see their deficiencies; Hawkins is intelligent, but 'an instance of the fatal fascination of splendid establishments' – an attraction from which Priestley was of course exempt, since his refusal to subscribe to the Thirty-Nine Articles barred him from both university education and a career in the church.[64] Of the four, the first and last are most substantial: to Knowles, Priestley is straightforwardly dismissive; to Barnard, more ingeniously so. To Barnard's claim that Unitarians were responsible for a rising crime rate, Priestley called for a check on the denominations of condemned prisoners: 'The usual *last dying speeches and confessions* of those wretches do not, I believe, throw any light upon the subject; but perhaps you will say that we bribe them all to be silent' (p. 104). But this *reductio ad absurdum* was followed by an olive branch, inviting Barnard to visit him. Horsley and Hawkins were opposites, however: Hawkins was an erstwhile friend who had unexpectedly gone to print against Unitarianism and Horsley was an enemy. Priestley's implacability was based on the Bishop's determination to attack him personally, to destroy his credit and the authority of his name, not least by disparaging Priestley's scientific achievements which he dismissed as 'lucky discoveries'. An outraged Priestley responded by ironically flattering the Bishop as an effective controversialist: 'After seeing your first set of *Letters* to me, I said to several of my friends, that if I could have dictated the whole of your performance myself, it should have been just what I found it to be' (p. 2). This epistolary paradox repositions him as knowingly on Horsley's side because Horsley is unwittingly on his – a theme that subsequently becomes important. On Horsley's stated aim to ruin his reputation, Priestley countered with the argument (for which there was wide support at the time) that controversy should avoid personal reflections:

> The real value of every work comes in time to be justly appreciated. Allowance is made for errors and imperfections, and due credit is given to every man, and to every production, for what is just and will bear examination. This is all that I desire... (pp. 4–5)

The question of credit is displaced from author to text by impersonal verbs: the man who makes ironic observations to his friends first disappears, then reappears, as if enacting a move against *ad hominem* writing and towards inquiry. Priestley gives short shrift to Horsley's declaration that he had not read his four-volume history of early opinions about Christ – because nobody should read it! and because it would bestow the oxygen of publicity on heresy. To one barred from libraries it was particularly galling to see those with access neglect the privilege. A comic turn in which Priestley wrote to the Bishop asking to borrow a book he is said to have misquoted was followed by an impassioned plea: 'if you have any generosity in your nature, lay open the stores of learning locked up at Oxford and Cambridge to us poor sectaries' (p. 72).

What makes Priestley's letters to the Bishop of St David's remarkable, however, is that he comes close to a discussion of the unconscious. He tries to explain why it is that controversies become virulent, how reason can be unreasonable too. He points to the presence of something unconscious – 'that *secret influence of motives*, of which the agent himself is not directly apprized' (p. 11) – which makes men who impartially seek truth become unconscious promoters of their own beliefs: 'the human mind is so complex a thing, that there is great room for self-deception, especially in cases where the passions and affections are strong' (p. 12). People who hold passionate beliefs or dislikes confuse arguments and persons because they are unconsciously driven: 'In many cases, I am satisfied, that the pure *love of truth* is on both sides absorbed into passions of a very different nature' (p. 14). Unusually, Priestley sees argument as a passionate exercise of reason; a love of truth is a paradox, since love is a passion that hinders the exercise of reason. Hence controversialists both insult their opponents and claim to be dispassionate. Priestley relates 'this *latent insincerity*' more particularly to religious controversy, in which people engage in '*direct prevarication*', that is, accusing their adversaries of deliberately telling lies. Priestley argued it would be more Christian at least to give others the benefit of the doubt about their intentions. These two strands, of the unconscious motives in controversy and unchristian accusations of intents to deceive, come together in letters. As Priestley wrote and interpreted them, they convey a sense of the person and a sense of the true person who cannot hide his self-deceptions. A bold, contemptuous and imposing manner might work in conversation, he told the Bishop, but 'it is attended with no lasting advantage in *writing*, when big words, and haughty airs, may be examined at leisure, and their insignificance seen through' (p. 61). It is as if Priestley had stumbled on the textual unconscious in and through letters.

Priestley's letters to Hawkins found another way to avoid the *ad hominem* pitfalls of religious controversy. In part his target was not Hawkins alone but anyone who subscribed to the Thirty-Nine Articles for reasons of expedience not conscience. Here a literal interpretation of the words clashed with a latitude of interpretation (which Hawkins advocated), a latitude which might be secured through metaphor. Like the deist who mocked the three Somewhats, Priestley had fun with Hawkins' metaphors for the Trinity (which included trees, royal titles and divisible polyps): 'It is a mere business of *Abracadabra* . . . we have neither *ideas* nor *words* for this curious distinction' of three persons in one (p. 166). Since Hawkins has otherwise an enlightened mind, Priestley concludes that he can only be driven to these tortured analogies by a perverted system: 'I now see that there is something in the church of England, which has more power than I was aware of, to blind the eyes of men, in other respects honest and ingenuous' (p. 183). The personal form of the letter holds the addressee personally responsible for his views, but the individual also represents a system which has its own unconscious drives.

Of all writers on religion in the eighteenth century, Tom Paine was the most controversial best-seller. Often misrepresented as an atheist, he was in fact a deist who viewed the Bible, especially the Old Testament, not as holy writ but a collection of corrupt and irrelevant texts. The title of Paine's *Age of Reason* (1793) seems to play on a familiar opposition between reason and revelation, but it also evokes a partnership between reason and ridicule that was understood in theological controversy. Many rushed into print to revile Paine or ridicule him in turn, but a carefully reasoned answer by Richard Watson deserves particular attention. Watson, a Regius Professor of Divinity at Cambridge, was Bishop of Llandaff at the time. Twenty years previously he had written an answer to Gibbon, *An Apology for Christianity*; the title of his letters to Paine, *An Apology for the Bible*, would have reminded older readers of this. The challenge facing Watson was how to counter Paine's populism, particularly amongst merchants, manufacturers and tradesmen, without resorting either to polemic or to arcane scholarship. Permitting himself a few moments of indignation at Paine's sarcasms on the Old Testament, Watson in his refutation manifested intellectual care, moral seriousness and a focus both on the details of Paine's arguments and on their wider implications. He was careful to respect the power of his target – 'I have no reluctance in acknowledging, that you possess a considerable share of energy of language, and acuteness of indignation'[65] – and epistolary form provided the perfect means for one mind to engage seriously with another. Although Watson committed himself to impersonal analysis and a generous belief that deists were sincere, he comes across less as one of two equals in debate and more like a don wearily dealing with a bright but wayward student. He makes concessions where he can, trying to enter into Paine's scepticism: 'I own it is strange, very strange [that God should have manifested himself to the Jews] . . . but what is there that is not strange? It is strange that you and I are here . . .' (p. 9). On possible interpellations to the Book of Moses he writes carefully, 'I admit this inference, but I deny its application. A small addition to a book does not destroy either the genuineness or the authenticity of the whole book' (p. 23). Emphasising a formal training in logic (with occasional references to his university background), he exposes Paine as unskilled. He cites earlier sceptics who have made the same criticisms and comes to sound like an irritated don marking a not-very-good essay: 'You certainly have read the New Testament, but not I think with much attention . . . you ought to have known that Luke was no apostle . . .' (p. 85).[66] Paine was self-educated but Watson refrains from remarking on this: other scholars are invoked not to remind ignorance of learning but to bring in thinkers on both sides of the cause whose greater care in argument shows up Paine as a loose cannon. Paine's would-be explosion of religion thus seems to tear holes in the whole fabric of investigative thought in a way that benefits no one.

The form of letters allows Watson moments of subjectivity, more as an elegiac representative of human fallibility than an ego intent on vanquishing an opponent:

> With a mind weary of conjecture, fatigued by doubt, sick of disputation, eager for knowledge, anxious for certainty, and unable to attain it by the best use of my reason in matters of the utmost importance, I have long ago turned my thoughts to an impartial examination of the proofs on which revealed religion is grounded, and I am convinced of its truth. (p. 43)

The Bishop presents himself as a reluctant controversialist, strictly an apologist; part of the difference, enhanced by the personal medium of letters, is an imaginative sympathy which shows he can put himself in his opponent's shoes even as he chastises the owner of those shoes for marching in the wrong direction. This is most evident in his use of political analogies, in which he shows awareness of the world and of Paine's world despite their intellectual differences. For example, Paine had contemptuously described the Book of Ruth as ' "an idle bungling story, foolishly told, nobody knows by whom, about a strolling country girl creeping slily to bed to her cousin Boaz" '. The Bishop makes a modern comparison straight off Paine's territory:

> The disturbances in France have driven many men with their families to America: if, ten years hence, a woman, having lost her husband and children, should return to France with a daughter-in-law, would you be justified in calling the daughter-in-law a strolling country girl? (p. 35)

Instead, he suggests, it is an interesting and affecting story, making it sound like a novel by their contemporary Charlotte Smith in which revolutionary turmoil and family loyalty intertwined. Most startling is his challenge to Paine on tithes. Here the head-to-head form of letters strips down identity to what is exchanged on the page:

> Husbandmen, artists, soldiers, physicians, lawyers, all let out their labour and talents for a stipulated reward: why may not a priest do the same? Some accounts of you have been published in England; but, conceiving them to have proceeded from a design to injure your character, I never read them. I know nothing of your parentage, your education, or condition in life. You may have been elevated, by your birth, above the necessity of acquiring the means of sustaining life by the labour either of hand or

head: if this be the case, you ought not to despise those who have come into the world in less favourable circumstances. If your origin has been less fortunate, you must have supported yourself, either by manual labour, or the exercise of your genius. Why should you think that conduct disreputable in priests, which you probably consider as laudable in yourself? (pp. 20–1)

The Bishop lectures Tom Paine, man of the people, for not being democratic enough! Reassuring that group of mercantile readers supposed to be most vulnerable to Paine's polemic, the letters stress a common denominator of self-help, unapologetically. Finding common ground with the republican in the idea that a labourer is worthy of his hire, Watson turns a priest-class away from being an ideological state-apparatus and into a group like any other on the labour market.

Although denominational lines were quite clearly drawn in the eighteenth century, Christians moved between churches, especially in the metropolis. Sermon-tasting, or sampling sermons at different churches, was a not uncommon practice, but there were economic ties between members of a congregation and their pastors which encouraged worshippers to stay with whatever group they contributed to financially. Even the well-organised Methodists ran into financial trouble periodically, forcing John Wesley to send out letters requesting extra donations in order to clear debts.[67] Poor Christians often struggled to find money to pay for letters,[68] but spiritual direction of the right kind was reckoned a valuable commodity. Letters were an important means of establishing communities and their leadership in ways that overlapped with but are not exactly mapped onto geographical centres. Religious fellowship was not simply a matter of locality: letter-writers acted as epicentres too.

Ministers of the gospel could elect to be epistolary epicentres and many were active correspondents, writing letters of spiritual direction and pastoral care. The character of a minister was much discussed in the eighteenth century.[69] It was also illustrated by collections of letters, often posthumous, which showed a minister both as a Christian like those under his care and as a leader or exemplar differentiated from them by his vocation. Thus he had to be both fraternal and paternal. Letters demonstrated the even tenor of his ways by testifying to his faith on specifically Christian occasions – that is, every day. There was a spectrum of types: at the meek end, one might instance John Savage, a nervous young man in charge of a dissenting congregation in Surrey. Offered as a role model to young Christians, his biographer claimed that his sacred fire 'did not burn only upon the public altar of the sanctuary; it was the same in his family, in his study, and in the closet'.[70] Savage was consistently timid: when he started preaching, it was 'like the snail attempting to gain the pole'.[71] His letters to parishioners stress his empathy with their doubts, difficulties and fears not from doctrinal uncertainty but from an anxious temperament. At the charismatic end of the spectrum was William Huntington, an avid controversialist whose letters promoted his authority as a minister. His collected works ran to twenty-six volumes and even George III read his writings. Huntington had a colourful life: a casual labourer at many jobs, including coal-heaving, he went to London to establish a congregation in the 1780s. This was a success: he told one opponent that he had above three thousand souls in his care and 'they are bomb-proof'.[72] Huntington preached an evangelicalism which many thought akin to Antinomianism, or the belief that sinners could be saved through their own efforts without the intercession of Christ. He secured an income of £2000 a year, an astonishing transformation for a man who had been so poor that for two years he and his family had lived on gleaned barley.[73] Easily offended, hard to placate and convinced of his own righteousness, Huntington had an inflammable disposition. Letters provided the perfect medium for his peculiar mix of scripture and aggression. As Southey put it, 'Huntington was a sort of evangelical Ishmaelite, and in that character considered himself at war, not only with the Church, but with all sects and denominations.'[74] The 1790s was a decade hospitable to messiahs and Huntington described himself in his epitaph as a prophet (though his predictions about Napoleon were infallibly wrong). He had to convince readers that he was not a false prophet and his letter-writing activities were crucial to this. Supremely self-confident despite or because of his lowly origins and sinful history, Huntington offended many: 'A man, who to the manners of a mountebank, unites the malignity of an assassin.'[75]

In his preaching and letter-writing, Huntington tapped into deep anxieties amongst Christians about the theatre. The stage was regularly reviled especially by evangelicals.[76] Their hostility is usually explained as pious opposition to worldly entertainments. It was also an anxiety about the potential *similarity* between the stage, actors and audiences and the pulpit, ministers and congregations. What linked them was declamation and body language. Some preachers were said to be popular only because of 'a bastard kind of oratory, stolen from the theatre'.[77] As a legitimate kind of oratory, one might compare the temperate language of a minister like Jonathan Dickinson, whose letters on religion to a not-fervent-enough gentleman combine civility and religious authority; his moves between 'pray, Sir' and 'Sir, pray' mark out a span between the optative and the imperative which characterised best practice in Anglican eighteenth-century religious exhortation. Moreover, although Dickinson's letters were addressed to a gentleman, his list of subscribers was class-inclusive, featuring reverends, farmers, shoemakers and sugarboilers.[78] Huntington assumed drama was normal and necessary because saving souls was a dramatic business, whereas people who preferred their religion to be prosaic hated the theatricality of his letters.

Many evangelicals travelled considerable distances to seek out ministers who answered their needs. And ministers travelled considerable distances to find them: Huntington had offshoot congregations in Sussex, Bristol and Lincolnshire. Believers who stayed put felt entitled to criticise, often by writing letters to the minister.[79] Some were unhappy as what they saw as an excess of polite reason or an absence of vital religion; they wanted to be stirred up more. Others felt shut out by a class-insensitive Anglicanism that preached the virtues of charity regardless of the desperate poverty of some of its adherents. Preferences were often organised around how strongly the word of God was delivered. Evangelicals were open to its provenance in mean instruments: as one put it, it was 'all one to Omnipotence, to work by Worms, or by Angels'.[80] This egalitarian belief made a coal-heaver as good a man of God as a university-educated established cleric; it also meant his critics could claim to be doing the Lord's work too. Huntington established his authority by keeping chapel government to himself and displaying extensive knowledge of scripture: known in later life as 'the walking Bible', he was hard to beat in correspondence although it was his power as a preacher that initially attracted adherents: 'I believe I was made the father of thirty souls, before I could distinctly read any one chapter in the Bible.'[81] A minister's authority was demonstrated in preaching and reinforced by letter-writing. Local approval depended on whether congregations liked their ministers to be one-like-us or one-better-than-us. Disapproval by outsiders often turned on class affiliations: some of the most violent attacks on Methodists were made by Anglicans appalled at their use of preachers from humble backgrounds. Many feared labourers could not be labouring class if they exchanged their trades for itinerant preaching and satirised them for sounding too working-class in their preaching: 'You may always find, either in their *Words* or *Actions*, or *both*, something which savours strongly of their *Trade*. Their chief *Flowers of Rhetoric* are for the most Part taken from *thence*.'[82] Even within Methodism, there was some doubt as to whether doing the Lord's work as a preacher should be a full-time occupation paid for centrally or whether preachers should support themselves by working during the week.[83] Running in parallel with this material question was a debate about the value of learning in a minister. At one end of the spectrum was a poly-math who could translate scripture immediately into any of thirteen sacred languages; at the other, a penitent alcoholic who wrote 'the *best Studying* is on our *Knees*'.[84] Basic literacy was obviously desirable because it enabled people, young and old, to read their Bible; hence numerous efforts to set up charity schools and Sunday schools.[85] For John Wesley, grace supplied 99 per cent of a minister's authority; 'learning may than have its place'.[86] Hunt-ington's only formal education was at dame-school; he put S.S. (for Sinner Saved) after his name to parody doctors of divinity, distinguished by D.D. His labouring-class background and lack of education potentially disquali-fied him from ministerial authority in some people's eyes; in others', these factors gave him authority. His correspondence was a showcase for his authority just as much as his sermons: through printing letters, Huntington expelled and welcomed members of his congregation. Many outsiders read those letters in a hostile way because of who the author was regardless of what he said; others sympathetic to the preacher found themselves caught in snares of theology when they entered correspondence. There was little room for neutral readings.

Huntington seems to have invented his epistolary character (he refers to no models) but people approached him with varied assumptions about what a minister should be and do. His letters, like those of Wesley, took up questions of class and education; how those letters were written was itself part of the argument. In the Anglican church which drew its clergy from the universities, ignorance was often construed as a cause of sin. Wesley made a significant distinction between the traditional evidence of Christianity which could be comprehended only by men of strong understanding, and inward evidence, which was 'so plain, that a peasant, a woman, a child may feel all its force'.[87] Huntington's hearers were not impressed if he used 'a great swelling word' and he had no pretensions to an educated congregation:

> the Lord's army, in London, is marshalled in *three* ranks. There are some professing nobility and gentry; these being learned, God sends gentlemen of eminent learning to preach to them. The second rank consists chiefly of mechanicks, of good education; and God sends such mechanics to preach to them. The third battalion consists of servants, journeymen, a great number of old chairwomen, together with some scavengers, lamp-lighters, and hod-men. Now you and I must be standard-bearers to this battalion of light infantry...[88]

Writing ostensibly to a younger preacher who wanted advice on whether he should go to an academy and acquire some qualifications, Huntington was pragmatic about class divisions between Christians. Learned ministers would not despise the self-taught providing they kept to their 'proper sphere', like grooms who belonged in a stable and should not meddle with side-boards (p. 45). But he also suggested his correspondent could go some-where where his origins as a shoemaker were not known, providing he could keep it quiet. This combination of pragmatism and craft he was happy to commit to print. It matched his colloquial yet eloquent language, a combi-nation that appealed to evangelicals far more than politeness.

Christians often approved a minister on the basis of his language. Evan-gelical discourse was heavily scriptural because by using authentically biblical language, a Christian could convey sincere belief and minimise error. As Huntington put it, 'let us preach as much scripture as possible, for the Bible is excellent language' (p. 45). Problems arose, however: quotation was necessarily bound to interpretation and differences in applying texts could not be settled simply by reference to those texts' common source in the Bible. As Locke observed, smarting in a controversy of his own, 'every one is orthodox to himself', and 'scripture serves but, like a nose of wax, to be turned and bent, just as may fit the contrary orthodoxies of different societies'.[89] Related to orthodoxy was the problem of inspiration, supposed to be a gift available to all believers, not just ministers, so Huntington's claims to superior knowledge were vain because others knew their scripture well and were equally entitled to divine assistance.[90] A third problem was that of contingency: putting together texts from different parts of the Bible could create a collage in which all the components might be scriptural but the combination unscriptural. Huntington was fond of this tactic and it made his homiletic letters hard to answer. Of a paragraph with no less than ten Biblical references, all footnoted, he claimed, 'I wrote it just as it came flowing on my mind' (p. 67). Arguing against men of learning who lacked grace, he declares (p. 21)

> They seemed with big heads (2), ricketty joints (3), wild, unscriptural notions (4), confused ideas (5), and a language half *Hebrew*, and half *Ashdod*...I fear all *such* children of Zion will, *instead of well-set hair, appear in baldness* (7).
>
> 2 Prov x. 8   5 Psalm v. 21
> 3 I Kings xviii. 21   7 Isaiah iii. 24
> 4 I Pet. i. 18

(This dig gained force from Huntington's singular wig-wearing habits.)[91] The peculiar language that pleased his congregation frustrated opponents because it mixed aggression and comfort: 'True repentance is not pressed, squeezed, nor extorted, by the workings and violent struggles of guilt and wrath, fear and torment; but it flows out under the sin-pardoning operations of the Spirit of Love.'[92] Huntington's discursive vehemence seemed at odds with soothing promises.

In this strange context, then, Huntington conducted many quarrels. One began when a troubled member of his flock consulted him on a point of theology. Thomas Hacker was puzzled by Huntington's pronouncements on the law (which in this context meant not the ten commandments, but the means by which a believer could be saved) and he wrote asking for clarification. Huntington replied rudely – 'either you are blind, or I am' – and demanded Hacker send his objections formally, so he could refute them in print. Hacker wondered politely how Huntington could be sure he could refute objections he had not yet seen. Huntington then accused him in a sermon of sinfully writing letters on the Sabbath. Following a scuffle in the vestry, during which Huntington tore up another letter, Hacker resignedly went to print, expecting to be anathematised but determined to have a hearing from his minister.[93] Another quarrel which this time Huntington took to print was with a Mr Bramah, who wanted to join Huntington's chapel and sent him money. Unfortunately Bramah had made the mistake of doubting the divinity of Christ and passing remarks on Huntington, who sent back the money with a curt note. Bramah demanded an apology and wrote a biblically rhapsodic letter of vengeance, to which Huntington replied with a formal note saying the correspondence was being printed, at Huntington's expense. When others tried to play biblical games, Huntington switched tack and became clinical: far from evading correspondence, he answered at inordinate length the cross and plodding letters of his detractor. His skill as a controversialist is measurable by his indefatigability as a letter-writer: he warned one adversary, 'you may depend upon having the last word in this controversy, if you are the longest liver', and his final words to Bramah, in a menacing postscript, are 'if you publish 10,000 letters, I will answer them, if God permit'.[94] Gone are the genteel appeals to candour of scholarly controversy; in the third battalion, hand-to-hand fighting took place through letters.

To deter the ungodly and parade his epistolary skills, Huntington published a set of exchanges with three correspondents, claiming weariness of controversy (but showing none). The first was with a Mr Loud who disagreed with Huntington about Christ: he thought the divine was converted into the human Christ, whereas Huntington believed human and divine were united in Christ. Loud's views were explained over two pages; Huntington's correction and admonishment occupies seventy-five pages, as if to drown him out. The next to be seen off was one J. Walker: grateful for a good sermon, he was unable to agree with Huntington that a rod and a sceptre were the same thing. His objections were politely put but Huntington treated him to a full display of ministerial authority: 'Hearers are no more infallible than preachers; and more frequently err in finding fault than the Lord's servants do in preaching.'[95] The last correspondent was a deferential foreigner who humbly begged the same sermon might be printed. Huntington responded positively, comparing the tractable Fixsen to the rebellious Loud: 'Mr. Loud must get into Satan's strong hold, while Fixsen, who sat in the prison-house, must go forth and shew himself.'[96] In Huntington's peculiar prose, this meant Loud should shut (himself) up, whereas Fixsen should not. The collection might be taken as evidence of Huntington's susceptibility to letters of flattery, but it also showed how ministers faced controversies, or enemies, in their own congregations. For Huntington's followers, purity of doctrine was more important than politeness. Wrathful letters were reassuring.

Huntington's voluminous publications include much gentler pastoral correspondence with adherents, especially later in life when his position was more secure. His polemical activities faltered after 1806 when an adversary charged him with libel (they settled out of court).[97] Two controversies involving women show how devotions got mixed up with hunting down error through letters. The first involved a published correspondence between Elizabeth Morton, an ex-Catholic converted by Huntington's preaching and correspondence, and Maria de Fleury, a writer of religious meditations who had taken issue with Huntington in a printed letter, charging him with error and spleen. Morton replied furiously on Huntington's behalf in ways that relentlessly gendered the controversy, from the epigraphs on, which included 1 Tim. ii. 12, 'But I suffer not a woman to teach, nor to usurp any authority over the Man, but to be in silence.' Morton demanded 'from what part of God's word you, as a *woman*, have found authority to take up your pen, and act as arbitrator and commander in chief in defence of an host of men... Who is this mighty Deborah, that *treads in the highways unoccupied?*'[98] In the third battalion, women could only be camp followers. She thought it pretentious of de Fleury to use 'heads' for her text, since it made her letter look like one by a divine; instead, women should put queries. Morton acknowledges a radical difference of discourse between them, apropos a passage in Ezekiel about shaving and hiding the hairs in skirts, which she construes metaphorically as an emblem of the elect, cut off from the flesh and hid in Christ's skirts: 'To you it may appear strange, but to me it seems scriptural.'[99] Morton had been converted by Huntington's letters and she copied his asperity. Her final sarcasms about de Fleury's becoming head of the church, a mother abbess, inventively rework tropes of dress conventionally associated with female vanity; she will be 'swaddled in candour, clothed with meekness, and ornamented with universal charity, and fleshly affections'.[100] This metaphor makes de Fleury, an evangelical, seem Catholic and Catholics seem hypocrites, an insult the more stinging because as an ex-nun, Morton had supposedly already detected one set of pious frauds.[101] Nuns and de Fleurys could stand in the more easily for each other since each was female and clothed in self-righteousness.

Maria de Fleury answered Morton by writing directly to Huntington, defending herself ('I love order and I don't know why it should be confined to divines')[102] and pointing out that Huntington's quickness to take offence did not show much Christian meekness. On Timothy's injunction she responded she was not preaching, but (quoting chapter and verse) the Bible showed women were 'at full liberty to converse of the things of God, both by speaking and writing, not only with private Christians, but also with the greatest ministers on earth' and this liberty still held: 'I and every converted woman under heaven have an equal right with them to converse with, or write to the greatest minister of the gospel existing.'[103] The question of women's authority in religious matters was a touchy one. In Methodism, women were not allowed to preach but they were allowed to speak of their experiences in large gatherings and in a few cases the line was blurred.[104] A generation earlier, when a discourse of rights and liberty was around less, Anne Dutton had resorted to a startling defence of her career as a published author of religious writings: she was not disobeying Timothy's injunction to women not to preach or address men in public, because although print was a medium produced in the public sphere, books were read in the private sphere, so really she had transgressed no boundary or decorum: 'Books...visit every one, and converse with them in their own *private Houses.*'[105] Maria de Fleury challenged Huntington's public representation of his credentials, especially on his elaborate title pages where he assumed a string of titles:

'formerly a pupil under Moses, and instructed in all the wisdom of Egypt...for twenty years a fellow of Grace College, in the university of Sion; fellow student with Jonah, Peter, Manasseh, Mary Magdalene,' (what! Mr. Huntington fellow student with a woman?) and John Bunyan...Now under-chaplain to her most excellent majesty the royal Sheba...[106]

Just as people wary of tertiary education promote the term 'university of life', so his mimicry shows an ambivalence about learning after all. Huntington first tried to argue that de Fleury's letter was written by a man. Then he resorted to open misogny: he wielded a sword, de Fleury shook a duster.[107] De Fleury stood her ground against Huntington's railing: 'such rebellion...such DARING INSOLENCE...this DAUGHTER OF THE DEVIL'[108]; his abusiveness proved her point. Scripturally sanctioned misogynist stereotypes of Jezebels and witches, with populist and Miltonic overtones, could in the eyes of an educated genteel readership (the first and second battalions) be defeated by cool reason. Letters served all enlisted Christians: their polite displays of logic suited Christians who valued reason; to those who preferred revelation, letters clothed faith in rhetorical power. Hence letters confirmed boundaries between the educated and the vulgar as well as dissolving them.

Even a united congregation could be torn apart by letters when different ways of reading them put pressure on a common character of Christian. The final controversy I wish to discuss arose over a preacher who stood in for Huntington at his chapel. The congregation liked him and raised a hundred pounds as a thank you. When Huntington returned, far from being pleased at his flock's generosity, he revealed a debt of three hundred pounds of his own, which they duly paid. Huntington then accused Mr Wilkinson, the preacher, of infecting his wife with venereal disease: the source of this story was a boy called E. Body, who said he had it from his mother who had attended Mrs Wilkinson in childbirth. In the subsequent storm of letters, one of the congregation wrote to Mrs Wilkinson who replied that the story was a malicious lie invented by the Body family as revenge for her husband not marrying their daughter. As God was her witness, she wrote, she had no disease and was happily married to a faithful and pious man. Her correspondent, not satisfied, wrote to Mr Wilkinson proposing the matter be cleared up before witnesses. The scandal reached the newspapers, attracting others who wrote in claiming to have been slandered for obstructing Huntington's interests and to have suffered financially in consequence.

Some correspondents expressed pleasure at seeing Huntington in trouble and 'that he who had been the porcupine, the adder, the cockatrice of Religion, was himself to be tried'; others pointed out that given his own past as a fornicator, it hardly behove Huntington to cast stones at sinners.[109] On the one hand, correspondents advanced a rational, legal and secular paradigm, that people were innocent until proven guilty; on the other, they debated how far an individual's sinfulness invalidated him as a minister and how far hypocrisy was endemic to a congregation led by a difficult, charismatic man. In the flurry, a gently dignified letter from Wilkinson protesting his wife's perfect health, and a letter from her doctor testifying that her only complaint was a touch of arthritis on the knee, went more or less unobserved, displaced by Huntington as a cause célèbre. Was he '*A sheep without, a wolf within*' or a true prophet whose honour was naturally doubted in his own country? Letters defending Huntington were suspected to have originated in his own closet; as in criminal cases, how texts were handled became a measure of deception. The usual accusations of Antinomianism were aired, as a supposed disbelief in the law of Christ became a trope for disorderliness or being beyond any law. Body's son retracted his slander: the only person involved who had clearly committed a sin, he was least discussed, subsumed into the drama of Huntington as controversialist, for once unable to write himself into authority through letters. The collision of secular testimony with Biblical analogues or the problem of Christians bearing false witness which could not be allayed by the meekness of the injured, showed letters in the service of acerbic controversy and pastoral care, creating and confirming the eighteenth-century character of Christian.

Devotional letters

The designation, CHRISTIAN, comprehends much. – John Monro

Reading and writing letters contributed to a sense of Christian community. This section starts with a discussion of how individuals related to their immediate community, a community on paper as much as a geographical locality, and to a wider readership which defied earthly laws of time and space to unite those seeking the promised land. There was some common reading – the letters of Elizabeth Rowe, the meditations of James Hervey and the poetry of Edward Young were popular. Christians' familiarity with scripture also contributed to interdenominational uses of letters and memoirs. Deathbed literature was especially relevant since it was said that what distinguished Christians from others was, first and last, their confidence in the jaws of death. Through letters, particular subcultures are visible – indeed, letters helped create them, although the relationship between beliefs and epistolary publicity of those beliefs is not a simple story of cause and effect. These subcultures were distinguished from each other by various features.

One of the most important was the significance accorded to the figure of Christ: to what degree was he divine or mortal or a composition of both and what was his role as an intercessor for sinners? In religious controversy, these arguments were identifiable through labels – that is, people announced themselves (or more usually denounced others) as Socinians or Antinomians. Hence John Wesley's reluctance to accept the label of Methodist for those who followed his lead, because to have a label was to be flagged for attack. In devotional letters, these labels mattered less; instead, letters testified to practical religion. That they were also a medium widely used for speculative theology was not a problem; they took on doctrinal colour and were certainly marketed to specific groups, but were also read in terms of a general Christian identity. The term 'devotional letters' indicates a large field which one might describe as pastoral, except that the term already has a use in literary history so I think it is best avoided. By 'devotional' I mean letters in which people showed care of each other's souls, whether ministers or ordinary believers who shared with their correspondents a desire to be classed among sheep rather than goats on Judgment Day. Devotional letters also provided a form through which people paid their devotions to God. They did so through epistolary means of praise, comfort and despondency, especially important concepts to evangelicals. This is an area in which women writers are well represented. I end with looking at Methodists in detail because they more than others made letter-writing an active part of their identity and community and because their emphasis on Christ connected to views about the body and its utterances which gave letters a distinctive role. The contours of the Methodist world can be read through letters, which were understood at the time to be a medium for the religion of the heart.

To be a Christian was to join a fellowship: 'the worship of Heaven is *social*'.[110] This fellowship was natural, like warmth, but required agents: 'As one live coal kindles two cold ones, so one warm lively Christian, by his converse and prayers, is apt to set several cold hearts a glowing about Christ and spiritual things.'[111] Epistolary converse was an analogue to the communion of saints:

While I write, the idea of the saints' communion strikes me with pleasure; and I cannot forbear indulging the reflection. – It is a communion which absence does not prevent; for often 'at once they sing, at once they pray.' Around the throne resorted to by all, they have fellowship one with another. And frequently, though they know it not, they hold a near communion in fears, expectations, and delights. Their minds made kindred by a Power Divine, muse on the same subjects, and take the same retired walks within. A course tending to the heavenly land they are all agreed to run in; and thus they tread the same path, though sometimes with unequal steps. Their blest communion death cannot interrupt; for as to the saints in glory, among their numbers, in their lays, we even *now* thirst to join; yea, we pant to praise. And as the happy family, one after another, arrive there, their communion is rendered complete, and its duration secured for eternity.[112]

Letters played out etymological connections between communion, communication and community. Able to cross time and space even as they were products of a moment and a place, letters acted out a Christian soul's aspiration to escape earthly constraints. They manifested religion's power to change boundaries. The living longed to be united with those who have passed over: for many writers, ties of kinship were replaced by indissoluble Christian bonds. 'I find my relations in the spirit are nearer and dearer to me than my relations in the flesh.'[113] Tropes of the family taken from scripture provided eighteenth-century correspondents with an image of closeness and licence to speak freely, which was important given that spiritual urgency required the suspension or reverse of epistolary decorums. 'You see, I have addressed you with an unreserv'd freedom and familiarity. I have... treated you as if we were in the same State of Equality now, as we shall quickly find ourselves before the Tribunal of our glorious Judge.'[114] A discourse of good government within the family merged with that of the state for Christians across eighteenth-century culture: '*there is nothing more* Civil, *nothing more* Humane, *nothing more* gentle *and* governable, *than a* mature *and* well-grown Christian'.[115] This discourse deflected anxieties about the role of religion in civil society's broils; it also proposed that to be a good Christian was to be a good person in any station or situation of life. In this a Cambridge Platonist of 1710 could agree with a Methodist of 1760, who declared, 'The sacred principles within [the letters he was prefacing]... diffuse a lustre over their several relations and characters in life, and hence they are good husbands, wives, parents, brethren, sisters, members of churches, subjects to their princes, and citizens of mankind.'[116]

Christian identity was a communicative one. Letters were the best fuel to light a fire to send incense to God and warm herself, wrote Mary Astell. Communication was not just upward and inward but outward too: 'those that truly love God are desirous to have others love him too'.[117] Communicative desire could become compulsive: souls in a state of grace 'cannot spend one day without some converses with their God and Saviour, some holy traffic with the world of glory in a free and uninterrupted exchange of prayers hopes humiliations confessions praises thanksgivings on their side'.[118] Here letters overlapped with diaries and prayers, but their inclusion of a second party allowed those conversations to be supported by Christian fellowship: 'I really think myself a subject too mean for a letter... but when on the other hand I consider the truly christian spirit that delights in hearing of the mercies and goodness of God... I am encouraged to speak of his gracious dealings to me.'[119] Secular epistolary decorums had to be adjusted since Christians wrote within a three-way relationship of self–God–other rather than the usual self–other. It was understood that to write as a Christian meant being impolite in so far as worldly people regarded religion as a duty rather than a passion, if they regarded it at all, but the committed Christian held up otherworldly standards, like one excusing herself for not congratulating a newly married friend: 'I can no more allow myself to write trifling letters, than I can to speak idle words, all of which I must be accountable for at the great audit.'[120] The idea of audit that permeated Christian culture owed much to a mercantilist civil society; Christians also generated their own discourse of fellowship. Christians were to encourage, comfort and advise one another, share joys and sorrows, and join with one another in religious exercises, 'in a word, to keep up...the communion of saints in the most intimate manner'.[121] By writing letters Christians could reach those 'in many dark corners of the country, ready to perish with lack of knowledge'.[122] Likewise, reading letters enabled Christians to review the Lord's work in others as well as themselves, to partake of their vicissitudes and struggles and to take comfort from their triumphs. So one collection offered its readers 'a Cordial for the Faint, a Staff for the Lame, and abundant consolations for those under temptations'.[123] Time and space became metaphors for moral progress and letters a means of expending and measuring Christian energy: 'Remember a christian cannot stand still; he must go either forwards or backwards; and if you have not made some advances towards heaven since the clock struck last, you have gone back towards the contrary road.'[124] To be writing or reading letters meant being active.

Letter-writing promoted a sense of similitude between Christians. It showed that 'Good men...had like passions; they were in the same contagious world; yet they were holy and heavenly in their affections and actions.'[125] It was a commonplace that examples were more efficacious than precepts, because they showed *how* one might fulfil divine commands. Curiously, given the articulating power of letters, excellent examples were praised as 'silent' reproofs – the idea being that the reader was shown what had to be done and left to apply it. In the genre of sacred biography, biographers and editors were keen to list their subjects' epistolary skills:

> Mr. *Parker* had all the qualifications requisite in a christian correspondent; ardent piety, sound wisdom, great experience, tender sympathy, unaffected sincerity, and a steady and persevering attachment to those who were favoured with his friendship. What an acquisition is such a friend! He improved his leisure moments for many years of his life, in writing letters of instruction, admonition or consolation, to those for whose welfare he had the most solicitous concern. And a word in season how good it is![126]

What is striking about these testimonials is how they supply a genealogy, a set of characteristics mediated by the biographer who thus tends the community from which the letter-writer has departed. A letter-writer's abilities comprehended God-given talents, and a Christian's improvement of them, measured by investment in writing time or spread of epistolary networks. So Elizabeth Bury's biographer reported

> In writing of Letters she had a great aptness and felicity of language, and was always thought so close and pertinent, and full to the purpose, and withal so serious, spiritual and pungent, that her correspondence was greatly valued by some of the brightest minds, even in very different countries.[127]

A second feature of these genealogies is their formality, often at odds with the letters themselves. As introductions, like the formality of prescripted prayers, they put readers into a suitably serious frame of mind. A long address to a 'Christian Reader' which prefaced one volume of letters demonstrated how sermonising editors presented exemplary Christians as like-us and not-like-us. The writer, John Monro, was a person of limited education and great piety, 'So that here thou has no less than a valuable Jewel, tho' in a very homely Case.' The title's survey of duties and graces pointed to practical applications for the reader, who was also to be 'instructed in the Wiles of Satan' by the letters. Tensions between pedagogy and autodidacticism are defused by the editor's personal affirmation – 'I was instructed, convinced, humbled, excited and encouraged by them', thanks to the Holy Ghost, by whose means Christians 'speak of the great Things of God, in a very pointed and distinct Manner, and with an elevated Frame and spiritual Dialect'.[128] Letters united soul and voice with a trace of body, as if anticipating the life of the spirit after death; the ghost of the writer returned through the Holy Ghost.

The gendering of Christian community was erratically inclusive – that is, although communities included women, they tended to be subsumed into the discursive embrace of brotherhood. Collections of letters usually specify the sex, though not always the full identity of women letter-writers, and they rarely remarked on the sexual politics of correspondence between women and men in the way that secular collections did. (Omission of names was perhaps a formal way of abjuring the world, as if Christian identity could dispense with the vanity of names as well as titles.) Brotherhood was a discourse which had to absorb differences, as the circular letters put out by Baptist Associations show. These were letters which were printed following annual meetings of local churches; they reviewed the year's work, reported its tally of souls gained and lost, and enlarged on a spiritual theme for the edification of those unable to attend. They were presented as collectively authored, for although they were written by one person, the topic was agreed beforehand and screened before being read aloud to the assembly. The letter was not just an instrument but a symbol which evoked St Paul's epistles: 'We wish to see you living epistles of Christ, known and read of all your acquaintance.'[129] Two examples show how they used letters symbolically to promote community and brotherhood. The Baptists who met at Salisbury in 1798 were conscious of their dwindling numbers and energies but declared that since scripture truths were eternal, they could recycle past years' letters. Quoting Hervey's dictum that a Christian should write something about Christ every day, they meditated on how letters united the living and the dead. Johnson's remark that we will receive no letters in the grave did not mean they could not be sent:

> Some of the letters you have received on those occasions, were written by our dear departed Brethren, whose lips and hands are now mouldered to dust; but by your looking over again the letters they wrote, they will, though dead, yet speak again to you.

An elegy for a community of thirty years' standing became a monument of faith for the living and a symbol of communication in a future state:

> Death hath sealed up the hands of most of the writers, and closed the eyes of most of the first readers of these letters; as well as emptied the pulpits, and pews, in most of our places of worship. The writers and readers of this letter will probably soon close their correspondence in this world. May a better correspondence be opened between them in a better world![130]

The Baptists who met at Northampton in 1793 had meant to write on zeal but had been pre-empted by the Yorkshire Association, so they discussed missionary activities instead. Two brethren had gone to India, so they printed a farewell letter of encouragement to them and letters of support from other groups. The enterprise had been initiated by letters – 'The *Hindoos* had written to us for missionaries, while we were forming our plan' – and instead of an epistolary sermon, they printed a *Letter to the Indian Christians*.[131] This was addressed to 'all in *India* who call upon the name of *JESUS CHRIST* our *LORD*, both their's and our's', the separate pronouns registering difference even as they promoted union. One brother had warned that heathens would judge God and Christianity by what they saw of Christians' character, so the letter had to be written to support that character. In the exhortation which follows, awareness of difference is uppermost – the difference between Indian Christians and other Indians. 'Expect persecutions and reproaches ... Consider who it is that maketh you differ.' As consolation, the Baptists offered likeness to themselves, particularised in letters to individual converts like 'Dear brother *Ram Ram Boshoo*' who had written a hymn which they assured him was sung by thousands in Britain: 'Your sentiments and feelings are ours! We feel that we are brethren!' Another, who had evidently been backsliding, had fraternity offered to him as a carrot: 'Might we add (surely we may) dear brother *Mohun Chaud*?' Letters, like prayers, were acts of remembrance whose reciprocity ('Let us have your's for us in return') enacted Christian equality.

The affinity between brothers as Christians pervaded unpublished letters too. One such relationship, between Richard and George Cumberland, illustrates how letters expressed the nuances of practical religion. Richard was a vicar in the Cotswolds who in many respects fitted a stereotype of Anglican clergy as complacent: he had problems with local farmers over tithes, enjoyed the company of his books and a brace of spaniels and took on a parish whose spiritual neglect was evinced by the filthy, damp and half-ruined state of its church, which he compared to Goldsmith's deserted village and blamed on the negligence of the landlord class.[132] But this he deplored and set about its restoration. George worked in London in an insurance office which he hated; pursuing many artistic and scientific interests, his diversions also included writing sermons anonymously for the press. They corresponded regularly, confiding their views of life, romantic involvements and states of mind – not without friction since the lively George got impatient with Richard's ponderousness and Richard sometimes found his brother too frivolous. Interestingly the clergyman wrote little about religion other than the cares and duties of his parish; it was the nominally secular brother whose letters meditated on the discontents of worldliness:

> I often cry out when alone and filled with careful thoughts, am I never to find rest? must paultry concerns for ever disquiet me?...Assuredly I was not sent here to be unhappy – In this manner I reply – Cease to be depressed at every opposition to thy wishes – desire nothing which is unlikely to be, magnify thy good fortune, submit to thy bad, call the ills that befall thee common events and thou wilt be happy...I will plan a life of real usefulness [including doing good and forgiving offences] – Charmed with these delightful resolutions, I retire to my Chamber, address myself to the Almighty with the utmost humility, and fall asleep fill^d with the pleasing vision...[133]

Although his good resolutions wear off, this Christian self-catechism with its liturgical echoes shows how letters provided an outlet for spiritual questions, here framed by a rather English stoicism and play between melancholy and good-humour. This letter is like a sermon, addressed to himself in the intimate vocative; it is also a form of Anglican confession, as he debates whether to send it to his brother:

> why is it that we are afraid to divulge these sensations that do us most honour? Wherefore should I conceal from my best, *real* friend, that I sometimes resolve well tho I do not always act so – Good Heaven! that example should teach us to appear so unlike ourselves – How different

this World and the next! What we blush to reveal here, is what we shall be proud to acknowledge there...[134]

Writing thus fortified his mind, he noted; it also shows that interiority exists as much in the letters of reticent Anglicans as in the less-abashed discussions of the 'inward man' amongst Methodists.

Correspondence was better than conversation at exploring spiritual needs because it presumed a contract to follow through discussions and allowed monologue. Although letters by Christians cover a range of preoccupations, three discourses feature across the board: praise, comfort and what I will call gloom. These represent respectively the Christian as elect, human and sinner and although they also feature in non-epistolary genres there are particular reasons why letters were hospitable to them. These discourses were historically inflected: satirists thought gloom endemic amongst Methodists and the Methodist Conference of 1741 worried about a doctrinal emphasis productive of despair. 'Q. Do not some of our assistants preach too much of the wrath, and too little of the love of God? A. We fear that they have leaned to that extreme.'[135] But Methodists were the most active in producing a culture of comforting texts and many of Charles Wesley's hymns were written 'for Believers Rejoicing'.[136] If prose was the preferred medium for divine anger, and song for rejoicing, letters connected them. 'The language of men is too weak to describe the deep things of God', opined John Wesley,[137] but letters could accommodate plainness, lyricism and everything in-between. The devotional registers of praise, comfort and gloom had particular dynamics: praise involved longing; comfort, an active closeness; gloom, paralysis. Praise moved outward and upward, wafting like incense to the Lord; comfort moved more on a level, like an embrace; gloom moved inward and downwards. Between the elevated language of praise and the 'low worm' who felt gloom lay a language of mood which it was understood letters could express. Moreover, the process of sending a letter (outward), exchanging a letter (on a level) and absorbing a letter (inward) had parallels with the dynamics of praise, comfort and gloom. I shall discuss each in turn.

Epistolary resistance to closure made letters a good vehicle for praise of God, which ideally was endless. Boundaries were suspended as the soul yearned to be one with God. In a correspondence with John Norris, published in 1695 as *Letters Concerning the Love of God*, Mary Astell found it hard to stop writing on the subject: 'yet I find like its divine Object, it has no Bounds'.[138] The power of praise to lift the soul away up out of the body made the body potentially abject: all other delights in comparison were like faeces, she declared, although a body was needed in order to register the energy-field of praise, for instance by trembling: 'All true Lovers of GOD being like excited needles, which cleave not only to him their *Magnet*, but even to one another.'[139] Astell had initiated the correspondence and its double act was appropriate: 'Were I to deal only with the rational Part of Man, I should think that half of what has been said would be enough', wrote Norris, but letters allowed Astell's rhapsodies to complement his reasonings.[140] This is not to figure the feminine as gushing – Norris was fervent in his praise of Astell's rhetorical power – but the repetitions between their letters allowed for doubling rather than division of the discursive work of paying tribute. The joint epistolary enterprise becomes an emblem of the soul's motion towards other believers and towards God; each can enlarge upon the other's words. Moreover, as the love of God inspired love of one's neighbour, the correspondence brings them closer to God by being close to each other through letters. Praise often seems to start from a point of enclosure which it breaks through, seeking outlets. A methodist was one who had the love of God shed abroad in his heart, wrote John Wesley;[141] this notion of 'abroad' was often figured in relation to the enclosures of home, literally, the closet in which many Christians performed their devotions. Margaret Andrews, who died aged 13, was an exemplary figure because she prayed three times a day in her closet, for two hours in the sharpest winter weather, and 'she made every room in the house an oratory'.[142] The Rev. John Parker, also held up as an example for his gifts in prayer, declared 'when it is well with me in the closet, I long most of all to tell others what I see and feel'.[143] If the body was a stronger trope of enclosure, the closet worked as a protected space, ideally as uninterruptable as christian love itself.[144] But praise was more vocal than prayer, and loud, as in shouts of joy. Sometimes discursive decibels were literal: early Methodists frequently had to contend with noisy opposition, like banging of drums outside the window, which shouts of joy might drown out.[145]

In the later eighteenth century, the language of praise occasioned some debate. The Psalms were recommended as the vehicle for praise because they were the language of inspiration. This became increasingly at odds with the simplicity cultivated by hymn-writers like Watts and Charles Wesley and it was compounded by the uncomfortable rhythms of poetic paraphrases of the Psalms – what Paine called English prose run mad. Rowland Hill agreed: 'Is it metre? Is it poetry? Is it English? Why, for such a reason, are we to serve God in such distorted language... yet attempt a style so different when we preach and pray?'[146] Strictly speaking it was not English but Hebrew anglicised. It had little space for narrative and so it attracted writers enraptured by adjectives and adverbs. Letters, in contrast, were clearly vernacular. They allowed narrative without being prosaic and they allowed meditation with lyricism. The success of this combination gave rise to an eighteenth-century sub-genre, the rhapsodic survey, for example in Richard Pearsall's *Contemplations of the Ocean* and *Contemplations on Butterflies* in which God the Creator was praised through his works.[147]

Where praise was talking to God, comfort was talking to a friend in the temporary absence of God. The friend who offered concern and commiseration was active in spirit, like the Holy Ghost the Comforter, although comfort was premised on equal inadequacy: 'let us sympathize with each other in sorrow or joy, and provoke unto love, and to good works'.[148] Comfort required the self to be open, to unfold its cares, suiting the open, unfolding form of the letter. Like confessions, the presence of a listener compelled letter-writers to try to be honest. Comforted by the thought that through such letters someone might be moved to pray for him when he could not pray for himself, John Newton wrote 'my confessions rather express what I know I ought to think of myself, than what I actually do'.[149] Letters offered attentions that were especially soothing to troubled souls like John Haime who preached in the army before becoming one of Wesley's preachers. He suffered from a strange burning illness that aggravated his despair: 'Feeling I wanted help both from God and man, I wrote to Mr. Wesley', whose speedy answer, 'God is on your side', was the first of many comforting letters.[150] Given the violence of much eighteenth-century medicine, those afflicted in body were grateful for soothing words; those afflicted in mind welcomed epistolary reasonings. George Trosse had an early life as restless as a protagonist in a Defoe novel and became an alcoholic before being converted, not least by his landlady:

> She was very well acquainted with the Scriptures, insomuch, that I sometimes receiv'd a Letter from her with a Hundred and odd Proofs in the Margin, fitted in good Measure to comfort poor *tempted* and *dejected Souls*. She had great Compassion upon me; would many times sit and discourse with me, would give me good Directions, and offer me considerable Encouragements.[151]

Two factors came together in comfort: the inspiring examples of others and 'a word in season' – the right text at the right time, which might arise in a sermon or arrive in a letter. So Hannah Ball was comforted by letters from her former maid and Agnes Smyth was comforted by the printed letters of Jane Cooper.[152] In the latter case, comfort was oblique but can be teased out: Smyth came from a genteel family and initially found the working-class company of her fellow Methodists a shock. She got over this, but seems to have struggled against doing her own housework, partly because it reduced the time she could devote to religious activities. The Biblical precedent of Martha was some help; it may be that Cooper's letters comforted her because they were written by a servant. They impressed John Wesley so much that he recommended they should be supplied to all Methodist societies.[153] 'A word in season' comforted by excluding doubt, which meant the word had to be emphatic: hence John Wesley's remark that 'In writing practically I seldom argue concerning the meaning of texts; in writing controversially, I do.'[154] The word could also be picked out by readers, like Wesley's correspondents who added their own underlinings to his letters.[155]

The power of examples came to letter-writers through their acquaintance, through print and through letters. Sacred biography promoted letters over funeral sermons because they were less prone to flattery and because they made Christian interiority available to others, encouraging imitation. The young John Savage was mindful on his deathbed that his letters could be compared to John Newton's widely read collection and told his uncle 'that he had his *Cardiphonia*, – they were all *from the heart*'.[156] That an epistolary community was co-extensive with a Christian one was recognised by John Wesley. Stressing it was a new departure for a spiritual magazine, he put lives and letters at the heart of his *Arminian Magazine* because they contained 'the marrow of experimental and practical religion'.[157] Complementing prose accounts of pious deaths, letters offered pious lives.

One common manifestation of comfort came in the form of questions and answers. Eighteenth-century Christians were keen on questions, from catechism to dialogue to quizzing servants about sermons[158] to interrogating parishioners.[159] John Wesley's most durable correspondences turned on the enquiry, 'how is it with your soul?' and to his favoured correspondents he wrote short, urgent letters of pointed questions. His wife thought these too comforting, rifled his pockets, stole his letters and eventually published some as evidence of her husband's over-attachment to young women. Questions were something a friend could put – ironically Wesley thought friends and their questions were a good defence against temptation – but they were also a form of the voice of conscience. The Dissenter Joseph Williams wrote in 1746 to comfort a doubting young gentleman, 'Go on asking, seeking, knocking' for everyone who did so would be answered; in 1747, he tried to reclaim a dissolute friend: 'I wrote him a long letter last week, in which I put many searching questions to him, desiring him to put them close to his conscience.'[160] A variation on questioning was the Methodist practice of 'telling faults', in which a friend would offer home truths. 'I have long seen a mixture of pride and vanity even in the best of your perform-ances' wrote Mrs Lefevre, puncturing her friend's reputation for humility; 'Look upon yourself as a *poor, lost, helpless, miserable creature*...' This may be to the same friend who defied her advice, went to the pleasure gardens of Vauxhall and, worse, enjoyed it, which earned a stern rebuke: 'What a frightful distance is there still between you and a christian!'[161] Questions put a Christian on guard against enemies within. It was said of John Wesley that he was vulnerable to sycophants and others besides his wife objected to his conduct with respect to women. When one of his assistants plucked up courage to address him on the matter, he cleverly used a conceit of a band-meeting, in which telling faults was accepted business: 'Now, Sir, will you suppose yourself to be a band-leader and that I meet in band with you? And will you allow me to tell you what I have in my heart, what I know, what I believe, what I fear?'[162] (Wesley replied he was not offended, but evaded the reproofs.) Comfort could either mimic the protection of God against danger without or warn against that danger within which arose from not seeing danger outside. God was simultaneously all-powerful and made ineffectual by a sinner's negligence. Letters warned, challenged and helped especially by directing the addressee to turn to Christ for support. A discourse of props and helps ran through Christian thought – in Locke's phrase, Christ was an Almighty arm to lean upon.[163] This support was related to literal, bodily weakness in illness, and to a metaphorical faintness which could be comforted by food – comfort-eating, as it were, with the gospel's promises offered as cordials and scripture as a feast. Props also related to that discourse of lowness which kept a proper distance between a believer and God, a distance bisected by the crucified Christ.

Eighteenth-century genres such as graveyard poetry and meditations among tombs posit a living voice among the dead. Gloom does not quite fit this literary crepuscular culture: it expresses a deadness among the living, and to those outside it, it seems puzzling. Susanna Wesley wrote to her son John that she thought Methodists were too keen on gloom, although Wesley urged them to make new chapels light and airy buildings, and to avoid melancholy: 'Every believer ought to *enjoy life*.'[164] Methodists were unafraid of gloomy places shunned by others, like prisons, and, British weather permitting, their open-air preaching took them to light places. Gloom was not exclusive to Methodists, but particularly associated with them because of their preoccupation with sin and themselves as miserable sinners. By sin they meant to stress not their state as subjects so much as objects – it was not that they were unhappy people, but that all people were wretched because humanity was fallen and sinful. Christ the Redeemer had ransomed people from sin but to be saved required more effort on the believer's part, including recognition of the intensity of Christ's sufferings and the enormity of the obligation that entailed. Since Christ was a man of sorrows, people should eschew gaiety.[165] One might arrive at an earthly state of readiness for salvation but the ideal was impossible to achieve: 'The whole life of a christian is founded on a hope which cannot be accomplished but by dying.'[166] First, one needed grace for atonement; second, justification by faith; third, regeneration, in which the image of God returned to the soul as if in a new birth.[167] Those regenerated might slip back into sin; those seeking the new birth could blame only their own deficiencies if it eluded them. In John Wesley's words, 'darkness (unless in the case of bodily disorder) seldom comes upon us but by our own fault'.[168] A culture of accountability and monitoring in the regular meetings in classes, bands and societies, reinforced by a culture of reading pious texts and writing diaries and letters, meant that Methodists were accountable for every moment. Hence they seem more susceptible to a complaint of 'wandering thoughts' which tempted many Christians during formal worship. In contrast, other Anglicans for whom salvation lay in good works could rest assured that unless they were engaged in wrong-doing, they were not sinners. Hence the hostility between the two: one thought the other was overdoing it and the other thought the one was not doing nearly enough.

Methodist consciousness of sin permeated letters and led into a very particular subculture. Doctrinally complex and textually influential, it featured a discourse of pain which linked a Christian's body with Christ's body. I depend here upon the work of Elaine Scarry, who has suggestively connected forms of torture, belief and manufacture in ways that exceed my argument here. Parts of her model help map a Christian identity peculiar to the eighteenth century, I think. Scarry proposes that belief happens when an object created by you is described as if it created you. Christians may reject this premise, but it leads to a valuable distinction between two classes of object: the weapon, by which a bodiless Old Testament God proves his existence to believers by hurting their bodies, and the tool, by which believers make their faith real by turning their bodies into instruments of witnessing.

> As in the Old Testament scriptures, in the New the human body substantiates the existence of God, but rather than that bodily verification occurring in the bodily alteration of pain, it occurs in the bodily alteration of sensory apprehension, not the hand of a woman turning leprous but the hand of a woman touching Jesus, not the thousands cut and killed in the desert beneath Horeb but the thousands who 'watch, hear,' and then follow in order to sustain this perceptual privilege.[169]

The Cross is a narrative midpoint, which becomes a focal point for Christians over time. It is a weapon for wounding Christ and a tool, the means of redemption. Scarry's argument has particular implications for eighteenth-century society which was both militarist and manufacturing, and which redesigned many tools. 'In scenes of both reproduction and wounding, the graphic image of the human body substitutes for the object of belief that itself has no content and thus itself cannot be represented.'[170] In scenes of witnessing, as God acquires a body and humanity acquires a voice, 'continual exchange between the categories is not simply permitted but *required* in the very act of belief'.[171] Avid readers of both Old and New Testaments, eighteenth-century Christians took up both discourses. My final section explains how useful this model is for reading Methodist letters.

Behind much of the hostility to Methodism lay a discourse of the body which Methodism was thought to pervert. Tropes of sourness were common, invoking a wrinkled nose and screwed-up mouth, a face of distaste projected *onto* Methodists. Methodism, wrote one critic, was 'A system of faith for souring the temper.'[172] Others criticised evangelicals' strange body language: 'their carriage in prayer being with their eyes for the most part shut, and their arms stretched out in a yawning posture, their hearers might, by a very pardonable error, be induced to think they were talking in their sleep'.[173] The image of hypocrisy as a mask played into this sense of a body unnatural, although the violently visceral discourse of religious enthusiasm was not confined to Methodists. So Joseph Williams related the effects of a sermon: 'In the discourse, how did my heart throb? How did every bowel within me roll?'[174] But Methodism had particular antipathies to the body, summed up in Susanna Wesley's advice to her son: 'whatever increases the strength and authority of your body over your mind; that thing is sin to you'.[175] The body was not clearly abject but it was clearly problematic, as in Hester Ann Rogers' ambiguity: 'I find I need not drop the body to enjoy the presence of my God...yet my desires are insatiable: I long to plunge deeper into God.'[176] Christians generally were ambivalent about the body: as flesh, it was heir to ills, prone to temptation and deserved to be mortified, but it could be pressed into God's service too. The exercise of faith drew on images taken from bodily movement: 'hence we speak of standing, walking, living by faith'.[177] Partly to differentiate spiritual ills from carnal illness, John Wesley took a deep interest in bodily sickness, diagnosing his correspondents' ailments and advising his preachers not to drink tea (it created wind, he thought).[178] His compendium of home remedies, *Primitive Physick*, went into 40 editions[179] and he was almost as keen to promote it as any of his doctrinal works. Indeed, insofar as it promoted a healing ministry, it *was* a doctrinal work. His followers tried to treat somatic pain spiritually: Agnes Smyth had upper back problems, which she thought was God's way of breaking her stiff-necked pride; Mary Mahony eased agonising rheumatism by contemplating the crucified Christ's pains in his hands and feet; Hester Ann Rogers relieved a feverish sore throat by being swallowed up in praise.[180] These suggestive reversals of body and soul tended to occur when believers were sick. Merging their sufferings with those of Christ, sick Christians were invited to pray 'Let my present Condition be so Sanctified, that my Sufferings may be united to those of my Saviour.'[181] But they also drew on an idea of an inward body whose faculties were spiritualised. So John Wesley pondered the heavenly music heard by dying Christians: 'May we conceive that this is literally the music of angels? Can that be heard by ears of flesh and blood?'[182]

Letters helped articulate a discourse of the body even as they substituted for it. A comparison with prayer is helpful here because prayer required certain bodily postures (bended knees, bowed head, a submissive heart) and it too materialised the voice in complex ways. Eighteenth-century Christians used speaking prayer (prescripted and extempore), written prayers, silent prayer and secret prayer. Henry More recommended short prayers accompanied by deep sighs following which the believer inhaled the pure air of God.[183] An aspiring body expressed an aspiring soul. Secret prayer could be performed vocally in a closet or silently in company, where believers' devotions were sometimes evident because they moved their lips noiselessly. 'A sigh or groan is equal to a thousand words'[184]: likewise, letters were obviously articulate but at the same time they testified to the body's inexpressiveness. Agnes Smyth began a letter to her sister-in-law, 'THIS comes from one, groaning under a sense of corruption, and yet not finding power to cry to God for relief.'[185] Christians' letters are full of complaints of dullness in prayer. Where channels of prayer were blocked, letters might divert the voice. Groaning was significant to Methodists for two reasons. First, it erased distinctions dependent on education, putting confidently chattering classes on a level with the humbly inarticulate; second, it returned believers to a body with signifying powers, but restricted that power to signify pain. John Wesley felt discomfort amongst fashionable Methodists: 'On this account the North of England suits me best, where so many are groaning after redemption.'[186] Groaning did such precise discursive work that Wesley resisted alternatives: when one of his preachers took up screaming, Wesley emphatically discouraged him.[187]

The somatic nature of spiritual pain was a way of representing belief in Christ's pain, returning it to the believer's body. Both weapon and tool, the Cross functioned as the place where believers wounded Christ through sin and the site where Christ became the instrument of sinners' salvation. The Father wounded, the Son was wounded and the believer re-enacted that wounding through ontological violence located in the inward, spiritualised body. This dynamic helps explain a culture of textuality too: part of evangelicals' openness to texts, and their restless quest for relevant words, was an investment in text as something which could project divine hurt back. Thus John Wesley told a correspondent, 'I wish we also felt the arrows of the Lord . . . that piercing sense.'[188] A more familiar form of this is the idiom of being *struck* by an idea. Psychoanalysis relates this to the somatic preoccupations of the unconscious; eighteenth-century Christians explained it as divine agency. So sinners stayed sinners until the word took on potency:

> But if once the blessed Spirit undertakes the work, he will . . . open their eyes . . . Though they could before sit under the most powerful ministry from year to year, without care, fear, or sensible apprehension of their danger: Yet now an ordinary sermon, or a particular passage in a sermon, which perhaps they had heard hundreds of times before without concern, shall awaken their sleepy consciences, and make them, with trembling and astonishment, cry out, *What shall I do to be saved?*[189]

Again and again Methodist memoirs testify to efficacious texts whose accidental appearance is construed as providential. Perhaps the strangest was Thomas Taylor's experience. One of Wesley's preachers, he was used to isolated circuits in Wales and Scotland. Riding in a lonely place, he came across a strip of paper on the ground; on it was written a message that Christ's love was a correcting love.[190] Correction here means simultaneously bringing back from error and the infliction of physical pain, and for evangelicals being hurt was a sign of being right. As Charles Wesley put it in a hymn,

> Dear dying Lamb, for whom alone
> We suffer pain and shame and loss,
> Hear thine afflicted people groan,
> Crushed by the burden of Thy cross...[191]

Texts had a protective power too – Hervey carried a Bible with him even to meals and the Wesley brothers taught themselves to read aloud whilst walking (which is tricky).[192] The word of God as manifested in Christians' letters was both 'oil and wine, and balm for the healing of those who are wounded, and a hammer to break into pieces the obstinate and obdurate heart'.[193] The power of text to comfort made its transformation into a weapon all the more striking, so to speak.

The most violent scene of bodily hurt in Methodism was that of the 'new birth', which occasioned much debate. Like the twentieth-century charismatics' Toronto Blessing, it required a public setting; like actual birth, it involved pain and production. 'On Saturday evening Ann Allen (a young woman) was seized with the pangs at Weavers' Hall. They did not continue long before the snare was broken, and her soul delivered.'[194] Paradoxically, images of childbirth broke the ties of flesh. Two bodies were produced, one hurt, or 'cut to the heart', in Wesley's phrase, and one healed, 'restored to peace'. Not all were so delivered, which Wesley attributed to the Holy Ghost being displeased, and they could continue for weeks in a state of heaviness, 'so that sometimes their bodies almost sink under the weight of the wounded spirit'.[195] What triggered the fit was often a wounding text:

> some single sentence, often taken from the Holy Scripture, which suddenly pierced their soul like a dart, so that they lost all command of themselves in that moment. The subjects were various, but always bordering upon the love of Christ to lost sinners.[196]

George Whitefield disapproved of the new birth, arguing that it took people away from the written word, and Charles Wesley, also suspicious, wanted those who experienced it to write down an account.[197] John Wesley was sufficiently concerned to wonder if this was a diabolical phenomenon, and he wrote to evangelists in Scotland enquiring if they had had comparable experience. One reported collective weeping, congregations in floods of tears, suggestively reminiscent of Scarry's observation that God in the Old Testament is disembodied but appears through fire or flood. Wesley's account stressed outward signs:

> Some of them drop down as dead, having no strength or appearance of life left in them. Some burst out into strong cries and tears, some exceedingly tremble and quake; from some great drops of sweat fall to the ground, others struggle as in the agonies of death, so that four or five

strong men can hardly restrain a weak woman or child from hurting themselves or others.[198]

In contemporary culture, scenes of transformation in which mortals acquire supernatural powers mostly stress painlessness. Bruce Wayne becomes Batman or Clark Kent becomes Superman through donning a costume; an outfit in reality immensely uncomfortable for an actor to wear is represented as a (literally) seamless transition.[199] Methodists represented Christ's saving of them through scenes of pain which mimicked the Crucifixion. John Wesley drew the line in some cases, expelling those who claimed to feel the blood of Christ running down their arms and throats.[200] Sceptics of these accounts stressed the presence of women, as if to explain them away as the productions of hysterical females, but they affected men too: 'Many young, strong men have roared out, through the anguish of their spirit.'[201] That men were made weak and women and children strong confirms Scarry's observation that 'to be intensely embodied is the equivalent of being unrepresented and...is almost always the condition of those without power'.[202] The human body analogically verifies God through scenes of hurt, Scarry argues, which are occasioned by doubt: hence the violence, rhetorical or literal, which punishes the (dis)believer. It may seem odd to read the new birth as an expression of doubt rather than conviction, but it articulated something somatically which was more complex than God speaking through the human body. If the word was God, and humans were voiceless, writing was one place in which that voicelessness could be expressed, just as Christ's body was the word made flesh. Methodist letter-writing took up the challenge.

Written accounts of new births are strangely full of mouths, as if the human projection of voice as the prerequisite of God had become overdetermined. Agnes Smyth's experience began with

> an uncommon faltering in my voice, and beating at my heart...I, then, burst out into roaring...Part of the time, I think I scarce knew whether I was *in the body, or out of the body*. After continuing so for near an hour, the Lord opened my mouth with praise, and filled it with laughter.[203]

She laughed for two hours. Her mouth fails in its function of speech and succeeds in being an outlet for laughter, which she represents as coming from outside her. An account with some parallels was given by Grace Murray, the woman John Wesley nearly married. After hearing one of his sermons,

> my Heart was as hard as a Stone so yt I was quite amazed at Myself. As I step'd off ye Bench in order to go Home, suddenly I was struck down, & fell to ye Ground. I felt as if my Heart was bound round with an Iron

Girdle; I knew myself to be a lost, damn'd Sinner, without Xt [Christ], without Faith, hanging over ye Mouth of Hell, & yet sustain'd in an inexpressible manner by I knew not what or whom. I cd not speak nor cry out, but only groan to God. Thus I continued for half an hour. When I was a little recover'd, two of our Sisters made a shift to lead me Home.[204]

She then begged Charles Wesley to pray for her strength to increase 'till Death is swallowed up in Victory'. The trunk of her body is paralysed and suspended, but again the discourse has strongly oral features. The mouth of hell, the jaws of death: threatening forms of orality could be fended off by making the believer's mouth neutral, unable to frame words, but open and able to let laughter or groans pass through.

Another component of Methodism's particular character that affected the role of letters was the significance accorded to Christ as a divine person in human form who mediated between God and sinners. Wesley argued that Methodists believed only in 'the blood of the everlasting covenant...the grace or free love of God, for the alone merits of His Son Jesus Christ'.[205] Although Wesley was scornful of Calvinist gospel-sermons in which preachers 'bawl out something about Christ and His blood',[206] his own adherents enthused about blood: 'See the God of angels: O look at his precious bleeding side – his hands, his head, his feet! Behold him gasping, groaning, dying, that you might be made clean!'[207] The figure of Christ was condensed to a fluid, blood. In humans, blood is normally abject,[208] but the power of Christ's blood to cleanse marks it out as non-abject, indeed anti-abject. For Catholics, this blood usually has specific points of emanation – Christ's five wounds; for Protestants, it streams in the firmament. Perhaps to compensate for this, they use a discourse for their own bodies that breaks them into parts or re-orders them as a blazon. These blazons fit the second part of Scarry's model, in which the New Testament re-ordering of relations between human and divine makes the human body function as a witness, an instrument (rather than a site of wounding by a weapon). Ears, lips, mouth, eyes, breast, heart: body parts are treated separately even as they share a function of witnessing or giving praise. Methodist blazons stressed heart consciously (Methodism was the religion of the heart, in Wesley's phrase) and mouth subconsciously, perhaps to counterbalance that orthodox Anglican discourse of good works which privileged the hand as a body part – the open hand, the helping hand of charity.

The mouth plays an important role in Christianity through ingesting the body and blood of Christ in communion. In Smollett's *Humphry Clinker*, the Indians among whom Lismahago has lived are unimpressed by French missionaries: 'when they pretended to create God himself, to swallow, digest, revive and multiply him ad *infinitum*, by the help of a little flour and water, the Indians were shocked at the impiety of their presumption'.[209] Convicted of making, unmaking and reproducing God at will, the missionaries are condemned to the stake. Smollett's joke is primarily anti-Catholic, or anti-French, but perhaps also against the free-thinking Lismahago's audience, the Methodist-inclined Tabitha Bramble and Humphry Clinker. Anglican clergy were often caricatured as well fed: from the same novel, at Bath are seen 'great overgrown dignitaries and rectors, with rubicund noses and gouty ancles, or broad bloated faces, dragging along great swag bellies; the emblems of sloth and indigestion'.[210] A long tradition of corpulence as the symbol of church excess (Robin Hood's friend Friar Tuck is its jolliest representative) had in the eighteenth century a thin counterpart – Methodists. Obviously thinness drew on the Methodist struggle against fleshly appetite, but there was more to it than that. I wish to end by exploring aspects of the discourse of food which connects faith, the mouth and letter-writing, bearing in mind that there are modern equivalents.[211]

Fasting was part of the established church's ritual in the eighteenth century. There were national fast days, usually at times of war or mourning, and dietary restrictions during Lent. These could be interpreted creatively, as illustrated by the dissenting minister who wittily justified dining on roast beef during Lent because it put him in mind that all flesh was grass.[212] Strict fasting was one of the early hallmarks of Methodism and John Wesley followed an austere diet, eschewing meat.[213] His mother thought this would keep his passions low, but she remarked in the same letter that to contemplate God made nature faint; we feel swallowed up.[214] Not eating, or not eating meat, redirected belief to God incarnate, that is, Christ. The Wesley brothers became committed vegetarians: when Charles married, his wife had to promise she would never interfere with his diet, nor, later, their son's.[215] One of the attractions of their going as missionaries to Georgia was the simplicity of its food, but this was not just a matter of bodily nourishment: as John Wesley put it, 'an Indian hut affords no food for curiosity'.[216] Curiosity led to enquiry which led to controversy; just as meat fed the sinful body, the mind was corrupted by food for thought. Taking in the milk of the word, and vegetables, the soul was freed from flesh.[217] Though Methodist fasting declined over the years, Wesley went on recommending it[218] and denying accusations of compensatory binge-eating.[219] Often preaching four or five times a day, Wesley practised an oral faith, in which his mouth became an instrument of spreading the word which was God. To put meat into that same mouth was to recorporealise it. An intriguing incident while Wesley was at Oxford sheds light on this. In 1734 he wrote to his old mentor William Law asking for advice on the case of a young man called John Robson who had abandoned religion.[220] Wesley had advised him to give up meat, which he refused since he was an athletic type. Wesley had then advised him to spend less time on the classics, but Robson refused to give them up either. Shortly afterwards he stopped taking communion, saying he was not remotely bothered about the state of his soul. Wesley was mystified. Robson's choice of meat, classics and no communion was the reverse of Wesley's vegetables, divinity and the sacrament as matter fit for a Christian to inwardly digest. Renouncing flesh, reading the word and consuming the word made flesh: each fed his faith.

The mouth is something material and a means of producing the voice. As mouth is to body, text is to writer – something which dematerialises the body yet re-inscribes it. Texts of scripture pierced evangelicals and condensed their bodies to speaking parts and dumb mouths. Christians of both sexes compared themselves to babes and sucklings, suggesting a quest for the good breast that psychoanalysis, following Melanie Klein, proposes as a powerful unconscious drive in adults. Believing, Wesley told a correspondent, involved listening to 'the inward voice which says, "Open thy mouth and I will fill it." '[221] The systematic orality of Wesley's letters is more than an extreme form of the common metaphor of letter-writing as 'talking on paper'. The common description of letters as 'talking on paper' here acquires special significance for correspondents who had already dematerialised their bodies into mouths open for religious texts. Even critics recognised the discursive variety of this single-mindedness: Methodists 'Groan, weep, rave, rant, confess, exhort and sing'.[222] Letters made a special space for mediation between the body and God; they sublimated and rematerialised the word of God. Scriptural utterance and its reception became a cycle of pain and relief through letters especially. 'I fear I shall tire you with my tale of affliction so often repeated. But out of the abundance of the heart the mouth speaks, and the pen writes.'[223] Talking on paper had never been so versatile.

Postscript

Postscripts are the written equivalent of afterthoughts. Or are they? One novelist declared 'ladies, and lovers, generally postpone their most material business, to their postscripts';[1] having got this far, readers will no doubt hope the business is done. Critics like closure; letter-writers resist it. Both know no subject can ever be finished: as Lady Mary Wortley Montagu wrote in 1755, 'where we love we have allways something to say'.[2] Writing this book has made me aware of how important letters were to eighteenth-century literature and culture – indeed, they were a principal medium through which literature and culture interacted. The letters I have discussed are a tiny fraction of what was written, posted and printed in the period, yet they indicate why the eighteenth century has the best claim to be the great age of letter-writing and letter-reading.

It is important to remember we perceive eighteenth-century letters through filters that cut out some kinds of letters and shift others forward. Our readings are mediated by technologies which date: 'Letter-writing, like so many time-honoured institutions, is becoming a lost art: it seems to have fallen into disuse with the quill pen', lamented an early twentieth-century critic.[3] Epistolary form is often seen as being overpowered by new technologies, especially ones that shrink space – the telegram, the telephone, even (as in this quotation) the railways are blamed. Conversely, frames of mediation insert distance between old letters and modern readers. Many nineteenth-century editors of eighteenth-century letters stressed the quaintness of the previous age and pitied its letter-writers for living in a world with fewer commodities and conveniences. Twentieth-century editors of anthologies praised letters for their human interest, their window on interiority. Early twenty-first century scholars incline to seeing letters in a context of performativity, a concept which, following Judith Butler's work, informs all social occasions and exchanges. 'Like personal letters, conversation might on occasion purport to reveal the heart, but – also like letters – it more often constructed a social mask.'[4] Letters become performances; correspondents take up roles. The main attraction of incorporating letters into theories of

332 *Eighteenth-Century Letters and British Culture*

social acting is that theatricality, freed from the confines of a literal stage, becomes a metaphor, even a medium, which acknowledges the agency and artifice present in letter-writing through writerly consideration of content. But then if social acting is performative, what distinguishes the epistolary actor? And epistolary audience? Some letters are improvisational; some follow a script. Performativity in itself does not get us very far.

One version of performativity that seems to be useful is the analogue of masking or masquerading. Historicising and dramatising the self through what was undoubtedly a significant form of cultural expression in the eighteenth century, tropes of masquerading are useful for letters because they allow for changes of costume, so to speak, and because both masks and costume combine expressiveness with concealment.[5] But like the general metaphor of performativity, comparisons to masquerading do not really help illuminate motive. Why are masks necessary? 'I almost think the same skin/For one without, has two or three within': Byron gestures to a multiplicity within subjectivity which ironically gets covered over by metaphors of masking. Metaphors of masquerading also beg questions concerning the meaning of clothes in eighteenth-century society where most people had limited wardrobes. Critics have been interested in politeness partly because it supplies reasons for masking: people are polite and write polite letters because to do so helps secure social position. But plenty else besides politeness was shaping eighteenth-century Britain and even if an ideal of politeness informed social interaction influentially, its practice was often imperfect. Angry letters and letters of argument go against the grain of politeness in explicit and sanctioned ways; aggression has conventions too. Such letters need to be understood not only in terms of a projection of a letter-writer's identity, or even a dynamic written into and through correspondence, but also in terms of how letter-writers challenge each other's identities.

What one critic has described as 'The common critical assumption that the writer's sense of a specific audience shapes epistolary prose' locates letter-writing in the realm of the conscious.[6] It also posits 'sense' as the mechanism by which the genre's properties are chosen and applied. Letters are a genre of second thoughts too: hence leaving a letter unsent or wishing it rewritten or simply disowning it, like Darcy in *Pride and Prejudice*, who says of his letter to Elizabeth that he thought it was written when he was cool and collected, but was later convinced it was written in a dreadful bitterness of spirit. If letters are to be taken as emanations of the self, models of that self need to accommodate self-contradiction, alienation and change. Letters do not reveal an inner man or woman or an inmost self. Letters disclose inner personations, in which history is one variable and temperament another. The process is not artifice but acculturation through form.

One eighteenth-century letter-writer wrote with fascination about his pet chameleon; its ability to change surface colouration stands in as a symbol for a variable self, actively reactive to context.[7] Yet although such a symbol, like masking, suggests the absence of a deep self in the eighteenth century at least in certain communicative contexts, letters depend on 'sense' in intuitive as well as rational ways – specifically, they tap into the unconscious. There is an unconscious present in letters that invites further exploration. Love-letters have unconscious wishes as well as conscious desires; religious letters speak to conscious fears and unconscious terrors; letters of remonstrance, protest and quarrel manifest aggression. Letters of argument that appeal to reason cast the shadow of unreason too. Passions shadow the Enlightenment: the eighteenth century was a period of war as well as reason. Reason in the so-called Age of Reason was tested through letters more than any other genre because they included the structural possibility of an answer: like letter-writing, reason is process as much as product. Epistolary contestation and disagreement foreground conflict and potential irreconcilability which complicate an idea of letters as a genre that 'adumbrates a new kind of community, that of the like-minded'.[8] The unlike-minded were also newly visible, in newspapers and periodicals for instance. Letter-writers may be thought of as testing for like-mindedness; failures to find it showed the limits of politeness. However many eighteenth-century letter-writers aspired to be polite, one should not overlook epistolary situations in which politeness faltered, failed or was never attempted, and the many occasions shaped by ahistorical drives – oedipal dramas, traumas, desires, boundaries, the shadow of death. Psychoanalysis is as useful as history in accounting for epistolary practices. Moreover, psychoanalysis can help explain what goes right in letter-writing as well as what goes wrong. Letters can be read in terms of historically constructed and sanctioned forms of social relations; they can also be interpreted as expressions of emotions produced by a collective unconscious.[9] Gratitude, obedience, conformity and other states of mind create the social practices that also express them. Moulded and remoulded by age, sex, class and the like, they can be tracked through epistolary conventions – and departures from them – as important signs of off-the-page emotions that structured people's social identities. The history of emotions is hard to recover; letters provide access to cultural forces at group and individual levels.

'What is identity? Scholars of eighteenth-century Britain aren't sure, but they think they know it when they see it.'[10] Kathleen Wilson argues that modern psychological notions of identity are useful for understanding the period even if they are a little anachronistic and even though eighteenth-century people 'or at least those to whom we have access, tended to assess themselves less though their internal lives (although their state of virtue, sin and morality was important to many) than through their behavior, social position and reputation'.[11] The interdependence of internal and external identity was in the eighteenth-century often expressed through the idea of approbation. Self-approbation turns on internalisation of views in awareness of others who may or may not hold the same values; approbation by others offers individuals a version of values which they may share or resist. When Johnson wrote that no man sat down to write a letter without considering the figure he would make, he suggested the letter was a genre of self-editing, looking inward; his remark also suggests that letters express identity in relation to social process, looking outward. Scott Paul Gordon has argued that 'eighteenth-century individualism exists alongside a counter-tradition that resists "autonomy" and that defers agency from the individual to external nature'.[12] Letters connect self to other and self to a world that does not necessarily recognise self in the same terms; hence letters show self is fluid.

The I and you singular of personal correspondence is one of several paradigms of epistolary writing in which pronouns assume changeable relations, impersonal as well as personal. Identity, in other words, is manifested in relationships. One way to explore this through letter-writing is to look at subscriptions. A common subscription in the twenty-first century is 'Yours sincerely'. Why do we advance sincerity as our default? Why do we guard against being thought insincere, especially in many letters, like letters of business, where sincerity could be said to be merely a gloss on transactions? If Žižek is right and an ideology is socially effective only if individuals participating in it are not fully aware of its proper logic,[13] 'sincerity' functions as a sign of non-knowledge, a pretence that after all capitalism cares what we think. To some extent it does: capitalism needs emotional investments, as in brand loyalty, in order to distract from its heartlessness. To what equivalent priorities do eighteenth-century subscriptions point? One common subscription was 'Your humble servant'. It lasted long and was widely used – more than one might expect. It turns up in letters of friendship between equals, for instance, and at the end of the century when familiar letter-writers were freer to be less formal. It connected an older discourse of literal service and figurative duty with a newer discourse of politeness; it echoed religious discourses that gave believers an identity as servants of Christ. Like 'Yours sincerely', it was a rhetorical convention, a usefully neutral formula which could be open to light irony. Nonetheless, the choice of humility is significant. 'Your humble servant', like 'Your obedient servant', represents a letter-writer as lowly in relation to the addressee. In many contexts, this lowliness functions as a posture of submission in relation to power. Foucauldian ideas of power have had a deep influence on scholars of the eighteenth century; here, I want to suggest subscriptions of humility should alert us to the importance of authority in eighteenth-century culture. Many letters were sent between people of unequal authority even within the same class. Did people subscribe themselves in submissive terms to compensate for an assertion of self through writing letters? And in a world where class difference was important, what were the relations between an actual class of servants, a cross-class discourse of service and an epistolary preference for representing letter-writers as servants?

If subscriptions of humility and service underline the importance of hier-archy in eighteenth-century culture, letters also testify to a counter-move-ment: anyone can have their say by writing a letter. The eighteenth century can be described as an Age of Opinion, and letters were central to it. 'We live in an Age... where every Man supposes that he has a Right of thinking as he pleases on any Question, and writing and speaking whatever he thinks', one commentator at the mid-century grumbled, adding 'this Spirit of Licentiousness... has of late mixed itself with some graver Characters, and infected... even the *Divine* and the *Antiquarian*'.[14] Like clubs, letters aired opinions and made them proliferate. 'Opinionated' is a seventeenth-century coinage meaning 'obstinate in belief'; in the eighteenth century, stronger investments in reason meant obduracy could be overcome by the persuasive power of reasoning. The liberty of the press was a discursive ideal important to constructions of national identity, however fictitious in practice; letter-writing and reading contributed to the visibility and exchange of opinions, testing the frontiers of free-thinking. Awareness of letters changes an under-standing of what scholars routinely refer to as the expansion of print culture. Print culture expanded in large part because letter-writing expanded. There was an expansion of *writing* culture, part of which ended up in print. There would be no expansion of print culture in the eighteenth century without its reservoir of letter-writing, just as the Internet expanded thanks to its symbiotic relation with email. I do not wish to replace a story of the rise of the novel with the rise of the letter – letters were an important constituent of fiction and literary genres are not soufflés – but to argue that scholars of the eighteenth century should read with a commitment to remembering that where texts are in letter-form, it matters. Letters were more important than the novel to eighteenth-century culture.

The story of an expanded print culture offers another way to see the significance of letters. It has been suggested that the early modern period experienced an information overload. Especially between 1550 and 1750, Daniel Rosenberg suggests, people thought there were more books (whether there were or not) and developed ways of dealing with the phenomenon.[15] Responses included anxiety, delight and what one might call neutral responses, re-organising information so that it could be accessed differently, for instance through indexes and encyclopaedias. Rosenberg suggests 'it may be that the very devices created to "contain" information overload are the devices that "create" it in the first place'.[16] I think letters benefit from being seen in this context. Though obviously letters like pieces of string could be any length, and some kinds were constrained by material consider-ations like the price of postage, nonetheless they were a form that made information relatively manageable. Letters to newspapers inclined to the short; letters to friends could extend to the long. Epistolary genre is stretchy. Rosenberg suggests it is not quantity of information so much as the qualities by which information is presented that create perceptions of load and overload. Epistolary form divided narratives into small stores of knowledge; it made writings less weighty whilst preserving their seriousness. It gave people a reasonable space in which to have their say and it encouraged more people to have a say through its provision of reasonable space.

'Critics have started to reflect on the letter as a cultural institution with multiple histories.'[17] As one of those critics, I am naturally in favour of reflections on multiple histories. I am also in favour of promoting *letters*, rather than *the letter*, as a way of foregrounding diversity within the genre. Methodological closeness between some literary critics and historians means creatively sharing new knowledges about letters; nonetheless, I think letters are best read in ways that add to epistolary histories without making historicity the only goal. Subscriptions express both conventions and the agency: they allow letter-writers to define themselves and relationships through a range of options limited by social conventions. So I end, sincerely, with a wish to have served the subject of eighteenth-century letters: your humble servant.

Notes

A Letter of Introduction

1. The Eighteenth Century Short Title Catalogue. Of course there are many more epistolary texts which do not announce themselves as such in their titles. There were more than a thousand titles using 'A Letter', 1801–15, according to Paul Magnuson, *Reading Public Romanticism*, Princeton, Princeton University Press, 1998, p. 37. Place of publication for all texts cited is London unless stated otherwise.
2. See *Essex Pauper Letters, 1737–1837*, ed. Thomas Sokoll, Oxford, Oxford University Press for the British Academy, 2001.
3. See Mary A. Favret, 'War Correspondence: Reading Romantic War', in *Correspondences: A Special Issue on Letters*, eds Amanda Gilroy and Wil Verhoeven, *Prose Studies*, Vol. 19, No. 2, 1996, pp. 173–85.
4. See Anne Goldgar, *Impolite Learning: Conduct and Community in the Republic of Letters, 1680–1750*, New Haven and London, Yale University Press, 1995.
5. See Kate Teltscher, 'The Sentimental Ambassador: The Letters of George Bogle from Bengal, Bhutan and Tibet, 1770–1781', in *Epistolary Selves: Letters and Letter-Writers, 1600–1945*, ed. Rebecca Earle, Warwick Studies in the Humanities, Aldershot, Hants and Brookfield VT, Ashgate, 1999, pp. 79–84; *William Robertson and the Expansion of Empire*, ed. Stewart J. Brown, Cambridge, Cambridge University Press, 1997; Tim Fulford's work on Joseph Banks.
6. See Donna T. Andrew, ' "To the Charitable and Humane": Appeals for Assistance in the Eighteenth-Century London Press', in *Charity, Philanthropy and Social Reform from the 1690s to 1850*, eds Hugh Cunningham and Joanna Innes, Houndsmill, Macmillan, 1998, pp. 87–107.
7. Frances Brooke in her 1764 periodical *The Old Maid*, p. 39, joked about the academic rejection letter:

    N.B. We are obliged to A.B. for his *Dissertation* (or his *Letter*; or his &c &c.) but as we have *already* spoken to that subject (See Vol. xxxix.) or, as C.D. seems to us more *scientifical*, and not intermixed with *personal reflections*, we hope that A.B. will not take it ill, if we *cannot* insert it.

8. 'If there is a limitation to this method, it arises from the plenitude of possible connections that one could trace, not from an absence of connections...'. Magnuson, *Public Romanticism*, p. 37.
9. Claudia Benthein, *Skin on the cultural border between self and the world*, trans. Thomas Dunlap, New York, Columbia University Press, 2002, p. 13.
10. Nathaniel Wraxall, *Cursory Remarks Made on a Tour Through Some of the Northern Parts of Europe, Particularly Copenhagen, Stockholm, and Petersburgh*, 1775, p. 307; William Hunter, *Travels in the Year 1792 Through France, Turkey, and Hungary, to Vienna: Concluding with an Account of that City*, 2 vols, 2nd edition, 1798, Vol. II, p. 363.
11. Susan E. Whyman, *Sociability and Power in Late-Stuart England: The Cultural Worlds of the Verneys 1660–1720*, Oxford, Oxford University Press, 1999, p. 7. Anna Bryson, *From Courtesy to Civility: Changing Codes of Conduct in Early Modern*

England, Oxford, Clarendon Press, 1998, pp. 155–7, also argues that letters were courtesies in the seventeenth century from the 1630s onwards.

12. For other views, see Lawrence E. Klein, *Shaftesbury and the Culture of Politeness: Moral Discourse and Cultural Politics in Early Eighteenth-Century England*, Cambridge, Cambridge University Press, 1994, passim but especially pp. 3–8; Paul Langford, *A Polite and Commercial People: England 1727–1783*, Oxford and New York, Oxford University Press, 1992, pp. 59–71; Dina Goodman, *The Republic of Letters: A Cultural History of the French Enlightenment*, Ithaca, Cornell University Press, 1994.

13. [Philip] Thicknesse, *Père Pascal, a Monk of Montserrat Vindicated: In a Charge Brought against Him by a Noble Earl of Great Britain*, 1783, p. 33.

14. On letters and duelling, see my article 'Duelling by Sword and Pen: The Vauxhall Affray of 1773', in *Correspondences*, eds Gilroy and Verhoeven, *Prose Studies*, Vol. 19, No. 2, pp. 160–72.

15. 'Introduction', *Epistolary Selves*, ed. Earle, p. 8.

16. Thomas O. Beebee, *Epistolary Fiction in Europe, 1500–1850*, Cambridge, Cambridge University Press, 1999, p. 15.

17. William Merrill Decker, *Epistolary Practices: Letter Writing in America before Telecommunications*, Chapel Hill and London, University of North Carolina Press, 1998.

18. One should also remember that 'friends' in the eighteenth century did not mean quite what it does now. See Naomi Tadmor, *Family and Friends in Eighteenth-Century England: Household, Kinship, Patronage*, Cambridge, Cambridge University Press, 2001, especially ch. 7.

19. Properly, *Letters Written to and for Particular Friends, on the Most Important Occasions*, 1741, but as well known by this, its running title.

20. Harriet Guest, *Small Change: Women, Learning, Patriotism, 1750–1810*, Chicago and London, University of Chicago Press, 2000, pp. 5–26; p. 11.

21. So a correspondent told Hester Lynch Piozzi that Elizabeth Montagu was 'monstrously proud of your letter and shews it every where'. *The Piozzi Letters: Correspondence of Hester Lynch Piozzi (formerly Mrs. Thrale) 1784–1821*, eds Edward A. Bloom and Lillian D. Bloom, London and Toronto, Associated University Presses, 1989, p. 197.

22. Lawrence E. Klein, 'Gender and the Public/Private Distinction in the Eighteenth Century: Some Questions about Evidence and Analytic Procedure', *Eighteenth Century Studies*, Vol. 29, No. 1, 1995, pp. 97–109, p. 99.

23. Brooke, *The Old Maid*, p. 280. This is in essay No. 34 which was not written by Brooke.

24. Earle, *Epistolary Selves*, p. 3, treats the term 'personal' as a substitute for 'private' and, like it, unsatisfactory. I propose it as an alternative, which is not to be divided off from a sense of the public. Conversely, the 'public' is composed of a collection of people who can be individuated and known through print or acquaintance.

25. Cecile M. Jagodzinski, *Privacy and Print: Reading and Writing in Seventeenth-Century England*, Charlottesville and London, University of West Virginia Press, 1999, pp. 75–6, hints at dialectic: 'For seventeenth-century readers (many of them newly literate), the publication of letters became occasions to reflect upon the legitimacy of personal privacy ... publication ... become[s] the means by which the private comes to have value.'

26. Paul Magnuson uses the term 'public letter' for general purposes, though he argues for attention to the particularities of epistolary discourse.

27. Jacques Derrida, *Archive Fever: A Freudian Impression*, trans. Eric Prenowitz, Chicago and London, University of Chicago Press, 1996, p. 90.
28. In conversation, Boston, 1999.
29. Amanda Vickery, *The Gentleman's Daughter: Women's Lives in Georgian England*, New Haven and London, Yale University Press, 1998, pp. 29–30.
30. Whyman, *Sociability and Power*, p. 65.
31. Thus Derrida, *Archive Fever*, p. 90: 'With the irreplaceable singularity of a document to interpret, to repeat, to reproduce, but each time in its original uniqueness, an archive ought to be idiomatic, and thus at once offered and unavailable for translation, open to and shielded from technical iteration and reproduction.'
32. The term limbo comes from the Latin *limbus*, hem: as if on the dress of thought, such letters are at the edge. Electronic cataloguing and digitisation allow us to bring them back.
33. Philip Gaskell, *A New Introduction to Bibliography*, Oxford, Clarendon Press, 1972 repr. 1979, p. 38.
34. George Bickham, *The Universal Penman*, 1733–41. Compare, now, the difference between signing your name and 'printing' it.
35. *The Tatler*, 3 vols, ed. Donald Bond, Oxford, Clarendon Press, 1987, Vol. II, p. 31 (No. 178). John Dyer also used this kind of in-between font. See *Tatler*, Vol. I, p. 150.
36. Stanley Morison, *Ichabod Dawks and his News-Letter with an Account of the Dawks Family of Booksellers and Stationers 1635–1731*, Cambridge, Cambridge University Press, 1931, p. 25 and passim.
37. Thus William Shenstone to Thomas Percy in 1762: 'I am making a sett of *boxes* y^t are to appear on ye outside like books...As these books are *really* boxes to contain ye Letters of some chosen Correspondents, I shall Letter ye Backs wth my Friends' names.' *The Letters of William Shenstone*, ed. Marjorie Williams, Oxford, Blackwell, 1939, pp. 618–19.
38. Shorthand had existed earlier; compare Pepys' *Diaries*. Byrom's system was published posthumously in 1767. See *John Byrom: Selections from his Journals and Papers*, ed. Henri Talon, Rockcliff, 1950, pp. 7–9. Richardson's explanation of shorthand as the means by which lengthy scenes in *Sir Charles Grandison* (1753) are supposedly conveyed verbatim is thus not implausible (as is often assumed) but rather modish.
39. James Raven, *Judging New Wealth: Popular Publishing and Responses to Commerce in England, 1750–1800*, Oxford, Clarendon Press, 1992, p. 64. Does the double column arrangement mimic the turning of a sheet of paper?
40. William Mason, *Gray's Poems and Memoirs of His Life and Writings*, 2nd edition, 1775, p. 5.
41. Merrill Decker, *Epistolary Practices*, p. 5.
42. Roger Chartier, Alain Boureau and Cecile Dauphin, *Correspondence: Models of Letter-Writing from the Middle Ages to the Nineteenth Century*, trans. Christopher Woodall, Cambridge, Polity Press, 1997, p. 14.
43. Methodist societies had regular 'letter-days' in which correspondence from fellow believers was read out. *The Works of John Wesley*, Vol. 25, *Letters*, Vol. I, 1721–39, ed. Frank Baker, Oxford, Clarendon Press, 1980, p. 80. Baker suggests the practice may have come from the Moravians.
44. These routes, like their epistolary traffic, were liable to obstruction. On the awfulness of eighteenth-century roads, see Anne D. Wallace, *Walking, Literature*

and English Culture: The Origins and Uses of Peripatetic in the Nineteenth Century, Oxford, Clarendon Press, 1993, p. 24.

45. Vickery, *Gentleman's Daughter*, pp. 60 and 70. She also notes the role of essays in 'linguistic models'.
46. See Jones DeRitter, *The Embodiment of Characters: The Representation of Physical Experience on Stage and in Print, 1728–1749*, Philadelphia, University of Pennsylvania Press, 1994, and Margaret Anne Doody, *A Natural Passion: A Study of the Novels of Samuel Richardson*, Oxford, Clarendon Press, 1984.
47. *The Genuine History of Mrs Sarah Prydden, usually called Sally Salisbury, and Her Gallants*, 1723, p. 3.
48. Rogier Chartier, '*Secrétaires* for the People? Model Letters of the Ancien Régime: Between Court Literature and Popular Chapbooks' in Chartier, Boureau, Dauphin, *Correspondence*, pp. 59–111; p. 95.
49. Ibid., p. 100.
50. Whyman, *Sociability and Power*, p. 97 stresses female agency in how, for instance, aunts taught forms of duty to the next generation.
51. For further discussion, see Paul Baines, *The House of Forgery in Eighteenth-Century Britain*, Aldershot, Ashgate, 1999, especially ch. 4. By the 1780s there were mechanical means of copying available.
52. Famously, Austen's Marianne thinks Willoughby a good thing because he shares her literary tastes.
53. Marjorie Reeves, *Pursuing the Muses: Female Education and Nonconformist Culture 1700–1900*, Leicester and Herndon VA, Leicester University Press, 1997, p. 19. The young John Wesley and some of his friends also corresponded under romance signatures. Rowe may well have known Katharine Philips's *Letters from Orinda to Poliarchus* (1705). Examples of women poets mid-century who used a persona in poetic epistles include Mary Jones and Mary Leapor.
54. Elizabeth Heckendorn Cook, *Epistolary Bodies: Gender and Genre in the Eighteenth-Century Republic of Letters*, Stanford, Stanford University Press, 1996, p. 16.
55. Beebee, *Epistolary Fiction*, pp. 9–11.
56. Chartier, *Correspondence*, p. 94. See also Toby L. Ditz, 'Formative Ventures: Eighteenth-Century Commercial Letters and the Articulation of Experience', in *Epistolary Selves*, ed. Earle, pp. 59–78.
57. Vickery, *Gentleman's Daughter*, p. 80.
58. Reeves, *Pursuing the Muses*, pp. 34–5, p. 38.
59. The parliamentary privilege of sending letters for free was commonly extended beyond its legitimate remit. Securing this benefit preoccupied many correspondents. Stratagems for evading payment were common.
60. *The Percy Letters*, 8 vols, eds David Nichol Smith and Cleanth Brooks, 1940–85, Louisiana State University Press, Yale University Press, Vol. I, pp. 130–1. Malone claimed he had carefully weighed his letter so it must either have gained by the damp of the mail or been overcharged by the Post Office (a common occurrence). Percy tactfully replied that he hoped his correspondent would not lessen his effusions, but use thinner paper.
61. *Letters of the Late Ignatius Sancho, an African*, 2 vols, 1782, Vol. 1, pp. 28–9.
62. Evidence of the unreliability of the post is plentiful; that it deterred people from writing is doubtful. Some alternative means of conveyance were strange but efficient, like the Quaker messenger who could trot faster than a horse, whom William Dyer paid three guineas to deliver a letter by an agreed deadline. See Carl B. Estabrook, *Urbane and Rustic England: Cultural Ties and Social*

Spheres in the Provinces 1660–1780, Manchester, Manchester University Press, 1998, pp. 233–4.

63. For details of postal arrangements in the eighteenth century, see Sir [George] Evelyn Murray, *The Post Office*, G.P. Putnam's Sons, 1927, pp. 1–22 and Howard Robinson, *Britain's Post Office: A History of Development from the Beginnings to the Present Day*, London, Geoffrey Cumberlege and Oxford University Press, 1953, especially chs iv–xi. Rowland Hill, who introduced the prepaid postage stamp in 1840, remembered his impoverished mother fearing the postman. Nancy Martin, *The Post Office: From Carrier Pigeon to Contravision*, J.M. Dent & Sons, 1969, p. 13.

64. Michel Foucault, 'What is an Author' in *The Foucault Reader*, ed. Paul Rabinow, Harmondsworth, Penguin, 1984, pp. 101–20, pp. 107–8. The disappearance of personal signatures in the early twenty-first century and their replacement by digital signatures means this argument is evolving again.

65. Whyman, *Sociability and Power*, p. 10.

66. The 'Town' in question is not always London; the title features in several texts published in Edinburgh and concerned with Scottish matters.

67. Magnuson, *Public Romanticism*, p. 50: 'Influential works rarely appear without address, precise location, and explicit or implicit signature, even though all may create a disguise'. See also pp. 24–37.

68. See Aileen Douglas, *Uneasy Sensations: Smollett and the Body*, Chicago and London, University of Chicago Press, 1995; *The Gentleman's Magazine*, 16 vols, ed. Thomas Keymer, Pickering and Chatto, 1998, Vol. I, p. xvi: 'its annual prefaces boast about its many correspondents residing in remote counties'; p. xxvii, 'From 1735 onwards the annual title-page advertised "Dissertations and Letters from Correspondents" as a key feature.' Keymer also notes how the magazine connected readers in Britain and the colonies.

69. Thus *The Friendly Couriere: By Way of Letters from Persons in Town to Their Acquaintance in the Country. Containing Whatever is Curious or Remarkable at Home or Abroad*, 1711. The recipients are distinguished by their interests – religious, political, literary, military, social; the subscribers are alphabetical entities, AB, CD, dispensing with proper names.

70. 'Clerical pamphlets and mass mobilization are not the same thing', claims one historian – but they may be closer than he implies. Bruce P. Lenman, 'Political Identities and the Languages of Liberty in the Eighteenth Century', *Journal of British Studies*, July 1996, Vol. 35, No. 3, p. 409.

71. Decker, *Epistolary Practices*, p. 8.

72. When Johnson wrote of letter-writing that no man sat down to depreciate his own character by design, his immediate reference was to Pope; his own lack of ease with letter-writing has a bearing on it too. *The Lives of the English Poets*, 3 vols, ed. George Birkbeck Hill, Oxford, Clarendon Press, 1905, Vol. III, p. 207.

73. Decker, *Epistolary Practices*, p. 8.

74. *Letters Written by Sir William Temple, Bart. And other Ministers of State, Both at Home and Abroad, Containing an Account of the Most Important Transactions that Pass'd in Christendom from 1665–1672*, ed. Jonathan Swift, 1701, 1703, 3 vols, Vol. I, Publisher's Epistle to the Reader.

75. See Patricia Meyer Spacks, *Gossip*, New York, Knopf, 1985 and Cynthia Lowenthal, *Lady Mary Wortley Montagu and the Eighteenth-Century Familiar Letter*, Athens GA and London, University of Georgia Press, 1994, ch. 2.

76. Cited by Mason, *Life of Gray*, p. 4.

77. *The Works of the Late Ingenious Mr. George Farquhar: Containing All His Poems, Letters, Essays and Comedies, Publishe'd in his Lifetime*, 2 vols, 6th edition, 1728, Vol. 1, p. 43; Alvaro Ribeiro S.J., 'The "Chit-Chat way": The Letters of Mrs Thrale and Dr Burney', in *Tradition in Transition: Women Writers, Marginal Texts and the Eighteenth-Century Canon*, eds Alvaro Ribeiro S.J. and James G. Basker, Oxford, Clarendon Press, 1996, p. 31.

78. Reviewing his own letters, Pope describes them as 'thoughts just warm from the brain, without any polishing or dress, the very dishabille of the understanding'. *Letters of Mr Pope & Several Eminent Persons*, 5 vols, 1735, Vol. 1, p. 39. 'Dress' here slides into its more general sense as an all-purpose verb for making or processing (as in hairdressing).

79. John Lettice, *Letters on a Tour Through Various Parts of Scotland, in the Year 1792*, 1794, p. 435: 'concluding his letter with "it is the will of yours". – What dignity!'

80. Participants in this debate include Hester Chapone, *Letters on the Improvement of the Mind*, 1773; Hester Cartwright, *Letters on Female Education*, 1777; Helen Maria Williams, *Letters from France*, 1790; Laetitia Hawkins, *Letters on the Female Mind*, 1793; Maria Edgeworth, *Letters for Literary Ladies*, 1795. See also Kathryn Sutherland, 'Writings on Education and Conduct: Arguments for Female Improvement', *Women and Literature 1700–1800*, ed. Vivien Jones, Cambridge, Cambridge University Press, 2000, pp. 25–45.

81. *The Polite Politician: Or, Entertaining Correspondent*, 2 vols, 1751, Vol. I, pp. 110–11 [mispag for 140–1]; Vol. II, pp. 62–5. The title's word-play shows how people understood politeness to be strategic.

82. Alain Boureau, 'The Letter-Writing Norm, a Medieval Invention', in *Correspondence*, Chartier, Boureau, Dauphin, p. 24.

83. Ribeiro, 'Chit-Chat', p. 30.

84. Catherine Gallagher, *Nobody's Story: The Vanishing Acts of Women Writers in the Marketplace 1670–1820*, Berkeley, Los Angeles, University of California Press, 1994, p. xiii. For further discussion, see my article 'Varieties of Women's Writing', in *Women and Literature 1700–1800*, ed. Jones, pp. 285–302.

85. *Epistolary Histories: Letters, Fiction, Culture*, eds Amanda Gilroy and W.M. Verhoeven, Charlottesville VA and London, University Press of Virginia, 2000, p. 1.

86. Klein, 'Gender and the Public/Private Distinction', p. 101.

87. E.P. Thompson, *The Romantics: England in a Revolutionary Age*, Merlin Press, 1997, p. 101.

88. For instance, on the letter's importance in politics long before the French Revolution. On women and political letter-writing, see my article 'Armchair Politicians: Elections and Representations, 1774', in *Tulsa Studies in Women's Literature*, Vol. 17, No. 2, Fall 1998, Political Discourse/British Women's Writing, 1640–1867, pp. 269–82; Elaine Chalus, 'That Epidemical Madness': Women and Electoral Politics in the Late Eighteenth Century', in *Gender in Eighteenth-Century England: Roles, Representations and Responsibilities*, eds Hannah Barker and Elaine Chalus, London and New York, Longman, 1997, pp. 151–78; Mary A. Favret, *Romantic Correspondence: Women, Politics and the Fiction of Letters*, Cambridge, Cambridge University Press, 1993.

89. E.P. Thompson, *The Romantics*, p. 34.

90. Deidre Shauna Lynch, *The Economy of Character: Novels, Market Culture and the Business of Inner Meaning*, Chicago and London, University of Chicago Press, 1998, p. 11.

91. Klein, 'Gender and the Public/Private Distinction', p. 101.

92. Peter Linebaugh, *The London Hanged: Crime and Civil Society in the Eighteenth Century*, Harmondsworth, Penguin, 1991, pp. xxiv, and xxvi. See also Vic Gattrell, *The Hanging Tree: Execution and the English People 1770–1868*, Oxford, Oxford University Press, 1994, p. ix, on how distress affects scholars. For immense epistolary affect, see Olivier Blanc, *Last Letters: Prisons and Prisoners of the French Revolution 1793–1794*, trans. Alan Sheridan, New York, Noonday Press, 1989. Written by people about to be executed, these letters mix heart-breaking farewells to loved ones with instructions to pay debts owed – often small sums, but the meticulousness with which they are remembered invests them with all the mortal significance of honour.

93. See Norma Clarke, *The Rise and Fall of the Woman of Letters*, Pimlico, 2004, and *Bluestocking Feminism: Writings of the Bluestocking Circle, 1738–1790*, 6 vols, ed. Gary Kelly, Pickering and Chatto, 1999.

94. Carolyn Steedman, 'A Woman Writing a Letter' in *Epistolary Selves*, ed. Earle, pp. 111–33, p. 123, noting that what goes on in painting does not necessarily happen in engravings. Early modern paintings of women with letters have important similarities with nineteenth-century paintings of women reading, for which see Kate Flint, *The Woman Reader 1837–1914*, Oxford, Clarendon Press, 1993, pp. 320–30. Cecile Dauphin, *Correspondence*, p. 121 finds that nineteenth-century manuals show men writing letters; the act of receiving letters has become feminine. The scene of writing is also gendered: men stand at desks to write, women use tables or their knees. For a good example of eighteenth-century conventions, see a small pair of paintings by a Danish artist, Niclas Lafrensen, 'Le Roman' and 'La Lettre', in the Cognacq-Jay collection, Paris.

95. See Ros Ballaster, *Seductive Forms: Women and Amatory Fiction 1684–1740*, Oxford, Clarendon Press, 1992 and Linda Kauffmann, *Discourses of Desire: Gender, Genre, and Epistolary Fictions*, Ithaca, Cornell University Press, 1986.

96. Pamela, Clarissa, Fanny Hill, Julie – all male-authored fictions. See *Writing the Female Voice: Essays on Epistolary Literature*, ed. Elizabeth C. Goldsmith, Pinter, 1989, and my article 'Le Roman par Lettres', in *Lettres Européennes: Histoire de la Littérature Européenne*, eds Annick Benoit et Guy Fontaine, Paris, Hachette, 1992, pp. 533–7.

97. *Love-Letters between a Certain late Nobleman and the Famous Mr. Wilson* (1723) ed. Michael S. Kimmel, New York, Haworth Press, 1990, also as *Journal of Homosexuality*, Vol. 19, No. 2.

98. *The British Spy*, Saturday 8, January 1757.

99. As reported by *The London Chronicle*, reprinted in *Con Men and Cutpurses: Scenes from the Hogarthian Underworld*, ed. Lucy Moore, Harmondsworth, Penguin, 2000, pp. 72–3.

100. John Wesley to Ann Bolton, May 13, 1774: 'Now you write like a woman of business. They commonly leave out the *I*, and say, "Shall come. Shall do so," not *I* shall'. *The Letters of the Revd. John Wesley M.A.*, 8 vols, ed. John Telford, Epworth Press, 1931, Vol. 6, p. 85.

101. Compare Lady Mary Pierrepoint's terse correspondence with Edward Wortley in Wortley Montagu, *Letters*, ed. Halsband, Vol. I, p. 64: 'People in my way are sold like slaves, and I cannot tell what price my Master will put on me'; also p. 55, resisting commodification. See also the discussion of marriage in Whyman, *Sociability and Power*, ch. 5, and courtship in Vickery, *The Gentleman's Daughter*, ch. 2.

102. W.F. Bynum, 'Health, Disease and Medical Care', in *The Ferment of Knowledge: Studies in the Historiography of Eighteenth-Century Science*, eds G.S. Rousseau and

Roy Porter, Cambridge, Cambridge University Press, 1980, pp. 211–44, p. 212. John Wiltshire, *Samuel Johnson in the Medical World: The Doctor and the Patient*, Cambridge, Cambridge University Press, 1991, p. 74, cites Johnson's description of his doctor's letters as cordials.

103. John Wesley was asked so frequently that he published a handbook, *Practical Physick*, 1747, which became a bestseller (cold water or roast apples were his common nostrums).

104. On doctors, see Penny Corfield, *Power and the Professions in Britain 1700–1850*, London and New York, Routledge, 2000, pp. 137–73. Of course correspondence also testifies to patients disputing with doctors – for instance, Hester Thrale in Wiltshire, *Johnson and the Medical World*, p. 90. Bartholomew Ruspini added letters from satisfied users testifying to the efficacy of his styptic solution to the eighth edition of *A Treatise on the Teeth*, 1797.

105. Vickery, *Gentleman's Daughter*, ch. 3 passim. She notes women's letters are rich in references to pregnancy, but laconic about labour, pp. 102, 110.

106. Steedman, 'A Woman Writing a Letter', in *Epistolary Selves*, ed. Earle, p. 120.

107. Heckendorn Cook, *Epistolary Bodies*, p. 12. She sees letters as 'between manuscript and print, private correspondence and published text', circulating in an 'oscillation between private and public, which is also implicitly an oscillation between a corporealized, gendered writing subject and the disembodied voice of the citizen-critic'.

108. Many titles of works using personae made it clear who or what the author was arguing against.

109. George M. Ella, *William Huntington: Pastor of Providence*, Darlington, Evangelical Press, 1994, p. 13 calls him a 'saint of the writing desk'.

110. The prevalence of Anglicanism in polite circles also squeezed out female fervency; Vickery describes her subjects' 'unenthusiastic Anglicanism' and moves swiftly on. *Gentleman's Daughter*, p. 32.

111. See Bruce Redford, *The Converse of the Pen: Acts of Intimacy in the Eighteenth-Century Familiar Letter*, Chicago, University of Chicago Press, 1986, pp. 1–7. He sees allusion as an equivalent to the performance of conversation, although what he describes as the resources of an actor are also all acts of body language, pp. 5–6.

112. Robert Dodsley, *The Preceptor: Containing a General Course of Education*, 2 vols, 1748, Vol. I, p. 208.

113. Robert Bolton, *Letters and Tracts on the Choice of Company and Other Subjects*, 1761, p. 10: 'we may be said, with equal propriety, to converse with books, and to converse with men'.

114. Dissimilarities between writing and impolite talking were discussed, however: compare Addison's story of a man who had an amanuensis take down an evening's conversation at a party of swearers. Cited in *The Correspondent*, 2 vols, 1796, Vol. I, p. 108.

115. John Hawkesworth, 'Essay Toward the Art of Thinking', *The Selector*, No. 1, 1776, n.p., discusses 'free conversation with sensible persons' as a process dependent on thought, a habit assisted by book and pen. Like Cowper, he noted that conversation required effort. Other eighteenth-century conversationalists struggled to write letters: thus Gibbon and Boswell. See Bruce Redford, 'The Converse of the Pen': Letter Writing in the Age of Johnson, Catalogue of an Exhibition at the Beinecke Rare Book and Manuscript Library, Yale University, Sept through Nov 1984, n.p.

116. [George North], *An Answer to a Scandalous Libel, Entitled The Impertinence and Imposture of Modern Antiquaries Display'd*, 1741, p. 2.

117. George Steiner, 'The Distribution of Discourse', *On Difficulty and Other Essays*, Oxford, Oxford University Press, 1978, pp. 61–94, p. 73; *A New Miscellany for the Year 1738*, pp. 1–4 discussed at length registers of formality in conversation and different kinds of letters, comparing writing a public letter to dancing minuets, and writing to a friend to walking in stout shoes.

118. Lennard J. Davis, 'Conversation and Dialogue', in *The Age of Johnson*, ed. Paul Korshin, AMS Press, New York Vol. 1, 1987, pp. 347–74, p. 363 and pp. 357–8 on Boswell's interest in a new musical system, devised by Joshua Steele, to represent a person's conversation through musical denotation – a system tested satisfactorily on Garrick's conversation.

119. Cicero and Seneca made close connections between letter-writing and conversation. In his *Moral Epistles*, Seneca suggests epistolary argument restrains body language: 'Etiam si disputatem, nec supploderem pedem nec manum iactarem nec attolerem vocem, sed ista oratoribus reliquissem...' [Even if I were arguing a point, I should not stamp my foot, or toss my arms about, or raise my voice; but I should leave that sort of thing to the orator...] Abraham J. Malherbe, *Ancient Epistolary Theorists*, Scholars Press, Atlanta GA, 1988, p. 29.

120. So on 15 August 1741, the Duchess of Portland was trying to write to Elizabeth Montagu while two lords read out different newspapers to her. *Conversations, or the Bas Bleu, Addressed to Mrs Vesey: An Exhibition at the Houghton Library, Cambridge, Massachusetts, 1977*, ed. Sidney Ives, The Stinehour Press, n.d., p. 28.

121. C. Aspinall-Oglander, *The Admiral's Wife: Being the Life and Letters of the Hon. Mrs. Boscawen from 1719–1761*, Longmans, Green & Co., 1940, p. 81.

122. Thomas Brown et al, *Letters from the Dead to the Living*, 1702, Elizabeth Singer Rowe, *Friendship in Death*, 1728 – both popular works. They also take up late seventeenth-century dialogues of the dead, especially ones by Fontanelle and Fénelon.

123. As spelled out in the title of John Newton's *Cardiphonia: Or the Utterance of the Heart; in the Course of a Real Correspondence*, (1781), 2 vols, Edinburgh, 1825.

124. Patrick Brydone, *A Tour through Sicily and Malta*, 1773, p. 286. He was addressing William Beckford.

125. *The Letters and Prose Writings of William Cowper*, 5 vols, eds James King and Charles Ryskamp, Oxford, Oxford University Press, 1979–86, Vol. I, pp. 369–70.

126. See Betty A. Schellenberg, *The Conversational Circle: Rereading the English Novel, 1740–1775*, Lexington, University of Kentucky Press, 1996; Sylvia Harcstark Myers, *The Bluestocking Circle: Women, Friendship, and the Life of the Mind in Eighteenth-Century England*, Oxford, Clarendon Press, 1990; Elizabeth Eger, ' "The noblest commerce of mankind": Conversation and Community in the Bluestocking Circle' in *Feminism and Enlightenment*, eds Barbara Taylor and Sarah Knott, Palgrave, 2004, pp. 288–305. J.H. Plumb saw eighteenth-century social life as a matter of circles, remarking 'Wherever there are highly fashionable circles, men and women will want to break into them.' *Georgian Delights*, Weidenfeld and Nicholson, 1980, p. 147.

127. Greg Laugero, 'Infrastructures of Enlightenment: Road-making, the Public Sphere, and the Emergence of Literature', *Eighteenth-Century Studies*, Vol. 29, No. 1, 1995, pp. 45–67; p. 58. When Ralph Allen reformed cross-post and bye-post (i.e. those letters which, unlike 'London letters' and 'country letters', did not pass through London) he fixed barriers across roads used by people who were bypassing official routes. *Ralph Allen's Own Narrative 1720–1761*, ed. Adrian E. Hopkins, intro. Foster E. Bond, *The Postal History Society*, special series No. 8, n.p. 1960, p. 25.

128. Diane Cousineau, *Letters and Labyrinths: Women Writing/Cultural Codes*, Newark, University of Delaware Press and London, Associated University Presses, 1997, p. 30.

129. See Terry Castle, *Masquerade and Civilisation*, Methuen, 1986. Bruce Redford discusses Gray and Walpole in a section entitled 'Love in Several Masques', in *Converse of the Pen*. On the performativity of conversation, see Erving Goffman, *Forms of Talk*, Blackwell, 1981.

130. For example, on the fashion for all things Hanoverian, as HORATIUS VALPOL-HAUSEN; on vacant bishoprics, as THE ABBOT OF STRAWBERRY. *Horace Walpole's Correspondence*, 48 vols, ed. W.S. Lewis, Yale University Press, 1937–83, 9.222; 40:125.

131. On costume, see Aileen Ribiero and Celina Fox, *Masquerade*, exhibition catalogue, Museum of London, 1983, and Castle, *Masquerade and Civilisation*, pp. 58–78.

132. David Nokes, *John Gay: A Profession of Friendship*, Oxford, Oxford University Press, 1995, pp. 545–6; Julius Bryant, *Mrs Howard: A Woman of Reason 1688–1767*, exhibition catalogue, English Heritage, 1988, pp. 14–15.

133. *The Letters and Diplomatic Instructions of Queen Anne*, ed. Beatrice Curtis Brown, Cassell & Co., 1935. Queen Anne's letters show a spectrum of naming, from personae from Lee's play *Mithridates* (p. 4) to 'Mansell' for James II (a phrenonym?), to 'the spider' and 'the monster' for various enemies (pp. 34, 60).

134. Because editors add lists of 'characters' or dramatis personae to Shakespeare's plays; compare Richardson's 'Men, Women and Italians' at the beginning of *Sir Charles Grandison*. Lynch, *Economy of Character*, p. 14.

135. *The Works of the late Reverend James Hervey*, 1789, Newcastle upon Tyne, p. 547. Shaftesbury's *Characteristics of Men, Manners, Opinions, Times*, 1711, assumed and explored the idea of character in diverse ways.

136. Lynch, *Economy of Character*, pp. 45, 57, 75 and passim.

137. Paul Langford, *Englishness Identified: Manners and Character 1650–1850*, Oxford, Oxford University Press, 2000, p. 318.

138. *The Spectator*, 5 vols, ed. Donald Bond, Oxford, Clarendon Press, 1965, Vol. IV, p. 491 [No. 555].

139. On different kinds of probability in relation to character, see Paul J. Korshin, 'Probability and Character in the Eighteenth Century', in *Probability, Time, and Space in Eighteenth Century Literature*, ed. Paula R. Backscheider, New York, AMS Press, 1979, pp. 63–77.

140. Redford, *Converse of the Pen*, pp. 49–92.

141. *The Journals and Letters of Fanny Burney (Madame D'Arblay)*, 12 vols, eds Joyce Hemlow et al, Oxford, Clarendon Press, 1972–84, Vol. 1, p. 11.

142. For instance, Jane Brereton, *Poems on Several Occasions*, 1744 and Mary Masters, *Familiar Letters and Poems on Several Occasions*, 1755; David Bellamy, *The Young Lady's Miscellany*, 1723; Sylviana Sola, *Various Essays*, 1752; *Matrimony, or the Road to Hymen made Plain, Easy and Delightful*, 1791 and Charles Dibdin, *The Musical Tour of Charles Dibdin*, 1788.

143. On origins, see Beebee, *Epistolary Fiction*; John J. Richetti, *Popular Fiction before Richardson: Narrative Patterns 1700–1739*, Oxford, Clarendon Press, 1969; on endings, see Favret, *Romantic Correspondence*; Nicola J. Watson, *Revolution and the Form of the British Novel 1790–1825*, Oxford, Clarendon Press, 1994; Leah Price, *The Anthology and the Rise of the Novel: From Richardson to George Eliot*, Cambridge, Cambridge University Press, 2000.

144. Susan Gubar, *Critical Condition: Feminism at the Turn of the Century*, New York, Columbia University Press, 2000, p. 23, quoting Miller, *Getting Personal*, 1991, p. 20.

145. Janet G. Altman, *Epistolarity: Approaches to a Form*, Columbus, Ohio State University Press, 1982, p. 194, on the novel: 'In general, the German letter writer is a diarist, the English correspondent a witness, and the French *épistolier* a verbal duelist.' Quoted by Beebee, *Epistolary Fiction*, p. 16, who notes, p. 15, 'the letter not only records social reality but also helps constitute it'.
146. See Barbara J. Shapiro, *A Culture of Fact, England, 1550–1720*, Ithaca, Cornell University Press, 2000, especially ch. 4, ' "News," "Marvels," "Wonders," and the Periodical Press', pp. 86–104; Fritz Levy, 'The Decorum of News', in *News, Newspapers, and Society in Early Modern Britain*, ed. Joad Raymond, Portland, Oregon and London, Frank Cass, 1999; Lennard Davis, *Factual Fictions: The Origins of the English Novel*, New York, Columbia University Press, 1983.
147. F. Gordon Roe, *Women in Profile: A Study in Silhouette*, John Baker, 1970, p. 54: by Mrs Elizabeth Pyburg, of William III and Queen Mary.
148. Compare Lady Mary Wortley Montagu comparing a dull letter to tent-stitch. Richardson's comment that a pen was as pretty an instrument in the hands of a lady as a needle can thus be read as a story about technologies of the self rather than simple femininities. Needles were also the prime tools of etchers.
149. Richard C. Sha, 'Expanding the Limits of Feminine Writing: The Prose Sketches of Sydney Owenson (Lady Morgan) and Helen Maria Williams' in *Romantic Women Writers: Voices and Countervoices*, eds Paula R. Feldman and Teresa M. Kelley, Hanover and London, University Press of New England, 1995, pp. 194–206.
150. See James Vernon, 'Who's afraid of "the Linguistic Turn"?' 'Social History and its Discontents', *Social History* 19, 1994, pp. 81–97; also John Brewer, *Sentimental Murder: Love and Madness in the Eighteenth Century*, HarperPerennial, 2005, pp. 280–93.

1 Learning to Write

1. *The New Art of Letter-Writing*, 2nd edition, 1762, p. 1.
2. Ibid., p. 9.
3. Ibid., pp. 2–3.
4. Daniel Defoe, *The Compleat English Gentleman*, ed. Karl D. Bülbring, London, David Nutt, 1890, pp. 127–32.
5. Daniel Defoe, *The Complete English Tradesman, in Familiar Letters, Directing him in all the Several Parts and Progressions of Trade*, 1726, p. 22.
6. *The Complete Letter-Writer, or Polite English Secretary*, 11th edition, 1767, preface.
7. *The Complete Letter-Writer*, Edinburgh, 1768, p. 36.
8. Dorothy Kilner, *Dialogues and Letters on Morality, Oeconomy, and Politeness, for the Improvement of Young Female Minds*, 1780, pp. 38–40.
9. *Letters from Bath 1766–1767 by the Rev. John Penrose*, eds Brigitte Mitchell and Hubert Penrose, Gloucester, Alan Sutton Publishing Ltd, 1983, p. 135. On Penrose and other aspects of politeness in Bath, see Philip Carter, *Men and the Emergence of Polite Society, Britain 1660–1800*, Harlow, Longman, 2001, pp. 175–83.
10. Ibid., pp. 143–4; 157.
11. *The New Art of Letter-Writing*, p. 4.
12. Richard Hooker, *The Weekly Miscellany*, 21 April 1738, n.p.
13. Cowper, *Letters*, eds King and Ryskamp, Vol. II, p. 35.
14. Ibid., Vol. I, pp. 367–8.
15. Michèle Cohen, *Fashioning Masculinity: National Identity and Language in the Eighteenth Century*, Routledge, 1996, p. 50.

16. Anne Goldgar, *Impolite Learning*, p. 6:

> Although we can identify the general social origins and milieu of most scholars as bourgeois, that does not mean they were self-consciously members of a bourgeoisie, and indeed their whole ethos entailed a redefinition of status according to the norms of their own community...the only 'public' my scholar cared about was each other.

17. Rev. George Brown, *The English Letter-Writer; or the Whole Art of Correspondence*, c.1775.
18. *The Ladies Complete Letter-Writer; Teaching the Art of Inditing Letters on every Subject that can call for their Attention, as Daughters, Wives, Mothers, Relations, Friends, or Acquaintance*, Dublin, 1763.
19. Ibid., p. 2.
20. *The Correspondent, A Selection of Letters from the Best Authors*, 2 vols, 1796, Vol. I, p. 53.
21. Thomas Goodman, *The Experienc'd Secretary: Or: Citizen and Countryman's Companion*, 4th edition, 1707, p. 42.
22. *New Art of Letter-Writing*, p. 3.
23. Ibid., p. 11: 'Epistolas debere interdum hallucinari'.
24. *Rambler*, 152, cited in *Correspondent*, Vol. I, p. 5.
25. *Complete Letter-Writer*, p. 2.
26. Samuel Johnson [no relation] *A Compleat Introduction to the Art of Writing Letters*, 1758, p. 148.
27. For example, *Epistles Elegant, Familiar and Instructive* (1791) was composed of four books. The first sampled Cicero and Pliny, the second, historical English letters, the third, late seventeenth-century wits and Pope and the fourth, other eighteenth-century writers. It included no examples from French letter-writers.
28. See Isobel Grundy, *Samuel Johnson and the Scale of Greatness*, Athens, Georgia, Georgia University Press, 1986, links Johnson's appreciation of minuteness and detail to letter-writing: p. 70, on his 'delight in trivia for their own sake', for instance, in a letter to Hester Thrale: 'My love to all / Both great and small.'
29. *Rambler*, 152, in *Correspondent*, p. 5.
30. This is discussed further below.
31. Painful subjects like illness, death or disgrace were certainly present in printed letters other than manuals.
32. *Ladies Complete Letter-Writer*, p. 2.
33. *The Correspondent*, Vol. I, p. ix.
34. Ibid., p. 14.
35. Ibid., p. 282; in 'To a Young Lady on her Marriage'. The association between women's letters, amorous discourse and uncultured orthography turns up as late as 1897 in Bram Stoker's *Dracula*, where Jonathan Harker records in his journal 'Here I am, sitting at a little oak table where in old times possibly some fair lady sat to pen, with much thought and many blushes, her ill-spelt love-letter.' Ed. A.N. Wilson, World's Classics, Oxford and New York, Oxford University Press, 1983, p. 36.
36. *The Cumberland Letters 1771–1784*, ed. Clementina Black, Martin Secker, 1912, p. 160.
37. [Richard and Elizabeth Griffith], *A Series of Genuine Letters between Henry and Frances*, 2 vols, 2nd edition, 1761, Vol. I, p. xviii.
38. *Verney Letters of the Eighteenth Century from the MSS. at Claydon House*, 2 vols, ed. Margaret Maria Lady Verney, LL.D., Ernest Benn Ltd, 1930, Vol. I, p. 42.

39. Diary entry, quoted by M. Phillips and W.S. Tomkinson, *English Women in Life & Letters*, Oxford, Oxford University Press, 1926, p. 72.
40. Samuel Richardson, *Clarissa, or the History of a Young Lady*, ed. Angus Ross, Harmondsworth, Penguin, 1985, p. 1468.
41. Printed variously in several manuals; also in Howard Erskine-Hill, *Alexander Pope: Selected Letters*, Oxford, Oxford University Press, 2000, p. 110.
42. Tobias Smollett, *The Expedition of Humphry Clinker*, ed. Angus Ross, Harmondsworth, Penguin, 1967 repr. 1980, for instance Win Jenkins, 'We were yesterday three kiple chined, by the grease of God, in the holy bands of mattermoney' (pp. 394–5); in a letter from Bristol, Lydia uses the word 'agreeable' four times in one paragraph (p. 55).
43. Elizabeth Steele, *Memoirs of Mrs. Sophia Baddeley, late of Drury Lane Theatre*, 6 vols, 1787, Vol. I, pp. 120–1.
44. Cohen, *Fashioning Masculinity*, pp. 30–1, with particular reference to the 1720s.
45. Ibid., p. 14.
46. Ibid., p. 33.
47. Edmund Sexton, *Letters from an Arminian in Ireland*, 1757, p. 55.
48. Richardson, *Clarissa*, pp. 1467–8.
49. John Gilbert Cooper, *Letters Concerning Taste*, 1755, pp. 116–18. Ease in Voiture's letters comes from their author having been 'polish'd by that advantageous Collision with the brightest Part of our Species'.
50. Despite the common formula of 'A Letter from a Gentleman in the Town to a Friend in the Country', urbanity in English letters was a state of mind rather than a geographical fact.
51. *Ladies Complete Letter-Writer*, p. 154. Also, as a version of Voiture, in *Familiar and Courtly Letters to Persons of Honour and Quality*, 2 vols, 3rd edition, 1701, Vol. I, p. 167.
52. In Wettenhall Wilkes, *A Letter of Genteel and Moral Advice to a Young Lady* . . . , 4th edition, 1746, pp. 186–90, advice about handwriting is shortly followed by an injunction never to appear in company without stays.
53. *Correspondent*, Vol. I, p. 33.
54. Catherine Ingrassia, *Authorship, Commerce and Gender in Early Eighteenth-Century England*, Cambridge, Cambridge University Press, 1998, p. 41.
55. Ibid., p. 42; pp. 64–5.
56. Ingrassia's reading, like mine, stresses the importance of homosociality: ibid., ch. 2 passim. We differ in that I want to emphasise its epistolary workings. See also Carolyn D. Williams, *Pope, Homer and Manliness: Some Aspects of Eighteenth-Century Classical Learning*, Routledge, 1993, ch. 2.
57. Charles Gildon, *The Post-Boy Robb'd of his Mail: Or, the Pacquet Broke Open*, 2 vols, 2nd edition, 1706, Vol. 1, p. 349.
58. Ibid.
59. *Some Letters between Mr. Locke, and Several of his Friends*, 1708, n.p.
60. Maynard Mack, *Alexander Pope: A Life*, New Haven and London, Yale University Press, 1985, p. 657. Howard Erskine-Hill cites as precedents Cicero, Pliny the Younger, Erasmus, Spenser and Milton, thus studiously avoiding eighteenth-century examples. *Pope: Selected Letters*, p. xiv.
61. See Kathleen M. Swaim, 'Matching the "Matchless Orinda" to Her Times' in *1650–1850: Ideas, Aesthetics, and Inquiries in the Early Modern Era*, III, eds Kevin L. Cope and Laura Morrow, New York, AMS Press, 1997. Swaim argues that Katherine Philips secured publication of her letters by stratagems as devious as any attributed to Pope; no wonder, since the market was so hard for women to break into.

62. Cited by Mack, *Life of Pope*, p. 654. Pope's fears were increased by a bill for renewing copyright, put to the House of Lords in the spring of 1735, which Pope called 'a Booksellers Bill' because he thought it gave too much power to booksellers at the expense of authors and the public. Pope claimed the unauthorised publication of his letters by Curll helped turn opinion against the Bill. See Mack, ibid.

63. For instance, Voiture, *Familiar and Courtly Letters*, 1701; translations by Dryden, Cheek, Dennis, Cromwell and others were followed by original letters from Dryden, Congreve, Wycherley, Dennis and others.

64. Ibid., n.p.

65. *The Works of the Celebrated Monsieur Voiture*, 2 vols, 1715, Vol. I, p. x.

66. Exceptions were men like Lord Chesterfield and Horace Walpole whose correspondence with French women was gallant in a continental way and Pope, who for all his adoption of the persona of a rake as a young man was not physically cut out for it. Mack notes, *Life of Pope*, p. 150, that, like Pope, Voiture was small. See also James Anderson Winn, *A Window in the Bosom: The Letters of Alexander Pope*, Hampden, Connecticut, Archon, 1977, p. 136, and Valerie Rumbold, *Women's Place in Pope's World*, Cambridge, Cambridge University Press, 1989, pp. 2–6.

67. *Letters of Mr Pope and Several Eminent Persons, from the Year 1705, to 1711*, 5 vols, 1735, Vol. III, p. xv. For instance, Pope's to a lady with a book of drawings drew heavily on Voiture's to Mme. Rambouillet with a book of prints.

68. Dennis left out or altered those of his *Original Letters* written when in a state of war with Pope: Winn, *A Window in the Bosom*, p. 131.

69. 'Letters of Friendship' in Voiture, *Familiar and Courtly Letters*, Vol. I, p. 43; p. 41; p. 19.

70. Ibid., Vol. I, p. 43. Compare James Thomson to Aaron Hill: 'I will not affect a moderate Joy at your Approbation, your praise: It pleases, it delights, it ravishes me!' *A Collection of Letters Never Before Printed: Written by Alexander Pope, Esq; and other Ingenious Gentlemen, to the late Aaron Hill, Esq.*, 1751, p. 55.

71. 'Letters from 1711–15', *Letters of Mr. Pope*, Vol. I, p. 74 (different sections have separate pagination).

72. Ibid., p. 43.

73. Kaja Silverman, *Male Subjectivity at the Margins*, Routledge, 1992, p. 360. My discussion owes much to ch. 8, 'A Woman's Soul in a Man's Body: Femininity in Male Homosexuality', especially pp. 360–4.

74. Ibid., p. 363.

75. *Letters of Mr. Pope*, Vol. II, p. 74.

76. On how gender is worked into allegorical figures, compare the debate about the French Revolution's Marianne: was she an overdetermined female figure, a phallic figure, or a bisexual androgynous figure in feminine form? Discussed in *Language and Rhetoric of the Revolution*, ed. John Renwick, Edinburgh, Edinburgh University Press, 1990, p. 42.

77. Silverman, *Male Subjectivity*, p. 362.

78. See Philip Carter, 'Mollies, Fops and Men of Feeling: Aspects of Male Effeminacy and Masculinity in Britain, c.1700–1780', D.Phil. thesis, University of Oxford, 1995, p. 328: 'Historians who identify effeminacy as synonymous with a particular aspect of male sexual activity are in danger not only of writing an overly teleological history of male sexuality but also of reducing the history of eighteenth-century masculinity to a parade of sexual practices.'

79. Mark Breitenberg, *Anxious Masculinities in Early Modern England*, Cambridge, Cambridge University Press, 1996, p. 8.
80. Pope, 'Letters from 1711–15', p. 109.
81. James Heywood, *Poems and Letters on Several Occasions*, 1722, pp. 77–8.
82. Winn, *A Window in the Bosom*, p. 60. Swift told Laetitia Pilkington that he thought Pope was not as candid to the merits of other writers as he should have been. See Claudia N. Thomas, *Alexander Pope and His Eighteenth-Century Women Readers*, Carbondale and Edwardsville, Southern Illinois University Press, 1994, p. 107.
83. Wycherley to Pope, *Letters of Mr. Pope*, Vol. I, p. 38.
84. *A Pacquet from Will's*, 1701, pp. 49–50.
85. *Letters of Pope*, Vol. I, p. 53. Women poets asked for criticism tentatively. Compare Katherine Philips, *Letters from Orinda to Poliarchus*, 1705, pp. 93, 118: 'lay aside the Courtier, and tell me frankly your real Thoughts of my weak Performances.'
86. Ibid., p. 42.
87. Walsh, *Works*, p. 16.
88. Lady Mary Wortley Montagu's letters were not printed until after her death in 1763. Some were in circulation earlier but my argument about the intersection of class, gender and commodification concerns constructs in print.
89. Voiture, *Works*, p. 219.
90. *Letters of Mr. Pope*, Vol. V, p. 172.
91. Ibid., pp. 245–6.
92. Ibid., Vol. III, p. vii. 'Simplex munditiis', unaffected by manners: Horace, Ode I, 1.5. Curll is playing Pope at his own game of Horace. The murky story of the letters' publication is covered by Winn, *A Window in the Bosom* and by Ingrassia, *Authorship, Commerce and Gender*.
93. Ibid. Granville and Manley may have had political connections.
94. Jonathan Richardson's portrait of Pope c.1718, reproduced in Mack, *Life of Pope*, p. 675, shows Pope in a fully unbuttoned coat; the Hoare portrait (Mack's cover illustration) shows the top two buttons done up. Compare also Kneller's portrait of Arbuthnot, writing in informal dress, ibid., p. 194.
95. [Charles Gildon], *Memoirs of the Life of William Wycherley, Esq., With a Character of His Writings*, 1718, p. 19.
96. Wendy L. Jones, *Talking on Paper: Alexander Pope's Letters*, English Literary Studies Monograph No. 50, University of Victoria, British Columbia, Canada, 1990, p. 49.
97. Pope, *Selected Letters*, ed. Erskine-Hill, p. xxii.
98. *Letters by Several Eminent Persons Deceased*, 3 vols, 1772, Vol. I, preface.
99. *The Letters of Samuel Johnson*, 5 vols, ed. Bruce Redford, Princeton, New Jersey, Princeton University Press, 1992–94, Vol. I, p. 197.
100. Hester Lynch Piozzi, *Letters to and from the late Samuel Johnson, LL.D.*, 2 vols, 1788, Vol. I, p. 62.
101. Johnson, *Letters*, ed. Redford, Vol. I, p. 197.
102. Johnson, *Letters*, ed. Piozzi, Vol. II, p. 410.
103. Dustin Griffin, *Literary Patronage in England 1650–1800*, Cambridge, Cambridge University Press, 1996, p. 244.
104. Compare Samuel Richardson as a 'man of letters' enabled by female correspondents.
105. Johnson, *Letters*, ed. Redford, Vol. I, p. 96.
106. James Boswell, *The Life of Samuel Johnson, LL.D.*, 2 vols, 1791, Vol. I, p. 142.

107. Ibid., p. 143.
108. Johnson, *Letters*, ed. Redford, Vol. I, pp. 260–1.
109. Walter Jackson Bate, *Samuel Johnson*, Chatto & Windus, 1978, p. 257.
110. Sir Andrew Anecdote, *A Collection of Interesting Biography*, Dublin, 1792, pp. 133–4. This text is an abridgment of Boswell's *Life*. In 1760, Burney generously sent a further relic – some bristles from Johnson's hearth broom. On hearing this, Johnson took pity on him, sent him a set of the *Lives of the Poets* and later met him. Shortly afterwards the admirer died (perhaps affected by excitement).
111. *Letters, Written by the late Jonathan Swift, D.D.*, ed. Sir John Hawkesworth, 3 vols, 1766, Vol. I, p. ix.
112. Ibid., p. x.
113. Esther Schor, *Bearing the Dead: The British Culture of Mourning from the Enlightenment to Victoria*, Princeton, New Jersey, Princeton University Press, 1994, pp. 48–72; p. 48.
114. No. 60; Johnson, *Letters*, ed. Redford, Vol. I, p. 266, n. 4.
115. Peter Pindar [John Wolcot], *Bozzy and Piozzi, A Pair of Town Eclogues*, 1786, p. 17.
116. Some collections of anecdotes were epistolary: thus Burney's 'Windsoriana'.
117. William Mason, *Gray's Poems and Memoirs of His Life and Writings*, 2nd edition, 1775, p. 5.
118. Johnson, *Letters*, ed. Piozzi, Vol. I, pp. v–vi.

2   Writing as a Parent

1. Thus Toni Bowers, *The Politics of Motherhood: British Writing and Culture, 1680–1760*, Cambridge, Cambridge University Press, 1996, sees Augustan ideals of virtuous motherhood 'universally imposed on women' and demanding mothers be 'invisible, inaudible' (pp. 28–30). She does see maternal agency in Pennington's letter of advice to her daughter – although she relates its publication to 'the transgressions of the epistolary novelist', p. 225.
2. See Naomi Tadmor, *Family and Friends in Eighteenth-Century England: Household, Kinship, and Patronage*, Cambridge, Cambridge University Press, 2001, especially chs 5 and 7.
3. *The Young Lady's Pocket Library, or Parental Monitor* (hereafter *YLPL*), introduction by Vivien Jones, *For Her Own Good: A Series of Conduct Books*, Bristol, Thoemmes Press, 1790 repr. 1995, p. vi.
4. See *The Ideology of Conduct: Essays in Literature and the History of Sexuality*, eds Nancy Armstrong and Leonard Tennenhouse, New York and London, Methuen, 1987.
5. *The Young Gentleman and Lady Instructed in such Principles of Politeness, Prudence, and Virtue, As will Lay a Sure Foundation in This Life, and Eternal Happiness in a Future State; Interspersed with such Observations and Maxims, As Demonstrate the Danger and Folly of Vice, and, the Advantage and Wisdom of Virtue*, 2 vols, 1747.
6. Robert Dodsley, *The Preceptor: Containing a General Course of Education*, 1748. It was licensed under Chesterfield's hand.
7. *The Crisis of Courtesy: Studies in the Conduct-Book in Britain, 1600–1900*, ed. Jacques Carré, Brill's Studies in Intellectual History, Vol. 51, Leiden, E.J. Brill, 1994, p. 5.
8. Ibid.

9. For instance, *Spectator* No. 263. A supposed correspondent sends thoughts on the mutual consideration that should subsist between fathers and sons, and encloses a rebuke from a widowed mother to her son for begrudging her jointure. The son's short reply is a model of penitence, illustrating the ideal power of letters to regulate family relationships.

10. Carré, *Crisis of Courtesy*, p. 3.

11. Wettenhall Wilkes, *A Letter of Genteel and Moral Advice to a Young Lady: Being a System of Rules and Informations; Digested into a New and Familiar Method, to Qualify the Fair Sex to be Useful and Happy in Every Scene of Life*, 4th edition, 1746; Preface, n.p. He argued fictionality made no difference to moral truth, but said he did have a niece.

12. See Robin Kent, *Aunt Agony Advises: Problem Pages through the Ages*, W.H. Allen, 1979.

13. In 1791 when Elizabeth Smith, aged 12, was confirmed, a friend of her mother's wrote earnestly to her about principles of faith. After confirmation, she wrote, 'we must be considered as thinking and acting for ourselves; though still subject to the commands, and happy in the advice, of our parents'. *Fragments in Prose and Verse: By a Young Lady, Lately Deceased*, 7th edition, 1809, p. 168.

14. Vivien Jones, 'The Seductions of Conduct: Pleasure and Conduct Literature', in *Pleasure in the Eighteenth Century*, eds Roy Porter and Marie Mulvey Roberts, Basingstoke and London, Macmillan, 1996, especially p. 115 and pp. 123–4.

15. Courtney Melmoth [Samuel Jackson Pratt], *The Pupil of Pleasure*, 2 vols, 1777; Vol. 1, pp. 28–32.

16. T.G.A. Nelson, *Children, Parents, and the Rise of the Novel*, Newark and London, Associated University Presses, 1995, p. 27.

17. Linda Pollock, *A Lasting Relationship: Parents and Children over Three Centuries*, Hanover and London, University Press of New England, 1987, p. 11. On the historiography of childhood, see pp. 11–13. Nelson, *Children, Parents*, pp. 15–17 and Introduction discusses the problems of using fiction and first-person writings as evidence for *practices*.

18. Mr Rowell (trans.), *The Marchioness De Lambert's Letters to her Son and Daughter, on True Education, &c. &c. &c.* [sic], 1749. Subscribers included Edward Wortley Montagu, a famously disappointing son.

19. Arabella Davies, *Letters from a Parent to Her Children: Written to Them while under Tuition at School*, 1788, epigraph (Proverbs xxii 6).

20. Robert Dodsley, *The Oeconomy of Human Life*, 9th edition, 1758. First published in 1750, it had gone through 200 editions by 1800; in America there were 48 editions by 1800. See Harry M. Solomon, *The Rise of Robert Dodsley: Creating the New Age of Print*, Carbondale and Edwardsville, Southern Illinois University Press, 1996, p. 139.

21. Sarah Pennington, *An Unfortunate Mother's Advice to her Absent Daughters, in a Letter to Miss Pennington*, Dublin, 1790; YLPL, p. 55.

22. *The Letters of Eliza Pierce 1751–1775*, ed. Violet M. Macdonald, The Haslewood Books, 1927, pp. 92–3.

23. Rosamond Bayne-Powell, *The English Child in the Eighteenth Century*, John Murray, 1939, pp. 304–5.

24. Jonathan Curling, *Edward Wortley Montagu 1713–1776: The Man in the Iron Wig*, The Rogues Gallery, Andrew Melrose, 1954, p. 84.

25. *Pierce*, p. 112.

26. John Martin, *Some Account of the Life and Writings of the Rev. John Martin, Pastor of the Church Meeting in Store Street, Bedford Square,* 1797, p. 18.
27. Davies, *Letters,* p. v.
28. [John Sherbrooke], A Tradesman, *Serious Advice of a Parent to His Children, Concerning the Errors of the Day,* Nottingham, 1734, p. 4.
29. *Susanna Wesley: The Complete Writings* ed. Charles Wallace Jr, Oxford, Oxford University Press, 1997, pp. 40, 53, 57, 71.
30. Raymond Lister, *Samuel Palmer: A Biography,* Faber and Faber, 1974, p. 172.
31. *Excellencies United,* 1787; *Encyclopaedia of Manners and Etiquette, comprising Chesterfield's Advice to His Son,* 1850.
32. For instance, Sarah Cowper copied Lord Burghley's ten precepts to his son, widely available in print. Pollock, *A Lasting Relationship,* p. 247.
33. Arabella Davies, *Letters,* p. 117.
34. J. Taylor, *A Summary of Parental and Filial Duties, or an Interesting Description of what Parents and Children Owe to Each Other: Inculcating, also, the most Valuable Requisites for a Liberal Education,* Sheffield, 1805, p. 25.
35. *The Polite Philosopher; or An Essay on the Art which Makes a Man Happy in Himself and Agreeable to Others,* 2nd edition, 1787, p. 2.
36. George Savile, Lord Marquess of Halifax, *The Lady's New-Year's-Gift or: Advice to a Daughter,* 1700, repr. Stamford, Connecticut, Overbrook Press, 1934, p. 2.
37. Ibid., p. 3.
38. Cited by Vivien Jones (from *The Vindication of the Rights of Woman*), YLPL, p. xxiv.
39. Davies, *Letters,* p. 47.
40. George Bickham, *Selected Plates from The Universal Penman,* Cambridge, W. Heffer & Sons Ltd, [1943] n.p.
41. Davies, *Letters,* pp. 23–4.
42. *A Father's Advice to his Son, Laying Down Many Things which have a Tendency to Direct and Fix the Mind in Matters of the Greatest Importance,* 1736, p. vi.
43. John Tavernier, *The Newest and most Compleat Polite Familiar Letter-Writer,* 4th edition, Berwick, 1768, p. 53.
44. Nicholas Carew (BL Add. Mss 29599 f 312) reproduced in Pollock, *A Lasting Relationship,* pp. 184–5. The child's script follows pre-marked lines on the paper; compare later punishments for children of writing 'lines', as in the title sequence to *The Simpsons.*
45. Lady Mary Wortley Montagu, *Letters,* ed. Halsband, Vol. II, pp. 491–2. That 'ought' is still didactic.
46. Taylor, *Summary,* p. 40.
47. Davies, *Letters,* p. 31.
48. Chua Wee Hian, *'Dear Mum and Dad...': How to Honour Your Parents,* Leicester, Inter-Varsity Press, 1984, p. 93. This text puts the onus on children to write (it assumes a Christian student readership, away from home). Some postmodern parents prefer e-mail to phones because it allows advice to be frequent, uninterrupted and invites a considered response.
49. *Advice from a Father to a Son, Just Entered the Army, and about to Go Abroad into Action,* 1776, pp. 24–5, p. 73.
50. Jane Davis, *Letters from a Mother to Her Son, on His Going to Sea,* 3rd edition, Stockport, [1799], pp. 22, 32, 55.
51. Ibid., p. 37.
52. *The Parish Nurse,* n.d. [1795–7] In the late twentieth century, the telephone occupied an analogous space: compare 'Childline' and other 'help' lines. The state acted surprisingly promptly to help James Richardson, an English sailor

who was kidnapped and impressed into the Prussian military. In May 1767, he smuggled out a letter to George III; six weeks later his release had been secured. T.H. White, The *Age of Scandal: An Excursion through a Minor Period*, Harmondsworth, Penguin, 1950, pp. 111–12.

53. *Sophronia, or Letters for the Ladies*, 1761, p. 181.
54. John Wilkes, *Letters from the Year 1774 to the Year 1776, of John Wilkes, Esq.*, 4 vols, 2nd edition, 1805, Vol. II, p. 89.
55. Michèle Cohen, *Fashioning Masculinity: National Identity and Language in the Eighteenth Century*, Routledge, 1996, p. 57.
56. Compare *The Pembroke Papers (1734–1780): Letters and Diaries of Henry, Tenth Earl of Pembroke and His Circle*, ed. Lord Herbert, Jonathan Cape, 1942, pp. 51–3: instructions for the young Lord Herbert including admonitions about diet, exercise, dental care. He, his companion and his tutor were each enjoined to write to Lord Pembroke once a month, on regular days. They did so and corresponded just as actively with Lady Pembroke.
57. Helen Sard Hughes, *The Gentle Hertford: Her Life and Letters*, New York, Macmillan, 1940, p. 271.
58. Ibid., p. 284.
59. Ibid., p. 36. Lady Betty did, by an epistolary error: on her marriage she sent the old Duke a dutiful letter asking to be allowed to come and pay respects. Assuming he would refuse, she set off north. The Duke in fact accepted her visit but by the time the letter caught up with her, it was too late and he was implacably offended.
60. Compare one modern editor: 'Mrs. Piozzi of Bath and Brynbella has not the same interest as Mrs. Thrale of Streatham'. *The Queeney Letters Being Letters Addressed to Hester Maria Thrale by Doctor Johnson, Fanny Burney and Mrs. Thrale-Piozzi*, ed. the Marquis of Lansdowne, Cassell & Company, 1934, p. 127. Subsequent references are to this edition and are incorporated in the text.
61. *Marchioness de Lambert's Advice from a Mother to Her Son and Daughter*, 1729, p. 84.
62. Richard Murray, *Alethia: or, a General System of Moral Truths, and Natural Religion; Contained in Letters from Selima, Empress of the Turks, to Her Daughter Isabella, at Grand Cairo*, 2 vols, 1747, Vol. I, p. 35.
63. H.T. Barnwell, *Two Modes of Parental Correspondence: Mme de Sévigné and Lord Chesterfield*, Institute for Advanced Research in the Humanities, University of Birmingham, 1997, p. 4.
64. Ibid., p. 6.
65. *Lady Bessborough and Her Circle*, eds The Earl of Bessborough, with A. Aspinall, John Murray, 1940, p. 3.
66. Ibid., p. 161.
67. Ibid., p. 31.
68. Ibid., p. 133.
69. Ibid., p. 159.
70. Ibid., p. 262.
71. Halifax, *New-Year's Gift*, p. 59.
72. Peter Wagner, 'Hogarth's *Industry and Idleness*: Subversive Lessons in Conduct', in *Crisis of Courtesy*, ed. Carré, p. 57. See also Joan Lane, *Apprenticeship in England, 1600–1914*, Routledge, 1996.
73. Solomon, *Dodsley*, p. 10.
74. Stephanie Fysh, *The Work(s) of Samuel Richardson*, Newark, University of Delaware Press and London, Associated University Presses, 1997, pp. 45, 55.
75. Tavernier, *Letter-Writer*, p. 42.

76. Ibid., p. 45.
77. G.B., *The Last Advice of an Old Father, Being a Letter from a Father in the Country to his Son in Town*, [1793]. G.B. stands for Great Britain; the reformist son, like a Jacobite rebel, is called James.
78. Patricia Meyer Spacks, ' "Always at Variance": Politics of Eighteenth-Century Adolescence', in Spacks and W.B. Carnochan, *A Distant Prospect: Eighteenth-Century Views of Childhood: Papers Read at a Clark Library Seminar*, 13 October 1979, William Andrews Clark Memorial Library, U.C.L.A., 1982, p. 3.
79. Cited by, for instance, Thomas Sheridan, *British Education: Or, the Source of the Disorders of Great Britain*, 1756, repr. Scholar Press, 1971, p. 31.
80. Frank Brady, *James Boswell: The Later Years 1769–1795*, Heinemann, 1984, p. 10.
81. Erasmus Jones, *The Man of Manners: Or, Plebian Polish'd*, 2nd edition, 1737, p. 18.
82. John Aubrey, *Brief Lives*, 2 vols, ed. Andrew Clark, Oxford, Clarendon Press, 1898, Vol. I, p. 42.
83. Edmund Rack, *Essays, Letters, and Poems*, Bath, 1781, p. 245.
84. William Cowper, *Adelphi*, in *Letters*, Vol. I, pp. 4–48; p. 27.
85. F.T. Travell, *The Duties of the Poor; Particularly in the Education of their Children; in an Address from a Minister to his Parishioners*, 5th edition, 1799, p. 36.
86. For instance Dr John Gregory, YLPL, p. 11.
87. See John Bender, *Imagining the Penitentiary: Fiction and the Architecture of Mind in Eighteenth-Century England*, Chicago and London, University of Chicago Press, 1987: 'supervision: an imaginative projection in the subject's consciousness of the jailer's eye watching, as if eternally, from a centrally placed, curtained observation tower in full view of every cell', pp. 23–4.
88. Compare Big Brother is watching you.
89. *Sophronia*, p. 68. This novel genially challenges the double standard but requires a trade-off: wives are to be more good-humoured and tolerant.
90. Halifax, *New-Year's-Gift*, p. 89.
91. Mr Cresswick, *The Lady's Preceptor; or a Series of Instructive and Pleasing Exercises in Reading*, 1792, p. 180. By 1725, more than half the inventories of gentry and middling tradesmen recorded ownership of mirrors: Lorna Weatherill, *Consumer Behaviour and Material Culture in Britain 1660–1760*, 2nd edition, Routledge, 1996, p. 186.
92. Ibid., p. 134.
93. *The Mirror*, 2 vols, 4th edition, Dublin, 1782, Vol. I, pp. 33–5. Written by Henry Mackenzie and others, this periodical originally appeared in Edinburgh, 1779–80.
94. See Spacks, *Privacy*, ch. 4.
95. Brady, *Boswell*, p. 186.
96. *Eliza Pierce*, p. 117.
97. *Marchioness de Lambert*, 1729, pp. 34, 45.
98. Peter Peckard, *A Sermon Preached at St. James's, Westminster, Sunday, April 24, 1775*, 2nd edition, 1776. This sermon denounced Chesterfield for supposedly prescribing hypocrisy.
99. *Marchioness de Lambert*, 1729, p. 151.
100. Halifax, *Advice*, pp. 37, 74.
101. *Marchioness de Lambert*, 1729, pp. 46–7.
102. *An Apology for the Life of Colley Cibber*, ed. B.R S. Fone, Ann Arbor, University of Michigan Press, 1968, p. 12.
103. Taylor, *Summary*, pp. 75–7.
104. Nelson, *Children, Parents*, p. 213; pp. 208–18 on *The History of the Human Heart* (1749).
105. Taylor, *Summary*, p. 69. He draws on the earlier observations of Pierre Charron.

106. Dodsley, *The Preceptor*, p. 14.
107. *Epistle to a Footman* (1732), quoted by Solomon, *Dodsley*, pp. 16–17.
108. For further discussion, see Philip Carter, *Men and the Emergence of Polite Society*, passim; Klein, 'Gender'; Cohen, *Fashioning Masculinity*.
109. Philip, second Earl of Chesterfield, P.C., D.C.L. (Oxon), F.R.S. *Some Short Observations for the Lady Mary Stanhope Concerning the Writing of Ordinary Letters*, ed. W.S. Lewis, Farmington, Connecticut, privately printed, 1934, p. 10.
110. Colin Franklin, *Lord Chesterfield: His Character and Characters*, Aldershot, Scolar Press, 1993, p. 61. Dr Dodd's professions of devotion did not stop him from shortly afterwards forging a bill upon the godson for £4200. Intriguingly, Franklin notes this was the same sum which Chesterfield told his godson he had cost him since he went abroad.
111. Franklin, *Chesterfield*, p. 11. He reads Chesterfield as 'insensitive', p. 18, and the son as 'rather heroic than feeble', p. 74.
112. Ibid.
113. *The Letters of Philip Dormer Stanhope 4th Earl of Chesterfield*, 6 vols, ed. Bonamy Dobrée, Eyre & Spottiswoode, 1932, p. 1773. Pagination is continuous. Subsequent page references will be included in the text. Conventions of naming are awkward since Chesterfield's son and godson were both called Philip.
114. On the publication history, see Dobrée, p. 223; Franklin, *Chesterfield*, pp. 29–37. Eugenia sold James Dodsley the copyright for £1575.
115. Chesterfield did advise his son to write regularly to his mother (p. 2509); he also advised Lord Huntingdon to do so too (p. 1386).
116. Quoted by Pollock, *A Lasting Relationship*, p. 44.
117. *Bessborough*, p. 73.
118. When the boy was older, Chesterfield imagined his responses through dialogue, casting Philip as bored with the hectorings of an old prig (e.g. p. 1395). Arguably, dialogue seems a more invasive appropriation of the son's voice.
119. *Lord Chesterfield's Letters*, ed. David Roberts, Oxford, Oxford World's Classics, 1998, p. xxiii.
120. H.T. Barnwell, *Two Modes*, p. 15.
121. A Man of the World, *Free and Impartial Remarks upon the Letters Written by the Late Right Honourable Philip Dormer Stanhope, Earl of Chesterfield, to his Son Philip Stanhope, Esq.*, 1784, p. 39.
122. A Gentleman of Cambridge, *The Lady's Preceptor*, 3rd edition, 1745, p. 8. This advice does not seem parodic.
123. Edmund Burke, *A Philosophical Enquiry into the Origin of our Ideas of the Sublime and Beautiful*, ed. Adam Philips, World's Classics, Oxford and New York, Oxford University Press, 1990, p. 109.
124. Chesterfield was short with a big head and black teeth; Philip Stanhope was described as 'an individual who combined intelligence, reserve, clumsiness, squatness, and portliness in equal proportions.' Roberts, *Chesterfield's Letters*, p. xiv, quoting William Hayley.
125. Chesterfield did talk specifically about courts, so I follow his use of courtier although some of his applications are to politicians and diplomats (the separation is mine not his).
126. Thomas Hunter, *Reflections Critical and Moral on the Letters of the Late Earl of Chesterfield*, 2nd edition, 1777, p. 247.
127. Ibid., pp. 19, 70, 149. See also Roberts, pp. x–xiii.
128. As one mother sensibly observed, 'if I must chuse I had rather have my Son have the Virtues without Graces than the Graces without Virtues'. *Eliza Pierce*, pp. 104–5.

129. Roberts, p. xii. Sterne's *Sentimental Journey* and Richard Graves' *The Spiritual Quixote* indicate the taste.

130. A Man of the World, *Free and Impartial Remarks upon the Letters Written by the Late Right Honourable Philip Dormer Stanhope, to his Son Philip Stanhope, Esq.*, 1784, p. 32.

131. Hunter, *Reflections*, pp. 142, 146.

132. But Lady Pembroke, who probably read Chesterfield's *Letters* (her husband did), took a similar view. In 1776 she wrote to her son's tutor that they should try to avoid him first falling in love in Italy, because its society was so morally lax it would be too easy for him. Conceding she was writing 'a little odly' and on 'rather a difficult subject for me', her views sound very like Chesterfield's (until the last phrase): 'the very best thing that can happen to a very young man, is to fall desperately in love with a woman of fashion who is clever, & who likes him enough to teach him to endeavour to please her, & yet keep him at his proper distance'. *Pembroke Papers*, p. 71.

133. Boswell's *Life of Johnson*, ed. George Birkbeck Hill, rev. L.F. Powell, Oxford, Clarendon Press 1934, 6 vols, Vol. ii, pp. 340–1. Chesterfield had read *Clarissa*: he told Mme du Boccage that Richardson lacked style but knew the heart (p. 1589).

134. Melmoth, *The Pupil of Pleasure*.

135. p. 2272. Lady Suffolk's reply is in Horace Walpole's hand.

136. p. 1686. He then cites lines by Dryden on his mistress as applicable to a minister.

137. An Amateur du Bon Ton [X.Y.Z.], *An Apology for Mrs. Eugenia Stanhope, Editor of the Earl of Chesterfield's Letters to Philip Stanhope Esq*, 1775, p. 83. In 1774 the Tahitian Omai was in London, which concentrated people's minds on comparisons between savage and polite.

138. On fops, see Carter, *Men and the Emergence of Polite Society*, ch. 4, and Cohen, *Fashioning Masculinity* pp. 38–41. Cohen questions (p. 5) whether effeminacy meant the same in the eighteenth century as it does now.

139. Gothic villains also tried to compose their faces to masks, but stayed transparent. Compare the face of Montoni in Ann Radcliffe, *The Mysteries of Udolpho*, World's Classics, Oxford, p. 122. Portraits of Chesterfield do show his face as smooth.

140. Melmoth, *Pupil of Pleasure*, p. 156.

141. For discussion of Chesterfield's indulgence of instincts in the dogs he kept, and visitors' complaints about their unsocial behaviour, see my article 'Fume and Perfume: some eighteenth-century uses of smell', *Journal of British Studies*, Vol. 43, October 2004, pp. 444–63, pp. 454–5.

142. p. 1345, p. 363. Philip was fond of food, especially gooseberries and cream. A sad story tells how, during a visit to his father, when a half-finished dish was being removed from table, he seized it and ate it messily. His enraged father ordered the servant to take him away and shave him, since he had lathered his face with cream. The Earl of Charlemont, source of this story, described Philip Stanhope as 'a perfect Tony Lumpkin'. Franklin, *Chesterfield*, pp. 80–1.

143. Chesterfield lost large sums of money at cards, which he regretted.

144. *Rambler* 98, quoted by Cohen, *Fashioning Masculinity*, p. 51. Johnson claimed he was polite because he did not interrupt people, listened attentively and did not hold forth at length. Still he had a reputation for rudeness. Boswell, *Life of Johnson*, Vol. v, p. 363.

145. Chesterfield did have a mistress, Fanny Shirley. On the classification of courtiers, compare Lady Mary Wortley Montagu's division of people into men, women and Herveys.

146. Burke thought fathers could not be loved because of their authority, whereas grandfathers were freer. Chesterfield's grandparenting was warmer in many respects and he saw the child much more.
147. Hunter, *Reflections*, p. 92.
148. Amateur, *Apology*, p. 35.
149. On the overlap between language teaching and speech communities, see Niels Haastrup, 'The Courtesy Book and the Phrase Book in Modern Europe', *Crisis of Courtesy*, ed. Carré pp. 65–80.
150. Compare Virginia Woolf's Judith Shakespeare. I have not been able to discover what became of her.
151. Cohen, *Fashioning Masculinity*, p. 97.
152. Johnson, *A Journey to the Western Islands of Scotland*, ed. R.W. Chapman, Oxford, Oxford University Press, 1970, p. 50.
153. I take the categories from Lévi-Strauss but note that one could read Swift's *A Modest Proposal* in these terms too.

3 Writing as a Lover

1. Roland Barthes, *A Lover's Discourse*, trans. Richard Howard, Harmondsworth, Penguin, 1978, p. 212.
2. Edith Roelker Curtis, *Lady Sarah Lennox: An Irrepressible Stuart 1745–1826*, The Woman's Book Club, n.p., n.d., p. 54, re Lord Newbottle.
3. *The Road to Hymen*, 1790, p. 44.
4. The idea of the companionate marriage has been attractive partly because it connects representation and practice relatively simply. See William C. Horne, *Making a Heaven of Hell: The Problem of the Companionate Ideal in English Marriage Poetry, 1650–1800*, Athens GA, University of Georgia Press, 1993, pp. 1–31.
5. Elizabeth Heckendorn Cook, *Epistolary Bodies*, p. 33.
6. Catherine Jemmat, *The Memoirs of Mrs. Catherine Jemmat, Daughter of the late Admiral Yeo of Plymouth*, 2 vols, 2nd edition, 1762, Vol. I, p. 148. A budding poet, she was impressed by poetically influenced love-letters – and received them.
7. Eliza Heywood, *Love-Letters on All Occasions*, 1730, p. 90.
8. *The Lover's Manual*, 1753, p. 90.
9. *The Lover's Best Instructor; or the Whole Art of Courtship*, Wolverhampton, 1770, pp. 42–3.
10. *The Academy of Pleasure*, 1656, pp. 7, 35. Collections like this one were still read in the eighteenth century; they did not exactly date, though they are historically specific.
11. Thus *The Academy of Compliments*, c.1770, borrowed from *Le Jardin d'Amour*.
12. *The Art of Courtship, or The School of Love*, n.d., p. 3.
13. *Love Letters of Famous Men and Women of the Past and Present Century*, 2 vols, ed. J.T. Merydew, Remington & Co., 1888, Vol. I, p. 11.
14. *The Whole Pleasures of Matrimony Interwoven with Sundry Comical and Delightful Stories with the Charming Delights, and Ravishing Sweets of Wooing and Wedlock, in all it's Diverting Enjoyments*, n.d., p. 6.
15. Curtis, *Lennox*, p. 65.
16. *The Lover's Pacquet; or The Marriage-Miscellany, with the Newest Mode of Courtship; Containing the Mysteries and different sorts of Corporeal Love*, 1733, p. 3.

17. Kristina Straub, *Sexual Suspects: Eighteenth-Century Players and Sexual Ideology*, Princeton, New Jersey, Princeton University Press, 1992, ch. 1. She notes, however, 'such a hierarchy does not guarantee a stable and fixed order of looking, especially in the playhouse. The theater's discursive space both makes a particular demand for "rules" of spectating and foregrounds the difficulty of fixing those rules' (p. 7).

18. *The Lover's Pacquet*, p. 31.

19. Sir Richard Steele, *The Lover* (No. 7, 11 March 1714), 1725, pp. 37–42.

20. *The Maidens Faithfull Counsellour: or, The Speediest Way to get Good Husbands*, n.d., p. 20.

21. Curtis, *Lennox*, p. 68.

22. Henry Mackenzie, *Julia de Roubigné, A Tale*, 2 vols, 2nd edition, 1778, Vol. I, pp. 49–50.

23. *The Academy of Compliments*, 1715, p. 15.

24. *The Ladies Cabinet, or A Companion for the Toilet*, 1743, pp. 21–2.

25. Aristanaetus, *Letters of Love and Gallantry* [1698], pp. 1–2.

26. See Anne Vincent-Buffault, *The History of Tears: Sensibility and Sentimentality in France*, Houndmills, Macmillan, 1991, p. 7: 'between the letter novel and the love letter there was a phenomenon of imitation, of impregnation. The pages, whether printed or manuscript, appear well sprinkled with tears.'

27. Sir Walter James, *The Letters of Charlotte During her Connexion with Werter*, 2 vols, 1786, Vol. I, p. 45.

28. *The Lover's Best Instructor*, p. 21; *The Lover's Manual*, p. 99.

29. [G. Gaylove], *A Select Collection of the Original Love Letters of Several Eminent Persons, of Distinguished Rank and Station, Now Living*, 1755, p. 36.

30. See Lee Clark Mitchell, *Westerns: Making the Man in Fiction and Film*, Chicago and London, Chicago University Press, 1996, ch. 6, 'A Man is being Beaten'.

31. S.M., *The Female Critick: Or Letters in Drollery from Ladies to their Humble Servants*, 1701, p. 22.

32. Jean-Jacques Rousseau, *Eloisa: Or, a Series of Original Letters Collected and Published by J-J. Rousseau*, 4 vols, 1761, Vol. III, p. 58.

33. Judith Halberstam, *Skin Shows: Gothic Horror and the Technology of Monsters*, Durham NC, Duke University Press, 1995, p. 141; citing Carol Clover, *Men, Women and Chain Saws: Gender in the Modern Horror Film*, Princeton NJ, Princeton University Press, 1992, p. 46.

34. Barthes, *A Lover's Discourse*, p. 67.

35. Aristaenetus, *Letters of Love and Gallantry*, p. 86.

36. Ibid., p. 102.

37. John Robinson, *Love Fragments*, 1782, p. 33.

38. Jonathan Swift, *Journal to Stella*, 2 vols, ed. Harold Williams, Oxford, Clarendon Press, 1948 repr. 1963. For instance, Vol. I, p. 57.

39. Richard and Elizabeth Griffith, *A Series of Genuine Letters between Henry and Frances*, 6 vols, 2nd edition, 1761–66, Vol. II, p. 342. I refer to them by their real or literary names as context requires. This is 'Frances'.

40. Roy Roussel, *The Conversation of the Sexes: Seduction and Equality in Selected Seventeenth- and Eighteenth-Century Texts*, New York and Oxford, Oxford University Press, 1986, p. 69.

41. Ibid., p. 70.

42. Curtis, *Lennox*, pp. 86–7. The evidence comes from a letter from George III to Lord Bute.

43. Excerpted in *The Correspondent: A Selection of Letters from the Best Authors*, 2 vols, 1796, Vol. II, pp. 343–4. For discussion of the letter as an alternative to food, see Maud Ellmann, *The Hunger Artists: Starving, Writing and Imprisonment*, Virago Press, 1993, especially p. 70: 'The bodies of the starvers dwindle as their texts expand, as if they were devoured by their prose. Since food and words are circulating currencies, the faster, by refusing one such form of interchange, seems to be impelled to look for satisfaction in the other. It is *circulation*, therefore, that underlies the art of hunger . . .'. The figure of the lover is normally appetitive, just not necessarily for food.

44. *Love Letters*, ed. Merydew, Vol. I, pp. xv–xix. See also Peggy Kamuf, *Fictions of Feminine Desire: Disclosures of Heloise*, Lincoln and London, University of Nebraska Press, 1982, pp. xii–xiii, on the eighteenth-century disturbances of Abelard and Heloise's tomb, opened in 1768 and their remains exhumed and transferred in 1780, 1792, 1800, 1807 and 1817.

45. Laurence Sterne, *Letters from Yorick to Eliza*, 1775, p. 15; hereafter cited as *LYE*.

46. Chief among Sterne's imitators was William Combe, a complex figure. See Harlan W. Hamilton, *Dr Syntax: A Silhouette of William Combe, Esq. (1742–1823)*, Chatto and Windus, 1969, especially pp. 46–8 and pp. 113–18.

47. Some argue this sensibility is mocked in *A Sentimental Journey*. See Ian Jack's edition of both, Oxford, Oxford University Press, 1968, pp. 130–1. Hamilton, *Dr Syntax*, p. 118, says of the letters making up the *Second Journal to Eliza*, in fact by Combe, 'It was unnecessary to think them really Sterne's, and apparently no one did so; it was enough that they were in Sterne's manner – his worst manner, perhaps, but at the moment his most popular.' Combe's authentic forgeries, or inventions based on good sources, were even more successful in his *Letters of the Late Lord Lyttleton*, 1780. Hamilton notes, p. 134, Combe's 'unerring sense for the current clichés.'

48. *LYE*, p. 181 (11 July 1767).

49. *Letters Written Between Yorick and Eliza with Sterne's Letters to his Friends*, 1788, p. 68; hereafter cited as *LBYE*.

50. *Letters of Laurence Sterne*, ed. Lewis Perry Curtis, Oxford, Clarendon Press, 1935, p. 15. The idea was that Wilkes, having destroyed Sterne's letters to him, could replace them.

51. Ibid., pp. 12–14. He concedes it is possible that Sterne used his earlier letter as a 'source'.

52. Ibid., p. 138.

53. *LYE*, p. 68.

54. Sterne, *Letters*, ed. Curtis, p. 460.

55. *LBYE*, p. 41.

56. Vincent-Buffault, *History of Tears*, p. 158 cites an 1834 novel by Balzac in which a cynical male alludes to sprinkling drops of water onto writing paper to give his love-letters more effect.

57. *The Lover's Pacquet*, pp. 6–7.

58. *LBYE*, p. 40.

59. Ibid., pp. 45–6.

60. Ibid., p. 43.

61. Mary Masters, *Familiar Letters and Poems*, 1755, letters I–XII.

62. Paula R. Backscheider, ' "I Died for Love": Esteem in Eighteenth-Century Novels by Women', in *Fetter'd or Free? British Women Novelists 1670–1815*, eds Mary Anne Schofield and Cecilia Macheski, Athens, Ohio and London, Ohio University Press, 1986, pp. 152–69, p. 153.

63. Catherine Jemmat, *Memoirs*, Vol. I, p. 54; Elizabeth Gooch, *The Life of Mrs Gooch*, 3 vols, 1792, Vol. I, p. 30.
64. Elizabeth Griffith, *The Delicate Distress* (1769), eds Cynthia Booth Ricciardi and Susan Staves, *Eighteenth-Century Novels by Women*, Lexington, The University of Kentucky Press, 1997, p. 140.
65. See Peter Fenves, 'Politics of Friendship – Once Again', *Eighteenth-Century Studies* Vol. 32, No. 2, Winter 1998/99, pp. 133–55, especially pp. 136–42.
66. Jacqueline Pearson, *Women's Reading in Britain 1750–1835: A Dangerous Recreation*, Cambridge, Cambridge University Press, 1999, p. 26.
67. Sterne, *Letters*, ed. Curtis, p. 120.
68. *LYE*, p. 75.
69. *The Lover's Pacquet*, pp. 1–2.
70. Steele, *The Lover*, 1715, p. 146.
71. For one contentious reading, see Jennie Wang, *Novelistic Love in the Platonic Tradition: Fielding, Faulkner and the Postmodernists*, Lanham, Maryland and Oxford, Rowman and Littlefield, 1997.
72. *Love's Academy*, 1709, p. 5.
73. Martha Fowke, *The Epistles of Clio and Strephon*, 1720, p. xxxii. For biographical information, see Roger Lonsdale, *Eighteenth-Century Women Poets: An Oxford Anthology*, Oxford, Oxford University Press, 1990, pp. 84–5; also Christine Gerrard, *Aaron Hill: The Muses' Projector 1685–1750*, Oxford, Oxford University Press, 2003, ch. 3. Sansom died in 1736; a first-person memoir of her life was published in 1752.
74. Fowke, *Epistles*, p. xxviii.
75. Ibid., p. xliii.
76. Ibid., pp. xxxviii, 45.
77. Ibid., p. 68.
78. *Sentimental Beauties and Moral Delineations from the Writings of the Celebrated Dr Blair . . .*, [1782], p. 29.
79. But compare the ambiguity of Charlotte Lennox's *The Female Quixote*, 1752.
80. For instance, *The Art of Engaging the Affections of Wives to their Husbands*, 2nd edition, 1745, pp. 86–7; Elizabeth Griffith, *The Delicate Distress*, p. 166. See also her play *The Platonic Wife*, 1765, in which a separated wife is deluded into seeking a sentimental male friend before being reunited with a tender husband.
81. Amanda Vickery, *The Gentleman's Daughter*, p. 9.
82. 'J.J. Rousseau' [a pseudonym] *Letters of an Italian Nun and an English Gentleman*, 1781, p. xiii, hereafter cited as *Italian Nun*. Some reviewers thought it was by Rousseau, but Harlan W. Hamilton, *Dr Syntax*, p. 131, attributes it to William Combe. He notes Combe wrote another epistolary novel with a nun-in-love plot.
83. Henry Mackenzie, *Julia de Roubigné*, 2 vols, 1777, Vol. I, p. 59.
84. Sarah Herbold, 'Rousseau's Dance of Veils: The *Confessions* and the Imagined Woman Reader', *Eighteenth-Century Studies*, Vol. 32, No. 3, 1999, pp. 333–53, pp. 342–3. Interestingly, 'expunge' is now a verb used in commands to delete unwanted e-mail.
85. Sir Walter James, *The Letters of Charlotte, During her Connexion with Werther*, 2 vols, 1786, Vol. I, p. 48.
86. J-J. Rousseau, *Eloisa, or a Series of Original Letters*, 4 vols, 1761, Vol. II, p. 189. I have deliberately used the text available to eighteenth-century English readers. But I refer to Julie (rather than Eloisa) as the heroine and the novel as *La Nouvelle Héloïse* (rather than *Eloisa*), according to what suits the context best.

87. Mira Morgenstern, *Rousseau and the Politics of Ambiguity: Self, Culture and Society*, University Park PA, Pennsylvania State University Press, 1996, pp. 95–107, 199–227. See also Stephen G. Salkever, 'Interpreting Rousseau's Paradoxes', *Eighteenth-Century Studies*, Vol. 11, No. 2, 1977–78, pp. 204–26.

88. Tania Modlieski, *Loving With A Vengeance: Mass-produced Fantasies for Women*, Methuen, 1982, and Roger Dadoun, 'Fetishism in the Horror Film', in *Fantasy in the Cinema*, ed. James Donald, BFI, 1989, pp. 39–59, especially pp. 50–4 on the *imago* of the archaic mother.

89. Rousseau, *Eloisa*, Vol. III, p. x.

90. Julia Kristeva, *Tales of Love*, trans. Leon S. Roudiez, New York, Columbia University Press, 1987, develops other theoretical readings of lovers.

91. Rousseau, *Eloisa*, Vol. IV, p. 143 – sounding very like Barthes!

92. Ibid., Vol. II, p. 16.

93. Ibid., Vol. III, p. 178.

94. Ibid., Vol. III, p. 193.

95. *The Correspondent*, Vol. I, p. 245.

96. John Matthews, *Eloisa en Dishabille: Being a New Version of that Lady's Celebrated Epistle to Abelard*, 1801, p. 18.

97. On the Portuguese Nun and Heloise, see Peggy Kamuf, *Fictions of Feminine Desire*, chs 1 and 2, and Linda Kauffman, *Discourses of Desire: Gender, Genre and Epistolary Fictions*, Ithaca and London, Cornell University Press, 1986, pp. 91–117, especially pp. 95–6.

98. Again nomenclature is tricky. Eighteenth-century writers tend to refer to Eloise or Eloisa; I use Heloise where appropriate.

99. *Abelard to Eloisa, Leonora to Tasso, Ovid to Julia, Spring, and Other Poems*, 4th edition [c.1780], advertisement.

100. The Rev. Joseph Berington, *The History of the Lives of ABEILLARD and HELOISA; Comprising a period of eighty-four years, from 1079 to 1163*, Birmingham, 1787, p. 241.

101. *Letters of Abelard and Heloise*, trans. John Hughes, 6th edition, 1736, p. 115.

102. *Italian Nun*, p. 64.

103. Kamuf, *Fictions*, p. 41.

104. Eve Kosofsky Sedgwick, *The Coherence of Gothic Conventions*, Methuen, 1986, ch. 4.

105. *Italian Nun*, p. 39.

106. Marjorie Garber, *Vested Interests: Cross-dressing and Cultural Anxiety*, New York, Routledge, 1992, 1997, p. 218.

107. Ibid., p. 139.

108. Chloë Chard, 'Women who transmute into tourist attractions: spectator and spectacle on the Grand Tour', *Romantic Geographies*, ed. Amanda Gilroy, pp. 109–26, p. 113. Compare that staple of orientalism, enclosed and veiled women in harems.

109. Rousseau, *Eloisa*, Vol. III, p. 178.

110. Hughes, *Eloisa*, p. 131.

111. Ibid., p. 139.

112. Ibid., p. 154.

113. Compare Keats's 'veiled Melancholy' in his *Ode on Melancholy*.

114. Kamuf, *Fictions*, p. 98.

115. A story originating in the early thirteenth century and 'a testimony of the extent to which the two lovers had become a romantic legend' according to

Peter Dronke, *Abelard and Heloise in Medieval Testimonies*, University of Glasgow Press, W.P. Ker Lecture No. 26, 1976, p. 23.
116. Rousseau, *Eloisa*, Vol. IV, p. 219.
117. Ibid., Vol. II, p. 217.
118. Ibid., Vol. IV, p. 13.
119. Ibid., p. 145.
120. Ibid., p. 135.
121. Ibid., p. 138.
122. Ibid., p. 140.
123. Ibid., p. 157.
124. Ibid., Vol. II, p. 246.
125. Ibid., Vol. IV, p. 14.
126. Hughes, *Eloisa*, p. 263.
127. Rousseau, *Eloisa*, Vol. III, p. xiii.
128. See Toni Bowers, *The Politics of Motherhood*, 1996, especially pp. 1–28.
129. R. Adams Day, *Told in Letters: Epistolary Fiction before Richardson*, Ann Arbor, The University of Michigan Press, 1966, p. 38.
130. Hughes, *Eloisa*, p. 107.
131. Judith Madan, 'Abelard to Eloisa', *The Unfortunate Lovers; Two Admirable Poems: Extracted out of the Celebrated Letters of Abelard and Eloisa*, 1756, p. 17. Madan wrote the poem in 1720, according to Roger Lonsdale, *Eighteenth-Century Women Poets*, p. 93.
132. Hughes, *Eloisa*, p. 50.
133. Griffith, *Genuine Letters*, Vol. III, p. 166.
134. Compare a print showing Elizabeth Montagu and William Mason as Heloisa and Abelard, satirising their intellectual pretensions. Reproduced in Jonathan Wordsworth and Stephen Hebron, *Romantic Women Writers*, The Wordsworth Trust, 1994, p. 12.
135. Griffith, *Genuine Letters*, Vol. I, pp. 185, 200. Subsequent references are included in the text.
136. Elizabeth Kowaleski-Wallace, *Their Fathers Daughters: Hannah More, Maria Edgeworth and Patriarchal Complicity*, Oxford, Oxford University Press, 1991, pp. 11–12.
137. Laurence Stone, *The Family, Sex and Marriage in England, 1500–1800*, Weidenfeld and Nicholson, 1977, p. 222.
138. Tristran and Isolde, Romeo and Juliet – or Inkle and Yarico, very popular in the eighteenth century, from Steele's *Spectator* (13 March 1711) and George Colman's 1787 opera.
139. Berington, *History*, p. 57.
140. *The Love-Letters of William Pitt First Lord Chatham*, ed. Edward Ashton Edwards, Chapman and Hall, 1926; 21 October 1754. Pitt was 46.
141. Ibid., p. 108.
142. Ibid., p. 81.
143. Popular till the mid-century, the play had had 147 performances by 1776. *The Plays of Richard Steele*, ed. Shirley Strum Kenny, Oxford, Clarendon Press, 1971, p. 265.
144. *The Correspondence of Richard Steele*, ed. Rae Blanchard, Oxford, Clarendon Press, 1968, pp. 193, 196, 343.
145. Ibid., p. 360.
146. *The Tatler*, 3 vols, ed. Donald F. Bond, Oxford, Clarendon Press, 1987, Vol. II, p. 138 (No. 104, 8 December 1709).
147. Halberstam, *Skin Shows*, p. 168.

4 Writing as a Criminal

1. J.M. Beattie, *Crime and the Courts in England 1660–1800*, Oxford, Clarendon Press, 1986, pp. 15–25; J.A. Sharpe, *Crime in Early Modern England 1550–1750*, Longman, 1984, pp. 41–72.
2. Ian A. Bell, *Literature and Crime in Augustan England*, Routledge, 1991, chs 1 and 2 passim.
3. Ibid., p. 65.
4. *The Hamwood Papers of the Ladies of Llangollen and Caroline Hamilton*, ed. Mrs G.H. Bell, Macmillan, 1930, pp. 83–5.
5. Ibid., p. 198.
6. On writing as an innocent, see my article ' "The Tribunal of the Public": 18th-century letters and the politics of vindication', in *Gender and Politics in the Age of Letter-Writing, 1750–2000*, eds Caroline Bland and Máire Cross, Aldershot, Ashgate, 2004. Paralegal uses of letters to refute allegations, challenge institutions and corporations, and restore reputations show the characters of innocent and guilty have fluid and contested relations.
7. Compare the case of William Gregg who copied correspondence from Queen Anne left lying open in Harley's office. *The Malefactors Register; or, New Newgate and Tyburn Calendar*, 7 vols, 1779, Vol. I, p. 112.
8. Bell, *Literature and Crime*, p. 15.
9. Paul Baines, *The House of Forgery in Eighteenth-Century Britain*, Aldershot, Ashgate, 1999, p. 50.
10. Ibid., p. 20.
11. *The Malefactors Register*, Vol. I, p. 133.
12. *The Trial of Mrs. Rudd*, 1776, p. 17. For a full study of the case, see Donna T. Andrew and Randall McGowen, *The Perreaus and Mrs Rudd: Forgery and Betrayal in Eighteenth-Century London*, Berkeley and Los Angeles, University of California Press, 2001.
13. *The Case of Col. Francis Chartres, for a Rape Committed on the Body of Anne Bond*, in *A Collection of Remarkable Trials*, Glasgow, 1739, pp. 121–8.
14. *A Genuine Account of the Proceedings on the Trial of Florence Hensey MD*, 1758, p. 51.
15. *The Trials of Robert and Daniel Perreau's* [sic], 1775, p. 10.
16. *Mr. Nash's Narrative*, Bath, 1767, p. 8. Conversely Sir Herbert Croft declared of the letters of Junius, 'The original letters are clearly written in a female hand.' *The Love-Letters of Mr.H. & Miss R. 1775–1779*, ed. Gilbert Burgess, 1895, p. 195.
17. *The Genuine Trial between the Rt. Hon. Geo. Onslow, Esq; and the Rev. Mr. John Horne*, 1770, p. 28.
18. *The Malefactors Register*, Vol. I, p. 232.
19. Ibid., p. 293.
20. James Bevell, *An Authentic Narrative of the Methods by which the Robbery Committed in the House of the Earl of Harrington, in the Stable-Yard, St. James's, was Discovered*, 1765, p. 3.
21. *The Genuine History of the Inhuman and Unparalell'd* [sic] *Murders committed on the Bodies of Mr. William Galley and Mr. Daniel Chater*, 1749. Context for this and related cases is discussed by Cal Winslow, 'Sussex Smugglers', pp. 119–66 in Hay, Linebaugh, Rule, Thompson and Winslow, *Albion's Fatal Tree: Crime and Society in Eighteenth-Century England*, 1975, repr. 1988, Harmondsworth, Penguin.
22. See Ruth Perry, *Women, Letters and the Novel*, New York, AMS Press, 1980, ch. 1 passim.

23. See Vic Gattrell, *The Hanging Tree: Execution and the English People 1770–1868*, Oxford, Oxford University Press, 1994.
24. Alexander Smith, *A Complete History*, 1719; quoted by Peter Linebaugh, *The London Hanged: Crime and Civil Society in the Eighteenth Century*, Harmondsworth, Penguin, 1991, p. 28.
25. For instance, *The Last Letters of Thomas Potts*, Paisley, 1797, whose sale Potts hoped would make his wife a little money.
26. Cotton Mather, *Useful Remarks*, New London, 1723, p. 42.
27. Rev. Thomas Maxfield, *A Short and Authentic Account of the Particular Circumstances of the last Twenty-Four Hours of the Life and Death of William Davies*, 1776, p. 24.
28. *The Malefactors Register*, Vol. I, p. 405. These letters, and one to his mother, might well be fictional. They can be read in *Authentic Memoirs of the Life and Surprising Adventures of John Sheppard*, reprinted in Horace Bleackley, *Jack Sheppard*, 1933, William Hodge and Company, pp. 188–9. For a helpful general discussion of the genre, see Bell, *Literature and Crime*, ch. 2, 'Representing the Criminal', pp. 47–91.
29. James Collard, *The Life, and Extraordinary Adventures of James Molesworth Hobart*, 2 vols, 1794, Vol. II, p. 218.
30. *The Life of Mr. John Stanley*, 1723, p. 3.
31. *An Authentic Account of the Life and Memoirs of Mr. William Smith*, 1750, p. 19.
32. Ibid., pp. 23–4.
33. Ibid., p. 33.
34. Thomas Harris, *The Real, Genuine, and Authentic Narrative of the Proceedings of Capt. James Lowrey*, 1752.
35. Susan Sage Heinzelman, 'Guilty in Law, Implausible in Fiction: Jurisprudential and Literary Narratives in the Case of Mary Blandy, Parricide, 1752', pp. 309–36, in *Representing Women: Law, Literature, and Feminism*, eds Susan Sage Henzelman and Zipporah Batshaw Wiseman, Durham NC, Duke University Press, 1994, p. 331.
36. *The Unhappy Case of Samuel Orton, Addressed to the Reverend Mr.——*, 1767, p. 21.
37. A Scottish mob rioted for two nights in her cause, according to the DNB, and in 1750 the king gave her a pension of £300 p.a. Lord Douglas was finally persuaded to settle his estate on the surviving son.
38. *Letters of the Right Honourable Lady Jane Douglas; with several other Important Pieces of Private Correspondence*, 1767, p. i.
39. Ibid., p. vii.
40. Ibid., p. 65.
41. Ibid., p. 64.
42. See Maud Ellmann, *The Hunger Artists*, Virago, 1987, on starvation, imprisonment and writing.
43. Spatial fantasy in prison letters could work in reverse, to accentuate masculine bodily desires: in *The Double Captive, or Chains Upon Chains*, 1718, a Jacobite prisoner fantasises from Newgate about dalliance in Kensington Gardens with his mistress.
44. The editor of the Douglas letters is adamant that they are not criminals.
45. See Linebaugh, *The London Hanged*, ch. 1.
46. [Thomas Watling], *Letters from an Exile at Botany-Bay, to his Aunt in Dumfries*, Penrith, 1793, pp. 22–3.
47. Rev. Dr Allen, *An Account of the Behaviour of Mr. James Maclaine*, 1750, pp. 18–25.
48. John Brewer, *Sentimental Murder: Love and Madness in the Eighteenth Century*, Harper Perennial, 2005, p. 159.
49. Ibid., pp. 152–72.

50. *Mr. H. and Miss R.*, ed. Burgess, p. 176.
51. On the significance of fragments, see Elizabeth Wanning Harries, *The Unfinished Manner: Essays on the Fragment in the Later Eighteenth Century*, Charlottesville, University Press of Virginia, 1994.
52. *Mr. H. and Miss R.*, ed. Burgess, p. 167.
53. Ibid.
54. Ibid., p. 164.
55. Ibid., p. 173.
56. Ibid., p. 147. Scent-hounds were used to hunt down runaway slaves on eighteenth-century plantations, so Croft-as-Hackman's allusion may also be colonial.
57. The debate became intense after Goethe's epistolary and ambiguous portrait of Werter. Croft thought all suicides were mad because they inflicted the pain of their discovery on those they loved.
58. *Mr. H. and Miss R.*, p. 231.
59. *Leicester and Nottingham Journal*, Saturday, 10 August 1771.
60. *Mr. H. and Miss R.*, pp. viii–xvi.
61. Robert Miles discusses Croft as an intriguing figure (in both senses) in relation to Chatterton in 'W.H. Ireland, the Shakespeare Forgery, and New Forms of Romantic Authority', unpublished paper.
62. *Mr. H. and Miss R.*, p. 214.
63. James Foster, *An Account of the Behaviour of the Late Earl of Kilmarnock*, 1746, pp. 30–1.
64. *The Last Letters of Thomas Potts*, p. 12.
65. Johann Katte, *The Three Last Letters written by the late Unhappy Mons. De Catte*, 1734.
66. Paul Kléber Monod, *Jacobitism and the English People 1688–1788*, Cambridge, Cambridge University Press, 1989, pp. 107–11.
67. *Matter of Fact, being A Short but True Account of the Birth, Education, and Ordination of William Paul, Clergyman*, n.d., p. 22.
68. *The Case of William Paul, a Clergyman, and John Hall, Esq.*, 1716, pp. 18–19.
69. *A Full and Authentick Account of the Intended Horrid Conspiracy and Invasion*, 1715, pp. 22, 30.
70. *The Malefactors Register*, Vol. 1, p. 251. On how threatening letters and how they rewrite this picture of gentlemen writing quietly, see E.P. Thompson, 'The Crime of Anonymity', *Albion's Fatal Tree*, pp. 255–344.
71. For instance, the Babington Plot and the Popish Plot. The significance of letters in such plots is sustained by their attraction for eighteenth-century historians.
72. Gerald MacLean, 'Re-siting the Subject', in *Epistolary Histories: Letters, Fiction, Culture*, eds Amanda Gilroy and Wil Verhoeven, Charlottesville, University Press of Virginia, 2000, pp. 176–97, p. 185. On the significance of *The King's Cabinet Opened* (1645), see ibid. and Diane Purkiss, 'Gender, Power and the Body: Some Figurations of Femininity in Milton and Seventeenth-Century Women's Writing', D. Phil. thesis, Oxford University, 1991, pp. 397–407.
73. *An Account of the Proceedings in Scotland against David Baillie, with Relation to the Plot*, 1704, p. 21.
74. Monod, *Jacobitism*, p. 119.
75. Ibid., pp. 102, 104.
76. Ibid., pp. 121–5 on letter-writing and Jacobitism. See also Murray G.H. Pittock, *Jacobitism*, Macmillan, 1998, ch. 3.

77. William Sampson, *The Trial of the Rev. William Jackson...for High Treason*, Dublin, 1795, p. 30.
78. Ibid., p. 74. That such paranoia was not confined to the British Isles can be seen from the letters of Lady Mary Wortley Montagu, where references to family were scrutinised for coded meanings by the Venetian authorities.
79. *Trial of Florence Hensey MD*, p. 54.
80. Ibid., p. 39.
81. *Genuine Memoirs of the Lives of Messieurs D. and R. Perreau*, 1775, p. 60.
82. *The Genuine Case of Mrs. Rudd*, in Sir John Fielding, *Forgery Unmasked, or Genuine Memoirs of the Two Unfortunate Brothers, Rob. And Daniel Perreau, and Mrs. Rudd*, 1775, p. 30.
83. Heinzelman, 'Guilty in Law'; Margaret Anne Doody, 'The Law, the Page, and the Body of Women: Murder and Murderesses in the Age of Johnson', *The Age of Johnson*, ed. Paul Korshin, New York, AMS Press, 1987, Vol. 1, pp. 127–60, especially pp. 151–60 on Blandy; Alexander Welsh, *Strong Representations: Narrative and Circumstantial Evidence in England*, Baltimore, Johns Hopkins University Press, 1992.
84. Welsh, *Strong Representations*, p. 26.
85. *Memoirs of the Life and most Memorable Transactions of Capt. William Henry Cranston*, 1753, 2nd edition, p. 6.
86. *Memoirs*, p. 13.
87. *Miss Mary Blandy's own Account of the Affair between Her and Mr. Cranstoun*, 1752, p. 18. This is by her.
88. Ibid., pp. 23–4.
89. *The Case of Miss Blandy and Miss Jeffreys Fairly Stated and Compared*, 1752, p. 18.
90. *The Secret History of Miss Blandy*, 1752, p. 16.
91. Taken from the original reproduced in *Trial of Mary Blandy*, ed. William Roughead, Edinburgh, William Hodge and Company, 1914, facing p. 24. *Memoirs of...Cranston*, p. 25 printed a version with slight but significant variations: an exclamation mark after the salutation, more even syntax. These make the text more polite and melodramatic.
92. *The Tryal of Mary Blandy, Spinster; for the Murder of her Father, Francis Blandy, Gent.*, 1752, p. 7.
93. *Miss Blandy's Narrative*, in *A Letter from a Clergyman to Miss Mary Blandy, Now a Prisoner in Oxford Castle; with her Answer Thereto*, 1752, p. 18.
94. James Caulfield, *Blackguardiana*, 1793, n.p.
95. *Memoirs of the Life of William-Henry Cranstoun, Esq. in which His Education and Genius are Consider'd*, 1752, p. 52. The variant spelling of his name distinguishes it, just, from the short title of the other *Memoirs*.
96. *A Genuine and Impartial Account of the Life of Miss Mary Blandy*, 1752, p. 16.
97. Ibid., p. 7.
98. Margaret Anne Doody, 'Voices of Record: Women as Witnesses and Defendants in the *Old Bailey Sessions Papers*', pp. 287–308 in *Representing Women*, eds Henzelman and Wiseman, p. 292.
99. Rev. Dr James Allen, *An Account of the Behaviour of James Maclaine*, 1750, p. 4.
100. *A Letter from a Clergyman*, p. 13.
101. P. Elkington, *The Case of Miss Blandy*, Oxford, 1752, title page.
102. *An Impartial Enquiry into the Case of Miss Blandy*, 1752, p. 4.
103. *Impartial Account*, p. 13.
104. A Gentleman of Oxford, *A Candid Appeal to the Publick, Concerning the Case of the Late Miss Mary Blandy*, 1752, p. 9.

105. *An Impartial Enquiry into the Case of Miss Blandy*, 1752, p. 4.
106. *Secret History*, p. 77.
107. Ibid., pp. 78, 81.
108. *Tryal*, p. 46.
109. Welsh, *Strong Representations*, pp. 15–18.
110. Ibid., p. 7. Eighteenth-century commentators voiced some reservations about this process of reading signs: compare a letter to *The Gentleman's Magazine* contemporary with the Blandy case, concerning another (fictional?) murdered father: bloody footprints in the snow matched the print of shoes belonging to his son, who was duly hanged; later, his sister confessed to having committed the crime, wearing her brother's shoes. *Gentleman's Magazine*, Vol. XXII, April 1752, pp. 125–6.
111. *Tryal*, p. 45.
112. Cited by Henzelman, 'Guilty in Law', p. 322. The discourse here is affected by poison's invisibility. One should also remember Mary Blandy did not deny it was by her hand her father died; the point was whether she knew the powders she gave him were poison.
113. *Memoirs of... Cranston*, pp. 30–1.
114. *Memoirs of... Cranstoun*, pp. 49–50.
115. *Narrative*, p. 15.
116. James Boswell, *Journal of a Tour to the Hebrides*, Tuesday, 7 September 1773, ed. R.W. Chapman, Oxford, 1924 repr. 1978, p. 262.
117. *Captain Cranstoun's Account of the Poisoning the Late Mr. Francis Blandy*, 1752.
118. Ibid., p. 7.
119. Ibid., p. 10.
120. Ibid., p. 11.
121. Ibid., p. 12.
122. Cranstoun lived for some years quietly in Flanders. His death was immensely painful, his body so swollen that people thought he would burst. Local priests claimed him as a Catholic and gave him a grand funeral.
123. *Original Letters To and From Miss Blandy and C—— C——*, 1752, title page.
124. *Original Letters*, p. 36.
125. Henzelman and Doody both discuss judicial hostility to Blandy, demonstrated by the Lord Chancellor's interest in whether she could be tried for petty treason and his pre-trial assumption of her guilt.
126. *The Case of Miss Blandy*, p. 18. The prosecution noted that Cranstoun had rented a house in Henley called 'The Paradise'; Henzelman, 'Guilty in Law', p. 312.
127. *The Genuine Lives of Capt. Cranstoun and Miss Mary Blandy*, 1753, p. 62.
128. *Miss Mary Blandy's Own Account*, p. 45.
129. *A Genuine and Impartial Account*, p. 16.
130. *The Case of Miss Blandy*, p. 13.
131. *Authentick Memoirs of the Wicked Life and Transactions of Elizabeth Jeffryes, Spinster*, 1752, 2nd edition, p. 8.
132. Ibid., pp. 5–6.
133. *A Genuine and Impartial Account*, p. 11.
134. *The Case of Miss Blandy*, p. 20.
135. For a reading of the case's medical testimony, see Julia Rudolph, 'The Body of Sarah Stout: Science, Gender and Status in a Seventeenth-Century Murder Trial', paper presented at the 'Tales from the Old Bailey: Writing a New History from Below' conference, University of Hertfordshire, 5–6 July 2004.

136. *The Tryal of Spencer Cowper, Esq; and John Marson, Ellis Steven and William Rogers, for the Murder of Mrs. Sarah Stout, a Quaker*, 1699, p. 19. He was the younger brother of the Lord Chancellor, later a judge, and father of the poet Judith Madan.

137. Ibid., p. 29.

138. Ibid.

139. Ibid., p. 30.

140. Ibid.

141. Ibid., p. 31.

142. Ibid., p. 36.

143. Laetitia Pilkington, Teresia Constantia Phillips, Elizabeth Justice and others used letters outside the law in order to challenge corrupt or hostile representations of themselves in law. See my article, 'Women, Scandal and the Law', in *Women, Texts and Histories 1575–1760*, eds Clare Brant and Diane Purkiss, Routledge, 1992, pp. 242–70.

144. *The Hertford Letter: Containing Several Brief Observations on a Printed Tryal, Concerning the Murder of Mrs. Sarah Stout*, 1699, p. 13.

145. *A Reply to the Hertford Letter*, 1699.

146. On available legal options, see Lawrence Stone, *Road to Divorce: England 1530–1987*, Oxford 1990, and Bridget Hill, *Women, Work and Sexual Politics in Eighteenth-Century England*, Oxford, 1989.

147. *A New and Compleat Collection of the Most Remarkable Trials for Adultery*, 2 vols, 1780, p. 148. The trial date is 1765. The cases I refer to are with a few exceptions included in either this publication or *Trials for Adultery*, 9 vols, 1779. Wherever possible I shall simply give short titles.

148. John P. Zomchick, *Family and the Law in Eighteenth-Century Fiction: The Public Conscience in the Private Sphere*, Cambridge, Cambridge University Press, 1993, p. 3.

149. *The Trial of Fanny Wilmot*, 1792, p. 36. The presents were money, new clothes, an elegant gold ring with a lock of her hair, a heart-shaped nutmeg grater and a bottle of eau-de-cologne.

150. *Trial of William Atkinson*, 1789, p. 23.

151. Ibid., p. 5.

152. Phillip Cade against Catherine Cade, 1772.

153. *The Trial of Richard Lyddel*, in *A Collection of Remarkable Trials*, Glasgow, 1739.

154. Lord Ligonier against Lady Ligonier, 1771, p. 48.

155. Ibid., p. 39. Lady Ligonier retained some control over these intimate texts in that it was she who organised their collection and formal identification through her father, pp. 61–3.

156. Ibid., p. 42.

157. Rt. Hon. Lord Viscount Bellfield vs. Hon. Arthur Rochfort, p. 27.

158. *A Collection of Remarkable Trials*, p. 53.

159. Ibid., p. 61.

160. Edith Roelker Curtis, *Lady Sarah Lennox, An Irrepressible Stuart 1745–1826*, The Woman's Book Club, n.d., p. 151.

161. *A Full and Complete History of His R——l H—— the D—— of C——d and Lady G——r, the Fair Adultress*, 2 vols, 3rd edition, 1770, Vol. I, p. 207.

162. Sadly he did not. She died not long after the case, supposedly from grief at his forsaking her. He too died young.

163. *The Tryal between Sir W——m M——rr——s and Lord Augustus Fitzroy*, 1742, p. 11.

164. Ibid., p. 21.

165. Ibid., p. 44.
166. Ibid., p. 25.
167. Ibid., pp. 46–7.
168. *The Trial of the Right Honourable Maria Bayntun*, pp. 30, 80.
169. Curtis, *Lennox*, pp. 186–7. On scandal as prime copy, see Cindy McCreery, 'Keeping up with the *Bon Ton*: the *Tête-à-Tête* series in the *Town and Country Magazine*', pp. 207–29, in *Gender in Eighteenth-Century England*, eds Barker and Chalus, p. 228, 'It was both gossip column and moral commentary.'
170. All quotations are from Bayntun, pp. 101–3.
171. Richard Draper against Elizabeth Drapper [sic], 1771, p. 17.
172. Ibid. References to his letters are pp. 12–15.
173. Ibid., pp. 21–2.
174. Ibid., p. 17.
175. Richard Heatley against Arabella Heatley, 1770, p. 57.
176. Ibid.
177. Ibid., pp. 63, 75, 78.
178. *Trial of Mr. Samuel Euclid Oliver, for Incestuous Adultery with Miss Elizabeth Jane Hoskings his Wife's Sister*, 1774, in *A New and Complete Collection*, Vol. II, p. 243. 'Thing' was a term recognised as describing behaviour thought to be against natural as well as civil law. Compare *Love Letters between a certain late Nobleman & the famous Beau Wilson*, 1723: 'The Thing speaks itself', preface.
179. Ibid.
180. Ibid., p. 244.
181. Ibid., p. 245.
182. *The Trial of the Rev. Mr. James Altham of Harlow, in the County of Essex, for Adultery, Defamation and Obscenity*, 2 vols, 1785, Vol. II, p. 62.
183. Ibid., Vol. II, p. 4.
184. *A New and Compleat Collection*, Vol. II, p. 76.
185. *The Trial of Andrew Robinson Bowes, Esq. for Adultery and Cruelty*, 1789, p. 24.
186. Ibid., pp. 40–1.
187. John Worgan against Sarah Worgan, 1768, in *Trials for Adultery*, 1780, Vol. VII, p. 85.
188. *The Trial of Lord Grey*, p. 72.
189. A Civilian, *Free Thoughts on Seduction, Adultery and Divorce*, 1771, p. 202.
190. *The Trial of Mrs Ann Wood*, p. 30.
191. *The Trial of Mrs Elizabeth Leslie Christie*.
192. *The Trial of Mrs Harriet Errington*.
193. *Narrative of the Trial of Harriot Brooke*, 1767, pp. 160–1. This was not an isolated instance: compare *The Trial of Katherine Earle*, 1765.
194. No. 28, May 6–13, 1746; quoted in Bruce Robbins, *The Servant's Hand: English Fiction from Below*, New York, 1986, p. 13.
195. *Trial of Sir Francis Blake Delaval*, preface.
196. *Free Thoughts*, p. 178.
197. Ibid., pp. 178–9.
198. *The Trial of Captain Gambier*, pp. 8, 29.
199. *The Trial of Catherine Degen*, p. 8.
200. *The Marquis of Carmarthen* v. *the Marchioness of Carmarthen*, pp. 15–16.
201. Ibid., p. 45.
202. Ibid.
203. Ibid., p. 20.

204. *A Full and Complete History*, Vol. I, p. 33.
205. Ibid., Vol. II, p. 54.
206. Ibid., p. 44.
207. Ibid., p. 68.
208. *Free Thoughts*, p. 186.
209. *A Full and Complete History*, Vol. II, p. 61.
210. Ibid., p. 77.
211. Ibid., Vol. I, pp. 198–9.
212. *Trials for Adultery*, Vol. IV, pp. 72–103.
213. *Free Thoughts*, p. 183.
214. Ibid., pp. 205–6.
215. Ibid., p. 263.

5 Writing as a Citizen

1. Jonas Hanway, *Letters Admonitory and Argumentative from J. H——y, Merchant, to J. S——r, Merchant, In Reply to Particular Passages, and the General Argument, of a Pamphlet, entitled, Further Considerations on the Bill, &c.*, 1753, p. 204.
2. Linda Colley, *Britons: Forging the Nation 1707–1837*, New Haven and London, Yale University Press, 1992, pp. 277–8.
3. Paul Keen, *The Crisis of Literature in the 1790s: Print Culture and the Public Sphere*, Cambridge, Cambridge University Press, 1999, p. 14.
4. Ibid., pp. 82–3.
5. Cowper, *Letters*, Vol. II, p. 350.
6. Anna Clark, 'The Chevalier d'Eon and Wilkes: Masculinity and Politics in the Eighteenth Century', *Eighteenth-Century Studies*, Vol. 32, No. 1, 1998, pp. 19–48; p. 21.
7. Pierre Bourdieu, *Acts of Resistance: Against the Tyranny of the Market*, trans. Richard Nice, New York, New Press, 1998, p. vii.
8. Ibid., p. 9.
9. Ibid., p. 25.
10. *An Essay on Parties and a Free Government, in the Character of an Ancient Trimmer*, n.d., preface. In Smollett's *Launcelot Greaves* (1762) when the quixotic hero stumbled into an election and proposed a third party take over from the Whigs and Tories, they pelted him out of town together.
11. A Gentleman at Oxford, *Animadversions of the Conduct of the Opposers of the Present Administration*, n.d., p. 2.
12. John Trenchard and Thomas Gordon, *Cato's Letters*, 4 vols, 1724, Vol. I, p. xi.
13. Joseph Galloway, *Letters from Cicero to Catiline the Second*, 1781, pp. 72–3.
14. *The Letters of Junius*, ed. John Cannon, Oxford, Clarendon Press, 1978, p. xxvi.
15. Dror Wahrman, *Imagining the Middle Class: The Political Representation of Class in Britain, c.1780–1840*, Cambridge, Cambridge University Press, 1995, p. 12. 'Public opinion' has its own history in political language; I use it as a historically stable term to show up other instabilities.
16. Of course opinions were formed through conversation as well as print; compare Smollett's humorous variant on the pow-wow in *Launcelot Greaves* when some characters in a pub conduct a wow-wow.
17. Thus a verse in 1640: 'News is conveyed by letter, word, or mouth, / And comes to us from north, east, west, and south.' Quoted by Alexander Andrews, *The History of British Journalism, from the Foundation of the Newspaper Press in England*

to the Repeal of the Stamp Act in 1855, with Sketches of Press Celebrities, 2 vols, 1859, Richard Bentley, Vol. I, p. 18.

18. *A Collection of Letters on Patronage and Popular Election*, Edinburgh, 1783, pp. iii–iv.
19. *A Letter to the Right Hon Wm. Pitt, on the Restriction of the Regent's Authority*, 1789, p. 5.
20. Capel Lofft, *Three Letters in the Question of the Regency*, 1788, advertisement. The term 'public reason' is Montaigne's.
21. John Brewer, *The Sinews of Power: War, Money and the English State 1688–1783*, Routledge, 1989, ch. 8 passim.
22. *A Letter from an Irish Gentleman in London to the People of Ireland on the Limitations of the Regency*, 1789, p. 8.
23. Nicholas Rogers, *Whigs and Cities: Popular Politics in the Age of Walpole and Pitt*, Oxford, Clarendon Press, 1989, p. 404.
24. Kathleen Wilson, *The Sense of the People: Politics, Culture, and Imperialism in England, 1715–1785*, Cambridge, Cambridge University Press, 1995, p. 41.
25. On periodical letters, see Katherine Shevelow, *Women and Print Culture: The Construction of Femininity in the Early Periodical*, Routledge, 1989.
26. For example, 'Probus' was a persona used by Charlotte Forman in newspaper letters of 1756–60 and 1773–75. See *Eighteenth-Century Popular Culture: A Selection*, eds John Mullan and Christopher Reid, Oxford, Oxford University Press, 2000, p. 261.
27. Anna Clark, 'Chevalier d'Eon', pp. 39–40, argues gender lines harden thanks to Wilkes and other radicals' distinctions between different public and private behaviours for the sexes. On relations between liberty and libertinism, see my article 'Armchair Politicians: Elections and Representations, 1774' in *Tulsa Studies in Women's Literature*, Political Discourse/British Womens' Writing, 1640–1867, Vol. 17, No. 2, Fall 1998, pp. 269–82.
28. [John Perceval, Earl of Egmont], *The Nature of the Present Excise, and the Consequence of its Further Extension, Examined*, 1733, p. 15.
29. *A Letter to the Right Honourable Charles James Fox, on the Late Conduct of his Party*, 2nd edition, 1789, p. 1.
30. Ibid., p. 6.
31. See, inter alia, Linda Colley, *In Defiance of Oligarchy: The Tory Party 1714–1760*, New Haven, Yale University Press, 1989; J.C.D. Clark, *English Society 1688–1832*, Cambridge, Cambridge University Press, 1985; Frank O'Gorman, *Voters, Patrons, Parties: The Unreformed Electoral System of Hanoverian England 1734–1832*, Oxford, Oxford University Press, 1989; Paul Langford, *A Polite and Commercial People 1727–1783*, Oxford, Oxford University Press, 1989; Nicholas Rogers, *Whigs and Cities* and *Crowds, Culture and Politics in Georgian Britain*, Oxford, Oxford University Press, 1998; Kathleen Wilson, *The Sense of the People*; John Brewer, *The Sinews of Power*; Richard Price, *British Society 1680–1880: Dynamism, Containment and Change*, Cambridge, Cambridge University Press, 1999.
32. 'Atticus', *London Journal*, Saturday, 22 March 1728–29.
33. A Gentleman of Wiltshire, *Country Common Sense*, Gloucester 1739, p. 96.
34. *The Polite Politician: Or, Entertaining Correspondent*, 2 vols, 1751, Vol. I, p. 369.
35. A Gentleman at Guadaloupe, *Reasons for Keeping Guadaloupe at a Peace*, 1761, p. 65.
36. *The Political Beacon: Or the Life and Character of Oliver Cromwell, Impartially Illustrated*, 1770, p. 3.
37. John Almon, *Memoirs of a Late Eminent Bookseller*, 2 vols, 1790, Vol. I, p. 175.
38. *The Prospect Before Us*, 1788, n.p.
39. 7 May 1770, in *Repository*, Vol. I, p. 474.
40. Matthew Concanen, *The Speculatist*, 1730, p. 225.

41. Tobias Smollett, *The History and Adventures of an Atom* in *The Works of Tobias Smollett*, 8 vols, ed. James P. Browne MD, 1872, Vol. VI, p. 308.
42. *Cato's Letters*, Vol. II, p. 163.
43. Nathaniel Wraxall, *Memoirs of My Own Times*, 2 vols, 1815, Vol. I, p. 490.
44. *Authentic Papers concerning a late Remarkable Transaction*, 1746.
45. John Robins, *A Bone to Pick, Recommended to the Several Water Companies of this Metropolis; or a Check to Avarice, Tyranny and Oppression in Two Parts*, 1790.
46. Bourdieu, *Acts of Resistance*, p. 4, citing an unnamed German author.
47. Wilson, *The Sense of the People*, p. 32.
48. *Faithful Copies of all the Letters that have Appeared in the General Advertiser, under the Signatures of Scourge, and W. Bennett, Camberwell*, 1781, p. 6. Atkinson was eventually pilloried, reviled and left the country.
49. Ibid., p. 57.
50. Deborah Baker Wyrick, *Jonathan Swift and the Vested Word*, Durham, NC, University of North Carolina Press, 1988, reprinted in *Jonathan Swift*, ed. Nigel Wood, Longman, 1999, pp. 70, 72.
51. Ibid., p. 71.
52. Hannah Barker, *Newspapers, Politics, and Public Opinion in Late Eighteenth-Century England*, Oxford, Clarendon Press, 1998, p. 40.
53. Castle, *Masquerade and Civilization*, p. 131 reads this as a carnivalesque contradiction.
54. Barker, *Newspapers*, p. 38.
55. There were some letter-writing ghosts, interestingly – letters as if from ghosts of actual people (Shaftesbury, Voltaire) and ghosts of personae (Alfred, the Drapier) were published in the eighteenth century. There are a few seventeenth-century instances too.
56. Nathaniel Glasgow, *A Copy of Two Letters to the Magistrates and Town-Council of Glasgow*, n.p., 1725, p. 13.
57. For instance, Timothy Nabber asking to replace Jack Ketch in *The Original Weekly Journal with Fresh Advices, Foreign and Domestick*, 23–30 June 1716.
58. See Julie Ellison, *Cato's Tears and the Making of Anglo-American Emotion*, Chicago, University of Chicago Press, 1999, and Lisa A. Freeman, 'What's Love Got to Do with Addison's *Cato*?', *Studies in English Literature 1500–1900*, Vol. 39, No. 3, Summer 1999, pp. 463–82 for further discussion of Cato.
59. John Keane, *Tom Paine: A Political Life*, Bloomsbury, 1995, pp. 130–3 discusses the controversy between Tom Paine and a 'Cato' in Philadelphia.
60. *Cato's Letters*, Vol. III, p. 89.
61. See James Sambrook, *The Eighteenth Century: The Intellectual and Cultural Context of English Literature, 1700–1789*, Longmans, 1986, pp. 207–8.
62. Hannah Barker, 'Press, Politics and Reform 1779–1785', Oxford D. Phil. thesis, 1994, p. 221.
63. Ibid., p. 229.
64. A Freeholder, *A Letter to Sir Richard Hill, Esq.*, 1782, p. 26. Conversely Capel Lofft announced he was not afraid to sign his polemical *Three Letters on the Question of a Regency*, 1788, pp. 34–5.
65. An Honest Man, *The Secret Springs of the Late Changes in the Ministry Fairly Explained*, 1766, p. 4.
66. Thomas Cooke, *The Letters of Atticus, as Printed in the London Journal, in the Years 1729 and 1730 on Various Subjects*, 1731, p. 13.
67. These three all featured in Concanen's *The Speculatist* (1730). Peregrine Ramble suggestively anticipates Smollett's protagonists Roderick Random and Peregrine Pickle.

68. Concanen, *Speculatist*, p. 117.
69. *A Collection of Letters on Patronage and Popular Election* ... Edinburgh, 1783, p. 42.
70. Cooke, *Atticus*, p. 11. On the cult of Raleigh, see Christine Gerrard, *The Patriot Opposition to Walpole: Politics, Poetry, and National Myth, 1725–1742*, Oxford, Clarendon Press, 1994, pp. 157–61.
71. Galloway, *Letters*, 1781, Advertisement.
72. Ibid., p. vii.
73. Reported by Smollett to Whitefoord, 18 May 1779; quoted by Barker, 'Press, Politics and Reform', p. 16.
74. Concanen, *Speculatist*, p. 267.
75. David Erskine, *Letters of Albanicus to the People of England, on the Partiality and Injustice of the Charges Brought against Warren Hastings, Esq., Late Governor of Bengal*, 1786, p. 5. Erskine prefers letters to courts as a means of constituting 'the tribunal of the public' precisely because the show trial of Hastings proves courtroom justice is no justice.
76. David Nokes, *Jonathan Swift: A Hypocrite Reversed*, Oxford, Oxford University Press, 1985, p. 283.
77. Cato Ultonensis, *A Word of Advice: or A Friendly Caution to the Collectors of Ireland, in Relation to Wood's Brass-Money*, Dublin, 1724, p. 4.
78. Ibid., p. 5.
79. Raymond Williams, *The Country and the City*, Hogarth Press, 1985, p. 104.
80. *A Letter to the Shopkeepers, Tradesmen, Farmers, and Common-People of Ireland, Concerning the Brass Half-Pence Coined by Mr. Woods, with a Design to have them pass in this Kingdom*, Dublin, n.d., p. 15.
81. Wyrick, *Jonathan Swift*, pp. 75–6, cites Jack Gilbert's suggestion that M.B. may stand for Marcus Brutus, whom Swift admired; she thinks 'M.B.' is pronounced 'am, be' – an existential declaration. I think the initials bear comparison with the *Journal to Stella*, in which people Swift cares about are condensed into the initials 'M.D.', usually glossed as 'My Dear' or 'My Dears'.
82. James Thompson, *Models of Value: Eighteenth-Century Political Economy and the Novel*, Durham and London, Duke University Press, 1996, p. 65. See also pp. 37–86 on paper currency vs. coin.
83. [Swift], *A Letter to the Shopkeepers*, p. 30.
84. In a ghastly case of contested lunacy c.1749, a wife tried to prove her husband was sane. He was given £30 pounds in coins from different countries and told to make them add up. He lost the case, his wife lost him. *To the Humane and Compassionate of all Ranks, especially the Fair Sex, Is with the greatest Deferrence Adressed* [sic], n.d.
85. M.B. Drapier, *Some Observations upon a Paper, Call'd The Report of the Committee of the Most Honourable the Privy Council in England, Relating to Wood's Half-pence*, Dublin, n.d. [1724], p. 3.
86. M.B. Drapier, *A Letter to the Whole People of Ireland*, Dublin, 2nd edition, 1724, pp. 3–4.
87. Jonathan Swift, *The Drapier's Letters*, ed. Herbert Davis, Oxford, Clarendon Press, 1935, p. 19.
88. Drapier, *Letter to the Whole People*, p. 16.
89. Warren Montag disputes 'the received truth that Swift was a champion of Irish liberty ... absolutely hegemonic in literary circles', with reference to the Drapier's letters. See 'Warrant Montag replies to Carole Fabricant', *Eighteenth Century Fiction*, Vol. 9, No. 1, 1996, pp. 101–2.

90. William Drennan, *The Letters of Orellana, an Irish Helot; to the Seven Northern Counties not represented in the National Assembly of Delegates, held at Dublin, October, 1784, for Obtaining a More Equal Representation of the People in the Parliament of Ireland*, n.p., 1785, p. 7.
91. Ibid., p. 19.
92. *Examinator's Letters, or a Mirror for British Monopolists and Irish Financiers*, Dublin, 1786, p. 79.
93. Their boldest success was arguably the appearance of Richardson's novel *Sir Charles Grandison* (1753) in advance of the author-printer's own edition.
94. On patriots, see Gerrard, *Patriot Opposition*, pp. 4–6.
95. *Cato* in Addison, *Miscellaneous Works: Poems and Plays*, ed. A.C. Guthkelch, G. Bell and Sons, 1914, p. 342. Ellison, *Cato's Tears*, discusses other eighteenth-century plays featuring Romans, including Thomson's *Sophonisba* (1730); she proposes that Addison's Cato provides the Whigs with a legitimising narrative.
96. Addison, *Cato*, ed. Guthkelch, p. 349.
97. Ellison, *Cato's Tears*, pp. 50–62.
98. There are Shakespearian complications here, obviously.
99. Addison, *The Freeholder*, ed. James Leheney, Oxford, Clarendon Press, 1979, p. 183.
100. Ibid., p. 237.
101. Almon, *Memoirs*, Vol. 1, p. 74.
102. Ellison, *Cato's Tears*, p. 189.
103. *Cato's Letters*, Vol. I, p. xv.
104. Ibid., p. xx.
105. Ibid., p. xllvii.
106. Ibid., p. xxix.
107. Ibid., p. xlvii. Compare clubs as analogue. Marie Mulvey Roberts argues that 'Fictional clubs were normally devised as a way of attacking opponents in the world of letters, journalism or politics.' 'Pleasures Engendered by Gender: Homosociality and the Club' in *Pleasure in the Eighteenth Century*, eds Roy Porter and Marie Mulvey Roberts, Houndmills, Macmillan, 1996, pp. 48–76; p. 63.
108. Ellison, *Cato's Tears*, p. 18: 'What has conventionally been defined as the late eighteenth-century Age of Sensibility is, in fact, sensibility's second act.'
109. Ibid., Vol. I, p. 303
110. Ibid., Vol. II, p. 207.
111. Ibid., Vol. III, p. 32.
112. Discussed by Shevelow, *Women and Print Culture* and Madeleine Kahn, *Narrative Transvestism: Rhetoric and Gender in the Eighteenth-Century English Novel*, Ithaca and London, Cornell University Press, 1991, ch. 1.
113. *The Letters of the Celebrated Junius*, 2 vols, 1783, Vol. I, p. 179.
114. *The Letters of Junius* ed. C.W. Everett, Faber and Gwyer, 1927, p. 352.
115. For example, Pope's *Moral Essays* or Johnson's *Vanity of Human Wishes*.
116. *The Censor Censur'd: or, Cato turn'd Catiline*, 1722, p. 13.
117. *Cato's Letters*, Vol. I, p. 28.
118. Bourdieu, *Acts of Resistance*, p. 4.
119. *Cato's Letters*, Vol. I, p. 309.
120. See John Carswell, *The South Sea Bubble*, 1960 rev. 1993, Stroud, Glos., Allan Sutton Publishing Ltd, chs 13 and 14.
121. Classical frugality also appealed to Trenchard: he was interested in the Cynics and published some letters under the signature Diogenes. Comparativism

lasted: Charles James Fox was fond of comparing the 1790s to the first century BC. See L.G. Mitchell, *Charles James Fox*, Harmondsworth, Penguin, 1997, p. 186: 'he liked to think of himself as Brutus, saving representative institutions'. Catherine the Great admired Fox as an orator and planned to put his bust in her gallery between Cicero and Demosthenes. Ibid., p. 118.

122. John Trenchard and Thomas Gordon, *A Collection of Tracts*, 2 vols, 1751, Vol. II, p. 23.

123. *A Letter from a Member of Parliament for a Borough in the West, to a Noble Lord in his Neighbourhood there, concerning the Excise-Bill and the Manner and Causes of Losing it*, 1733, p. 29.

124. *The Censor Censur'd*, p. 25.

125. Matthew Tindall, *A Defence of our Present Happy Establishment*, 1722, p. 5.

126. Ellison, *Cato's Tears*, p. 68.

127. Wraxall, *Memoirs* Vol. I, p. 445.

128. See George Hardinge, *Chalmeriana, or a Collection of Papers Literary and Political*, 1800, pp. 62–6. Wraxall says Sir William Draper, Junius's chief target, was anxious to know who Junius was almost to his deathbed. Most commentators now agree in thinking Junius was Sir Philip Francis, a clerk in the War Office.

129. [John Bowdler], *Reform or Ruin: Take Your Choice!*, 1797, p. 1.

130. *Junius*, ed. Everett, p. 366, p. 259.

131. Ibid., p. 317.

132. Ibid., pp. 192–3; from *Thoughts on the late Transactions respecting Falkland's Islands*.

133. Ibid., p. 192.

134. See John J. Burke, Jr, 'When the Falklands First Demanded an Historian: Johnson, Junius, and the Making of History in 1771', *The Age of Johnson*, ed. Paul Korshin, Vol. 2, New York, AMS Press, 1989, pp. 291–310, p. 301. Isobel Grundy, *Samuel Johnson and the Scale of Greatness*, Athens, Georgia, University of Georgia Press, 1986, p. 86, notes Johnson had not used this kind of contempt in his *Rambler* or *Idler*, which strengthens the case for it being a borrowed idiom.

135. Herbert M. Atherton, *Political Prints in the Age of Hogarth: A Study of the Ideographic Representation of Politics*, Oxford, Clarendon Press, 1974, p. 259, p. 229.

136. Ibid., plate 61. Atherton points out, p. 229, that actual statuary was political: 'The Temple of British Worthies' at Stowe was the Cobhamite Patriots' ironic satire on Robert Walpole.

137. *Junius*, ed. Everett, p. 193.

138. Ibid., p. 190.

139. Ibid., p. 100.

140. Decimus Junius Juvenalis, satirist; Marcus Junius Brutus, Caesar's friend, opponent, assassin, who was married to Cato's daughter, which provides Junius with a nice kinship to Cato, the republican letter-writer. There was also a Junius who was a heretic professor in the Continent on the 15th century. See Ellison, *Cato's Tears*, pp. 57–9 on Nathaniel Lee's *Lucius Junius Brutus* (1680) and successors on stage.

141. See Elaine Chalus, 'That epidemical madness' in *Gender in Eighteenth-Century England*, eds Barker and Chalus.

142. See Rogers, *Crowds, Culture and Politics*, passim and H.T. Dickinson, *The Politics of the People in Eighteenth-Century Britain*, Houndmills, Basingstoke, Macmillan, 1994, pp. 125–58.

143. Rogers, *Whigs and Cities*, p. 400.

144. Ibid., p. 350.

145. Paul Langford, *The Excise Crisis: Society and Politics in the Age of Walpole*, Oxford, Clarendon Press, 1975, p. 138.
146. William Combe, *A Letter from a Country Gentleman, to a Member of Parliament, on the Present State of Public Affairs*, 7th edition, 1798, p. 28.
147. Rogers, *Whigs and Cities*, p. 230.
148. Mitchell, *Fox*, p. 34.
149. Rogers, *Whigs and Cities*, p. 366.
150. John Toland, *The Danger of Mercenary Parliaments*, 1722, p. i.
151. Ibid., p. iv.
152. Cato Redivivus, *Patriotism, A Political Satire*, 1767, p. vii.
153. Rogers, *Whigs and Cities*, p. 283; p. 299; p. 325.
154. Ibid., p. 190.
155. A Plain Common Freeholder, *Letters to Sir William Beauchamp Proctor*, 1768, p. 14; *The Election Magazine, or Repository of Wit and Politics*, Norwich, 1784, p. 30.
156. John Wilkes, *Two Letters to the Rt Hon Sir John Cust, Speaker*, Edinburgh, 1764. It was one of Cato's virtues that he had been first in and last out of the Senate every day.
157. *A Genuine and Authentic Account of the Proceedings at the Late Election for the City and Liberty of Westminster*, 1749, p. 54.
158. *A Collection of Advertisements, Letters and Papers, and some other Facts, Relating to the Last Elections at Westminster and Hasting* [sic], 2nd edition, 1722, p. 46.
159. The success of this fiction of popular request can be seen in its use in America up until the 1850s at least, as the way in which presidential candidates declared themselves. David M. Potter, *The Impending Crisis 1846–1861*, New York, Harper and Rowe, 1976, pp. 69–70.
160. *Flagel: or A Ramble of Fancy through the Land of Electioneering*, 1768, pp. 9–10.
161. Michael J. Franklin, *Sir William Jones*, Cardiff, University of Wales Press, 1995, p. 35: 'Jones did not help matters by enclosing printed copies of his pro-American 'Ad Libertatem' in his own letters to staid Oxford acquaintances.' Whyman, *Sociability and Power*, p. 163, notes awkward letters helped John Verney come last in a county election in 1696.
162. Barker, *Newspapers*, argues political content helped to sell newspapers. See also Christine Ferdinand, *Benjamin Collins and the Provincial Newspaper Trade in the Eighteenth Century*, Oxford, Clarendon Press, 1997.
163. Marcus Wood, *Radical Satire and Print Culture 1790–1822*, Oxford, Clarendon Press, 1998, pp. 12–13.
164. Ibid., ch. 1, on various genres and mock-genres, especially the parodic advertisement, also discussed by Jon Mee, 'The Political Showman at Home: Reflections on Popular Radicalism and Print Culture in the 1790s' in *Radicalism and Revolution in Britain, 1775–1848*, ed. Michael T. Davis, Macmillan, 2000, pp. 41–55.
165. Raymond O'Malley, 'Flowers in the Valley: Folk-Songs in Britain' in *18th Century Britain*, ed. Boris Ford, The Cambridge Cultural History of Britain, Vol. 5, 1992; pp. 95, 99.
166. *Election Magazine*, p. 5.
167. *Journal of the Proceedings at the Election of the Knights of the Shire to Represent the County of Norfolk in Parliament*, 1784, p. 22.
168. Ibid., p. 61.
169. *Election Magazine*, p. 4.
170. Ibid., p. 16.
171. Ibid., p. 3.

172. *The Bristol Contest, Containing A Particular Account of the Proceedings of both Parties . . .*, Bristol, 1781, p. 38.
173. On Robert Merry, Della Cruscan and democrat, see Mee, 'The Political Showman', pp. 46–8.
174. *The Bristol Contest*, p. 34.
175. Anti-semitism in 1753 was exacerbated by arguments about sacred history, discussed in ch. 7.
176. *The Bristol Contest*, p. 23. There were plenty of Jacobites in Wales and Phillips is counted a Jacobite by one historian of Jacobitism, Paul Monod.
177. Ibid., p. 27.
178. Ibid., p. 10.
179. As the poll books suggest and Rogers confirms in *Whigs and Cities*, ch. 8 passim.
180. Ibid., p. 294.
181. Ibid., p. 299.
182. H.T. Dickinson, ' "The Friends of America": British Sympathy with the American Revolution' in *Radicalism and Revolution*, ed. Davis, pp. 1–29, notes support in large cities, including Bristol, pp. 5–6.
183. *The Bristol Contest*, 1781, p. 30.
184. Hannah More, *Village Politics, Addressed to all the Mechanics, Journeymen, and Labourers in Great Britain*, 1792. 'Will Chip' sounds like a relation of William Hint and William Plain.
185. *The Bristol Contest*, 1781, p. 30.
186. More, *Village Politics*, pp. 59–60. On fables earlier in the century, see Jayne Elizabeth Lewis, *The English Fable: Aesop and Literary Culture 1651–1740*, Cambridge, Cambridge University Press, 1996.
187. A Ship's Carpenter in *The Bristol Contest*, 1781, p. 32.
188. Ibid., pp. 26–7.
189. Ibid., 1781, p. 68.
190. *The Wit of the Day, or the Humours of Westminster*, 1784, p. 95.
191. *The Cirencester Contest*, [1750 ?], p. 60.
192. Sir Richard Hill, *Hard Measure, or A Real Statement of Facts, in a Letter to the Burgesses, and Freemen Burgesses, of the Town of Shrewsbury*, Shrewsbury, 2nd edition, 1795, p. 31.
193. Ibid., p. 1.
194. An impression reinforced by his portrait which still hangs at Attringham Hall in Shropshire.
195. Ibid., p. 42, p. 38.
196. Ibid., p. 45.
197. *Measure for Measure, An Answer to the Last Edition and Supplement of 'Hard Measure', in a Letter to the Electors of Shrewsbury*, 2nd edition, 1796, p. 73.
198. Ibid., p. 78.
199. *Letters between Sir Richard Hill, Baronet, John Hill, and Edward Burton, Esquires*, Shrewsbury, 1796. In the end, John Hill conceded to his nephew – really for financial reasons, since he had 13 children to support.
200. Balaam's Ass, *Shrewsbury Election* [sic], Shrewsbury, 1796, p. 9.
201. Paul Langford, *The Excise Crisis*, 1975.
202. Brewer, *Sinews of Power*, p. 247.
203. *A Letter from a Member of Parliament for a Borough in the West*, p. 9.
204. Ibid., p. 10.
205. Langford, *Excise*, p. 152.

206. *The Nature of the Present Excise, and the Consequences of its Farther Extension, Examined*, 1733, p. 40.
207. Langford, *Excise*, p. 48.
208. *A Letter from a Member of Parliament to his Friends in the Country, Concerning the Duties on Wine and Tobacco*, 1733, pp. 9–13.
209. *The Budget Opened*, p. 18.
210. *Excise: Being a Collection of Letters, &c.*, n.d., p. 30.
211. Ibid., p. 12.
212. Langford, *Excise*, p. 56.
213. *A Letter... to a Noble Lord*, p. 15.
214. Ibid., p. 21.
215. Langford, *Excise*, p. 49.
216. *A Review of the Excise Scheme*, p. 4.
217. Mitchell, *Fox*, pp. 25, 99.

6 Writing as a Traveller

1. Donna Landry, 'Love Me, Love My Turkey Book: Letters and Turkish Travelogues in Early Modern England', in *Epistolary Histories*, eds Gilroy and Verhoeven, pp. 51–73, p. 51.
2. Thus Lady Mary Wortley Montagu expects her correspondent to be relating her account of fabulous jewels in Turkey to the world of the *Arabian Nights*. She confirms fiction as a relevant model. *Letters*, ed. Halsband, Vol. I, p. 385.
3. Landry, 'Love Me', p. 55.
4. Edward Young, *The Centaur Not Fabulous*, 1755, p. xv.
5. Ibid., p. 325.
6. Shaftesbury, *Characteristics*, ed. Klein, p. 39. See also Frantz Fanon, *Black Skin, White Masks*, Pluto, 1986.
7. Voltaire, 'A Conversation with a Chinese', in *Philosophical Tales, Romances and Satires*, n.d. Voltaire's *Letters Concerning the English Nation* (1733) was written in the subtle persona of an English author. See Nicholas Cronk, World's Classics edition, 1999, pp. xiv–xxvii.
8. W. Daniel Wilson, 'Turks on the Eighteenth-Century Operatic Stage and European Political, Military, and Cultural History', *Eighteenth Century Life*, IX No. 2, January 1985, pp. 79–92, p. 83.
9. Richard Dyer, *White*, Routledge, 1997, p. 45.
10. Homi K. Bhabha, *The Location of Culture*, Routledge, 1994, p. 89.
11. The exception that one could argue proves the (colonial) rule is India, which produced few personae. Anglo-Indians were ridiculed through the stereotype of the nabob.
12. Bhabha, *Location*, p. 70.
13. Ibid.
14. Ibid.
15. Oliver Goldsmith, *The Citizen of the World* in *Collected Works of Oliver Goldsmith*, 5 vols, ed. Arthur Friedman, Oxford, Clarendon Press, 1966, Vol. II, p. 166.
16. *An Answer from Lien Chi, in Pekin, to Xo Ho, the Chinese Philosopher in London, To which is annexed A Letter from Philo-Britain to Lien Chi*, 1757, p. 5.
17. Sir James Prior, *Life of Goldsmith*, 2 vols, 1837, Vol. I, p. 360, quoted in Goldsmith, *Collected Works*, ed. Friedman, pp. ix–x. Richard C. Taylor, *Goldsmith As Journalist*, Associated University Presses, 1993, p. 110, suggestively connects Goldsmith's

development of a traveller-persona to his 'Irishness', which gave him 'an acute sense of himself as a cultural outsider in London'.

18. Charles Johnston, *The Pilgrim: or, A Picture of Life. In a Series of Letters, Written mostly from London by a Chinese Philosopher, to his Friend at Quang-tong*, 2 vols, Dublin, 1775, Vol. I, p. 69.
19. Goldsmith, *Citizen*, p. 15.
20. Marquis D'Argens, *Lettres Chinoises*, translated as *Chinese Letters. Being a Philosophical, Historical, and Critical Correspondence between a Chinese Traveller at Paris, and his Countrymen*, 1741.
21. Goldsmith, *Citizen*, p. 14; Letter VII. A selection of Confucius's writings had been available in English since 1691.
22. Bhabha, *Location of Culture*, p. 77.
23. Goldsmith, *Citizen*, Preface; Johnston, *Pilgrim*, Vol. I, p. 35.
24. David Porter, 'Monstrous Beauty: Eighteenth-Century Fashion and the Aesthetics of the Chinese Taste', *Eighteenth-Century Studies*, Vol. 35, No. 3 (2002), pp. 395–411, p. 400.
25. Goldsmith, *Citizen*, pp. 146–7.
26. Johnston, *Pilgrim*, p. 43.
27. Goldsmith, *Citizen*, p. 103.
28. Ibid., pp. 13–14.
29. *Travels of the Jesuits, Into Various Parts of the World*, 2 vols, trans. John Lockman, 1743, Vol. I, p. 145.
30. Horace Walpole, *A Letter from Xo Ho, a Chinese Philosopher at London, to his Friend Lien Chi at Peking*, 1757, p. 2. On Walpole and chinoiserie in general, see David Porter, 'From Chinese to Goth: Walpole and the Gothic Repudiation of Chinoiserie', *Eighteenth Century Life*, Vol. 23, No. 1, February 1999, pp. 46–58.
31. Walpole, *Xo Ho*, p. 5.
32. Ibid., p. 2.
33. Montesquieu's *Lettres Persanes*, 1721. Various English translations were in print throughout the century.
34. John Andrews, *Letters to a Young Gentleman on his Setting out for France*, 1784, p. 153.
35. Lord Lyttleton, *Letters from a Persian in England to his Friend at Ispahan*, 1735, p. 78.
36. Ibid., pp. iv–v.
37. Ibid., p. v.
38. Lyttleton, *Letters from a Persian*, p. 27.
39. *The Persian Letters Continued*, 1736, 3rd edition, p. iv.
40. Elizabeth Heckendorn Cook notes that intellectual historians reading the *Lettres Persanes* as a cultural critique omit the harem material and literary critics reading the text as a novel focus on it. *Epistolary Bodies*, p. 23.
41. Goldsmith, *Citizen*, p. 142. Compare Montesquieu's claim to have relieved his reader of oriental turns of phrase which would have 'bored him sublimely'. *Persian Letters*, ed. C.J. Betts, Harmondsworth, Penguin, 1973 repr. 1993, p. 39.
42. Ros Ballaster, *Seductive Forms: Women's Amatory Fiction from 1684 to 1740*, Oxford, Clarendon Press, 1992, especially pp. 114–23 apropos Manley.
43. Compare Eliza Haywood, *Letters from the Palace of Fame*, 1727, which mixes 'translation' from an Arabian manuscript with letters sent by Ariel, 'First Minister in the Regions of Air, to an Inhabitant of this World', Alla, advising women about conduct and Richard Murray's *Alethia: Letters from Selima, Empress of the Turks to her daughter Isabella*, 1747, discussed in 'Writing as a Parent.'

44. On their role thus in juvenile literature, see Samuel F. Pickering Jr, *Moral Instruction and Fiction for Children, 1749–1820*, Athens, Georgia, University of Georgia Press, 1993, pp. 1–31.

45. For example, Ange Goudar, *The Chinese Spy, or Emissary from the Court of Pekin, Commissioned to Examine into the Present State of Europe*, 6 vols, 1765 (translated from the French).

46. William H. Epstein suggests spying and letter-writing are linked by the phrase 'under cover' which derives from the practice of addressing a letter to one person under a cover addressed to another. OED does not confirm this link, but it is suggestive. See 'Assumed Identities: Gray's Correspondence and the "Intelligence Communities" of Eighteenth-Century Studies', *The Eighteenth Century*, Vol. 32, No. 3, Fall 1991, pp. 274–88, p. 279. Epstein notes, p. 278, a letter from Gray to Walpole in January 1735 in the persona of the Turkish Spy, passing on 'intelligence' about Cambridge.

47. Lyttleton, *Letters from a Persian*, numbers 45–7.

48. *The Life of Cassem, the Son of Hamid, A Noble Arabian*, 1746, n.p.

49. One of the characteristics of the Turkish Spy is that he is well read in (world) history.

50. *Cassem*, p. 43.

51. Wilson, 'Turks', p. 80.

52. Peter Miles, 'Smollett, Rowlandson, and a Problem of Identity: Decoding Names, Bodies, and Gender in Humphry Clinker', *Eighteenth Century Life*, Vol. 20, No. 1, February 1996, pp. 1–23, p. 11. Miles notes p. 16 Smollett thought of the Jesuits as sodomites too.

53. Timothy Mowl, *Horace Walpole: the Great Outsider*, John Murray, 1996, pp. 91–2.

54. Montesquieu discusses the threat of castration to one character, Letters 41–43.

55. Terry Castle, *Masquerade and Civilization*, p. 74: 'much of the masquerade's popularity undoubtedly came from the fact that it offered a *Spielraum*, an environment where repressed impulses could be acted out safely'.

56. Lyttleton, *Letters from a Persian*, p. 81.

57. Wortley Montagu, *Letters*, ed. Halsband, Vol. I, p. 328.

58. William Hunter, *Travels in the Year 1792 through France, Turkey, and Hungary, to Vienna*, 2 vols, 2nd edition, 1798, Vol. II, pp. 261–2.

59. Jack P. Greene, 'Empire and Identity from the Glorious Revolution to the American Revolution', *The Oxford History of the British Empire*, ed. Wm. Roger Louis, Vol. II, *The Eighteenth Century*, ed. P.J. Marshall, Oxford and New York, Oxford University Press, 1998, pp. 208–30, p. 219. This is tricky terrain: Goldsmith's title category of 'Citizen of the World' is significantly non-nationalist but was not necessarily understood as embracing countries beyond Europe. In *Journal of a Tour to the Hebrides* (14 August 1773) Boswell describes himself as a citizen of the world because he has felt at home in six countries, but they are all European.

60. But as Roy Foster argues, 'attitudes best called colonial' were demonstrably in abundance. Quoted in Colley, *Britons: Forging the Nation 1707–1837*, New Haven and London, Yale University Press, 1992, p. 8. Thomas Bartlett, ' "This Famous Island Set in a Virginian Sea": Ireland in the British Empire, 1690–1801', *The Oxford History of the British Empire*, Vol. II, pp. 253–75, describes 'an untidy jumble [of] "kingdom", "colony", "dependency", and, faintly, "nation"', p. 254.

61. Thomas Campbell, *A Philosophical Survey of the South of Ireland*, 1777, p. 466.

62. Robert Hellen (or Viscount Edmund Sexton Pery), *Letters from an Armenian in Ireland*, pp. 13–14. Compare Frederic Jebb, *The Letters of Guatimozin*, 1779, in which an

Irish author uses an indeterminately foreign persona to abuse the Scots as England's colonial lackeys.

63. *Armenian*, p. 58. For economic details, see Bartlett, 'This famous island', pp. 254–62.
64. Campbell, *Philosophical Survey*, p. 121.
65. Ibid., p. 131.
66. Ibid., p. 127.
67. Ibid., pp. 155–6.
68. Ibid., p. 253.
69. Ibid., p. 253.
70. See *Diary of a Visit to England in 1775 by an Irishman* [Thomas Campbell], Sydney, 1854, p. v.
71. *Diary*, pp. 42–3. My reading may of course be affected by my Englishness.
72. Bhabha, *Location of Culture*, p. 70. When coloniser and colonised share the same skin colour, the nature of the persona as mask changes. Compare Noel Ignatiev, *How the Irish Became White*, Routledge, 1995, p. 3: 'In becoming white the Irish ceased to be Green.'
73. Balanchandra Rajan, 'Feminizing the Feminine: Early Women Writers on India' in *Romanticism, Race, and Imperial Culture, 1780–1834*, eds Alan Richardson and Sonia Hofkosh, Bloomington and Indianapolis, Indiana University Press, 1996, pp. 149–71, p. 153.
74. William Dalrymple, *White Mughals: Love and Betrayal in Eighteenth-Century India*, Flamingo, 2003.
75. Philip Dormer Stanhope, *Genuine Memoirs of Asiaticus In a Series of Letters to a Friend*, 2nd edition, 1785, p. 130. Rajat Kanta Ray, 'Indian Society and the Establishment of British Supremacy, 1765–1818', *Oxford History of the British Empire*, Vol. II, pp. 508–29, p. 519, notes 'There was no political discourse in eighteenth-century India to construe resistance to the foreigners as a national war for the defence of the country.' 'Annals of English tyranny' shows 'Asiaticus' recognised the usefulness of English political discourse for resistance to English rule.
76. Michael H. Fisher, *The First Indian Author in English: Dean Mahomed (1759–1851) in India, Ireland, and England*, Delhi, Oxford University Press, 1996, p. 216. I agree with Fisher that the writer's voice is not exclusively European; I also agree with Suvir Kaul's review, *Textual Practice* Vol. 11, Issue 3, Winter 1997, pp. 252–6, that '*The Travels* does not provide us with a model of authentic "Indianness"', p. 555.
77. Sake Dean Mahomet, *The Travels of Dean Mahomet, a Native of Patna in Bengal*, 2 vols, Cork, 1794, Vol. I, p. 180.
78. *Mahomet*, Vol. I, p. 173.
79. Compare John Bull (and contrast Mickey Mouse).
80. See the discussion of political personae in 'Writing as a Citizen'.
81. John Shebbeare, *Letters on the English Nation by Battista Angeloni a Jesuit, Who Resided Many Years in London*, 2 vols, 1755, Vol. I, p. 140.
82. Ibid., p. vii.
83. *Travels of the Jesuits, Into Various Parts of the World*, 2 vols, 1743, trans. John Lockman, Vol. I, pp. vi–viii.
84. Ibid., p. viii.
85. *The Travels of Several Learned Missioners of the Society of Jesus, into Divers Parts of the Archipelago, India, China and America*, 1714, p. 186. See also Barbara Widenor Maggs, '"The Jesuits in China": Views of an Eighteenth-Century Russian Observer',

Eighteenth-Century Studies, Vol. 8, No. 2, Winter 1974–75, pp. 137–52, especially pp. 141–6 and Kate Teltscher, *India Inscribed: European and British Writing on India 1600–1800*, Oxford University Press, Delhi, 1997, especially pp. 75–97 on Jesuits (and Lutherans) in India.

86. Shebbeare, *Angeloni*, p. liv.
87. Lockman, *Travels*, Vol. I, p. xii.
88. Ibid., p. viii.
89. Samuel Madden, *Memoirs of the Twentieth Century*, 1733, p. 131.
90. Ibid., p. 180.
91. Ibid., p. 283.
92. *Letters from an American in England to His Friends in America*, 1769; the text is the same as that circulating in 1781 under the title *Anticipation, or the Voyage of an American to England in the Year 1899* (though the story is explicitly set at the end of the eighteenth century).
93. Martin Thom, *Republics, Nations and Tribes*, Verso, 1995, p. 5.
94. Stuart Sherman, *Telling Time: Clocks, Diaries, and English Diurnal Form, 1660–1785*, University of Chicago Press, 1996, pp. 113–14.
95. John Andrews, *Letters*, p. 25.
96. Ibid., p. 555.
97. Ibid., p. 574.
98. Charles Cordiner, *Antiquities and Scenery of the North of Scotland, in a Series of Letters to Thomas Pennant, Esqr.* 1780, p. 3. Pennant's name in the title would help it to sell.
99. Edward Clarke, *Letters Concerning the Spanish Nation*, 1763, p. ii.
100. John Williams, *An Account of some Remarkable Ruins, Lately Discovered in the Highlands, and Northern Parts of Scotland*, Edinburgh, 1777, p. 73.
101. Ibid., p. 11.
102. Thomas Windham, *An Account of the Glacieres or Ice Alps in Savoy, in Two Letters . . .* 1744, p. 27.
103. William Thomson, *Letters from Scandinavia, on the Past and Present State of the Northern Nations of Europe*, 2 vols, 1796, Vol. I, p. 74. Thomson was possibly writing these letters at home, hence imitating the wildness allowed to those writing on the road.
104. John Lettice, *Letters on a Tour through various parts of Scotland, in the year 1792*, 1794, p. 92.
105. Eyles Irwin, *A Series of Adventures in the Course of a Voyage up the Red-Sea . . . In Letters to a Lady*, 1780, p. 120.
106. Henry Rooke, *Travels to the Coast of Arabia Felix*, 2nd edition, 1784, p. 52.
107. Wortley Montagu, *Letters*, ed. Halsband, Vol. I, p. 284.
108. William Coxe, *Travels in Switzerland*, 3 vols, 1789, preface.
109. Compare Lichtenberg's admiration of Garrick, in *Lichtenberg's Visits to England as described in his Letters and Diaries*, translated and annotated by Margaret L. Mare and W.H. Quarrel, Oxford, 1938, p. 9.
110. Williams, *Ruins*, p. 26. Correspondents' replies are printed at the end.
111. Ibid., p. 45.
112. Patrick Brydone, *A Tour Through Sicily and Malta*, 2 vols, 1773, Vol. I, p. 99.
113. Richard C. Sha argues the sketch conflates 'the public and private spheres that it was intended to separate', and so is especially useful to women. 'Expanding the Limits of Feminine Writing: The Prose Sketches of Sydney Owenson (Lady Morgan) and Helen Maria Williams' in *Romantic Women Writers: Voices and Countervoices*, eds Paula R. Feldman and Theresa M. Kelley, Hanover and

London, University Press of New England, 1995, pp. 194–206, p. 194. I question this gendering, although I agree it is a less 'finished' genre and as such widely used by letter-writers, especially towards the end of the century when picturesque added value to roughness.

114. Lettice, *Letters*, p. 509.
115. Sir John Talbot Dillon, *Letters from an English Traveller in Spain, in 1778, on the Origin and Progress of Poetry in that Kingdom*, 1781, p. vi.
116. Dillon, *Letters*, p. iv. Compare Pope, *Epistle to a Lady* (1735): 'Some wand' ring touch, or some reflected light, / Some flying stroke alone can hit 'em right', ll. 153–4.
117. Dillon, *Letters*, p. vi.
118. Alexander Drummond, *Travels through Different Cities of Germany, Italy, Greece, and Several Parts of Asia, as far as the Banks of the Euphrates*, 1754, p. 11.
119. Ibid., pp. 1–2.
120. William Coxe, *Sketches of the Natural, Civil, and Political State of Swisserland*, 2nd edition, 1780, p. 47.
121. Ibid., p. 151.
122. Ibid., p. 46.
123. Christopher Hervey, *Letters from Portugal, Spain, Italy and Germany in the years 1759, 1760, and 1761*, 3 vols, 1785, Vol. II, p. 482.
124. Coxe, on the source of the Danube, *Sketches*, p. 2. Compare Jeremy Black, *The British Abroad: The Grand Tour in the Eighteenth Century*, Alan Sutton, Stroud, 1992, p. xiii: 'Letters written on the spot and at the time are a more accurate guide to experience than the polished prose of calm recollection, however quotable or literary the latter might be.' Literary critics may demur.
125. Hunter's travels may well have been written nowhere near the spot, which reinforces my point.
126. Edward Topham, *Letters from Edinburgh, Written in the Years 1774 and 1775, Containing some Observations on the Diversions, Customs, Manners and Laws, of the Scotch Nation, During a Six Months Residence in Edinburgh*, 1776, p. vii.
127. Thus Mary Wollstonecraft's *Letters Written During a Short Residence in Sweden, Norway, and Denmark*, 1796. Contractions of her title to *A Short Residence . . .*, as in the Penguin edition, suppress this genre-function, commonplace by 1796 (and used in the full title of Eliza Hamilton's *Letters of a Hindoo Rajah* the same year).
128. Drummond, *Travels*, p. 104.
129. *Sketches*, p. 2.
130. Samuel Sharp, *Letters from Italy, Describing the Customs and Manners of that Country, in the Years 1765, and 1766*, 1767, 2nd edition, p. 181.
131. Nathaniel Wraxall, *Cursory Remarks made in a Tour Through Some of the Northern Parts of Europe, particularly Copenhagen, Stockholm, and Petersburgh*, 1775, pp. 1–2.
132. A Virginian, *The American Wanderer, Through Various Parts of Europe, in a Series of Letters to a Lady*, 1783, pp. 89–90.
133. Wraxall, *A Tour through the Western, Southern and Interior Provinces of France, in a Series of Letters*, in *Memoirs of the Kings of France*, 2 vols, 1777, Vol. II, p. 201.
134. Anne Grant, *Letters from the Mountains; Being the Real Correspondence of a Lady Between the Years 1773 and 1803*, 3 vols, 1806, Vol. I, p. 98.
135. Ibid., Vol. I, p. 65.
136. Chloe Chard, *Pleasure and Guilt on the Grand Tour*, Manchester, Manchester University Press, 1999, p. 42.

137. Kate Teltscher, 'The Sentimental Ambassador' in *Epistolary Selves*, ed. Earle, pp. 79, 93.
138. Dillon, *Letters*, p. 15.
139. Grant, *Letters*, Vol. II, p. 82.
140. Topham thought this view 'the most picturesque and beautiful' of any in Europe. *Letters*, p. 29.
141. Lettice, *Letters*, p. 521.
142. John Sturch, *A View of the Isle of Wight, in Four Letters to a Friend*, Newport, Isle of Wight, 1794, 5th edition, p. 19.
143. Joseph Cradock, *Letters from Snowdon: Descriptive of a Tour through the Northern Counties of Wales*, 1770, p. 9.
144. Hervey, *Letters*, Vol. I, p. 260.
145. Henry Hodgson, *Letters to Mrs Kindersley*, 1778, p. 10.
146. Wraxall, *Cursory Remarks*, p. 82.
147. Sir Richard Sulivan [sic], *Observations made During a Tour through Parts of England, Scotland and Wales*, 1780, p. 1.
148. Sharp, *Letters from Italy*, p. 248.
149. Benedict Anderson, *Imagined Communities*, Verso, 1983 rev. 1991, p. 6.
150. Contrast Barbara Korte, *English Travel Writing: From Pilgrimages to Postcolonial Explorations*, Macmillan, 2000, Index, p. 216: 'foreignness, *see* otherness'.
151. It was a complex combination, including moral authority, practical responsibility, economic dependence, social inferiority and intellectual superiority. Many tutors were also clergy, which threw spiritual authority and equality into the mix.
152. Wortley Montagu, *Letters*, ed. Halsband, Vol. III, p. 15.
153. See, inter alia, Katherine Turner, *British Travel Writers in Europe 1750–1800*, Ashgate 2001; Linda Colley, *Britons*; Paul Langford, *Englishness Identified: Manners and Character, 1650–1850*, Oxford, Oxford University Press, 2000; Jeremy Black: *The British Abroad: The Grand Tour in the Eighteenth Century*, Allen Sutton, Stroud, 1992; Chloe Chard, *Pleasure and Guilt on the Grand Tour; Romanticism and Colonialism: Writing and Empire, 1780–1830*, eds Timothy Fulford and Peter J. Kitson, Cambridge, Cambridge University Press, 1998; Mary Louise Pratt, *Imperial Eyes: Travel Writing and Transculturation*, New York, 1992; Sara Mills, *Discourses of Difference: An Analysis of Women's Travel Writing and Colonialism*, Routledge, 1991.
154. Vilashini Cooppan, 'W(h)ither Post-colonial Studies? Towards the Transnational Study of Race and Nation' in *Postcolonial Theory and Criticism*, eds Laura Chrisman and Benita Parry, *Essays and Studies* 1999, Vol. 52, pp. 1–35, p. 9.
155. Colley, *Britons*, p. 6.
156. Chard, *Pleasure*, pp. 42–7.
157. Coxe, *Sketches*, p. 463.
158. Hunter, *Travels*, Vol. I, p. 170.
159. Charles Dupaty, *Sentimental Letters on Italy*, 1785 trans. 1789, p. 96.
160. Hunter, *Travels*, Vol. II, pp. 136–7.
161. Sharp, *Letters from Italy*, p. 171.
162. Hunter, *Travels*, Vol. I, p. 165. For further discussion of women in travel writing, see my article 'Climates of Gender' in *Romantic Geographies*, ed. Gilroy, especially pp. 135–41.
163. Hunter, *Travels*, Vol. I, p. 188.
164. Irwin, *Adventures*, p. 390.

165. Thus Alexander Drummond, writing in 1744, reckoned that Padua had 116 churches, 25 monasteries, 23 convents and 16 hospitals. *Travels*, p. 84.
166. Ibid., p. 80.
167. Ibid., p. 195.
168. Ibid., p. 118.
169. Sharp, *Letters from Italy*, p. 194; pp. 123–5.
170. William Eddis, *Letters from America, Historical and Descriptive; Comprising Occurrences from 1769, to 1777, Inclusive*, 1792, p. 115.
171. Chloe Chard, 'Women who transmute into tourist attractions: spectator and spectacle on the Grand Tour' in *Romantic Geographies*, ed. Gilroy, pp. 109–26.
172. Brydone, *Tour*, Vol. I, p. 148.
173. Ibid., pp. 149–50. Beckford later became a devotee of St Anthony.
174. *Correspondence of Thomas Gray*, 3 vols, eds Paget Toynbee and Leonard Whibley, Oxford, 1935 repr. 1971, Vol. I, p. 130.
175. Drummond, *Travels*, p. 173. Compare Smollett's *Letters from France and Italy* (1766) and Philip Thicknesse's Francophile corrections of Smollett and others in *Observations on the Customs and Manners of the French Nation* (1766).
176. For a helpful discussion, see Kathleen Wilson, *The Island Race: Englishness, Empire and Gender in the Eighteenth Century*, Routledge, 2003, Introduction.
177. Irwin, *Adventures*, p. 48.
178. John Luffman, *A Brief Account of the Island of Antigua*, 2nd edition, 1789, p. 34.
179. Jemima Kindersley, *Letters from the Island of Teneriffe, Brazil, the Cape of Good Hope and the East Indies*, 1777, p. 263.
180. Hervey, *Letters*, Vol. II, p. 521. Did the denouement vary between countries, one wonders? On taciturnity as a national characteristic, see Langford, *Englishness Identified*, pp. 175–84; as a gendered characteristic, see Cohen, *Fashioning Masculinity*, p. 104. She points out many Englishwomen were fluent in other languages, making them more competent travellers than men who were monoglot or only au fait with dead languages.
181. Kindersley, *Letters*, p. 244.
182. Coxe, *Travels*, Vol. III, p. 324.
183. Thomas Nugent, *The Grand Tour, Or, A Journey through the Netherlands, Germany, Italy, and France*, 4 vols, 3rd edition, 1778, Vol. I, preface.
184. Rooke, *Arabia Felix*, p. 90.
185. Ibid., 'Translation of a Firman of the Ottoman Porte'.
186. Alexander Cluny, *The American Traveller: Or, Observations on the present State, Culture and Commerce of the British Colonies in America . . . by an Old and Experienced Trader*, 1769, Advertisement.
187. Ibid., p. 21.
188. Ibid., p. 112.
189. Ibid., p. 20.
190. Ibid., p. 3.
191. Ibid., p. 4.
192. Ibid., p. 5.
193. Ibid., p. 20.
194. *Mercator's Letters on Portugal and its Commerce*, 1754, p. viii.
195. Arthur Gray and Frederick Brittain, *A History of Jesus College Cambridge*, Heinemann, 1960, p. 141. Clarke's travels were later published.
196. Wilson, *The Island Race*, p. 18.
197. Ibid., p. 10.

7   Writing as a Historian

1. Goldsmith, *Collected Works*, ed. Friedman, Vol. I, p. 269.
2. Gilbert Stuart, *A View of Society in Europe*, 1778, Edinburgh, p. v.
3. Alexander Tytler, *Plan and Outline of a Course of Lectures on Universal History, Ancient and Modern, Delivered in the University of Edinburgh*, pp. 4, 5.
4. Laird Okie, *Augustan Historical Writing: Histories of England in the English Enlightenment*, Lanham, New York and London, University Press of America, 1991, p. 9. Alternatively one can consider a continental model of *érudits* and *philosophes*. Anne Goldgar, *Impolite Learning: Conduct and Community in the Republic of Letters, 1680–1750*, Yale University Press, 1995, posits a shift in mid-century, when savants think learning is in peril; she relates this to a new culture of politeness, in which the scholar's social status falls as the author's rises. See pp. 226–42.
5. In this I disagree with Thomas Beebee, who argues writing history is the 'least appropriate' task for epistolary form, because it is to-the-moment. *Epistolary Fiction in Europe*, p. 298.
6. Francis Squire, *Remarks upon Mr. Carte's Specimen of his General History of England: very proper to be read by all such as are Contributors to that great Work*, 1748, p. 11.
7. Ibid., p. 6.
8. Gilbert Stuart, *The History of Scotland, from the Establishment of the Reformation, Till the Death of Queen Mary*, 2 vols, 1782, Vol. 1, Advertisement.
9. M. de Voltaire, *The Philosophy of History*, 1766, p. 1.
10. Stuart, *History*, pp. vi–vii.
11. Cited by William Nicolson, *The English, Scotch and Irish Historical Libraries*, 3rd edition, 1736, p. 28. The image is also alchemical.
12. William Hayley, *An Essay on History; in Three Epistles to Edward Gibbon, Esq. with Notes*, 1780, p. 13.
13. Ibid., p. 29. On the relationship between history and natural history, see Joseph Levine, *Doctor Woodward's Shield: History, Science and Satire in Augustan England*, Ithaca and London, 1991, passim but especially p. 32 on fossil shells.
14. John Whitaker, *Gibbon's History of the Decline and Fall of the Roman Empire, in Vols. IV, V, and VI, Quarto, Reviewed*, 1791, p. 255.
15. George Sewell, *A Second Letter to the Bishop of Salisbury, upon the Publication of his New Volume of Sermons*, 1713, p. 8.
16. *Discourse, delivered by the Right Honourable Earl of Buchan*, 1778, pp. 23–4. Metaphors of heaviness helped exclude women, the lighter sex. There were no women admitted to Erskine's society and few women feature as donors to the collection of books and objects it quickly amassed. The Duchess of Portland was an exception to the general exclusion of women from historical collecting (she was also an exceptional collector). The learned Society of Roman Knights founded in 1722 did include women: Stuart Piggott describes this as 'unprecedented'. *William Stukeley: An Eighteenth-Century Antiquary*, 1950 rev. 1985, Thames and Hudson, New York, pp. 53–5.
17. Another powerful set of metaphors concerned painting, which I have no space to discuss here but note accusations of varnish and false colouring worked like accusations of luxuriance.
18. Quoted in Hayley, *Essay on History*, p. 147: 'Une imagination sage, & fleurie, qui peigne les actions, qui deduise les causes, & qui presente les reflexions avec clarté & simplicité; quelquefois avec feu, mais toujours avec gout & élégance.'
19. Thomas Carte, *A General History of England*, 4 vols, 1747, Vol. 1, p. xii.

20. *The Critical History of England, Ecclesiastical and Civil*, 2nd edition, 1726, p. 154.

21. *Letters on various Subjects, Literary, Political, and Ecclesiastical, to and from William Nicolson, DD.*, 2 vols, ed. John Nicols, 1809, Vol. I, p. 142.

22. See Mary Douglas, *Purity and Danger: An Analysis of the Concept of Pollution and Taboo*, Routledge and Kegan Paul, 1966, and Carolyn Steedman, *Dust*, Manchester, Manchester University Press, 2001. Dust is also at odds with polish and so expresses anxiety about the place of the scholar in polite society.

23. I make this generalisation in spite of my chapter on the importance of letters in politics, because in the context of the republic of letters scholarly differences were supposed to be addressed without reference to political or religious differences. See Goldgar, *Impolite Learning*, p. 227, arguing the intrusion of politics meant people failed. But still, they tried.

24. *Directions for a proper Choice of Authors to Form a Library, which May both Improve and Entertain the Mind, and be of real Use in the Conduct of Life*, 1766, p. 14; Goldsmith, *Collected Works*, Vol. 1, p. 45.

25. Quoted by J.E. Norton, *A Bibliography of the Works of Edward Gibbon*, Oxford, 1940, p. 70.

26. Goldsmith, *Collected Works*, Vol. V, p. 288.

27. Ibid., p. 284. The relevant passage in Polybius is corrupt but that makes Goldsmith's motives more evident.

28. Goldsmith was paid £21 for his *History of England in a series of Letters from a Nobleman to his Son at University* (1764), discussed below. See Ralph M. Wardle, *Oliver Goldsmith*, Archon Books, 1969, p. 148.

29. Walpole, *Correspondence*, ed. Lewis, 15 March 1783, 15: 173, quoted by Peter Sabor, 'Horace Walpole as a Historian', *Studies in the Eighteenth Century* 6, eds Colin Duckworth and Homer le Grand, special issue of *Eighteenth Century Life*, 11, No. 1, February 1987, pp. 5–17, p. 7.

30. Alexander Campbell, *An Examination of Lord Bolingbroke's Letters on History*, 2nd edition, 1753, pp. 136–7; p. 45. Compare Philalethes Rusticus, *The Impertinence of Modern Antiquarians Displayed*, 1739, p. 20, attacking notions of an invisible smith to whom Wayland's Smithy in Oxfordshire might have been a memorial: 'are they not all Stories much fitter for a Nurse than a Doctor?'

31. John Whitaker, *The Genuine History of the Britons Asserted against Mr Macpherson*, 1773, 2nd edition, p. 306.

32. Thus Gilbert Burnet, *The History of the Rights of Princes*, 1681, p. 39, criticises Maimbourg's history of Arianism for being more like a novel than history and was in turn accused of preferring fictional chimeras, by George Sewell, *A Review of Three Letters Written to the Bishop of Salisbury*, 1714, p. 7.

33. Quoted by George Sewell, *The Third Letter to the Bishop of Salisbury*, 1714, p. 67.

34. *The Letters of Samuel Johnson*, 4 vols, ed. Bruce Redford, Princeton NJ, Princeton University Press, 1992; to Boswell, 27 October 1779, Vol. III, p. 200.

35. See Gerald MacLean, 'Re-siting the Subject' in *Epistolary Histories*, eds Gilroy and Verhoeven, pp. 176–91, especially pp. 180–91 for an illuminating discussion of secrecy. *The King's Cabinet Opened* is a key text here.

36. The expression is John Rushworth's: *Historical Collections of Private Passages of State*, 8 vols, 1659–1701, Vol. I, 1659, Preface, n.p.; Vol. V, 1692, title page.

37. See Ros Ballaster, *Seductive Forms: Women's Amatory Fiction from 1684 to 1740*, Oxford, Clarendon Press, 1992, especially pp. 42–60. Her terminology of romance, amatory fiction and political engagement connects women's fiction and politics; I discuss here only the ways in which secret history and history used letters differently.

38. Paris, 1689, p. 18, p. 5.
39. For example, Hugh Speke, *The Secret History of the Happy Revolution in 1688*, 1715; Count Mirabeau, *The Secret History of the Court of Berlin*, 2 vols, 1789.
40. *The Fair Concubine: Or, the Secret History of the Beautiful Vanella*, 3rd edition 1752, p. 35.
41. Madame de Villedieu in *The Secret History of the Court of Augustus Caesar*, 1729, daringly took as her subject the love life of Ovid (which turns out to be all talk).
42. Compare Ballaster, *Seductive Forms*, p. 43 on bienséance (decorum) and vraisemblance (truth to nature) in seventeenth-century French romances by women.
43. *The Secret History of an Old Shoe*, 1734, p. 6.
44. *Concubine*, p. 17.
45. See *Novel and Romance 1700–1800: A Documentary Record*, ed. Ioan Williams, Routledge and Kegan Paul, 1970.
46. *Collected Works*, Vol. I, p. 80.
47. *The Life of Richard Nash, Esq; Late Master of Ceremonies at Bath*, 1762, 2nd edition, p. 3.
48. John Evelyn, *Letters . . . to and from William Nicolson*, Vol. I, p. 143.
49. Ibid., p. 144.
50. Jayne Elizabeth Lewis, 'Mary Stuart's "Fatal Box": Sentimental History and the Revival of the Casket Letters Controversy' in *The Age of Johnson*, ed. Paul Korshin, New York, AMS Press, Vol. 7, 1996, pp. 427–73, p. 432.
51. Campbell, *Examination*, p. 14.
52. *Directions for a proper Choice*, p. 13.
53. Goldsmith, *Collected Works*, Vol. V, pp. 288, 338.
54. A Fellow of the Antiquary Society, *A Sketch of the Materials for a History of Cheshire*, 1771, p. 39.
55. *Monthly Review*, October 1773, p. 305. Gower offered his plates, which cost him 50 guineas, free to any interested historian.
56. The project did not progress and eventually the materials were dispersed.
57. Okie, *Augustan Historical Writing*, pp. 17–18 on the late 17th century and pp. 118–19 on the 1740s, which saw the publication of, amongst others, Ormonde papers and the Earl of Stafford's letters in 1739; Thurloe papers in 1742 (7 vols mostly of letters from the interregnum period), Burleigh papers in 1742, Sidney papers in 1746, Harleian papers 1744–46 and the Somers Tracts 1748–52. Okie concludes, p. 119, 'In the late Augustan period, printed sources were still far more accessible to historians than manuscript materials.'
58. Ibid., p. 9. Okie concedes the existence of chairs in history at the universities of Oxford and Cambridge but claims the professors did no work.
59. Burnet, *An Introduction to the Third Volume of the History of the Reformation of the Church of England*, 2nd edition, 1714, pp. 7–8.
60. See Goldgar, *Impolite Learning*, pp. 231–5 on how scholars found writing dedicatory epistles increasingly repugnant and how, ironically, the ending of patronage benefitted belle lettrists rather than scholars.
61. Thomas Arnold, *Sketches from the Carte Papers*, Dublin, 1888, p. 4. There were initially 153 large bundles, to which Carte added the mass of letters found in 14 wicker bins at Kilkenny Castle.
62. Macpherson, *Original Papers*, 2 vols, Dublin, 1775, Vol. 1, p. 5.
63. 'Philalethes', *Impartial Reflections upon Dr. Burnet's Posthumous History*, 1724, n.p.
64. Gilbert Burnet, *Some Account of the Life and Writings of Gilbert Late Lord Bishop of Sarum*, 1715, p. 7.
65. This is not a simple antithesis: q.v. Gibbon, who admired Livy greatly.

66. Goldsmith, *Collected Works*, Vol. V, pp. 283–4.
67. *The English, Scotch and Irish Historical Libraries*, 3rd edition, 1736 was Nicolson's national survey of collections, both public and private. Concerning the history of Oxford University, for instance, the Cotton Library had 21 vols of charters, orders, statutes, decrees, letters etc.; p. 150.
68. Ibid., p. 247.
69. Where there appeared fewer, it was possibly only because the papers were not yet organised. The Cotton Library had 43 vols of treaties between the English, Scots and French and as many more in an unbound state.
70. Nicholson, *English... Libraries*, p. 246.
71. Ibid., pp. 246–7.
72. Carte, *A General History of England*, Vol. III, p. iii.
73. Oldmixon, *Critical History*, p. 240.
74. Macpherson, *Original Papers*, Vol. I, p. 9.
75. Horatio Walpole, *An Answer to the Latter Part of Lord Bolingbroke's Letters on the Study and Use of History*, 1762, p. 7.
76. William Russell, *The History of Modern Europe*, 1779–84, pt 1, p. iii.
77. On Macaulay as historian, see Bridget Hill, *The Republican Virago: The Life and Times of Catharine Macaulay, Historian*, Oxford, Clarendon Press, 1992, ch. 2; also Devoney Looser, *British Women Writers and the Writing of History, 1670–1820*, Baltimore and London, Johns Hopkins University Press, 2000, ch. 5.
78. Towards the end of the century, women were more visible as writers of educational literature, including history. This is usually for (and about) children being educated at home by their mothers. Dialogues joined letters as an unpretentious form of pedagogy. Compare Hannah Neale's *Sacred History in Familiar Dialogues*, 1796.
79. Macaulay, *The History of England from the Revolution to the Present Time in a Series of Letters to a Friend* [the Reverend Dr Wilson], Bath, 1778, Vol. 1 (no more published) p. 271.
80. Macaulay, *The History of England from the Accession of James I to that of the Brunswick Line*, 8 vols, 1763–83, Vol. 1, 1763, p. xiii.
81. See Henry Rowlands' preface to *Mona Antiqua Restaurata*, Dublin, 1723, for elaborate solar metaphors.
82. Stuart Piggott, *Ancient Britons and the Antiquarian Imagination: Ideas from the Renaissance to the Regency*, New York, Thames and Hudson, 1989, pp. 20–1.
83. Compare *The Universal Librarian for April, May, June*, 1751, pp. 146–9 on a coin inscribed 'Oriuna', depicting a woman, and whether her name was derived from Oriens or Orion.
84. Goldgar, *Impolite Learning*, p. 17. See also p. 65 on how journals took up many of these functions. For a good example, see *The Correspondence of Thomas Blount (1618–1679): A Recusant Antiquary*, ed. Theo Bongaerts, Amsterdam, Holland University Press, 1978.
85. Rowlands, *Mona Antiqua*, p. 335. Compare Levine, *Woodward's Shield*, passim, on Lhywd and antiquarian feuds and alliances.
86. Nicolson, *Letters*, Vol. 1, p. 39. Cabinets of coins and other objects, even more than collections of papers, were in private ownership.
87. Blount, *Correspondence*, p. 95. Two of the three examples given show Wood's source to be Blount, who had the information by letters from others. See similarly Gilbert White, *The Natural History and Antiquities of Selbourne, in the County of Southampton: with Engravings, and an Appendix*, 1789, which joins natural history and local antiquarianism in letters drawing on gentlemanly correspondence.

88. Goldgar, *Impolite Learning*, pp. 161, 163.
89. Piggott, *Ancient Britons*, pp. 136–39 discusses it but with no consideration of the role of letters.
90. Francis Wise, *A Letter to Dr. Mead*, Oxford, 1738, p. 4.
91. George North, *An Answer to a Scandalous Libel, Entitled The Impertinence and Imposture of Modern Antiquarians Display'd* ... 1741, p. 38.
92. W.B. Carnochan, *Gibbon's Solitude: The Inward World of the Historian*, Stanford, Stanford University Press, 1987, p. 38.
93. Ibid., p. 39.
94. Philalethes, *Impertinence*, p. 17.
95. Macpherson, *Original Papers*, Vol. I, p. 1. He thought it was a particularly English trait.
96. Oldmixon, *Critical History*, p. 176, describing with irony Echard's *History*: 'see what *Heroes* and Saints are lifted on King *Charles*'s Side; what *Cravens* and *Scoundrels* on the Side of the Parliament'.
97. Charles Owen, *The Danger of the Church and State from Foreigners*, 1750, 3rd edition, pp. 4–9. Compare the more familiar Whig argument which saw no contradiction in executing or deposing particular kings in order to safeguard the monarchy.
98. Langford, *Englishness Identified*, p. 1.
99. Besides Rupert Green, *Abstract*, see Jane Austen's *The History of England* (written 1791).
100. *The Conclusion of Bishop Burnet's History of his own Life and Times*, 1724, p. 37.
101. Hayley, *Essay on History*, p. 83.
102. Goldsmith, *Collected Works*, Vol. V, p. 278.
103. John Clubbe, *The History and Antiquities of the Ancient Villa of Wheatfield, in the County of Suffolk*, 1758, p. iv.
104. Nicolson, *Libraries*, p. 181.
105. *Love-Letters from King Henry VIII*, 1714, p. xxii.
106. Macpherson, *Original Papers*, Vol. II, p. 503. Sarah Churchill denied this in her *Memoirs*.
107. In John Breval, *The History of the House of Nassau, from its earliest Known Origin, continued Down to the Present Times*, 1734.
108. Abraham Lemoine, *A Defence of the Sacred History*, 1753, p. 8; Thomas Hunter, *A Sketch of the Philosophical Character of the late Lord Viscount Bolingbroke*, 1770, pp. 113–16.
109. Robert Clayton, *A Vindication of the Histories of the Old and New Testament*, Dublin, 1752. These ideas led later to him falling out with the church.
110. Compare D.J. Womersley, 'Lord Bolingbroke and Eighteenth-Century Historiography' in *The Eighteenth Century: Theory and Interpretation*, Vol. 28, No. 3, Fall 1987, pp. 217–34: 'An exile in France from 1715 to 1723, he is a medium through whom Continental ideas about the writing of history were introduced into English', p. 218.
111. Hunter, *Sketch*, n.p.
112. Ibid., p. 67.
113. A Free-Thinker, *Miscellaneous Observations on the Works of the late Lord Viscount Bolingbroke* ... 1755, p. 24.
114. *Critical Remarks upon the late Lord Viscount Bolingbroke's Letters on the Study and use of History, As far as they regard Sacred History*, 1754, p. 8.
115. Peter Whalley, *A Vindication of the Gospels*, 1753, p. 12.
116. Hunter, *Sketch*, p. 119.

117. *Critical Remarks*, p. 64.
118. Campbell, *Examination*, p. ii.
119. Ibid., p. 30.
120. Ibid., p. 41.
121. A version of Chesterfield's letters did circulate as a history textbook: *Letters Upon Ancient History, in French and English; Chiefly written by the late Earl of Chesterfield To his Son, Philip Stanhope, Esq. Now published for the use of Schools and Private Pupils*, 1783.
122. *The Roman History, in a Series of Letters from a Nobleman to his Son*, 2 vols (c.1774), Vol. I, p. 2.
123. Ibid., Vol. I, p. 12. The father–son model also has classical precedents. 'Frederick' may be allusive; it was the name of the eldest son of George II, who died in 1751.
124. Ibid., p. 7.
125. Keryl Kavanagh, 'Paradigms of Pleasure and Virtue: Oliver Goldsmith's Fictive Histories', *Studies in the Eighteenth Century 6*, pp. 163–9, sees the persona's appeal as simple snobbery: 'given the society in which he lived, [it] allowed his judgment to be accepted', p. 165. I think this is too simple.
126. *An History of England, in a Series of Letters from a Nobleman to his Son* in *Collected Works*, Vol. I, p. 293.
127. William Zachs, *Without Regard to Good Manners: A Biography of Gilbert Stuart 1743–1786*, Edinburgh, Edinburgh University Press, 1992, p. 13.
128. Catharine Macaulay, *History of England from the Accession of James I*, Vol. 1, 1763, p. vii.
129. Ibid., p. ix.
130. The association goes back of course to Filmer's *Patriarcha* and Locke's *Two Treatises on Government*, texts some eighteenth-century writers still had in mind.
131. On eighteenth-century historians' uncomfortable engagement with secret history in queenly history, see my article, 'Love Stories? Epistolary Histories of Mary Queen of Scots', *Epistolary Histories*, eds Gilroy and Verhoeven, pp. 74–98.
132. *Athenian Letters: or, the Epistolary Correspondence of an Agent of the King of Persia, Residing at Athens during the Peloponnesian War*, 1781, p. x.
133. Ibid., p. 443. Anxieties about effeminacy are here obviously also connected to orientalism. Though the Persian Cleander is the main character, the *Letters* are not Persian – not just to avoid confusion with Montesquieu's but to promote Hellenism.
134. Ibid., p. 457.
135. Ibid., p. 458.
136. Ibid., p. 338. Compare the last two lines of Mary Leapor's poem 'Man the Monarch', also written in the 1740s: 'ev'ry Cottage brings / A long Succession of Domestic Kings.'
137. *The Works of the late Miss Catherine Talbot*, ed. Rev. Montagu Pennington, 9th edition, 1819, p. 235 (Dialogue II.)
138. Sabor, 'Walpole as Historian', p. 5; Mowl, *Walpole*, p. 2.
139. Sabor, 'Walpole as Historian', pp. 13–14.
140. Ibid., p. 13.
141. Mowl, *Walpole*, p. 23; Sabor, 'Walpole as Historian', p. 15.
142. Clifford Siskin, *The Work of Writing: Literature and Social Change in Britain, 1700–1830*, Baltimore and London, The Johns Hopkins University Press, 1998, p. 47.
143. Quoted by Siskin, ibid., p. 48.

144. Ibid., pp. 48, 49. For a response to Hume which addressed distinctions between philosophy, history, religion and politics, see Daniel MacQueen, *Letters on Mr Hume's History of Great Britain*, Edinburgh, 1776.
145. Walpole, *Correspondence*, ed. Lewis, 25 August 1784; 25.520.
146. Wilmarth S. Lewis, *Rescuing Horace Walpole*, New Haven, Yale University Press, 1978, p. 142.
147. 9 May 1778; 24.379.
148. 'Political climate' is a twentieth-century idiom, but perhaps hinted at here.
149. Thus Mowl, *Walpole*, p. 23 on his 'determination to treat letter-writing almost as a career'; Bruce Redford, *The Converse of the Pen*, ch. 4.
150. 21 January 1767; 22.480
151. To Montagu, 6 November 1756; 9.203.
152. To Gibbon, 14 February 1776; 41.335–6. He refers to the Roman emperors treated by Gibbon in the first volume of *Decline and Fall*.
153. 3 February 1760; 21.368.
154. Compare Gilbert White's use of oral history in the form of old people's memories.
155. 5 December 1760; 21.459.
156. 12 May 1783; 15.180.
157. 17 July 1755; 35.236.
158. 28 February 1769; 23.94.
159. To Mann, 26 June 1765; 22.306.
160. *Lennox*, p. 51 (July 1761).
161. Nathaniel Wraxall, *Memoirs of the Courts of Berlin, Dresden, Warsaw and Vienna*, 2 vols, Dublin, 1799, Vol. I, pp. 1–2.
162. Lady Mary Wortley Montagu burnt her memoirs sheet by sheet as she wrote them; Samuel Johnson burnt his on completion.
163. To Boswell, 9 September 1769; *Letters*, ed. Chapman, Vol. III, p. 329.
164. *Memoirs of King George II*, 3 vols, ed. John Brooke, New Haven and London, Yale University Press, 1985, Vol. II, p. 2.
165. 30 September 1785; 16.282.
166. To Mann, 30 August 1782; 25.3122.
167. 26 July 1745; 19.78.
168. 20 August 1742; 18.29.
169. Stuart Sherman, *Telling Time: Clocks, Diaries and English Diurnal Form, 1660–1785*, Chicago and London, Chicago University Press, 1996, p. 12. He discusses diaries, newspapers and journal-letters, but not letters *per se*, interestingly.
170. Compare *Census of British Newspapers and Periodicals, 1620–1800*, eds Ronald S. Crane, F.B. Kaye and M.E. Prior, 1927 repr. 1966, Holland Press, 1979. See also Davis, *Factual Fictions*, on the instability of news as a discourse.
171. 7 May 1760; 21.403.
172. 30 January 1757; 21.52.
173. 23 March 1782; 29.207. Sherman, *Telling Time*, p. 12, notes that in discussing relations between chronography and narrative, Paul Ricoeur's key verb is 'emplot'.
174. To Mann, 9 May 1779; 24.471.
175. 22 March 1771; 23.281–2.
176. 13 September 1759; 21.328–9.
177. 1 November 1764; 38.455.
178. To William Cole, 21 June 1782; 2.329.
179. To Lady Ossory, 13 September 1798; 34.64.
180. To Mann, 18 January 1781; 25.116.

181. To the Earl of Hertford, 5 October 1764; 38.443–4.
182. To Mason, 18 February 1778; 28.357.
183. 18 June 1758; 21.212.
184. To Mann, 9 April 1772; 23.400.
185. Alexander Pettit, 'Lord Bolingbroke's Remarks on the History of England and the Rhetoric of Political Controversy', *The Age of Johnson*, Vol. 7, ed. Paul Korshin, New York, AMS Press, 1996, pp. 365–95, p. 365.
186. To Henry Seymour Conway, 29 October 1762; 38.187–8.
187. 13 February 1768; 14.171.
188. To the Earl of Strafford, 27 November 1781; 35.363.
189. 18 November 1771; 23.350.
190. 17 November 1763; 22.185–6.
191. To Mason, 12 May 1778; 28.393.
192. 22 March 1762; 10.22.
193. To Mann, 9 June 1768; 23.32.
194. 30 March 1781; 25.141–2. Compare to Mann, 3 October 1762 (22.85) on heroes: 'How many must be wretched, before one can be renowned!' He is most sarcastic about empires in *Memoirs*, Vol. II, pp. 15–16.
195. To Lady Ossory, 8 January 1780; 33.158. Contrast John Brooke's otherwise suggestive verdict on Walpole, *Memoirs*, Vol. I, p. xxvii: 'He was insensitive to ideas, but acutely sensitive to personalities.' I suggest his own personality is an idea.
196. John Sekora, *Luxury: The Concept in Western Thought, Eden to Smollett*, Baltimore and London, Johns Hopkins University Press, 1977, p. 89.
197. To Mann, 28 December 1761; 21.558–9.
198. 21 December 1773, 23.536; 12 May 1778, 28.392.
199. To Mann, 26 May 1762; 22.39.
200. Ibid.
201. Johnson planned both a military dictionary and a history of war. He never wrote them but the contingency of interests is suggestive. See *Letters*, ed. Chapman, Vol. I, p. 21.
202. To Mann, 31 December 1769; 23.166.
203. To Mann, 16 July 1776; 24.228.
204. To Mann, 18 January 770; 23.176.
205. Ibid., 11 November 1774; 24.55.
206. To Mason, 5 April 1777; 28.295.
207. 30 November 1761; 15.73.

8 Writing as a Christian

1. See Isabel Rivers, *Reason, Grace and Sentiment: A Study of the Language of Religion and Ethics in England, 1660–1780*, Vol. I: *Whichcote to Wesley*, Cambridge, Cambridge University Press, 1991, p. 3.
2. *The Letters of John Wesley*, 8 vols, ed. John Telford, Standard Edition, Epworth Press, 1931, Vol. 1, p. xviii. Cited hereafter as Wesley, *Letters*.
3. On Methodism, see Kenneth Hylson-Smith, *The Churches in England from Elizabeth I to Elizabeth II*, 3 vols, SCM Press, 1997, Vol. II: 1689–1833, ch. 4, especially pp. 158–68; David Hempton, *The Religion of the People: Methodism and Popular Religion c.1750–1900*, Routledge, 1996 and *Methodism: Empire of the Spirit*, New Haven, Yale University Press, 2005; D.W. Bebbington, *Evangelicalism in Modern Britain: A History from the 1730s to the 1980s*, Routledge, 1989 repr. 1993, especially chs 1 and 2.

4. Isaac Carter, *The Tomb Stone of the Late Rev. Huntington, A Monument of Unequalled Arrogance and Insult to the Whole Protestant Church in the British Empire*, Portsea, Hants, 1813, p. 35 – not an admirer!

5. Rowland Hill, *Journal of a Tour through the North of England and Parts of Scotland*, 1799, pp. 13, 98, 166.

6. John Willison and John Bonar, *The Duty and Advantage of Religious Societies, Proven from Scripture and Reason: With proper Directions to all who either are or may be engaged in such Societies*, Kilmarnock, 1783, p. 83.

7. *The Pre-existence of Souls and Universal Restitution Considered as Scripture Doctrines*, Taunton, 1798, p. 25. The Burnham Society was modelled on the interdenominational college of Trevecca in Wales, founded by the Countess of Huntingdon.

8. Ibid., p. 58.

9. *The Evangelical Magazine*, January 1798, p. 7.

10. *Susanna Wesley: The Complete Writings*, ed. Charles Wallace Jr, New York and Oxford, Oxford University Press, 1997, p. 33: the editor on her letters in relation to her husband, brother and sons.

11. Wesley, *Letters* 2: 174.

12. Ibid., 4: 24; to Dr Free who wanted Wesley to answer privately the criticisms he had made publicly.

13. Ibid., 4: 90.

14. Ibid., 1: 40.

15. Beilby Porteus, *A Review of the Life and Character of the Right Rev. Dr. Thomas Secker, Late Lord Archbishop of Canterbury*, 5th edition, 1797, p. 68.

16. Joseph Proud, *An Impartial Account of a Public Disputation on Water Baptism, held on the 25th Day of October, 1787, at the general Baptist Chapel, in Bar-Street, Norwich, between John Bousell, a Speaker amongst the People called Quakers, and Joseph Proud, Pastor of the general Baptist Congregation, in Ber-Street, With some further Observations in Vindication of that Sacred Ordinance*, Norwich, n.d., p. 2.

17. Ibid., pp. 10, 11, 13.

18. Ibid., p. 29.

19. Ibid., pp. 31–2.

20. John Bousell, *The Ram's Horn Sounded Seven Times: Being a Visitation of Divine Love to those Merchants of Babylon who have taken upon themselves the office of Teachers among the people called Baptists, whose mountain, built in their own wisdom, will be destroyed by the stone cut out of the mountain without hands (the wisdom and power of God), with every other mountain in the kingdom of Babylon – The false church shall fall, and the true Church be built again*, Norwich, [1787]; pt II, p. 39.

21. Ibid., p. 3.

22. Ibid., p. 11.

23. Ibid., pt I, p. 41.

24. Ibid., pt II, pp. 25–6.

25. Isaiah Birt, *A Vindication of the Baptists, in Three Letters, Addressed to a Friend in Saltash*, Bristol, 1793.

26. George Whitefield, *A Letter to the Right Reverend the Bishop of London, and the other the Right Rev. the Bishops, Concern'd in the Publication of a Pamphlet, entitled, Observations upon the Conduct and Behaviour of a certain Sect usually distinguished by the Name of Methodists*, 1744.

27. Ibid., p. 6, p. 22.

28. Samuel Dampier, *A Letter to Mr. Thomas Coad, of Stoford, Occasioned By a Prayer of his, in the Presbyterian Congregation in Yeovil*, Bristol, 1740, pp. 4, 25.

29. Henry Dodwell, *A Preliminary Defence of the Epistolary Discourse, Concerning the Distinction between Soul and Spirit*, 1707, 'An Address to my Adversaries', n.p. Part of what makes Dodwell's prose so perplexed is his unusual underlinings. His 1706 text was *An Epistolary Discourse, Proving, from the Scriptures and the First Fathers, that the Soul is a Principle naturally Mortal, But Immortalised Actually by the Pleasure of God, to Punishment; or, to Reward, by its Union with the Divine Baptismal Spirit.*
30. *Preliminary Defence*, n.p.
31. Samuel Clarke, *A Third Defense of an Argument Made use of in a Letter to Mr Dodwel[l], to prove the Immateriality and Natural Immortality of the Soul*, 1708, p. 68.
32. Thomas Milles, B.D. *The Natural Immortality of the Soul Asserted, and Proved from the Scriptures, and First Fathers: In Answer to Mr Dodwell's Epistolary Discourse, in which he Endeavours to Prove the Soul to be a Principle Naturally Mortal*, Oxford, 1707, p. xx. Like Dodwell's, a 500 page book.
33. John Norris, *A Letter to Mr. Dodwell, Concerning the Immortality of the Soul of Man*, 4th edition, 1722; To the Reader, n.p., p. 15.
34. Henry Dodwell, *A Letter from the Learned Mr. Henry Dodwell to the Right Reverend the Bishop of Sarum, in which he owns his Spiritual Character, but not his Temporal*, 2nd edition, 1712, pp. 15–16. Sarum is an ecclesiastical name for Salisbury.
35. *Four Letters which Passed between the Right Reverend the Lord Bishop of Sarum and Mr. Henry Dodwell, Printed from the Originals*, 1713, p. 37.
36. George Sewell, *The Clergy and the Present Ministry Defended*, 3rd edition, 1713, p. 2. See also *A Second Letter to the Bishop of Salisbury, Upon the Publication of His New Volume of Sermons*, 1713, p. 7.
37. Benjamin Hoadly, *Some Considerations Humbly Offered to the Right Reverend the Lord Bishop of Exeter*, 3rd edition, 1709, p. 5.
38. Benjamin Hoadly, *A Humble Reply to the Right Reverend the Lord Bishop of Exeter's Answer*, 1709, p. 4.
39. Ibid., p. 67.
40. *The Lord Bishop of Exeter's Answer to Mr. Hoadly's Letter*, 2nd edition, 1709, p. 56.
41. John Wesley, *An Earnest Appeal to Men of Reason and Religion*, 5th edition, Dublin, p. 14.
42. *Theatrical Entertainments Consistent with Society, Morality, and Religion*, 1768, p. 19.
43. A Moral Philosopher, *Deism Fairly Stated, and Fully Vindicated, from the Gross Imputations and Groundless Calumnies of Modern Believers*, 1746, p. 44.
44. See Arthur Skevington Wood, *Revelation and Reason: Wesleyan Responses to Eighteenth-Century Rationalism*, n.p. The Wesley Fellowship, 1992, and Rivers, *Reason, Grace and Sentiment*, pp. 207–8 on Wesley.
45. Henry Dodwell, *Christianity Not Founded on Argument; and the True Principle of Gospel-Evidence Assigned: in a Letter to a Young Gentleman at Oxford*, 1741, p. 4. Subsequent page references are incorporated into the text.
46. Quoted by, amongst others, Anne Dutton, *Divine, Moral, and Historical Miscellanies in Prose and Verse*, 3 vols, 1761–63, Vol. I, p. 51.
47. Quoted by Benedict Anderson, *Imagined Communities: Reflections on the Origin and Spread of Nationalism*, Verso, 1983 rev. 1991, 1996, p. 24.
48. Sceptical time may hope for a hereafter but doubts the heretofore, or 'In the beginning'. Deists were most critical of scripture's version of prehistory.
49. Thomas Mole, *The Grounds of Christian Faith Rational: In Answer to Christianity Not founded on Argument*, 1743, p. 5.
50. Henry Etough, *A Letter to the Author of Christianity Not Founded on Argument, &c. By a Young Gentleman of Cambridge*, 1742, p. 13.

51. John Leland, *Remarks on a Late Pamphlet, entitled Christianity not founded on Argument*, 1744, p. 70.
52. Etough, *A Letter*, pp. 4, 27.
53. John Brine, *The Christian Religion Not Destitute of Arguments Sufficient to Support it*, 1743, p. 1.
54. George Benson, *The Reasonablenesse* [sic] *of the Christian Religion, As Delivered in the Scriptures*, 1743, p. iv.
55. *The Oxford Young Gentleman's Reply to a Book entitled, Christianity not Founded on Argument, &c.*, 1743, p. 29.
56. Ibid., p. 33.
57. Philip Doddridge, *The Perspecuity and Solidity of those Evidences of Christianity, To Which the generality of its Professors among us may attain, Illustrated and Vindicated; in a letter to the Author of a late Pamphlet, intitled, Christianity not founded on Argument, &c.*, 1742, p. 6. On Doddridge's reluctance in controversy, see Rivers, *Reason, Grace and Sentiment*, pp. 180–204.
58. Ibid., p. 56.
59. Ibid., p. 30.
60. Philip Doddridge, *A Second Letter to the Author of a Pamphlet, Intitled, Christianity Not founded on Argument, &c.*, 1743, p. 59; *An Answer to a late Pamphlet, Intitled Christianity not founded on Argument, &c.*, 1743, p. 61.
61. Jon Mee, *Dangerous Enthusiasm: William Blake and the Culture of Radicalism in the 1790s*, Oxford, Clarendon Press, 1992, p. 14.
62. Ibid; see also pp. 162–3 on Paine's hostility to the authority of the Bible.
63. He also used the *Gentleman's Magazine* for this purpose, which created further epistolary ripples. Compare *GM* Vol. LIX (1789) pt 2, pp. 706–7.
64. Joseph Priestley, *Defences of Unitarianism for the Years 1788 & 1789*, Birmingham, n.d, p. vii. Subsequent page references are included in the text.
65. R. Watson, *An Apology for the Bible, in a Series of Letters Addressed to Tom Paine, Author of a Book entitled, The Age of Reason, Part the Second, being an Investigation of True and of Fabulous Theology*, 4th edition, 1796, p. 1. Subsequent references are included in the text.
66. Paine wrote the first part of *The Age of Reason* in difficult circumstances in revolutionary France, without access to a Bible and under threat of imprisonment or worse. *The Life and Major Writings of Thomas Paine*, ed. Philip S. Foner, New York, Citadel Press, 1945, pp. 514–15: 'notwithstanding which, I have produced a work that no Bible believer, though writing at his ease, and with a library of Church books about him, can refute'. Paine repeated some of his principles in a letter to Samuel Adams of 1803 whose publication brought him much trouble. See John Keane, *Tom Paine: A Political Life*, Bloomsbury, 1995, p. 47: 'the letter to Adams felt like a knife in the heart of Christianity'.
67. Wesley, *Letters*, 5: 68.
68. Thus Susanna Wesley wrote to John in 1726: 'it seemed a palpable piece of cruelty to make you pay for a letter unless I could send money too'. *Complete Writings*, p. 126.
69. See W.M. Jacob, *Lay People and Religion in the Early Eighteenth Century*, Cambridge, Cambridge University Press, 1996, ch. 2.
70. Joseph Jefferson, *The Young Evangelist; Exemplified in a Life of the Late Rev. John Savage*, Southampton, n.d. (but published in a shortened version in the *Evangelical Magazine* of December 1798), p. 35.
71. Ibid., p. 26.

72. William Huntington, S.S. *A Letter to the Rev. T. Joss*, 1794, p. 12.
73. *Huntingtonia*, 1796, p. 40. See also Ebenezer Hooper, *The Celebrated Coalheaver; or Reminiscences of the Rev. William Huntington, S.S.*, London, Gadsby, 1871, and his sequel, *Facts, Letters and Documents (chiefly unpublished), Concerning William Huntington, his Family & Friends: Forming an Addenda to 'The Celebrated Coalheaver.'* Gadsby, 1872. Huntington died in 1813, aged 69, but was still arousing controversy in the 1850s.
74. Hooper, *Celebrated Coalheaver*, p. 43.
75. *Huntingtonia*, p. 40.
76. Agnes Smyth, for instance, choked with rage at the sight of a lord going in a coach to the playhouse; *The Religion of the Heart, Delineated in a Series of Letters, Written by Mrs. Agnes Smyth*, 1783, p. 19. Rowland Hill, *Journal*, p. 146, referred to the playhouse as Satan's synagogue.
77. *Some Account of the State of Religion in London: in Four Letters to a Friend in the Country*, 1774, p. 6.
78. Jonathan Dickinson, *Familiar Letters to a Gentleman, upon a variety of seasonable and important Subjects in Religion*, Dublin, 1752.
79. Anne Dutton, *Miscellanies*, Vol. I, p. 97. On the characteristics of evangelicalism, see D.W. Bebbington, *Evangelicalism: A History from the 1730s to the 1980s*, 1989, p. 3, and Hylson-Smith, *Churches in England*, pp. 183–4.
80. Anne Dutton, *A Letter to Such of the Servants of Christ, who May have any Scruple about the Lawfulness of Printing any Thing Written by a Woman: To Shew, That Book-teaching is Private, with Respect to the Church, and Permitted to Private Christians; Yea, Commanded to Those, of Either Sex, Who are Gifted for, and Inclin'd to Engage in This Service*, 1743, p. 11. For worms, see Psalm XXII, v.6.
81. William Huntington, S.S., *Letters on Ministerial Qualifications*, 2nd edition, 1788, p. 41.
82. [William Combe], *The Fanatic Saints; or Bedlamites Inspired*, 2nd edition, 1778, p. 19.
83. John Wesley favoured the former, Charles Wesley the latter. In 1752 they nearly fell out about it. See Mabel Richmond Brailsford, *A Tale of Two Brothers: John and Charles Wesley*, Rupert Hart-Davis, 1954, p. 236.
84. George Stonhouse, as reported in *The Pre-existence of Souls*, p. 43; George Trosse, in *The Life of George Trosse, Late Minister of the Gospel in the City of Exon, who died January 11th, 1712/13*, Exeter, 1714, p. 89.
85. A Clergyman of Wales [Griffith Jones], *Welsh Piety; or, the Needful Charity of Promoting the Salvation of the Poor*, 1740; Beilby, *A Letter to the Clergy of the Diocese of Chester, Concerning Sunday Schools*, 2nd edition, 1786, especially p. 16, where he points out that children who learn to read can teach their illiterate parents about religion.
86. Wesley, *Letters*, 3: 175.
87. Wesley, *Letters*, 2: 384.
88. Huntington, *Letters on Ministerial Qualifications*, pp. 42–3. Subsequent page references are included in the text.
89. John Locke, *A Second Vindication of the Reasonableness of Christianity, &c.*, in *The Works of John Locke in Nine Volumes*, 12th edition, 1824, Vol. VI, pp. 377, 275.
90. *The Barber's Mirror; Or a Portrait of the Rev. William Huntington, Drawn from Real Life: Being Remarks on that Gentleman's Pamphlet entitled 'the Barber:' With an Account of his Strange and Deplorable FRENZY*, 1791, pp. 10–11.
91. He sported a black wig.
92. William Huntington, S.S., *Discoveries and Cautions from the Streets of Zion, by a Watchman of the Night: in a Sermon, delivered at Providence Chapel, October 22, 1798* ... 2nd edition, 1802, p. 12.

93. Thomas Hacker, *Believers Entanglement by the Moral Law, Proved Inconsistent with the Abolition of the Law*, 1794, pp. 11, 48.

94. William Huntington, S.S., *A Letter to the Rev. Caleb Evans, M.A. Master of the Seminary at Bristol*, 2nd edition, 1798, p. 105; *A Feeble Dispute with a wise and learned Man*, 1793, p. 40.

95. William Huntington, S.S., *The Mystery of Godliness; in a Letter to an Erroneous Man*, 1794, p. 93. These questions connect to key doctrinal arguments; they were not the Enlightenment equivalent of how many angels could fit on a pinhead.

96. Ibid., p. 102.

97. Huntington had compared 'Onesimus', alias Garnet Terry, to Paine. Others thought Paine and Huntington were similar, in damaging Christianity. See Hooper, *Facts, Letters and Documents*, pp. 31, 49.

98. Elizabeth Morton, *The Daughter's Defence of her Father; or, An Answer to the letter addressed to Mr. Huntington, Written by Madame (de Mara) Flora, & Co*, 1788, p. 8.

99. Ibid., p. 17.

100. Ibid., p. 52.

101. In order to show Huntington her conversion was sincere, Morton sent him strips of her nun's robes to use as shaving cloths!

102. Maria de Fleury, *An Answer to the Daughter's Defence of her Father, Addressed to her Father Himself*, 1788, p. 7.

103. Ibid., pp. 13–14.

104. Wesley, *Letters*, 5: 257, 311.

105. Anne Dutton, *A Letter to such of the Servants of Christ*, 1743, p. 4.

106. de Fleury, *An Answer*, p. 50.

107. William Huntington, S.S. *The Broken Cistern, and the Springing Well: Or, the Difference Between Head Notions and Heart Religion, Vain Jangling and Sound Doctrine*, 2nd edition, 1800, p. vi, p. 91.

108. de Fleury, *A Serious Address to the Rev. Mr. Huntington; containing some Remarks on his Sermon, entitled 'The Servant of the Lord, described and vindicated.'*, 1788, p. 21.

109. *Huntingtonia*, p. 19.

110. Dutton, *Miscellanies*, II: 72.

111. Willison and Bonar, *Religious Societies*, p. 12.

112. Jefferson, *Life of John Savage*, pp. 115–16.

113. *Spiritual Letters: By Several Eminent Christians*, Chester, 1767, p. 80. The writer was a Methodist preacher, excusing himself from a visit to his family whom he had not seen for 18 years.

114. Dickinson, *Familiar Letters*, p. 9.

115. Richard Ward, *The Life of the Learned and Pious Dr. Henry More, Late Fellow of Christ's College in Cambridge. To which are annex'd Divers of his Useful and Excellent Letters*, 1710, p. 211.

116. *Living Christianity Delineated in the Diaries and Letters of Two Eminently Pious People lately Deceased; viz. Mr. Hugh Bryan, and Mrs. Mary Hutson, Both of South Carolina*, 1760, p. viii.

117. Mary Astell, *Letters Concerning the Love of God, between the Author of the Proposal to the Ladies and Mr. John Norris: Wherein his late Discourse, shewing That it ought to be intire and exclusive of all other Loves, is further cleared and justified*, 1695, preface, n.p.

118. *Living Christianity*, p. v.

119. *Spiritual Letters: By Several Eminent Christians*, Chester, 1767, p. 35.

120. Ibid., p. 106.

121. Willison and Bonar, *Religious Societies*, p. 36.
122. William Huntington, S.S., *A Correspondence Between Noctua Aurita, of the Desert, and Philomela, of the King's Dale*, 1809, p. 4.
123. *Spiritual Letters*, p. 6.
124. Mrs Lefevre, *An Extract of Letters*, Bristol, 1769, p. 75.
125. *Letters to his Friends, By the Rev. John Parker, Late Minister of the Gospel at Wainsgate, in Wadsworth, near Halifax, Leeds*, ed. John Fawcett, 1794, p. 7.
126. Ibid., p. 43.
127. Thomas Gibbons, *Memoirs of Eminently Pious Women, Who were Ornaments to their Sex, Blessings to their Families, and Edifying Examples to the Church and World*, 2 vols, 1777, Vol. II, p. 358.
128. Monro, *A Collection of about Fifty Religious Letters, Expressing the various Duties and Exercises of, and Crosses, Trials and Discouragements in the World, the Graces, Abilities and Consolations in Christ, attending the Christian in this Life: Written to diverse Persons, Ministers and others, some yet alive*, Edinburgh, 1722, pp. iii–v.
129. *The Elders, Ministers, and Messengers of the Several Baptist Churches, met in Association, at Exeter May 25 and 26, 1796*, n.p., 1796, p. 5.
130. *The Circular Letter from the Elders, Ministers and Messengers, of the Several Baptist Churches of the Western Association, Assembled at Salisbury, May 30 and 31, 1798*, n.p., 1798, pp. 10–11.
131. *The Circular Letter from Baptist Ministers and Messengers, Assembled at Northampton, June 4, 5, and 6, 1793*, n.p., 1793, pp. 2, 9.
132. *The Cumberland Letters 1771–1784*, ed. Clementina Black, Martin Secker, 1912, pp. 274–5.
133. Ibid., p. 165.
134. Ibid., p. 166
135. Quoted in Mabel Richmond Brailsford, *A Tale of Two Brothers: John and Charles Wesley*, Rupert Hart-Davis, 1954, p. 145.
136. Ibid: 68 (out of 770-odd) are designated thus in his *Hymns for the Use of People called Methodists*, 1779.
137. Wesley, *Letters*, 6: 25.
138. Astell, *Letters Concerning the Love of God*, p. 250.
139. Ibid., p. 259; preface, n.p.
140. Ibid., p. 217.
141. John Wesley, *The Character of a Methodist*, 10th edition, 1786, p. 6.
142. Gibbons, *Memoirs of Eminently Pious Women*, Vol. II, p. 10.
143. Parker, *Letters to his Friends*, p. 186.
144. Ibid., p. 123: 'Christian love will be 'perfect in its measure, uninterruped in its operation, and perpetual in its continuance ...'
145. Joseph Cole, *Memoirs of Miss Hannah Ball, of High Wycomb, in Buckinghamshire*, York, 1796, p. 42.
146. Hill, *Journal*, p. 174.
147. Richard Pearsall, *Contemplations on the Ocean, Harvest, Sickness and the Last Judgment, in a Series of Letters to a Friend*, 1753, and *Contemplations on Butterflies . . . . In a Series of Letters to Several Friends*, 1758.
148. *Living Christianity Delineated*, p. 37.
149. John Newton, *Cardiphonia: or The Utterance of the Heart; in the Course of a Real Correspondence*, 2 vols, Edinburgh, 1825, Vol. II, p. 38.
150. John Haime, *A Short Account of God's Dealings with Mr. John Haime, late soldier in the Queen's Regiment of Dragoons*, 1799, pp. 11, 31.

151. Trosse, *Life*, p. 58.
152. Cole, *Memoirs*, p. 42; Smyth, *Religion of the Heart*, p. 282.
153. Wesley, *Letters*, 4: 312. This was in 1764.
154. Ibid., 2: 57.
155. *The Works of John Wesley*, ed. Frank Baker, Vol. 25, *Letters I 1721–1739*, Oxford, Clarendon Press, 1980, p. 50.
156. Jefferson, *The Young Evangelist*, p. 57.
157. Wesley, *Letters*, 6: 295.
158. For example, Gibbons, *Pious Women*, on Elizabeth Bury, Vol. II, p. 379.
159. John Wesley's father made an annual circuit of his parish asking people about the state of their souls; he wrote the answers in a book. Wesley, *Letters*, 2: 11.
160. *Extracts from the Diary, Meditations and Letters of Mr. Joseph Williams of Kidderminster, who died December 21, 1755, aged 63*, Shrewsbury, 1779, pp. 159, 173.
161. Lefevre, *Letters*, pp. 7–9, 10–12.
162. Wesley, *Letters*, 6: 360.
163. John Locke, *The Reasonableness of Christianity, as delivered in the Scriptures*, in *Works*, 1824, Vol. VI, p. 151.
164. Brailsford, *A Tale*, p. 62; Wesley, *Letters*, 7: 392.
165. *Spiritual Letters*, p. 13.
166. Thomas Coke, *A Funeral Sermon, Preached in Spitalfields-Chapel, London, On Sunday, October 26, 1794, on the Death of Mrs. H.A. Rogers*, Bristol, 1796, p. 7.
167. Hester Ann Rogers, *Spiritual Letters Written by Mrs H.A. Rogers, Written Before and After Her Marriage, Peculiarly Calculated to Illustrate and Enforce Holiness of Heart and Life*, Bristol, 1796, pp. 3–5.
168. Wesley, ed. Baker, *Letters I*, p. 98.
169. Elaine Scarry, *The Body in Pain: The Making and Unmaking of the World*, Oxford University Press, 1985, repr. 1988, p. 212.
170. Ibid., p. 198.
171. Ibid., p. 219.
172. Crosse, *A Letter*, p. 20, quoting Price's *Discourse on the Love of our Country*.
173. *Theatrical Entertainments*, p. 18.
174. Williams, *Extracts*, p. 152.
175. Wesley, *Letters I*, ed. Baker, p. 166.
176. Rogers, *Spiritual Letters*, pp. 13–14.
177. Mole, *Grounds of Christian Faith*, p. 17.
178. Wesley, *Letters*, 7: 306. Compare 5: 132, his eight rules for a preacher in Ireland are predominantly bodily, including, eat milk or gruel for supper, keep clothes clean and mended, get rid of lice and the itch, avoid tobacco, snuff and drams.
179. Brailsford, *A Tale*, p. 289.
180. Smyth, *Religion of the Heart*, p. 199; Coke, *Funeral Sermon*, p. 51, Rogers, *Spiritual Letters*, p. 58.
181. James Ellesby, *The Sick Christian's Companion: Consisting of Prayers, Meditations and Directions*, 1729, p. 6.
182. Wesley, *Letters*, 3: 111. This discourse has implications for Wordsworth's 'inward eye'. Wesley's father thought it was unintelligible.
183. Ward, *Life of More*, pp. 102–3.
184. *Spiritual Letters*, p. 208.
185. Smyth, *Religion of the Heart*, p. 104.
186. Wesley, *Letters*, 5: 93.
187. Ibid., 6: 308.

188. Ibid., 4: 8–9.
189. Jonathan Dickinson, *Sermons and Tracts, Separately Published at Boston, Philadelphia, &c.,* Edinburgh, 1793, p. 216.
190. Thomas Taylor, *Redeeming Grace Displayed to the Chief of Sinners; Being a Short Account of GOD's Dealings with Thomas Taylor,* 4th edition, Leeds, 1785, p. 51.
191. Brailsford, *A Tale,* p. 143, from *Hymns on Several Occasions.* The occasion here was to encourage converts in Wiltshire who were being persecuted, that is, having hurts inflicted on them.
192. *The Life of the Reverend James Hervey, Rector of Weston-Favell, in Northamptonshire,* Berwick, 1770, p. lvii; Wesley, *Letters I,* ed. Baker, p. 281.
193. *Spiritual Letters,* p. 6.
194. Wesley, ed. Baker, *Letters I,* p. 665.
195. Ibid., p. 680.
196. Ibid., p. 690.
197. Brailsford, *A Tale,* p. 166.
198. Wesley, *Letters I,* ed. Baker, p. 680.
199. Adam West with Jeff Ronin, *Back to the Batcave,* Titan Books, 1994, pp. 61–2.
200. Wesley, *Letters 5:* 365.
201. Smyth, *Religion of the Heart,* p. 77.
202. Scarry, *The Body in Pain,* p. 207.
203. Smyth, *Religion of the Heart,* p. 89.
204. Quoted in Brailsford, *A Tale,* p. 176.
205. Wesley, *Letters,* 2: 39. It is suggestive that Wesley suffered from nosebleeds.
206. Ibid., 6: 326.
207. Rogers, *Spiritual Letters,* p. 31.
208. Horror films and science fiction films make this point clearer: the green slime which emanates from aliens or the demonically possessed is an abjected inversion of red blood.
209. Tobias Smollett, *The Expedition of Humphry Clinker,* 1771, Harmondsworth, Penguin, 1967 repr. 1980, pp. 231–2.
210. Ibid., p. 103.
211. On the connections between intellectuals, the mouth and smoking, see Richard Klein, *Cigarettes are Sublime,* Durham and London, Duke University Press, 1993, especially pp. 30–40 on Sartre.
212. Voiture, *Letters,* p. 176.
213. Anita Guerrini, 'The Hungry Soul: George Cheyne and the Construction of Femininity', *Eighteenth-Century Studies,* Vol. 32, No. 3, 1999, pp. 279–91, relates Wesley's ideas on the 'nexus of food, flesh and spirit' to those of Cheyne, whose spiritual, mental and physical well-being were managed through a largely vegetarian diet.
214. Wesley, *Letters I,* ed. Baker, p. 383.
215. Brailsford, *A Tale,* p. 170. John Wesley resumed eating meat for a brief span, but gave it up again, ostensibly on medical advice. *Letters* 2: 285.
216. Ibid., p. 139.
217. Guerrini, 'The Hungry Soul', p. 286, argues for an association between meat and masculinity, and milk and femininity. This may well be, but one should not forget the terms' significance in religious discourse.
218. In 1785 he declared it 'well-nigh forgotten' as a practice; *Letters,* 7: 259.
219. Ibid., 4: 27.
220. Wesley, *Letters I,* ed. Baker, p. 385.

221. *Letters*, 5: 255.
222. [Combe], *Fanatic Saints*, p. 9.
223. Parker, *Letters to His Friends*, p. 186.

Postscript

1. Elizabeth Griffith, *The Delicate Distress*, (1769), eds Cynthia Booth Ricciardi and Susan Staves, Lexington, University Press of Kentucky, 1997, p. 181.
2. Wortley Montagu, *Letters*, ed. Halsband, Vol. III, p. 90.
3. Ada M. Ingpen, *Women as Letter Writers*, Hutchinson & Co., 1909, p. iii.
4. Patricia Meyer Spacks, *Privacy: Concealing the Eighteenth-Century Self*, Chicago and London, University of Chicago Press, 2003, p. 12.
5. See Dror Wahrman, *The Making of the Modern Self: Identity and Culture in Eighteenth-Century England*, New Haven and London, Yale University Press, 2004.
6. Spacks, *Privacy*, p. 190.
7. Drummond, *Travels*, p. 175, with a mix of active and passive verbs and a delightful sketch.
8. Spacks, *Privacy*, p. 33.
9. See Frederic Jameson, *The Political Unconscious: Narrative as a Socially Symbolic Act*, Routledge, 2002, and Jacqueline Rose, *On Not Being Able to Sleep: Psychoanalysis and the Modern World*, Chatto and Windus, 2003, for different models.
10. Kathleen Wilson, *The Island Race: Englishness, Empire and Gender in the Eighteenth Century*, Routledge, 2003, p. 1.
11. Ibid., p. 2.
12. Scott Paul Gordon, *The Power of the Passive Self in English Literature, 1640–1770*, Cambridge, Cambridge University Press, 2002, p. 5.
13. Ibid., p. 11, quoting Slavoj Žižek, *The Sublime Object of Ideology*, Verso 1989, pp. 20–1.
14. *A Complete Vindication of the Mallard of All-Souls College*, 2nd edition, 1751, pp. 13–14.
15. *Journal of the History of Ideas*, Vol. 64, No.1, January 2003, special issue on Early Modern Information Overload, ed. Daniel Rosenberg, Introduction, pp. 1–9; p. 1.
16. Ibid., p. 9.
17. *Epistolary Histories*, eds Gilroy and Verhoeven, p. 4.

Short Bibliography

For reasons of space, this bibliography lists a small fraction of texts cited, some with shortened titles. Full details of all primary texts and secondary reading are given in 'Notes' section. Apologies for any inconvenience. Place of publication for all texts is London unless specified otherwise.

Abelard to Eloisa, Leonora to Tasso, Ovid to Julia, Spring, and Other Poems, 4th edition, [c.1780].

The Academy of Compliments, [1750].

Addison, Joseph, *Miscellaneous Works: Poems and Plays*, ed. A.C. Guthkelch, 1914.

Advice from a Father to a Son, Just Entered the Army, and About to go Abroad into Action, 1776.

Allen, Rev. Dr. James, *An Account of the Behaviour of Mr. James Maclaine*, 1750.

Almon, John, *Memoirs of a Late Eminent Bookseller*, 2 vols, 1790.

An Account of the Proceedings in Scotland against David Baillie, with Relation to the Plot, 1704.

An Amateur du Bon Ton [X.Y.Z.], *An Apology for Mrs. Eugenia Stanhope*, 1775.

An Answer from Lien Chi, in Pekin, to Xo Ho, the Chinese Philosopher in London, To Which is Annexed A Letter from Philo-Britain to Lien Chi, 1757.

An Answer to a late Pamphlet, Intitled Christianity not Founded on Argument, &c., 1743.

An Answer to the Latter Part of Lord Bolingbroke's Letters on the Study and Use of History, 1752.

An Authentic Account of the Life and Memoirs of Mr. William Smith, 1750.

Andrews, John *Letters to a Young Gentleman on his Setting out for France*, 1784.

Anticipation, or the Voyage of an American to England in the Year 1899, 1781.

Argens, Jean Baptiste de Boyer, Marquis d', *Chinese Letters. Being a Philosophical, Historical, and Critical Correspondence between a Chinese Traveller at Paris, and his Countrymen*, 1741.

Aristanaetus, *Letters of Love and Gallantry*, [1698].

Arnold, Thomas, *Sketches from the Carte Papers*, Dublin, 1888.

The Art of Courtship, or The School of Love, n.d.

Astell, Mary, *Letters Concerning the Love of God*, 1695.

Athenian Letters: or, the Epistolary Correspondence of an Agent of the King of Persia, Residing at Athens during the Peloponnesian War, 1781.

Authentick Memoirs of the Wicked Life and Transactions of Elizabeth Jeffryes, Spinster, 2nd edition, 1752.

B.[ritain], G.[reat], *The Last Advice of an Old Father, Being a Letter from a Father in the Country to his Son in Town*, [1793].

Balaam's Ass, *Shrewsbury Election* [sic], Shrewsbury, 1796.

The Barber's Mirror; Or a Portrait of the Rev. William Huntington, Drawn from Real Life: Being Remarks on that Gentleman's Pamphlet entitled 'the Barber:' With an Account of His Strange and Deplorable FRENZY, 1791.

Behn, Aphra, *Love Letters between Polydorus the Gothick King, and Messalina, Late Queen of Albion*, 'Paris' [i.e. London], 1689.

Berington, the Rev. Joseph, *The History of the Lives of ABEILLARD and HELOISA* . . ., 1787.

Birt, Isaiah, *A Vindication of the Baptists, in Three Letters, Addressed to a Friend in Saltash*, Bristol, 1793.

Blackall, Offspring, *The Lord Bishop of Exeter's Answer to Mr. Hoadly's Letter*, 2nd edition, 1709.

Blandy, Mary, *Miss Mary Blandy's own Account of the Affair between Her and Mr. Cranstoun*, 1752.

Blount, Thomas, *The Correspondence of Thomas Blount (1618–1679): A Recusant Antiquary*, ed. Theo Bongaerts, Amsterdam, 1978.

Bolingbroke, Henry St John, *Letters on the Study and Use of History*, 2 vols, 1752.

Bolton, Robert, *Letters and Tracts on the Choice of Company and Other Subjects*, 1761.

Boswell, James, *The Life of Samuel Johnson LL.D*, 6 vols, ed. George Birkbeck Hill, rev. L.F. Powell, Oxford, 1934.

Bousell, John, *The Ram's Horn Sounded Seven Times: Being a Visitation of Divine Love to those Merchants of Babylon who have taken upon themselves the office of Teachers among the people called Baptists, whose mountain, built in their own wisdom, will be destroyed by the stone cut out of the mountain without hands (the wisdom and power of God), with every other mountain in the kingdom of Babylon – The false church shall fall, and the true Church be built again*, Norwich, [1787].

[Bowdler, John], *Reform or Ruin: Take Your Choice!*, 2nd edition, 1797.

Breval, John, *The History of the House of Nassau, from its earliest Known Origin, continued Down to the Present Times* . . ., 1734.

The Bristol Contest, Containing A Particular Account of the Proceedings of both Parties . . ., Bristol, 1781.

Broderick, Thomas, *Letters from Several Parts of Europe and the East*, 2 vols, 1753.

Brown, Rev. George, *The English Letter-Writer; or the Whole Art of Correspondence*, c.1775.

Brown, John, *Essays on the Characteristics*, 1751.

Brown, Thomas et al, *Letters from the Dead to the Living*, 1702.

Brydone, Patrick, *A Tour Through Sicily and Malta*, 2 vols, 1773.

Burnet, Gilbert, *The History of the Rights of Princes*, 1681.

——, *An Introduction to the Third Volume of the History of the Reformation of the Church of England*, 2nd edition, 1714.

——, *Some Account of the Life and Writings of Gilbert Late Lord Bishop of Sarum*, 1715.

——, *The Conclusion of Bishop Burnett's [sic] History of his own Life and Times*, 1734.

Burney, Frances, *The Journals and Letters of Fanny Burney (Madame D'Arblay)*, 12 vols, eds Joyce Hemlow et al, Oxford, 1972–1984.

Campbell, Alexander, *An Examination of Lord Bolingbroke's Letters on History*, 2nd edition, 1753.

Campbell, Thomas, *A Philosophical Survey of the South of Ireland*, 1777.

[Campbell, Thomas], *Diary of a Visit to England in 1775 by an Irishman*, Sydney, 1854.

Carte, Thomas, *A General History of England*, 1747, 4 vols.

The Case of Miss Blandy and Miss Jeffreys Fairly Stated and Compared, 1752.

The Case of William Paul, a Clergyman, and John Hall, Esq., 1716.

Cato Redivivus, *Patriotism, A Political Satire*, 1767.

Cato Ultonensis, *A Word of Advice*, Dublin, 1724.

The Censor Censur'd: or, Cato turn'd Catiline, 1722.

[Chesterfield] Philip, 2nd Earl of Chesterfield, *Some Short Observations for the Lady Mary Stanhope Concerning the Writing of Ordinary Letters*, ed. W.S. Lewis, 1934.

The Letters of Philip Dormer Stanhope 4th Earl of Chesterfield, 6 vols, ed. Bonamy Dobrée, 1932.

——, *Lord Chesterfield's Letters*, ed. David Roberts, Oxford, 1998.

The Circular Letter from Baptist Ministers and Messengers, Assembled at Northampton, June 4, 5, and 6, 1793, n.p., 1793.

The Circular Letter from the Elders, Ministers and Messengers, of the Several Baptist Churches of the Western Association, Assembled at Salisbury, May 30 and 31, 1798, n.p., 1798.

Clarke, Edward, *Letters Concerning the Spanish Nation*, 1763.

Clarke, Samuel, *A Third Defense of an Argument Made use of in a Letter to Mr Dodwell [sic], to Prove the Immateriality and Natural Immortality of the Soul*, 1708.

Clubbe, John, *The History and Antiquities of the Ancient Villa of Wheatfield, in the County of Suffolk*, 1758.

Cluny, Alexander, *The American Traveller*, 1769.

Collard, James, *The Life, and Extraordinary Adventures of James Molesworth Hobart*, 2 vols, 1794.

A Collection of Advertisements, Letters and Papers, and some other Facts, Relating to the Last Elections at Westminster and Hasting [sic], 2nd edition, 1722.

A Collection of Letters Never Before Printed: Written by Alexander Pope, Esq; and other Ingenious Gentlemen, to the late Aaron Hill, Esq., 1751.

A Collection of Letters on Patronage and Popular Election, Edinburgh, 1783.

A Collection of Remarkable Trials, Glasgow, 1739.

[Combe, William], *Letters of the Late Lord Lyttleton*, 1780.

The Complete Letter-Writer, Edinburgh, 1768.

The Complete Letter-Writer, or Polite English Secretary, 11th edition, 1767.

A Complete Vindication of the Mallard of All-Souls College, 2nd edition, 1751.

Concanen, Matthew, *The Speculatist*, 1730.

Cooke, Thomas, *The Letters of Atticus*, 1731.

Cooper, John Gilbert, *Letters Concerning Taste*, 1755.

Cordiner, Charles, *Antiquities and Scenery of the North of Scotland, in a Series of Letters to Thomas Pennant, Esqr.*, 1780.

The Correspondent: A Selection of Letters from the Best Authors . . ., 2 vols, 1796.

[Country Farmer], *Three Letters to a Member of the Honourable House of Commons, from a Country Farmer, Concerning the Price of Provisions, and Pointing out a Sure Method of Preventing Future Scarcity*, 1766.

Cowper, William, *The Task, a Poem in Six Books*, 1785.

——, *The Letters and Prose Writings of William Cowper*, eds James King and Charles Ryskamp, 5 vols, Oxford, 1979–86.

Coxe, William, *Sketches of the Natural, Civil, and Political State of Swisserland*, 2nd edition, 1780.

——, *Travels in Switzerland*, 3 vols, 1789.

Cradock, Joseph, *Letters from Snowdon: Descriptive of a Tour Through the Northern Counties of Wales*, 1770.

[Cranstoun], *Captain Cranstoun's Account of the Poisoning the Late Mr. Francis Blandy*, 1752.

Critical Remarks upon the late Lord Viscount Bolingbroke's Letters on the Study and Use of History, as far as they regard Sacred History, 1754.

The Cumberland Letters 1771–1784, ed. Clementina Black, 1912.

Davies, Arabella, *Letters from a Parent to her Children: Written to them while under Tuition at School*, 1788.

Davis, Jane, *Letters from a Mother to her Son, on his Going to Sea*, 3rd edition, Stockport, 1799.

Defoe, Daniel, *The Complete English Tradesman, in Familiar Letters*, 1726.

Dickinson, Jonathan, *Familiar Letters to a Gentleman*, Dublin, 1752.

Dillon, Sir John Talbot, *Letters from an English Traveller in Spain, in 1778*, 1781.

Doddridge, Philip, *The Perspecuity and Solidity of those Evidences of Christianity, To Which the generality of its Professors among us may attain, Illustrated and Vindicated; in a letter to the Author of a late Pamphlet, intitled, Christianity not founded on Argument, &c.*, 1742.

——, *A Second Letter to the Author of a Pamphlet, Intitled, Christianity not Founded on Argument, &c.*, 1743.

Dodsley, Robert, *The Preceptor: Containing a General Course of Education*, 2 vols, 1748.

——, *The Oeconomy of Human Life*, 9th edition, 1758.

Dodwell, Henry, *An Epistolary Discourse, Proving, from the Scriptures and the First Fathers, that the Soul is a Principle naturally Mortal, But Immortalised Actually by the Pleasure of God, to Punishment; or, to Reward, by its Union with the Divine Baptismal Spirit*, 1706.

——, *A Preliminary Defence of the Epistolary Discourse, Concerning the Distinction between Soul and Spirit*, 1707.

——, *A Letter from the Learned Mr. Henry Dodwell to the Right Reverend the Bishop of Sarum, in which he owns his Spiritual Character, but not his Temporal*, 2nd edition, 1712.

Dodwell, Henry [junior], *Christianity Not Founded on Argument; and the True Principle of Gospel-Evidence Assigned: in a Letter to a Young Gentleman at Oxford*, 1741.

The Double Captive, or Chains Upon Chains, 1718.

[Douglas, Lady Jane], *Letters of the Right Honourable Lady Jane Douglas*, 1767.

Drennan, William, *The Letters of Orellana*, Dublin, 1785.

Drummond, Alexander, *Travels through Different Cities of Germany, Italy, Greece, and Several Parts of Asia, as far as the Banks of the Euphrates*, 1754.

Dutton, Anne, *A Letter to Such of the Servants of Christ, who May have any Scruple about the Lawfulness of Printing any Thing Written by a Woman: To Shew, That Book-teaching is Private, with Respect to the Church, and Permitted to Private Christians; Yea, Commanded to Those, of Either Sex, who are Gifted for, and Inclin'd to Engage in this Service*, 1743.

——, *Divine, Moral, and Historical Miscellanies in Prose and Verse*, 3 vols, 1761–3.

Eddis, William, *Letters from America, Historical and Descriptive*, 1792.

The Elders, Ministers, and Messengers of the Several Baptist Churches, met in Association, at Exeter May 25 and 26, 1796, n.p., 1796.

Election Magazine, Norwich, 1784.

Elkington, P., *The Case of Miss Blandy*, Oxford, 1752.

Encyclopaedia of Manners and Etiquette, Comprising Chesterfield's Advice to his Son, 1850.

Epistles Elegant, Familiar and Instructive, 1791.

Erskine, David, *Letters of Albanicus to the People of England*, 1786.

An Essay on Parties and a Free Government, in the Character of an Ancient Trimmer, n.d.

Etough, Henry, *A Letter to the Author of Christianity Not Founded on Argument*, 1742.

Examinator's Letters, or a Mirror for British Monopolists and Irish Financiers, Dublin, 1786.

Excise: Being a Collection of Letters, &c., n.d.

The Fair Concubine: Or, the Secret History of the Beautiful Vanella, 3rd edition, 1752.

Faithful Copies of all the Letters that have Appeared in the General Advertiser, Under the Signatures of Scourge, and W. Bennett, Camberwell . . ., 1781.

The Farmers Address to their Representatives. Humbly Recommended to the Careful Perusal of Every Corn Farmer, and Every Honest Man in Great Britain, 1768.

Farquhar, George, *The Works of the Late Ingenious Mr. George Farquhar: Containing all His Poems, Letters, Essays and Comedies, Publish'd in His Lifetime*, 2 vols, 6th edition, 1728.

A Father's Advice to His Son, 1736.

Fielding, Henry, *The History of Tom Jones, A Foundling*. 6 vols, 1749.

——, *The True Patriot: And the History of our own Times*, 1745–6, in The Wesleyan Edition of the Works of Henry Fielding, *The True Patriot and Related Writings*, ed. W.B. Coley, 1987.

Fleury, Maria de, *A Serious Address to the Rev. Mr. Huntington; containing some Remarks on his Sermon, entitled 'The Servant of the Lord, described and vindicated.'*, 1788.

——, *An Answer to the Daughter's Defence of Her Father, Addressed to Her Father Himself*, 1788.

Four Letters which Passed between the Right Reverend the Lord Bishop of Sarum and Mr. Henry Dodwell, Printed from the Originals, 1713.

Fowke, Martha, *The Epistles of Clio and Strephon*, 1720.

A Freeholder, *A Letter to Sir Richard Hill, Esq.*, 1782.

Free-Thinker, A, *Miscellaneous Observations on the Works of the late Lord Viscount Bolingbroke . . .*, 1755.

A Friend to the Old Interest, *A View of the Cirencester Contest*, [1753].

The Friendly Couriere: By Way of Letters from Persons in Town to Their Acquaintance in the Country, 1711.

A Full and Complete History of His R——l H—— the D—— of C——d and Lady G——r, the Fair Adultress, 2 vols, 3rd edition, 1770.

Galloway, Joseph, *Letters from Cicero to Catiline the Second*, 1781.

[Gaylove, G.], *A Select Collection of the Original Love Letters of Several Eminent Persons, of Distinguished Rank and Station, Now Living*, 1755.

A Gentleman of Oxford, *A Candid Appeal to the Publick, Concerning the Case of the Late Miss Mary Blandy*, 1752.

The Gentleman's Magazine, 16 vols, ed. Thomas Keymer, 1998.

A Genuine Account of the Proceedings on the Trial of Florence Hensey MD, 1758.

A Genuine and Authentic Account of the Proceedings at the Late Election for the City and Liberty of Westminster, 1749.

A Genuine and Impartial Account of the Life of Miss Mary Blandy, 1752.

The Genuine History of the Inhuman and Unparalell'd [sic] Murders committed on the Bodies of Mr. William Galley and Mr. Daniel Chater, 1749.

Genuine Memoirs of the Lives of Messieurs D. and R. Perreau, 1775.

Gibbons, Thomas, *Memoirs of Eminently Pious Women*, 2 vols, 1777.

Gildon, Charles, *The Post-Boy Robb'd of his Mail: Or, the Pacquet Broke Open*, 2 vols, 2nd edition, 1706.

[Gildon, Charles], *Memoirs of the Life of William Wycherley, Esq.*, 1718.

Glasgow, Nathaniel, *A Copy of Two Letters to the Magistrates and Town-Council of Glasgow*, n.p., 1725.

Goethe, Johann Wolfgang Von, *The Sorrows of Werter* [sic], 2 vols, 1779.

Goldsmith, Oliver, *An History of England in a Series of Letters from a Nobleman to his Son at University*, 1764.

——, *Collected Works of Oliver Goldsmith*, 5 vols, ed. Arthur Friedman, Oxford, 1966.

Goudar, Ange, *The Chinese Spy, or Emissary from the Court of Pekin, Commissioned to Examine into the Present State of Europe*, 6 vols, 1765.

Grant, Anne, *Letters from the Mountains*, 3 vols, 1806.

Gray, Thomas, *Correspondence of Thomas Gray*, 3 vols, eds Paget Toynbee and Leonard Whibley, Oxford, 1935 repr. 1971.

Green, Rupert, *An Abstract of the History of England*, in *The Secret Plot*, 1779.

Griffith, Elizabeth, *The Delicate Distress*, 1769.

Griffith, Richard and Elizabeth, *A Series of Genuine Letters between Henry and Frances*, 6 vols, 3rd edition, 1770.

Hacker, Thomas, *Believers Entanglement by the Moral Law, Proved Inconsistent with the Abolition of the Law*, 1794.

Haime, John, *A Short Account of God's Dealings with Mr. John Haime*, 1799.

Hamilton, Eliza, *Translation of the Letters of a Hindoo Rajah; Written Previous to, and during the period of his Residence in England*, 2 vols, 1796.

The Hamwood Papers of the Ladies of Llangollen and Caroline Hamilton, ed. Mrs G.H. Bell, 1930.

Hanway, Jonas, *Letters Admonitory and Argumentative from J. H——y, Merchant, to J. S——r, Merchant*, 1753.

Harris, Thomas, *The Real, Genuine, and Authentic Narrative of the Proceedings of Capt. James Lowrey*, 1752.

Hayley, William, *An Essay on History; in Three Epistles to Edward Gibbon, Esq. with Notes*, 1780.

The Hertford Letter: Containing Several Brief Observations on a Printed Tryal, 1699.

Haywood, Eliza, *The Works of Mrs Eliza Haywood*, 4 vols, 1724.

——, *Letters from the Palace of Fame*, 1727.

Haywood, James, *Poems and Letters on Several Occasions*, 1722.

Hellen, Robert, *Letters from an Armenian in Ireland to his Friends at Trebizond*, 1757 [Sometimes attributed to Viscount Edmund Sexton Pery].

Hervey, Christopher, *Letters from Portugal, Spain, Italy and Germany in the years 1759, 1760, and 1761*, 3 vols, 1785.

Hervey, James, *Remarks on Lord Bolingbroke's Letters on the Study and Use of History*, 1752.

——, *The Works of the late Reverend James Hervey*, Newcastle upon Tyne, 1789.

Hill, Sir Richard, *Hard Measure, or A Real Statement of Facts*, Shrewsbury, 2nd edition, 1795.

Hoadly, Benjamin, *Some Considerations Humbly Offered to the Right Reverend the Lord Bishop of Exeter*, 3rd edition, 1709.

——, *A Humble Reply to the Right Reverend the Lord Bishop of Exeter's Answer*, 1709.

Hodgson, Henry, *Letters to Mrs Kindersley*, 1778.

An Honest Man, *The Secret Springs of the Late Changes in the Ministry Fairly Explained*, 1766.

Hooper, Ebenezer, *The Celebrated Coalheaver; or Reminiscences of the Rev. William Huntington, S.S.*, 1871.

Hunter, Thomas, *A Sketch of the Philosophical Character of the late Lord Viscount Bolingbroke*, 1770.

——, *Reflections Critical and Moral on the Letters of the Late Earl of Chesterfield*, 2nd edition, 1777.

Hunter, William, *Travels in the Year 1792 through France, Turkey, and Hungary, to Vienna: Concluding with an Account of that City*, 2 vols, 2nd edition, 1798.

Huntington, William, S.S., *Letters on Ministerial Qualifications*, 2nd edition, 1788.

——, *A Feeble Dispute with a Wise and Learned Man*, 1793.

——, *A Letter to the Rev. T. Joss*, 1794.

——, *The Mystery of Godliness; in a Letter to an Erroneous Man*, [1794].

——, *The Broken Cistern, and the Springing Well: Or, the Difference between Head Notions and Heart Religion, Vain Jangling and Sound Doctrine*, 2nd edition, 1800.

——, *A Correspondence Between Noctua Aurita, of the Desert, and Philomela, of the King's Dale*, 1809.

An Impartial Enquiry into the Case of Miss Blandy, 1752.

Irwin, Eyles, *A Series of Adventures in the Course of a Voyage up the Red-Sea . . . In Letters to a Lady*, 1780.

James, Sir Walter, *The Letters of Charlotte During her Connexion with Werter*, 2 vols, Dublin, 1786.

Jebb, Frederic, *The Letters of Guatimozin*, Dublin, 1779.

Jefferson, Joseph, *The Young Evangelist; Exemplified in a Life of the Late Rev. John Savage*, Southampton, n.d. [1799].

Jemmat, Catherine, *The Memoirs of Mrs. Catherine Jemmat*, 2 vols, 2nd edition, 1762.

Johnson, Samuel, *The Letters of Samuel Johnson*, 5 vols, ed. Bruce Redford, 1992–4.

Johnson, Samuel, [no relation] *A Compleat Introduction to the Art of Writing Letters*, 1758.

Johnston, Charles, *The Pilgrim: or, A Picture of Life. In a Series of Letters, Written Mostly from London by a Chinese Philosopher, to His Friend at Quang-tong*, 2 vols, Dublin, 1775.

Journal of the Proceedings at the Election of the Knights of the Shire to Represent the County of Norfolk in Parliament, 1784.

Junius, *The Letters of the Celebrated Junius*, 2 vols, 1783.

——, *The Letters of Junius*, ed. John Cannon, Oxford, 1978.

Katte, Johann, *The Three Last Letters written by the late Unhappy Mons. De Catte*, 1734.

Kindersley, Jemima, *Letters from the Island of Teneriffe, Brazil, the Cape of Good Hope, and the East Indies*, 1777.

The Ladies Complete Letter-Writer, Dublin, 1763.

[Lambert, de] *The Marchioness De Lambert's Letters to her Son and Daughter, on True Education, &c. &c. &c.* [sic], trans. Mr Rowell, 1749.

Lefevre, Mrs, *An Extract of Letters*, Bristol, 1769.

Leland, John, *Remarks on a Late Pamphlet, entitled Christianity not founded on Argument*, 1744.

Lemoine, Abraham, *A Defence of the Sacred History*, 1753.

A Letter from a Clergyman to Miss Mary Blandy, 1752.

A Letter from a Member of Parliament to his Friends in the Country Concerning the Duties on Wine and Tobacco, 1733.

Letters from an American in England to his Friends in America, 1769.

A Letter to the Right Honourable Charles James Fox, on the Late Conduct of his Party, 2nd edition, 1789.

A Letter to the Right Hon Wm. Pitt, on the Restriction of the Regent's Authority, 1789.

A Letter to the Shopkeepers, Tradesmen, Farmers, and Common-People of Ireland, Dublin, n.d.

Letters between Sir Richard Hill, Baronet, John Hill, and Edward Burton, Esquires, Shrewsbury, 1796.

Letters by Several Eminent Persons Deceased, 1772.

A Letter from a Member of Parliament for a Borough in the West, to a Noble Lord in his Neighbourhood there, concerning the Excise-Bill, and the Manner and Causes of Losing it, 1733.

Letters of Abelard and Heloise, trans. John Hughes, 6th edition, 1736.

Letters Upon Ancient History, in French and English, 1783.

Lettice, John, *Letters on a Tour through various parts of Scotland, in the year 1792*, 1794.

The Life of Cassem, the Son of Hamid, A Noble Arabian, 1746.

Living Christianity Delineated in the Diaries and Letters of Two Eminently Pious People, 1760.

Locke, John, *Some Letters between Mr. Locke, and Several of his Friends*, 1708.

——, *The Works of John Locke in Nine Volumes*, 12th edition, 1824.

Lofft, Capel, *Three Letters on the Question of Regency*, 1788.

Love Letters of Famous Men and Women of the Past and Present Century, 2 vols, ed. J.T. Merydew, 1888.

Love-Letters between a certain late Nobleman and the Famous Mr. Wilson, (1723), ed. Michael S. Kimmel, New York, 1990.

Love-Letters from King Henry VIII, 1714.

The Love-Letters of Mr. H. & Miss R. 1775–1779, ed. Gilbert Burgess, 1895.

The Lover's Best Instructor; or the Whole Art of Courtship, Wolverhampton, 1770.

The Lover's Manual, 1753.

The Lover's Pacquet, 1733.

The Lover's Secretary, 1692.

Lyttleton, Lord, *Letters from a Persian in England*, 1735.

M. S., *The Female Critick: Or Letters in Drollery from Ladies to their Humble Servants*, 1701.

Macaulay, Catharine, The *History of England from the Accession of James I to that of the Brunswick Line*, 8 vols, 1763–83.

——, *The History of England, from the Revolution to the Present Time, in a Series of Letters to a Friend* [the Revd Dr Wilson], Bath, 1778.

Mackenzie, Henry, *The Man of Feeling*, 1771.

——, *Julia de Roubigné, A Tale*, 2 vols, 2nd edition, 1778.

Macpherson, James, *Original Papers, Containing the Secret History of Great Britain from the Restoration, to the Accession of the House of Hanover*, 2 vols, 1775.

MacQueen, Daniel, *Letters on Mr Hume's History of Great Britain*, Edinburgh, 1776.

Madan, Judith, 'Abelard to Eloisa' in *The Unfortunate Lovers; Two Admirable Poems: Extracted Out of the Celebrated Letters of Abelard and Eloisa*, 1756.

Madden, Samuel, *Memoirs of the Twentieth Century*, 1733.

Mahomet, Sake Dean, *The Travels of Dean Mahomet, a Native of Patna in Bengal*, 2 vols, Cork, 1794.

The Maidens Faithfull Counsellour: Or, The Speediest Way to get Good Husbands, n.d.

The Malefactors Register; or, New Newgate and Tyburn Calendar, 7 vols, 1779.

A Man of the World, *Free and Impartial Remarks upon the Letters Written by the Late Right Honourable Philip Dormer Stanhope, Earl of Chesterfield, to his Son Philip Stanhope, Esq.*, 1784.

Martin, John, *Some Account of the Life and Writings of the Rev. John Martin*, 1797.

Mason, William, *Gray's Poems and Memoirs of his Life and Writings*, 2nd edition, 1775.

Masters, Mary, *Familiar Letters and Poems on Several Occasions*, 1755.

Matter of Fact, being A Short but True Account of the Birth, Education, and Ordination of William Paul, Clergyman, n.d.

Matthews, John, *Eloisa en Dishabille: Being a New Version of that Lady's Celebrated Epistle to Abelard*, 1801.

Maxfield, Rev. Thomas, *A Short and Authentic Account of the Particular Circumstances of the last Twenty-Four Hours of the Life and Death of William Davies*, 1776.

Measure for Measure, An Answer to the Last Edition and Supplement of 'Hard Measure', in a Letter to the Electors of Shrewsbury, 2nd edition, 1796.

Melmoth, Courtney [Samuel Jackson Pratt], *The Pupil of Pleasure*, 2 vols, 1777.

Memoirs of the Life and most Memorable Transactions of Capt. William Henry Cranston, 2nd edition, 1753.

Memoirs of the Life of William-Henry Cranstoun, Esq. in which His Education and Genius are Consider'd, 1752.

Mercator's Letters on Portugal and its Commerce, 1754.

Milles, Thomas, B.D. *The Natural Immortality of the Soul Asserted, and Proved from the Scriptures, and First Fathers: In Answer to Mr Dodwell's Epistolary Discourse, in which he Endeavours to Prove the Soul to be a Principle Naturally Mortal*, Oxford, 1707.

Mirabeau, Count, *The Secret History of the Court of Berlin*, 2 vols, 1789.

The Mirror, 2 vols, 4th edition, Dublin, 1782.

Monro, John, *A Collection of about Fifty Religious Letters*, Edinburgh, 1722.

Montagu, Lady Mary Wortley, *The Complete Letters of Lady Mary Wortley Montagu*, 3 vols, ed. Robert Halsband, Oxford, 1965–7.

Montesquieu, *Persian Letters*, ed. C.J. Betts, 1973 repr. 1993.

More, Hannah, *Village Politics, Addressed to all the Mechanics, Journeymen, and Labourers in Great Britain*, 1792.

Morton, Elizabeth, *The Daughter's Defence of her Father; or, An Answer to the letter addressed to Mr. Huntington, Written by Madame (de Mara) Flora, & Co*, 1788.

Muralt, Béat Louis de, *Letters Describing the Character and Customs of the English and French Nations*, 1726.

Murray, Richard, *Alethia: or, a General System of Moral Truths, and Natural Religion*, 2 vols, 1747.

The Nature of the Present Excise, and the Consequences of its Farther Extension, Examined, 1733.

A New and Compleat Collection of the Most Remarkable Trials for Adultery, 2 vols, 1780.

The New Art of Letter-Writing, 2nd edition, 1762.

Newton, John, *Cardiphonia: Or the Utterance of the Heart; in the Course of a Real Correspondence*, (1781), 2 vols, Edinburgh, 1825.

Nicolson, William, *The English, Scotch and Irish Historical Libraries*, 3rd edition, 1736.

——, *Letters on various Subjects, Literary, Political, and Ecclesiastical, to and from William Nicolson, DD.*, 2 vols, ed. John Nicols, 1809.

Norris, John, *A Letter to Mr. Dodwell, Concerning the Immortality of the Soul of Man*, 4th edition, 1722.

North, George, *An Answer to a Scandalous Libel, Entitled The Impertinence and Imposture of Modern Antiquarians Display'd*, 1741.

Oldmixon, John, *The Critical History of England, Ecclesiastical and Civil*, 2nd edition, 2 vols, 1726–30.

Original Letters To and From Miss Blandy and C——C——, 1752.

Orton, Samuel, *The Unhappy Case of Samuel Orton, addressed to the Reverend Mr.——*, 1767.

The Oxford Young Gentleman's Reply To a Book entitled, Christianity not Founded on Argument, &c., 1743.

A Pacquet from Will's, 1701.

Paine, Thomas, *The Age of Reason. Being an Investigation of True and Fabulous Theology*, 1793.

——, *The Life and Major Writings of Thomas Paine*, ed. Philip S. Foner, New York, 1945.

Parker, John, *Letters to his Friends, By the Rev. John Parker*, ed. John Fawcett, 1794.

Pearsall, Richard, *Contemplations of the Ocean, Harvest, Sickness and the Last Judgment*, 1753.

——, *Contemplations on Butterflies, on the Full Moon, and in a Walk Through a Wood*, 1758.

The Pembroke Papers (1734–1780): Letters and Diaries of Henry, Tenth Earl of Pembroke and His Circle, ed. Lord Herbert, 1942.

Pennington, Sarah, *An Unfortunate Mother's Advice to Her Absent Daughters, in a Letter to Miss Pennington*, Dublin, 1790.

Penrose, John, *Letters from Bath 1766–1767 by the Rev. John Penrose*, eds Brigitte Mitchell and Hubert Penrose, Gloucester, 1983.

Percy, Thomas, *The Percy Letters*, 8 vols, eds David Nichol Smith and Cleanth Brooks, Louisiana and New Haven, 1940–85.

The Persian Letters Continued, 3rd edition, 1736.

A Person in Business, *Two Letters on the Flour Trade, and Dearness of Corn*, 1766.

Philalethes, *Impartial Reflections upon Dr. Burnet's Posthumous History*, 1724.

Philips, Katherine, *Letters from Orinda to Poliarchus*, 1705.

Pierce, Eliza, *The Letters of Eliza Pierce 1751–1775*, ed. Violet M. Macdonald, 1927.

Piozzi, Hester Lynch, *Anecdotes of the late Samuel Johnson LL. D. During the Last Twenty Years of his Life*, 1786.

——, *Letters to and from the late Samuel Johnson, LL.D.*, 2 vols, 1788.

Pitt, William, *The Love-Letters of William Pitt First Lord Chatham*, ed. Edward Ashton Edwards, Chapman and Hall, 1926.

A Plain Common Freeholder, *Letters to Sir William Beauchamp Proctor*, 1768.

The Polite Politician: or, Entertaining Correspondent, 2 vols, 1751.

Pope, Alexander, *Eloisa to Abelard*, 1719.

——, *Letters of Mr Pope and Several Eminent Persons, from the Year 1705, to 1711*, 5 vols, 1735.

——, *The Correspondence of Alexander Pope*, 5 vols, ed. George Sherburn, Oxford 1956.

——, *Alexander Pope: Selected Letters*, ed. Howard Erskine-Hill, Oxford, 2000.

Potts, Thomas, *The Last Letters of Thomas Potts*, Paisley, 1797.

Priestley, Joseph, *Defences of Unitarianism for the Years 1788 & 1789*, Birmingham, n.d.

Proud, Joseph, *An Impartial Account of a Public Disputation on Water Baptism, held on the 25th Day of October, 1787, at the general Baptist Chapel, in Bar-Street, Norwich, between John Bousell, a Speaker amongst the People called Quakers, and Joseph Proud, Pastor of the general Baptist Congregation, in Ber-Street, With some further Observations in Vindication of that Sacred Ordinance*, Norwich, n.d.

Pulteney, William, *The Budget Opened*, 1733.

——, *A Review of the Excise-Scheme*, 1733.

The Queeney Letters Being Letters Addressed to Hester Maria Thrale by Doctor Johnson, Fanny Burney and Mrs. Thrale-Piozzi, ed. the Marquis of Lansdowne, 1934.

A Reply to the Hertford Letter, 1699.

Richardson, Samuel, *Pamela, or Virtue Rewarded*, 2 vols, 1740.

——, *Letters Written to and for Particular Friends on the Most Important Occasions*, 1741.

——, *Clarissa, or the History of a Young Lady*, 1747–49, ed. Angus Ross, 1985.

——, *The History of Sir Charles Grandison*, 7 vols, 1753–4.

Robins, John, *A Bone to Pick, Recommended to the Several Water Companies of this Metropolis; or a Check to Avarice, Tyranny and Oppression in Two Parts*, 1790.

Robinson, John, *Love Fragments*, 1782.

Rogers, Hester Ann, *Spiritual Letters Written by Mrs H.A. Rogers*, Bristol, [1796].

The Roman History, in a Series of Letters from a Nobleman to his Son, 2 vols, [1774].

Rooke, Henry, *Travels to the Coast of Arabia Felix*, 2nd edition, 1784.

Rousseau, Jean-Jacques, [*La Nouvelle Héloïse*] *Eloisa: Or, a Series of Original Letters Collected and Published by J.J. Rousseau*, 4 vols, 1761.

'Rousseau, J.J.' *Letters of an Italian Nun and an English Gentleman*, 1781.

Rowe, Elizabeth Singer, *Friendship in Death: Twenty Letters from the Dead to the Living*, 1728.

Rowlands, Henry, *Mona Antiqua Restaurata*, Dublin, 1723.

Rushworth, John, *Historical Collections of Private Passages of State*, 8 vols, 1659–1701.

Russell, William, *The History of Modern Europe*, 1779–84.

Rusticus, Philalethes, *The Impertinence of Modern Antiquarians Displayed*, 1739.

Sampson, William, *The Trial of the Rev. William Jackson . . . for High Treason*, Dublin, 1795.

Sancho, Ignatius, *Letters of the Late Ignatius Sancho, an African*, 2 vols, 1782.

Savile, George, Lord Marquess of Halifax, *The Lady's New-Year's-Gift or: Advice to a Daughter*, 1700, repr. Stamford, Connecticut, 1934.

The Secret History of an Old Shoe, 1734.

The Secret History of Miss Blandy, 1752.

Sévigné, Mme de [Marie de Rabutin-Chantal], *Court Secrets: or, The Lady's Chronicle Historical and Gallant*, 1727.

——, *Selected Letters*, trans. Leonard Tancock, 1982.

Sewell, George, *A Second Letter to the Bishop of Salisbury*, 1713.

——, *The Third Letter to the Bishop of Salisbury*, 1714.

——, *A Review of Three Letters Written to the Bishop of Salisbury*, 1714.

Sharp, Samuel, *Letters from Italy, Describing the Customs and Manners of that Country, in the Years 1765, and 1766*, 2nd edition, 1767.

Shebbeare, John, *Letters on the English Nation by Battista Angeloni a Jesuit, Who Resided Many Years in London*, 2 vols, 1755.

Shenstone, William, *The Letters of William Shenstone* ed. Marjorie Williams, Oxford, 1939.

[Sherbrooke, John], A Tradesman, *Serious Advice of a Parent to his Children*, Nottingham, 1734.

Smith, Elizabeth, *Fragments in Prose and Verse: By a Young Lady, Lately Deceased*, 7th edition, 1809.

Smollett, Tobias, *Letters from France and Italy*, 1766.

——, *The Expedition of Humphry Clinker*, 1771, ed. Angus Ross, 1967 repr. 1980.

——, *The Works of Tobias Smollett*, 8 vols, ed. James P. Browne M.D., 1872.

Smyth, Agnes, *The Religion of the Heart, Delineated in a Series of Letters*, 1783.

Some Account of the State of Religion in London: in Four Letters to a Friend in the Country, 1774.

Sophronia, or Letters for the Ladies, 1761.

Spiritual Letters: By Several Eminent Christians, Chester, 1767.

Squire, Francis, *Remarks upon Mr. Carte's Specimen of his General History of England*, 1748.

Stanhope, Philip Dormer, *Genuine Memoirs of Asiaticus In a Series of Letters to a Friend*, 2nd edition, 1785.

Steele, Elizabeth, *Memoirs of Mrs. Sophia Baddeley, late of Drury Lane Theatre*, 6 vols, 1787.

Steele, Richard, *The Tender Husband: or, The Accomplish'd Fools*, 1705.

——, *The Correspondence of Richard Steele*, ed. Rae Blanchard, Oxford, 1968.

——, *The Plays of Richard Steele*, ed. Shirley Strum Kenny, Oxford, 1971.

Sterne, Laurence, *The Life and Opinions of Tristram Shandy*, 9 vols, 1759–67.

——, *Letters from Yorick to Eliza*, 1775.

——, *Letters Written Between Yorick and Eliza with Sterne's Letters to his Friends*, 1788.

Stuart, Gilbert, *The History of Scotland, from the Establishment of the Reformation, Till the Death of Queen Mary*, 2 vols, 1782.

Sturch, John, *A View of the Isle of Wight, in Four Letters to a Friend*, 5th edition, Newport, Isle of Wight, 1794.

Swift, Jonathan, *The Hibernian Patriot: Being a Collection of the Drapier's Letters to the People of Ireland, Concerning Mr. Wood's Brass Half-pence*, 1730.

——, *Letters Written by the late Jonathan Swift, D.D.*, 3 vols, ed. Sir John Hawkesworth, 1766.

——, *The Drapier's Letters*, ed. Herbert Davis, Oxford, 1935.

Talbot, Catherine, *The Works of the late Miss Catherine Talbot*, ed. Rev. Montagu Pennington, 9th edition, 1819.

Tavernier, John, *The Newest and most Compleat Polite Familiar Letter-Writer*, 4th edition, Berwick, 1768.

Taylor, J., *A Summary of Parental and Filial Duties*, Sheffield, 1805.

Taylor, Thomas, *Redeeming Grace Displayed to the Chief of Sinners*, 4th edition, Leeds, 1785.

Temple, William, *Letters Written by Sir William Temple, Bart. And other Ministers of State*, 3 vols, ed. Jonathan Swift, 1701, 1703.

Thicknesse, Philip, *Observations on the Customs and Manners of the French Nation*, 1766.

Thomson, James, *The Seasons*, 1730.

Thomson, William, *Letters from Scandinavia, on the Past and Present State of the Northern Nations of Europe*, 2 vols, 1796.

Topham, Edward, *Letters from Edinburgh, Written in the Years 1774 and 1775*, 1776.

Travels of the Jesuits, into Various Parts of the World, trans. John Lockman, 2 vols, 1743.

The Travels of Several Learned Missioners of the Society of Jesus, 1714.

Trenchard, John and Gordon, Thomas, *Cato's Letters*, 4 vols, 1724.

Trial of Mary Blandy, ed. William Roughead, Edinburgh, 1914.

The Trial of Mrs. Rudd, 1776.

The Trial of the Rev. Mr. James Altham of Harlow, 2 vols, 1785.

Trials for Adultery, 9 vols, 1779.

Trosse, George, *The Life of George Trosse*, Exeter, 1714.

The Tryal of Mary Blandy, Spinster; for the Murder of Her Father, Francis Blandy, Gent., 1752.

The Tryal of Spencer Cowper, Esq., 1699.

Verney Letters of the Eighteenth Century from the MSS. at Claydon House, 2 vols, ed. Margaret Maria Lady Verney, LL.D., 1930.

Voiture, Mons. de, Vincent, *Familiar and Courtly Letters to Persons of Honour and Quality*, 2 vols, 3rd edition, 1701 [for 1702].

——, *The Works of the Celebrated Monsieur Voiture*, 2 vols, 1715.

Voltaire, *The Works of M. de Voltaire*, 5 vols, 1779–80.

Walpole, Horace, *The Correspondence of Horace Walpole*, ed. W.S. Lewis, 48 vols, 1937–83.

——, *A Letter from Xo Ho, a Chinese Philosopher at London, to his Friend Lien Chi at Peking*, 1757.

[Watling, Thomas], *Letters from an Exile at Botany-Bay, to his Aunt in Dumfries*, Penrith, 1793.

Watson, Richard, *An Apology for the Bible, in a Series of Letters Addressed to Tom Paine*, 4th edition, 1796.

Wesley, John, *The Letters of John Wesley*, 8 vols, ed. John Telford, 1931.

Wesley, Susanna, *Susanna Wesley: The Complete Writings*, ed. Charles Wallace Jr, Oxford, 1997.

Whiteaker, John, *The Genuine History of the Britons Asserted against Mr Macpherson*, 2nd edition, 1773.

——, *Gibbon's History of the Decline and Fall of the Roman Empire . . . Reviewed*, 1791.

White, Gilbert, *The Natural History and Antiquities of Selbourne, in the County of Southampton: With Engravings, and an Appendix*, 1789.

Whitefield, George, *A Letter to the Right Reverend the Bishop of London, and the Other the Right Rev. the Bishops*, 1744.

Wilkes, John, *Letters from the Year 1774 to the Year 1776, of John Wilkes, Esq.*, 4 vols, 2nd edition, 1805.

Wilkes, Wettenhall, *A Letter of Genteel and Moral Advice to a Young Lady . . .*, 4th edition, 1746.

Williams, John, *An Account of some Remarkable Ruins, Lately Discovered in the Highlands, and Northern Parts of Scotland*, Edinburgh, 1777.

Williams, Joseph, *Extracts from the Diary, Meditations and Letters of Mr. Joseph Williams*, Shrewsbury, 1779.

Willison, John, and Bonar, John, *The Duty and Advantage of Religious Societies . . .*, 1783.

Windham, Thomas, *An Account of the Glacieres or Ice Alps in Savoy*, 1744.

Wise, Francis, *A Letter to Dr. Mead Concerning Some Antiquities in Berkshire . . .*, Oxford, 1738.

The Wit of the Day, or the Humours of Westminster, 1784.

Wollstonecraft, Mary, *Letters Written During a Short Residence in Sweden, Norway, and Denmark*, 1796.

Wraxall, Nathaniel, *Cursory Remarks Made on a Tour Through Some of the Northern Parts of Europe, Particularly Copenhagen, Stockholm, and Petersburgh*, 1775.

——, *Memoirs of My Own Times*, 2 vols, 1815.

[Young, Edward], *The Complaint, or Night-Thoughts on Life, Death & Immortality*, 1742.

Young, Edward, *The Centaur Not Fabulous*, 1755.

The Young Gentleman and Lady Instructed, 2 vols, 1747.

The Young Lady's Pocket Library, or Parental Monitor, 1790, ed. Vivien Jones, Bristol, 1995.

Index

Printed in the United States
63876LVS00002B/13

9 781403 994820

PR.915

.B73

2006